Oxford Read

Homer's *Iliad*

M000283819

Oxford Readings in
Homer's *Iliad*

Edited by
DOUGLAS L. CAIRNS

OXFORD
UNIVERSITY PRESS

OXFORD
UNIVERSITY PRESS

Great Clarendon Street, Oxford OX2 6DP

Oxford University Press is a department of the University of Oxford.
It furthers the University's objective of excellence in research, scholarship,
and education by publishing worldwide in

Oxford New York

Auckland Bangkok Buenos Aires Cape Town Chennai
Dar es Salaam Delhi Hong Kong Istanbul Karachi Kolkata
Kuala Lumpur Madrid Melbourne Mexico City Mumbai Nairobi
São Paulo Shanghai Taipei Tokyo Toronto

Oxford is a registered trade mark of Oxford University Press
in the UK and in certain other countries

Published in the United States
by Oxford University Press Inc., New York

© Oxford University Press 2001

The moral rights of the author have been asserted
Database right Oxford University Press (maker)

First published 2001

All rights reserved. No part of this publication may be reproduced,
stored in a retrieval system, or transmitted, in any form or by any means,
without the prior permission in writing of Oxford University Press,
or as expressly permitted by law, or under terms agreed with the appropriate
reprographics rights organization. Enquiries concerning reproduction
outside the scope of the above should be sent to the Rights Department,
Oxford University Press, at the address above

You must not circulate this book in any other binding or cover
and you must impose this same condition on any acquirer

British Library Cataloguing in Publication Data

Data available

Library of Congress Cataloging in Publication Data

Data applied for

ISBN 0-19-872183-8
ISBN 0-19-872182-X (pbk.)

3 5 7 9 10 8 6 4 2

Typeset in Photina by Newgen Imaging Systems (P) Ltd, Chennai, India
Printed in Great Britain
on acid-free paper by
Biddles Ltd., Short-Run Books, King's Lynn

PREFACE

The field of Homeric studies is a vast and vigorous one, and it has not been my intention, either in selecting the articles for inclusion in this volume or in introducing them, to make any pretence towards representative coverage of such a wide and diverse set of sub-disciplines. But neither are the articles simply a heterogeneous collection of greatest hits: taken together, they illustrate the conviction that the *Iliad* is no primitive, unidimensional artefact, but the finest fruit of a long and rich tradition, a poem peopled by characters who possess a past, a future, and an inner life, and who are embedded in an idealized but not entirely fantastic society, which, though it exists in a complicated relationship to that of its original audiences, none the less engages those audiences' deepest moral, social, and political concerns. A notable link between the articles is their determination to see the *Iliad* in context, whether the context be that of the society to which it is addressed, the tradition from which it emerged, the works and genres with which it competed, or the reception which it received in Archaic and Classical Greece. The pieces are arranged in the volume and discussed in the Introduction in such a way as to move from the general to the particular, from questions of origins, background, and general character to the specific artistry and individuality of the poem itself. In the Introduction I have tried to explore some of the connections between the different Chapters, to set them in a wider context, and to engage with their arguments. I have not attempted to provide a complete bibliography of all relevant studies which have appeared since the original publication of the pieces anthologized here; the reader may obtain helpful bibliographical orientation (most recently) from J. Latacz (ed.), *Zwei Hundert Jahre Homer-Forschung* (Stuttgart, 1991); I. Morris and B. Powell (edd.), *A New Companion to Homer* (Leiden, 1996); and R. Rutherford, *Homer* (*Greece & Rome* New Surveys in the Classics 26, Oxford, 1996); also from the extensive references provided in K. Stanley, *The Shield of Homer* (Princeton, 1993). For detailed study, the Cambridge commentary (G. S. Kirk *et al.* (edd.), *The Iliad: A Commentary* (Cambridge, 1985–1993)) is indispensable.

I am grateful to several friends and colleagues for assistance in the preparation of this book: for suggestions for inclusion to Alex Garvie and Robin Hankey; for editorial assistance to Noreen Humble; for secretarial help to Jennifer Murray; for commenting on a draft of the Introduction to Alex Garvie and Richard Rutherford; and for help in obtaining books and articles to Roger Brock, Francis Cairns, Malcolm Heath, and Elizabeth Pender.

D.L.C.

Glasgow
August 2000

CONTENTS

ABBREVIATIONS

Abbreviations of the names of ancient authors and works generally follow those given in the *Oxford Classical Dictionary* (3rd edn., Oxford, 1996). Abbreviations of periodicals, editions, collections of fragments, and works of reference are as follows:

Abh. Mainz	Abhandlungen der Akademie der Wissenschaften und der Literatur, Mainz
ABSA	*Annual of the British School at Athens*
ABV	J. D. Beazley, *Attic Black-Figure Vase-Painters* (Oxford, 1956)
AC	*L'Antiquité classique*
Add.²	T. H. Carpenter (ed.), *Beazley Addenda* (2nd edn., Oxford, 1989)
AJP	*American Journal of Philology*
Allen	T. W. Allen (ed.), *Homeri Opera* v: *Hymni, Cyclus, Fragmenta* etc. (2nd edn., Oxford, 1912)
Anc. Soc.	*Ancient Society*
Annales ESC	*Annales: économies, sociétés, civilisations*
Arch. Hom.	*Archaeologica Homerica*
ARV²	J. D. Beazley, *Attic Red-Figure Vase-Painters* (2nd edn., Oxford, 1963)
Bernabé	A. Bernabé (ed.), *Poetarum Epicorum Graecorum Testimonia et Fragmenta* (Leipzig, 1987)
Bethe	E. Bethe, *Homer: Dichtung und Sage* ii. 2 (2nd edn., Leipzig, 1929)
BICS	*Bulletin of the Institute of Classical Studies*
Boeckh	A. Boeckh (ed.), *Pindari Opera quae supersunt* (2 vols., Leipzig, 1811–21)
Cl. Ant.	*Classical Antiquity*
CJ	*Classical Journal*
Comp.	I. Morris and B. Powell (edd.), *A New Companion to Homer* (Leiden, 1997)
CP	*Classical Philology*
CQ	*Classical Quarterly*
CR	*Classical Review*

CW	*Classical World*
D	E. Diehl (ed.), *Anthologia Lyrica Graeca* (3rd edn., Leipzig, 1949–54)
Davies	M. Davies (ed.), *Epicorum Graecorum Fragmenta* (Göttingen, 1988)
DK	H. Diels and W. Kranz (edd.), *Die Fragmente der Vorsokratiker* (6th edn., Berlin, 1951–2)
Entretiens Hardt	Fondation Hardt: Entretiens sur l'antiquité classique
FGrH	F. Jacoby (ed.), *Die Fragmente der griechischen Historiker* (Berlin/Leiden, 1923–58; Leiden, 1994–)
FS	*Festschrift*
Gött. Nachr.	*Nachrichten von der Gesellschaft der Wissenschaften zu Göttingen*
G&R	*Greece & Rome*
GRBS	*Greek, Roman, and Byzantine Studies*
HSCP	*Harvard Studies in Classical Philology*
Il. Comm.	G. S. Kirk *et al.* (edd.), *The Iliad: A Commentary* (6 vols., Cambridge, 1985–93)
JHS	*Journal of Hellenic Studies*
JRS	*Journal of Roman Studies*
LIMC	*Lexicon Iconographicum Mythologiae Classicae* (8 vols., Zurich, 1981–97)
Lloyd-Jones	H. Lloyd-Jones, Appendix, in H. Weir Smyth (ed.), *Aeschylus* II (2nd edn., Cambridge, Mass., 1957)
L–P	E. Lobel and D. L. Page (edd.), *Poetarum Lesbiorum Fragmenta* (Oxford, 1955)
Maehler	H. Maehler (ed.), *Pindarus. Pars* II: *Fragmenta* (Leipzig, 1989)
MDAI(A)	*Mitteilungen des Deutschen Archäologischen Instituts, Athenische Abteilung*
MH	*Museum Helveticum*
Mnemos.	*Mnemosyne*
M–W	R. Merkelbach and M. L. West (edd.), *Fragmenta Hesiodea* (Oxford, 1967)
Njbb	*Neue Jahrbücher für das klassische Altertum, Geschichte und deutsche Litteratur*
OCT	Oxford Classical Texts
Od. Comm.	A. Heubeck *et al.* (edd.), *A Commentary on Homer's Odyssey* (3 vols., Oxford, 1988–92)
Paralipomena	J. D. Beazley, *Paralipomena: Additions to 'Attic Black-Figure Vase-Painters' and to 'Attic Red-Figure Vase-Painters' (Second Edition)* (Oxford, 1971)
PBA	*Proceedings of the British Academy*

PCPS	Proceedings of the Cambridge Philological Society
PdP	La parola del passato
Pf.	R. Pfeiffer (ed.), Callimachus (2 vols., Oxford, 1949–53)
PLLS	Papers of the Liverpool [superseded by: Leeds International] Latin Seminar
PMG	D. L. Page, Poetae Melici Graeci (Oxford, 1962)
PMGF	M. Davies (ed.), Poetarum Melicorum Graecorum Fragmenta (Oxford, 1991–)
P. Oxy.	Oxyrynchus Papyri
QUCC	Quaderni urbinati di cultura classica
Rabe	H. Rabe (ed.), Syrianus, In Hermogenem (2 vols., Leipzig, 1892–3)
Radt	S. Radt (ed.), Tragicorum Graecorum Fragmenta, vol. III Aeschylus (Göttingen, 1985), vol. IV, Sophocles (2nd edn., Göttingen, 1999)
RE	G. Wissowa et al. (edd.), Paulys Realencyclopädie der classischen Altertumswissenschaft (Stuttgart, 1893–1978)
REA	Revue des études anciennes
REG	Revue des études grecques
Rev. Phil.	Revue de philologie
RM	Rheinisches Museum für Philologie
Rz.	A. Rzach, Hesiodi Carmina (3rd edn., Leipzig, 1913)
SB Berlin	Sitzungsberichte der preußischen Akademie der Wissenschaften zu Berlin
SB Heidelberg	Sitzungsberichte der Heidelberger Akademie der Wissenschaften
SB Wien	Sitzungsberichte der Österreichischer Akademie der Wissenschaften zu Wien
Schrader	H. L. Schrader (ed.), Porphyrii Quaestionum Homericarum ad Iliadem Pertinentium Reliquias (Leipzig, 1880–2)
SCO	Studi classici e orientali
SEG	Supplementum Epigraphicum Graecum
Snell	B. Snell (ed.), Tragicorum Graecorum Fragmenta, vol. I, Didascaliae . . . et Fragmenta Tragicorum Minorum (Göttingen, 1971)
SO	Symbolae Osloenses
SVF	H. von Arnim (ed.), Stoicorum Veterum Fragmenta (4 vols., Leipzig, 1903–24)
TAPA	Transactions and Proceedings of the American Philological Association
UCPCP	University of California Publications in Classical Philology

Van der Valk	M. van der Valk (ed.), *Eustathii Archiepiscopi Thessalonicensis: Commentarii ad Homeri Iliadem pertinentes* (4 vols., Leiden, 1971–87)
West	M. L. West, *Iambi et Elegi Graeci* (2 vols., 2nd edn., Oxford, 1989–92)
WS	*Wiener Studien*
Wyss	B. Wyss (ed.), *Antimachi Colophonii Reliquiae* (Berlin, 1936)
YCS	*Yale Classical Studies*
ZPE	*Zeitschrift für Papyrologie und Epigraphik*

Introduction

I. ORIGINS AND EARLY RECEPTION

Of the first two contributions to this volume (Morris, Chapter 1, and Burkert, Chapter 2), the former argues that the culture represented in the Homeric poems is derived from and reflects the ideological concerns of the society in which the poems reached their final, 'monumental' form, while the latter seeks to trace, in the art and literature of the sixth century BC, the process by which the *Iliad* and the *Odyssey* became the classic texts that they are for us and were for Greeks of the Classical period. Thus, though neither deals systematically with questions of dating, composition, or textualization, each presupposes that the two poems reached their definitive (written) form at a relatively early period: the late eighth century, according to Morris, the first half of the seventh, according to Burkert. Some version of this general position is, I believe, the most plausible hypothesis, but not all contemporary Homerists would agree. Minna Skafte Jensen, for example, has made a powerful case for the composition of the poems at Athens, under Pisistratid patronage, in the sixth century, and several other scholars share her opinion that the poems did not achieve textual fixity until then.[1]

---

[1] M. Skafte Jensen, *The Homeric Question and the Oral-Formulaic Theory* (Copenhagen, 1980). Closest to Skafte Jensen in denying the existence of large-scale Homeric epics before the mid-6th cent. is R. Sealey, 'From Phemius to Ion', *REG* 70 (1957), 312–55. K. Stanley, *The Shield of Homer* (Princeton, 1993), 279–96, would locate complete textualization, involving reshaping of pre-existing material, in the same period; cf. A. Ballabriga, 'La Question homérique: pour une réouverture du débat', *REG* 103 (1990), 16–29, K. Dowden, 'Homer's Sense of Text', *JHS* 116 (1996), 47–61. G. Nagy, *Homeric Questions* (Austin, 1996), 29–112, *Poetry as Performance* (Cambridge, 1996), 107–14 (and the preliminary studies referred to in those works; cf. also R. Seaford, *Reciprocity and Ritual* (Oxford, 1994), 144–54) argues for 6th-cent. textualization of poems which had already achieved a high degree of fixity in the oral tradition (see n. 12 below). Approaches of this general type are anticipated not only in G. Murray, *The Rise of the Greek Epic* (3rd edn., Oxford, 1924), 306–16, but also in some of the earliest modern contributions to the Homeric Question: see A. Parry

The postponement of the textualization of the monumental *Iliad* has its attractions: since it rejects the idea that the poem was committed to writing at a date soon after the adaptation of the Phoenician alphabet to the writing of Greek, it avoids the difficulty of accounting for the coming to be of a written text of over 15,000 lines at a time when there was no audience for written literature;[2] since it also dispenses with the notion of a large-scale, orally transmitted predecessor of the written text, it avoids the difficulty of imagining a context for the performance of such a poem.[3]

There are, however, telling arguments against this hypothesis. First, Richard Janko's study of the development of epic diction has demonstrated that the language of the *Iliad* represents a relatively early stage in a tradition which evolved further in the *Odyssey*, the Hesiodic poems, and the Homeric Hymns;[4] its text must have been fixed at a time when oral composition of hexameter poetry was (and would long continue to be) the norm.[5] Now, although Janko believes that his schema best suits an eighth-century date for the Homeric poems,[6] the dates which his researches establish are relative, and only the support of absolute dating criteria would anchor them at any particular period; there is, however, no absolute date for any of the works studied in his book.[7] Yet even relative dating imposes

---

in M. Parry, *The Making of Homeric Verse* (Oxford, 1971), pp. xii–xv; H. Lloyd-Jones, 'Remarks on the Homeric Question', *Academic Papers: Greek Epic, Lyric, and Tragedy* (Oxford, 1990), 3–5.

  [2] See Murray (n. 1), 187; Sealey (n. 1), 350; the observation goes back to F. A. Wolf (*Prolegomena to Homer* (Eng. trans. Princeton, 1985), 116); cf. A. Ford, 'The Inland Ship: Problems in the Performance and Reception of Homeric Epic', in E. Bakker and A. Kahane (edd.), *Written Voices, Spoken Signs* (Cambridge, Mass. 1997), 84, 108. For various views on the practical problems in producing, copying, and distributing written works of such massive scale at a period not long after the introduction of the alphabet, see L. H. Jeffery in A. J. B. Wace and F. H. Stubbings (edd.), *A Companion to Homer* (London, 1962), 545–59, esp. 555–9, A. Heubeck, *Arch. Hom.* iii. x: *Schrift* (Göttingen, 1979), 150–6, W. Burkert, *The Orientalizing Revolution* (Cambridge, Mass., 1992), 30–3, W. V. Harris, *Ancient Literacy* (Cambridge, Mass. 1989), 46–7; Janko, *Il. Comm.* iv. 32–3, B. B. Powell, *Homer and the Origin of the Greek Alphabet* (Cambridge, 1991), 32, 181–2.

  [3] See Powell (n. 2), 229; contrast O. Taplin, *Homeric Soundings* (Oxford, 1992), 26–30, 39–41.

  [4] *Homer, Hesiod, and the Hymns* (Cambridge, 1982).

  [5] This, indeed, is accepted by Sealey (n. 1), 315–17, and Skafte Jensen (n. 1), 157, but without reference to the relative dating of other hexameter poetry.

  [6] See now Janko, 'The Homeric Poems as Oral Dictated Texts', *CQ* 48 (1998), 1, citing Powell (n. 2), 186–220.   [7] See Janko (n. 4), 195–6.

considerable restrictions on the potential for down-dating: late textualization of the *Iliad* entails even later textualization of the *Odyssey*, the Hesiodic poems, and the Hymns; if the first member of this series achieved its definitive written form only in the mid-sixth century, all other members must have achieved theirs even later; but (as we shall see presently) already at the end of the sixth century Homer and Hesiod were regarded as classics, the founding fathers of Greek poetry and thought. And it is not only extant hexameter poetry that one has to take into account here: for as the *Odyssey* complements and accommodates the (earlier) *Iliad*,[8] so the (Trojan) Epic Cycle (in its final, now lost, written versions) complemented and thus presupposed both;[9] these poems were well known in written form in the fifth century, and believed to have been composed by figures of the remote past (or by Homer himself).[10] Radical downdating of the *Iliad* would demand an impossible degree of haste in the production of what fifth-century authors already regarded as classic texts.

The conclusion that a text of the *Iliad* more or less as we know it antedated the incorporation of the poems into the Pisistratean Panathenaia thus seems unavoidable. (This is, after all, broadly what the testimonia on the 'Pisistratean recension' attest to.)[11] Given that oral transmission of the monumental poem prior to that date cannot explain the relative antiquity of the *Iliad*'s diction,[12] such a text must

---

[8] See below, this section, on Rutherford's Ch. 3 in this vol.

[9] Though perhaps not as seamlessly as Proclus' summaries would suggest: see M. Davies, *The Epic Cycle* (Bristol, 1989), 8, 60, 62. On the Cycle, see further in Section IV below.

[10] There are no reliable dates for the poems of the Cycle; M. Davies, 'The Date of the Epic Cycle', *Glotta* 67 (1989), 89–100 (cf. id. (n. 9), 3–4), dates the Cycle to the 6th cent.; but see R. Schmitt, 'Zur Sprache der kyklischen *Kypria*', in W. Görler and S. Koster (edd.), *Pratum Saraviense* (FS P. Steinmetz, Saarbrücken, 1990), 11–24, and cf. Janko, *Il. Comm.* IV. 14 n. 21.

[11] For testimonia and discussion, see T. W. Allen, *Homer: The Origins and the Transmission* (Oxford, 1924), 226–38; R. Merkelbach, 'Die pisistratische Redaktion der homerischen Gedichte', *RM* 95 (1952), 23–47; J. A. Davison, 'Peisistratus and Homer', *TAPA* 86 (1955), 1–21; G. S. Kirk, *The Songs of Homer* (Cambridge, 1962), 306–12; Skafte Jensen (n. 1), 128–58, 207–26; Janko, *Il. Comm.* IV. 29–32; cf. S. West, *Od. Comm.* I. 36–40.

[12] Kirk (n. 11), 98–101, 301–3, 316–25 (cf. Taplin (n. 3), 41–4) argues that the *Il.* was composed orally and transmitted orally for several generations. Cf. Nagy's hypothesis (n. 1) that the oral tradition of the Homeric poems crystallized in a relatively stable 'formative' period from the mid-8th to mid-6th cent.; but oral transmission makes modification and development inevitable, and consistent archaism on the scale required is surely impossible: see Janko (n. 4), 17, 192, 220–1, and (n. 6), I, 11–12. See also (in response to Kirk) A. Parry, 'Have We Homer's *Iliad*?' in *The Language of Achilles and Other Papers* (Oxford, 1989), 104–40.

have been a written one, though the further hypothesis that it must
have been dictated,[13] though certainly plausible, is not, despite what
its proponents claim, inevitable.[14]

The dating of the Homeric poems and the relation of the world
they depict to the society from which they finally emerged are two
separate issues, and it is the latter that is the proper subject of
Morris's paper. He stresses that the society and institutions of the
poem cannot simply be identified with those of a particular historical
period, chiefly because the poem uses the phenomenon of 'epic distance' imaginatively to recreate a lost heroic age and to retroject its
social preoccupations into an idealized heroic past.[15] After making
all due allowances for this phenomenon, however, the world of the
Homeric poems must (he argues) be rooted in that of their original
audience, for the reason that oral tradition continually remodels its
material in the light of the experiences and world-view of its contemporary listeners.[16] This thesis, amply supported by comparative
evidence, tells strongly against Finley's view that heroic society
represents a fossilized version of tenth- or ninth-century realities,
with a substantial chronological gap between the society that
received the poems and that which is depicted in them.[17] Recent
studies have shown that in their geographical orientation, political
development, and religious practices the poems exhibit numerous

[13] A. B. Lord, 'Homer's Originality: Oral Dictated Texts', *TAPA* 84 (1953), 124–34
and *The Singer of Tales* (Cambridge, Mass, 1960), 148–57; Skafte Jensen (n. 1), 81–95;
M. L. West, 'Archaische Heldendichtung: Singen und Schreiben', in W. Kullmann and
M. Reichel (edd.), *Der Übergang von der Mündlichkeit zur Literatur bei den Griechen*
(Tübingen, 1990), 33–50: Powell (n. 2), 228–30; R. Janko, *Il. Comm.* IV. 37–8; id.
(n. 6), 1–13.

[14] Janko (n. 6) argues that written composition would have removed inconsistencies and anomalies whose presence in our text is to be explained on the
assumption that a dictating poet could not return to passages already recorded; but
there is no reason to assume that the desire and capacity to revise what one has
written in the interests of consistency are inevitable concomitants of the ability to
write (as any university examiner can testify). For the hypothesis of written
composition, see e.g. A. Parry (n. 12); Lloyd-Jones (n. 1), 3–20; M. Reichel, *Fernbe-
ziehungen in der Ilias* (Tübingen, 1994), 372–6, amplified in 'How Oral is Homer's
Narrative?', *PLLS* 10 (1998), 1–22.

[15] The term is J. M. Redfield's: *Nature and Culture in the Iliad* (Chicago, 1975; new
edn., Durham, NC, 1994), 35–9; cf. H. van Wees, *Status Warriors* (Amsterdam, 1992),
6–21 on 'fantasy'.

[16] This was also M. Parry's view: see (n. 1) p. XLV. Cf. W. Kullmann, 'Homers Zeit
und das Bild des Dichters von den Menschen der mykenischen Kultur', in Ø. Andersen
and M. W. Dickie (edd.), *Homer's World* (Bergen, 1995), 59–60 (with refs.).

[17] Finley, *The World of Odysseus* (2nd edn., Harmondsworth, 1979), esp. 34, 47–8.

points of contact with the situation of the Greek world following the 'Greek Renaissance' of the eighth century BC;[18] but opinions differ as to how far into the Archaic period their accommodation of contemporary realities extends.

Certain features now seem to some scholars to fit better with what we know of the seventh century (though there is room for dispute both about the interpretation of the Homeric data and about the specific dating of the historical phenomena to which they supposedly refer);[19] there are also candidates for consideration as sixth-century features,[20] although these, like those which can plausibly be identified as Bronze Age survivals, are isolated; the bulk of the data presented by the poems suggests reflection of Greek society at some time in the eighth or seventh centuries.

Morris's thesis demands only that the poet's contemporary audience should be able to understand or construe the world of the poems in the light of its own, not that the culture of the heroes should be entirely remodelled after the world of the audience's experience, and accordingly some feel that he plays down the possibility that the imaginative reconstruction of a heroic age may incorporate identifiable features from earlier historical periods:[21] the process by which the tradition is refashioned in terms of the contemporary audience's

---

[18] See esp. J. P. Crielaard, 'Homer, History, and Archaeology', in id. (ed.), *Homeric Questions* (Amsterdam, 1995), 201–88; cf. Van Wees (n. 15), 53–8, 156–62.

[19] See W. Burkert, 'Das hunderttorige Theben und die Datierung der *Ilias*',*WS* 89 (1976), 5–21; M. W. Dickie, 'The Geography of Homer's World', in Andersen and Dickie (n. 16), 29–56; Kullmann, ibid. 57; Stanley (n. 1), 279–80 (arguing for a 'halt in the "homeostatic" adjustment of the poetic tradition to contemporary material culture' in the early 7th cent., with final textualization in 6th-cent. Athens); H. van Wees, 'The Homeric Way of War', *G&R* 41 (1994), 138–46; M. L. West, 'The Date of the *Iliad*', *MH* 52 (1995), 213–19.

[20] See Sealey (n. 1), 341, Skafte Jensen (n. 1), 167–71, Stanley (n. 1), 401 n. 32.

[21] E. S. Sherratt, 'Reading the Texts: Archaeology and the Homeric Question', in C. Emlyn-Jones, L. Hardwick, and J. Purkis (edd.), *Homer: Readings and Images* (London, 1992), 145–65 offers an 'evolutionary' version of Morris's thesis, accommodating his position that the poetic tradition served the needs of the present, but hypothesizing three distinct stages at which rapid social change precipitated a need to press the epic tradition into the service of contemporary ideology and arguing for 'stratigraphy' in the preservation of traces of these stages in the development of the epic *Kunstsprache*. Cf. C. G. Thomas, 'The Homeric Epics: Strata or a Spectrum?', *Colby Quarterly* 29 (1993), 273–82, C. M. Antonaccio, 'Lefkandi and Homer', in Andersen and Dickie (n. 16), 6, 20. But the process of recombination, reconstitution, and modification of traditional elements that is oral composition suggests that genuine fossilized survivals, i.e. ancient artefacts preserved in early linguistic forms (e.g. ξίφος ἀργυρόηλον: see Kirk, *Il. Comm.* 1. 118 on 2.45), will be few and far between. How Sherratt's theory might explain the survival of elements of non-material culture is even more difficult to imagine.

cultural presuppositions can leave untouched earlier features which remain comprehensible either in contemporary terms or in terms of an audience's understanding of its own past.[22] Such features, however, are likely to be few and isolated, and their existence would not greatly affect the essential point that it is to the needs and demands of its contemporary audiences that the *Iliad* responds.[23]

Burkert's concern in Chapter 2 is with the reception of the Homeric poems among later audiences; his specific thesis involves the hypothesis of competition to be regarded as inheritors of the narrative traditions of heroic epic between the creative choral lyric (or citharody) of Stesichorus and the hexameter poetry of the Chian rhapsodes who called themselves Homeridae—Stesichorus' poems incorporate epic themes, situations, and even language into a new kind of performance, while the Homeridae both affirm the classic status of the works of their 'ancestor' and use that status to enhance the prestige of their own productions. At the same time, Burkert's study constitutes a more general survey of the sixth-century reception of the Homeric poems and of the processes by which they achieved their classic status.

These processes may be traced in both art and literature. Though considerable problems, inherent in the relation between artistic and literary representations of myth, limit the extent to which artistic evidence may be used to trace the influence of the Homeric poems,[24] the earliest mythical representations in Greek art show that, from the earliest examples in the late eighth century until around the last quarter of the sixth, Iliadic and Odyssean scenes are comparatively rare, and that plausible candidates for consideration as depictions of

---

[22] K. Raaflaub has proposed that there will be a 'time-lag' in the tradition's adaptation to contemporary realities, and thus an overlap of old and new which an audience will accommodate in terms of its genuine folk-memory of events of up to three generations past; see 'Homer to Solon', in M. H. Hansen (ed.), *The Ancient Greek City-State* (Copenhagen, 1993), 45; *Comp.* 628; and 'A Historian's Headache: How to Read "Homeric Society"?' in N. Fisher and H. van Wees (edd.), *Archaic Greece* (London, 1998), 163–93; cf. W. Donlan, 'Political Reciprocity in Dark Age Greece', in C. Gill, N. Postlethwaite, and R. Seaford (edd.) *Reciprocity in Ancient Greece* (Oxford, 1998), 53. But I doubt very much (for the reasons Morris advances) whether the world of the poems as a whole, as opposed to particular aspects of it, should derive from the contemporary audience's cultural memory.

[23] See below, Section II.

[24] See A. M. Snodgrass, *Homer and the Artists* (Cambridge, 1998); cf. id., *Comp.* 560–82; also S. Lowenstam, 'The Uses of Vase-Depictions in Homeric Studies', *TAPA* 122 (1992), 165–98; id., 'Talking Vases: The Relationship between the Homeric Poems and Archaic Representations of Epic Myth', *TAPA* 127 (1997), 21–76.

the *Iliad* or the *Odyssey* are rarer still. At this period, artists are more likely to depict non-Trojan than Trojan myth, more likely to choose episodes treated elsewhere in the Trojan Cycle than scenes from the *Iliad* or the *Odyssey*, and just as likely to diverge from as to agree with the Homeric poems in the detail of scenes that do occur in the *Iliad* or the *Odyssey*. This shows us that the versions of events portrayed in our *Iliad* and *Odyssey* did not become canonical in the eyes of artists until (at least) the later sixth century. This has been variously explained: as a function of earlier artists' reliance on traditions and conventions independent of Homeric poetry or as a reflection of the as yet limited cultural authority exercised by monumental Homeric epics composed at an earlier date.[25] That it does not testify to late sixth-century artists' use of epic poems newly constituted, by virtue of their adoption as texts for performance at the Athenian Panathenaia, in the form in which we have them[26] is suggested by the literary evidence. For it is at precisely the point at which vase-painters begin to follow the Homeric poems more closely in their depiction of heroic scenes that we find a proliferation, in Simonides (born 556, died *c*.467), Xenophanes (? *floruit c*.540), and Heraclitus (*floruit c*.500), of indications of the status of Homer and Hesiod as seminal figures in Greek culture.[27] To this period, too, dates the first recorded work of Homeric scholarship, by Theagenes of Rhegium.[28] The incorporation of the *Iliad* and the *Odyssey* into Panathenaic performance, then, may have enhanced their prestige,[29] but it cannot be the cause of the enormous cultural authority to which the literary evidence attests; rather, it must itself have been motivated by a sense of the poems' existing prestige.

In earlier poetry, however, traces of the influence of Homer, or more specifically the *Iliad* and the *Odyssey*, are both scarce and

[25] The former explanation is favoured by Snodgrass (n. 24), the latter by Lowenstam in his 1997 article (n. 24). Cf. M. L. West, 'The Invention of Homer', *CQ* 49 (1999), 364–82.   [26] So Skafte Jensen (n. 1), 106, Stanley (n. 1), 267.

[27] Simonides: fr. 11. 15–18, frr. 19–20 West; cf. T 47k Campbell; Xenophanes: B 10–12 DK; Heraclitus: A 22, B 42, B 56 DK. Cf. West (n. 25), 376–9. Sim. 564 *PMG* (with its reference to Homer and Stesichorus as authors of poems on the funeral games of Pelias) is a reminder that 'Homer' in such contexts is not restricted to the *Il*. and the *Od*.

[28] On Theagenes, see R. Pfeiffer, *A History of Classical Scholarship from the Beginnings to the End of the Hellenistic Age* (Oxford, 1968), 10; N. J. Richardson, 'Aristotle's Reading of Homer and its Background', in R. Lamberton and J. J. Keaney (edd.), *Homer's Ancient Readers* (Princeton, 1992), 31 = *Il. Comm*. VI. 27.

[29] And it certainly represents a crucial stage in the transmission of their texts: see Janko, *Il. Comm*. IV. 29–37.

uncertain. Many of the alleged Homeric 'allusions' or 'quotations' in archaic poets are to be regarded instead as the exploitation of common poetic language and *topoi*.[30] A case for specific knowledge of the plot of the *Iliad* can, however, be made for Alcaeus fragment 44 L-P, which (lines 6–8) not only summarizes the events of the latter part of *Iliad* I (Achilles' appeal to his mother, her supplication of Zeus), but explicitly presents this as part of the story of Achilles' *mēnis* (wrath). For M. L. West, this fragment 'clearly presupposes the *Iliad*' and 'implies the whole framework of the epic'.[31] The conventional dating of Alcaeus would place this 'allusion' around 600 BC or not long thereafter; but the (reasonable) assumption that the fragment exhibits knowledge of our *Iliad* is open to the sceptical objection that all it demonstrates is knowledge of a 'wrath of Achilles' narrative which may originally have been an independent epic theme.[32]

The knowledge of the Homeric texts that Burkert attributes to Stesichorus (active in the first half of the sixth century) is also vulnerable to scepticism. Burkert's statement that Stesichorus fragment 209 *PMGF* 'reproduces almost word for word a crucial scene in the *Odyssey*' is a slight exaggeration; the fragment clearly stems from a version of the scene of Telemachus' departure from Sparta in *Odyssey* 15. 43–184, but the verbal similarities are limited to the occurrence of $\theta\epsilon\hat{\iota}o\nu$ $\tau\acute{\epsilon}\rho\alpha\varsigma$ ('divine portent', col. I. I; cf. *Odyssey* 15. 168, $\tau\acute{o}\delta$' $\acute{\epsilon}\phi\eta\nu\epsilon$ $\theta\epsilon\grave{o}\varsigma$ $\tau\acute{\epsilon}\rho\alpha\varsigma$, 'the god revealed this portent') and $o\grave{\upsilon}\delta$' $\grave{\epsilon}\gamma\acute{\omega}\nu$ σ' $\grave{\epsilon}\rho\acute{\upsilon}\xi\omega$ ('nor shall I detain you', col. I.10, cf. *Odyssey* 15. 68 $o\check{\upsilon}$ $\tau\acute{\iota}$ σ' $\grave{\epsilon}\gamma\acute{\omega}$ . . . $\grave{\epsilon}\rho\acute{\upsilon}\xi\omega$); yet these verbal parallels combine with similarities of detail as well as situation (in both Telemachus receives a silver bowl with a gold rim, col. II. I–2, *Odyssey* 15. 115–16) to make creative adaptation of a specific Homeric passage a plausible hypothesis.[33] But this is as good as it gets: the other Stesichorean candidates for consideration as references to our *Iliad*, the fragments of the *Geryoneis* discussed by Burkert, cannot bear so much weight. In one (fragment S 13) the monster Geryon's mother, Callirhoe, bares

---

[30] See R. L. Fowler, *The Nature of Early Greek Lyric* (Toronto, 1987), 20–52. Callinus 6 West (see Burkert, this vol., Ch. 2 n. 15) is dubious evidence: the attribution to Callinus depends on an emendation (in Pausanias 9. 9. 5), and we have only Pausanias' report of his source's opinion (that Homer composed the *Thebais*), not the source's *ipsissima verba*.   [31] (n. 19), 206–7.

[32] Skafte Jensen (n. I), 102–3.

[33] Against which the differences in detail (the order of events, the provenance of the bowl) noted by Skafte Jensen (n. I), 105, would be no obstacle.

her breast in an appeal to her son not to face death in combat, as does Hecuba to Hector in *Iliad* 22 (83); but in her description of herself as 'miserable in motherhood' (*alastotokos*, 2–3) she also calls to mind Thetis' striking epithet *dusaristotokeia* ('miserable mother of an outstanding son', *Iliad* 18. 54), which suggests that Stesichorus' poem bears a relationship to epic presentations of the 'hero and his mother' theme which is not simply that of copy to model. The use of the breast in maternal supplication, in any case, cannot be tied to one specific situation, and the form of words used ('If ever I presented my breast to you . . .') employs a standard formula of prayer liable to be used in any such situation. In the other passage (S 11. 8–24) Geryon does, as Burkert says, employ 'the syllogism of practical heroism' famous from Sarpedon's speech to Glaucus in *Iliad* 12 (322–8), that it is the fact of mortality which makes heroic achievement necessary and meaningful, but the appearance of similar reasoning in contexts where a Homeric flavour is (at least) not prominent suggests that it, too, is to be regarded as a *topos*.[34] If we accept (as I think we should) that a text of the Homeric poems predated the activity of Stesichorus, and if we further accept, as well we might, that fragment 209 shows Stesichorean knowledge of a specific passage of the *Odyssey*, then it is by no means impossible that S 11 and S 13 should exhibit an intertextual relation with our Homeric poems; the point is simply that such a conclusion does not impose itself on the basis of the texts of the fragments themselves.

Simonides quotes *Iliad* 2. 146 as the second line of fragment 19 West and attributes it to the 'Chian man'.[35] The use of this designation to identify Homer recalls the reference to the blind man of Chios in the conclusion to the Delian part of the *Homeric Hymn to Apollo* (165–78) which forms such an important part of Burkert's thesis. Both Burkert and Janko agree that this formulation is intended to place the performance of the hymn in the tradition of Homeric poetry, and both take the passage as evidence for the Chian Homerids' claim to custodianship of the Homeric legacy; both,

---

[34] See Alcaeus fr. 38A L–P, a drinking song which uses the example of Sisyphus to underline the message that our mortal condition requires that we enjoy life while we can; cf. Pindar, *Ol.* 1. 81–5, where Pelops is made to base the drive for glory on the inevitability of death.

[35] On the attribution (to Simonides, not Semonides), see M. L. West, *Studies in Greek Elegy and Iambus* (Berlin, 1974), 179–80, H. Lloyd-Jones, *Females of the Species* (London, 1975), 96–7.

moreover, would date the composite Delian–Pythian Hymn specifically to the Samian tyrant Polykrates' Pythian-and-Delian festival of
523 or 522 BC.[36] Burkert, however, relates the reference to the blind
man to the performance of the composite hymn—a Chian rhapsode
in 522 BC adverts to the classic status of his supposed ancestor and
places his own song, in contradistinction to the lyric performance of
a chorus of maidens, in the same tradition. Such a reference to a
classic Homer would not be unparalleled or surprising at such a date.
Janko, on the other hand, dates the Delian hymn, to which the
sphragis (seal) of 165–78 belongs, to a much earlier period on linguistic grounds, in which case the Chian Homerids' assimilation of
their own activity to that of their classic ancestor could be traced
back as far as the mid-seventh century. If that is so, it would be a very
isolated early acknowledgement of Homeric authority; for that
reason, some might be inclined, despite the evidence of Janko's sta-
tistics, to prefer Burkert's dating.

  In the context of the reception of the *Iliad* in other works of poetry,
special consideration must be given to the relation between the *Iliad*
and the *Odyssey*, as discussed here by Rutherford (Chapter 3). As he
is careful to point out, the question of the relation between two
products of a rich and long-lived oral tradition is a complex one, in
which easy assumptions of allusion or imitation are precluded by
the use and re-use in all such poems of traditional language, themes,
and story patterns. The presence of references to other stories or the
adoption of motifs which may have been taken from other stories
does not prove a debt to a pre-existing fixed text. But although
a sceptic could argue along these lines against every one of
Rutherford's alleged Odyssean responses to the *Iliad*, it is surely very
unlikely that the *Odyssey* does not exhibit awareness of the other
poem. Janko's relative dating makes the *Iliad* the older of the two (a
supposition shared by most), and if this is accepted it makes it very
likely that the monumental *Iliad* is the model for a monumental
Odyssey which appears to adapt and extend some of its compositional
principles. It is a well-known fact, enshrined in 'Monro's Law',[37] that
the *Odyssey* does not refer to any event which actually occurs in the

---

[36] See Burkert, this vol., Ch. 2, and in G. W. Bowersock, W. Burkert, and
M. C. J. Putnam (edd.), *Arktouros* (Berlin and New York, 1979), 53–62; Janko (n. 4),
112–15, 258–62; West (n. 25), 368–72.
[37] D. B. Monro, *Homer: Odyssey* vol. II (Oxford, 1901), 325.

Iliad; but given that both poems show considerable knowledge of a multiplicity of episodes from other epic traditions, this is more likely to be deliberate avoidance than ignorance, and, as Rutherford shows, the *Odyssey* seems in practice to accommodate the *Iliad* by working round it, yet bringing the audience up to date with the fates of its major characters. But though the *Odyssey* never refers to an event narrated in the *Iliad*, it does refer to events which are foreshadowed in that poem. It is, for example, Achilles' wish in the *Iliad* that his bones should be interred together with those of Patroclus (*Iliad* 23. 91–2, 243–4); the *Odyssey* takes the trouble to confirm that this wish was fulfilled (*Odyssey* 24. 76–9),[38] and *Odyssey* 24 in general refers back to the death of Achilles in a way that is fully in keeping with the foreshadowings of that event in the *Iliad*.[39] The composer of *Odyssey* 24 seems to have known our *Iliad* or something very like it; many, however, would argue that that book is a late addition to the poem.[40]

The Trojan Cycle looms far larger in the *Odyssey* than any other epic tradition, and it is a notable feature of the poem's artistic self-consciousness that its fixation on the Trojan War is a fixation on that event as a subject of song.[41] But this is (at least in part) a natural consequence of the *Odyssey*'s own position as one of the *Nostoi* which bring the Trojan saga to its close; and, of course, the *Iliad* was not the only poem about the Trojan War. This observation somewhat undercuts Rutherford's argument that the third song of Demodocus (*Odyssey* 8. 499–520), which 'describes the sack of Troy, so often foreshadowed in the later parts of the *Iliad*', presupposes knowledge of the latter poem, for the sack of Troy was itself the subject of the *Iliupersis*, oral versions of which no doubt predate both our *Iliad* and our *Odyssey*. Rutherford can, however, point to Demodocus' first song, *Odyssey* 8. 72–82, which, in linking a quarrel of 'the best of the Achaeans' with the 'plan of Zeus' in a manner which clearly hints at

---

[38] See Janko, *Il. Comm.* IV. 314; K. Usener, *Beobachtungen zum Verhältnis der Odyssee zur Ilias* (Tübingen, 1990), 105, 108.   [39] See Usener (n. 38), 104–8.

[40] For discussion and references see Heubeck, *Od. Comm.* VI on 23. 297, R. Rutherford, *Homer* (G&R New Surveys in the Classics 26, Oxford, 1996), 74–7, 81 n. 69.

[41] Thus not only the bards, Phemius and Demodocus, but also the Sirens sing of Troy: 1. 325–7, 8. 72–82, 499–520, 12. 189–90. On the close association between 'song' and 'Troy' in the *Od.*'s depiction of bards, cf. (e.g.) W. Marg, *Homer über die Dichtung* (Münster, 1957), 13–14; S. Goldhill, *The Poet's Voice* (Cambridge, 1991), 93–108; M. Finkelberg, *The Birth of Literary Fiction in Ancient Greece* (Oxford, 1998), 74, 142.

more than is said, may well suggest knowledge of the (or at least an) *Iliad*.[42]

II. SELF, SOCIETY, AND THE GODS

As we have seen, the question of where to locate the world of the poem is distinct from that of the poem's date. The *Iliad* is a poem of the past; but as the product of an oral tradition, the circumstances of its development mean that until it was recorded in writing it was much more responsive to the demands of its audience than any written production; it is reasonable to assume (with Morris) that in an oral tradition details which seem arcane or unintelligible to the audience will be filtered out, and that even though the poem offers no simple window to the world of any one historical period, nevertheless its social, political, and ethical concerns will be translatable into the terms of contemporary debate. Archaeological and linguistic evidence suggests that in the case of the *Iliad* this process of adaptation to the contemporary cultural environment came to an end in the early Archaic period. The world of its audience, then, is not that of the Classical *polis*, but nor is it that of the Dark Age, much less of some primitive pre-*polis* past. It is to the imagination of such an audience that the politics, ethics, psychology, and religion of the Homeric poems must make their appeal.

The work of M. I. Finley created an influential image of the Homeric world as a remote, *sui generis*, but none the less historical society.[43] In response, A. M. Snodgrass denied the historicity of Homeric society by emphasizing real or apparent contradictions in the poems' representation of material culture and social forms.[44] Such attempts to establish the uniqueness, strangeness, or ahistoricity of Homeric society have supported primitivist models which trace the development of the social, political, and ethical model of the Classical

---

[42] NB how this almost seems to be cued by *Il.* 19. 63–4—the quarrel will live in the oral tradition. On this case, see W. Marg, 'Das erste Lied des Demodokos', in *Navicula Chilonensis* (FS Jacoby, Leiden, 1956), 16–29; cf. O. Taplin, 'The Earliest Quotation of the *Iliad*?', in E. M. Craik (ed.), '*Owls to Athens*' (Oxford, 1990), 109–12, Goldhill (n. 41), 95–6, and Finkelberg (n. 41), 146–7; the allusion to the quarrel of the *Il.* is denied (*a priori*) by G. Nagy, *The Best of the Achaeans* (Baltimore 1979; revised 1999), 23–4, 42–3.   [43] Finley (n. 17).

[44] 'An Historical Homeric Society?' *JHS* 94 (1974), 114–25; for discussion, see K. Raaflaub in Fisher and Van Wees (n. 22), 174–7.

city-state from its antithesis in the Homeric poems. The primitivist–developmental approach can, however, also be detected in the search for the immature shoots of entire facets of western civilization—the concept of the individual, the notion of responsibility—in its supposed seedbed culture of early Greece. There are many objections to the cultural-determinist assumptions of this approach; but to refute it in detail, we need to discover what sort of results are yielded by an examination of the poems themselves which eschews the radical us/them antithesis and the *a priori* developmental assumptions of earlier interpreters.

A proper assessment of the psychology of Homer's characters is a necessity both for an understanding of the *Iliad*'s ethical and political background and for an appreciation of the extent to which we can expect a role for individual characterization and personal motivation in its narrative. Students coming to the topic for the first time may be surprised to discover that phenomena we take for granted as constitutive of individuality, such as a notion of one's self as a cause of action, even the notion of one's body as an organic unity, have been denied Homeric man. Focusing on the accounts of Homeric man's inability to reach a 'real' decision given by Christian Voigt and Bruno Snell, Richard Gaskin (Chapter 4) shows (on the one hand) that Homer's characters have all they need to make and to conceptualize decisions in the same way as we do (i.e. as responses to the relative desirability of the available options), and (on the other) that it is the Snellian rather than the Homeric notion of 'decision' that requires explanation.[45] The importance of this is not that Snell's approach has been widely accepted—he has had his followers, but most scholars have been content to dismiss his theories as extreme and counter-intuitive.[46] But together with this dismissal have gone both a feeling that there is indeed *something* primitive about Homeric

[45] Snell and Voigt demanded that a decision express the agent's self-consciousness of his ability to choose, and denied that status to choices reached on the basis of considerations of the advantageousness, attractiveness, or conventionality of the options; see Gaskin, Ch. 4 nn. 2–3, 20–4.

[46] Snell's claim that Homeric man possessed no concept of the body as such has recently been endorsed by P. du Bois, 'Archaic Bodies-in-Pieces', in N. B. Kampen (ed.), *Sexuality in Ancient Art* (Cambridge, 1996), 60; cf. Vernant (this vol., p. 326); for a pithy refutation see B. Williams, *Shame and Necessity* (Berkeley and Los Angeles, 1993), 23–5. Snell's doctrines on the lack of unity of both mind and body in Homer receive wholesale endorsement from H. Erbse, 'Zur Motivation des Handelns bei Homer', *Perspektiven der Philosophie* 10 (1984), 207–28; their influence may be traced in the recent and stimulating work of Finkelberg (n. 41), 34–61, 63–5. For

man's sense of self and an unwillingness to debate the intellectual
underpinnings of Snell's thesis. Thus more of the Snellian view survives even in his opponents than they might admit. Gaskin therefore
performs a service in demonstrating both that there is nothing
especially primitive or unfamiliar in Homeric decision-making and
that the Snellian approach rests on a model of the development of
notions of selfhood and responsibility towards a specific modern
philosophical position which esteems the autonomy of an uncondi-
tioned will above all else;[47] thus one must do more than point out,
against Snell, that Homeric characters do manifestly have a sense of
themselves and each other as responsible individuals or that they
clearly do make 'decisions' in the light of the available alternatives,
because neither the sort of 'autonomy' or 'selfhood' nor the notion of
'decision' identified by these objections would satisfy Snell's criteria;
only when we understand Snell's views in their intellectual context
can we recognize that they rest on presuppositions that most of us do
not share.

    Although it is necessary to establish the existence of a concept of
individuality in Homer which allows the modern reader to conceive
of Homeric characters in the sort of basic human terms without
which interpretation could barely get off the ground, consideration of
the psychology and ethics of the *Iliad*, and their embodiment in the
poem's social and political norms, must not stop there: the Homeric
concepts of selfhood, personality, responsibility, and obligation (and,
many would now argue, their modern counterparts too) must be
specified with reference to their embeddedness in real social relationships and institutions, rather than merely by consideration of the
subjectivity of individuals and the language in which it is expressed.
Paradoxically, perhaps, the first relationship to be considered in this
connection, that between man and god, is one which we might
describe as a metaphysical as well as a social one. In its original form,

discussion and refutation, see T. Jahn, *Zum Wortfeld 'Seele-Geist' in der Sprache Homers*
(Munich, 1987), 172–9; A. Schmitt, *Selbständigkeit und Abhängigkeit menschlichen
Handelns bei Homer*, Abh. Mainz 1990.5, 21–71 and *passim*; H. Pelliccia, *Mind, Body,
and Speech in Homer and Pindar* (Göttingen, 1995), 15–27, 214, and *passim*; M. Clarke,
Flesh and Spirit in the Songs of Homer (Oxford, 1999), 115–19.

[47] Gaskin retains a greater emphasis on 'autonomy' and 'self-consciousness' than
would be acceptable to the more thoroughgoing anti-Kantianism of C. Gill, *Personality in Greek Epic, Tragedy, and Philosophy* (Oxford, 1996), but it is clear that he sees
these notions as rooted in the agent's response to the conditions of everyday life,
rather than as components of an attitude of radical detachment from such conditions.

Lesky's piece (Chapter 5) started from the views of Snell regarding the autonomy of Homeric characters,[48] for as well as believing that Homeric man's freedom to act was limited by his lack of a clear view of what was in his power, Snell also saw the intervention of the Homeric gods in human affairs as a considerable limitation on humans' sense of their ability to initiate and answer for their actions.

Part of the utility of Lesky's discussion lies in its demonstration that divine influence on human action and decision takes many forms. In a number of cases, divine influence is no less readily explicable than human, as when a god offers advice, draws attention to a useful or attractive option which the character may not have considered, or gives reasons why the human interlocutor should be persuaded; though divine power and authority far exceed human, divine influence in such situations does not differ in kind from that which a mortal might exercise. Similarly, it is clearly very unwise to attempt to resist divine coercion, but in fact characters do attempt to do so, and thus demonstrate that the exercise of divine power in such circumstances is comparable to human attempts at coercion.

Lesky's taxonomy of forms of divine–human interaction represents a scale from cases in which the contribution of human and divine motives can be easily distinguished and separated to others in which he feels that divine and human factors coexist in an unreflective, pre-theoretical combination of causes, each of which is sufficient in itself to bring about the particular result. This is the point on which his argument has recently been criticized by Arbogast Schmitt.[49] Schmitt argues that Lesky is wrong to seek human autonomy only where divine influence is entirely lacking, and claims that he ends up corroborating Snell's thesis with his acceptance that, since divine and human factors can each constitute sufficient causes of one and the same act, Homer and his characters lack a clear distinction between 'I' and 'not-I', of what is and is not in the individual's power. Lesky's position is, on this view, incoherent, since it entails that Homeric man should be both aware and unaware that he is the source of his acts. The truth, according to Schmitt, is not that Homeric man has no very clear idea of what is and is not up to us, but that he draws the distinction differently, not at the point at which

---

[48] I have abridged Lesky's article in this regard, both to avoid overlap with Gaskin's and because Lesky's discussion of Snell has been superseded by later treatments.   [49] Schmitt (n. 46), 36–52, 72–114.

'inner' and 'outer' diverge, but within what post-Cartesian thought
would regard as the 'inner self' of the individual. The power or
influence of a god is always separable from a human being's sus-
ceptibility to it, and the combination of these two factors in causation
is a genuine partnership of complementary but distinct aspects; thus
Pandarus, the vehicle of Zeus' and Athena's plan to break the truce in
Iliad 4, is specifically sought out as an appropriate character for such
an enterprise; he is tempted, not compelled to shoot his arrow at
Menelaus; he is 'foolish' (4. 104). Equally, Agamemnon is just the
type to be deceived by false dreams and deluded by Ate; in these
cases, according to Schmitt, the divine, external force provides a great
deal in the way of motivation, but always focuses on aspects of the
individual acted upon for which that individual bears responsibility.

   Both Schmitt and Lesky acknowledge cases in which human and
divine factors combine in motivating an action, and both (incidentally) recognize that Homeric and modern thought alike identify
aspects of choice which seem not to be subject to the authority of
the individual. They differ only in respect of Schmitt's claim that
human and divine factors are separable in all cases. This is clearly
possible: when both Achilles (*Iliad* 9. 629) and the gods (636) are
said to put a savage *thumos* in Achilles' breast one could argue
that this presupposes Schmitt's distinction between external
impulse and individual response—the gods work with the character of Achilles as it already exists and Achilles endorses and
appropriates the feelings which result from the divine impulse. But
the text does not say this, and it is not clear that the position
should be rationalized in this way.

   More generally, it may be a mistake to follow the approach of
either Lesky or Schmitt too closely. Each takes the Homeric poems as
raw data in a psycho-historical enquiry, and considers all relevant
passages to be equally good evidence for implicit psychological and
theological attitudes. The problem with such an approach is that it
takes too little account (*a*) of the rhetorical strategies used by the
characters themselves in describing human–divine interaction and
(*b*) of the artistic practices of the poet in presenting such interaction.
The significance of the first point emerges when we examine Lesky's
and Schmitt's accounts of cases in which a given action or state
of affairs is attributed now to a human, now to a god, now to both.
In *Iliad* 3, for example, Priam tells Helen that he regards the gods,
not Helen herself, as responsible for the woes which followed her

abduction, but she is clearly not reassured, and blames herself, while in Book 6 similar self-reproach on her part is coupled with a reference to divine will.[50] Similarly, Agamemnon is reproached for his conduct in seizing Achilles' prize, and frequently accepts the legitimacy of others' criticism;[51] yet in Book 19 he describes himself as 'not responsible' and offers an elaborate paradigm to illustrate the vulnerability of all, even Zeus himself, to the divine force of Ate.[52] For Lesky, these cases illustrate stress in various degrees and at different times on what are in fact 'two sides of the same coin', an action caused by both human and divine factors; while Schmitt, too, believes that the passages are to be taken together to yield an overall picture in which divine and human contribute in different ways, so that he can argue that where only one factor is mentioned, the other is presupposed.[53] But the situation is more complicated than either of these approaches would suggest.

When Priam refers to the role of the gods in Helen's leaving of Menelaus he is neither presenting the action in one of two possible ways nor stressing only one of two motivating factors, for he says explicitly that he holds the gods *and not Helen herself* responsible for what has occurred. We cannot simply combine this explanation with Helen's indications of her own sense of responsibility and say that the true picture is that offered by Helen herself in Book 6 (344–58), that both divine and human factors are somehow involved, because Priam's choice of words specifically excludes such a manoeuvre. This formulation is surely not to be attributed to Priam's heterodox theology, but to the rhetorical function of his speech as a representation of his fondness for Helen (and as a foil for her own contrasting evaluation). Priam's words indicate that ascriptions of responsibility to gods or humans are at the mercy of the speaker's intention in context: even if we decide that the Homeric orthodoxy is indeed a combination of divine and human motivation, we cannot explain away Priam's words as referring only to a part of the whole.

The situation with regard to Agamemnon's culpability and his appeal to Ate is yet more complex. On the one hand, there is plenty of evidence that Agamemnon is held responsible for insulting Achilles;

---

[50] 3. 164–5, 172–80, 6. 344–58.
[51] See 1. 286, 2. 239–40, 375–8, 9. 104–11, 114–20, 13. 107–15, 14. 49–51, 19. 85–6, 181–3.   [52] 19. 86–138.   [53] Schmitt (n. 46), 109.

on the other, there is his own statement that he is not responsible
because he was deluded by Ate. There are also evaluations of his
conduct which combine the two factors. Once again, however, we
cannot simply treat these passages indiscriminately as evidence.
Agamemnon himself, in his 'Apology' of Book 19, intends his
explanation in terms of Ate to exculpate (the Achaeans reproach
him, but he is not responsible, 85–6): the intention of this utterance is
not to emphasize one of two aspects of causation—Agamemnon
wishes as far as possible to deny his own responsibility. None the less,
he sees himself as liable to make reparation (137–8), and this may be
felt to support a contention that the two elements, divine and human
responsibility, are indeed present, even though Agamemnon seeks to
play down the latter. Or one might prefer to take the Adkinsian line
that the episode illustrates the importance in Homeric society of strict
liability, regardless of intention, rather than 'moral responsibility'.[54]
But all this is to read the passage as an objective statement of psycho-
theological orthodoxy,[55] when it is clear that the issue of blame and
responsibility in Agamemnon's speech is subject to a considerable
degree of rhetorical manipulation conditioned by his sense of what
would be politically expedient in this important public context. This
is not Agamemnon's only reference to his *atē*: in Book 9 (115–20) he
accepts not only that he was deluded by *atē*, but also that this renders him a legitimate object of reproach, that he was at fault, and
that he is required to offer reparation to Achilles. These remarks are a
response to Nestor, who has pointed out that Agamemnon ignored
sound advice in taking Briseis from Achilles, and yielded instead to
his 'great-hearted *thumos*' (106–11); in accepting this diagnosis,
Agamemnon recognizes a reference to his *atai* (115), and admits that
he was indeed deluded (ἀασάμην, 116), because he relied on his
'wretched *phrenes*' (119); 'nor', he adds, 'do I deny it' (116); but why
would one deny being deluded by *atē* if this mitigated one's responsibility and exempted one from blame (Agamemnon's claim in Book

---

[54] See A. W. H. Adkins, *Merit and Responsibility* (Oxford, 1960), 51–2; M. Gagarin.
Aeschylean Drama (Berkeley, 1976), 6–11; Erbse (n. 46), 211–13. Erbse (212) contends
that Ag.'s explanation must be taken at face value, because no character disputes it in
the immediate context: this is not true, for Odysseus' warning (at 181–2) that Ag.
should be 'more just in future' is a claim that he was unjust, a legitimate object of
censure, in his dealings with Achilles; and there is no point in warning someone to
behave well in future if it is not in his power to do so.

[55] As does Finkelberg (n. 41), 65.

19)? In Book 9 Agamemnon's *atē* is precisely the point on which blame should focus,[56] while in 19 he is quite explicit that the Achaeans' blame is misplaced—he is not *aitios*, because he was deluded (85–6). The contribution of divine influence to human motivation and its effect of human culpability is not a settled issue, but subject to manipulation to suit the purposes of the speaker and the demands of the context ('private' in Book 9, 'public' in Book 19; Agamemnon is demoralized in 9, trying to re-establish his credibility in 19; and so on).[57] To be sure, the audience is firmly encouraged to judge Agamemnon's apology in the light of previous evaluations of his conduct, and to conclude that his attempt to save face is a failure, but still it does the passage scant justice to treat it merely as one piece of evidence among many.

As well as the aims of the characters in presenting their own and others' actions in a certain way, we also have to reckon with the artistic purposes of the poet. The presentation of divine intervention in the *Iliad* is inevitably affected by the stance of poetic omniscience, which means that the narrator can identify divine influence in ways in which no real human being could,[58] as well as by one of the fundamental premisses of the *Iliad*, that the action takes place in an age, long before and far superior to the present, when men and gods rubbed shoulders. Many of the forms of divine intervention in the poem would be unavailable as explanatory devices to its audience, which accepted that things just did not happen like that in their world. But it is to the world of the audience that the normative ethical, psychological, and theological categories of the poem must appeal; and thus the representation of a world in which the actions of gods and their influence on events can be securely identified is bound to create a degree of dissonance with the everyday assumptions of a real world in which divine interference, even if suspected, is never certain and rarely accepted as an excuse. It is far from certain that either the poet or his audiences would have reached any very clear or settled conclusion about how the representation of divine

[56] Cf. Achilles at 1. 411–12; also Achilles' bitter complaint at 367–77, which attributes Agamemnon's offence to *hubris* and *anaideiē*, and concludes contemptuously with the observation that Zeus deprived him of his wits; this is vituperation, not exculpation, and yet Agamemnon himself can conclude his 'Apology' with an almost identical reference to Zeus at 19. 137.

[57] For the importance of such considerations in Homeric characters' representations of their motivation, cf. Pelliccia (n. 46), 259–60.

[58] See M. M. Willcock, 'Some Aspects of the Gods in the *Iliad*', *BICS* 17 (1970), 1–10.

influence in narrative or in speech should be reconciled with the audience's everyday practice of holding individuals responsible for their actions.

Any 'theory' of divine–human interaction held by poet or audience is likely to have been vague and shifting; when embedded in the imaginative world of heroic fantasy and subjected to the rhetorical manipulations of individually drawn characters, each with their own agenda, it must have become vaguer still. In the end, whatever view we take of the coexistence of human and divine motivation in Homer, any sensible explanation will have to account for the fact that Homer's characters act consistently on the basis that they and others are legitimately held accountable for their actions. Whether they *should* act on this basis, given other beliefs which surface from time to time in the text, may be another matter, but the gulf between the pragmatic view that individuals are responsible for their acts and any watertight theoretical justification for such a view is, we must recognize, a feature of our own thinking about responsibility. Our own 'theories' in this matter are also highly malleable in practice, and we are all very familiar with the ways in which partiality or self-deception can alter one's representations of culpability. As Williams has shown,[59] as far as responsibility is concerned, Homeric man lives in a world which is configured in the same fundamental terms as our own. Factors other than the commands of our rational selves, both external and internal, influence our choices and our actions. When a Homeric character succumbs to a divinely inspired impulse such as *atē* there is a sense in which his experience is comparable to our own when we regard ourselves as subject to motives which we somehow feel are unauthorized by or distanced from our better judgement.[60] Any attempt to label these factors is liable to be metaphorical and personificatory; the Homeric gods which intervene in human choices and the various 'psychic organs' which engage Homer's characters in internal dialogue are personificatory constructs in the same way as are the ego, the superego, and the id, the conscious and the unconscious, or the rational and the non-rational self.[61]

[59] (n. 46), 21–40, 46–9, 50–6.

[60] On such 'self-distancing', see R. W. Sharples, '"But why has my spirit spoken with me thus?" Homeric Decision-making', *G&R* 30 (1983), 3; Pelliccia (n. 46), 206–11, 228–9, 236–7, 259–60; Gill (n. 47), 187–9, 200.

[61] (Quasi-)personification, and in particular metaphors of internal dialogue, are not only virtually indispensable in the description of mental activity, but may actually capture something of significance about that activity. A popular modern work on the

In holding their fellows responsible for their actions, Homer's characters do not simply express irritation towards those who annoy or frustrate them, but are capable of censuring those whom they believe to be deficient with regard to society's norms. Nor is this merely an incidental fact about the *Iliad*, for the notion that individual characters are subject to the evaluation of their peers is central to the concept of honour which is the driving force of Homeric values. In my chapter (Chapter 6), I attempt to demonstrate the significance of this concept of honour as the basis of ethical evaluation in Homer, arguing that the hitherto prevalent categorization of values as 'co-operative' or 'competitive' collapses in a world in which the dominant ethic is one of reciprocity and in which the motive of honour promotes both self- and other-regarding behaviour. Not only does the terminology of blame and dishonour straddle any supposed competitive *versus* co-operative distinction, but it also allows that censure of others for co-operative failure may be the reaction of the impartial as well as the complaint of the aggrieved party, and several contexts make explicit appeal to the notion that one should expect to be judged by the same standards as one employs in judging others. These are the standards which are internalized in the sense of *aidōs* (shame, respect) which protects both one's own honour and that of other members of one's group.[62] Thus the *Iliad* operates with a system of ethics which is intelligible to the modern reader as such; it is not true that its dominant values are agonistic and individualistic; the very issue of the poem is Agamemnon's breach of the communal ethic of reciprocity in initiating the quarrel with Achilles, and the issue of reparation for this offence underlies the poem's ethical structure until Achilles' anger at the dishonour he received at Agamemnon's hands is superseded by his anger at the death of Patroclus, an anger which arises from Achilles' own sense that he has failed in his obligations to a friend and which is finally assuaged

---

development of behaviour appends the following to its account of motivational conflict: 'Much of animal and human behaviour and physiology operates on the basis that considerable autonomy has seemingly been designed into each behavioural system or organ. Interaction necessarily occurs between them to prevent total breakdown when the different parts pull in different directions' (P. Bateson and P. Martin, *Design for a Life: How Behaviour Develops* (London, 1999), 97). (For a thorough investigation of what internal dialogue really amounts to in Homer, see Pelliccia (n. 46).)

[62] Cf. Williams (n. 46), 83–4.

by his recognition of the possibility of community even between enemies. The pursuit of self-interest regardless of others does not figure among the *Iliad's* ideals.[63]

Honour in the *Iliad* thus sustains the values of a society which lays great stress on equilibrium and the avoidance of unprovoked aggression, but which is peopled by heroes who are acutely sensitive to the slightest suggestion of an affront and naturally more concerned with the maintenance and enhancement of their own status than with the status of their rivals. The limitations on self-assertion inherent in the Iliadic discourse of honour are there because they are necessary. This inclusivity in the heroic code is an important theme in Schofield's study of the political character of the *Iliad* (Chapter 7). Schofield stresses the importance of rhetorical performance and excellence in counsel as sources of prestige, and demonstrates that focus on these abilities constitutes an invitation to the audience to respond evaluatively, in the light of their own political experience, to the political issues raised by the poem. Again, the quarrel between Achilles and Agamemnon is central. Not only does it arise from the conduct of an assembly, the poem's main political institution, but it also gives rise to subsequent major assemblies and parleys which deal with its consequences and (eventually) its resolution. These assemblies are the arena in which the *euboulia* (or otherwise) of the speakers is displayed.[64] There is an expectation that a good speaker will show strategic sense, as well as impress by the sheer attractiveness of his eloquence,[65] but there is also a focus on leadership qualities, including responsibility and concern for others, ability to take advice, and a concern for limit and appropriateness in one's dealings with other members of the group. Evaluated in these terms, Agamemnon fares badly; as Schofield points out, it is as a leader, not

---

[63] Cf. R. Osborne, *Greece in the Making* (London, 1996), 153: the *Il.*'s agonistic values are 'paraded to be questioned'.

[64] On the importance of rhetorical performance in the *Il.* (and its role in the individual characterization of speakers) see R. P. Martin, *The Language of Heroes* (Ithaca, NY, 1989); on the significance of assemblies (etc.), see M. Detienne, *Les Maîtres de vérité dans la Grèce archaïque* (2nd edn., Paris, 1973), 87–95. On the differentiation of speeches by character, cf. I. J. F. de Jong in *Comp.* 319, 324–5.

[65] Cf. the element of rhetorical connoisseurship (appreciated by schol. T on 3. 212) in the description of the styles of Menelaus and Odysseus at 3. 209–24, with K. J. Dover, *Lysias and the Corpus Lysiacum* (Berkeley, 1968), 176–8; cf. Martin (n. 64), 96.

as a fighter, that Agamemnon is judged and found wanting. In this he contrasts especially with Nestor and with Odysseus, both of whom voice criticism of his leadership.[66]

Nestor is particularly important in this regard, in that both his status (a function of his age and experience) and his style (his lengthy digressions, his use of incidents from his past as *exempla*) indicate authority.[67] The use of the exemplary style is one of the ways in which the epic steers the response of its audience, and it is no accident that it is most strikingly deployed at crucial points in the narrative by figures of accepted authority and status. With Nestor's interventions we should compare Phoenix's use of the Meleager paradigm in Book 9, where once again an aged, quasi-father-figure offers an extended *exemplum* in order to underscore the authority of his advice.[68] This is the kind of authority which Achilles himself assumes in Book 24, where, paradoxically, it is the younger man who deploys an extended paradigm (the example of Niobe) to console the older.[69] In the achievement of this degree of reflective authority Achilles contrasts with his vanquished opponent, Hector, who, as Schofield shows, is caught in the internal contradictions of the heroic code at the point at which the warrior values which the community inculcates for its own protection themselves become detrimental to the community, and the self-assertion which the pursuit of honour demands itself threatens dishonour.[70]

These reflections on the political aspects of the *Iliad* bring us back to the question of its appeal to its original audience. Clearly, the poem is addressed to an audience of 'political animals'. This might suggest that the Homeric poems can instruct us in the social and political ideologies of the Archaic period; and it is both true that the *Iliad* does invite such an ideological construction and likely that its original audience will have seen the poem as exemplary of current political ideals (whether or not every audience, or every member of every audience, accepted these ideals). But the hope that we can draw very

[66] Nestor: 9. 102–13, Odysseus: 14. 83–102, 19. 181–3; see O. Taplin, 'Agamemnon's Role in the *Iliad*', in C. B. R. Pelling (ed.), *Characterization and Individuality in Ancient Greek Literature* (Oxford, 1990), 60–82; Martin (n. 64), 113–19. On the leadership role of the hero, see now J. Haubold, *Homer's People: Epic Poetry and Social Formation* (Cambridge, 2000), esp. 52–68 on Ag.

[67] Cf. Martin (n. 64), 80, 101–9.

[68] See J. G. Howie, 'The *Iliad* as *Exemplum*', in Andersen and Dickie (n. 16), 152–4.

[69] See Martin (n. 64), 144–5, 201; cf. Willcock, this vol., Ch. 15, on paradigms.

[70] See above all Redfield (n. 15).

much that is specific from these conclusions is a forlorn one; for
although the *Iliad* meditates on kingship, it is by no means clear
whether it is for or against—there is an ideal kingship according to
the poem,[71] but it is an ideal which is not matched in practice by the
poem's highest office-holder, Agamemnon. Nor can we be sure that
the political institutions portrayed in the poem are identical or even
closely similar to those that its ideology might be used to support in
the real world; as Robin Osborne writes, 'Monarchical rulers too are
good to think with, even, perhaps especially, in a community that
lacks them.'[72]

III. POETICS

It is a short leap from discussion of Homeric society, ethics, and
psychology to consideration of Homeric poetics, because it is clear
not only that the *Iliad* is a work that demands ethical engagement,
socio-political reflection, and interest in character and motivation,
but also that these elements are inextricably linked: the Homeric
hero lives under the scrutiny of a community to which he owes
considerable obligations, which holds him responsible for his
achievements and his failures, and on which he depends for the
recognition he craves; his displays of prowess within this community
involve eloquence and judgement as well as military skills, and the
character of his judgement and extent of his eloquence are important
features of an individuality of style which is a major contributor to
Homeric characterization; and ultimately the hero's concerns—the
nature of his obligations to others and theirs to him, of friendship
and enmity, the limits, frustrations, and sufferings which experience
imposes on aspiration, the struggle to achieve recognition in life and
everlasting fame in death—these form the ethical fabric on which the
response of an audience rests.

Schofield's discussion of the inclusivity of the heroic code has
already raised the question of the tragedy of Hector, the character
most strikingly caught at the point where the demands of honour

[71] A significant issue in ancient responses to the poem; see O. Murray, 'Philodemus
on the Good King according to Homer', *JRS* 55 (1965), 161–82; F. Cairns, *Virgil's
Augustan Epic* (Cambridge, 1989), 10–11.

[72] Osborne (n. 63), 151. On the question of the ideology of the Homeric poems, see
Morris (this vol., Ch. 1) and his refs. (to which add A. Dalby, 'The *Iliad*, the *Odyssey*,
and their Audiences', *CQ* 45 (1995), 268–79; W. G. Thalmann, *The Swineherd and the
Bow: Representations of Class in the Odyssey* (Ithaca, NY, 1998)).

conflict, while Lesky's discussion of divine–human interaction prompts acknowledgement of the theme of human propensity to delusion. These themes are developed in Rutherford's account of the tragic 'flavour' of the *Iliad* (Chapter 8). The *Iliad*, several of the greatest tragedies of Aeschylus and Sophocles (less so Euripides), and Aristotle's theory of the tragic share a concentration on human beings' tendency to act in partial or total ignorance of the consequences of their actions, a tendency which is highlighted, both in tragedy and in Homer, by prophecies and foreshadowings and by contrast with the concept of a divine plan. The pattern of error, recognition, and reversal is, as Rutherford shows, particularly pronounced in the cases of Patroclus, Hector, and Achilles, each of whom realizes, too late, how much his conduct has cost him.[73] The fates of these characters are closely entwined: Hector's death is prophesied at the moment of Patroclus'; it both follows from it as a consequence and recalls it in the detail of its presentation; and Achilles is aware that revenge on Hector for the death of Patroclus will lead inevitably to his own demise. There is here, as Rutherford points out, an intensification of insight: we are repeatedly made aware of the imminence of Patroclus' doom, but when it comes it takes the character himself unawares; Hector, however, realizes his delusion and foresees his end, while Achilles not only sees all too clearly his own responsibility for the death of Patroclus but goes to his final confrontation with Hector in full knowledge that his own death will follow. Central to Rutherford's case is the significance of pity, the most important of the tragic emotions. The pattern of human error, ignorance, and fragility which the *Iliad* so powerfully exploits evokes 'not simply despair, but pity', for it is a condition which unites both characters and audience. Fittingly, Achilles' insight into his own condition culminates in his recognition of the community of suffering in which he and Priam participate, in spite of their enmity; as the final section of Rutherford's chapter shows, the Achilles–Priam scene in Book 24 is at once the culmination of the poem's tragic appeal to the sympathetic imagination[74] and a seminal statement of the Greek recognition that a proper sense of oneself and one's place in the world demands understanding of the humanity of others.[75]

---

[73] Especially Hector: see Redfield (n. 15), 128–59; M. Mueller, *The Iliad* (London, 1984), 36–44, 60–76.   [74] Cf. Macleod, this vol., pp. 308–10.
[75] Recent discussions of pity in the *Il.* may be found in G. Zanker, *The Heart of Achilles* (Ann Arbor, 1994); K. Crotty, *The Poetics of Supplication* (Ithaca, NY,

The importance of pity in Homeric poetics is also central to
Macleod's paper (Chapter 9), which in turn relates closely to
Rutherford's other contribution to this volume (Chapter 3) on the
relation between the *Iliad* and the *Odyssey*.[76] Macleod states his
position succinctly at the outset: 'If . . . the *Odyssey* is the same sort of
poem as the *Iliad*, and if it refashions and reconsiders the central
theme of the *Iliad*, we may expect its reflections on poetry to be
relevant to the earlier work.' It may be argued that the *Odyssey*'s self-
consciousness regarding song and suffering tells us only about the
poetics of that poem, but Macleod and Rutherford (Chapter 3) show
clearly how the *Odyssey*'s concern with song is a concern also with
Iliadic themes and subjects. Particularly relevant are the three songs
of Demodocus in *Odyssey* 8 (72–82, 266–366, and 499–520).[77] The
first of these, as we saw, probably alludes to the very episode which is
the *Iliad*'s starting-point, the quarrel of the 'best of the Achaeans'
prophesied to arise shortly before the fall of Troy. The third likewise
has a Trojan theme, narrating an event foreshadowed though not
narrated in the *Iliad*, the fall of Troy (through Odysseus' own stra-
tagem of the wooden horse). In both these cases there is a contrast
between the responses of the Phaeacians, who hear the songs with
pleasure, and of Odysseus, who weeps. Though there is disagreement
on the interpretation of this disjunction and its significance for
Homeric poetics,[78] I am convinced by Macleod's argument that the
diverging responses represent as distinct two elements, of detachment and of involvement, which are to be combined in the ideal
response.[79] Odysseus' sorrow characterizes the episode as painful,

1994); on Ach.'s gift for imaginative sympathy as a hallmark of his style, cf. Martin (n.
64), 139.

[76] On Homeric poetics in general see the classic studies of Marg (n. 41); G. Lanata,
Poetica preplatonica (Florence, 1963), 1–19; H. G. T. Maehler, *Die Auffassung des
Dichterberufs im frühen Griechentum bis zur Zeit Pindars* (Göttingen, 1963), 9–34;
W. Schadewaldt, *Von Homers Welt und Werk* (4th edn., Stuttgart, 1965), 54–86; cf.
more recently G. B. Walsh, *The Varieties of Enchantment* (Chapel Hill, 1984), 3–21;
Goldhill (n. 41), ch. 1 *passim*, esp. 57–68; C. P. Segal, 'Bard and Audience in Homer',
in Lamberton and Keaney (n. 28), 3–29; A. Ford, *Homer: The Poetry of the Past*
(Ithaca, NY, 1992); Finkelberg (n. 41).

[77] Demodocus' songs cannot be used as direct evidence for the performance of the
Homeric poems themselves (G. Nagy, *Pindar's Homer* (Baltimore, 1990), 21–4), but
this does not exclude the possibility that they have something to tell us about the
Homeric conception of poetry. See now Finkelberg (n. 41), 139–40.

[78] Walsh (n. 76: 5–6) would adopt Phaeacian detachment as the model for the
ideal audience response.

[79] On the Phaeacians' role as secondary narratees, see De Jong, *Comp.* 311.

whereas the Phaeacians' response is one of pleasure; the Phaeacians are a hedonistic people who inhabit a world somewhere between the real and the fantastic—they, perhaps, are too detached; Odysseus, who catches the allusion to the quarrel 'which caused ten thousand pains for the Achaeans' (*Iliad* 1. 2), is too involved, his tears repeatedly disturbing the pleasure of the feast in which all are supposed to share.[80] There is a closer approximation to the ideal audience reaction in 8. 521–30: again Odysseus weeps, and again (531–43) Alcinous is at pains to restore good cheer, a sign that Odysseus' response still exceeds that of any ordinary audience; yet at the same time Odysseus' grief now focuses not on his own sufferings, but on those of others; more particularly, one of the most remarkable of all Homeric similes compares the reaction of Odysseus, the source of Troy's woes, to the grief of a widowed mother, captured and enslaved in the sack of her city.[81] Odysseus, a participant in the action narrated, is none the less detached enough to sympathize with the fate of his defeated enemies, and does so in a manner comparable to the reaction of one whom this fate touches most pathetically. This imaginative identification with the sufferings even of one's enemies is precisely the experience of Achilles in *Iliad* 24, and this passage is indication enough that the poems share the same aesthetic. This seems to be confirmed even by the second song of Demodocus, the story of the adultery of Ares and Aphrodite, for as Walter Burkert has shown (and as Rutherford reiterates), this presentation of divine frivolity (an Iliadic, rather than an Odyssean characteristic) as a foil to the serious theme of the whole poem looks very much like the *Odyssey*'s knowing deployment of an Iliadic technique (as in the case of the divine quarrel in *Iliad* 1).[82]

Homeric poetry focuses on suffering, but its effect is a form of pleasure, the paradoxical pleasure of pity.[83] That this is not purely

[80] 8. 83–95; cf. 537–43, with W. J. Slater, 'Sympotic Ethics in the *Odyssey*', in O. Murray (ed.), *Sympotica* (Oxford, 1990), 213–20.

[81] On the simile, see H. P. Foley, 'Reverse Similes and Sex-Roles in the *Odyssey*', *Arethusa* 11 (1978), 7–26; for the pathos of the woman's fate, cf. *Il*. 6. 448–65, 9. 590–4, 22. 62, 65.

[82] See W. Burkert, 'The Song of Ares and Aphrodite', translated from *RM* 103 (1960), 130–44, in P. V. Jones and G. M. Wright (edd.), *Homer: German Scholarship in Translation* (Oxford, 1997), 249–62.

[83] The pleasure of expressing painful emotion is frequently acknowledged in the poems: *Il*. 23. 14, 108, 153, 24. 507, 513–14; *Od*. 4. 113, 183, 10. 398–9, 16. 215, 19. 249, 22. 500, 23. 231.

an Odyssean notion is suggested not only by the *Odyssey*'s repeated focus on Iliadic themes in its discourse on poetry, but also by the occasional, restrained appearance of a similar ethos in the *Iliad*. Alcinous' (detached) observation that human suffering is the gods' way of providing material for the songs of the future (*Odyssey* 8. 579–80) also forms part of Helen's bitter reflection on her own predicament (*Iliad* 6. 357–8), and a similar relation between suffering and art is discernible in the description of her weaving 'the trials of the Trojans and Achaeans, which they endured for her sake' at 3. 125–8.[84] A comparable degree of self-reflexivity is also apparent in the behaviour of Achilles at *Iliad* 9. 186–9, 'pleasing his heart' by singing 'the famous deeds of men' ($\kappa\lambda\acute{\epsilon}\alpha$ $\mathring{\alpha}\nu\delta\rho\mathring{\omega}\nu$)[85] to the accompaniment of a lyre he took as booty in the most frequently mentioned of his previous, extra-Iliadic exploits, the capture of Hypoplakian Thebe;[86] the scene vividly suggests Achilles' pre-occupation with the relation between success, glory, and song which he feels has been disturbed in his own case; here alone the *Iliad* manifests that closeness of hero and bard which is exploited so extensively in the *Odyssey*.

This very closeness provides the response to a possible criticism of Macleod's argument, that he conflates two kinds of performance, song and storytelling, which should be kept distinct.[87] *Qua* performance, one might argue, these will have features in common, but

---

[84] See Segal (n. 76), 13, on 'women's way of telling stories in the wordless medium of their world'. Finkelberg (n. 41: 77–88) observes that the transformation of suffering into song does not represent a comprehensive theory of what poetry is for, according to Homer, and establishes instead that 'historical significance' is the criterion for memorialization of a particular episode; the poet's stance is that of providing, thanks to the Muses' knowledge of the totality of events, authentic access to the truth; yet it is significant that suffering and artistic activity are so explicitly linked, and that the suffering can be said to be for the sake of the song, a formulation in which the artistic representation is prior to the 'historical' event (see Finkelberg 152).

[85] This is also the description of Demodocus' first song, *Od.* 8. 73, a song which, as we have seen, bears an oblique relation to the song that is the *Il.*; on the phrase, cf. Nagy (n. 42), 16–18, 21–2, 95–106, 111–17; but see also S. D. Olsen, *Blood and Iron* (Leiden, 1995), 2–3.

[86] On which see J. W. Zarker, 'King Eetion and Thebe as Symbols of the *Iliad*', *CJ* 61 (1965), 110–14; O. Taplin, 'Homer's Use of Achilles' Earlier Campaigns in the *Iliad*', in J. Boardman and C. E. Vaphopoulou-Richardson (edd.), *Chios* (Oxford, 1986), 15–19; cf. P. V. Jones, 'Poetic Invention: The Fighting around Troy in the First Nine Years of the Trojan War', in Andersen and Dickie (n. 16), 101–11.

[87] See H. Mackie, 'Song and Storytelling: An Odyssean Perspective', *TAPA* 127 (1997), 77–95; L. Edmunds in *Comp.* 416–17.

they are different sorts of performance and so their poetics will be different. The weakness of this line of argument, however, is precisely that the distinction between song and storytelling is so frequently elided by the *Odyssey*-poet. Odysseus himself is compared to a singer by both Alcinous (11. 367–9) and Eumaeus (17. 518–21);[88] for Eumaeus both the generic, divinely inspired singer and Odysseus the storyteller produce pleasure and enchantment in an audience (ἱμερόεντα, 519, ἔθελγε, 521), and the narrator himself tacitly makes the same comparison when he describes the enraptured silence which is the Phaeacians' response to Odysseus' tales (11. 333–4, 13. 1–2).[89] This, then, is why Eumaeus' responses to Odysseus' tales of woe, responses of pleasure (17. 515–21), but also of emotional engagement (14. 361–2), can serve as a paradigm for the response of the poetic audience.[90]

Any distinction between storytelling and poetry is further elided by the fact that the stories of Odysseus, and especially the narrative of his adventures in Books 9–12, are subsumed into poetry as extended secondary narratives;[91] we the audience hear exactly what the Phaeacians, Eumaeus, and Penelope hear, and their reactions guide our reactions. This closeness of bard and hero illuminates another aspect of Homeric poetics, the importance of autopsy as a guarantee of 'truth':[92] Odysseus compliments Demodocus that he sings of the sufferings of the Achaeans as though he himself had been present or heard from someone who was (*Odyssey* 8. 489–91); Odysseus, of course, was present, and thus vouches for the authenticity of Demodocus' art; Demodocus has this capacity because he is, like the whole 'tribe' of bards, taught by the Muses;[93] the Muses, according

---

[88] Cf. the stringing of the bow at 21. 405–9, with Goldhill (n. 41), 66.

[89] For pleasure and enchantment as audience responses to song, see Macleod, this vol., p. 301, Walsh (n. 76), 5–6, 14–15; H. Parry *Thelxis* (Lanham, Md., 1992), 153–4; Finkelberg (n. 41), 91, 94–5; cf. 1. 337–8: the singer's trade is in θελκτήρια ἔργα, 'works of enchantment'; Macleod notes the relevance of the Sirens here: cf. Schadewaldt (n. 76), 85, Goldhill (n. 41), 64–5; P. Pucci, 'The Song of the Sirens', in S. L. Schein, *Reading the Odyssey* (Princeton, 1996), 191–9; Finkelberg, 95–8.

[90] Cf. Eumaeus at 15. 398–402.

[91] But see I. J. F. de Jong, 'The Subjective Style in Odysseus' Wanderings', *CQ* 42 (1992), 1–11, on the ways in which Odysseus' secondary narrative remains a character-speech rather than becoming totally assimilated into the style of the primary narrator; cf. O. Jørgensen, 'Das Auftreten der Götter in den Büchern ι–μ der Odyssee', *Hermes* 39 (1904), 357–82, W. Suerbaum, 'Die Ich-Erzählungen des Odysseus', *Poetica* 2 (1968), 150–77.   [92] See Finkelberg (n. 41), 71–3.

[93] 8. 479–81; cf. 44–5, 63, 73, 488; also the statement of Phemius at 22. 347–8.

to the invocation at *Iliad* 2. 485–6, 'are present', and thus possess an absolute knowledge of events unavailable to mortals.[94] Demodocus, then, is in the same position as our poet, whose song comes directly from the Muses (*Iliad* 1. 1, *Odyssey* 1. 1); Odysseus, on the other hand, has a more limited, but still authentic form of first-hand, eyewitness knowledge. In invoking the Muse and in using his hero as a secondary narrator the poet is making two slightly different, but complementary claims for the 'truth' of his song.[95]

The closeness of poet and hero which we noted in the cases of both Odysseus and Achilles, especially in their relation to the 'glorious deeds of men', is something that may be traced in the praise-poetry of Pindar and Bacchylides, in which it is a pervasive notion that the glory of the *laudandus* is the material of the poet's song (thus the poet needs the victor), but also that the skill and reputation of the poet is the guarantee of the addressee's immortal fame (and so the victor needs the poet).[96] Homer does not use his own name or reputation to guarantee fame, but none the less the relation between song, success, and suffering is as intimate in Homer as it is in Pindar.[97] This is the central theme of Vernant's chapter (Chapter 10), which concentrates on the *Iliad*'s opposition between the beautiful death which is the condition for poetic immortality and the threat of mutilation or non-burial which would wipe out such immortal fame. Vernant shows how the search for heroic honour is represented as a means of overcoming death through the medium of 'a song of praise';[98] again the self-reflexivity of Achilles' performance of the κλέα ἀνδρῶν (9. 189) is indicative—the glory of the warriors who are the subject of Achilles' song survives through performances such as his, in the

---

[94] See Schadewaldt (n. 76), 82; Ford (n. 76), 49–51, 60–1, 72–9.

[95] Cf. Ford (n. 76), 121–5. But NB Od.'s lying tales indicate that a storyteller (secondary narrator) might lie, which is not a possibility that the *Od.*, unlike Hesiod's *Theogony*, admits in the case of the Muse-inspired poet (Finkelberg (n. 41), 129). This is an important difference between song and storytelling, and a significant element in the *Od.*'s theory of poetry; just as significant, however, are the closeness in expression of *Od.* 19. 203 and Hes. *Theog.* 27 (the as yet unrecognized Od. and Hesiod's Muses are capable of 'lies resembling truth') and the possibility that the practice of Od. the storyteller resembles that of the poet in ways that Homeric poetics does not admit; see further Walsh (n. 76), 20, Goldhill (n. 41), 67–8, Finkelberg 148–50, 156–60.

[96] Cf. Nagy (n. 77), 199–214.

[97] This is not to say that the construction and valorization of these factors is a constant across works, genres, and periods; see Goldhill (n. 41), 69–166.

[98] For this general approach, see Nagy (n. 42); but see also Goldhill (n. 41), 108.

same way as his will survive through performances of the *Iliad*. This immortality, as Vernant insists, is not merely literary, for the public performance of epic poetry preserves the hero's glory as an element in the collective memory of the culture, so that he continues, beyond the reach of death, to be 'present in the community of the living'. But the 'beautiful death' is not only a (paradoxical) way of overcoming mortality; its enemy is also 'harsh old age' (*Iliad* 8. 103, 23. 623), which in itself 'makes a man ugly and base' (as Mimnermus puts it, 1. 6 West), and whose unseemliness is compounded when an old man suffers violent death, as Priam emphasizes in contrasting the beautiful death of the young warrior in battle with the pitiful fate of an old man killed and mutilated in the sack of a city (22. 71–6). The way in which the beautiful death preserves the memory of the warrior at what the Greeks considered the most beautiful time of life, the 'flower of youth',[99] indicates that the adjective *kalos* (22. 73) has its full aesthetic significance in such applications; there is thus a further antithesis between the beauty of the kind of death which secures immortal fame and the ugliness of the mutilated corpse. It is here that the aesthetic nature of the *Iliad's* terminology of honour and shame reaches its deepest significance, as the heroes pursue that which is at once most honourable and most beautiful, while at the same time fearing for themselves and their *philoi* (yet seeking to inflict upon their enemies) that which is ugliest and least conducive to honour.[100] A further element of this concerns the role of the burial or non-burial of the corpse: Books 22 and 23 powerfully juxtapose the horror of non-burial and the importance of proper funeral rites, while Book 24 secures the latter, and thus the fame of a beautiful death, for Hector.[101] Proper funerary ritual, like

[99] Vernant's antithesis between the 'heroic' youth of figures such as Patroclus and the 'ordinary' youth of other young warriors will not survive consideration of the contribution of the deceased's youth to a feeling of pathos in the 'obituary notices' of minor as well as major warriors (J. Griffin, *Homer on Life and Death* (Oxford, 1980), 105–6, 123–30, 131–4). Similarly, I feel he is wrong to take Achilles' rejection of the ambassadors as indicative of a distinction between 'extraordinary' (or 'heroic') and 'ordinary' honour (see rather Gill (n. 47), 124–54).

[100] See Redfield (this vol., Ch. 16) on the intimation of this theme in the Prologue of Book 1.

[101] But also a different kind of *kudos* for Achilles (24. 110 with Macleod ad loc.; cf. Taplin, this vol., Ch. 11 n. 39), which contrasts sharply with his previous attempts to obliterate Hector's honour—attempts which threatened Ach.'s own honour (24. 33–54). As Vernant recognizes, the pursuit of one's own glory by means of the

heroic song, is a prerequisite for *kleos*:[102] both memorialize the
dead; the grave-marker or *sēma* ideally is a guarantee of *kleos* for
all time (e.g. 7. 89–91, the *sēma* of Hector's victim will testify to
Hector's own *kleos*), but this will only be the case if an oral tradition persists alongside the mute stones.[103]

The Shield of Achilles in *Iliad* 18 is regularly seen as a symbol of
the poem in which it embedded, as a model of the craftsmanship of
the poem itself.[104] For Taplin (Chapter 11), it functions as a microcosm, especially indicative of the poem's *ethos* in the way that, both
internally (in the contrast between the city at war and the city at
peace, 18. 491–540) and in relation to the rest of the poem, it sets the
war which is the poem's focal concern in the wider context of the
norms which have been disrupted by war, the benefits and institutions of civilization which war destroys. The shield presents the ideal
of the Homeric 'good life' which is represented in similar terms
throughout both Homeric poems (especially in the idyllic existence of
the *Odyssey*'s Phaeacians), and at the same time foregrounds the
benefits of peace which elsewhere surface only in similes and scattered reminders (e.g. the detail of the washing troughs in the midst of
the deadly pursuit of Hector at 22. 153–6). Taplin is aware of the
charge that his argument is merely 'the product of sentimental
pacifism', but makes a telling reply in his demonstration that the

elimination of that of one's opponent may have ambiguous consequences for the hero
(cf. Hainsworth, *Il. Comm.* III. 49). But 24. 110 shows that Iliadic *kudos* is elastic
enough to accommodate aspects other than those (the self-assertive and martial ones)
which are commonly regarded as typically heroic (cf. Hainsworth, *Il. Comm.* III. 53).

[102] On the role of death ritual in the conclusion of the *Il.*, see Seaford (n. 1), 159–90.
[103] NB 23. 332–4, where Nestor points to the *sēma* of a man who died long
ago, but cannot name him; cf. M. Lynn-George, *Epos: Word, Narrative, and the Iliad*
(Basingstoke, 1988), 265–6; Ford (n. 76), 144–5; Vernant, by contrast, takes the
'fixity' of the gravemarker (*Il.* 17. 432–5) at face value.
[104] On the thematic and compositional relation between the shield and the *Il.*, see
Stanley (n. 1), 3–6, 189–90, 293–6, with bibliography of modern discussion of the
shield at 303–4 nn. 1–7; A. S. Becker, *The Shield of Achilles and the Poetics of Ecphrasis*
(Lanham, Md., 1995), *passim*, with bibliography at 5 n. 9; cf. Edwards, *Il. Comm.* V.
200–9. For the shield as a symbol of the poet's craft, see K. Reinhardt, *Die Ilias und ihr
Dichter* (Göttingen, 1961), 401–11, Marg (n. 41), 21–37, Schadewaldt (n. 76),
352–74, Becker 4–5, 38–41, 51–86 *passim*, 106, 151–3; Ford (n. 76), 168–71, denies
any notion of the poet as craftsman; cf. Finkelberg (n. 41), 101, 11–21, 169 (and her
discussion of the shield at 112–16, 119–20), though she observes that the Homeric
poems may in fact (rather than in poetic theory) be analogues to works of
craftsmanship; Nagy (n. 42), 297–300, makes a plausible case for linking the
etymology of the name, Homeros, to the notion of poet as craftsman, but for different
views, see J. Latacz in *Der neue Pauly* v. 687; West (n. 25), 374–6.

'tensions, even contradictions, [which] are inseparable parts of a complex whole' surface most strikingly where the juxtaposition of peace and war creates a feeling of dissonance, as in the case of the simile which he cites from 21. 346–7, where the gladness of the gardener at the wind which dries his newly watered plot in autumn contrasts sharply with Hephaestus' fire which burns the corpses and parches the plain. It is this recognition of the miseries and losses of war in a poem which celebrates martial excellence that provides the material for Book 24's emphasis on the sympathy resulting from acceptance of the universality of human suffering.[105]

IV. THE ARTISTRY OF THE *ILIAD*: TRADITION AND INDIVIDUALITY

The final group of essays to be discussed deals broadly with questions of Homeric artistry, particularly against the background of the oral tradition of songs on Trojan and other themes. Griffin's contribution (Chapter 12) is the most general of these, and it comes out strongly in favour of the creative artistry of individual poetic genius. Griffin's reasons for this position lie in the unique quality of the *Iliad* and the *Odyssey* in comparison with the Epic Cycle, poems no longer extant whose traditions certainly antedate the composition of 'our' Homeric poems and emerged in written versions at some stage in the (?) later Archaic period,[106] probably under the stimulus of written versions of the *Iliad* and *Odyssey*.[107] The hallmark of this Homeric uniqueness, according to Griffin, is the Homeric poems' rejection of the elements of 'the fantastic, the miraculous, and the romantic' which appear to have been prominent in the Cycle.[108]

Of particular significance is the absence of miraculous invulnerability and of the possibility of real immortality in the *Iliad*; as we have seen, the inevitability of death and the miseries of old age help define the *Iliad*'s notion of heroism; eternal life and eternal youth are, as Griffin points out, reserved for the gods; even Heracles died

---

[105] Cf. M. S. Silk, *The Iliad* (Cambridge, 1987), 73–8.

[106] See n. 10 above.

[107] On the Cycle in general, see Davies (n. 9); J. Latacz in *Der neue Pauly* III. 1154–6.

[108] To this one would wish to add focus on a single and unifying theme, as noted by Aristotle, *Po.* 1459[b]2–7; also the Homeric epics' large proportion of direct speech, *Po.* 1460[a]5–11, with Kirk, *Il. Comm.* II. 28–33.

(*Iliad* 18. 117–19), and the immortality which gods occasionally confer on their offspring and their favourites, in the *Odyssey* as well as in the Cycle,[109] is never considered. The *Iliad*'s notion of the heroic, in fact, can be seen to entail a strong sense of what is and is not proper in a heroic character or a heroic poem, and much that is found in the Cycle is excluded from the *Iliad* as unheroic.[110]

Although there are, in fact, elements of the miraculous and the magical in Homer,[111] we can accept a general qualitative difference between the *Iliad* and *Odyssey*, on the one hand, and the Cycle on the other; but what accounts for it? Some of the comparative shortcomings of the Cycle (e.g. their episodic character) are no doubt due to the fact that the surviving fragments and summaries belong to poems composed with the aim of producing written complements to pre-existing texts of the *Iliad* and the *Odyssey*, and one might wish to argue that the earlier traditions from which these poems derived may have been closer in style to our Homeric poems.[112] But no one would argue that these earlier traditions contained anything like the *Iliad* or the *Odyssey* in scope, conception, or focus; in attaining such a stage of development, therefore, the Homeric poems have differentiated themselves from other traditions. At the same time, it is most unlikely that the comparatively greater interest in the fabulous, the romantic, and the sensational shown by the Cycle should have been introduced at a late stage in the development of the epic tradition, for the simple reason that the *Iliad* and the *Odyssey* themselves can frequently be shown to have been aware of or to have suppressed such elements.[113] Since the *Iliad* has thus rejected such aspects of its own tradition, one cannot surmise that the differences between it and the Cycle are to be attributed to a divergence in the

---

[109] *Od.* 4. 561 (Menelaus), 11. 601–4 (Heracles), *Cypria* p. 31. 31 Davies (Dioscuri; cf. and contrast *Od.* 11. 299–304), p. 32. 62 Davies (Iphigeneia), *Aethiopis* p. 47. 19 Davies (Memnon), p. 47. 27–8 (Achilles), *Telegony* p. 73. 24 Davies (Telegonus, Telemachus, and Penelope).

[110] One might call this the '*Parisurteil*-principle', after K. Reinhardt's famous essay, now in Jones and Wright (n. 82), 170–91; cf. Dowden (n. 1), 53.

[111] e.g. Achilles' immortal, talking horse, *Il.* 19. 404–17, Hephaestus' robotic maidservants, 18. 417–21; cf. e.g. the bag of winds, *Od.* 10. 19–47, and the magic of Circe, 10. 210–397.

[112] See Latacz (n. 107), 1155–6, Dowden (n. 1), 48–9; cf. more generally Hainsworth, *Il. Comm.* III. 44.

[113] e.g. the judgement of Paris (with Reinhardt); cf. the brand in the Meleager story (Hainsworth, *Il. Comm.* III. 131–2); see further below, nn. 144–6.

epic tradition.[114] Many will find it hard to believe that such a consistent idea of what is and is not in keeping with the ethos of the *Iliad* could be attributable to impersonal forces of historical development,[115] and will be more ready to consider the role of a single poet's design and overall conception of his work.[116]

One of the chief interests in the Cycle in recent Homeric scholarship has been as the basis for the school of criticism known as neoanalysis.[117] Its fundamental premisses are (first) that the *Iliad* as we have it contains a number of episodes which are patterned on episodes from elsewhere in the epic tradition and (second) that the adaptation of these episodes in such a way that an audience can recognize both the use of the model and its creative adaptation to its new context is a significant feature of Homeric artistry. In its earliest versions, neoanalysis assumed that the models in question would be pre-existing written poems, something which earned the movement the scorn (or at best the indifference) of oralists, but lately neoanalytic studies have accepted that these should rather be imagined as deriving from the oral traditions which later provided the material for the Cyclic epics known to us in fragmentary or summary form.[118] Neoanalysis thus raises the question of allusion in oral or oral-derived epic: for strict oralists, this question does not arise, for (they argue) in an oral tradition there can be no concept of a fixed text to which allusion could be made; poets make use of a stock of motifs common to many other narratives and traditions, but as 'tradition' exists only in so far as it is immanent in the current performance, no motif can be definitively associated with any particular narrative sequence, and the practice of composition in performance means that the attention of the audience is always on the present and thus

---

[114] Much less are they differences of genre (*pace* L. M. Slatkin, *The Power of Thetis* (Berkeley, 1991), 7); see the conclusion to Griffin, this vol., Ch. 12.

[115] Such is the premiss of Nagy's 'evolutionary model'; see (e.g.) *Homeric Questions* (n. 1), 92.

[116] That the excellence of the *Il.* is not to be attributed to the excellence of an entire tradition, or to that of a genre or style, is stressed by A. Parry (n. 12), 116, 134.

[117] For bibliographical surveys, see W. Kullmann, 'Zur Methode der Neoanalyse in der Homerforschung', *WS* 15 (1981), 5–32, 'Oral Poetry Theory and Neoanalysis in Homeric Research', *GRBS* 25 (1984), 307–23, and in J. Latacz (ed.), *Zweihundert Jahre Homer-Forschung* (Stuttgart, 1991), 425–55; M. E. Clark, 'Neoanalysis: A Bibliographical Review', *CW* 79 (1986), 379–94; M. W. Edwards, 'Neoanalysis and Beyond', *Cl. Ant.* 9 (1990), 311–25, and *Il. Comm.* v. 16–19; Willcock in *Comp.*, 174–89.

[118] See esp. Kullmann's *GRBS* article (n. 117).

on the use to which traditional motifs are put in the present context
alone.[119]

To this it has fairly been objected that 'It is . . . questionable
whether this extreme oral poetry has actually existed.'[120] That the
Iliad makes use of material which had already attained a degree of
textual fixity (though not necessarily in written form) cannot really
be doubted: the best evidence is the use of the dual number (which
Greek employs in speaking of a pair of persons or things) in the
narrative of the Embassy in Book 9, where the ingenuity of all
alternative efforts to explain how the dual can be used of a group of
three ambassadors fails in comparison to the most economical and
plausible explanation, that a pre-existing version of the episode
which contained two ambassadors has been reshaped into one that
includes three.[121] Nor can the strict denial of allusion in Homeric
poetry be maintained, for the simple reason that the *Iliad* and the
Odyssey are replete with summary references which presuppose
knowledge of other epic tales in a more or less standard form (for if
there is no more or less standard form of a particular story, a summary reference will not suffice). Thus the *Iliad* expects familiarity
with Theban stories,[122] with the deeds and sufferings of Heracles,[123]
with the story of Bellerophon,[124] and with the battle of Lapiths and
Centaurs.[125] Zeus' list of (some of) his liaisons and their resulting
offspring at 14. 315–28 alone contains summary allusions to the
offence and punishment of Ixion, the origin of the centaurs, the story

---

[119] See (e.g.) Nagy (n. 42), 42–3; J. M. Foley, *Immanent Art: From Structure to
Meaning in Traditional Oral Epic* (Bloomington, 1991); cf. id. in *Comp.* 167–73.

[120] Dowden (n. 1), 60 on Foley, *Immanent Art* (n. 119), 8.

[121] See *Il.* 9. 182–3, 185, 192, 196–8. For the possible explanations, see
Hainsworth, *Il. comm.* III. 85–7; the hypothesis of an earlier version is ruled out *a
priori* by Nagy, *Homeric Questions* (n. 1), 138–44, reprising (n. 42), 42–58; I find his
explanation—that the notion of 'two heralds' is a traditional norm—incredible.

[122] 4. 370–410, 5. 800–13, 13. 663–70, 14. 114–25, 323–5, 23. 346–7,
679–80.

[123] 5. 392–404, 638–42, 648–51, 8. 362–9, 11. 690–3, 14. 250–61, 266, 323–4,
15. 18–30, 639–40, 18. 117–19, 19. 95–133, 20. 145–8. With Heracles' role in the first
sack of Troy (5. 638–51, 14. 250–6, 15. 26–30, 20. 145–8), cf. the references to the
servitude of Apollo and Poseidon to Laomedon (7. 452–3, 21. 441–57), an earlier
episode in the same chain of events; see M. Lang, 'Reverberation and Mythology in
the *Iliad*', in C. A. Rubino and C. W. Shelmerdine (edd.), *Approaches to Homer*
(Austin, 1982), 140–64.

[124] 6. 152–211; NB the allusion to the trickery of Sisyphus, 152–3, and the
suppression, which is not the same as ignorance, of Pegasus and Bellerophon's
attempt to fly up to Olympus.   [125] 1. 263–8, 2. 740–4; with 741 cf. 14. 318.

of Perseus and Danae,[126] and the pursuit of Europa.[127] Familiarity is likewise assumed with various myths about the gods, notably those concerning the establishment of Zeus' authority: the division of the world between the three sons of Kronos, Zeus, Poseidon, and Hades (15. 185–93);[128] the Titanomachy (8. 478–81, 14. 203–4, 273–4, 278–9, 15. 224–5),[129] Typhoeus (2. 782–3);[130] Otus and Ephialtes (5. 385–91).[131]

One very striking feature of the *Iliad*'s allusions to other stories is the fact that they are typically embedded in direct speech; the external stories are thus presented as part of the past of the characters and draw much of their argumentative authority from their status as extended reminiscences, while at the same time acquiring the emotional charge which attaches more to secondary than to primary narrative in Homer. This is also an Odyssean technique: that poem also alludes to myths external to the Trojan Cycle,[132] but the majority of its allusions are to events between the point at which the *Iliad* ends and the departure of the Greeks following the sack of Troy, and the majority of these occur in the reminiscences of characters involved, particularly in the two Underworld scenes, but also in the scenes at Pylos and Sparta.[133] Thus the use of the past in the *Odyssey* serves to

[126] Cf. 5. 738–42, the only passage which might imply Perseus' slaying of Medusa.

[127] No reference to Zeus' metamorphoses in these last two cases.

[128] Contrast Hes. *Theog.* 73–4, 881–5, but the Iliadic version is not likely to be an invention; see Janko, *Il. Comm.* IV. 247 ad loc.

[129] Cf. the oath by the Styx, 14. 271, 15. 37–8, which presupposes the role of Styx in the Titanomachy (*Theog.* 389–401, 780–806).

[130] Cf. *Theog.* 820–68.

[131] The particular episode in this passage is otherwise unattested, but not necessarily incompatible with the version at *Od.* 11. 305–20. References to previous conflicts between Zeus and other Olympians (1. 396–406, 586–94, 14. 200–10, 250–61, 15. 18–30, 18. 394–9) are yet more problematic, since they are otherwise unattested in any form; cf. Zeus' threats of future violence at 5. 897–8, 8. 13–14, 19–27, 397–408, 14. 254–61, and see below on Slatkin's and Willcock's discussion of 1. 396–406.

[132] e.g. the Argonautica (12. 69–72), the story of Oedipus (11. 271–80), the career of Heracles (8. 224–8, 11. 266–8, 601–4, 21. 24–30).

[133] e.g. the trials of the Achaeans on their various *nostoi* (3. 130–98, 254–312, 4. 351–586), among which the sufferings of Agamemnon at the hands of Aegisthus and Clytemnestra, avenged by Orestes, are paramount (1. 29–31, 3. 303–10, 4. 512–37, 11. 405–61, 24. 24–34, 95–7). The poem also describes, mentions, or presupposes the death of Antilochus, and thus the conflict of Achilles and Memnon (3. 111–12, 4. 187–9, 11. 468, 11. 522, 24. 16); the disguised Odysseus' reconnaissance within the walls of Troy (4. 242–58, possibly developed from a tradition concerning the theft of the Palladium, with a degree of ad hoc elaboration; see West, *Od. Comm.* 1. 208–9 ad 242 ff.); the Wooden Horse and the Sack of Troy (4. 271–89, 8. 492–520, 11. 523–32);

locate both the characters themselves and the narrative to which they belong in a wider epic framework,[134] and (as we have noted) the poem virtually parades its intertextual engagement with the oral traditions of the Fall of Troy by embedding several of its references to earlier stages of the story in the songs of bards.[135] Defence of 'allusion' or 'intertextuality' in Homer need not entail culpable disregard of the poems' oral origins, but is in fact compatible with a view of the oral poet's art which recognizes the need for him to display his mastery of a wide repertoire and to convince audiences of his superiority to his competitors.[136]

The *Iliad* similarly includes previous stages of the Trojan story within its scope, but it also looks forward to a greater extent than does the *Odyssey*.[137] As Kullmann points out (Chapter 13), this is part of the technique by which the Wrath of Achilles truly becomes an *Iliad*, for, again, a major feature of the *Iliad*'s uniqueness vis-à-vis the Cycle, one singled out for comment since Aristotle (*Poetics* 1459[a] 30–[b]7), is its concentration on a single theme while at the same time including the rest of the war within its imaginative scope. Thus the *Iliad* takes us from the wedding of Peleus and Thetis and the Judgement of Paris,[138] *via* the early years of the war,[139] to the death

Helen's marriage to Deiphobus after the death of Paris (4. 276, 8. 517–18); the battle for the body of Achilles (5. 309–10, 24. 37–42); the role of Philoctetes in the taking of Troy (8. 218–20); the role of Neoptolemus (11. 505–37), including his slaying of Eurypylus (11. 519–22; cf. *Little Iliad* p. 52, 14–15 Davies); the judgement of the arms and Ajax's suicide (11. 541–67); the death and funeral of Achilles (24. 36–97).

[134] P. V. Jones, 'The Past in Homer's *Odyssey*', *JHS* 112 (1992), 74–90, argues that the *Od.* largely constructs a picture of the past to suit its own narrative needs, but he may mislead by limiting himself to the world of Ithaca before Odysseus' departure and during his absence.

[135] See n. 41 above. The 'Quarrel' in 8. 73–82 may be an 'invention', but, as we decided above, it is still very likely that it alludes to the greater quarrel between Achilles and Agamemnon in *Il.* 1.

[136] See Hainsworth, *Il. Comm.* III. 130; and cf. J. A. Notopoulos, 'Continuity and Interconnection in Homeric Oral Composition', *TAPA* 82 (1951), 93, Usener (n. 38), 205, Dowden (n. 1), 52.

[137] There is a degree of preparation for Odysseus' future in the prophecies of Tiresias (11. 121–37), picked up in Odysseus' reference to his future travails (23. 248–53), but these references are relatively meagre and cannot with any degree of certainty be regarded as exploiting knowledge of pre-existing traditions about Odysseus; the Cyclic continuation of the *Od.*, the *Telegony*, seems, in its fulfilment of the *Od.*'s forward references, rather to take the *Od.* itself as its point of departure; see Davies (n. 9), 87–94.

[138] Wedding: 16. 380–1, 867, 17. 195–6, 443–4, 18. 84–5, 432–4, 23. 276–8, 24. 60–3, 537; judgement: 24. 28–30.

[139] e.g. a raiding expedition leading to the sack of Thebe (1. 366–9, 2. 691, 6. 414–28, 9. 188, 16. 152–3, 23. 827–9; cf. *Cypria* fr. 22 Davies), Lyrnessos (2. 690–3, 19.

of Achilles and the sack of Troy.[140] No doubt some details common to the *Iliad* and the Cycle derive from the *Iliad* itself;[141] but equally there are details that attest to the Cycle's independence,[142] while the allusive nature of many of the *Iliad*'s references establishes its use of earlier traditions.[143]

But the *Iliad*'s orientation towards the past and future of the Trojan story, and the poetic traditions which tell that story, is more complex than any list of references to episodes attested in later poems would suggest. The *Iliad*, for example, may include details which overlap with, but also diverge from the Cycle in such a way as to define itself as a production of a different order, with distinct norms of decorum and propriety. A case in point would be the story of Achilles' early education at the hands of Chiron the centaur. The latter is present in the poem: at 4. 219 the physician, Machaon, treats Menelaus with drugs which the Centaur had once given his (Machaon's) father, Asclepius; at 11. 830–2 it is Achilles himself who is the beneficiary of Chiron's medical training, a detail which must suggest, allusively, the tradition that Achilles was deposited with the Centaur at an early age and reared by him rather than by his parents.[144] In the *Iliad*, however, Achilles' upbringing is normalized as

60, 19. 291–9, 20. 92, 191–2), and Pedasos (20. 92), as well as the capture of Aeneas' cattle on Mount Ida (20. 89–93, 187–94). Jones (n. 86), 101–12, points out how few these episodes are, and how inadequately they (and the other, less specific references he lists to the earlier years' fighting) fill the time available up to the opening of the *Il.* in the tenth year of the war. He concludes that there was no developed tradition of the first nine years' fighting at Troy, and agrees with Ø. Andersen ('The Making of the Past in the *Iliad*' HSCP 93 (1990), 25–45) that the *Iliad* generally creates its own version of the past.

[140] Death: 18. 96, 19. 416–17, 21. 110–13, 277–8, 22. 359–60; sack: see the fates of Cassandra and Astyanax (22. 62–4, 24. 732–9, with significant reference to Astyanax's being hurled from the walls of Troy in 735; cf. *Iliupersis*, fr. 3 Davies, *Ilias parva*, frr. 20–1 Davies); the death of Priam (22. 66; cf. *Ilias parva* fr. 17 Davies, but contrast *Iliupersis* p. 62. 19–20 Davies). Cf. the survival of the Aeneidae (20. 302–8; cf. *H. Ven.* 196–7, *Iliupersis* p. 62. 12–13 Davies).

[141] See Davies (n. 9), 48 on the *Cypria* summary, lines 79 ff.

[142] e.g. the divergence of *Cypria* fr. 21 Davies from *Il.* 2. 690–3, 19. 60, 291–9 regarding the provenance of Briseis.

[143] See W. Kullmann, *Die Quellen der Ilias* (Wiesbaden, 1960), 17. For a full list of references to earlier and later stages of the Trojan story, see Kullmann, 6–11, with further discussion at 227–357.

[144] See [Hes.] fr. 204. 87–9 M–W, Alcaeus fr. 42 L–P, Pind., *Pyth.* 6. 21–3, *Nem.* 3. 43–53; for Achilles' talents as a healer, cf. Proclus' summary of the *Cypria*, p. 32, 53–4 Davies; the tutelage of Chiron appears already in 7th-cent. art, *LIMC* I, Achilleus pl. 21; the *Precepts of Chiron*, a lost work of uncertain date, once attributed to Hesiod, must also have taken this situation as its starting point.

far as possible: to all intents and purposes, Thetis remains with her husband and child until Achilles' departure for Troy (1. 396–7, 16. 222–3, 570–6, 18. 57–60, 329–32, 438–41, 19. 422), and the infant Achilles grows up in his father's house, under the watchful eye of an entirely human surrogate father, Phoenix (9. 485–95).[145] As Griffin shows, the inclusion of Chiron is enough to suggest his role in Achilles' upbringing, but at the explicit level the poem eschews tales of a prodigious child brought up in the wilds by a divine creature of half-human, half-bestial appearance. Another possible example concerns Achilles' departure to join the expedition, recruited, quite unexceptionally, by Odysseus and Nestor (7. 127–8, 9. 252–9, 11. 765–90); yet the poem is also aware of a tradition linking Achilles (9. 666–8) and Neoptolemus (19. 326–7) with the island of Skyros, which may signal an exclusion of the story (attributed to 'the Cyclic poets' by a scholion on 19. 326) that Achilles was sent to Skyros by Peleus, who had received a prophecy that his son was fated to die at Troy, and concealed, dressed as a girl, among the daughters of Lycomedes, only to be discovered by a ploy of Odysseus, but not before he had impregnated Deidameia with Neoptolemus.[146] In contrast with this sort of thing, the *Iliad* employs a version of the departure of Achilles that is consistent with its own canons of heroic propriety: Achilles, brought up in his father's house, his mother and his tutor, Phoenix, in attendance, bids farewell to a home and father to which he will never return, accepting, his father's heroic precepts ringing in his ears, the challenge to fight at Troy; we may suspect that the poem's earliest audiences were encouraged to contrast this version of events with very different traditions regarding the role of Chiron and Peleus' attempts to save his son's life; but even if we prefer to see the latter as independent stories to which the *Iliad* does not allude, we can none the less appreciate how the *Iliad*'s construction of its own background constitutes an attempt to situate the poem with regard to other possible or competing versions. The *Iliad* clearly

---

[145] Chiron appears also at 16. 143–4 = 19. 390–1 as the source of Peleus' mighty ashen spear (for which cf. 20. 277, 21. 162, 22. 133, with Kullmann (n. 143), 232–6), which is specifically a wedding present in *Cypria* 3 Davies; on the poet's 'rationalizing genius' in playing down or effacing the miraculous aspect of Peleus' wedding gifts (immortal horses, originally invulnerable armour, a spear which returns to its owner), see Janko, *Il. Comm.* IV. 334 (cf. ibid. 310–11, 409).

[146] See Davies (n. 9), 45 and 66 for discussion of the location of this fr. in *Cypria* or *Ilias parva*; Griffin (this vol., Ch. 12) assumes location in *Cypria* = fr. 13.2 Bethe. On Iliadic traces of this tradition, cf. Hainsworth, *Il. Comm.* III. 145–6.

exists in a wider context of traditional stories and poems; it exploits, alludes to, and modifies this tradition, but in doing so establishes itself as more than simply one work among many.

The fact that the *Iliad* can be shown to exhibit a relation towards extra-Iliadic tradition means that, though one can never claim with certainty that knowledge of such tradition is tacitly presupposed, one also cannot rule out in advance the possibility that certain, not obviously allusive, passages are composed in such a way as to gain in significance if read with the wider tradition in mind. Thus, while the *Iliad* makes no mention of virgin sacrifice at Aulis, no one who knew of such a tradition could fail to construe 1. 106–8 (Agamemnon's complaint at Calchas' past prophecies) as a covert reference to the sacrifice of Iphigeneia.[147] The most poignant of such cases would require an audience to apply its knowledge of the destruction of Troy; the fate of Astyanax, for example, directly foreshadowed towards the poem's close,[148] infuses with pathos the scene between Hector and Andromache in Book 6, with all its hopes and fears for the future; equally, if foreshadowings of the fate of Priam and the future role of Neoptolemus presuppose the latter's killing of the former, knowledge of this must profoundly affect an audience's response to the Achilles–Priam scene, with all its stress on the father–son relationship, in Book 24.[149] Study of the *Iliad*'s relationship with other elements of the poetic tradition is thus no arid scholarly diversion, but a major contributor to the reconstruction of a fully engaged audience response.

Homer also brings the beginning and the end of war into the poem by including elements from those temporal stages within its compass. The beginning of the conflict is especially suggested by the inclusion (during the phase of retardation between Zeus' promise to aid the Trojans in Book 1 and the first real Trojan successes in Book 8) of episodes which function as though the early stages of the poem actually describe the early stages of the war. These include the Catalogue in Book 2 and the Teichoskopia (View from the Walls) and the duel of Paris and Menelaus in Book 3. In the case of the Catalogue and the Teichoskopia, in particular, there is a strong suspicion that they derive from an earlier poetic account, perhaps the *Iliad* poet's

---

[147] Cf. 1. 71–2: Calchas' prophetic skill 'led the Achaeans to Troy'; cf. Dowden (n. 1), 52–3.   [148] See n. 140 above.
[149] See M. Anderson, *The Fall of Troy in Early Greek Poetry and Art* (Oxford, 1997), 38–48.

own, which treated the progress of the war in diachronic sequence. Though the Catalogue has clearly been adapted to fit its current context, it is equally clear that such a passage suits the gathering of the fleet at Aulis better than a gathering of the forces in the tenth year of the war,[150] while the Teichoskopia seems to betray its origins in its form, in that it has Priam implausibly ask Helen to identify the major Greek leaders. The lack of fit between the scene and its context suggests a pre-existing version;[151] and the lack of any attempt to mitigate the implausibility of such a scene at this stage in the war suggests that the poet was happy to allow his audience to appreciate his technique in incorporating the whole war in his *Iliad*.

It is when we come to consider the incorporation of events belonging to later stages of the war within the action of the *Iliad* that we appreciate the most significant contribution of neoanalysis to Homeric studies. For it is established beyond any reasonable doubt that, in his presentation of the sequence of events leading from the entry of Patroclus into battle to the death of Hector, Homer follows a pattern established in traditional versions of the death of Achilles at the hands of Paris and Apollo, following Achilles' own killing of Memnon in revenge for the latter's killing of Achilles' companion, Antilochus.[152] It may be objected that, striking though the parallel between the two sequences is both in detail and in broad sweep, the similarities are to be attributed not to the deliberate borrowing which constitutes oblique reference, but merely to the use of typical scenes as a standard feature of the oral poet's art;[153] but surely even use of a type-scene in one context might remind an audience of its use in another, especially where the latter is a significant and familiar one.

[150] See Kullmann (n. 143), 157–67.
[151] As even Kirk, *Il. Comm.* I. 286–7 accepts.
[152] The main passages are: 16. 419–683, 466–76 (cf. 8. 80–129 with Pind. *Pyth.* 6. 28–9, and see M. M. Willcock, 'Antilochus in the *Iliad*', in *Mélanges É. Delebecque* (Aix-en-Provence, 1983), 482–3; Kirk, *Il. Comm.* II. 305, Janko, *Il. Comm.* IV. 379), 777–867, 17. 702–61, 18. 26–7 (with 16. 775–6 and *Od.* 24. 39–40, and see H. Pestalozzi, *Die Achilleis als Quelle der Ilias* (Erlenbach, 1945), 18, Schadewaldt (n. 76), 168, Kullmann (n. 143), 38), 35–69 (with *Od.* 24. 47–9, 58–9), 95–6 (with 16. 36–7, 49–51), 19. 404–24, 22. 208–13, 378–84, 23. 14 (with *Od.* 24. 84–6). See also 11. 369–78 (with Kullmann *GRBS* 1984 (n. 117), 307–23; contrast B. Fenik, *Typical Battle Scenes in the Iliad* (Wiesbaden, 1968), 234–5). For a brief summary and discussion see Davies (n. 9), 4–5, 55–9; detailed discussion with bibl. in Janko, *Il. Comm.* IV. 312–14, 371–3, 378–9, 395, 399, 408–10, 414, Edwards, *Il. Comm.* V. 16–19, 62, 90, 98, 132, 140–1, 149, 150–1, 158–9, 235; contrast their colleague, Kirk, at *Il. Comm.* II. 26–7, 304–5.
[153] See Fenik (n. 152), 231–40; cf. Hainsworth, *Il. Comm.* III. 42.

Where, moreover, a motif seems more appropriate in one context than another, there must be a presumption that it has been adapted from the context where it is more at home; thus, while it is true that Achilles goes to face both Hector and Memnon with the knowledge that his own death must follow, the statement of Thetis that it will follow 'straightaway' (18. 96) upon the death of Hector is simply not as true as it would be in the case of Achilles' confrontation with Memnon.[154] The poet of the *Iliad* wishes to place Achilles' decision to avenge the death of Patroclus on the same level of seriousness as the decision to avenge the death of Antilochus; but not only do we feel, through this parallel of motifs and the explicit foreshadowings of Achilles' death, that the death of Achilles is imminent;[155] we also experience it at one remove through the death and funeral of Patroclus, and especially through the sorrows of Thetis. Thus the death of Achilles is not merely foreshadowed, but powerfully present to the audience even as they follow the poet's representation of his life.

Neoanalysis, then, affords insight into the creative processes behind the epic's use of tradition, suggests something of an audience's expectations of a bard and his repertoire, and, most importantly, lays bare the techniques by which the poet exploits his audience's knowledge of the epic tradition in order to deepen their response to a narrative in which both past and future are powerfully present. Kullmann's article here builds on his neoanalytic researches, but its particular focus is on the way in which the characters' possession of a past and a future in the Trojan story and a certain degree of consistency in their presentation as characters throughout the Trojan Cycle contributes to their characterization. The characters' orientation towards the past and the future is thus a means of creating a sense of their individuality and inner psychological life: Helen, for example, is preoccupied with the past in a way which gives a strong impression of her remorse and wistful longing for the days before all the trouble started; at the other extreme, Hector is deeply concerned with his own image in the future, and with the status of

---

[154] See Seaford (n. 1), 155–8; Dowden (n. 1), 56–8.

[155] Foreshadowings of Achilles' death become more frequent and explicit as the poem nears its close: 1. 352, 415–18, 16. 709, 17. 406–7, 18. 59–60, 95–121, 330–2, 464–5, 19. 328–30, 416–17, 421–2. 21. 100–13, 277–8, 22. 359–60, 23. 80–1, 150, 24. 84–6, 91, 104–5, 131–2; *qua* preparation for the poem's sequel, cf. the prominence of Antilochus in bringing the news of Patroclus' death to Achilles in Books 17–18 and in the Funeral Games of 23.

his son as heir to his father's glory,[156] while Andromache's focus on both past and future is centred on the family, both the natal family destroyed by Achilles and the conjugal family which will be wiped out in the sack of the city; Andromache's present insecurity and concern in Book 6 is a product of her past experience and an accurate predictor of her fate in the future. Though it is no doubt true that the characters' orientation towards the past and the future could be a significant feature even if relevant elements of past and future had been invented, this case in particular shows how the audience's knowledge of events subsequent to those narrated in the poem can lend an extra dimension to their response.[157]

Neoanalysis is not inherently hostile to the notion of ad hoc invention; on the contrary, Kullmann is at pains to recognize this category and distinguish it from the exploitation of audience knowledge of pre-existing stories.[158] Nor should these be regarded as strict alternatives, for (on the one hand) pre-existing stories must normally be adapted to serve their Iliadic purpose, and (on the other) stories apparently invented for an Iliadic context do not arise *ex nihilo*—even the most original ad hoc invention must exist as part of a system of traditional elements, and (we might add) the techniques of oral poetry and storytelling strongly favour remodelling and reconfiguration of traditional elements rather than absolute innovation.[159] Thus there should be no question of our signing up for exclusive membership of one school of thought rather than the other;[160] we need to work with both categories, of invention and of adaptation; but in practice differences remain, both between those who in general favour one approach over the other and on the categorization of particular episodes as invented or as drawn from/ alluding to other traditions.[161]

[156] Cf. Martin (n. 64), 132–4, 136–9.

[157] For other perspectives on the uses of the past in Homeric poetry, see Kullmann in Andersen and Dickie (n. 16), 57–75; Jones ibid. 101–12 (=n. 86) and (n. 134); Andersen (n. 139).   [158] (n. 143), 13–17.

[159] Jones (n. 134) 78–9, 81, 87 distinguishes three types of invention: (I) *de novo* innovation; (II) 'creative elaboration, the application of material typical of oral epic to new circumstances'; (III) adaptation from one context to another; he concludes that the *Od.*'s version of the past largely conforms to type (II).

[160] *Pace* (e.g.) L. Muellner, *The Anger of Achilles* (Ithaca, NY, 1996), 118 n. 54: 'the whole concept of ad hoc invention is radically inconsistent with the principles of traditional poetic composition.'

[161] Pro-invention see: Willcock (this vol., Ch. 15) and 'Ad hoc Invention in the *Iliad*', *HSCP* 81 (1977), 41–53; B. K. Braswell, 'Mythological Innovation in the *Iliad*',

These positions are represented in this volume by Willcock and Slatkin (respectively). Slatkin (Chapter 14) is on firmest ground with her demonstration that the presentation of Thetis and her relationship with her son in the *Iliad* is determined by the poem's persistent emphasis on the mortality of its heroes; here the *Iliad* distinguishes itself from the Cycle, especially from the presentation of the doublet Memnon/Dawn, Achilles/Thetis in the *Aethiopis*. Thus the Iliadic Thetis, unlike Eos and unlike her Cyclic counterpart, who removes Achilles to the White Island, must be helpless to protect or rescue her son. But there is a concatenation of references to Thetis' protection and rescue of gods, including Zeus himself, as recounted in the passage of Book I in which Achilles asks Thetis to use her previous favour to Zeus as an argument in enlisting his support (1. 396–406).[162] Thetis loosed the bonds imposed on Zeus by Hera, Poseidon, and Athena, and used the hundred-hander, Briareos (whom men call Aegaeon), to keep the other gods at bay. This tale, which occurs in no other extant literary source,[163] clearly has (at least) a traditional core: the binding of the dominant god by his rivals is a motif that occurs in Hesiod's *Theogony*, in the context of myths of divine succession which culminate in the establishment of Zeus' authority. The *Iliad* refers directly to these traditions by its use of the figure of Briareos/Aegaeon, Zeus' ally in the Titanomachy,[164] which bears out Slatkin's contention that the motif of binding is to be construed as an application of Theogonic tradition.

Achilles' narrative thus highlights its debt to a pre-existing body of myth: the crucial questions, however, concern its details, especially the status of Thetis' contribution. First, though the opposition of

CQ 21 (1971), 16–26; Andersen (n. 139), Jones (n. 134), Jones (n. 86); anti-invention: Lang (n. 123); Slatkin (this vol., Ch. 14); G. Nagy, 'Mythological Exemplum in Homer', in R. Hexter, D. Selden (edd.), *Innovations of Antiquity* (New York 1992), 311–31 (now revisited in *Homeric Questions* (n. 1), 113–46); see also Edmunds, *Comp.* 428–34, distinguishing characters' innovations from the poet's.

[162] See also 6. 135–7 (rescues Dionysus), 18. 394–405 (rescues Hephaestus; cf. *h. Hom. Ap.* 319–20).

[163] Though Ion of Chios 741 *PMG* seems to have mentioned the summoning of Aegaeon to Olympus by Thetis, and schol. A *Il.* 1. 399 cite Didymus for a plot against Zeus on the part of Hera, Poseidon, Athena, and Apollo, foiled with the help of Briareos and resulting in the binding of Hera and the servitude of Poseidon and Apollo to Laomedon (for which cf. schol. bT on *Il.* 1. 400b); Lang (n. 123) uses this to construct a consistent narrative from scattered refs. to divine conflict; this is endorsed by Nagy (n. 161) and Edmunds, *Comp.* 432–3.

[164] *Theog.* 157–8, 501–2, 617–35, 817–19.

Hera, Poseidon, and Athena is paralleled, the threat which it poses to
Zeus' established superiority is not; elsewhere it is Zeus who threatens other gods with violence, binding, and ejection from Olympus,
not vice versa.[165] Accordingly, Willcock (Chapter 15) argues that the
particular occasion to which Achilles refers is an invented one; the
opposition of Hera, Poseidon, and Athena is to be explained not with
reference to a hypothetical mythical tradition, but in terms of the
exigencies of the immediate situation: 'It is precisely because these
are the three gods who support the Greeks in the *Iliad*, and who
would therefore most wish to prevent Zeus acceding to Thetis' request,
that they are made the opponents of Zeus in the invented myth.'[166]

This is not, however, the end of the line for Slatkin's argument, for
the status of Thetis' role in the narrative remains to be established: is
her importance in maintaining the supremacy of Zeus a function of
the invention employed in adapting traditional material to its present
purpose or is it itself a traditional element? That the latter is possible
is strongly suggested by the information given in line 404 that
Briareos 'is better in strength than his father'.[167] This detail, enigmatic in its context, seems to point to the story known to the author
of the *Prometheus Bound* and to Pindar that Zeus and Poseidon were
forced to avoid sexual congress with Thetis on account of a prophecy
that her son would be stronger than his father.[168] For Slatkin, this
story is the origin of the mortality of Achilles and of the grief of
Thetis, which (she claims) presupposes the goddess's wrath. The
argumentation here is somewhat schematic: Thetis' power to harm
is derived from the bivalence of her power to protect, and her wrath
is derived from her grief in accordance with a scheme devised by
G. Nagy for the case of Achilles. Yet Slatkin is persuasive in comparing Thetis to the wrathful Demeter of the Homeric Hymn, and the
premiss of her argument, that both the reference to Briareos *per se*

---

[165] Kirk, *Il. Comm.* I. 93–4; cf. T. N. Gantz, *Early Greek Myth* (Baltimore, 1993), 58–9.
[166] Willcock (this vol.), p. 439. Cf. schol. AbT on I. 400b.
[167] This may, puzzlingly, be an explanation of the name Aegaeon, or it may give
a reason for the choice of Briareos as ally; Briareos' father in Hesiod is Uranus
(*Theog.* 147–9), though in the *Titanomachy* the father of Aegaeon was Pontus,
according to schol. A. R. I. 1165 = *Tit.* fr. 3 Davies; but only if his father were
Poseidon would the γάρ-clause have particular point in explaining the enlisting of his
help as a means of subduing his father; but such a paternity is maintained only by
sources who draw that inference from this passage (schol. AD on I. 399, AT on I.
404, Eustath. 122. 36–7, 124. 4 = I. 182. 22–3, I. 191. 15 Van der Valk).
[168] *PV* 907–27, Pind. *Isthm.* 8. 26–48.

and the amplification that he is stronger than his father look beyond the text, is a plausible one.[169]

On the other hand, there are older versions of Thetis' relationship with Zeus than the account given by *Isthmian* 8 and alluded to in *PV*, for according to a papyrus fragment of Philodemus' *On Piety*, in the *Cypria* (fragment 2 Davies) and in the Hesiodic *Catalogue* (fragment 210 M–W) Thetis resisted Zeus' attentions because she did not wish to offend Hera, for which Zeus punished her by marrying her to a mortal. This does not prove Pindaric innovation, but it may give us pause before we assume that the audience of the *Iliad* knew the Pindaric myth.[170] It is a good hermeneutic principle that 'not mentioned' is not equivalent to 'unknown'; but in cases such as these argumentation that a given mythical variant was known and available for allusion must stop short of proof. However that may be, Slatkin's argument remains valuable, particularly in its emphasis on the *Iliad*'s consistent sense of its own ethos as a heroic poem. Even if we cannot be sure that the poem alludes to a particular tradition in which the stability of Zeus' hegemony was purchased at the price of Achilles' mortality, it remains true that the poem uses Thetis and her place in the world of the Olympians as a means of defining Achilles' mortality and thus his tragic fate; even if Achilles does not directly claim that his short life constitutes a sacrifice for Zeus' benefit which Zeus ought to recognize and requite,[171] still he emphasizes the gulf in

---

[169] Willcock (this vol., p. 440) compares the putative transformation of this motif from an application in a pre-existing myth with the appearance of the motif of petrifaction in the Niobe-paradigm, where the reference to the people's petrifaction (as an explanation for the non-burial of Niobe's children) is most probably influenced by the petrifaction of Niobe herself in the traditional story (ibid., text to n. 5). Though Slatkin sees Willcock as an opponent, his conception of invention would in this case allow her to retain much that is essential to her thesis.

[170] As J. March points out, *The Creative Poet* (*BICS* Suppl. 49, London, 1987), 8 (cf. *G&R* 40 (1993), 82) Thetis' refusal to offend Hera sits well with the detail given in *Il*. 24. 59–60 that Hera brought Thetis up—a detail which is offered as Thetis' motive for avoiding intercourse with Zeus by Apollod. 3. 13. 5. For Pindar as innovator in *Isthm*. 8 see March, ibid. 9–11, 23, A. Köhnken, 'Gods and Descendants of Aiakos in Pindar's Eighth Isthmian Ode', *BICS* 22 (1975), 25–36, and cf. Edwards, *Il. Comm.* v. 196; in favour of the antiquity of Pindar's version, see A. Lesky, *Gesammelte Schriften* (Berne, 1966), 401–9, Muellner (n. 160), 95–6, 121–2; cautious, but against the assumption of Pindaric innovation, G. A. Privitera, *Pindaro: Le Istmiche* (Milan, 1982), 121–2.

[171] Slatkin's rendering of 1. 352–4 ('Mother, since you did bear me to be short-lived | surely high-thundering Olympian Zeus ought to | grant me honour') is a mistranslation (cf. Vernant's version in Ch. 10 n. 3). 352 should be translated: 'since you [a goddess] are my mother, even though I am short-lived [mortal]'; i.e. it may be

status between himself and his mother as part of his claim to divine honour. This does not prove allusion to the *Isthmian* 8 story, but it does exploit the motifs of the closeness of Zeus and Thetis and of the status of Thetis' offspring which are central to that version. More generally, Slatkin well emphasizes the reticence and allusiveness of the *Iliad*'s treatment of the mythology of Thetis,[172] and we can be sure that, whatever the detail, this is a deliberate strategy that expresses the *Iliad*'s sense of its own artistic character. Finally, Slatkin has certainly demonstrated the importance of the *Iliad*'s location of gods as well as men in a present which presupposes a past and foreshadows a future both of which draw resonance from a wider corpus of myth and traditional stories.[173]

Willcock (Chapter 15) opposes Slatkin in arguing for ad hoc invention in the mythical exemplum of 1. 396–406, but he agrees with her in recognizing the presence of traditional material, albeit adapted to its Iliadic purpose by means of an invented detail. This, he argues, is typical of the persuasive use of mythical *exempla* or paradigms.[174] Willcock's main point is that the specific link between the situation of the paradigmatic figure and the Iliadic may in fact be invented for the sake of the parallelism itself; thus the motif of Niobe's eating in the Niobe paradigm is invented to provide the point of contact with Priam's refusal to take food in *Iliad* 24, and Meleager's anger, withdrawal, and belated return to battle (after an intensifying sequence of appeals on the part of his *philoi*) are tailored to the particular situation of Achilles in the paradigm offered by Phoenix in *Iliad* 9 (524–99). The Niobe-paradigm is indeed the test case, for the only plausible explanation for the detail of the sorrowing Niobe's partaking of food is Achilles' need to provide an argument for Priam also to do so. It is significant, however, that this is the only *de novo* invention in Achilles' version of the story; otherwise, his account of the Niobe myth is traditional, but for his explanation of the non-burial of her children as a result of the petrifaction of their potential buriers (24. 610–11), and this, Willcock well argues, is a transference of the motif of petrifaction (of Niobe herself) from the traditional

difficult to prevail upon Zeus to assist a mortal, but it should be easier when his mother is a goddess. (Cf. A. Ford's review in *CP* 89 (1994), 76.)

[172] Cf. Gantz (n. 165), 228–9.

[173] Cf. C. Emlyn-Jones, 'The Homeric Gods: Poetry, Belief, and Authority', in Emlyn-Jones, Hardwick, and Purkis (n. 21), 97.

[174] On the paradigmatic use of myth, cf. Edmunds in *Comp.* 418–20.

version. Other cases are less clear-cut, and one is often required to suspend definitive judgement on the proportion of innovative *versus* traditional material in a particular case. There is enough evidence, however, for us to conclude that some combination of tradition and invention exists in such cases, and to recognize that the study of mythological paradigmata and *exempla* in the *Iliad* is a study both of the poem's use of tradition and of the principles which guide the rhetoric of its characters.[175] Whether or not a paradigm is more invented than traditional (or vice versa), its general status and function as an argumentative tactic is clear: paradigmata are typically persuasive, sometimes consolatory, a form of authoritative speech which makes use of historical or mythical precedent to articulate norms of behaviour; the story itself is, by virtue of its presentation as a paradigm, endowed with authority, an authority which is often reinforced by the inherent status of the speaker (Nestor, Phoenix, Achilles himself in Book 24).

The most significant Iliadic paradigm is that of Meleager, whose aim is nothing less than to persuade Achilles to end his wrath and return to battle. Willcock points out how its introduction seems to place it in a wider tradition of extra-Iliadic epic, for in 524–8, Phoenix not only stresses the antiquity of the tale, but also presents it as one of the *klea* (reports, famous tales of glorious deeds) of heroes of old, using a phrase which is often taken as Homeric poetry's own term for the genre to which it belongs.[176] The familiarity of the mythical background is confirmed by the brevity of Phoenix's references to the cause of Artemis' anger, the sending of the Calydonian boar, and the expedition to kill the creature. The motif of Meleager's wrath, on the other hand, is treated expansively, and Willcock is able to point to several aspects of this expansive narrative which can be explained as results of the adaptation of the story of Meleager to its new argumentative context.[177] These include: Meleager's withdrawal from battle, in anger at his mother's curse; the reversal of his side's fortunes in battle during his absence;[178] the appeals of his people,

---

[175] Willcock (this vol., Ch. 15 n. 22) regards the technique as distinctive enough—it is not paralleled in the *Od.*—to be considered as an element of a particular poet's art. [176] Cf. n. 85 above.

[177] Cf. S. C. R. Swain, 'A Note on *Iliad* 9. 524–99', *CQ* 38 (1988), 271–6; Edmunds, *Comp.* 430 (though he does not accept the 'invention' of Meleager's anger).

[178] While Meleager fought, things went badly for their opponents, who 'could not, many though they were, remain outside the wall' (551–2). As Willcock points out

entreating him with gifts to give up his wrath, in an intensifying 'scale of affection';[179] and his obduracy, until finally persuaded by the person closest to him, his wife, Cleopatra. All these details suggest adaptation to fit not only the situation in which Achilles finds himself in Book 9, but also the broader sequence of events up to and after that point; the Meleager paradigm is emblematic of the development of Achilles' wrath in its relation both to the antecedents of his stance in Book 9 and to its consequences.

That the Meleager story required modification in order to serve as a paradigm is shown by its persistent inappropriateness for Phoenix's purposes, in spite of his best efforts to secure a match:[180] first, Phoenix uses the story as an argument to persuade Achilles to relax his anger; it performs the same function as his *exemplum* that even the gods relent (497);[181] yet it begins with the unassuageable anger of a goddess at a mortal's failure to include her in his sacrifices (533–8); more significantly, the story has an ending which Phoenix does not relate (as such) and which must have been well known to the audience—Meleager dies on his return to battle, killed either by sympathetic magic when his mother burns a log which symbolizes his life (Bacchylides 5, Phrynichus fragment 6 Snell, Aeschylus, *Choephori* 603–12; Pausanias 10. 31. 4) or by Apollo ([Hesiod] fragments 25. 9–12, 280. 2 M–W, and *Minyad* fragment 3 Davies). Phoenix cannot efface this detail entirely, but makes the mother's curse, a wish for her son's death, the cause of Meleager's anger, with a strong hint (in the reference to the Erinys' receipt of the message) to the curse's fulfilment (566–72). A version of Meleager's death, caused by his mother, Althaea, was certainly there in the version that Phoenix adapts: but we do not know whether Homer has turned the sympathetic magic of the log into a curse or adapted a version in which Meleager was killed by Apollo (a version which need not be incompatible with the motif of Althaea's curse).[182] If the latter were

---

(this vol., p. 448), 'The lines suit Achilles exactly. But they do not suit Meleager so well. Meleager was among the *defenders* of Calydon; the Curetes were the attackers (531–2).'

[179] See J. T. Kakridis, *Homeric Researches* (Lund, 1949), 141–54.
[180] See Hainsworth, *Il. Comm.* III. 130–1.   [181] Cf. Ajax at 632–8.
[182] Kakridis (n. 179), 13–16, and Hainsworth, *Il. Comm.* III. 131–2, are convinced that the motif of the log is an ancient one (contrast March (n. 170), 44–6, who regards it as originating with Stesichorus; cf. J. Bremmer, 'La Plasticité du mythe: Méléagre dans la poésie homérique', in C. Calame (ed.), *Métamorphoses du mythe en Grèce antique* (Geneva, 1988), 37–56). If old, the brand may have been omitted on

presupposed, then there would be a strong link between the Meleager paradigm and the death of Achilles and its foreshadowing in the death of Patroclus;[183] but even if the assumed knowledge of the circumstances of Meleager's death is vaguer than that, any audience would have been able to recognize that by returning to battle Meleager was hastening his own death, and will have seen the relevance of this when Achilles himself takes a decision to do precisely that. Thus the paradigm works on two levels and serves two purposes, that of Phoenix and that of the poet; the audience's knowledge of the pre-existing story both highlights its inappropriateness for Phoenix's purpose and is exploited for a wider artistic purpose which only becomes fully apparent as the *Iliad* progresses.[184]

Here we should consider another element of the paradigm which looks beyond its immediate function, namely the reference to Meleager's wife and her place in the 'scale of affection' (556–65, 590–6). Hers forms the culmination of the appeals of *philoi* which persuade Meleager to relent; but this is less part of Phoenix's argument (for his purpose is to place Meleager's comrades as high as possible in the hierarchy in order to provide a parallel to the current situation) than of the poet's, for whom Meleager's wife corresponds to Achilles' closest *philos*, Patroclus, whose appeal is decisive in Achilles' own case. This being so, many have commented on the fact that the names of these two figures, Cleopatra and Patroclus, are compounded of the same two elements. There is argument, first, as to whether this is significant: Willcock is sceptical in the article reproduced in this volume, but better disposed to the idea in his commentary on 556;[185] if the point is significant, then one name has presumably been invented to recall the other; and if this is so, then surely Cleopatra is the invention: she, after all, has another name (Alcyone, 562), and it seems that it is by this name that she is better known, as it occurs in a digression (557–64) on her parents whose allusiveness indicates its reference to a pre-existing myth.[186]

the *'Parisurteil*-principle'; but perhaps merely because it would make Meleager's death appear more present than it already is.

[183] NB also the conflict between the hero and Apollo in the digression on Idas and Marpessa in 557–64; see Edmunds, *Comp.* 431–2.

[184] See Edmunds, *Comp.* 426–8, 430–2.

[185] *Homer: Iliad* I–XII (London, 1978), 282.

[186] R. von Scheliha, *Patroklos* (Basle, 1943), 247, argued that Patroclus is an Iliadic invention; but see Janko, *Il. Comm.* IV. 312–14, Snodgrass, (n. 24) 72.

This digression, in fact, may have the purpose of rooting the innovation of the invented name in the authority of pre-existing mythology.[187]

The Meleager paradigm is thus paradigmatic also of the *Iliad*'s engagement with a wider poetic and mythological tradition: there is concise allusion to other well-known stories; reworking and reconfiguration of traditional material; and, ultimately, a version of an external story which is made to illuminate the *Iliad*'s own central concerns and to conform to its sense of itself as a poem of tragic heroism.

The chapters of Griffin, Kullmann, Willcock, and Slatkin have led us to consider the traditionality and the individuality of the *Iliad*; we close with two chapters (Redfield, Chapter 16, De Jong, Chapter 17) which not only illustrate significant literary approaches to the poem with reference to passages of Book 1, but which also in their way offer perspectives on the individuality of the poem's artistry. Both indicate in their different ways contemporary criticism's successful overcoming of oralist objections to the literary interpretation of epic:[188] oral theory's challenge to literary criticism (the demand for a new, 'oral poetics') fastened on a form of literary criticism that is no longer practised, one that focused on significant use of individual words, either in terms of traditional, belletristic connoisseurship or from a New Critical perspective (identifying long-range echoes, patterns, and ironies in the disposition of single terms).[189] Strict oralist objections can be countered on their own terms: it may be true that the formula rather than the single word is the lexical unit, but this does not deprive that unit of the potential for significant meaning;[190] the impression that Homeric lines compose themselves on the basis of their formulas has never been justified; and there exist examples enough of significant choice of epithet from

---

[187] See Hainsworth, *Il. Comm.* III. 130 on 561–3; contrast Edmunds, *Comp.* 431.

[188] See (e.g.) J. A. Notopoulos, 'Parataxis in Homer', *TAPA* 80 (1949), 1–23; id. 'Towards a Poetics of Early Greek Oral Poetry', *HSCP* 68 (1964), 46–65; F. M. Combellack, 'Milman Parry and Homeric Artistry', *Comparative Literature* 11 (1959), 193–208; cf. J. B. Hainsworth, 'The Criticism of an Oral Homer', *JHS* 90 (1970), 190–8 = Emlyn-Jones, Hardwick, and Purkis (n. 21), 65–75. On the implications of M. Parry's work for criticism, see A. Parry in M. Parry (n. 1), pp. L–LXII.

[189] Hence oralists make so much of the fact that there is no concept of the single 'word' in Serbo-Croat oral song: A. B. Lord, *The Singer of Tales* (Cambridge, Mass., 1960), 25, Foley in *Comp.* 151–3; cf. Finkelberg (n. 41), 123–4.

[190] See A. Parry in M. Parry (n. 1), p. LV.

a plurality of possibilities, as well as of significant application of stock combinations.[191]

But the real answer to the call for a distinct, non-literary, oral poetics is that no such thing is necessary.[192] Certainly, all interpreters of Homer need to have orality constantly in mind (especially in confronting the use of repetitions, type-scenes, themes, and formulas), but the constraints that this places on the forms of literary criticism chiefly employed today are minimal. As Janko points out, 'our basic notions of "literary" style have been decisively shaped by poems of oral origin'.[193] Beyond that, the many modern schools of criticism which focus on factors such as the poem's key themes and concepts, its relation to its tradition, its cultural context, its ideological orientation, its presentation of the story (etc.) have no need to be inhibited by considerations of orality. So much has the tide turned, in fact, that the onus is now on oralists to demonstrate that there is any significant way in which the status of the *Iliad* as an oral-derived text precludes or limits the application of familiar interpretative strategies.[194]

Redfield's detailed and wide-ranging discussion combines traditional classical scholarship with the tools of contemporary linguistics and with structuralist poetics and anthropology. Like Macleod, he stresses the importance of the proem as an indicator of the poem's theme and of its scope, and shows how it encapsulates *in parvo* the poem's movement from Achilles' wrath to the fate of those slain in battle, how it moves from focus on the individual hero to the community of the living and the dead and thence to the plan of Zeus, and how it takes the reader from the statement of the poem's theme and its significance to the initial point in the narrative. The proem, on Redfield's interpretation, both exhibits a formal structure of its own, encompassing a range of expressive poetic devices such as personification and metaphor, and presents *in nuce* the poem's concentration on human suffering and the location of human beings between beasts and gods. Homer's art, in the composition of this proem, lies

---

[191] See Redfield, this vol., Ch. 16, for this approach.

[192] See R. Thomas, *Orality and Literacy in Classical Greece* (Cambridge, 1992), 29–51.

[193] Janko, *Il. Comm.* IV. p. XI; developed in (n. 6), 11; this view is endorsed even by Foley in *Comp.* 173.

[194] See De Jong in Crielaard (n. 18), 134, quoting the preface to D. Shive's *Naming Achilles* (Oxford, 1987).

not in inventive departure from tradition, but in the deployment of familiar epic diction in striking ways.

The intersection of the various strands of Redfield's erudition is most striking in his defence and discussion of δαῖτα ('feast', the reading of Zenodotus), rather than πᾶσι ('all', sc. birds) in 1. 5. For Kirk (ad loc.) the former is merely 'a fussy change of the vulgate', and one might initially suspect that Redfield's preference is a symptom of the structuralist fixation on the 'alimentary code' as a significant element in the articulation of a culture's *mentalité*. But this would be unfair: as Redfield points out, δαῖτα seems to have been current in the fifth century, to judge from the imitation of the proem at Aeschylus, *Suppliants* 800–1; the reading thus deserves more consideration than Kirk gives it.[195] Redfield's analysis goes further, however, in its observation that δαῖτα is confirmed by τεῦχε, used here as the proper word for the preparing of a meal and governing ἑλώρια (prey) by a slight zeugma. There is therefore a distinct possibility that the proem, by conflating human consumption of cooked food in a civilized setting (δαῖτα) with birds' feeding on raw human flesh, does, in fact, look forward to the disruption in the alimentary code that is such a feature of later parts of the poem, as exposure and mutilation of bodies, their consumption by birds, dogs, and fish, and finally even cannibalism threaten to fulfil in extremes of savagery the negation of civilization implicit in civilization's practice of warfare. As Redfield well notes, the horror of the consumption of the unburied corpse is threatened, but never realized in the poem itself, yet it is presented as a factual consequence of the *mēnis* of Achilles in the proem; thus the proem prefigures the vividness and the reality with which the imminence of the threat is later presented to the audience.[196]

Redfield's remarks on the personification of the *mēnis* through the adjective οὐλομένην (as well as by its function as subject of the phrase 'which inflicted countless pangs on the Achaeans') make

[195] Its merits are acknowledged by Leaf and Willcock ad loc.; cf. Pfeiffer (n. 28), III–13, Haslam in *Comp.* 72; Janko, *Il. Comm.* IV. 23, regards it as an early emendation. Pfeiffer (III) compares (as well as Aesch. *Supp.* 800–1) also Soph. *Ant.* 29–30 and Eur. *Ion* 504–5, *Hec.* 1078; Soph. *Aj.* 830 and Ar. *Av.* 1117, on the other hand, may be thought to provide 5th-cent. evidence of the vulgate reading (see M. L. West's *apparatus* (Stuttgart, 1998) ad loc.).

[196] The topic is explored further by C. P. Segal, *The Theme of the Mutilation of the Corpse in the Iliad* (Leiden, 1971) and by Redfield himself in *Nature and Culture* (n. 15); cf. Vernant, this vol., Ch. 10.

use of an important distinction between character-language and narrative-language: οὐλόμενος is otherwise confined to speeches, and shares with other terms similarly restricted a subjective note of emotional engagement which is generally rare in the narrator-text.[197] This distinction has, since Redfield wrote, been the subject of more systematic study by Homeric narratologists, notably Irene de Jong, whose discussion of *Iliad* 1. 366–92 in Chapter 17 serves as an introduction to an approach which has borne considerable fruits in demonstrating the subtlety with which the Homeric narrative presents the point of view of narrator and characters as a means of guiding the reader's response.[198] De Jong's subject is a character-speech which is also itself a (secondary) narrative, namely Achilles' account to Thetis of the circumstances surrounding his withdrawal from the fighting, circumstances which have already been conveyed to the audience in the preceding narrative. Analysis of these two narratives in narratological terms demonstrates the artistry of the poet—the composer of both—in using direct speech and secondary narrative to convey Achilles' own perspective on the events which trigger the plot of the whole poem. For despite a degree of verbatim repetition that is typical of the oral style, and despite similarities in the modes of presentation of Achilles as narrator and of the primary narrator (especially in the former's temporary assumption of the latter's habitual 'omniscience'), Achilles' version demonstrates the higher degree of emotional engagement with what is related that is typical of speeches in general, and is to be seen not only in terms of the rhetoric of Achilles' request that his mother intercede with Zeus on his behalf, but also as

[197] See J. Griffin, 'Homeric Words and Speakers' (aka 'Words and Speakers in Homer'), *JHS* 106 (1986), 36–57, I. J. F. de Jong, 'Homeric Words and Speakers: An Addendum', *JHS* 108 (1988), 188–9, ead. in F. Létoublon (ed.), *Homage à Milman Parry* (Amsterdam, 1997), 293–302, Martin (n. 64). In her reply to Griffin in *JHS* 1988 (cf. *Comp.* 317), De Jong points out that passages of 'embedded focalization' (in which a character's point of view is embedded in the narrator-text) share some of the characteristics of speeches, and that the narrator-text, although largely bereft of the emotional and evaluative terms which are found in character-language, is none the less not to be regarded as absolutely 'objective', in the sense that it eschews the presentation of events in a manner designed to excite a particular evaluation.

[198] See esp. De Jong, *Narrators and Focalizers: The Presentation of the Story in the Iliad* (Amsterdam, 1987); S. Richardson, *The Homeric Narrator* (Nashville, 1990); L. E. Doherty, *Siren Songs: Gender, Audiences, and Narrators in the Odyssey* (Ann Arbor, 1995); cf. De Jong's 'Homer and Narratology', in *Comp.* 305–25.

an important contributor to his characterization at this crucial stage in the plot, and thus as a significant factor in the manipulation of the audience's sympathies by the poet.[199]

All of the articles included in this volume and discussed in this Introduction demonstrate that the *Iliad* is a poem which invites and demands interpretation on the part of any audience, ancient or modern. Evaluation of issues, acts, and individuals—emotional, ethical, and intellectual engagement—is essential to any satisfactory response. This engagement requires the fullest possible historical and cultural awareness, but cannot proceed on the basis of alienating strategies which categorize the poem and its contexts as radically other and primitive, or which presuppose an absence of commonality between different societies and different periods. One needs to acquire a range of skills and overcome a number of obstacles, both inherent in the material and erected by generations of professional experts, to get the most out of reading Homer's *Iliad*, but, as I hope the readings collected here demonstrate, the rewards fully justify the effort.

[199] As B. Heiden points out ('The Three Movements of the *Iliad*', *GRBS* 37 (1996), 11–12), Achilles' sequential narrative of events from their beginning in the raid on Thebe (1. 366–9) highlights by contrast the artistry of the poet in beginning with the *kephalaion* (principle point), the quarrel of Achilles and Agamemnon (1. 6–7).

I

The Use and Abuse of Homer

IAN MORRIS

I. INTRODUCTION

In this chapter, I make three main arguments.[1] First, I suggest that
the societies described in the *Iliad* and *Odyssey* tell us most about the
world Homer himself lived in. I make this argument by asking four
questions: how, when, why, and for whom were the *Iliad* and
Odyssey created? There are three ways to answer them: (*a*) through
information in the poems themselves; (*b*) through information in later
sources; and (*c*) through analogies with similar literature in better
documented societies. I conclude in section II that modern work on
oral poetry suggests that the basic cultural assumptions in the poems
derive from Homer's own society, and are not memories of vanished
worlds five, four, or even one century earlier. But comparative evidence is suggestive rather than decisive, and in section III, I consider
the most influential argument against this position, concluding that
it is not strong enough to undermine comparative expectations.

My second argument is that efforts to reconstruct *Homeric society*
are secondary to analyses of *Homeric culture*. By 'Homeric society',
I mean institutions and forms of behaviour; by 'Homeric culture',
I mean taken-for-granted attitudes about how the world works. In
sections IV and V I argue that Homer's heroic age is what *one poet* in
the eighth century BC thought that a vanished heroic age *ought* to be
like. Other poets had other ideas, now lost to us. These may have
been very different. I suggest that Homer's vision was transformed
into something like the texts we now have because it was a

---

[1] I have completely rewritten the original version of this chapter, shortening it,
clarifying the argument, and responding to new publications and critiques of my
essay. The main argument is much the same, but I distinguish more sharply between
social and cultural interpretations. I use Lattimore's translations.

particularly appealing one to aristocrats who had the resources both to transform it into written texts and to promote these fixed versions.

Understanding Homeric culture is vital for any larger history of Greek ideologies.[2] But my third argument is that we can go beyond such a history of ideologies to write a social history of the eighth century. Historians have tried to do this in three main ways: first, by simply treating the poems as sociological texts; second, by claiming to be able to 'sift' them for impurities; and third, by adding what Homer says to other sources (usually Hesiod) in the hope of producing a rounded picture. I argue in section VI that our best prospects come not from doing any of these things, but from making Homer part of a historical archaeology. The archaeological record is the residue of ritual actions in which people used material culture as a language for debating much the same questions as they discussed in contemporary poetry. Neither material nor poetic culture are transparent windows on to eighth-century reality; we cannot use either to check or test our interpretations of the other. Eighth-century words and things always come to us already shaped by ancient cultural concerns, but the ways in which the two records were formed were entirely different. By playing these different contexts off against one another—by translating back and forth between different early archaic language games—we can distinguish between what belonged to a particularly Homeric ideology and what formed part of the larger society.[3]

II. HOMER AS AN ORAL POET

(a) The Oral Composition Hypothesis

Milman Parry's first great achievement, in essays published between 1930 and 1933, was to find methods to study Homer's traditional

---

[2] The work of historians, archaeologists, and literary critics is converging in creating such a history: see J. Ober, *The Athenian Revolution* (Princeton, 1996), 3–12; I. Morris, 'Archaeology and Archaic Greek History', in N. Fisher and H. van Wees (edd.), *Archaic Greece* (London, 1998), 71–4; L. Kurke, *Coins, Bodies, Games, and Gold* (Princeton, 1999).

[3] In theoretical terms, this means recognizing the contributions of the new cultural history of the 1980s–90s without fully accepting its claims that social experience is radically discontinuous, which would make conventional kinds of social history impossible. See I. Morris, *Archaeology as Cultural History* (Oxford, 2000), 3–29.

language from the texts themselves. He concluded that 'Homer' was the representative of a long and anonymous oral tradition, with the result that 'the diction of the *Iliad* and *Odyssey*, being altogether traditional ... is filled with phrases emptier of meaning than any in Pope or Falconer'. Parry felt that an oral poet 'will do no more than put together for his needs phrases which he has often heard or used himself ... and he will recall his poem easily, when he wishes to say it over, because he will be guided anew by the same play of words and phrases as before ... the style which he uses is not his at all: it is the creation of a long line of poets or even of an entire people'. Consequently, 'his poetry remains throughout the sum of longer and shorter passages which he has heard'.[4] In these early works, Parry viewed oral poetry as rigid, composed mechanically, and largely memorized.

In 1933 Parry began fieldwork in Serbia to illustrate his theories, and immediately discovered that oral composition was more flexible. His colleague Albert Lord explained that 'oral ... does not mean merely oral presentation ... what is important is not the oral presentation but rather the composition *during* performance'.[5] Despite their claims to verbatim reproduction, Serbian performances varied enormously, and for Lord fluidity of themes, scenes, and wording was characteristic of oral poetry.[6] There are traditions where poets achieve some memorization, and Finnegan has collected examples from Somalia, Hawaii, Alaska, and the Appalachians.[7] But both Lord, working in Serbia, and Jack Goody, working in west Africa, concluded that large-scale memorization only appears in literate societies, where there is a fixed text to memorize, and a concept of its exact transmission.[8] Finnegan has downplayed boundaries between literate and oral culture, but notes that 'As soon as one looks hard at the notion of exact verbal reproduction over long periods of time, it becomes clear that there is very little evidence for it.'[9] Even the Indian *Rigveda*, often taken as the archetypal memorized text, has far

---

[4] M. Parry, *The Making of Homeric Verse* (Oxford, 1971), 370, 270, 335.

[5] A. B. Lord, *The Singer of Tales* (Cambridge, Mass., 1960), 5.

[6] Lord (n. 5), 20–9.

[7] R. Finnegan, *Oral Poetry* (Cambridge, 1977), 73–87, 135–9.

[8] J. Goody, 'Mémoire et apprentissage dans les sociétés avec et sans écriture', *L'Homme* 17 (1977), 42–9; A. B. Lord, 'Memory, Fixity, and Genre in Oral Traditional Poetics', in J. M. Foley (ed.), *Oral Traditional Literature* (Columbus, Oh., 1981), 460.

[9] Finnegan (n. 7), 140.

more variants than is generally recognized.[10] Strong claims of verbatim reproduction have been made for Xhosa poetry from South Africa, but in practice it rarely rises above 60 per cent accuracy from one performance to another.[11] Try as they might to keep a song the same, poets composing in performance inevitably recreate it differently; over time, it will change significantly.

Tracing changes in one song between performances in 1934–5 and 1950–1, Lord concluded that

the changes of which we have been speaking have been brought about, not by forces seeking change for its own sake, nor by pure chance, but by an insistent, conservative urge for preservation of an essential idea expressed in a single theme or group of themes.[12]

The oral-composition theory is now widely accepted.[13] The critics among classicists generally attack Parry's early works, rather than Lord's development of them. Some take offence at Parry's early claims that Homer's epithets carry no literary meaning, and refute this position by showing how flexible they could be. Others argue that Parry was blinded by his hostility to Romantic poetics, which made him unable to appreciate oral aesthetics.[14] But these arguments in no way contradict Lord's more developed oral-composition model, which remains compelling.

(b) The Past in Oral Poetry

Important consequences follow from Lord's model. If, as he says, oral poetry is constantly recomposed in performance, then it is unlikely that large blocks of poetry, and with them accurate accounts of centuries-old institutions or ideas, will be transmitted over long periods of time. It would be an exaggeration to say that oral societies float in a perpetual present, but ideas which are no longer relevant to

---

[10] W. J. Ong, *Orality and Literacy* (London, 1982), 66–8.
[11] J. Opland, *Xhosa Oral Poetry* (Cambridge, 1983).   [12] Lord (n. 5), 120.
[13] See J. M. Foley, *The Theory of Oral Composition* (Bloomington, Ind., 1988), and the journal *Oral Tradition*.
[14] e.g. N. Austin, *Archery at the Dark of the Moon* (Berkeley, 1975); P. Vivante, *The Epithets in Homer* (New Haven, 1982); D. Shive, *Naming Achilles* (Oxford, 1987); M. Lynn-George, *Epos: Word, Narrative, and the Iliad* (Basingstoke, 1988). See P. Zumthor, *Oral Poetry* (Minneapolis, 1990), on oral poetics and aesthetics.

the present do rapidly disappear. As Ong and Finnegan explain,

oral societies live very much in a present which keeps itself in equilibrium by sloughing off memories which no longer have present relevance . . . oral traditions reflect a society's present cultural values rather than idle curiosity about the past.[15]

Differently performed, or performed at a different time, or to a different audience or by a different singer, [an oral poem] is a different poem. In this sense, an oral poem is an essentially ephemeral work of art, and has no existence of continuity apart from its performance . . . In this respect, oral literature differs from our implicit model of written literature: the mode of communication to a silent reader, through the eye alone, from a definitive written text. Oral literature is more flexible and more dependent on its social context.[16]

For example, British authorities in Nigeria and Ghana found that Tiv and Gonja traditions changed considerably in less than two generations, to fit the needs of the present, and Lord found that the Novi Pazar had no way to keep track of how far their traditions were changing.[17] The performing poet continuously sloughs off unnecessary parts of the past, in interaction with his audience. Those dimensions of vanished institutions and conditions of action that no longer seem meaningful disappear. As Redfield says,

In telling a story the poet employs and persuades us to certain assumptions about the sources and conditions of action. He thus (in effect) takes a view of culture. And further: since he is telling his story to an audience, the meaning he conveys must be a meaning to them.[18]

Oral poetry must make sense to poet and audience; just as the poem was re-created in every performance, so too we can speak of a constantly re-created oral tradition. Far from being a repository of antiquated world-views, it is present-oriented, consisting only of what the parties to the performance think proper. Their sense of propriety is likely to include archaic artefacts and practices, and may actively resist what the poet and his audience think are recent innovations (see below on the 'epic distance'). But oral epic poetry tells us about the poet's and audience's imagination of what a heroic world *ought* to have been like, which is necessarily crafted from the materials of their own cultures.

---

[15] Ong (n. 10), 46–8.   [16] Finnegan (n. 7), 28–9.
[17] J. Goody and I. Watt, 'The Consequences of Literacy', in J. Goody (ed.), *Literacy in Traditional Societies* (Cambridge, 1968), 31–3; Lord (n. 5), 27.
[18] J. M. Redfield, *Nature and Culture in the Iliad* (Chicago, 1975), 23.

Homer's descriptions of poetic performances fit this picture.[19] His bards described heroic and divine actions that their audiences normally had not directly experienced. Yet the highest praise that a poet could receive was that he was absolutely truthful. As Odysseus said to Demodocus on Phaeacia,

> 'Demodocus, above all mortals beside I praise you.
> Surely the Muse, Zeus' daughter or else Apollo has taught you,
> for all too right following the tale you sing the Achaeans'
> venture, all they did and had done to them, all the sufferings
> of these Achaeans, as if you had been there yourself or had heard it
> from one who was.'

(Odyssey 8. 487–91)

How could the audience judge who was the best poet? It was easy for Odysseus, since he had been at Troy, but no one in Homer's or Demodocus' audiences had. Yet Demodocus could be judged λαοῖσι τετιμένον, 'the people's favourite' (8. 472). While a poet could sing about any theme (Phemius, *Odyssey* 1. 337–40; Demodocus, 8. 45), the audience's reaction determined his success, and their reports his reputation (e.g. 1. 351–2; 8. 496–8; cf. *Homeric Hymn to Apollo* 165–73; for bad results, *Odyssey* 1. 336–42; 8. 536–41).

Homer was clear that truthfulness came from the Muses (*Odyssey* 8. 488; 22. 346–8). The Muses taught poets about the heroic age (*Iliad* 1. 1–7; 2. 484–92; 11. 218–20; 14. 508; 16. 113–14; *Odyssey* 1. 1–10; 8. 73, 479–81, 496–8; 22. 346–8; cf. Hesiod, *Works and Days* 1; *Theogony* 22–8), but the audience judged the extent of the poet's inspiration and therefore the truth of his account. Homeric poetry had to satisfy its audiences; it had to conform to *their* ideas of how the heroic world had worked. It was not a recreation of a society that had vanished, or a composite made up from many chronological periods. It was part of a living culture.

That said, every society has constraints on what can legitimately be said about the past.[20] If Lord was right, Homer was trying both to transmit the received 'tradition' and to describe events he and his audience knew as having taken place in the distant past. The heroic age was different from his own, and he had to make sure everyone knew this. He used various devices to create what Redfield calls

---

[19] See, most recently, A. Dalby, 'Homer's Enemies: Lyric and Epic in the Seventh Century', in Fisher and Van Wees (n. 2), 196–200.

[20] A. Appadurai, 'The Past as a Scarce Resource', *Man* 16 (1981), 201–19.

'epic distance'.[21] He archaized, describing boars' tusk helmets, bronze weapons, and war chariots; he exaggerated, invoking untold wealth and impossible strength; and he invented, bringing in monsters and talking rivers and horses. Often the three methods blurred into each other.[22]

Oral poets in other cultures use similar techniques. Goody distinguishes between what he calls 'situations totales' and 'informations auditives'.[23] The former are poetic elements that had external *visual* referents—real places, roads that can be walked, etc. Thus Homer's Catalogue of Ships (*Iliad* 2. 484–759) listed major Bronze-Age centres accurately. In the eighth century, the power of Mycenae, Pylos, and Orchomenos was a thing of the past, but it retained a solid visual referent in the actual sites. 'Mycenae rich in gold' made sense to people, even if Mycenae was now a poor hamlet. Similarly, men no longer fought with bronze spears, but could understand such things. As the oral tradition was recreated, so too were the 'total situations' of epic distance.[24]

Goody's second class of situations, those without visual referents, is very different. Giant shields might not exist, but an audience could grasp what was meant. Similarly, for centuries poets kept singing about heroic kings fighting from chariots with bronze weapons and living in palaces. All these were concrete, imaginable entities. Chariots were still used in certain contexts; some bronze weapons remained in use (particularly in western Greece); and in addition to the crumbling ruins of actual Mycenaean palaces, it was not hard to visualize a big house. But Homer's warriors used their bronze swords and chariots very differently from the Mycenaeans, and the poet had no conception of Mycenaean palaces functioning as redistributive centres with professional scribes writing in a syllabic script. Only those elements of vanished institutions and practices which had a clear present referent remained meaningful. Those which did not

---

[21] Redfield (n. 18), 36–7.

[22] See H. van Wees, *Status Warriors* (Amsterdam, 1992), 16–21.

[23] Goody (n. 8), 37.

[24] Archaeologists have long treated the stratified nature of these total situations as evidence that the entire Homeric picture is a conflation of real elements drawn from different chronological periods (e.g. H. Lorimer, *Homer and the Monuments* (London, 1950); E. S. Sherratt, ' "Reading the Texts": Archaeology and the Homeric Question', *Antiquity* 64 (1990), 807–24). This misunderstands the nature of Homeric composition, as well as oversimplifying the material record (see I. Morris, 'Homer and the Iron Age', in *Comp.* 535–59).

disappeared from oral traditions just as they disappeared from Greek life.

Recently, however, William Sale has argued that the history of Serbian epic contradicts this. He suggests that

> Svetozar Koljević's *The Epic in the Making* ... shows how a body of poetry, known to be oral, at times reflects contemporary society, at times earlier society, and at times a blend of societies. Koljevic is able to determine reasonably well what is contemporary and what is earlier, and how much earlier, because we have a fair amount of information about medieval and renaissance Serbia and are even relatively well-informed about later periods.[25]

But Koljević's position was actually rather different. After explaining that he was analysing 'a complex give-and-take relationship between oral and literary culture' (unlike the situation in Dark-Age Greece), Koljević described poetic accounts of Serbia before the Turkish conquest as creating an idealized 'patriarchal never-never land', standing for 'the last times' before the infidel deluge. This image, Koljević argued, was 'rooted in the biblical idea of the Last Judgement'.[26] Eighteenth- and nineteenth-century singers reinvented fourteenth-century society in order to address their own ideological concerns. Nor is our knowledge of medieval Serbia as accurate as Sale suggests: the defining moment in most Serbian poetry is the battle of Kossovo in 1389, after which, according to V. S. Karadzić, the Serbs 'forgot everything that happened before and began henceforth to sing and spin their tales anew'.[27] Yet, as Koljević observes, 'there is no other major event in Serbian history about which so little is known'. Finally, in keeping with Goody's model, 'medieval facts and fantasies lived vividly for the later epic singers because they could see them on the fresco paintings of the Serbian churches and monasteries, together with some of their epic heroes'.[28]

(c) From Oral Performance to Written Text

If Lord's model of fluid oral composition in performance is sound, then Homer's assumptions about how the heroic world worked necessarily derive from the period when the *Iliad* and *Odyssey* were

---

[25] W. M. Sale, 'The Government of Troy', *GRBS* 35 (1994), 16–17.
[26] S. Koljević, *The Epic in the Making* (Oxford, 1980), 2, 103, 105.
[27] Quoted in Koljević (n. 26), 158.   [28] Koljević (n. 26), 105.

fixed in writing.[29] Lord suggested that this happened through dictation.[30] Our texts are not oral poetry, but *oral-derived* poetry.[31] Until dictated, the poems were constantly changing, with unwanted elements disappearing. Most historians put Homer around 750–700 BC, though the basis for this is weak. There are six groups of evidence:[32]

(I) External authority. Herodotus (2. 53) dated Homer and Hesiod four hundred years before his own time, so around 825 BC. Elsewhere (2. 145) he used a forty-year generation, and his date may mean 'ten generations'. This would leave Homer around 725, but the argument is hardly compelling. The other main literary sources are Cicero (*De oratore* 3. 137) and pseudo-Plato (*Hipparchus* 228b). They tell of a Pisistratid recension, dating the first authoritative texts of Homer after 550 BC, though they do not deny the existence of pre-Pisistratid texts.

(II) Internal evidence. Some scholars wish to date the poems like archaeological layers, by the latest datable objects in them. Pointing to the prominence of Egyptian Thebes, Athena's lamp, hoplite warfare, etc., they often suggest a point around 650 BC.[33] Again, the arguments are tenuous, given the clear evidence for changes in the texts in Alexandria. To extend the archaeological metaphor, Homer does not provide sealed deposits.

(III) Vase paintings. Assuming that artists would respond to the texts of Homer, some classicists look for the earliest 'Homeric' scenes. Some see them in the eighth century; others see none before the sixth. And in any case, as Snodgrass shows, there is no reason to assume any direct link between texts of our *Iliad* and *Odyssey* and artistic traditions.[34]

[29] G. Nagy (*Poetry into Performance* (Cambridge, 1996), 29–112; *Homeric Questions* (Austin, 1996), 107–225) has argued that the poems were only written down in the 6th cent., but had already reached substantially the form we know today in the 8th, crystallizing in oral performance. I attach much more importance to writing, but since Nagy agrees that our texts are close to the 8th-cent. versions, his arguments do not undermine my main conclusions about Homeric culture.

[30] A. B. Lord, 'Homer's Originality: Oral-Dictated Texts', *TAPA* 48 (1953), 34–54; cf. R. Janko, 'The Homeric Poems as Oral-Dictated Texts', *CQ* 48 (1998), 1–13.

[31] See J. M. Foley, *Immanent Art* (Bloomington, Ind., 1991), on the distinction.

[32] The evidence is reviewed in detail by B. Powell, *Homer and the Origin of the Greek Alphabet* (Cambridge, 1991), 187–220.

[33] e.g. M. L. West, 'The Date of the *Iliad*', *MH* 52 (1995), 203–19.

[34] A. M. Snodgrass, *Homer and the Artists* (Cambridge, 1998).

(IV) Nestor's Cup. Powell suggests that the reference to Nestor scratched on a cup in Pithekoussai gr. 168, around 725–700 BC, is a joke based on *Iliad* 11. 632–7. He concludes that 'these Euboian far-wanderers evidently knew Homer's poem well'.[35] However, it is just as likely (perhaps more so) that we see here a reference to the general heroic tradition, rather than to a text of the actual *Iliad* that we have.

(v) Tomb cult. Coldstream[36] suggested that the sudden interest in Mycenaean tombs after 750 BC was a response to Homer. But as Snodgrass points out, 'the contrast between the cremation, covered by a tumulus, that Homer describes and the multiple inhumations in rock-cut chamber tombs where most of the cults were instituted is so complete that it positively excludes familiarity with Homer—or, at least, identification of the object of the cult with a "Homeric hero" '.[37]

(VI) Language. Janko's statistical analysis suggests that the *Iliad* and *Odyssey* reached their current forms before Hesiod or the Hymns, and makes it very likely that they are substantially older than other archaic poetry.[38] The dates he suggests, in the eighth century, are only guesses, but they are the best we can do.

No piece of evidence is decisive, but the late eighth century seems most plausible, with further significant editing in the sixth. Snodgrass points out that an 'attitude of deference to the heroic past was an important element in the revolution that was sweeping through Greek life' around 750–700 BC.[39] This provides the most likely context for Homer's activity.

Further, a date around 750–700 seems to coincide with the invention of the Greek alphabet, without which there could be no written text. Linear B disappears after 1200 BC, and the earliest example of the alphabet may be four or five signs scratched on a flask in gr. 482/3 at Osteria dell'Osa in Latium, around 800–775, though this may not actually be Greek.[40] The word *Alikoeos* was scratched on a sherd dating c. 775 found on Naxos, but may postdate the pot's

[35] Powell (n. 32), 167. The grave is published in G. Buchner and D. Ridgway, *Pithekoussai* I (Rome, 1993).

[36] J. N. Coldstream, 'Hero Cults in the Age of Homer', *JHS* 96 (1976), 8–17.

[37] A. M. Snodgrass, *An Archaeology of Greece* (Berkeley, 1987), 161; see also C. Antonaccio, *An Archaeology of Ancestors* (Lanham, Md., 1995).

[38] R. Janko, *Homer, Hesiod, and the Hymns* (Cambridge, 1982).

[39] A. M. Snodgrass, *Archaic Greece* (London, 1980), 77.

[40] A. M. Bietti Sestieri, *The Iron Age Community of Osteria dell'Osa* (Cambridge, 1992), 184–5; E. Peruzzi, 'Cultura greca a Gabii nel secolo VIII', *PdP* 47 (1992), 459–68.

manufacture.[41] But several inscriptions definitely date 750–725, and by 700 writing was common.

These chronological coincidences suggest that Homer was active in the mid- or late eighth century, and that his poems were dictated soon after writing returned to Greece after a four-century break. Some Semiticists, however, argue that although the oldest inscriptions from Greece are eighth-century, their letter forms are derived from Phoenician signs of the eleventh century.[42] They conclude that writing was known in Greece across the Dark Age, but was used in archaeologically invisible ways. A bronze bowl with a short Phoenician inscription was found in a Knossian tomb of about 900 BC, showing that at least some Greeks knew of the concept of writing.[43]

This is an important point. Whether we accept the Lordian model of oral composition and the eighth-century date for Homer or not, *if* writing existed in Greece across the Dark Age, and *if* it was used to record heroic poetry on perishable materials like parchment or papyrus, and *if* this influenced Homer, this transforms historical interpretations of the *Iliad* and *Odyssey*. But this argument piles up ifs. The question comes down to weighing up the positive and negative evidence. The early transmission thesis rests on positive evidence of letter forms, but the total corpus of pre-500 BC Phoenician inscriptions is fewer than a dozen, and the distinctions between letter forms are subtle. The late transmission thesis is an argument from silence, but the number of post-700 inscriptions is now large, and there is still no sign of pre-800 BC Greek writing. The arguments for an eighth-century invention seem stronger to me,[44] although a single new find might completely change historical interpretations of Homer.

[41] V. Lambrinoudakis, 'Anaskaphi Naxou', *Praktika* 1981, 294, with Powell (n. 32), 131.

[42] J. Naveh, *Early History of the Alphabet* (Jerusalem, 1982).

[43] M. Sznycer, 'L'Inscription phénicienne de Tekke, près de Cnossus', *Kadmos* 18 (1979), 89–93. The 9th-cent. horse ornaments inscribed with Aramaic dedications to king Hazael of Damascus found at Eretria and Samos (F. Bron and A. Lemaire, 'Les Inscriptions araméennes de Hazaël', *Revue d'Assyriologie* 83 (1989), 35–44; I. Eph'al and J. Naveh, 'Hazael's Booty Inscriptions', *Israel Exploration Journal* 39 (1989), 192–200) were only deposited in the late 8th cent. (A. Charbonnet, 'Le Dieu aux lions d'Érétrie', *Annali del Istituto Orientale di Napoli* 8 (1986), 117–73; H. Kyrieleis and W. Rölling, 'Ein altorientalischer Pferdeschmuck aus dem Heraion von Samos', *MDAI(A)* 103 (1988), 37–75), and may not be relevant to Greek knowledge of writing before 750.   [44] See particularly Powell (n. 32).

I summarize the argument so far as four connected hypotheses:

1. The *Iliad* and *Odyssey* are oral-dictated texts.
2. The oral poems our texts derive from were composed in performance, as in Lord's model.
3. The poems were dictated around 750–700 BC.
4. There was little or no writing in Greece between 1200 and 750 BC.

If these hypotheses can be accepted,[45] then we must assume that the outlooks expressed in the poems derive from those current in Homer's own world of the eighth century BC.

III. HOMER AND THE EIGHTH CENTURY

Historians have taken a tremendous variety of positions on how to interpret Homer, but in the 1990s there has been a shift towards assuming an eighth-century Homeric society.[46] Few Homerists now believe that the *Iliad* and *Odyssey* tell us much about Mycenaean society.[47] More assume that its institutions and ideologies conflate elements drawn from a millennium of history, though this too is now a minority position.[48] But Finley's proposition that the world of Odysseus reflects Greece around 900 BC is still influential. So far, I have based my case on comparative expectations about Homeric composition. To fly in the face of these expectations, Finley's evidence would need to be strong indeed. In this section, I argue that there is nothing in the poems to rule out the eighth century as the source of heroic attitudes.

Finley believed that the world of the poems was too primitive to belong in the eighth century, and suggested that 'If, then, the world

---

[45] The fourth hypothesis is not strictly necessary, if we assume that Homer, like many modern oral poets (see § v), simply ignored the possibilities of writing, and went on composing orally.

[46] e.g. C. Ulf, *Die homerische Gesellschaft* (Munich, 1990); Van Wees (n. 22); K. Raaflaub, 'Homeric Society', in *Comp.* 624–48; 'A Historian's Headache: How to Read "Homeric Society"?', in Fisher and Van Wees (n. 2), 169–93; W. Donlan, 'The Homeric Economy', in *Comp.* 649–67.

[47] See J. Bennet, 'Homer and the Bronze Age', in *Comp.* 511–34.

[48] In the original version of this essay (pp. 104–15) I offered a detailed critique of this position, concentrating on Snodgrass, 'An Historical Homeric Society?', *JHS* 94 (1974), 114–25. The theory still has advocates (e.g. Sale (n. 25)), particularly among archaeologists (Sherratt (n. 24); J. Whitley, 'Social Diversity in Dark Age Greece', *ABSA* 86 (1991), 341–65).

of Odysseus is to be placed in time, as everything we know from the comparative study of heroic poetry says that it must, the most likely centuries seem to be the tenth and ninth.'[49] He supported the possibility of a 'frozen' poetic society by drawing an analogy with the *Song of Roland*, dating around AD 1100. This describes (very inaccurately) a campaign in 778, but Finley claimed that 'the background of Roland is the France of about a century before the poet's own time'.[50]

There have been heated debates over whether *Roland* was an oral composition dictated to a scribe, much like Lord's model for Homer, or whether it was created by a literate cleric who, if he chose to, could use Carolingian texts as models.[51] On the whole, studies of the for-mulae make the first theory more likely. But few historians share Finley's belief that *Roland* reflects an earlier society. Medievalists regularly interpret it as a guide into twelfth-century ideologies of good and bad knighthood, or even, as Zumthor suggests, 'not so much a reflection of reality or of past experience as a meditation on itself... it thus takes upon itself the diffuse ideology of a geo-graphically widely dispersed community'.[52] Similarly, early medieval Germanic heroic poems set in the great population movements at the end of the Roman empire seem to tell us more about the periods of their composition than about the heroic ages in which they are ostensibly set.[53]

The core of Finley's argument against an eighth-century back-ground was the absence of institutions which he believed must have existed in the poet's own age. There are two reasons why we might simply bypass it. First, if we use what we know of early Greek institutions to date Homeric society, then use Homeric

[49] M. I. Finley, *The World of Odysseus* (2nd edn., Harmondsworth, 1979), 48.

[50] Finley (n. 49), 47.

[51] J. Duggan, *The Song of Roland* (Berkeley, 1973); 'La Théorie de la composition orale des chansons de geste', *Olifant* 8 (1981), 238–55; 'Le Mode de composition des chansons de geste', *Olifant* 8 (1981), 286–316; W. Calin, 'L'Épopée dite vivante: reflexions sur le prétendu caractère oral des chansons de geste', *Olifant* 8 (1981), 227–37; 'Littérature médiévale et hypothèse orale', *Olifant* 8 (1981), 256–85; W. M. Sale, 'Homer and the *Roland*', *Oral Tradition* 8 (1993), 87–142, 381–412; id. (n. 25), 16, correcting the original version of this essay (p. 95).

[52] e.g. M. Keen, *Chivalry* (New Haven, 1984), 103; B. F. Cook, *The Sense of the Song of Roland* (Ithaca, NY, 1987); H.-E. Keller, *Autour de Roland* (Paris, 1989), 77–92 (calling it 12th-cent. royal propaganda); P. Haidu, *The Subject of Violence: The Song of Roland and the Birth of the State* (Bloomington, Ind., 1993); P. Zumthor, *Toward a Med-ieval Poetics* (Minneapolis, 1991), 277.

[53] Finnegan (n. 7), 247–50; Foley (n. 13), 65–74, 76–82.

society as a source for knowing about early Greek institutions, the argument is circular. Second, I am not suggesting that Homer can be used as a direct source for institutions. But if, as I suggest, Homer constructed a heroic culture from norms and expectations common in his own times, it would be surprising if no hint of contemporary institutions and practices crept in. I therefore review Finley's position in some detail.

Finley suggested that 'neither poem has any trace of the *polis* in its political sense', adding that in Homer we find 'no Ionia, no Dorians to speak of, no writing, no iron weapons, no cavalry in the battle scenes, no colonization, no Greek traders, no communities without kings', no overpopulation, and no Olympic games.[54] Finley notes elsewhere that those who claim that Homer reflects eighth-century realities faithfully often get into circular arguments, since so much of what we think we know about the eighth century comes from Homer;[55] but claiming the opposite is just as circular. This is misty territory, and the best we can do is to spell out the arguments as clearly as possible.

The question of *polis* institutions is the most serious, and I leave it till last. Nothing else on Finley's list makes a compelling argument for a tenth- or ninth-century world. The Dorians, Ionians, iron weapons, and cavalry were as present in Greece in the tenth century as in the eighth,[56] and their exclusion does not weigh against either date. All these absences belong to epic distancing, reminding the audience that this was not their world.

As already noted, writing was probably a new technique in Homer's day (I return to this below). I assume that he and his audiences felt that such novelties did not belong in the heroic age, although Homer betrays some knowledge of it (*Iliad* 6. 168–70).

Colonization is more complicated. Homer's description of the Cyclops' island (*Odyssey* 9. 116–41) is often taken as a blueprint for the sites favoured by eighth-century colonists, and his description of Scheria (6. 7–10) as a model for setting up an *apoikia*.[57] Finley

[54] Quotations from Finley (n. 49), 34, 48; population and games, id., *The Ancient Greeks* (Harmondsworth, 1963), 26.   [55] Finley (n. 49), 154.

[56] Though J. Hall, *Ethnic Identity in Greek Antiquity* (Cambridge, 1997), points out the complexities of Greek ethnogenesis. Weapons and cavalry: A. M. Snodgrass, *Early Greek Armour and Weapons* (Edinburgh, 1964).

[57] See C. Dougherty, *The Poetics of Colonization* (New York, 1993), 21–4. F. Hartog (*Mémoires d'Ulysse* (Paris, 1996)) even calls the *Odyssey* the first Greek ethnography, written against the background of the 8th-cent. colonial movement.

explained away the latter by saying it 'could equally reflect the first Greek settlements in Ionia about or soon after 1000 BC' as eighth-century foundations; but if so, then—as with iron and cavalry—colonization is no more of an argument against the eighth century than the tenth. Recent finds in Chalcidice suggest that there were long-distance relocations around 1100 and 900.[58] The eighth-century foundations may have been of a different order, but the issue is less clear-cut than Finley claimed.

While Greek traders are rare in Homer, the heroes were certainly at home with oriental luxury goods (e.g. *Iliad* 4. 141–5; 23. 740–8; *Odyssey* 5. 71–85, 120–32, 226–32, 613–19; 15. 113–19). Their familiarity with the east and the prominence of Egypt in the story (*Odyssey* 14. 425–58; 17. 424–7) in fact makes more sense in the eighth century than around 900; so too the ubiquitous Phoenicians (e.g. *Iliad* 23. 741–4; *Odyssey* 13. 272–86; 14. 288–9; 15. 415–16, 448–9, 459–70).[59] And while Greek trade with the rest of the Mediterranean declined in the tenth century, Levantine and perhaps even Egyptian objects were being buried at Lefkandi by 925. By 900 they also occur in graves at Athens and Tiryns, and Greek objects appear again in the Near East.[60] The absence of Greek traders is odd for an eighth-century setting, but we should remember that Odysseus was mistaken for a trader in Scheria (*Odyssey* 8. 159–64). As that episode reveals, commodity exchange was a charged issue, and we cannot rely on it as a neutral dating tool.[61]

Finley found in Homer 'no communities without kings', and treated this as evidence that the poems could not reflect the eighth century. Sale, however, suggests that Priam was so weak that Troy was really governed by an oligarchy of eighth-century type, while the Achaeans had 'absolute monarchies', distorted memories of Mycenaean times.[62] There is little agreement on Homeric kingship. There are hereditary sole rulers, but Drews translates *basileus* as

[58] A. M. Snodgrass, 'The Euboians in Macedonia', in B. d'Agostino and D. Ridgway (edd.), *Apoikia: Scritti in onore di Giorgio Buchner* (Naples, 1994), 87–93.

[59] See the excellent discussion of I. Winter, 'Homer's Phoenicians', in J. Carter and S. P. Morris (edd.), *Ages of Homer* (Austin, 1995), 247–71.

[60] Morris (n. 3), 208–11, 238–46, with references.

[61] See S. von Reden, *Exchange in Ancient Greece* (London, 1995), 58–76; D. Tandy, *Warriors into Traders* (Berkeley, 1997), 59–83.

[62] Sale (n. 25), esp. pp. 53–4. The word 'absolute' is an unfortunate choice, given the very different connotations early modern historians attach to it (see e.g. Q. Skinner, *The Foundations of Modern Political Thought* II (Cambridge, 1978)); nor

'highborn leader', seeing oligarchies of competing *basileis* leading Homeric communities.[63] Discussions have perhaps been too constitutionalist, not making enough allowance for what Weber called charismatic authority[64] and the tactics a would-be leader would need to maintain power in an unstable coalition of chiefs. As Aristotle noted (*Politics* 1285^{a}1–3), kingship came in many forms. We should not automatically assume that the differences between Priam and Agamemnon reflect historical layers rather than exigencies of plot and character.

Two other factors complicate using kingship to date Homeric society. First is our uncertainty about developments in the eighth century. According to tradition, kingship ended in 753/2 BC in Athens and 747 in Corinth, although (even excluding Sparta) it continued into the seventh and sixth century elsewhere. Looking outside the texts will not resolve this issue, particularly when we consider the second problem, the likelihood that heroic poets excluded contemporary developments to create epic distance. This eighth-century poet believed that there were kings in the heroic age; yet the kingship he imagined was a weak institution, constantly breaking down.

Finley's claim that Homeric Greece is not so 'over-populated' as eighth-century Greece is also hard to evaluate. The eighth century certainly saw rapid growth. Most Dark-Age Greeks probably lived in hamlets of no more than a few dozen souls, but the largest towns, like Athens, Argos, and Knossos, probably never fell below 1,000 inhabitants. By 700 BC, villages a few hundred strong were common, and 5,000 people may have lived at Athens.[65] Homer never gives population sizes, but Van Wees estimates that he imagined about

does Aristotle's *pambasileia* ('absolute monarchy') correspond to the Homeric situation, as he himself observed (*Politics* 1285^b).

[63] For recent competing interpretations, see R. Drews, *Basileus* (New Haven), 1983; P. Carlier, *Les Royautés en Grèce avant d'Alexandre* (Strasbourg, 1984); W. Donlan, 'Social Groups in Dark Age Greece', *CP* 80 (1985), 293–308; id., 'The Pre-State Community in Greece', *SO* 64 (1989), 5–29; Ulf (n. 46), 223–31; Van Wees (n. 22), 281–94; J. Lenz, 'Kings and the Ideology of Kingship in Early Greece', Unpublished Ph.D. diss., Columbia University, 1993; and Sale (n. 25), 39–45.

[64] M. Weber, *Economy and Society* (New York, 1968), 212–16, 226–54.

[65] Whitley (n. 48); I. Morris, 'The Early Polis as City and State', in J. Rich and A. Wallace-Hadrill (edd.), *City and Country in the Ancient World* (London, 1991), 28–57.

600 people in Ithaca town, with the largest Homeric towns probably running to 4,000 people, which would not be out of place in the eighth century.[66] Van Wees concludes that 'a Homeric town represents real Greek towns as they were from the eighth century onwards'.[67] Finley would doubtless have dismissed the huge armies in the *Iliad* (2. 494–877; 8. 562–5),[68] the 4,500 men sacrificing with Nestor at Pylos (*Odyssey* 3. 7–8), and the swarm of suitors (16. 247–50) as poetic exaggerations, and he was probably thinking of the general pattern of settlement on Ithaca. There was unoccupied land available for cultivation (*Odyssey* 24. 206–7); but Hesiod says the same for Boeotia (*Works and Days* 635–40), and archaeological surveys suggest that in many places there was no shortage of land until well into Archaic times.[69]

Homer's silence on the Olympic games is hardly surprising. According to Hippias of Elis, the first Olympic victor from outside the western Peloponnese was Diocles of Corinth in 728, and the first from outside the Peloponnese were Orsippos and Menos of Megara in 720 and 704. The games had a very local character until the seventh century. Homer only mentions Olympia and Delphi in passing (*Iliad* 2. 459–66; 20. 403–5; *Odyssey* 6. 162–7). If we are right to date Homer to the late eighth century, this too is unsurprising, given that the sanctuaries were only winning panhellenic standing at the very end of the century.[70]

The most important test is civic institutions. Finley did not explain what exactly he expected to find in Homer as evidence of 'the *polis* in its political sense', saying only that 'the social organisation of the world of Odysseus was inadequate for the tasks we know some *poleis* contemporary with Homer to have performed'.[71] Although it is hard to falsify such a broad statement, I think Finley was mistaken.

Throughout *The World of Odysseus* Finley emphasized the dominance of the *oikos* (household) in Homeric life, although he

[66] Van Wees (n. 22), 269–71.

[67] S. Scully, *Homer and the Sacred City* (Ithaca, NY, 1990); Van Wees (n. 22), 25–31; quotation from p. 54.

[68] 50,000 Trojans, and, by Sale's calculation (n. 25:55), 63,000 Achaeans.

[69] e.g. J. Cherry, J. Davis, and E. Mantzourani (edd.), *Landscape Archaeology as Long-Term History* (Los Angeles, 1991); M. Jameson, C. Runnels, and T. van Andel, *A Greek Countryside* (Stanford, 1994); B. Wells (ed.), *The Berbati-Limnes Archaeological Survey 1988–90* (Stockholm, 1996); J. L. Davis (ed.), *Sandy Pylos* (Austin, 1998).

[70] C. Morgan, *Athletes and Oracles* (Cambridge, 1990).

[71] Finley (n. 49), 156.

recognized that the agora and *themis* (law-session) were familiar
concepts in Ithaca.[72] Distinctions between public and private matters
were understood (*Odyssey* 2. 32, 44–5). No assembly had been called
on Ithaca in nineteen years, but the plot required that political life
had gone into suspended animation. When the assembly did meet, its
powers were considerable.[73] It could have fined Haliserthes heavily
(2. 192–3), and conceivably have exiled all the suitors (16. 381–2).
The Ithacans, acting outside the assembly, had acted against the
anti-Thesprotian policy of Antinous' father, who would have been
lynched but for Odysseus' intervention (16. 424–30).

The warriors' assembly at Troy was less powerful, but represents
a different political context. It made its wishes felt through applause
and cheers (*Iliad* 1. 22–3), but the *basileis* monopolized decisions
(e.g. 1. 376–9). The assembly could even be dissolved, yielding to
a gathering of nobles making decisions over dinner (9. 68–70). In
Scheria, Alcinous tells his elders to return the next day to discuss
Odysseus' passage home (*Odyssey* 7. 189–96), but when they do,
Alcinous simply tells them what he has decided (8. 28–40).

The Ithacans had no desire to send out a colony, and we have little
idea what else eighth-century assemblies did. But this is no argument
against an eighth-century basis. Indeed, public acclamation and
the nobles' ability to ignore decisions recalls nothing so much as
Plutarch's account of the Spartan assembly (*Lycurgus* 6), which
probably dates to the seventh century;[74] yet Sparta founded Taras in
706 with a political organization probably little more evolved than
Homeric Ithaca's.

Finley also argued that the world of Odysseus was one 'of strictly
private rights privately protected',[75] with the *oikos* acting largely
independently of higher-level institutions. This is an important
claim. Social evolutionists commonly define the state as 'a form of
sociopolitical organization that has achieved a monopoly over the
means of violence within a specified territory',[76] and in Hesiod we
certainly see supra-household dispute-settling institutions (*Works
and Days* 247–64; *Theogony* 81–90). If dispute-settlement really
was at the *oikos* level, this would undermine the assumption

---

[72] Finley (n. 49), 79.   [73] See Raaflaub in *Comp.* (n. 46), 641–5.
[74] See E. Flaig, 'Die spartanische Abstimmung nach der Lautstärke', *Historia* 42
(1993), 139–60; 'Das Konsensprinzip im homerischen Olymp', *Hermes* 122 (1994),
13–31.   [75] Finley (n. 49), 110.
[76] S. Sanderson, *Social Transformations* (Oxford, 1995), 56.

that Homer drew on eighth-century norms in imagining heroic
society.

But in Homer we see three levels of dispute-settlement. The first
is through interpersonal strife. Men flee their homes to escape the
vengeful kin of murder victims (e.g. *Odyssey* 1. 298–300; 16. 97–8);
but fourth-century authors could still claim that violent revenge
was normal (e.g. Plato, *Laws* 874b–d; Lysias 1. 2).[77] MacDowell[78]
suggested that *Iliad* 12. 421–4 shows two farmers settling a dispute
by fighting it out. But even if δηριάασθον in line 421 literally means
'fighting', all we see here is two squabbling farmers; Homer does not
suggest this was a legitimate way to settle disputes. *Iliad* 23. 553–4,
Antilochus' offer to fight for his prize in Patroclus' funeral games, is
more serious. Homer says that Achilles was delighted by Antilochus'
offer of violence (23. 557). More serious still is the crisis over
the suitors on Ithaca. Leocritus asserted that no one could stop the
suitors, because they were too strong (*Odyssey* 2. 242–51). On
his return, Odysseus surprised the suitors and killed them, rather
than appealing to legal authorities; and until Athena's intervention,
the suitors' families were planning violent revenge (22. 1–477;
24. 412–548).

At the second level of integration, disputes could be settled by
private agreements between the litigants (e.g. *Iliad* 9. 632–6;
Odyssey 21. 15–30); and at the third level, an outside arbiter could
intervene, like a *basileus* (*Iliad* 2. 205–6; 9. 98–9; 18. 497–508;
23. 485–7; *Odyssey* 3. 244–5) or a group of elders, often under the
gaze of the *dēmos* (*Iliad* 1. 237–9; 11. 807; 16. 387; 18. 497; *Odyssey*
12. 439–40).

Finley recognized all three levels, but dismissed the ten third-party
resolutions (eleven if we count *Odyssey* 2, where the *dēmos*'s intervention failed) as anachronisms 'which slipped by the poet',[79] leaving only a 'primitive' level of settlement at the *oikos* level.

Such special pleading, separating out 'early' and 'late' strata, is
always arbitrary. I suggest that all three levels coexisted in the eighth

---

[77] There is little agreement, though, over the significance of these passages. See
G. Herman, 'Tribal and Civic Codes of Behaviour in Lysias 1', *CQ* 43 (1993), 406–19;
'How Violent was Athenian Society?' in R. Osborne and S. Hornblower (edd.), *Ritual,
Finance, Politics* (Oxford, 1994), 99–117.

[78] D. M. MacDowell, *The Law in Classical Athens* (London, 1978), 11–12.

[79] Finley (n. 49), 110.

century. A fistfight or blow from a weapon would settle some
disputes, but others were resolved by discussion between the parties,
and where this failed, a third party might step in. The Shield of
Achilles shows part of this progression. The defendant wished to
settle out of court, as it were, paying a fine (*Iliad* 18. 499), but the
wronged party had refused this, with the result ἄμφω δ' ἰέσθην ἐπὶ
ἴστορι πεῖραρ ἐλέσθαι ('both then made for an arbitrator, to have a
decision', 18. 501). Hesiod's story (*Works and Days* 37–9) is another
example: after he and Perses had divided their *klēros* (estate), an
agreement within the *oikos*, Perses seized the greater part. When
they could not find a solution, their dispute became a public matter,
and the δωροφάγοι βασιλῆες were called in. For all we know they
also went through the stage of the two farmers in *Iliad* 12. 421–4,
wrangling over the *horoi*, before the *basileis* reached settlement
favourable to Perses.

In real life, all three levels always operate. The crucial question is
the balance between them. Even in Classical times, law and order
could break down just as in Odysseus' Ithaca under the stress of civil
war (e.g. Thucydides 3. 70–84). And far from suppressing lower
levels of dispute resolution, litigants could manipulate Athenian law
as one more tool to use in open-ended quarrels which could extend
across generations.[80] Homeric society was more violent than Classical Athens, but we need not assume that Homeric dispute resolution reflects a world lost in the mists of the Dark Age. Van Wees has
concluded that the use of private force in Homer is compatible with
eighth-century assumptions.[81]

We cannot say decisively whether Homeric political and legal
institutions are too primitive to be derived from eighth-century
norms. But given the expectations created by the comparative evidence, the burden of proof is on Finley. He claimed that what we
know of the eighth century and the institutions in the *Iliad* and
Odyssey 'are simply not the same',[82] but this cannot be upheld.
Homeric society was cruder and more violent than Classical Athens;
but so too was eighth-century Greece.

---

[80] R. Osborne, 'Law in Action in Classical Athens', *JHS* 105 (1985), 40–58;
D. Cohen, *Law, Violence, and Community in Classical Athens* (Cambridge, 1995); cf.
S. Johnstone, *Disputes and Democracy* (Austin, 1999).

[81] H. van Wees, 'Greeks Bearing Arms', in Fisher and Van Wees (n. 2), 333–78.

[82] Finley (n. 49), 33–4.

IV. POETRY AND SOCIETY

In section II, I argued from comparative evidence that in creating the heroic age, Homer drew on his own expectations about how the world worked but used distancing effects to remind his audience that this world was not their own. This would make Homer an outstanding source for eighth-century attitudes and mentalities, and some of the time a good source for eighth-century institutions. But the evidence from a particular historical context does not always fit into models based on cross-cultural regularities, and in section III, I examined Finley's argument that Homer in fact describes the Greek world around 900 BC. I concluded that Finley's arguments are not strong enough to make us go against the comparative expectations.

But saying that Homer based his heroic age on his own world is only the starting point. The next question is how he drew on his own and his audience's experiences and expectations in creating the heroic age.

There was probably much variation in the heroic ages that eighth-century poets created. At the most basic level of plot, Nagy suggests that Demodocus' song (*Odyssey* 8. 72–82) reveals knowledge of a different *Iliad*, focusing not on Achilles' anger against Agamemnon but on a quarrel with Odysseus; and Lord even claimed that there was an *Iliad* where the embassy to Achilles succeeded.[83] Herodotus (2. 112–20) knew yet another story, that instead of sailing to Troy, Helen spent ten years in Egypt. Herodotus says he learned this from Egyptian priests, but Stesichorus (fragment 192 *PMGF*) already knew it in the sixth century, and another fragment mentioning it may be Hesiodic (fragment 358 M–W).

Given such variation, can we assume that all poets represented heroic society in the same way? Some classicists would answer yes. Arthur Adkins argued that

Homeric values... suit Homeric society, inasmuch as they commend those qualities which most evidently secure its existence... we discover a society whose highest commendation is bestowed upon men who must successfully exhibit the qualities of a warrior, but must also be men of wealth and social position; men, too, who must display their valour both in war and peace

---

[83] G. Nagy, *The Best of the Achaeans* (Baltimore, 1979), 65; Lord (n. 5), 194.

to protect their dependents [*sic*] . . . it is reasonable to assume that such a
scale of values was generally acceptable.[84]

As Van Wees sums it up, 'the touchiness of Homeric men is their most
striking trait of character'.[85] They are acutely aware of status, constantly looking out for insults; and they respond to slights with deadly
violence. The poet criticizes men for weakness, but not for going too far.

Does this mean that eighth-century Greece was a place of towering heroes and cowering masses? Not necessarily. Other readers of
Homer see a very different ethos. Long argued that in fact excess
was criticized (e.g. *Iliad* 1. 276; 18. 334–7; 24. 46–54), suggesting
that Adkins had only used part of the evidence available. Adkins
replied that '*Aischron* [disgraceful] is the only word powerful enough
[to condemn a 'good man', an *agathos*]; and this is never used to
decry injustice in Homer', but Long argued that other terms, equally
strong in their own ways, condemned *hubris* and *huperbasiē*.[86]

This thirty-year-old debate raises important issues. The *Iliad* creates a strong impression of a world of unrestrained violence and
competition; but there is also a substratum of praise for co-operation,
generating a calibrated 'ethics of anger',[87] dictating how heroes
should act. Adkins and Long looked at the poems in different ways.
The competitive ethic *is* highly praised; but on occasion, different
attitudes show through.

Like Finley, Adkins placed his atomized Homeric society—'more
an agglomeration of "Cyclopean" households than an integrated
community'[88]—in the earlier Dark Age. It is certainly hard to imagine it founding Syracuse; but it is hard to imagine it founding
Torone or Mende either (n. 58 above). Adkins's model of an undec-
lared war between *oikoi*, the *oikos* surviving only if its *agathos* is
stronger than other *agathoi*, has no place in the real world. In fact, it
bears a striking resemblance to Hobbes's picture of the 'natural' stage
of human evolution in his *Leviathan*:

For WARRE, consisteth not in Battell only, or the act of fighting; but in a tract
of time, wherein the Will to contend by Battell is sufficiently known: and
therefore the notion of Time, is to be considered in the nature of Warre; as it

---

[84] A. W. H. Adkins, *Merit and Responsibility* (Oxford, 1960), 55, 34; Finleyan date:
57 n. 3.   [85] Van Wees (n. 22), 109.
[86] A. A. Long, 'Morals and Values in Homer', *JHS* 90 (1970), 121–39; A. W. H.
Adkins, 'Homeric Values and Homeric Society', *JHS* 91 (1971), 9.
[87] Van Wees (n. 22), 126–38.   [88] Adkins (n. 84), 54.

is in the nature of Weather. For as the nature of Foule Weather, lyeth not in a shower or two of rain; but in an inclination thereto of many days together; So the nature of Warre, consisteth not in actual fighting; but in the known disposition thereto, during all the time there is no assurance to the contrary. All other time is PEACE.[89]

'Warre', as Hobbes observed, was not an empirical reality, but an ideal type to contrast with functioning societies to clarify the essence of the state. Warre exists nowhere, because the members of society surrender their right to wage it. Did a state of Warre really exist in early Greece? Probably not; and Long's analysis shows that beneath the Warre, Homeric society followed 'the First, and Fundamental Law of Nature: which is, to seek Peace, and to follow it'.[90] Warre is a big part of Homer's vision of the Heroic Age. But it is part of a selective vision, not of a balanced overview. No real world can work this way; and in fact, the *Iliad* and *Odyssey* show us just why heroic society did not work this way either.

Hobbes theorized that state-sanctioned force ruled out Warre, but ethnography has shown that in fact the mechanisms involved are very different. In his classic essay *The Gift*, Mauss examined the exchange of gifts, often unsolicited, in pre-capitalist societies. Mauss noted that 'although the prestations and counterprestations take place under a voluntary guise they are in essence strictly obligatory, and their sanction is private or open warfare... To refuse to give, or to fail to invite, is—like refusing to accept—the equivalent of a declaration of war.'[91] Even the most agonistic groups subsume rivalry into exchange, burying Warre along the lines of Hobbes's and Adkins's constructs deep beneath the surface.

This is significant. Gift exchange is a striking feature of Homeric society. Gifts are constantly given, with the express purposes of establishing friendly relations between individuals and households (*Odyssey* 15. 54–5), normalizing social relations (8. 401–5), or marking status gradations (*Iliad* 23. 534–49). As in many cultures, giving is simultaneously competitive and harmonious, tying givers and takers together even as they vie for prestige.[92] Gift-giving is problematic and the assumptions of the parties involved always open

---

[89] Quoted from M. Sahlins, *Stone Age Economics* (Chicago, 1972), 172.
[90] Hobbes, quoted in Sahlins (n. 89), 177.
[91] M. Mauss, *The Gift* (London, 1966), 3, 11.
[92] Finley (n. 49), 45–6; *Economy and Society in Ancient Greece* (London, 1981), 213–45. Van Wees (n. 22: 228–37) downplays competitive giving. See also the essays

to question,[93] but the institution permeates the poems. It was probably a significant feature of eighth-century society, which Homer projected back on to the heroic age. But in doing so, he chose to make the harmonious aspects of gift-giving less prominent than the violent, competitive side which, he felt, characterized the heroic age.

Homer was not trying to describe eighth-century customs and manners. He modelled the heroic age on what he and his audiences took for granted about the world; but his portrayals of conflict and gift-giving suggest that he did so by exaggerating some elements and downplaying others, leading scholars like Adkins and Long to reach radically different interpretations of the basic ethos of Homeric society. Some historians conclude that we should reject the evidence of Homer as an artificial amalgam. But they are forgetting that the epics were produced by and for real people, acting in pursuit of their own goals in an age of bewildering change. They assume that Homer should be a mirror to an external reality, then find him a defective one. They reduce the historian's task to smoothing out his distorting surface to produce a clear reflection. But the epic is not some kind of bad history. It was a poetic creation, what *some* eighth-century Greeks thought the heroic world *ought* to have been like. In the next section, I discuss the perspective from which Homer took premisses to create the heroic age: that is, what elements of reality he incorporated into his imagined world, and whose reality this was.

V. LOCATING HOMER

We only have the epics because, at some point(s) in the eighth century, someone decided to write down 28,000 lines of poetry. This was surely an awesome task, not to be undertaken lightly, or without good reason. It is hard to imagine writing so much on wood, bronze, or clay tablets; papyrus, which Homer knew of (*Odyssey* 21. 391), is the most likely material, but even in the fifth century that was

in C. Gill, N. Postlethwaite, and R. Seaford (edd.), *Reciprocity in Ancient Greece* (Oxford, 1998).

[93] See R. Seaford, *Reciprocity and Ritual* (Oxford, 1994), 13–25; von Reden (n. 61), 13–49.

expensive.[94] Recording the *Iliad* and *Odyssey* was an epic task in its own right. We have to wonder why a great oral poet would want his works recorded in writing at all.

Lord held that writing destroys oral composition, but also noted that some Serbian poets in the 1920s were literate, yet made no use of these skills in composing.[95] The same is true in Albania, where poets ignore written versions of their own songs, continuing to compose freely in performance.[96]

It is unlikely that a poet anything like modern Balkan bards or those Homer describes would feel much need for written texts. Whether Homer wrote himself or dictated to a scribe, each poem required days of work. When in 1935 Avdo Mededović dictated the 12,000-line *Wedding of Smailagić Meho* to Parry and sang the 13,331-line *Osmanbey Delibegović and Pavicević Luka* into a microphone, it was, as Kirk notes, 'elicited by Parry's *specific and well-paid request* for the longest possible song'.[97] Parry had good reasons for wanting long, high-quality songs: they would support his thesis about Homeric composition. He had already advanced from Drake University to Harvard on the strength of this thesis: Mededović could give him the closest thing he could get to proof. This made it worth Parry's while to prevail on Mededović to sing four hours each day for a week, until his voice gave out; then after a week of rest and medication, to sing for another week.[98]

But what could have motivated a similar episode in the eighth century? The event is still more monumental if the alphabet was in its infancy, as suggested in section II. Homer's dates and the date of the alphabet's invention are hypotheses which may need revision, but the coincidence of our best guesses is striking—particularly when we note that the Greeks created a true alphabet rather than a syllabary, as used in Cyprus, or a consonantal script, like their west Semitic models.[99] Half a century ago, Wade-Gery mused that 'It would seem that the Greeks needed [alphabetic writing], the others did not . . . What function? . . . To serve as a notation for

[94] W. V. Harris, *Ancient Literacy* (Cambridge, Mass., 1989), 94–5; Powell (n. 32), 32.

[95] Lord (n. 5), 129, 132.

[96] M. Skafte Jensen, *The Homeric Question and the Oral-Formulaic Theory* (Copenhagen, 1980), 83–6.

[97] G. S. Kirk, *The Songs of Homer* (Cambridge, 1962), 274.

[98] A. B. Lord, 'Homer and Huso III: Enjambement in Greek and Southslavic Heroic Song', *TAPA* 79 (1948), 42.   [99] See Powell (n. 32), 68–118.

Greek verse.'[100] The idea that Greeks invented their alphabet specifically to record heroic poetry is not as far-fetched as it sounds; Powell
has shown that a high proportion of the earliest Greek inscriptions,
down to 650 BC, are poetic, often in hexameter, like Homer.[101] And
most early Greek poetry is heroic, theogonic, or genealogical.
Giddens calls writing a technique for 'stacking' the past, in the sense
of making information from an earlier time available in the present.[102] This is a particularly apposite way to think about eighth-
century Greek writing. Devoted to poetry of the past, it was from the
start a tool for bridging the gulf between the present and a better,
vanished time.

Wade-Gery suggested that the drive to invent the alphabet and
record Homer's vast epics came from the ruling elite of Chios' desire
to be celebrated at the *panēgureis* (festivals) springing up in the late
eighth century.[103] Wade-Gery's sources are poor, but he was right to
ask why someone wealthy enough to fund such an experiment
would bring together the greatest poet in Greece and the newest
technology in sittings that must have gone on for weeks, to produce
poems that could never be recited in full.

We do not have to look far for such a stimulus in the eighth
century. Society was in turmoil. Everything was changing. Starr
speaks of an 'Age of Revolution', and Snodgrass of a structural
revolution.[104] There is much dispute over just what was happening.
Snodgrass sees a population explosion leading to more warfare,
concentration of wealth, and the formation of state institutions,
legitimized through cultural transformations ranging from the
invention of writing to temple-building. I have argued that in fact
we see the collapse of Dark Age aristocracies before pressure from
the poor, and the creation of a new concept of the city-state as a
community of equal middling men. But both models agree
that every significant relationship in Aegean Greece—class, age,
gender, cosmology, ethnicity—was turned on its head in the

[100] H. T. Wade-Gery, *The Poet of the Iliad* (Cambridge, 1952), 13; cf. Snodgrass
(n. 39), 82–83; Powell (n. 32). R. D. Woodard, *Greek Writing from Knossos to
Homer* (Oxford, 1997), makes different arguments.
[101] Powell (n. 32), 119–86.
[102] A. Giddens, *A Contemporary Critique of Historical Materialism* (Stanford, 1981),
39, 94–95.
[103] Wade-Gery (n. 100), 6–9.
[104] C. G. Starr, *The Origins of Greek Civilization* (New York, 1961); Snodgrass (n. 39),
15–84.

eighth century.[105] The Greeks' world was expanding at a dizzying rate as travel became easier. Greeks had to deal with new cultural influences from east and west alike. Some embraced them; others resisted fiercely. If there was ever an age of revolution in antiquity, this was it.[106] Further, as Snodgrass concluded, 'it begins to look as if [an] attitude of deference to the heroic past was an important element in the revolution that was sweeping through Greek life.'[107]

What role did Homer play in rethinking relationships to the heroic past? That is the central question. Homer's function in later centuries is clear enough: 'Historically "real" or not, the epic system of values was very real to the Greeks of the Archaic and Classical periods . . . for the post-Homeric Greeks, especially those of higher status, the norms of individual behavior contained in the Homeric warrior ideal constituted a paradigm they accepted as right and proper.'[108] I have

---

[105] A. M. Snodgrass, *The Dark Age of Greece* (Edinburgh, 1971); *Archaeology and the Rise of the Greek State* (Cambridge, 1977); *Archaic Greece* (n. 39); 'The Rise of the Polis', in M. H. Hansen (ed.), *The Ancient Greek City-State* (Copenhagen, 1993), 30–40; I. Morris, *Burial and Ancient Society* (Cambridge, 1987); 'Archaeology and Archaic Greek History' (n. 2); *Archaeology as Cultural History* (n. 3), 257–306. Cf. Morgan (n. 70); J. Whitley, *Style and Society in Dark Age Greece* (Cambridge, 1991); R. Osborne, *Greece in the Making* (London, 1996), 70–214; Tandy (n. 61); S. Langdon (ed.), *New Light on a Dark Age* (Columbia, Mo., 1997); A. Mazarakis Ainian, *From Rulers' Dwellings to Temples* (Jonsered, 1997). Some scholars have suggested that the importance of the 8th cent. has been exaggerated (e.g. H. van Effenterre, *La Citè grecque* (Paris, 1985); P. Carlier, 'La Procédure de décision politique, du monde mycénien à l'époque archaïque', in D. Musti *et al.* (edd.), *La transizione dal miceneo all'alto arcaismo* (Rome, 1991), 85–95; S. P. Morris, *Daidalos and the Origins of Greek Art* (Princeton, 1992); 'Introduction', in G. Kopcke and I. Tokumaru (edd.), *Greece between East and West* (Mainz, 1992), pp. XIII–XVIII; J. Papadopoulos, 'To Kill a Cemetery', *Journal of Mediterranean Archaeology* 6 (1993), 175–206), but I do not think that these revisions address the evidence adequately (I. Morris, 'The Kerameikos Stratigraphy and the Character of the Greek Iron Age', *Journal of Mediterranean Archaeology* 6 (1993), 207–21; (n. 2), 71–3; 'Burial and Ancient Society after Ten Years', in S. Marchegay, M. T. Le Dinahet, and J.-F. Salles (edd.), *Nécropoles et pouvoir* (Lyons, 1998), 21–36; (n. 3), 100–6).

[106] See e.g. W. Burkert, *The Orientalizing Revolution* (Cambridge, Mass., 1992); Kopcke and Tokumaru (n. 105); I. Malkin, *The Returns of Odysseus* (Berkeley, 1998); I. Morris, 'The Art of Citizenship', in Langdon (n. 105), 9–43; (n. 3), 257–61; H. Niemeyer (ed.), *Phönizier im Westen* (Mainz, 1982); D. Ridgway, *The First Western Greeks* (Cambridge, 1992); M. Shanks, *Art and the Early Greek State* (Cambridge, 1999); G. R. Tsetskhladze and F. De Angelis (edd.), *The Archaeology of Greek Colonisation* (Oxford, 1994); M. L. West, *The East Face of Helicon* (Oxford, 1997); J. Whitley, 'Protoattic Pottery: A Contextual Approach', in I. Morris (ed.), *Classical Greece: Ancient Histories and Modern Archaeologies* (Cambridge, 1994), 51–70.

[107] Snodgrass (n. 39), 77.

[108] W. Donlan, *The Aristocratic Ideal in Ancient Greece* (Lawrence, Kan., 1980), 1–2, 183 n. 1.

argued that we can divide Archaic literature into two broad systems
of values, the 'elitist', promoting the idea of an aristocracy of culture
linked more closely to the gods, the heroes, and the kings of the
east than to the peasants of their own *poleis*, and the 'middling',
representing the *polis* as a homogeneous community cut off from
external sources of authority. The elitist vision appropriated Homer's
picture of the heroic age.[109]

But was this how the *Iliad* and *Odyssey* functioned in eighth-
century Greece? I believe that it probably was: that the poems were
simultaneously great art and a powerful ideological weapon in conflicts tearing Greek communities apart. They offered a vision of the
heroic age as a time when everyone had depended on a few great men
for their very survival. Without the heroes, poor men and women of all
classes would be reduced to servitude; and their *poleis* would be
devoured by enemies. This was how it had been in the great days when
gods walked among men. It was not so now, but that was a cause for
regret. Knowing that the most divinely inspired poet of all said it used
to be so would have been a wonderful thing for eighth-century aristocrats. Oral poetry often plays an important part in ideological
struggles in modern times,[110] but its great problem is its fluidity. It is a
two-edged sword: there is no guarantee that a particular poet will
continue to present the heroic age in just the right way, or that poets in
neighbouring villages will agree on how it used to be. Written down, it
is different. It is there for everyone to see: the greatest poet, the one
most inspired by the Muses, says it was so, and therefore it was so.

I suggest that the wealthy individuals who brought together
Homer and a master of the new technology of alphabetic writing
and/or funded these marathon sessions were aristocrats who found
Homer's vision of the heroic age particularly appealing. They probably did not consciously say to themselves that they were forging
a new weapon in the struggle against the lower orders and the
corrosive forces of change. More likely they were proud of the imagination they were showing in fixing the text, and pleased to be
giving the world a great gift. Warm feelings of nostalgia for the heroic

---

[109] Morris (n. 3), 178–80. Dalby assumes a 7th-cent. date for Homer, but he is
surely right to conclude that 'The heroic values of the *Iliad* and *Odyssey*, the village
satire of Archilochus, the collectivism of Solon and Tyrtaeus, the destructive politics of
Alcaeus, . . . all were somehow relevant to contemporary audiences. From startlingly
different perspectives, they are indeed visions of the same world' (n. 19: 206).

[110] Finnegan (n. 7), 242–3.

age and self-satisfaction in doing the right thing are always more powerful than cynical self- or class-interest. But they fixed a poetic vision that was grounded in the assumptions of the eighth century BC, but coloured by a strongly pro-aristocratic bias, and embellished by epic distancing. As Van Wees puts it, 'the poet turns the ideals of the present into the reality of the imaginary heroic past.'[111]

In the heroic age, it seems, the ruling class was maintained by 'gifts' from their subjects (e.g. *Iliad* 4. 259–60; 5. 78; 9. 149–56, 479–84; 17. 225–6, 248–50; 18. 290–2; *Odyssey* 1. 392–3; 13. 8; 14. 205). In return, they fought bravely (*Iliad* 12. 310–21); and even the 'gifts' are often represented as the people paying their leaders back for heavy spending in the public good (e.g. *Iliad* 1. 133–6; *Odyssey* 2. 74–8; 13. 13–15; 19. 194–8; 22. 55–8; 23. 356–8). This surely seemed a very satisfactory arrangement to eighth-century nobles. The warrior class could also expect fairly immediate obedience from the lower orders, another agreeable situation. The leading heroes had personal relationships with individual gods; and they were more handsome, cleverer, braver, and more eloquent than anyone else.

All this must have seemed excellent, making the heroic age a fine model for the troubled eighth century. But patrons have never yet worked out how to get great artists to deliver simple ideological messages. Homer was no different. The *Iliad* focuses on fractures within the ruling elite: Agamemnon and Achilles appeal to different sources of authority, and their inability to resolve their conflict tears the Achaean army apart. Nicolai sees Homer as pointing out the shortcomings of uncontrolled individuals, and promoting *boulai* of aristocrats.[112] Rose accepts the same division but sees Homer taking a different position:

Rather than a simple dichotomy of elite and mass, I see a more complex struggle *within* the ruling element over the issue of one-man rule vs. the collective exercise of power by aristocrats who view themselves as formal equals...I have posited in the ideological thrust specific to the poem a strong attachment...to the image of the monarchic warrior-chief, the true *basileus*, who based his claim to authority not on dubious claims of genealogy but on demonstrated prowess on the field and generosity in his direct relationship with his followers.[113]

[111] Van Wees (n. 22), 253.

[112] W. Nicolai, 'Rezeptionssteuerung in der Ilias', *Philologus* 127 (1983), 1–12.

[113] P. Rose, 'Ideology in the *Iliad*', *Arethusa* 30 (1997), 181, 192, criticizing what he takes to be the central argument of the original version of this essay.

Nicolai and Rose are not alone in privileging conflicts within the ruling elite over those between the aristocracy and the poorer members of their communities,[114] but I see three reasons to modify these claims.

First is the clear evidence in Archaic sources for the importance of mass/elite conflicts. This is sharpest in accounts of the Athenian crisis around 600 BC, including Solon's own poetry, but is also apparent in the assembly in *Odyssey* II, and in other Archaic poets' references to tyrants. Tyrants represented themselves as the scourges of aristocratic *hubris*,[115] and Solon and Theognis worried that they would unite with the poor and hungry.

Second, Homer does not speak with one voice. Even while exposing the terrors of a world of unregulated heroes, he asserts that the *basileis* represent the will of Zeus. Nestor reminds Achilles that 'a sceptre-bearing *basileus*, to whom Zeus gives *kudos* [glory], has more than his equal share of *timē* [honour]' (*Iliad* I. 278–9). Consequently, as Calchas observes, 'a *basileus* is the stronger one when he is angry with a common man; for even if the *basileus* keeps his wrath from rising on that day, afterwards he preserves his ill-will in his heart until he is able to settle the matter' (I. 80–3). Examples could be multiplied. Odysseus describes for Penelope the *kleos* (fame) of 'the blameless *basileus*, who is god-fearing, ruling over many men and upholding justice; through his good rule, the black earth bears wheat and barley, the trees are heavy with fruit, the flocks quickly produce young, and the sea yields fish; and the people flourish under him' (*Odyssey* 19. 109–14; cf. Hesiod, *Works and Days* 225–47). Martin has shown that Homer (particularly *Odyssey* 8. 166–77) and Hesiod (*Theogony* 81–103) drew on a common tradition of hexameter advice-poetry idealizing *basileis* as Zeus' representatives and the sources of divine order.[116] For both poets, the problems in the world—whether at Troy or at Ascra—were the results of real-life

[114] e.g. F. de Polignac, 'Repenser "la cité"?' in M. Hansen and K. Raaflaub (edd.), *Studies in the Ancient Greek Polis* (Stuttgart, 1995), 7–19; 'Entre les dieux et les morts', in R. Hägg (ed.), *The Role of Religion in the Early Greek Polis* (Stockholm, 1996), 31–40; 'Offrandes, mémoire et compétition ritualisée dans les sanctuaires grecs à l'époque géométrique', in P. Hellström and B. Allroth (edd.), *Religion and Power in the Ancient Greek World* (Uppsala, 1996), 59–66.

[115] See J. McGlew, *Tyranny and Political Culture in Ancient Greece* (Ithaca, 1993), 52–123, though McGlew avoids social analysis.

[116] R. P. Martin, 'Hesiod, Odysseus, and the Instruction of Princes', *TAPA* 114 (1984), 29–48.

basileis failing to live up to these standards. But Homer did not speak straightforwardly for either oligarchic-minded aristocrats or individual rulers.

Third, and most important, this is not an either/or proposition. I have argued elsewhere that mass/elite conflicts played into and fed off conflicts within the ruling class.[117] Indeed, following Skocpol's arguments, I have suggested that without fatal fissures within the ruling class, endemic rural agitation would never have led to the permanent, revolutionary changes of the eighth century.[118] The entire Mediterranean basin went through similar processes of population growth, state formation, and increased competition over resources in the eighth and seventh centuries.[119] But, I have argued, only in Greece did conflicts between would-be tyrants and defenders of a Dark-Age internally egalitarian aristocracy lead to alliances with the ordinary citizens which were so strong that the notion of a community of equal men was generalized to include all free-born males.[120]

The most obviously ideological dimension of the poems is the virtual absence of the poor. Fifty years apart, Calhoun and Geddes concluded that Homer imagined a world of heroic warriors,[121] but given the thousands of regular troops at Troy, this cannot be right. Rather, as Van Wees suggests, 'in the heroic world the social distance between prince and "common" man is such that personal contact between them is infrequent, or regarded as insignificant, or both, and deemed an unsuitable topic for a story'.[122]

The major exception is the Thersites episode (*Iliad* 2. 211–78). Thersites, 'the ugliest man who came beneath Ilion' (2. 216), was the paradigmatic *kakos* (base individual), standing up in the assembly to abuse the *basileis*. Odysseus beat him with a sceptre, reducing him to tears, and threatening worse. The troops laughed and praised Odysseus. 'So the multitude (*plēthus*) spoke', Homer

[117] Morris (n. 3), 161–85.
[118] Morris (n. 105), 202–10, following T. Skocpol, *States and Social Revolutions* (Cambridge, 1979).
[119] Morris (n. 2).
[120] Morris (n. 2), 75–6; 'Iron Age Greece and the Meanings of "Princely Tombs"', in P. Ruby (ed.), *Les Princes de la protohistoire et l'émergence de l'état* (Naples, 1999), 68–71.
[121] G. M. Calhoun, 'Classes and Masses in Homer', CP 29 (1934), 192–208, 301–16; A. G. Geddes, 'Who's Who in "Homeric" Society?' CQ 34 (1984), 17–36.
[122] Van Wees (n. 22), 81.

comments (2. 278). 'These final words, "thus spake the multitude",
protest too much', Finley observed.[123] Here, in the crudest way,
Homer idealizes the heroic world. Even in the darkest days of the
war, the ordinary soldiers rejoice when Odysseus dishonours the
only one of them who dared criticize Agamemnon's incompetence.
Yet some literary scholars have read into this episode subtle resistance to the warrior elite,[124] as if by having Thersites speak at all
Homer questioned the *status quo*. This strikes me as over-reading.
Throughout the *Iliad* and *Odyssey* Homer takes it for granted that
there are assemblies which all free men can attend and even speak at,
just as later sources say was the case in Archaic Sparta and Solonian
Athens. This, to him, was a fact of life about how communities
worked. Perhaps in the eighth century there were more critical
voices than before; but Homer was at pains to show that in the heroic
age, such carping was treated the way it deserved.

We have no direct evidence for how eighth-century audiences
reacted to Homer's songs, or who commissioned and then used the
texts. Deducing responses and from them the poems' sociological
functions is a highly subjective exercise. Yet we have to undertake it.
I suggest that if we impute rational motives and a reasonable
understanding of their own interests to actors in eighth-century
Greece, we should assume that this image of the heroic age appealed
particularly to those wealthy men who saw all that they held dear
collapsing in a time of revolutionary change. It offered them a
reassuring anchor in the past: the most talented and therefore most
divinely inspired singer held that the world of Odysseus had been one
where great men had protected their followers, punishing upstarts
and enemies. For these services they were respected and honoured.
The age of heroes was gone but not forgotten: the noble few in the
present could recapture its glories, and it provided a moral beacon in
these dark days.

VI. CONCLUSION: HOMERIC CULTURE

This essay is not a blueprint for reconstructing Homeric society.
I argue that the *Iliad* and *Odyssey* are two eighth-century versions of

---

[123] Finley (n. 49), 111.
[124] P. Rose, 'Thersites and the Plural Voices of Homer', *Arethusa* 21 (1988), 5–25;
W. G. Thalmann, 'Thersites: Comedy, Scapegoats, and Heroic Ideology in the *Iliad*',
TAPA 118 (1988), 1–28.

the heroic age.[125] Judging from the comparative evidence on oral composition, Homer imagined the heroic age in terms of the assumptions he and his audiences shared about how the world worked, and of how the heroic world had differed from the contemporary. I tried to show that there is nothing in the poems to contradict this thesis. In section v, I argued that this was not 'the' Greek image of the heroic age, but one which was partial and coincided with the interests of particular sections of the eighth-century upper classes—so much so that they went to the trouble of having Homer dictate versions of his stories. Homer is less a direct source for eighth-century society than for eighth-century culture. The distinction is significant.

Between 750 and 650 BC, the Greeks who lived around the shores of the Aegean turned the world on its head. Some historians write as if they could check their interpretations of Homeric society against the facts of the archaeological record, but those who do this have not grasped the complexity of this archaeological record, and do not understand what it is telling us. Its variety means that there is no way to use it to date Homeric society. At any moment, the material remains from different parts of the Greek world vary radically, indicating significant regional sociological differences.[126] The Greeks were experimenting with new ways of relating to the gods, the past, and the east. The recording of heroic, theogonic, and genealogical poetry was part of these experiments; so too were the rituals which created most of our archaeological record. The excavated record is not a transparent window onto the material culture in use at any specific time in the past: it is the product of ritual languages just as complex as Homer's, and then garbled by the vicissitudes of transmission.

What this means is that we can read the poems and the artefacts as two kinds of ritualized discourses on the form of the good society: we cannot use one to prove or disprove claims based on the other. Just as there were other poets offering slightly (or wildly) different visions of the heroic age from Homer's, so too the people who deposited the objects we dig up disagreed on how their rituals should

---

[125] Throughout this chapter, I conflate the two poems for the sake of convenience. I believe that both were composed by one poet, but the differences between them are often significant. A more thorough analysis would need to distinguish between the poems.   [126] Whitley (n. 48); Morris (n. 24).

represent the world. The Greeks who visited Mycenaean tombs and left offerings there behaved in a tremendous variety of ways, and perhaps did not even agree on who was in the tombs. Similarly, the horizon of 'heroizing' burials in these years suggests intense debate over what it meant to say that a recently deceased man deserved heroic honours.[127]

When we read Homer as a source for early Archaic history, we are necessarily engaged first and foremost in cultural, not social or economic, history. The poems are about superhuman heroes acting outrageously. The institutions they operated within may reflect those of the eighth century, but they may equally well be largely invented—the creation of poets who knew that the Achaeans had great kings, but could not begin to imagine a Mycenaean palace and its bureaucracy; poets who knew that the cowering lower classes jumped to obey their overlords, yet took it for granted that there had to be assemblies where all free men took part.

Twentieth-century historians have developed three main ways of reading Homer. He might be reflecting his own age; he might be remembering some earlier time (Mycenaean or Dark Age); or he might be conflating different ages or just making the whole thing up. That learned scholars have defended each suggests that each is, in a sense, correct. But none of them really captures what is going on. The basic problem lies in assuming that we can move directly from epic to social history. We cannot.

Robert Darnton, a leading scholar of Old Regime France, explains his historical methods as follows:

All of us, French and 'Anglo-Saxons', pedants as well as peasants, operate within cultural constraints, just as we all share conventions of speech. So historians should be able to see how cultures shape ways of thinking, even for the greatest thinkers. A poet or philosopher may push language to its limits, but at some point he will hit against the outer frame of meaning. Beyond it, madness lies—the fate of Hölderlin or Nietzsche. But within it, great men can test and shape the boundaries of meaning. Thus there should be room for Diderot and Rousseau in a book about *mentalités* in eighteenth-century France.[128]

---

[127] I set out my views on these issues in Morris (n. 105), 189–91; 'Tomb Cult and the "Greek Renaissance": The Past in the Present in the Eighth Century BC', *Antiquity* 62 (1988), 750–61; (n. 3), 267–72. Antonaccio (n. 37) reviews the evidence.

[128] R. Darnton, *The Great Cat Massacre and Other Episodes in French Cultural History* (London, 1984), 6.

Reading Homer as a source for the eighth century is an exercise in cultural history: it is about understanding representations and ideologies. We learn about how certain groups imagined the heroic age; and we can speculate about who those groups were, what it meant for them to cast the heroes in this light, and how other groups may have reacted.

Some cultural historians assert that all historiography is like this: we are trapped in the textuality of our sources, which never offer direct access to the past. Every presentation of facts is really a re-presentation; and all historians do is play off one (mis)re-presentation against another. Our reference to sources is no different from the intertextuality that literary scholars analyse.[129] I do not agree, and believe that we can in fact move from cultural to social and economic history.[130] But in the case of the eighth century, the nature of our evidence confronts us with formidable problems.

Homerists often say that the poems are full of distortions, archaisms, and Bronze-Age memories, which we can sift out if we are careful enough. But this common-sense methodology will not do. We need more sophisticated methods to move from Homeric culture to eighth-century society, and the only way to do this is to play Homer off against Hesiod and the archaeological evidence. All these sources are the products of culture-making; they are models *for* as well as models *of* reality. None offers us a bedrock of prediscursive fact against which we can test theories. But each kind of evidence was produced by *different* language games. By manipulating contexts we can clarify the different ideological arguments of the eighth century, and what was shared by all. It may not be social history of the type Finley believed he could write from Homer, but it is the foundation for a more realistic approach to Homeric history.

[129] See e.g. K. Jenkins (ed.), *The Postmodern History Reader* (London, 1997); A. Munslow, *Deconstructing History* (London, 1997); M. Poster, *Cultural History + Postmodernism* (New York, 1997). [130] Morris (n. 2), 74–9; (n. 3), 12–17.

2

The Making of Homer in the Sixth Century BC: Rhapsodes versus Stesichorus

WALTER BURKERT

The unique position of Homer in Greek civilization is so firmly established that we sometimes forget to wonder about it and to realize that it is in itself a unique phenomenon. Even the role of Shakespeare for the English is not closely analogous. One might be tempted to call Homer the Bible or the Koran of the Greeks, which brings out the basic difference that Homer is not, and never was, a religious reve- lation demanding submission and worship but rather literature that invited, and still invites, literary criticism, although he was to form the model and common reference point for the Greek mind. This phenomenon is strange in several respects: there is a strangeness of quality, of age, and of acceptance. I am not going to praise the quality of the *Iliad* and the *Odyssey* here, though I think they are better poems than any considerations of probability would suggest; nor shall I dwell on the fact that these compositions apparently come right at the beginning of Greek literacy and are a monumental achievement, rather than the first and uncertain steps one would expect. Hardly less surprising is the success of Homer among the Greeks, a dashing and lasting success that is not a necessary or natural cosequence of either age or quality; age is liable to go out of fashion, and quality is always debatable. Thus it is not enough to state or to postulate that there was one genius, or possibly two, who created these superb pieces of art, the *Iliad* and the *Odyssey*. An equally monumental problem is how the public was made to accept these texts as standard, in combination with a single author's name, *Homeros*, to the exclusion of other, similar texts that fell into neglect and were thus lost to posterity.[1] It is not the question of production but of 'reception' that will be the focus here.[2] In other words, I shall not deal with the Homeric question in the traditional sense, i.e. when and through what contributions, alterations, intermediate stages, and manipulations the texts we read came into existence. (I, for one, imagine the first written *Iliad* as a set of leather scrolls in the first half of the seventh century, emerging from an oral tradition that had been flourishing mainly in the eighth.[3]) The question will rather be: How did it happen that these texts were singled out with the name of *Homeros* attached to them, and were given absolute authority? This evidently was the first making of a classic in Greek literature, and it seems mainly to have been a process of the second half of the sixth century BC.

To begin by working backward. The special authority of Homer, i.e. basically the *Iliad* and the *Odyssey* bound to this author's name, was well established by the fifth century BC. 'Divine Homer', $\vartheta\epsilon\hat{\imath}os$ "Ομηρος, a formula in Homeric metre, resounds from Aristophanes' *Frogs* (1034), where it gives the impression of being familiar to the audience; it also recurs several times in the *Certamen* of Hesiod and Homer.[4] Herodotus has repeated references to Homer, some of which

[1] This is not the place to indulge in bibliography on Homeric problems. For such, see D. W. Packard and T. Myers, A *Bibliography of Homeric Scholarship, 1930–1970* (Malibu, 1974); A. Lesky, 'Homeros', *RE* Suppl. XI (1967), 687–846 (where part XI, 'Nachleben', was planned, but never published); A. Heubeck, *Die homerische Frage* (Darmstadt, 1974); J. Latacz, *Homer. Eine Einführung* (Munich, 1985); G. S. Kirk, 'The Making of the *Iliad*' in *Il. Comm.* I. 1–16; A. Heubeck, 'General Introduction' in *Od. Comm.* I. 1–23. On the name *Homeros* and the works attributed to him, see U. von Wilamowitz-Moellendorff, *Homerische Untersuchungen* (Berlin, 1884), 328–80; id. *Die Ilias und Homer* (Berlin, 1914), 356–76; F. Jacoby, 'Homerisches I: Der Bios und die Person', *Hermes* 68 (1933), 1–50 = *Kleine philologische Schriften* I (Berlin, 1961), 1–53; E. Schwartz, 'Der Name Homeros', *Hermes* 75 (1940), 1–9.
[2] The term and programme of *Rezeptionstheorie* go back to H. R. Jauss, *Literaturgeschichte als Provokation der Literaturwissenschaft* (Konstanz, 1967); id. *Toward an Aesthetic of Reception* (Minneapolis, 1982); W. Barner, 'Neuphilologische Rezeptionsforschung und die Möglichkeiten der klassischen Philologie', *Poetica* 9 (1977), 499–521; P. L. Schmidt, 'Reception Theory and Classical Scholarship: A Plea for Convergence', in W. M. Calder (ed.), *Hypatia: Essays in Classics, Comparative Literature and Philosophy Presented to H. E. Barnes* (Boulder, 1985), 67–77. The interrelations between production, performance, and reception are investigated by W. Rösler, *Dichter und Gruppe* (Munich, 1980); B. Gentili, *Poetry and its Public in Ancient Greece* (Eng. trans., Baltimore, 1988).
[3] Cf. W. Burkert, 'Das hunderttorige Theben und die Datierung der Ilias', *WS* 89 (1976), 5–21; on leather scrolls, see id. *The Orientalizing Revolution* (Eng. trans., Cambridge, Mass., 1992), 30–3; for problems of Homeric text transmission, see S. West, *Od. Comm.* I. 33–48.

have become famous. He discusses Homer's age and the attribution
to him of *Cypria* and *Epigonoi*, which is contested; and he uses
Homer's art of storytelling as a model—a striking case is the introduction of a baneful dream that prompts Xerxes to war, as the οὖλος
ὄνειρος did Agamemnon.[5] The text of the Derveni papyrus,
the author of which I guess might have been Stesimbrotus of
Thasos,[6] writing about 420 BC, shows Homeric philology surprisingly well developed, with a discussion of single forms and meanings
and quotations readily assembled. Earlier, possibly towards the
middle of the century, Protagoras had made the pun that Homer
used the imperative in prayer where he should have used the opta-
tive;[7] this has its full effect only if it refers to the very first line of the
classical author: μῆνιν ἄειδε θεά ('sing, goddess, of the wrath'). We
reach the first half of the fifth century with the inscription on one of
the herms of the stoa of herms in Athens, attributed to the epoch of
Cimon: it explicitly refers to the praise Homer spent on Menestheus,
king of Athens, as being 'the best to arrange horses and shield-
bearing men' (Plutarch, *Cimon* 7. 6). References to Athenians in the
Iliad are sparse, to put it mildly; to pick out this line and to com-
memorate it in public is indicative of a feeling that Athens simply
could not do without Homer.[8] Aeschylus is credited with the saying
that his tragedies were just 'slices cut from the great meals of
Homer'.[9] Anecdotes of this kind cannot be trusted, but the metaphor
is original: amid the competition that characterized Greek poetry,
it shows deference to the unique classic of the past. For Pindar,
too, Homer was a classic suited for ready quotation: 'This too is a
word of Homer...', he says in the *Fourth Pythian* (277),[10] and

---

[4] *Certamen* cd. T. W. Allen, *Homeri Opera* v (OCT, 1912), 214, 309, 338.

[5] Hdt. 2. 53. 2; 2. 117; 4. 32; he quotes the title, '*Iliad*', at 2. 116. 2, '*Odyssey*', at
4. 29; on 5. 67 see below, n. 16; dream: 7. 12–18; cf. *Il.* 2. 1–40.

[6] Preliminary edition in ZPE 47 (1982); cf. W. Burkert, ZPE 62 (1986), 1–5.
Parallel is Metrodorus, no. 61 in DK; even earlier Theagenes (no. 8 in DK).

[7] Protagoras 80 A 29 DK.

[8] The ref. is to *Il.* 2. 522–4, as also in Hdt. 7. 161. 3; Menestheus is named amid Trojan
warriors on an Attic black-figure kantharos, Berlin 1737, of c.575–550 BC; *Paralipomena*
72. 1, *Add.*[2] 49; K. Friis Johansen, *The Iliad in Early Greek Art* (Copenhagen, 1967), fig.
37. On Menestheus in the *Il.*, see Kirk, *Il. Comm.* 1. 179–80, 206–7.

[9] Aeschylus T 112 in S. Radt, *Tragicorum Graecorum Fragmenta* III (Göttingen,
1985).

[10] The ref. is to *Il.* 15. 207. In *Pyth.* 3. 81–2 he quotes *Il.* 24. 527 ff.,
misunderstanding the text; see also below, nn. 20, 39. The plot of the *Il.* and characteristic scenes are evoked by Bacch. 13. 105–69.

he alludes to the epithet of $\vartheta\epsilon\hat{\iota}os$ Ὅμηρος, in the *Fourth Isthmian* (55–7).

We get to the transition from the sixth century to the fifth with Heraclitus and Xenophanes, whose grim criticisms of Homer are an indirect tribute to his special status within the Greek world. Heraclitus also produces the oldest testimony to the Homeric legend, referring to the riddle of the lice that killed Homer at Ios.[11] Somewhat older, because he, too, was criticized by Heraclitus, is Xenophanes,[12] whose moral, theological, and epistemological criticism of the gods of Homer and Hesiod has remained famous; it was not even earnestly contradicted in antiquity. But if Xenophanes wished to replace the 'fictions of the ancients' with more sensible poetry, he was fighting in vain. A famous fragment of his says: 'From the beginning following Homer, because they all have learned...'; this is an incomplete sentence (B 10) that leaves open exactly what people learned and what they did in consequence; it nevertheless remains the earliest and most comprehensive statement of the authority of Homer as *praeceptor Graeciae*.[13] It bears testimony to a success already established.

Beyond the date of Xenophanes, the picture becomes blurred; only fragments of literature survive, which present their own problems of interpretation. Much depends on whether the fragment of an elegy which quotes the lines about the race of men being like leaves of a tree is to be attributed to Semonides in the seventh century or to Simonides at the end of the sixth century BC; the text says these are the most beautiful lines by the man of Chios.[14] I am inclined to side with Martin West against the earlier *communis opinio* and attribute the fragment to Simonides. Simonides also refers to 'Homer and Stesichorus', who 'sang to the people' about a detail of Meleager's role at the funeral of Pelias (564 *PMG*), an incident not to be found in our Homer. There remains what seems to be the oldest and most isolated testimony for the name of Homer: in the first half of the seventh century Callinus attributed the *Thebais* to Homer.[15]

[11] Heraclitus B 56; cf. B 42; A 22 DK.

[12] Xenophanes, *Silloi*, esp. B 11–12 DK; 'fictions of the ancients' B 1. 22 DK; criticized by Heraclitus B 40 DK.

[13] '[Homer] educated Hellas' is an established slogan in Pl. *Resp.* 606e.

[14] Semonides fr. 29 Diehl = Simonides fr. 19 West; cf. M. L. West, *Studies in Greek Elegy and Iambus* (Berlin, 1974), 179–80; the ref. is to *Il.* 6. 146 (cf. Mimnermus fr. 2 West). For Simonides' view of Homer as a unique classic, see now fr. 11. 15–18 and fr. 20 in M. L. West, *Iambi et Elegi Graeci* 11 (2nd edn., Oxford, 1992).

[15] Callinus fr. 6 West = Paus. 9. 9. 5 (the MS tradition has KALAINOS); cf. J. A. Davison, *From Archilochus to Pindar* (London, 1968), 81–2.

Herodotus has an interesting and much debated story about Clisthenes, tyrant of Sikyon about 570 BC. He put an end to the contests of rhapsodes in the city because the epic of Homer was always in praise of Argos and the Argives and, curtailing the cult of Adrastus, he transferred 'tragic choruses' to Dionysus.[16] Adrastus would again point to the *Thebaid*. This seems to be the first testimony as to 'rhapsodes', if we can be sure that the terminology had not been modernized by Herodotus or some intermediate source. There are, in addition, stories about the authority of Homer having been used in arbitration of political conflicts in the sixth century: Herodotus, in a passage with uncommonly garbled chronological problems, says the Athenians claimed possession of Sigeion at the Hellespont against the Lesbians because of their participation in the Trojan War, as attested by Homer (5. 94, cf. Aristotle, *Rhetoric* 1370^b30).[17] It is true that the Aeolian and Ionian colonization, and hence Aeolian Lesbians, are conspicuously absent from the *Iliad*, but more could be made of the role of Demophon and Acamas, sons of Theseus, in the *Little Iliad* and the *Iliupersis*. Another case was the quarrel about whether Ajax and Salamis belonged to Megara or Athens. In this case, the very passage in the *Iliad* on which the Athenian claim was based, 2. 558, was impugned by the adversaries as an interpolation by either Pisistratus or Solon. This shows a certain autonomy of the literary feud; it can be traced back to Dieuchidas in the fourth century, but not necessarily beyond that date.[18]

In all these cases we are dealing with later accounts; there always remains the problem of how much remodelling of the tradition has occurred since the sixth century, and what exactly was done, said, or believed then. The name of Homer is presumed to have been around, but it was not necessarily our *Iliad* that was at the centre of interest.

---

[16] Hdt. 5. 67, a passage heavily discussed in all studies of the beginnings of tragedy; see, among more recent studies, A. Lesky, *Greek Tragic Poetry* (Eng. trans. New Haven, 1983), 20–2; J. Svenbro, *La Parole et le marbre* (Lund, 1976), 44–5, who argues that Clisthenes' decree presupposes fixed texts, i.e. rhapsodes; E. Cingano, 'Clisthene di Sicione, Erodoto e i poemi del ciclo tebano', *QUCC* 20 (1985), 31–40.

[17] Cf. W. W. How and J. Wells, *A Commentary on Herodotus* II (2nd edn., Oxford, 1928), 56. Acamas and Demophon and their Trojan adventures appear in vase-painting from Exekias onwards: U. Kron, *Die zehn attischen Phylenheroen* (Berlin, 1976), 147–70, esp. pl. 19, 2, neck-amphora, Berlin F 1720, *ABV* 143, 1.

[18] The evidence for this quarrel and the theory of a Pisistratean redaction of Homer is collected and discussed in R. Merkelbach, *Untersuchungen zur Odyssee* (2nd edn., Munich, 1969), 239–62; Dieuchidas, 485 F 6 *FGrH* = Diog. Laert. I. 57. For Menestheus (*Il.* 2. 552), see above, n. 8.

The same is true for the epic tradition in various transformations in the poetry of Sappho and Alcaeus: there are Hector and Andromache, the model couple from Book 6 of the *Iliad*, or Thetis emerging from the sea to listen to her son, from Book 1; but the wedding of Peleus from the *Cypria*, or the *Iliupersis* with Ajax and Cassandra, are hardly less important.[19] Even for Pindar, Achilles' fights with Cycnus and Memnon, from the *Cypria* and the *Aethiopis*, respectively, are on equal footing with the Hector theme, and for him the tragedy of Ajax is testified to by Homer.[20]

There is another, and in fact much richer, corpus that tells us about the themes of epic poetry in the seventh and sixth centuries: Greek art, which is characterized by the development of epic iconography or *Sagenbilder*, in this very period. It has been more than fifty years since the book of Friis Johansen on the *Iliad* and early Greek art first appeared; much new evidence has come to light since then, and new controversies have arisen.[21] These cannot be explored in any depth by a philologist, and least of all would I embark on the problem of stylistic affinities between Homer or stages of Homeric poetry and the development of Greek Archaic art, as has notably been done in repeated attempts by Karl Schefold.[22] Fascinating as these studies are, it will be uncommonly difficult to reach agreement in such a field. I shall try to confine myself to some rather simple and obvious remarks.

As soon as Greek art begins to illustrate myth, about 700 BC, it shows familiarity with Trojan themes, though other themes, such as Heracles and Perseus and the Gorgons, are also important. The

---

[19] Hector and Andromache: Sappho fr. 44 L-P; Thetis: Alc. fr. 44 L-P; wedding of Peleus: Alc. fr. 42 L-P; Locrian Ajax: Alc. fr. 298 L-P; see D. Meyerhoff, *Traditioneller Stoff und individuelle Gestaltung: Untersuchungen zu Alkaios und Sappho* (Hildesheim, 1984).

[20] Cycnus, Hector, Memnon: Pind. *Ol.* 2. 81–3; cf. *Nem.* 3. 62; 6. 50 (Memnon); Homer honouring Ajax, *Isthm.* 4. 35–9, most probably refers to the *Aethiopis*, fr. 2 Allen = Schol. ad loc.

[21] Friis Johansen (n. 8); K. Schefold, *Frühgriechische Sagenbilder* (Munich, 1964); K. Fittschen, *Untersuchungen zum Beginn der Sagendarstellung bei den Griechen* (Berlin, 1969); R. Kannicht, 'Poetry and Art: Homer and the Monuments Afresh', *Cl. Ant.* 1 (1982), 70–86.

[22] K. Schefold, 'Archäologisches zum Stil Homers', *MH* 12 (1955), 132–44; id. 'Das homerische Epos in der antiken Kunst', *Atti del convegno 'La poesia epica e la sua formazione'*, Accad. Naz. dei Lincei, quad. 139 (Rome, 1970), 91–116, revised in Schefold, *Wort und Bild* (Basle, 1975), 27–42; cf. B. Andreae and H. Flashar, 'Strukturaequivalenzen zwischen den homerischen Epen und der frühgriechischen Vasenkunst', *Poetica* 9 (1977), 217–64.

earliest incontrovertible Trojan theme seems to be a wheeled Trojan horse on a Boeotian fibula.[23] A climax is attained with the amphora from Mykonos, which has the great tableau of an Iliupersis: the wooden horse with the warriors looking out, the infanticide, and Menelaus threatening Helen. These details, however, are neither in the *Iliad* nor in the *Odyssey*.[24] For compensation we have the famous illustrations of the Cyclops story, as contained in Book 9 of the *Odyssey*, which appear in Argive, Attic, and Euboean vase-painting.[25] Yet this episode is, in contrast to, say, Nausicaa or Eumaeus, a special case, a widespread type of folktale which, even if it were ultimately dependent on some *Odyssey*, owed its success to its intrinsic structure and dynamics, and not to special poetical skill. Thus we cannot be at all sure which form of an *Odyssey* was known to the artists in the first half of the seventh century. One early iconographic type depicts two women standing behind two fighting heroes; among epic themes this composition uniquely fits the duel of Achilles and Memnon, assisted by their divine mothers, Thetis and Eos, respectively.[26] An attractive theory of 'neoanalysis' postulates that this is an earlier tale and in some respects the model of the *mēnis* tale that forms the plot of our *Iliad*; the importance of Memnon for Pindar has already been mentioned. Other Trojan subjects prominent in seventh-century art are the Judgement of Paris and the Pursuit of Troilus by Achilles.[27]

All this points to the conclusion that it was not the unique text of the *Iliad* as the one great classic that made its impression on seventh-century art, but a more variegated complex of Trojan themes. This may be taken together with what is indicated by the literary

[23] Schefold (n. 21), pl. 6a; Fittschen (n. 21), 182.

[24] Schefold (n. 21), pls. 34, 35; Fittschen (n. 21), 182–3; C. Zindel, *Drei vorhomerische Sagenversionen in der griechischen Kunst* (Diss. Basle, 1974), 87–92.

[25] Fittschen (n. 21), 192–4; Schefold (n. 21), fig. 15, pls. I and 16, pl. 37; Cyclops and folktale, see D. L. Page, *The Homeric Odyssey* (Oxford, 1955), 1–20; W. Burkert, *Structure and History in Greek Mythology and Ritual* (Berkeley, 1979), 31–4 (with further bibliography).

[26] Fittschen (n. 21), 178–9; the type already occurs on the Geometric stand, Munich 8936, mentioned by Fittschen, p. 69, for the Molione. H. Pestalozzi, *Die Achilleis als Quelle der Ilias* (Erlenbach, 1945); W. Schadewaldt, 'Einblick in die Erfindung der Ilias' in *Von Homers Welt und Werk* (4th edn., Stuttgart, 1965), 155–202; cf. W. Kullmann, 'Zur Methode der Neoanalyse in der Homerforschung', *WS* 94 (1981), 5–42; id. 'Oral Poetry and Neoanalysis in Homeric Research', *GRBS* 25 (1984), 307–23.

[27] Paris: Chigi Vase, Schefold (n. 21), pl. 29b; Troilus: Zindel (n. 24), 30–80.

testimonia but for the fact that Heracles is nearly absent from what we know about literature of the period, and Theban themes are absent from early iconography.[28] The parallelism of art and literature cannot be pressed. As to the special plot of the *Iliad*, there still seems to be just one monument of the seventh century, the Euphorbus plate with its inscriptions that identify a scene from Book 17 of the *Iliad*. Euphorbus appears only to serve the narrative needs in the scene of Patroclus' death: he is doubling as himself and Apollo and at the same time he is mirroring Paris' role at the death of Achilles. The painter of the Euphorbus plate presumed his clients to be familiar with this story in considerable detail, though close scrutiny has revealed divergences from the version contained in our *Iliad*.[29] I feel sure the vase-painter had not read about this in a book, but more or less exactly remembered what he had heard.

By about 580/570, however, the whole of the *Iliad* appears to have been widely known, including those parts that are labelled later additions by the analysts: Phoenix, Dolon, the Games of Patroclus (as depicted by the vase-painter, Sophilus), and the Ransom of Hector. Even the last book of the *Odyssey* seems to have been around.[30] Athenians showed interest in Menestheus (cf. note 8). This did not encroach on the popularity of the *Cypria*[31] and other *Troika*. Some decades later, among the works of the Amasis Painter, there is the cup from the Norbert Schimmel collection, which has Poseidon urging the two Ajaxes and Teucer to battle, a scene from Book 13 of the *Iliad*; this cup is dated to 540/530 by the specialists. It was Friis

---

[28] I. Krauskopf, *Der thebanische Sagenkreis und andere griechische Sagen in der etruskischen Kunst* (Mainz, 1974), shows that representations of the Theban cycle were more popular in Etruria, but even there they became numerous only towards the end of the 6th cent. BC.

[29] London A 749; Schefold (n. 21), pl. 75; cf. Schefold in *Wort und Bild* (n. 22), 33–4; a hypothesis about the name Euphorbus on the basis of the Memnonis theory (n. 26 above) by H. Mühlestein, 'Euphorbos und der Tod des Patroklos', *Studi micenei ed egeoanatolici* 15 (1972), 79–90.

[30] Phoenix on a Corinthian cup, *c.*580 BC, Basle, private collection, *LIMC* I, Aias I 122; Dolon and Phoenix on a Corinthian cup, Brussels, *LIMC* 3, Dolon I; Friis Johansen (n. 8), 71, figs. 15, 16; Schefold (n. 21), 83, fig. 36; Ransom of Hector, Friis Johansen 49–50, 127–38; cf. Schefold (n. 21), pl. 76b; Sophilus fragment in Athens, *ABV* 39, 16 and Schefold (n. 21), pl. VI; amphora as Dionysus' wedding present for Thetis on the François Vase, Schefold (n. 21), pl. 48a, cf. E. Simon, *Die griechischen Vasen* (Munich, 1976), 70–1, in accordance with *Od.* 24. 74–5, rather than with Stesich. 234 *PMGF*.

[31] Request for the Return of Helen on a Corinthian krater in the Vatican in Rome, Schefold (n. 21), pl. 72.

Johansen's finding that the true efflorescence of *Iliad* scenes in Attic vase-painting was only reached by about 520 BC,[32] and this is largely still accepted. He did not know the magnificent Euphronius krater now in the Metropolitan Museum in New York, which takes its inspiration from Book 16 of the *Iliad*: Zeus weeping tears of blood at the impending death of Sarpedon and ordering Sleep and Death to take care of the body. With Euphronius we come close to the epoch of Xenophanes. Whether all this was 'Homer' to the artists, they chose not to tell us.

It remains to take account of the picture of epic poetry and poets as contained in the Homeric texts themselves.[33] The direct evidence comes mainly from the *Odyssey*: two epic singers, Phemius at Ithaca and blind Demodocus among the Phaeacians, are introduced in this poem and described with an affectionate care that makes one think of a self-portrait of the composer; Phemius is spared, of course, by Odysseus. Both singers have telling names—Phemius Terpsiades, the 'narrative tradition that is meant to please', and Demodocus, 'accepted by the public'. These are singers in the full sense, accompanying their song on a string instrument, the *phorminx*. They normally perform in the hall of the king after meals, as an ornament to the feast, although Demodocus also sings in the agora (*Odyssey* 8. 254 ff.) at the public festival given in honour of Odysseus. Phaeacian civilization has several traits more modern than the normal Homeric setting.

The subject of the singer's song in the largest sense is κλέα ἀνδρῶν, the glorious deeds of men. In practice this means the Trojan cycle, for Phemius as well as for Demodocus: Phemius sings the Return of the Achaeans, and Demodocus the Quarrel of Odysseus and Achilles and the Wooden Horse. The second Nekyia contrasts, from a vantage point in the beyond, the song of Achilles, the song of Clytemnestra, and the song of Penelope, i.e. *Achilleis* or *Iliad*, *Achaiōn Kathodos*, and the author's own *Odyssey*.[34] The audience is supposed to be familiar with the outlines of the tales, but the singer must find his special way in each case; part of his skill is to choose the point

---

[32] D. von Bothmer, *The Amasis Painter and his World* (Malibu, 1985), 217 no. 60 (referring to *Il*. 13. 45 ff.); Friis Johansen (n. 8), 223–41.

[33] Cf. W. Schadewaldt, 'Die Gestalt des homerischen Sängers', *Von Homers Welt und Werk* (n. 26), 54–86; H. Maehler, *Die Auffassung des Dichterberufs im frühen Griechentum bis zur Zeit Pindars* (Göttingen, 1963); Latacz (n. 1), 40–2.

[34] Cf. A. T. Edwards, *Achilles in the Odyssey* (Meisenheim/Glan, 1985), 86–93.

of departure—from where to start the story, ἀμόθεν (from some point or another). Phemius even claims to be *autodidaktos*, 'self-taught', for a god has given him various modes of song; this sets him apart not from divine inspiration but from merely reproductive performance of epic song.[35] That such a distinction should have been emerging is of great interest. Normally, the *aoidos* as portrayed by Homer is a creative and a traditional singer at the same time, moving within an accepted frame of traditional themes but generating his text afresh for each performance in the formulaic technique, as was discovered by Milman Parry.[36] The themes are known to singer and audience by catchwords such as 'the wooden horse'; but there are no fixed texts, and there is no author's name. The interest of a naive audience would have concentrated on the contents of the tale, a world of fancy believed to be basically 'true'; the singer or author is an obstacle to the imagination. In fact the problem of the individual author seems to be non-existent in pre-Greek or non-Greek literature: there is no author for *Gilgamesh*, for instance. Pre-Greek tradition and the analysis of the Greek formulaic style thus combine to encourage the statement that Homer does not presuppose Homer in the sense of the individual creative author of a fixed and potentially classical text.

Conditions had changed in a remarkable way by the end of the sixth century. At the time of Xenophanes, apparently the challenge was no longer to 'sing the Wooden Horse', or even 'the Mēnis of Achilles' but to 'recite a passage of Homer'. What had happened was that rhapsodes had replaced singers, *aoidoi*, a momentous change indeed. Creative improvisation had given way to the reproduction of a fixed text, learned by heart and available also in book form. The wrong etymology of the word *rhapsōdos*—from *rhabdos*, 'staff'—which is already used by Pindar (*Isthmian* 4. 38), bears witness to their custom, also identifiable in vase-paintings since the beginning of the fifth century: rhapsodes no longer used a *phorminx* for accompaniment, but the same staff as a speaker in the assembly; they did not sing, but recited. This is borne out by the word formation, correctly understood: in contrast to *kitharōdos, aulōdos, tragōdos, kōmōdos*, who

---

[35] *Od.* 23. 347. The singer's claims to inspiration and to telling the truth preclude the full concept of an author; cf. W. Rösler, 'Die Entdeckung der Fiktionalität', *Poetica* 12 (1980), 283–319, esp. 293–8.

[36] M. Parry, *The Making of Homeric Verse* (Oxford, 1971); A. B. Lord, *The Singer of Tales* (Cambridge, Mass., 1960).

are 'singers' in connection with lyre, flute, goat, or revel, *rhapsōdos* is
of the *terpsimbrotos* type, rephrasing ῥάπτειν ᾠδήν, 'to sew a song',
an external pre-existing object. The designation may have been a
joke originally, but it hit at some peculiarity.[37] The rhapsode was not
a singer in the full sense. For further distinction, rhapsodes are not
normally described as performing at the banquets of nobles in a
closed hall, but at public festivals in the form of well-organized
agōnes. This is presupposed and thus documented by Heraclitus' acid
remark that Homer deserved to be thrown out of the *agōnes* and to be
flogged (B 42). This was a most momentous change: rhapsodes did
not claim to produce texts of their own in public performance, but
were bound to the name of one author of the past, Homer.

Let us move carefully, since there has been much controversy on
'Homer' and the 'Homerids'. Detailed, if somewhat ironical, pictures
of rhapsodes are given by Plato and Xenophon;[38] Ion especially, in
Plato's dialogue, is ridiculed for his comprehensive and absurd claims
as to the all-round excellence and omniscience of his patron, Homer.
It is clear that this name is the trademark on which the rhapsodes
were professionally dependent; no wonder they were engaged in
Homeric propaganda; We are taken back to the beginning of the fifth
century with Pindar: for him the connection between rhapsodes and
Homer was already established beyond question. He makes
Homer himself a rhapsode, 'singing to the staff', and he introduces
Homeridai as ῥαπτῶν ἐπέων ἀοιδοί, 'singers of sewn verses'.[39]
Heraclitus adds the reference to *agōnes*.[40]

To sum up the facts: rhapsodes, reciting 'Homer', appeared in public
contests by the last third of the sixth century—possibly earlier—but
they were unknown to Homer. There remains the problem of what

---

[37] See H. Patzer, 'Rhapsodos', *Hermes* 80 (1952), 314–24; R. Sealey, 'From Phemios
to Ion', *REG* 70 (1957), 312–55; G. F. Else, 'The Origin of *ΤΡΑΓΩΙΔΙΑ*', *Hermes* 85
(1957), 17–46, esp. 27–34; G. Tarditi, 'Sull' origine e sul significato della parola
Rapsodo', *Maia* 20 (1968), 137–45. For the word formation, see T. Knecht, *Die
Geschichte der griechischen Komposita vom Typ* τερψίμβροτος (Diss. Zürich, 1946);
cf. Hes. fr. 357 M-W, Pind. *Nem.* 2. 2. The standard picture of a rhapsode with his staff
is the neck-amphora, London E270, *ARV²* 183, 15.
[38] Pl. *Ion*; cf H. Flashar, *Der Dialog Ion als Zeugnis platonischer Philosophie* (Berlin,
1958), 21–7; Xen. *Symp.* 3. 5–6; *Mem.* 4. 2. 10.
[39] Pind. *Isthm* 4. 34; *Nem* 2. 1; the scholium on the latter passage is the *locus
classicus* for rhapsodes and Homerids, cf. below, n. 41, and W. Burkert, 'Kynaithos,
Polycrates, and the Homeric Hymn to Apollo', in G. W. Bowersock, W. Burkert, and
M. C. J. Putnam (edd.), *Arktouros: Hellenic Studies Presented to B. M.W. Knox* (Berlin,
1979), 53–62, esp. 54–8.   [40] Heraclitus B 42 DK.

exactly the term *Homeridai*, used by Pindar, means. Acusilaus, a contemporary of Pindar, says this was a family from Chios. In spite of Detlef Fehling's criticism, I think it is most economical to combine Pindar and Acusilaus and to conclude that for a while a family from Chios—organized in a form comparable to the Asclepiads from Kos, the family of doctors—was organizing the recitation of Homer as their special craft,[41] referring to the text of the epics as their hereditary possession. The *Kreophyleioi* from Samos, who appear in the Pythagoras tradition, are a parallel from the same period, whose patrimony is the epic about Heracles and Oechalia.[42]

Modern studies of early Greek literature have rightly insisted on the close connection between production and performance in poetry.[43] Still rooted in an oral culture, the poem existed for and through the performance; the literary *genera* in fact reflect different conditions of performance. This is true for the epic singer as portrayed in the *Odyssey*, and it holds for the singers of *iamboi* and elegies, of monodic lyrics and of choral odes, and even for tragedy and comedy. But it does not apply to rhapsodes; or rather, in terms of performance there was a break between Homeric *aoidoi* and rhapsodes. Here, and here alone, we find a separation of production and performance, by the last third of the sixth century at the latest, which seems curiously deviant in the lively field of Greek poetic productions. In Thucydidean terms, *ktēma* (possession) has been dissociated from *agōnisma* (competition-piece). A frozen classic has appeared in the background, a fixed text, a set of books no doubt, even if it was possible to memorize the whole. This is the making of Homer in the sixth century, possibly due to *Homeridai* of Chios.

This much is certain for simple practical reasons, though it is not always acknowledged: there never could be a question of reciting the complete text of the *Iliad* at a rhapsodic contest.[44] To recite the whole of the *Iliad* alone, not to mention the *Odyssey* and all the other works still attributed to Homer, would take thirty to forty hours,

[41] Acusilaus, 2 F 2 *FGrH*; A. Rzach, 'Homeridai', *RE* VIII. 2145–2182; D. Fehling, 'Zwei Lehrstücke über Pseudo-Nachrichten (Homeriden, Lelantinischer Krieg)', *RM* 122 (1979), 193–210, esp. 193–9.
[42] Cf. W. Burkert, 'Die Leistung eines Kreophylos', *MH* 29 (1972), 74–85.
[43] Esp. Rösler and Gentili (n. 1).
[44] This is still often assumed, e.g. *Der kleine Pauly* s.v. 'Rhapsoden': 'die ganze Il. und Od.' The attested length for the Panathenaia is four days; schol. Aristides 196 Dindorf; cf. J. D. Mikalson, *The Sacred and Civil Calendar of the Athenian Year* (Princeton, 1975), 34.

more than the time available for all the tragedies and comedies at the
Great Dionysia, which clearly was the more important literary event
in Athens. Homerids could only produce selections from the huge
thesaurus that remained in the background. It is here that the
well-known testimony of the Platonic *Hipparchus* comes in (228b):
Hipparchus, son of Pisistratus, 'was the first to bring the Homeric
epics into this country [i.e. to Athens] and forced the rhapsodes at the
Panathenaia to go through them in due order, one taking the cue
from the other, as they still do today'. The separation of production
and performance is expressly stated here: rhapsodes are 'going
through' a pre-existing text, which has been 'brought' and which is
used to control what they are doing. The author of the text of course,
is Homer. It is not implied in this 'Panathenaic law' that the whole of
Homer had to be gone through; the regulation evidently was just
meant to ensure that Hector's Death came after Hector and Andromache and not vice versa. The festal occasion for the *agōn* was the
Panathenaia—the Great Panathenaia which the Athenians strove to
bring to Panhellenic importance in the sixth century. A parallel text
in Diogenes Laertius gives the name of Solon instead of Hipparchus
as author of the 'law' about the due order of recitation. Probably, the
name of the lawgiver has ousted the name of the tyrant.[45] The name
of Hipparchus gives a date roughly between 530 and 514, the year
of his assassination. Friis Johansen thought the evidence from
Athenian vase-painting confirmed the Hipparchean date.

It may appear that with the name of Pisistratus and the Panathenaic recitation we are drawn back into the maelstrom of Homeric
controversies. It has been about a hundred years since Wilamowitz's
Homerische Untersuchungen appeared and 190 years since Wolf's
Prolegomena, and we cannot claim to have any new foundations for
decisive progress.[46] I shall not discuss these problems. What I shall
try to do—and what has not always been done—is to call attention
to the interplay of the different *genera* of early Greek literature,
especially of epic and choral lyric, keeping in mind that these were
competing forms of performance that should be seen in relation to
the intended public. It is in this context that we can hail a remarkable

[45] Diog. Laert. I. 57; Lycurg. *Leoc.* 102: the Athenians 'made it a law to rhapsodize
every five years at the Panathenaia the verses of Homer among all the other poets';
see Friis Johansen (n. 8), 223–41.
[46] For recent surveys, see n. 1 above; for the Pisistratean redaction, see n. 18
above.

discovery that is less than twenty years old: the reappearance of
Stesichorus. I vividly recall the surprise when this happened in 1967.
There was first the impact of the metrical reconstruction of the
Geryoneis by W. S. Barrett and D. L. Page; fragments from an *Iliupersis* and a Wooden Horse and from a *Thebais* have followed suit.[47]
Part of the surprise was the sheer size of the *Geryoneis* as it emerged
from a stichometric sign and Barrett's calculations: more than
thirteen hundred lines, i.e. about the length of an Attic tragedy.
Equally surprising was the amount of Homerizing style, particularly
in a poem dealing with a monster. Geryon the 'roarer', master of
animals, with three heads to be killed three times, turns out to be
a hero of human, nay Homeric, dimensions. As he takes the word to
speak to his divine mother or to his comrade, the dialogues can be
reconstructed from unpromising scraps because they transcribe
nearly verbatim well-known passages of the *Iliad*: 'If I ever presented
you my breast', Callirhoe says to Geryon, as Hecabe says to Hector.
The syllogism of practical heroism is also copied: 'If we could be
immortal, not even I would go to battle; but since we have to die
anyhow, well, let us see . . .'.[48] Another fragment that had become
known earlier, apparently from Stesichorus' *Nostoi* (209 *PMGF*),
reproduces almost word for word a crucial scene from the *Odyssey*:
Telemachus taking leave of Helen and Menelaus at Sparta.[49] In
this passage the Telemachy and the main narrative of the *Odyssey*
are woven together in such a way that the seams show, but Stesichorus evidently knew exactly the Homeric text that we read.
Stesichorus has thus become the clearest *terminus ante quem* for the
text of Homer as we know it.

There is not much evidence for securely dating Stesichorus. The
testimony of Simonides groups him with Homer as an authority for
the mythic-epic tradition; chronographers hence place his death in
556, when Simonides was born, and this cannot be too far off the
mark: after Alcman but before Ibycus and well before Simonides. The

---

[47] The new fragments from *Geryoneis, Iliupersis,* and the Wooden Horse are
available in D. L. Page, *Supplementum Lyricis Graecis* (Oxford, 1974), 1–147, and
in Davies, *PMGF*; cf. M. L. West, 'Stesichorus redivivus', *ZPE* 4 (1969), 135–49;
D. L. Page, 'Stesichorus: The *Geryoneis*', *JHS* 93 (1973), 138–54; id. 'Stesichorus:
The "Sack of Troy" and "The Wooden Horse"', *PCPS* 19 (1973), 47–65; the *Thebais*
in P. J. Parsons, 'The Lille Stesichoros', *ZPE* 26 (1977), 7–36.

[48] Stesich. S. 13. 5; cf. *Il.* 22. 83; Stesich. S 11. 8–24; cf. *Il.* 12. 322–8.

[49] Stesich. 209 *PMGF*; cf. *Od.* 15. 160–78, 68.

influence of Stesichorus on figurative art that has been assumed, in particular for the reliefs of Foce del Sele and for some Chalcidian amphorae, would agree well with this.[50]

But it is less the individuality of a poet that matters in our context than the rediscovery of a special *genos* of Archaic Greek poetry—the big mythic-epic narrative in lyrical form. According to what has been said, this means the development of a special form of performance in the first half of the sixth century BC. It is wrong to censure Stesichorus for lack of originality and slavish dependence on the Homeric epics if his real aim and achievement was to readapt these to new forms of production. Unfortunately, it is precisely the form of performance which has become controversial: Martin West and Bruno Gentili, not negligible experts, have voted for kitharodic performance, one singer accompanying his song on the lyre.[51] Yet the triadic structure routinely used in the Stesichorean poems—*strophē, antistrophos, epōdos*—is a strong argument for choral production: we are told, and it makes sense, that this triadic structure had its functional origin in the dance.[52] Kitharody, by contrast, could even do without strophic responsion. The argument to follow favours choral presentation but it is not wholly dependent upon this hypothesis.

There is one feature of Stesichorean poetry which contrasts with what we find in Alcman and Ibycus as in Pindar and Bacchylides: there is no overt reference to a specific place, person, or audience, no Hagesichora at Sparta, Polycrates at Samos, or Hieron at Syracuse.[53]

---

[50] Cf. M. Robertson, 'Geryoneis: Stesichorus and the Vase-Painters', CQ 19 (1969), 207–21; P. Brize, Die Geryoneis des Stesichoros und die frühgriechische Kunst (Würzburg, 1980); a new pre-Stesichorean representation of Geryon: P. Brize, 'Samos und Stesichoros: Zu einem früharchaischen Bronzeblech', MDAI(A) 100 (1985), 53–90.

[51] M. L. West, 'Stesichorus', CQ 21 (1971), 302–14, esp. 307–13; Gentili (n. 2), 122, following C. O. Pavese, Tradizioni e generi poetici della Grecia arcaica (Rome, 1972), 239–40.

[52] We only have late sources for this: Syrian., In Hermog. I, p. 62, 1–10 Rabe; schol. rec. Pind. p. 11 Boeckh, etc.; see W. Mullen, Choreia: Pindar and Dance (Princeton, 1982), 225–30, who tries to trace the effect of dance, esp. 'epodic arrest', in Pindar's texts. The triadic system was proverbially connected with Stesichorus; see Zenobius Athous I. 23, with M. E. Miller, Mélanges de littérature grecque (Paris, 1868), 351. (Doubts about the interpretation of the proverb have been raised, after O. Crusius, by M. Davies, JHS 102 (1982), 206–10, although he shows that the textual basis for Crusius' conclusions was wrong.) Cf. Suda s.v. 'Stesichorus'.

[53] M. L. West, 'Stesichorus in Sparta', ZPE 4 (1969), 142–9, deals with P. Oxy. 2735, which has references to place and persons; Page, however, in his Supplementum (n. 47), 166, ascribes the text to Ibycus.

This means that these compositions could be performed everywhere in the Greek world without change, and they obviously were designed for this purpose. It is a Panhellenic fantasy-world of heroic myth that forms the contents of these poems, mentioning certain landscapes or families—an artistic whole in itself and thus acceptable and interesting in all places. Its counterpart in society must have been travelling professionals who presented these songs in various places.

Stesichorus himself is said to have come from Sicily; his activities are connected with Southern Italy as well as with Sparta, which must have inspired the notorious Helen Palinody; but he did not hold a local appointment, as Alcman had at Sparta. If these were choral performances, we must imagine travelling groups of *technitai* appearing wherever a public festival presented the occasion for a production.[54] It was outdoor singing that fit a chorus, in contrast to the domestic scene for kitharodic *skolia* and other symposiac poetry, and for earlier epic. With the full development of *polis* communities, even music and art moved from the *oikos* of the nobles to the agora. *Mousikoi agōnes* were organized in the wake of the earlier athletic contests. The reorganization of the Pythian Games in 582 must have been an important event in this respect. This was the epoch of Stesichorus.

We have at least one piece of testimony that professional foreign musicians performed in Athens in the sixth century: the 'Old Oligarch'—i.e. Pseudo-Xenophon, *Athenaiōn Politeia*—states that 'the *dēmos* has abolished here [sc. at Athens] those who performed sports and music. They decreed this was not honourable, because (in reality) they knew (but too well) that they could not do this (themselves).' They established choregies and gymnasiarchies instead to make the rich pay for the mob, and thus 'the *dēmos* thinks it proper to get money for singing, running and dancing'.[55] Stripped of its polemical overtones, this remains an interesting account of musical events before the democratic revolutions. In fact we know that the

[54] There is no direct evidence for travelling groups in the 6th cent.; one might as well imagine a travelling *didaskalos* selecting his chorus for training on the spot, but we know chorus training was a long process. Paus. 5. 25. 2–4 describes a 5th-cent. monument of a boys' chorus with *didaskalos* who drowned on a journey from Messina to Rhegion.

[55] Ps.-Xen. *Ath. Pol.* 1. 13; I do not agree with M. Treu, 'Eine Art von Choregie in peisistratischer Zeit', *Historia* 7 (1958), 385–91, who, however, has a good discussion of earlier interpretations of this passage.

production of dithyrambs was reorganized in 508 to represent all the ten Cleisthenian *phylai* in the performance,[56] and we also know that only Athenian citizens formed the choruses of tragedy. The 'Old Oligarch' was looking back at an earlier period when alien professionals showed their expertise—choruses of professionals, I would suppose. This would seem to coincide with the period of Stesichorus' activities; it also raises interesting questions as to the chorus of Thespis.[57]

If this picture of Stesichorean choruses travelling through Greece to perform in their new style at *polis* festivals must remain hypothetical to some extent, this much is clear from the texts: the new *genos*, style, and performance were meant to replace the old epic song. There are the same narratives about Thebes and Troy, Odysseus and Agamemnon; epic style with all its antiquated words and formulae is freely adapted; and even the heroic timbre, the stance of facing death with dignity, is taken over. At the same time there is an effervescence of ornamental diction in more variable metrical forms, and a more emotional, even larmoyant appeal; music, and possibly dancing, must have made quite a contrast to the more austere epic singers. As to content, the restrictions of epic realism are discarded as well; there is room for monsters and for miracles, the cup of Helios and the Erinyes pursuing Orestes. All these effects would have combined to make the traditional singer of tales look rather jejune and antiquated. What was most precarious in face of the new rivals was the art of improvisation of the creative-traditional *aoidos*. In the Stesichorean enterprise, especially if these were choruses, premeditation and training were everything; the result was to sweep the lonely singer from the marketplace. Stesichorean production must have been a success, at least for a while. At Sikyon, Clisthenes abolished epic for the benefit of 'tragic choruses'.[58] The dependence of Aeschylus on Stesichorus is a telling fact, as is the verse of Simonides that puts Stesichorus side by side with Homer (564 *PMG*).

Yet Stesichorean style, or rather Stesichorean performance, was not to last. If it had tried to outdo the epic singers by pushing forth the

---

[56] *Marm. Par.* 239 A 46 FGrH; cf. A. W. Pickard-Cambridge, *Dithyramb, Tragedy, and Comedy* (2nd edn., Oxford, 1962), 15; G. A. Privitera, *Laso di Ermione* (Rome, 1965), 86–8.

[57] U. von Wilamowitz-Moellendorff takes 'einen attischen Bürgerchor' into his definition of tragedy, *Einleitung in die griechische Tragödie* (Berlin, 1889) = id. (ed.), *Euripides Herakles* I (repr. Darmstadt, 1959), 108.   [58] See n. 16 above.

elements of music, of emotion, of fantasy, and probably the multiple voices of a chorus, the answer of epic was reduction to the essentials of a narrative text: rhapsodic recitation. This meant abandoning the element of music and the element of improvisation in favour of a fixed text that would stand through the contests. In other words, it is the Stesichorean transposition of mythic-epic narrative to some form of oratorium that explains the gap between the old epic singers and the rhapsodes of the sixth century. It is as a reaction to Stesichorean production that the success of the rhapsodes should be seen. Ousted from the field of music by the new virtuosi at the same time that the setting was changing from the domestic to the public field, epic had to resort to the power of the spoken word to secure its place in the *agōnes*. This was an opportunity for the rhapsodes, and they made the best of it. They had texts good enough to stand the test: Homerids brought Homer to the foreground, and their success turned out to be more lasting than the Stesichorean fashion had been. We thus comfortably arrive at the epoch of Pisistratus and his sons who 'brought Homer' to Athens—that is, Homeric recitation as the reassertion of an older *genos* in new circumstances, in a new form of performance.

The same epoch saw the emergence of another *genos* in Athens which was to dominate the Greek world: the *tragōdoi* of Thespis, who first performed about 534 BC. No texts of Thespis survive, and we cannot be sure about details of his achievement,[59] but this much is clear: tragedy was a combination of choral lyrics and spoken verse, taking up both the tradition of Stesichorus—including the Doric style of the chorals—and of Ionic–Attic *iambos*. The latter, however, was stripped of its musical accompaniment—the flute that had belonged to it—just as the rhapsode had given up the *phorminx*. The actor, like the rhapsode, recited verse with his individual voice in front of a large public in such a way that the text was clearly understood in all its details. It could be that the special acoustics provided by the natural slope in the precinct of Dionysus south of the Acropolis was decisive for this new form of performance, but the place for the first productions of tragedy is hotly debated,[60] and we do not know anything about the place for rhapsodic contests. Acting and rhapsodic

[59] All the evidence is now collected in B. Snell (ed.), *Tragicorum Graecorum Fragmenta* I (2nd edn., Göttingen, 1986), no. I.
[60] See now F. Kolb, *Agora und Theater, Volks- und Festversammlung* (Berlin, 1981), 26–58, with the review by R. Seaford in *CR* 33 (1983), 288–9.

recitation may also be seen as opposites, as were assigned to the two
'great' festivals organized in sixth-century Athens, the Dionysia and
the Panathenaia. The actor, wearing a mask, identified with the
mythical character he was presenting; the rhapsode, quoting from
a text composed ages ago, brought the past to life while maintaining
his distance from it. What was still common was the separation of
author and performer. It had long been recognized by that time, due
to the self-consciousness of many remarkable poets, that every poetic
production had an individual author. Even if the success of a tragedy
depended very much upon the actors, the chorus, and the appurte-
nances, one did not forget to ask for the man who 'did it', the *poiētēs*.
Improvisations on well-trodden paths of traditional heroic scenery
no longer had a chance in an age of competitive professionals. But
the making of a classic had.

We probably have one direct document from this situation, a passage from the Homeric *Hymn to Apollo*. This composition consists of
a Delian and a Pythian part, separable in background and style but
analogous in structure and thus clearly belonging together. This
fact, which has given rise to much debate, is especially puzzling in
terms of performance: a situation requiring a composite hymn is
almost inconceivable, since no singer or rhapsode could ever be
present at Delos and Delphi at the same time. An explanation comes
from the fact that once, and only once, Polycrates, tyrant of Samos,
organized a festival, *Pythia kai Delia*, at Delos, probably in 522 BC: it
is here that the composite hymn uniquely fits, and this should
establish its date. This suggestion has been made independently by
Richard Janko and by myself.[61] Parts of the text may well be older,
but the arrangement belongs to the Polycrates festival, including the
description of the Delian festival itself contained in the text. At that
time, while Asia Minor had fallen to the Persians and Pisistratus had
died, Polycrates was claiming the leadership of the Ionians through

---

[61] See Burkert (n. 39); R. Janko, *Homer, Hesiod, and the Hymns: Diachronic Devel-
opment in Epic Diction* (Cambridge, 1982), 109–14; problematic elaborations by F. De
Martino, *Omero agonista in Delo* (Brescia, 1982); A. M. Miller, *From Delos to Delphi:
A Literary Study of the Homeric Hymn to Apollo* (Leiden, 1986), has nothing on the
historical setting. A. M. Bowie in his review of Janko, *CR* 35 (1985), 242, finds it a
problem that Rheneia (Thuc. 3. 104) is not prominent in the hymn. Ps.-Hes. fr. 357
M–W probably is dependent on the hymn, in combination with *Op.* 654–5.
Pisistratus, too, had installed a sanctuary of Pythian Apollo in Athens, in addition
to the old cult of Delian Apollo, *Suda* s.v. *Python*.

his patronage of the Delian sanctuary. The so-called hymn is a *prooimion*, as Thucydides calls it, the preface of a rhapsode with reference to the local deities, to be followed by recitation of Homer. In the crucial passage in which the composer turns to praise the *hic et nunc* of the Delian festivities and also to introduce himself, he goes to some length to pay tribute to a chorus performing at Delos, a chorus of girls (156–65). They begin, he says, with a hymn to Apollo, Leto, and Artemis, and then, to the delight of the audience, they sing a song about 'ancient men and women, recalling them from memory'. This is heroic myth in the form of choral lyrics, in other words, a Stesichorean production—taking 'Stesichorean' to refer to *genos* and style, not to authorship. In this production, the girls 'know to imitate the voices and chatter of all people: everybody would say he was speaking himself' (162–5). This is enigmatic. Contrary to what both others and I myself have written,[62] I am inclined now to take this as indicating mimetic elements in this very performance of choral lyrics. The Stesichorus texts we have are full of direct speech and dialogues, and we wonder how this came out in performance. It would be tempting to distinguish between voices, to make Geryon sound different from his doleful mother and from Heracles (remember that the *tragōdoi* of Thespis had made their appearance by this date). I would not suggest that the *Hymn to Apollo* gives a clue to the normal production of Stesichorean lyrics. Rather, it indicates a peculiar experiment made by this one Delian chorus to take up mimetic elements that had proved so successful in the other *genos*. Be that as it may, the composer of the hymn is full of admiration, and he promises to carry the fame of this singular production abroad. In return for this he asks for a similar favour: 'You must also remember me in the future', he says, demanding that every stranger arriving at Delos be told about his achievement. In other words, the rhapsode is suggesting to his rivals, the chorus, a joint enterprise of mutual advertisement.

There follows a notorious and enigmatic passage: if anybody asks you, the bard says, 'which man comes here as the sweetest of singers for you, and who gives you most pleasure' (169–70), your answer

---

[62] W. Burkert, *Greek Religion: Archaic and Classical* (Oxford, 1985), 110, following H. J. Tschiedel, 'Ein Pfingstwunder im Apollonhymnos', *Zeitschrift für Religions- und Geistesgeschichte* 27 (1975), 22–39. W. Rösler has drawn my attention to Alcm. 39 *PMGF* for mimetic elements in choral lyrics.

should be: 'a blind man, living in rocky Chios; all songs of this man are
the best among posterity' (172–3). For some readers of the text,
including Thucydides, the rhapsode was Homer in person, speaking
about himself; others have held the hymn to be a fake for the very
reason that it introduces legendary Homer. Wilamowitz-Moellendorff
pushed the realistic hypothesis that some anonymous rhapsode,
accidentally blind, was introducing himself, and even suspected that
his name had been secondarily ousted from the text.[63] Yet it is quite
an extraordinary claim that is made for the anonym: 'all the songs' of
this man of Chios 'are the best among posterity', *metopisthen*—the
same word is used in the no less notorious prophecy in the *Iliad*
about the offspring of Aeneas.[64] This is the clearest expression in epic
diction of the notion of a classic, an absolute classic, that I can
imagine. This is meant to be Homer.

Are we then dealing with mystification, or is it possible to understand the text without the hypothesis of imposture? It is a kind of
riddle; it need not be a fake. One observation is important in this
respect: the problem is totally different for readers of the text, such as
we are and Thucydides was, and for the actual audience at the performance, say at Delos in 522.[65] The bard performing there either
was or was not blind, and the public saw and knew which was the
case. If he was blind, he made absurd claims about posterity. But
suppose he was not—and nothing in the text speaks for a blind
composer—then it was clear that he was not referring to himself
when he introduced the 'blind man of Chios'. Since the additional
information contained in the situation of performance *hic et nunc* has
vanished and only the pure, written text has remained, the modern
reader is led astray, as was Thucydides. The text of the hymn is not
straightforward and simple, but the reason for this is the very phenomenon that has been in focus here—the separation of performer
and author. The joint-enterprise suggestion of the rhapsode would

---

[63] Wilamowitz, *Ilias und Homer* (n. 1), 453. The textual evidence for line 171 is
discussed by Burkert (n. 39), 61.

[64] I do not find much discussion of line 173. It is perhaps characteristic that
A. L. T. Bergren, without discussion, translates 'All of his songs will be supreme
hereafter' ('Sacred Apostrophe: Re-Presentation and Imitation in the Homeric
Hymns', *Arethusa* 15 (1982), 83–108, esp. 93). Aeneas: *Il.* 20. 308.

[65] For a similar argument, see W. Rösler, 'Persona reale o persona poetica?
L'interpretazione dell' "io" nella lirica greca arcaica', *QUCC* 19 (1985), 131–44,
esp. 140.

draw attention to his person: I am singing your praise, you sing mine, and if anyone asks which is the best singer, please name— 'me', one would expect, but instead there comes the strange word *aphēmōs* (171). I understand it to mean: 'anonymously', 'don't mention a name'.[66] It is indeed not the name of the performer which matters, but another, that of the 'blind man in Chios'. Metrically, *Homeros* would fit. One may still find difficulties with the present tense 'he lives', οἰκεῖ (172); it would indeed be no change to read imperfect, οἴκει,[67] but the present tense may rather be timeless; Cleobulus just remains Λίνδου ναιέτας (an inhabitant of Lindos) (Simonides 581 *PMG*). Homer's home is Chios; though he was active long ago, he is still present among posterity, he regularly 'comes' to the contests—from which he should be thrown out, according to Heraclitus—and he has 'come' to Delos as he had been brought to Athens. Earlier in the text, in a list of Aegean place-names, it is Chios alone that gets a line of praise (38): '... which as the most brilliant of islands is lying in the sea'. The composer is alluding to his own special relations to Chios and to the absolute classic of Chios represented in his performance. We are drawn to the conclusion that in this text, the *HymntoApollo*, we hear the voice of a representative of Chian Homerids performing at Delos in 522. He strives to establish the art of rhapsodic recitation of Homer by politely endorsing the rival form of choral, Stesichorean representation, and yet by also stressing the unique status of the classic of the past. The *Hymn to Apollo* is parallel and contemporary to Hipparchus introducing 'Homer' and rhapsodic contests at the Panathenaia. The two testimonies reinforce each other. The revival of epic in the form of rhapsodic recitation takes place in confrontation with choral lyrics of Stesichorean type, and it implies the proclamation of Homer as the absolute classic, τοῦ πᾶσαι μετόπισθεν ἀριστεύουσιν ἀοιδαί (all of whose songs are the best among posterity).

It is tempting to add some general reflections on the situation in which this first making of a classic occurred. This is a period when in other fields of Greek civilization we also find expansion and experiment coming to an end, to be followed by concentration on what has

---

[66] Burkert (n. 39), 61, following a suggestion of Wilamowitz, *Ilias und Homer* (n. 1), 454.

[67] οἴκει, not ὤκει, would be the correct form: P. Chantraine, *Grammaire Homérique* I (Paris, 1958), 483.

been achieved. This is true for Greek colonization and also for the canon of the Greek temple. At the same time there are thoroughgoing changes in the economy, with the rapidly spreading use of money; in politics, with the Persian onslaught; and in the realm of thought and literature, as we see emerging what was later to be called philosophy, which in fact marked the end of the monopoly that poetry had held on wisdom. I shall not pursue these associations and perspectives, but wish rather to point to the uncertainties still surrounding the Homeric texts we have. I frankly do not know why and under what conditions the *Iliad* was originally written down, nor who originally read and preserved the scrolls, nor when recitation of fixed texts first began to replace the improvising singers of tales. One is still free to imagine Homer himself sitting down to record his poem because it was so great, or his family and friends piously preserving the text and learning it by heart; what is missing in this picture are the complications and coincidences in which real history is so rich. I have tried to call attention to phases of the public's reception, to different forms of production coming to prominence in successive epochs.

Another unsolved problem is the reduction of Homer's oeuvre to the *Iliad* and the *Odyssey*—and, sometimes, the *Margites*[68]— instead of the larger group of epics still acknowledged by Pindar. At any rate, there is reason to insist on a second and no less momentous step in making Homer a classic, after the declaration of rhapsodizing Homerids: the establishment of Homer as a school text. This is another story, an important and a fascinating one, though the early evidence is little more than scanty. A place of pride is occupied by the Douris cup in Berlin, datable to about 490, with its school scene, in which a boy is reading a nonsense epic verse from a scroll.[69] An earlier picture by Phintias depicts a music lesson without scrolls. The establishment of elementary schools, notably in Athens, must have made significant progress with the advent of democracy. The introduction of the institution of *ostrakismos* in 508(?)[70] presupposes

---

[68] Purportedly attributed to Homer by Archilochus fr. dub. 303 West, but I share West's scepticism (ad loc.) as to this testimony.

[69] Cup, Berlin F2285, *ARV²* 431, 18. Phintias, hydria, Munich 2421, *ARV²* 23, 7. Cf. G. Nieddu, 'Alfabetismo e diffusione sociale della scritture nella Grecia arcaica e classica: pregiudizi recenti e realtà documentaria', *Scrittura e civiltà* 6 (1982), 233–61, esp. 255–6.

[70] For evidence and problems, see R. Thomsen, *The Origins of Ostracism* (Copenhagen, 1972).

that the skill of writing was common among citizens. Nonsense inscriptions disappeared from Attic vase-painting about the same time.

The choice of Homer as a schoolbook is strange: it can hardly be justified on pedagogical grounds. In fact Near Eastern civilizations had been using the traditional epics as schoolbooks, too.[71] Elementary school texts need to be moderately attractive, and narrative texts are preferable: songs are unsuitable, for the children will learn them by heart rapidly and thus never learn to read. It may Simply be that Homer was the most readily available set of books at that time. Tragedies were not yet available as books—hence the eclipse of Thespis—and prose treatises in a jejune or idiosyncratic style, such as Hecataeus or Heraclitus, were hardly a choice. It was the rhapsodes who could say: λαβέ τὸ βιβλίον (take the book). At any rate, it is a fact that the *Iliad* was chosen as a schoolbook at an early date,[72] and since nothing is more conservative than school tradition—up to the twentieth century, at least—it has remained a schoolbook. It is not without reason that more modern local tradition of Chios has Homer sitting on a rock teaching schoolboys at Daskalopetra, which in reality had been a Cybele sanctuary.[73] The use of Homer in school must also have been responsible for Ionian orthography finally replacing the old Attic orthography, which was practised in bureaucracy down to 403 BC.[74] The Xenophanean phrase ἐξ ἀρχῆς καθ' Ὅμηρον (B10 DK: 'Since from the beginning all have learnt from Homer . . .') came true. We may still credit the rhapsodes with protecting Homer from total absorption into school dust: live performances by specialists competing for the favour of the

[71] E. Reiner in W. Röllig (ed.), *Altorientalische Literaturen*, Neues Handbuch der Literaturwissenschaften 1 (Wiesbaden, 1978), 157.

[72] H. I. Marrou, *Histoire de l'éducation dans l'antiquité* (6th edn., 1964; repr. Paris, 1981) says very little on Homer as a school text; for one detail see vol. 1. 230. Cf. E. Pöhlmann, 'Die Schriftreform in Athen um 403 und ihre Implikationen', in L. Kriss-Rettenbeck and M. Liedtke (edd.), *Erziehungs- und Unterrichtsmoden im historischen Wandel* (Bad Heilbrunn, 1986), 51–60. It is interesting that *Od.* 9. 39 appears as a graffito in 5th-cent. Olbia, *SEG* 30, 933. A boy reading the beginning of the eighteenth Homeric hymn from a scroll: red-fig. lekythos, *ARV²* 452, 677, 7; J. Dörig (ed.), *Art antique: collections privées de Suisse romande* (Geneva, 1975), no. 214. Alcibiades reading Homer as a schoolboy: Plut. *Alc.* 7.1.

[73] See now F. Graf. *Nordionische Kulte* (Rome, 1985), 107–15.

[74] Cf. Pöhlmann (n. 72), and A. Heubeck, *Schrift*, Archaeologica Homerica III. x (Göttingen, 1979), 161–9.

public, with the books of the one great classic in the background, were to remain a factor in Greek intellectual life for many generations. It was only towards the end of the fifth century that wealthy and educated people began to acquire private books, and Homer began to reach the third and final stage of a classic: the classic on a shelf.

3

From the Iliad *to the* Odyssey

R. B. RUTHERFORD

Graecorum iste morbus fuit quaerere quem numerum Vlixes remigum habuisset, prior scripta esset Ilias an Odyssia, praeterea an eiusdem esset auctoris, alia deinceps huius notae, quae sive contineas, nihil tacitam conscientiam iuvant, sive proferas, non doctior videaris sed molestior.

(Seneca, *de brevitate vitae* 13. 2)

'[Homer] wrote a sequel of Songs and Rhapsodies, to be sung by himself for small earnings and good cheer, at Festivals and other days of Merriment; the Ilias he made for the men and the Odysseis for the other sex.'

(Richard Bentley, *Remarks on a Late Discourse of Free Thinking* (1713))

I

The relation of the *Odyssey* to the *Iliad* has always been problematical. In ancient times, although a minority school of separatists, the *chōrizontes*, did exist, the general consensus was that the two epics were composed by a single master poet, 'Homer'. The reverse is the case today: although there have been distinguished voices on the other side, most scholars favour separate authorship.

Versions of this chapter were read to friendly audiences in London and Manchester. I am grateful to all who commented on these occasions, to Christiane Sourvinou-Inwood for helping me improve a second draft, and also to Nicholas Richardson and Oliver Taplin for letting me read relevant parts of their own work on the *Iliad*. Some parts of my argument overlap with two sections in the introduction to my commentary on *Odyssey* 19 and 20 (Cambridge University Press, 1992), but I hope that there is enough new material, and sufficient difference of emphasis, to justify this separate essay. Some of the informality of the lecture format has been preserved, partly to make clear that this is not intended to be a definitive treatment of the subject.

One poet or two, however, the comparison of the two epics raises important questions concerning the character and special quality of each—so alike in many ways, yet so very different. The difference has been variously described:[1] for Aristotle, the *Iliad* was simple in construction whereas the *Odyssey* was complex; the former resembled tragedy, the latter, with its satisfying and successful resolution, was closer to comedy (*Poetics* 13, 1453^{a}30–39, 24, 1459^{b}13–16). For 'Longinus' the *Odyssey* was the sadly deficient product of Homer's old age: like the setting sun, it lacked force, intensity, passion: *pathos* (emotion) was supplanted by *ēthos* (character) (*On the sublime* 9. 13–15). To Samuel Butler, the *Odyssey* showed signs of a woman's interests and intellect; for T. E. Lawrence, the author was a 'bookish, house-bred man', a great lover of the *Iliad* but falling far short of that poem in conception and gifts of characterization. Comparison breeds evaluation: the *Odyssey* has often suffered by comparison with the *Iliad*, and it is only recently that a majority of interpreters have begun to recognize that this poet is attempting something on the same scale, but in a different mould, and to see the two great epics as complementary, each giving a rich but partial vision of human society and heroic ideals.[2]

Ancient and modern readers naturally tend to assume that the two poems are connected—either the work of one mind, or one poem

[1] I owe much to earlier treatments. See esp. F. Jacoby, 'Die geistige Physiognomie der Odyssee', *Kleine philologische Schriften* I (Berlin, 1961), 107–39 (originally publ. in *Antike* 9 (1933), 159–94); A. Heubeck, *Der Odyssee-Dichter und die Ilias* (Erlangen, 1954); K. Rüter, *Odysseeinterpretationen* (Hypomnemata 19, Göttingen, 1969), 24–34, 64 ff. etc.; W. Burkert, 'Das Lied von Ares und Aphrodite', *RM* 103 (1960), 130–44 [trans. in P. V. Jones and G. M. Wright (edd.), *Homer: German Scholarship in Translation* (Oxford, 1997), 249–62]; J. Griffin, *Homer. The Odyssey* (Cambridge, 1987), 63–70. J. M. Redfield, 'The Making of the *Odyssey*', in A. Yu (ed.), *Parnassus Revisited* (Chicago, 1973), is a stimulating general essay. Although there are interesting ideas in P. Pucci, *Odysseus Polytropos* (Ithaca, 1987), his approach differs so much from mine that I have found it difficult to follow him in many of his conclusions. Here I would only comment that I am resistant to the conception of the *Il.* and *Od.* as fluid entities influencing one another intertextually, as if historical context and chronology were irrelevant as well as unknowable. This paper was already submitted to *BICS* when I obtained a copy of Knut Usener's monograph, *Beobachtungen zum Verhältnis der Odyssee zur Ilias* (Script-Oralia Reihe A, Bd. 5, Tübingen, 1990), which will swiftly establish itself as a standard work. I am happy to find that we agree considerably in our general approach, although there is surprisingly small overlap in the specific correspondences which we discuss. Some parallel observations in his study are referred to below, in the appropriate places.

[2] Amongst the most eloquent of recent voices I should cite N. Austin, *Archery at the Dark of the Moon* (Berkeley and Los Angeles, 1975), a work of real insight and sophistication, despite its eccentricities. See also W. G. Thalmann, *Conventions*

composed with an eye on, or in competition with, the other. The advent of 'oral' studies, however, has altered the terms of this debate. Since the work of Milman Parry and his followers, it has become clear that the Homeric poems did not spring into being from the imagination of one bard or even one generation. They are the product of a long tradition of oral poetry treating comparable subject matter in a recognizable style—a tradition which employed a poetic language of formulae and repeated story-patterns, which utilized a whole repertory of material, now beyond quantification, and which produced many other epics now lost. If, then, the *Iliad* and the *Odyssey* are two among many poems narrating events of the heroic age, it is less easy to assume that one is composed in direct emulation of the other. More specifically, the concept of 'allusion', in such a tradition, may itself be called into question. A poet in a predominantly oral culture, composing for oral performance even if employing writing himself, cannot (it is argued) echo or adapt the words or motifs of a fellow-practitioner in the subtle manner of a Euripides or a Callimachus; nor, even if he did so, could he suppose that his audience would appreciate such allusions. In response to these doubts and uncertainties, some critics now prefer to speak of an Achillean tradition, or of Iliadic poetry, regarding the extant poems, for all their beauties, as representative of only one stage in a continuously fluid poetic tradition.

In this area as elsewhere, it seems likely that too much ground has been conceded to the oralists. While some arguments for imitation or deliberate echoes of one poem by another must now be abandoned, and others treated with greater caution, the question of the relation between the *Iliad* and the *Odyssey* remains open, and our knowledge of the conditions under which they were produced is not such as to permit us to rule out in principle the possibility (to put it no more strongly) that a poet might quote or allude to an earlier poem. The aim of this chapter is set out a number of arguments for the *Odyssey* being later than, and conceived as a sequel to, the *Iliad*, and to list a number of passages in the *Odyssey* which seem to involve significant allusion to the *Iliad*, in the sense that such a passage calls to mind some prominent episode or feature of the *Iliad*, and may be

of Form and Thought in Early Greek Epic Poetry (Baltimore, 1984), ch. 6; E. K. Borthwick, *Odyssean Elements in the Iliad* (inaug. lecture, n.d., Edinburgh 1985?); A. Heubeck, general introd. to the Oxford *Odyssey*, I (Oxford, 1988), 3–23.

thought likely to remind an audience with experience of epic performances of that aspect of the *Iliad*. The argument is cumulative and tentative: it makes no claim to be exhaustive, and is indeed intended to stimulate further discussion. My own preference is for separate authorship of the two epics, but I have tried to present my argument in such a way that it may have something to offer the committed advocate of single authorship. Two other preliminary assumptions should also be explicitly mentioned: (1) I take it for granted that, with the exception of certain limited sections of the text, each poem is essentially a unified creation by a single mind (which is not to deny that both poems make use of stories and episodes already familiar to their audiences). (2) I assume that, whether or not the poets made use of writing in the process of composition, they were not 'primitive' oral bards incapable of artistic shaping of their work—that is, they were premeditating and planning their works, not improvising them, and they made use of cross-reference, foreshadowing, careful plotting and sequences of scenes, and many other poetic devices which serve to integrate and ornament a long narrative poem.

II

More precise examination of the relation between the two epics can usefully start from the fact that the *Odyssey* never refers to the main narrative events of the *Iliad*, the wrath of Achilles over Briseis, the fresh anger against Hector, the death of Troy's noblest defender.[3] This silence has been interpreted in different ways. The late Sir Denys Page held that the *Odyssey* was a wholly independent poem, composed by a poet working in a different place and in a different tradition from the poet of the *Iliad*, one who did not even know the story recounted in the *Iliad*.[4] This was a challenging proposition, but eccentric and perhaps wilfully provocative; it has itself been challenged on a number of levels and can by now be considered refuted.[5]

---

[3] This is sometimes called 'Monro's Law': see D. B. Monro, in one of the Appendices to his commentary on *Od.* 13–20 (Oxford, 1901), 325.

[4] *The Homeric Odyssey* (Oxford, 1955), ch. 6, esp. 149–59.

[5] See T. B. L. Webster, *From Mycenae to Homer* (London, 1958), 275–83; D. Young, 'Miltonic Light on Page's Homeric Theory', *G & R* 6 (1959), 96–108 (cf. A. Morpurgo, 'Omero, Milton e la filologia', *Riv. cult. class. med.* 2 (1960), 204–8); J. B. Hainsworth,

A more plausible position would be that the *Odyssey* deliberately neglects the central story of the *Iliad* because it could not be surpassed, could not be challenged direct. The *Odyssey* does, however, perform some of the functions of a sequel or epilogue (as Longinus and other ancient critics already noted).[6] That is, it does do a most efficient job of filling in the story since *Iliad* 24. The death of Achilles, the dispute over the armour, the Wooden Horse, the sack of Troy, the recovery of Helen, the murder of Agamemnon, the misfortunes of the other Greeks on the homeward voyage, all find a place somewhere. Few characters are left unaccounted-for, few questions unanswered. This would be a remarkable coincidence if the *Odyssey*-poet had never heard or encountered the *Iliad*.

Some of the more detailed arguments for the *Odyssey* being conceived as a sequel can be conveniently presented in terms of comparison between the poems. First, the *Iliad* and the *Odyssey* are more like one another in length than they are like any of the other early epics known to us as the Epic Cycle.[7] These Cyclic poems were, it appears, considerably shorter. The *Oedipodeia* had only 6,600 lines, as opposed to the *Iliad*'s 15,689 and the *Odyssey*'s 12,110. The *Thebais* was a little longer, with 7,000. Sometimes the summaries tell us the number of books rather than the number of lines: the *Aethiopis* had only five books, the *Iliupersis* a mere two. Only the *Cypria*, which had eleven books, would have any real chance of rivalling the Homeric epics in scale, and that only if each of its books were as long as the longest of Homer's, about a thousand lines.

More important is the resemblance between the poems in terms of structure and design. Both poems deal only with a part of their nominal subject. The *Iliad* is not the tale of the whole war of Troy but of a central episode, a matter of days, which is treated with exceptional fullness and made to include or imply an account of the Trojan

'No Flames in the *Odyssey*', *JHS* 78 (1958), 49–56; H. Erbse, *Beiträge zum Verstandnis der Odyssee* (Berlin, 1972), 177–229 ([trans. in Jones and Wright (n. 1), 263–320] on the 'Continuation', but valuable in showing some of the general weaknesses of Page's observations on vocabulary). Cf. also R. Janko, *Homer, Hesiod and the Hymns* (Cambridge, 1982), 83–4 and 191, whose detailed studies of diction lead him to the conclusion that the *Odyssey* is later than the *Iliad*, but need not be far from it in date and may even be by the same author.

[6] See 'Longinus', *On the Sublime* 9.12, with W. Bühler, *Beiträge zur Erklärung der Schrift vom Erhabenen* (Göttingen, 1964), 46–7.

[7] On the Cycle generally J. Griffin, 'The Epic Cycle and the Uniqueness of Homer', *JHS* 97 (1977), 39–53 [= this vol., Ch. 12]; M. Davies, *The Epic Cycle* (Bristol, 1987).

war as a whole. The *Odyssey* extends this technique: it does not narrate Odysseus' adventures sequentially, bringing him from Troy to Ithaca, but concentrates on the final stages, again treating a few crucial days in detail, but embracing retrospective accounts of the earlier episodes. Both poems, then, begin *in mediis rebus*; both end with the hero's future known but awaiting fulfilment. The resolution of the themes of the poem does not coincide with the end of the tale. This structural principle permits both expansive narration and a broader perspective. The mode of narration adopted by the cyclic epics seems to have been markedly different: in poems such as the *Cypria* and the *Iliupersis*, it appears that events followed one another sequentially, without a clear central figure or primary focus to the action. There is no single hero of the *Cypria*: in the summary of Proclus, the action moves from Paris to Menelaus, from Telephus to Agamemnon and Iphigenia to the marooning of Philoctetes, with Achilles only entering the limelight towards the end of the poem, when the war at last begins. Our direct quotations from and summaries of these early epics are late and of doubtful value, but the verdict of Aristotle and Horace confirms that they lacked the coherence and structural unity of the *Iliad* and the *Odyssey*.

   Other common features of the *Iliad* and the *Odyssey* will strike any reader; I offer only a partial list, many items of which again bring out the difference between the extant epics and what we know of the Epic Cycle. They both include extensive speeches of great rhetorical and emotional quality: the personalities of the heroes are revealed far more through their own words than by any comments or descriptions by the poet.[8] Both poems are rich in extended similes, often employed for thematic purposes as well as ornamentation. In both, scenes of anguish and grief are presented in language that is vivid without being extravagant; nor do the many scenes of violent death lapse into sadistic self-indulgence. The poems repeatedly dramatize moral dilemmas and issues of moment, but the poet himself declines the role of a moralist: although the blindness and folly of humanity are often portrayed in the *Iliad* and the *Odyssey*, there is little overt comment and less explicit moral judgement.[9] The complexity

---

[8] See further J. Latacz, 'Zur Forschungsarbeit an den direkten Reden bei Homer', *Grazer Beiträge* 2 (1974), 395–422, and my commentary on *Od.* 19–20, introd. 4(c).

[9] Cf. J. Griffin, 'Words and Speakers in Homer', *JHS* 106 (1986), 36–57; I. J. F. de Jong, *Narrators and Focalizers* (Amsterdam, 1987), a landmark study.

of human conflicts and personal relationships is not crudely over-simplified. What simplification there is arises from the selection and stylization necessary for the poet to enhance our sense of the dignity and nobility of his characters when confronted with the prospect of death, dishonour, or bereavement. Finally, the action of both epics is conducted under the observant eyes of the Olympian gods, who in both intervene to aid their favourites, and who also, to a degree which is not fully defined, concern themselves with the fulfilment of fate's decrees and the upholding of the moral order. For all the differences in their presentation, the gods in both epics serve to define more clearly the achievements and the limitations of mortal men.[10]

A further reason for the supposition that the *Odyssey* is a sequel or follow-up to the *Iliad* lies in the nature of the story it tells: the contrast of the heroes in each epic, and the contrasting outcome of each tale. The *Iliad* is a poem of war, the *Odyssey* one of peace. The former has as its hero a man of violent and passionate action, doomed to an early death, while the hero of the latter is an older and cannier figure, a master strategist and gifted orator, who despite a life of wandering and endurance will eventually meet a peaceful death, surrounded by his people and family. The *Iliad* is intense and sublime, the *Odyssey* more diffuse and diverse; the geographical range of the poems reflects these qualities, with the human action of the *Iliad* concentrated, with increasingly unbearable intensity, on the Greek camp, the plain of battle and the city of Troy, whereas the first half of the *Odyssey* offers constant changes of scene and characters, human and supernatural. The *Iliad* ends on a deeply tragic note, with both Achilles and Troy doomed by the will of the gods, though there is a saving magnanimity in Achilles' surrender of Hector for burial; the *Odyssey*, by contrast, has a happy ending, though not untinged with sadness at the years Odysseus and Penelope have lost from their life together, and at the prospect of future parting when the great traveller must renew his journeying, undertaking a voyage to placate Poseidon. As the ancient critics saw, the *Iliad*, with its stress on the plan of Zeus, the malignant will of the gods, and the consequent suffering of men, points the way to the greatest achievements of

---

[10] On the gods see W. Kullmann, 'Gods and Men in the *Iliad* and *Odyssey*', *HSCP* 89 (1985), 1–23; H. Erbse, *Untersuchungen zur Funktion der Götter im Homerischen Epos* (Berlin, 1986).

fifth-century tragedy,[11] while the *Odyssey*'s happy resolution, like its attention to personal relationships, recognition between *philoi*, and loyal or treacherous retainers, bring that poem, especially in its second half, closer to the gentler melodrama of Euripides, and to comedy, especially the New Comedy of Menander. Thus on the level of plot the tale the *Odyssey* tells is radically different from and opposed to that of the *Iliad*. There seems to be a deliberate contrast and indeed opposition between Odysseus and Achilles, the planner and the warrior, the pragmatist and the romantic—already hinted at in *Iliad* 9 and 19, it is developed further in the *Odyssey*, especially in Books 11 and 24.

Turning to matters of detail, we can, in my view, discern parallels and significant resemblances between the *Iliad* and the *Odyssey* in structure, specific episodes, and sometimes specific passages even on a close verbal level. The rest of this chapter will be an attempt to defend this proposition, which naturally confronts serious objections in view of the oral-formulaic style. In written literature, if a passage of any length occurs in identical or similar form in two different works, then there is an overwhelming likelihood that one of these is imitating or alluding to the other. But of course Homeric repetitions cannot be straightforwardly treated as evidence of imitation in this way.[12] It is always possible to claim that a phrase, or a series of lines, or a motif, used in both poems is simply part of the traditional language of poetry, the stock-in-trade of any average bard-in-the-street. In particular, we should exclude from consideration the so-called 'typical scenes', stock lines used or slightly modified when certain standard narrative events occur: when a feast is held, a ship

---

[11] Cf. Rutherford, 'Tragic Form and Feeling in the *Iliad*', *JHS* 102 (1982), 145–60 [= this vol., Ch. 8]; J. Gould, 'Homeric Epic and the Tragic Moment', in T. Winnifrith, P. Murray, and K. W. Gransden (edd.), *Aspects of the Epic* (London, 1983), 32–45; P. E. Easterling, 'The Tragic Homer', *BICS* 31 (1984), 1–8. R. Garner, *From Homer to Tragedy* (London, 1990), has considered this inexhaustible subject at a more detailed level of verbal reminiscence.

[12] That repetition of this kind *must* indicate a direct relationship between the passages involved is the basic premiss of K. Sittl, *Die Wiederholungen in der Odyssee* (Munich, 1882); cf. W. Diehl, *Die wörtlichen Beziehungen zwischen Ilias und Odyssee* (Diss. Greifswald, 1938), which I have not seen. More recent approaches are illustrated by G. M. Calhoun, 'Homeric Repetitions', *UCPCP* 12 (1933), 1–26; M. van der Valk, 'The Formulaic Character of Homeric Poetry and the Relation between the *Iliad* and the *Odyssey*', *AC* 33 (1966), 5–70; H. Bannert, *Formen des Wiederholens bei Homer* (WS Beiheft 13, Vienna, 1988). For an interesting study of Virgil's repetitions, which pays some attention to general issues, see W. Moskalew, *Formulaic Language and Poetic Design in the Aeneid* (*Mnemos.* Suppl. 73, Leiden, 1982).

launched, a sacrifice performed, an assembly summoned. Such
scenes occur several times in our two epics; they might recur in any
poem of this kind. We need therefore to consider how close, and how
prominent, a resemblance needs to be in order to prove, or at least
make it plausible, that an audience might detect significant allusion
from one poem to the other.

Some modern scholars deny the very possibility of 'allusion' in a
supposedly oral tradition: thus Anthony Edwards in a recent
monograph insists that 'Mere repetition of a phrase is inadequate
evidence from which to infer that there is allusion in one context to
another',[13] while Gregory Nagy is even more emphatic: 'when we
are dealing with the traditional poetry of the Homeric (and Hesiodic)
compositions, it is not justifiable to claim that a passage in *any* text
can refer to another passage in another text'[14] (my italics). The
caution is important, but the absolute ruling out of the very possibility of such reference seems excessively dogmatic. First, we do not
actually know that the *Iliad* and the *Odyssey* are themselves oral as
opposed to drawing on a previous oral tradition.[15] I myself find it
hard to believe in such lengthy works being composed in a wholly
oral culture: how could they ever be performed as the wholes that
they are?[16] I would prefer to see the *Iliad* as committed to writing at
the start, or intended for that; the *Odyssey* follows its lead, whether
or not it is by the same poet (I accept that downdating—increasingly
attractive on other grounds—may be the necessary corollary).
Second, even if this is not right, the denial of the very *possibility* of
allusion to another oral poem, however important, well-known, and

---

[13] Edwards, *Achilles in the Odyssey* (Beitr. zur klass. Philol. Bd. 171, 1985), 7.

[14] *The Best of the Achaeans* (Baltimore, 1979), 42. Cf. his n. 3 on that page. See
further J. A. Davison, 'Quotations and Allusions in Early Greek Literature', *Eranos* 53
(1955), 125–40 [=Davison, *From Archilochus to Pindar* (London, 1968), 70–85];
J. B. Hainsworth, *Homer* (*G&R* New Surveys 3, 1969), 2 and 30. M. M. Willcock, *CR*
38 (1988), 4 and *CR* 40 (1990), 207–8, takes a much more moderate view. For Hesiod
see P. Walcot, 'Allusion in Hesiod', *REG* 73 (1960), 36–9.

[15] Cf. Adam Parry in Milman Parry, *The Making of Homeric Verse* (Oxford, 1971),
lxi n. 1; A. Parry, 'Have we Homer's *Iliad?*', in *YCS* 20 (1966), 175–216, now repr. in
The Language of Achilles and Other Papers (Oxford, 1989), 104–40. A similar position is
taken e.g. by Heubeck (n. 2), 11–12.

[16] Oliver Taplin, in the first chapter of a forthcoming book pointedly entitled
Homeric Soundings, of which he has kindly let me read the typescript, restates the
case for an oral 'artistic' Homer, assuming either transmission through the guild of
Homeridai or early dictation to scribes [*Homeric Soundings* (Oxford, 1992), 31–44]. I
am not convinced, but see the former suggestion as the most promising alternative to
a literate *Iliad*-poet.

influential, goes much too far, particularly in view of our total ignorance of the context and conditions of performance, the expectations and enthusiasms of the audience, the frequency with which they demanded repetition of a favourite tale, and so on. Third, recent study of Homeric motifs and of the poet's adaptation of 'stock' themes, or his capacity to give 'typical' material in a new form and a sharper point, suggests that the epic poets' audience was alive to such innovation and variation *within* a work,[17] and it is not a very long step to the presumption that they could draw comparisons of this kind between works, particularly if prominent similarities of character, theme, language, and situation encouraged them to do so. The enthusiasm and interest of an unknown audience should not be curtailed by the *a priori* assumptions of modern theory.

If guesses about audiences are highly speculative, conjectures about the motivations and thought-processes of poets are both unfashionable and methodologically suspect. It may nevertheless be useful to advance a possible scenario which may render more credible the creation of the *Odyssey* as a work conceived as a sequel to the *Iliad* even within an oral tradition. Needless to say, this is not advanced as any more than an unverifiable hypothesis. Suppose the *Iliad*-poet had created a version of his great poem not too different from the poem we read today; suppose he had sung it again and again throughout a great part of his career, to popular acclaim; suppose this was the song he was chiefly associated with, the one everybody thought of as the best song of the best local bard. Hesiod speaks of 'competition' (*eris*) between bards (*Works and Days* 26); the poet of the *Homeric Hymn to Apollo* (or part 1 of it) wants his listeners to tell others that 'his songs are best' (line 173). Is it implausible that another bard, perhaps younger, perhaps even a disciple or companion, both admiring and jealous of the great singer's achievement, could conceive the idea of a poem on the same scale, dealing with some of the same characters, ten years on—how the heroes ended up; a poem which would be in competition with the *Iliad*, and so would naturally deal with many of the same themes from a different standpoint? This is of course pure speculation, but perhaps provides a working hypothesis. For those who would prefer to think of the *Iliad* and the *Odyssey* as being the creation of the

---

[17] See e.g. M. W. Edwards, 'Topos and Transformation in Homer', in J. M. Bremer, I. J. F. de Jong, and J. Kalff (edd.), *Homer: Beyond Oral Poetry* (Amsterdam, 1987), 47–60.

same poet, I offer a slightly different scenario: a poet who has grown impatient with his reputation as the *Iliad*-poet, who is weary of being asked for it, or parts of it, again and again, and who begins to weave a new poem, one which will replace the stark simplicity of the heroic world, the world of open combat and tragic death, with a subtler and more complex world of deception and guile. Whichever version you choose, my main point is that if there is a relationship of any kind between the *Iliad* and the *Odyssey*, if they are not just random survivals from a morass of epic song, then allusion cannot be ruled out and may be of the essence. The problem of identifying an allusion remains: as a general principle I would suggest that simple verbal repetition is not enough of itself: there should also be some similarity in context, in situation, or in the thematic aspects of a given episode; perhaps also (as in some of my examples), a similarity of placing within the overall form of the epic.

III

I begin from some obvious general resemblances, before turning to some possibly significant links, parallels or echoes. I do not, of course, place any weight on the fact that both epics are divided into 24 books, as that is a later editorial arrangement.[18]

Both poems, as already mentioned, plunge *in medias res*, into a situation which is very well advanced; in both, the first few hundred lines set the scene and commence the action with a sure and lively narrative, effortlessly introducing a wide range of characters and changes of scene; the role of the gods as observers who can intervene for good or ill is quickly established (thus Athene intervenes to calm Achilles in *Iliad* 1 and to stimulate Telemachus to action in *Odyssey* 1). After these swift and intriguing openings, both poems employ retardation and introduce sub-plots, delaying the anticipated climaxes: in the *Iliad*, the fulfilment of Zeus' promise to Thetis; in the *Odyssey*, the release and indeed the first appearance of Odysseus. Instead lesser figures fill the stage, and the scope of the poem is broadened.

---

[18] That the existing book-divisions are not only later than the classical period but also seriously misleading even to the modern reader who is aware of this fact is an important part of Taplin's argument in the work cited in n. 16 above [pp.13, 285–93].

Both poems also begin with an invocation of the Muse, leading into a brief statement of theme which emphasizes suffering (*Iliad* 1. 2 μυρί᾽ . . . ἄλγε᾽ ἔθηκε, 'it brought countless sorrows'; *Odyssey* 1. 4 πολλὰ . . . πάθεν ἄλγεα, 'many sorrows he suffered') and the destructive influence of the gods (*Iliad* 1. 5, *Odyssey* 1. 8–9). The most striking thing here, however, is that in both the *Iliad* and the *Odyssey* that statement embraces only part of the poem's full scope: in the *Iliad*, the poet announces that his subject will be the wrath of Achilles against Agamemnon, but does not give any hint of the later wrath against Hector, and its cause and consequences; indeed, the proem gives no hint of the prominence of the Trojans in the *Iliad*. In the *Odyssey*, the proem refers to the journeyings and homecomings of the hero without his companions, but in such a way as to suggest that his arrival home is the poet's main goal; there is as yet no mention of the fresh sufferings which await him in his own country.[19]

In Book 2 of the *Iliad*, Agamemnon summons an assembly of the whole Greek army, hoping to test their morale and to find it high; in fact his test is a disaster and he himself is almost humiliated. It is in this episode that we learn for the first time that the Greek army has been at Troy for almost ten years, and Odysseus reminds them of the optimistic omen which they saw at Aulis when they set out, an omen which the prophet Calchas had interpreted as foretelling the sack of Troy in the tenth year. In Book 2 of the *Odyssey*, the analogies are close. Encouraged by Athene's visit, Telemachus calls an assembly on Ithaca in the hope of shaming, or forcing, the suitors out of his home. In fact the assembly is passive, the suitors have things their own way, and Telemachus is humiliated. It is in this episode that we learn how long it is since the war of Troy ended, how long Odysseus has been lost—once again, ten years. Of course this could be a coincidence, for ten is always a convenient round number; but it is interesting that here too we have an auspicious omen—this time foreshadowing Odysseus' homecoming and revenge; and the prophet Halitherses, who interprets the sign, also refers to an earlier prophecy he made, at the beginning of the war, that Odysseus would return in the twentieth year.

---

[19] M. L. West, *Hesiod: Works and Days* (Oxford, 1978), 44, supposes this to be the consequence of the gradual evolution of the poems ('we can often see them having new ideas as they go . . . '), but this in my view grossly underestimates the control that the poets have over their material.

In both the *Iliad* and the *Odyssey* the narrative reaches its long-awaited climax in what is for us Book 22: *Iliad* 22, the killing of Hector by Achilles; *Odyssey* 22, the killing of the suitors by Odysseus, with 'Iliadic' warfare transferred to the domestic setting. The denial of mercy to the suppliant Leodes seems to recall the scene between Achilles and Lycaon in Book 21 of the *Iliad*.[20] But in both epics, the hero's triumph is followed by gentler scenes of reconciliation and reintegration: in the *Iliad*, the funeral games for Patroclus and the scene of pity and companionship between Achilles and Priam; in the *Odyssey*, the reunion of husband and wife, and (if we look to Book 24) the aversion of conflict in Ithaca.

A comparison of three key passages takes us further: two of these come in the *Iliad* (9. 385 ff., 22. 349 ff.), one in the *Odyssey* (22. 61 ff.). In Book 9 of the *Iliad*, the Greeks offered Achilles vast wealth and lands if he would only return and aid them in battle: but he defied them with unforgettable eloquence in the central speech of that book, esp. 378 ff.:

I hate Agamemnon's gifts, I value him at a straw's worth. Not if he were to give me ten or twenty times as much as he now possesses, and more thereafter, whatever he could get, not if he gave me all the wealth of Orchomenos or Egyptian Thebes . . . not if he were to give me gifts as numerous as the sand or the dust, not even so would Agamemnon persuade my heart, not before he pays back to me all the injuries that bring pain to my heart.

This speech is echoed in *Iliad* 22, where Hector begs for burial. If Achilles must kill him, so be it, but at least let him accept ransom from Priam, and surrender his body to receive due honour. But now Achilles' new wrath against Hector and Troy is as great as his old, and his words follow the same syntactical pattern as in the earlier speech in Book 9:[21]

Not if they were to bring here ransom tenfold or twentyfold, and promised more hereafter, not even if Dardanian Priam were to order your body to be weighed against gold for your ransom, not even so would your lady mother mourn over you as she sets you on a bier, you whom she bore—but the dogs and the birds shall divide your body among them. (22. 349–54)

So too in the *Odyssey*, when the suitors recognize who Odysseus is, they beg his forgiveness and promise him compensation, but their

[20] There are more detailed comparisons in B. Fenik, *Studies in the Odyssey* (Wiesbaden, 1974), 196–7; Pucci (n. 1), 128–9; Usener (n. 1), 131–40.

[21] Cf. C. W. Macleod (ed.), *Homer: Iliad XXIV* (Cambridge, 1982), 20–1.

pleas are dismissed with angry contempt:

Eurymachus, not even if you gave me all that you inherited from your father, all that is yours now and anything you might add from any source, not even so would I hold back my hands from slaughter, not before you suitors have paid to the full for your wrongdoings. (22. 61–4)

Thus we see that, however different and less glamorous, less of a conventional hero Odysseus may be, he can rise to the same heights of eloquence and heroic wrath as Achilles, greatest of the heroes. Here again, the parallelism could be coincidental, simply the traditional formulae for an angry speech in epic, but here again I doubt if that is a sufficient explanation; indeed, here above all I am convinced that the *Odyssey* imitates the *Iliad*.

If Book 24 of the *Odyssey* is substantially genuine, the conclusions of the two poems also invite a comparison, in two respects. First, both epics give prominence at the end to burial and funeral rites[22]—the funeral games of Patroclus and finally the burial of Hector in the *Iliad*, and the reminiscences of Achilles' funeral and the underworld scene of *Odyssey* 24 (where it is made clear that Achilles' and Patroclus' wish to be buried together was fulfilled: compare *Iliad* 23. 91–2 and 243–4 with *Odyssey* 24. 75 ff.). Second, the last episodes of the poem give special emphasis to the relationship between father and son. In *Iliad* 24 this is achieved only imperfectly and by analogy: Priam recovers Hector, but only his corpse, and Priam's age and misery reminds Achilles of his own father Peleus, with the consequence that, although they must remain enemies, they eat together, sharing their grief. By contrast in *Odyssey* 24, Odysseus and Laertes really are reunited and a meal follows, but this one is a celebration. But in view of the questionable status of *Odyssey* 24[23] these points should perhaps not be pressed. It may still be said, however, that the composer of the concluding scenes of the *Odyssey*, whether or not he was also the composer of the earlier part of the poem, had the *Iliad* in his mind.[24]

---

[22] Cf. D. Wender, *The Last Scenes of the Odyssey* (*Mnemos*. Suppl. 52, Leiden, 1978), 38–40; O. Whitehead, 'The Funeral of Achilles', *G & R* 31 (1984), 119–25.

[23] See now S. West, 'Laertes Revisited', *PCPS* NS 35 (1989), 114–43, and for a general account of the problems, with bibliography, Heubeck's commentary on 23. 297 ff. (pp. 317–20 of the Italian edition [= *Od. Comm.* 342–5]).

[24] See further Heubeck's commentary on 24. 472–88, for references and bibliography on possible echoes of *Il.* 4. 1–74 in the closing scenes of the *Od.*

Naturally, not all the resemblances fall so precisely into place at equivalent points in the poems. In a different category come a number of features at the opening of the *Odyssey* which bear similarity to aspects of the *end* of the *Iliad*.[25] These too are of a kind which seem appropriate to a 'sequel'. First, both Book 24 of the *Iliad* and Book 1 of the *Odyssey* begin with a contrast between the rest of the Greek host, reconciled or back home, and the hero, whose special status and isolation are emphasized: Achilles has not purged his grief and anger; Odysseus has not completed his journey home. Second, in both works a divine council follows, in which a majority of gods pity a human's situation (*Iliad* 24. 23, *Odyssey* 1. 19). One deity protests at the present situation, and Zeus takes steps to bring about a resolution of the problem. In both, the justice of the gods is called into question, and the piety of the victim (Hector in the *Iliad*, Odysseus in the *Odyssey*) is stressed: this virtuous behaviour imposes an obligation on the gods to set matters to rights. In both *Iliad* 24 and the *Odyssey*, Hermes is an important intermediary who takes steps to advance the decision of the gods: in the *Odyssey*, however, Hermes' role is postponed until Book 5, and the activities of Athene with Telemachus displace the anticipated encounter with the poem's hero. Athene, however, plays a part at first reminiscent of Hermes': in particular, she dons winged sandals normally worn by the latter (*Odyssey* 1. 96–8, cf. *Iliad* 24. 340–2, *Odyssey* 5. 44–6).[26] More loosely, the object achieved by the divine conference in each poem may be seen as comparable: in the *Iliad* they will command Achilles to release Hector's body, so that it may be brought home for burial; in the *Odyssey*, they will force Calypso to release Odysseus and enable him to return home. Both actions demonstrate the belated but real generosity and justice of the gods; in neither case is there divine unanimity, nor is partisan feeling absent.

[25] I am indebted here to Nicholas Richardson, who allowed me to read his discussion in volume 6 of the Cambridge *Iliad* commentary ahead of publication [published 1993: see pp. 21–4]. The similarities discussed here have of course sometimes been invoked as evidence that the last book or books of the *Il.* are of a later date than the rest, and even that the *Odyssey*-poet played a part in patching them in to an earlier version of the *Il.*; see e.g. Leaf's commentary (London, 1888), II. 536. I take it that it is by now unnecessary to argue for the view that Book 24 is the fitting and essential conclusion of the *Il.*: see G. Beck, *Die Stellung des 24. Buches der Ilias in der alten Epentradition* (Diss. Tübingen, 1964), Macleod, *Iliad* xxiv (n. 21), 16–35, and Richardson's commentary.

[26] On the parallels concerning Hermes see now Usener (n. 1), 165–82.

In the opening scene of the *Odyssey*, Zeus' reflections on human beliefs about the gods have often been interpreted as some kind of 'reaction' to the *Iliad*, and in particular to Achilles' disillusioned statements in Book 24.[27] In that book, Achilles offered Priam the bitter comfort that their unhappy destinies were not unique, but part of the human condition: Zeus (he says) brings misfortune to all men, sometimes mixed with good fortune, sometimes undiluted. In the allegory of the jars, no human receives unmixed blessings from the jar of good things (24. 525–33).[28] In Book 1 of the *Odyssey* Zeus complains that humans 'say that their misfortunes come from us. But they themselves also have sorrow beyond their portion through their own rash folly—as Aegisthus has just recently . . .' (1. 33–5). Clearly, this is a more straightforward, less tragic vision of the gods, which suitably introduces a number of important themes of the *Odyssey*. The theology here is different from that which dominates the *Iliad* as a whole, though it would be excessive to argue that the passage introduces ideas wholly alien to the *Iliad* or ethically more advanced. It is not clear to me, however, that this is a specific allusion to the *Iliad*. The allusion, if there is one, is insufficiently signalled, the polemic too generalized. What the passage clearly does do is establish the ethical tone of the *Odyssey*, with its emphasis on righteous dealing rewarded and rash or wicked behaviour as self-destructive; in other words, it sets out principles which will be normative, though not universal, in the narrative that follows. But this seems to me to be a case of the poet selecting from the traditional options one which suits the type of story he has to tell: Zeus' speech sets the *Odyssey* in contrast with more negative presentations of the gods (and more tragic presentations of mankind) in general, rather than in opposition to the *Iliad* in particular.

IV

I turn now to passages which shed more light on the nature of the imitation: the differing character of the *Iliad* and the *Odyssey* as poems, and the attitude of the poet of the *Odyssey* to the *Iliad*

---

[27] See S. West, *Od. Comm.* 1 on 1. 32 ff., and add Kullmann (n. 10); Erbse (n. 10), 237–41.

[28] E. R. Dodds, *The Greeks and the Irrational* (Berkeley and Los Angeles, 1951), 29, goes so far as to say that in these lines 'Achilles . . . pronounces the tragic moral of the whole poem'.

(whether or not they share the same author). Fundamental to the contrast between *Iliad* and *Odyssey* is the fact that in the *Iliad* the hero is going to die young, while in the *Odyssey*, although much is made of the grief and pain felt by his wife, son, and friends at the apparent death of Odysseus, we know that in the end he will indeed return beyond all hope, in the hour of greatest need. The grief and foreboding felt by Thetis on Achilles' behalf are fully justified; her prediction to Hephaestus is unambiguous and accurate (*Iliad* 18. 440–1):

$$\tau \grave{o} \nu \ \delta' \ o \grave{v} \chi \ \grave{v} \pi o \delta \acute{\epsilon} \xi o \mu a \iota \ a \grave{v} \tau \iota s$$
$$o \check{\iota} \kappa a \delta \epsilon \ \nu o \sigma \tau \acute{\eta} \sigma a \nu \tau a \ \delta \acute{o} \mu o \nu \ \Pi \eta \lambda \acute{\eta} \ddot{\iota} o \nu \ \epsilon \check{\iota} \sigma \omega.$$

I shall not welcome him back again on his return to his home, back into the house of Peleus.

But when Penelope uses similar language at *Odyssey* 19. 257–8, addressing her disguised husband who is already home and in her presence, the situation is paradoxical and the effect ironic: although her mood is one of despair, the movement of the plot is optimistic. The shared phraseology here is probably, however, too simple and inconspicuous to constitute an allusion. It is more rewarding to consider the actual portrayal of the heroes of the two poems, Achilles and Odysseus, within the *Odyssey*.

Both Achilles and Odysseus make a crucial choice of lives. As we learn in *Iliad* 9, his divine mother has told Achilles that 'twin destinies carry me to the end of death. If I remain here, and fight around the city of the Trojans, then my homecoming is gone, but my glory will live forever. But if I go home to my own native land, then my noble glory is lost for me, but my life will be long, and the doom of death will be slow to come to me' (9. 411–16). Of course, he remains and dies. Odysseus' choice, presented in *Odyssey* 5, is quite different: he can live forever with Calypso, and become an immortal consort, and be forgotten—concealed by her, forever, as her name implies. Or he can take to the sea once more, suffer further hardships and misfortunes, in the hope of coming home at last and living a mortal life with Penelope, who (as he tactfully admits) is inferior to Calypso in beauty and stature. Lost homecoming *versus* the choice to return home: the choices are different, and yet not perhaps totally opposed, for both Achilles and Odysseus fulfil their best nature rather than sinking into inglorious—and anonymous—ease.

By Book 24 of the *Iliad* Achilles knows that he will not live to see the taking of Troy, that he will never return to Greece or see once more his aged father Peleus, whom he imagines as alone and persecuted by his neighbours, without the protection that he, Achilles, should be providing (*Iliad* 16. 15–16, 18. 330–2, 19. 321–5, and esp. 24. 534–42). In Book 11 of the *Odyssey*, where Odysseus in the underworld encounters his former comrades-in-arms, Achilles is among them—very clearly, I feel, the Achilles of the *Iliad*, accompanied by Patroclus and Antilochus (11. 468).[29] Odysseus responds to his greeting with a speech of self-pity, complaining that he has still not come near to Greece (in fact an exaggeration: 10. 29), and his words also include flattery and admiration of Achilles; how fortunate he is, honoured like a god in life and like a great lord among the dead. Achilles' bitter response is one of the most famous passages in Homer (11. 488–91):

Odysseus, do not gloss over death to me. I would rather be alive as a worker on the land, slaving as a poor serf for another, a man with no property and livelihood, than be king over all the lifeless dead.

But equally notable is the way the speech continues, with Achilles harking back to his father and his inability to help him—again, perhaps a standard motif, but one which surely here recalls the Iliadic passages on this theme, and in particular *Iliad* 24—in a sense, Achilles' last appearance before the 'sequel' (11. 494–503):

And tell me also what news you have of noble Peleus. Is he still honoured among the thronging Myrmidons, or do they despise him in Hellas and Phthia, because old age fetters his limbs? If only I might return to help him, return to the sunlight as once I was, when in the wide land of Troy I fought for the Argives and slew the bravest of the enemy host. If in that manner I could return, even for a brief moment, to my father's house, then I would make my strength and my unapproachable hands hateful to any man who does him violence or thrusts him from his proper place of honour.

This is what Achilles *wishes* he could do, but it is also what Odysseus can and will do for his own father Laertes, and for his whole family. The men of violence, whom Achilles imagines dishonouring his father, correspond to the suitors, who ravage Odysseus' lands and seek to steal his wife and throne. Achilles also

---

[29] In later books of the *Il.* Antilochus is in many ways taking over the role of Patroclus as Achilles' closest comrade: see further M. M. Willcock, 'Antilochus in the *Iliad*', in *Mélanges É. Delebecque* (Aix-en-Provence, 1983), 479–85.

feels sorrow at his separation from his son Neoptolemus; again, this recalls the *Iliad*, in which he thought of him as well as Peleus when he knew that he must die (19. 326–37), and again there is a contrast with Odysseus, who will be reunited with his son as well as his father.

V

The *Odyssey* is a much more self-conscious poem than the *Iliad*, in the sense that it includes more overt reference to the powers and practitioners of poetry, and specifically heroic epic. Poets appear in the cast of characters, other songs are alluded to. The hero himself is compared to a bard and takes up his own tale where the Phaeacian minstrel Demodocus had left off; similarly, the 'poetic' qualities of his lying narratives are remarked upon by his Ithacan hearers (14. 361–2, 17. 518–20, cf. 19. 589–90). The borderline area between poetry and lies, of which the Muses told Hesiod, is familiar terrain to the poet of the *Odyssey*. Although the heroes of the *Iliad* hope for glory and remembrance after death, poetic self-reference does not figure so prominently, and takes less ingenious form, in the martial world of action. A memorable exception is the bitter comment of Helen in *Iliad* 6. 355–8, where she remarks to Hector that she and Paris will be remembered not gloriously, but with ignominy: 'hardship has come upon you most of all because of me, bitch that I am, and because of the folly of Alexandros: Zeus put an evil doom on us, so that we might be a subject for song even for men who come after us.' This line is echoed, it seems, in a less tragic and less personal context in the *Odyssey*, when Alcinous sympathetically encourages the weeping Odysseus to explain his distress and recount his experiences. The king's long speech includes the fatalistic comment that 'the gods made that misfortune for them [the Argives and Trojans], and wove destruction for men, so that there might be a song for those who come after' (*Odyssey* 8. 579–80). The essential difference is that Alcinous is an outsider, detached from the sufferings which he enjoys in poetry. The Phaeacians, a society remote from the rest of mankind and unheroic in life-style,[30] serve as an idealized audience for heroic

---

[30] On the life-style of the Phaeacians and on ancient evaluations of them see M. Dickie, 'Phaeacian Athletes', *PLLS* 4 (1983), 237–76. I am unconvinced by the defence offered by Hainsworth, *Od. Comm.* 1. 341–6.

song. What is agonizing memory for Odysseus (and present cause of guilt and regret for Helen) is delightful entertainment for them. This is another way in which the poet shows us the different perspectives from which the Trojan war, once over, can be viewed. It also, perhaps, hints at his perspective on the *Iliad*: a monumental achievement, but distant and unrepeatable, part of the great past.[31]

However that may be, it is widely accepted that the Phaeacian episode also includes more direct allusion to the *Iliad*, through the distorting mirror of the bard Demodocus.[32] Each of his three songs (8. 72–82, 266–366, 499–520) recalls aspects of the story of the *Iliad* without narrating any episode in its precise Iliadic form. The first and most allusive refers to a quarrel between two Greek heroes, misunderstood by Agamemnon as the fulfilment of a prophecy which in fact predicted his own far deadlier conflict with Achilles, still in the future. The motifs of Agamemnon's error, delusive prophecy, and the will of Zeus, all recall important themes of the *Iliad*.[33] The second song describes the love-affair of Ares and Aphrodite and Hephaestus' trapping of the adulterous pair: the whimsical and immoral behaviour of the gods, and their sensuality, remind us of the love-scene between Zeus and Hera on Ida (*Iliad* 14. 292–351). Moreover, looking beyond the song itself, we can observe analogies between the plotting Hephaestus, his apparent absence and his unexpected return, and the role of Odysseus later in the *Odyssey*. The way in which the divine action reflects more serious events on the human plane is typically Iliadic.[34] The third song describes the sack of Troy, so often foreshadowed in the later parts of the *Iliad*: as in the *aristeia*

---

[31] J. Griffin, 'Homer and Excess', in Bremer, de Jong, and Kalff (n. 17), 102, even suggests that the horrific martial scenes on Heracles' swordbelt in *Od.* 11. 609–14, and the hero's awed comment in his narration 'may he who designed it never design such a work again!', is an ingenious allusion to the author of the *Il.* itself!

[32] See esp. W. Marg, 'Das erste Lied des Demodokos', in *Navicula Chilonensis* (FS F. Jacoby, Leiden, 1956), 16–29; C. W. Macleod, 'Homer on Poetry and the Poetry of Homer', *Collected Essays* (Oxford, 1983), ch. 1 [= this vol., Ch. 9], and *Iliad XXIV* (n. 21), 1–8; O. Taplin, 'The Earliest Quotation of the *Iliad*?', in *Owls to Athens* (FS Sir Kenneth Dover, Oxford, 1990), 109–12. [See now A. F. Garvie (ed.), *Homer: Odyssey* VI–VIII (Cambridge, 1994), 248–55.]

[33] Nagy (n. 14), 42–58, interprets this passage along different lines, but less convincingly, to my mind. See also Usener (n. 1), 183, who sees the reference to the Διὸς βουλή (plan of Zeus) as a very fragile connection, but does not consider the wider context.

[34] See further Burkert (n. 1) [and Garvie (n. 32), 293–5, along with the detailed notes which follow].

of Hector, Trojan overconfidence leads to final defeat. The simile illustrating Odysseus' reaction to this song also reminds us of the bereaved women of Troy, especially Andromache, and of the cruelty that accompanies the sack of a city (cf. *Iliad* 9. 590–4, 24. 728–38). The inclusion of all three songs here, as already indicated, suits the hedonistic world of the Phaeacians. The songs also form a fitting backdrop to the events of the eighth book in which Odysseus is gradually restored to his heroic statue, and regains the energy and confidence he needs to recount his past and to confront the further trials that lie ahead of him.[35]

VI

If the *Iliad* is the poem of Ilium, the poem of the Trojan war, then the *Odyssey* is in part the poem of the aftermath of that war (particularly, though not exclusively, from the Greek side). The war is the most important thing in everybody's past. It is already the subject of poetry: Phemius sings in Book 1 of the sorrowful homecoming of the Greeks from Troy, and Demodocus, as we have just seen, recounts in Book 8 'the lay whose fame was at that time reaching the heavens', an episode from the early part of the war. Still more striking is the way the participants recall the conflict—not as their greatest triumph or as a victory over insuperable odds, but as a time of hardship and great suffering, culminating in terrible losses. Listen to Nestor, now at home in Pylos in his prosperous old age, in peacetime, surrounded by his wealth and his loyal sons (3. 103–19, largely Shewring's trans.):

My friend, your words have brought back to me what wretchedness we endured at Troy, indomitable though we were in spirit—what we endured on shipboard too, roving to plunder over the misty sea, wherever Achilles led the way, and then all our fighting round the great city of King Priam. There it was that the bravest of us fell. There lies the warrior Ajax, there lies Achilles, there Patroclus, equal to the gods as a counsellor, and there also lies my own dear son, Antilochus, so strong and so noble, so swift a runner, so bold a fighter. And beyond their loss we suffered many calamities: what mortal man could recount them all? No; if you stayed here five years, or six, searching out the tale of all the troubles the noble Achaeans bore—no, your patience would fail you first, and you would make for home. Nine long years, with every kind of

---

[35] Cf. W. Mattes, *Odysseus bei den Phäaken* (Würzburg, 1958), esp. 129 ff.

deceitful trick, we schemed for the downfall of the Trojans, and only after
much toil and pain did the son of Cronos bring fulfilment.

To hear Nestor talk, one would hardly think the Greeks had *won* the
war! And there is the same melancholy note in Menelaus' reminiscences in Book 4. Many of the Greek leaders died at Troy; others
perished on the journey home (the lesser Ajax), or on their return
(Agamemnon); but even those who have come home safely live on
with memories of what they have lost. Nestor and Menelaus, for all
their security, still have sorrows: Nestor grieves for his dear son
Antilochus, killed defending him at Troy, while Menelaus has no
legitimate heir (4. 10–14), and still feels the loss of his friends, who
endured so much for his sake in order to recover Helen. There is an
undertone of guilt in this scene as he glumly tells Telemachus that
money does not bring happiness (4. 90–112, 169–82).[36] Similarly
with Odysseus, there is perhaps a symbolic side to the fact that he has
lost on his voyages all the loot and treasure he brought from Troy.
More significant still is the wonderful scene in Phaeacia, where the
bard Demodocus sings of the Trojan horse and the sack of Troy—
Odysseus' greatest triumph, but according to Demodocus, his 'most
dreadful fight' (8. 519). In that scene Odysseus weeps for the past,
and the simile describing his grief, which compares him with a
bereaved wife in the midst of the brutal sacking of a city, surely
suggests that he grieves not only for his own sufferings, but also
for those he has inflicted (8. 521 ff.). In describing his encounter with
the intractable Ajax in the underworld, he again regrets his past
triumphs, in this case his having defeated Ajax in the contest for the
armour of Achilles: 'Would that I had never been victorious in such
a contest! Because of it, the earth closed over heroic Ajax . . .'
(11. 548–9).

The *way* in which the events of the war itself are remembered is
also interestingly different from the *Iliad*'s presentation of the war in
progress. Nestor speaks of the Greeks weaving (ῥάπτομεν) the
downfall of Troy by all kinds of trickery (παντοίοισι δόλοισι, 3.
118–19)—hardly the picture we get from the *Iliad*. Similarly,
Demodocus and others refer to the part played by the Wooden Horse,
a *dolos* (deceptive trick), Odysseus' and Athene's own conception—a
device to which the *Iliad*, with its more direct and heroic picture of
combat, never alluded. It is perhaps inevitable that the stories which

[36] Cf. also 24.95 (Agamemnon): was it all worth it?

Menelaus and Helen recount to Telemachus, to bring home to him
his father's great virtues, illustrate his powers of deception, disguise,
and self-discipline, rather than more martial qualities; more suggestive is the yarn that the beggar Odysseus spins to Eumaeus the
swine-herd, in a scene where he has not been identified as Odysseus
(14. 457 ff.), a yarn which describes a night-time ambush in which
the beggar was allegedly involved, and which lays much emphasis
on the wind and the cold and the ice and the hail, and what a pity he
hadn't brought his trusty sou'wester—the *discomforts* of the war, a
very different thing from the heroic suffering central to the *Iliad*. This
more down-to-earth, almost plebeian image of the Trojan war, suits
the lower-class social setting in which the beggar finds himself:[37]
but that is not the whole explanation. It is not, I think, too much to
say that the *Odyssey*-poet has a different attitude to war and heroic
prowess from the *Iliad*-poet. Indeed, there are even some scenes in
which heroic—Iliadic?—material or attitudes are reworked and
treated more lightheartedly: heroism with a smile. Here discussion of
allusion comes close to questions of possible parody.[38] Parody is
another concept which oralist criticism has barred from Homeric
scholarship, and it is certainly true that it is hard to identify with
certainty in so formal and regular a style. But when viewed alongside
other indicators of allusion it may perhaps reveal itself more clearly.

One fairly clear example of an allusion which is also in effect a
parody is *Odyssey* 6. 130 ff.[39] This is a lion simile, which is verbally
close to *Iliad* 12. 299 ff., but does not parody any specific lion simile
in the *Iliad*; rather, it pokes a little fun at that whole genre of comparisons. Odysseus is shipwrecked naked in Phaeacia; he hears the
sound of Nausicaa and her maids at play; diffidently, he tries to hide
his nakedness with a branch. 'Then he advanced like a mountain
lion, sure of his strength, who goes his way with blazing eyes

[37] Cf. the 'economic' account of war in general as a result of the demands of the
stomach (17. 285–9). For complaints about life under canvas cf. esp. the herald of
Agamemnon in Aesch. *Ag.* 555 ff.
[38] Cf. Monro (n. 3), 328 ff.; for criticism and scepticism see A. Shewan, 'Does the
Odyssey Imitate the *Iliad?*', *CQ* 7 (1913), 234 ff., W. B. Stanford (ed.), *The Odyssey of
Homer* (2nd edn., London, 1965) on *Od.* 14. 22, etc., Hoekstra, *Od. Comm.* II on 14. 3,
10 (but in his n. on 14. 192 he is more receptive); Hainsworth (n. 14), 2, asking 'Can
the grim meal of the Cyclops parody the formal dinners of heroic chiefs if there is only
one form in which such banquets can be conceived or expressed?'
[39] Cf. Pucci (n. 1), 158. Usener (n. 1), 195–7, groups this among his 'non-significant
parallels'.

through wind and through rain, hunting the wild deer or ranging among sheep or cattle. If flocks are penned in a strong-built fold, his hungry belly makes him go after them even there.' Here the phrase κέλεται δέ ἑ γαστήρ (his hungry belly urges him on) replaces the Iliadic κέλεται δέ ἑ θυμὸς ἀγήνωρ ('his proud heart urges him on', 12. 300), and this is wittily apt, as Odysseus has not eaten for twenty days and will shortly be guzzling from Nausicaa's picnic basket, 'avidly', says the poet (ἁρπαλέως) (249–50, where his long starvation is emphasized). The appetite of Odysseus is a recurrent motif in the *Odyssey*, one which ancient commentators found shocking but which we may enjoy as humorously realistic.[40] Moreover, the lion simile is wittily handled in itself: instead of the Iliadic pattern, where a warrior attacking his foes is compared with a wild lion attacking flocks, while a warrior reluctantly retreating is compared with a lion driven from the fold by dogs and shepherds, we have here an incongruity in the comparison of the humble suppliant Odysseus to a lion: this is only how he *appears* to the terrified girls.[41]

Another probable example of Iliadic reference also verges on parody, though in this case the allusion is repeated and perhaps more significant. In *Iliad* 6. 485–93, at the end of the moving scene between Hector and Andromache, Hector sends his wife home to her work at the loom and the distaff, kindly but firmly dismissing her from the sphere of war. His speech ends with the lines (6. 492–3):

$$\text{πόλεμος δ' ἄνδρεσσι μελήσει}$$
$$\text{πᾶσι, μάλιστα δ' ἐμοί, τοὶ Ἰλίῳ ἐγγεγάασιν.}$$

War will be the concern of the men, of all of those who dwell in Ilium, but chiefly myself.

These lines became proverbial, even notorious.[42] Similar language is used in the *Odyssey* in two passages in which Telemachus seeks to

---

[40] Cf. W. B. Stanford, *The Ulysses Theme* (2nd edn., Oxford, 1963), 67–71.

[41] See further R. Lattimore, introd. to his translation of the *Od.* (New York, 1965), 22.

[42] See esp. Ar. *Lys.* 520, 538. Cf. Kirk, *Il. Comm.* ii on 6. 490–3: '[The four lines] seem to have been so well known in this Iliadic context that their Odyssean recurrences were quotations, almost: in this case a single lost archetype, or typical use, is improbable.' Alternatively, we might suppose that the Iliadic phrase was already a commonplace (it is clearly the most 'natural' of the three), but that the *Od.* is still quoting its occurrence in the *Il.* S. West (*Od. Comm.* i) in her note on the passage in Book 1 is less happy with the idea of allusion here, but her doubts partly arise from a more favourable evaluation of Telemachus' actions and words in these earlier books (cf. pp. 55 and 67 of her commentary). See now Usener (n. 1), 47–66.

assert his authority over his mother: in Book 1, when he rebukes her for silencing Phemius' song about the return of the Achaeans from Troy, and in Book 21, when he takes steps to remove her from the scene of the contest with the bow, so that the episode may reach its bloody conclusion without endangering her. In both cases his speech of dismissal ends with the same phrases about loom and distaff (1. 356–8a, 21. 350–2a), then the lines continue with the Iliadic *polemos* replaced by *muthos* (word/story-telling) in Book 1, *toxon* (bow) in Book 21:

τόξον

μῦθος δ' ἄνδρεσσι μελήσει

πᾶσι, μάλιστα δ' ἐμοί· τοῦ γὰρ κράτος ἔστ' ἐνὶ οἴκῳ.

The bow/the tale will be the concern of the men, of all of them, but chiefly myself, for mine is the power in the house.

The likelihood that this is a reminiscence of the *Iliad* is increased by the inappropriateness of the phrase in 1. 356 = 21. 350, ἀλλ' εἰς οἶκον ἰοῦσα ('but proceeding to your home', cf. οἶκονδε, 'homeward', in the line which follows the speech); for Penelope, unlike Andromache, is already in her own home.[43]

If this allusion is accepted, we must still consider the effect of the adaptation. The poet himself gives us some guidance, in that in both cases Telemachus' speech is described as πεπνυμένον, 'wise'. So indeed the speeches are: in Book 1 he defends the validity of poetry on tragic themes, in Book 21 he openly declares himself both host and heir, and for the audience his prudence in protecting his mother is self-evident. Nevertheless, to Penelope his words bring amazement and distress: her reaction is not unambiguous admiration, and her silent obedience does not simply represent proper womanly behaviour; rather, her submission forms a part of the subtle presentation of tension and unease between mother and son which is sustained throughout the Ithacan books.[44] If it is accepted that this repetition of the 'man's concern' motif would probably be taken as an allusion to the *Iliad*, it seems that it must be read as an indication of the

---

[43] The other passage which needs consideration in this context is *Od.* 11. 352–3, where the repeated portion is, however, less extensive. It looks as though the *Odyssey*-poet associates this motif with scenes in which women are 'put in their place'; that does not, of course, exclude other reasons for using it.

[44] Cf. Rutherford, 'At Home and Abroad: Aspects of the Structure of the *Odyssey*', *PCPS* NS 31 (1985), 147 n. 20.

difference between Andromache and Penelope, between wartime
and peacetime conditions, and between the authority of a husband
and that of a son: in short, it illustrates the different and more
positive role of women in the *Odyssey*, which Telemachus in his
brash assertiveness underrates.[45] Book 23, in which Telemachus
again upbraids his mother (esp. 97 μῆτερ ἐμή, δύσμητερ, 'mother
mine, no true mother'), and is quietly reprimanded by both his
parents, provides the culminating scene in which Penelope is vin-
dicated, proving herself a worthy wife to Odysseus, as a paragon of
wifely fidelity and also of matching intelligence. The contrast with
Andromache's passive role as obedient sufferer shows us why peace
and homecoming are preferable to war and heroic death, for the
women of the *Odyssey* as well as for the men.

There are other passages in the *Odyssey* in which Iliadic vocabulary or motifs are employed in contexts which may seem amusing
or incongruous to ancient audiences and to ourselves. Humour is
surely undeniable in *Odyssey* 8, where Odysseus absurdly over-
reacts to the challenge to his athletic abilities from the tactless
Euryalus, hurls the discus much further than any of those present
could have managed, and makes a long, boastful speech asserting his
superiority at any sport they care to name; an embarrassed throat-
clearing silence follows. The drubbing which the disguised Odysseus
gives to the real beggar Iros similarly plays with the situation which
so fascinates the poet of the *Odyssey*: not warriors facing one another
openly as near-equals, but a true hero disguised and unsuspected
among lesser men.[46] In this case the resulting combat is not a duel
but a walkover, in which Odysseus has to force himself to hold back
for fear that his real strength might pulverize the inept opponent and
lead the suitors to suspect his real identity (18. 90–4; cf. 17. 235–8). It
is important not to overdraw the contrast between the two epics:
certainly there is humour in the *Iliad* too, not least in the funeral
games for Patroclus, where the extrovert, competitive impulses of the
Greeks are given full rein in a more controlled and ritualized environment than the battlefield; but it is still, I feel, a more affectionate
and enthusiastic humour than the ironic smile of the *Odyssey*-poet.
More objectively, it is fair to say that Achilles, his demands and his
emotions, are never treated with humour in the *Iliad*, whereas the

---

[45] Cf. esp. J. Winkler, *The Constraints of Desire* (London and New York, 1990),
129–61.   [46] Cf. Fenik (n. 20), 1–60.

hero of the *Odyssey* can be and often is the object of the poet's amused play—an ironic play which often embraces the efforts of Odysseus to play an old heroic role. What the poet of the *Odyssey* presents with greater sympathy is not the Iliadic outspokenness and braggadocio—the claim to be conqueror of Troy cuts little ice, we recall, with the Cyclops—but Odysseus' powers of endurance and self-restraint. Heroic self-assertion is kept in check even in the moment of triumph (22. 411 ff.): Odysseus himself rebukes his nurse for her exultation over the dead. Only during the actual slaughter does something of the old heroic love of battle for its own sake and for the glory it brings well up in the hero, and even there, it has been suggested, the Iliadic battle-motifs are exaggerated close to the point of parody.[47] Heroic combat in the *Odyssey*, I should argue, is seen as tragic in the past, but often grotesque in the present: in both lights its value is questioned. At the very least, we may say that in the *Odyssey* the hero's eyes are much less firmly fixed on glory.

It may be worth adding that the notion that men of the epic world, the world of heroes, were greater than we are now, that they could lift rocks (etc.) 'such as two men on the earth today could not lift', occurs in formulaic terms seven times in the *Iliad*, never in the *Odyssey*. We are dealing with a changed world.

Before summing up, I offer a final contrast which seems also to be an allusion. At *Iliad* 18. 239 ff., after the seemingly endless day of fighting by the ships has ended with the recovery of Patroclus' body, 'then Hera the ox-eyed queen sent down the unwearying sun to the streams of Ocean, against its will. So the sun set, and the noble Achaeans had respite from the cruel battle and the warfare common to all.' With this we may compare *Odyssey* 23. 243 ff., where we find Odysseus and Penelope, newly reunited, in one another's arms: 'rosy-fingered dawn when she appeared might have found them still weeping happily, if grey-eyed Athene had not thought of another plan. She held back the night to linger long at the horizon, checking Dawn of the golden throne at the edge of Ocean, and not allowing her as yet to yoke the rapid horses that bring men light, Lampus and Phaethon, the young steeds of Dawn.' The two passages have clear similarities: a patron goddess befriends the heroes at a moment of crisis, in the one case by accelerating sunset, in the other by delaying

---

[47] Cf. D. J. Stewart, *The Disguised Guest* (Lewisburg, 1976), 101 n.—a questionable position, however.

sunrise.[48] But what a difference in mood and elaboration. In the Iliadic passage this is a brief respite from further slaughter, and the night will be given up to mourning and anger; in the *Odyssey*, the night is extended for the pleasure of Odysseus and Penelope in lovemaking and conversation, as the hero recounts his adventures to his admiring wife, not without a touch of conceited self-praise. In the *Iliad* Hera shows her sympathy for the whole Greek army, exhausted and hard pressed; in the *Odyssey*, Athene's favour, though generous and affectionate, is for her special protégé, and just as the occasion is amusingly light-hearted, so the mythological detail is more baroque, with the added details of the horses of Dawn and the near-dramatic picture of Athene holding the impatient goddess back: all this presumably a development of the one word 'unwilling' ($\mathring{\alpha}\acute{\epsilon}\kappa o\nu\tau\alpha$) to describe the sun—the sole touch of personification in the starker Iliadic passage. Some have considered the *Odyssey's* use of the motif an ignoble absurdity: 'as if [the cartoon character] Li'l Abner were clad in Goliath's armour'.[49] It is better to acknowledge the different character and ethos of the later poem, which by such daring imitation and transformation presents its admiring riposte to the *Iliad*. As George Steiner wrote in a memorable essay, describing the contrast between the *Iliad* and the *Odyssey*: 'The old fires of the heroic are banked, and the muscular simplicity of life around Troy has yielded to all manner of irony and complication.'[50]

The ideals of peace, home, domestic and political harmony, which run through the *Odyssey*, make it not only a different, but almost an opposite kind of epic compared with the *Iliad*. Achilles' great choice was a glorious death, Odysseus' is a mortal life. Achilles' story is that of a man increasingly isolated from his own society, for even at the end of the wrath he still sits and dines apart from the rest of the host. The *Odyssey* tells of a man and wife reunited, a family and kingdom restored to peace and order. The heroic yields place to the domestic and civic, the warrior to the bringer of peace and prosperity.

---

[48] The compassion and sympathy of the goddesses in both the Homeric passages may be contrasted with the grim episode in the biblical book of Joshua, which employs the same motif: 10. 12–14, esp. 13, 'and the sun stood still, and the moon stayed, until the people had avenged themselves upon their enemies'.

[49] Van der Valk (n. 12), 22: it should be noted that he does not himself endorse this description.

[50] 'Homer and the Scholars', in *Language and Silence* (London, 1967), 207.

From that perspective the awesome intensity of the *Iliad* begins to look a little single-tracked: the youthful passion of Achilles impressive, yet self-destructive. The glory and grandeur of the Trojan war have now become a subject for song, but the memory of those days brings sorrow and a sense certainly of loss, possibly of waste. The homecoming of Odysseus is set in sharper relief—is shown to be the triumph which it is—by the contrast with those who have lost their homecoming or whose return is tinged with unhappiness.

ADDITIONAL NOTE (2000)

Another paper which discusses the matter of Odyssean imitation of the *Iliad* is by D. N. Maronitis, 'Références latentes de l'Odyssée à l'Iliade', in *Mélanges É. Delebecque* (Aix-en-Provence, 1983), 277–91.

G. Nagy has continued to publish on the development of the Homeric poems: see recently *Homeric Questions* (Austin, 1996), building on an article of the same title in *TAPA* 122 (1992), 17–60. In general he sees the poems as much more fluid in form, much less text-based, than my own treatment implies.

On the question of down-dating of the poems' composition, the provocative paper by M. L. West, 'The Date of the Iliad', *MH* 52 (1995), 203–19, is now essential reading. West criticizes several traditional arguments and presents a case for the *Iliad* in something like its present form being a creation of the period after 688 BC. More radical arguments for a late date for the ending of the *Iliad* are offered by R. Seaford, *Reciprocity and Ritual* (Oxford, 1994), ch. 5.

On competition in Greek society, and especially literary rivalries (see the end of my second section), see now M. Griffith, 'Contest and Contradiction in Early Greek Poetry', in M. Griffith and D. Mastronarde (edd.), *Cabinet of the Muses* (New York, 1990), 185–207.

One more general point which may need comment is my use of the term 'allusion' and my avoidance of the term 'intertextual' and its cognates except with reference to Pucci (n. 1). 'Intertextuality' is a term which has gained hugely in popularity amongst classicists in recent years, but which is often applied in a rather casual and unhelpful way. Sometimes, following Kristeva, who coined the term, it is used to refer to a universal and inescapable chain of relationships between all texts; sometimes more restrictedly, as though 'intertextual reference' is synonymous with 'allusion' (in which case the newer term is redundant); sometimes to indicate some looser relation which depends more on the critic's two-way comparisons than on the author's irrecoverable intentions. For a lucid and helpful account of these questions see L. P. Edmunds, 'Intertextuality Today', *Lexis* 13 (1995), 3–22. Since my paper was concerned with the *Odyssey* as in part a response to or even a critique of the *Iliad*, the assumption that deliberate imitation and specific allusion were involved was inevitable, and I do not regret the repeated use of these terms. Since I take the *Odyssey* to be later in date, the authorial allusion can only be one-directional; any two-way comparison is the product of the critic's juxtaposition and re-reading of these texts together. The distinction is an obvious one, but the determination of many critics to eradicate any implication that we might be aiming at an understanding, however imperfect, of authorial intention has led to much conflation of the two types of enquiry. See, however, for more recent statements of an approach to these issues which offers much stimulus (even though sceptics may still have doubts), the valuable book by S. Hinds, *Allusion and Intertext: Dynamics of Appropriation in Roman Poetry* (Cambridge, 1998), esp. 47–51 on the authorial issue; D. Fowler, *Roman Constructions: Readings in Postmodern Latin* (Oxford, 2000), 115–37 (repr. from *Materiali e discussioni per l'analisi dei testi classici* 39 (1997), 13–34), with the more recent comments on 111–14.

4

Do Homeric Heroes Make Real Decisions?

RICHARD GASKIN

I

Bruno Snell has made familiar a certain thesis about the Homeric poems, to the effect that these poems depict a primitive form of mindedness.[1] The area of mindedness concerned is agency, and the content of the thesis is that Homeric agents are not agents in the fullest sense: they do not make choices in clear self-awareness of what they are doing; choices are made *for* them rather than *by* them; in some cases the instigators of action are gods, in other cases they are forces acting internally on the agent and over which he has no control. Homeric heroes act in the way Descartes thought an animal acts: 'agitur, non agit'.[2] Such agents 'handeln nicht eigentlich (d.h. mit vollem Bewußtsein eigenen Handelns), sondern sie reagieren'.[3] The model of the agent which we moderns have is of a self which determines, rather than is determined to, action; the self arrives at this determination by considering available reasons for action in the

For their help with the original or the revision the author would like to thank Douglas Cairns, Michael Morris, Walter Nicolai, and Arbogast Schmitt.

[1] Especially in the following: *Aischylos und das Handeln in Drama* (*Philologus*, Suppl. 20, 1928), to be read with the review by E. Wolff in *Gnomon* 5 (1929), 386–400; 'Das Bewußtsein von eigenen Entscheidungen im früheren Griechentum' (repr. in his *Gesammelte Schriften* (Göttingen, 1966), 18–31; 'Göttliche und menschliche Motivation im homerischen Epos' (repr. in *Ges. Schr.*, 55–61); *Die Entdeckung des Geistes* (Hamburg, 1948); *Szenen aus griechischen Dramen* (Berlin, 1971). See also H. Fränkel, *Dichtung und Philosophie des frühen Griechentums* (Munich, 1962), 83–103 [trans. as *Early Greek Poetry and Philosophy* (Oxford, 1975)], and recently H. Erbse, 'Nachlese zur homerischen Psychologie', *Hermes* 118 (1990), 1–17.

[2] Snell, *Ges. Schr.* (n. 1), 61.

[3] C. Voigt, *Überlegung und Entscheidung: Studien zur Selbstauffassung des Menschen bei Homer* (Beiträge zur klass. Philol. 48; Meisenheim/Glan, 1972), 106.

light of its overall purposes,[4] and it moves to action in full self-consciousness of what it is doing, and why. This model of action, Snell claims, is not present in Greek literature before the tragedians. I think anyone ought to concede that there is *some* difference between the way Homer portrays decision-making and the way it is portrayed in tragedy (with further differences among the tragedians themselves); but has Snell located the difference in the right place? I shall argue in this chapter that he has not.

One of the main difficulties in pursuing this question has been the vagueness and uncertainty of the terminology. Snell himself has been a prime offender in this regard: talk about consciousness, self-consciousness, autonomy, and so on is of no help unless it is rendered precise in some way. It is not enough to claim that Homeric heroes do not make proper decisions, or do not act with full self-consciousness. What do these words mean? What exactly is it that they cannot do? I shall examine three more precise formulations of the general claim to be found in Snell's (and his follower Voigt's) writings.

II

In the first place, Snell argues that Homer has no word for the self, and since he has no word for it, it follows that as far as he is concerned the thing does not exist: only a 'naive realism' would read into Homer something for which he himself has no name.[5] In default of possessing a unitary self, Homeric man consists of a collection of various organs, each with its assigned function, but with no organizing principle rendering them coherent. Put like that, the claim seems outrageous. For it is not as if Homer represents his figures as *incoherent* assemblages of different organs: Achilles does not trip up every so often because his eye and his foot are unsynchronized. But it

---

[4] Reasons and purposes engage with one another: there is no *general* antecedence of one to the other. An Aristotelian—as opposed to a Humean—model of action allows for situations in which overall purposes are *shaped* by occurrent perceptions of features of the world as constituting reasons for action. See here D. Wiggins, 'Deliberation and Practical Reason' reprinted in A. Rorty (ed.), *Essays on Aristotle's Ethics* (Berkeley, 1980), 221–40.

[5] *Die Entdeckung des Geistes* (n. 1), ch. 1. Snell relies on the earlier work by J. Böhme, *Die Seele und das Ich im homerischen Epos* (Göttingen, 1929).

is quite true that Homer has no word for the self.[6] What has gone wrong?

One mistake Snell has made is to read too much into the modern concept of selfhood, and consequently to approach Homer with inappropriate expectations. Talk of the self is no more than talk about the coherence of the mental activities of a single person. The self is delimited as just that thing whose defining characteristic it is to organize and unite those activities. In any normal person those activities will be organized and united, and the word 'self' is just a label we attach to the person in his capacity as mentally endowed unitary being. There is accordingly no more to a self than that which is referred to using a personal pronoun or proper name, both of which linguistic devices are of course to be found in Homer.[7] The concept of self is just the concept of whatever is referred to using one of these devices. Hence without possessing a word for the concept of the self, Homer nevertheless thinks of his characters—and must so think of them, since he represents them in a coherent, lifelike way— as unitary agents.[8]

---

[6] That is, he has no *one* word for the *Gesamtgemüt*, as Böhme (n. 5) showed. In particular, the word *psuchē* does not discharge this function, since it denotes no more than the life or consciousness of a man, in the sense of that which is taken away when he swoons or dies. O. Regenbogen showed (in his "Δαιμόνιον ψυχῆς φῶς", repr. in his *Kleine Schriften* (Munich, 1961), 1 ff.) that the *psuchē* is not to be thought of as materializing at the moment of death, but rather as accompanying a man throughout his life and deserting him at death. I think Regenbogen succeeds in showing that the *psuchē* is the 'im Lebenden conditio sine qua non aller körperlichen, geistigen und emotionalen Regungen' (p. 20). But there is a difference between the life-principle of a man, which the *psuchē* may well be taken to represent, and the unitary nature of his self, which the *psuchē* cannot, as such, be taken to represent.

[7] Cf. R. Sharples, '"But why has my spirit spoken with me thus?": Homeric Decision-making', *G&R* 30 (1983), 1–7, who correctly points out that Snell's picture of Homeric man as an assemblage of various lobbying groups better fits Plato's model of the soul in *Republic* 4, or the myth of the charioteer in the *Phaedrus*. Sharples also alludes to a similarity between Homer and Aristotle—and the divergence of both of them from Plato—on the subject of *akrasia*, which I discuss below.

[8] See the interesting piece by C. Gill ('Did Chrysippus Understand Medea?', *Phronesis* 28 (1983), 136–49, in which he argues that the Medea of Eur. *Med.* 1078–80 must be thought of as a unitary agent. That was the line taken by Chrysippus, who argued that Medea's impulse to kill her children was contrary to reason in the sense that it was unreasonable, not in the sense that it was arational, as a Platonic model of the soul would have it. For Chrysippus, *hormai, pathē* etc. are rational in the sense that they are *conceptual* mental states: they involve judgements. He apparently used Homeric examples to justify his view that the soul functions in a unified way (Galen, *De Placitis Hippocratis et Platonis*, ed. P. De Lacy (Berlin, 1978–84), III. 2. 10–20). Galen takes a Platonic line on Medea's struggle (III. 3. 13. 22), describing her

A second, but related, mistake in Snell's theory is indicated by Böhme's classic study (note 5), on which Snell relied heavily in his claim that Homer had no word for the self. For it was part of Böhme's thesis that, although Homer has no *one* word for the self, he has an array of words (in particular *noos* and *thumos*) which can do duty for 'I'. Böhme explicitly drew the right conclusion from this observation (pp. 91–2): the fact that these different words are, in doing duty for 'I', interchangeable, shows that the organic coherence of the functions which the relevant words can otherwise denote was presupposed. In the case of *noos* and *thumos*, the coherence of the intellectual and the appetitive elements in the human mind is simply presupposed to the possibility that either word may go proxy for a word denoting the self, i.e. that which *unites* the various functions of mind.

A striking illustration of this occurs in the often-cited passage in *Iliad* 11 where Odysseus comes under increasing pressure from the Trojans after Diomedes' withdrawal, and wonders whether to retreat:

> And troubled, he spoke to his own great-hearted spirit (*thumos*):
> 'Ah me, what will become of me? It will be a great evil
> if I run, fearing their multitude, yet deadlier if I am caught
> alone; and Kronos' son drove to flight the rest of the Danaans.
> Yet still, why does the heart (*thumos*) within me debate on these things?
> Since I know that it is the cowards who walk out of the fighting,
> but if one is to win honour in battle, he must by all means
> stand his ground strongly, whether he be struck or strike down another.'
>
> (403–10, trans. Lattimore)

Homer first says (403) that Odysseus spoke to his *thumos*, and Odysseus' first words make it clear, if it needed making clear, that it is his *self* which is speaking. Odysseus suggests to his *thumos* that while flight would be cowardly, to be taken by the enemy would be worse; then he asks 'But why has my *thumos* spoken to me thus?' It would be absurd to object here that Homer is confused; that he has inconsistently ascribed Odysseus' words first to his self (addressing his *thumos*), and then to his *thumos* (addressing his self). What we have is simply a dialogue of the self with itself. The fact that

---

deliberation as an inner dialogue between *logismos* and *thumos*. But he introduces—
as anyone who wishes to make sense of Medea must do—a self (*autē*) separate from
these parts of the soul, and alternately under the hegemony of each.

Odysseus' mind is *not* an incoherent assemblage of unrelated functions is vividly conveyed by the emergence of one of those functions, *thumos*, first as hearer and then as speaker in this self-dialogue. The 'inconsistency' precisely subserves the purpose of representing Odysseus as an integrated whole.[9]

Methodologically speaking, the above discussion demonstrates the inadequacy of the so-called lexical method, upon which Snell relies, namely the principle that if a culture lacks a word for a thing, then it does not recognize that thing's existence.[10] Dodds subscribes to this principle when he writes that 'to ask whether Homer's people are determinists or libertarians is a fantastic anachronism: the question has never occurred to them, and if it were put to them it would be very difficult to make them understand what it means'.[11] But he himself, at the end of the same paragraph, describes Patroclus' death as 'overdetermined'. Of course Homer did not possess a *word* for the phenomenon of overdetermination. But that he did possess the *concept* of overdetermination is shown by his making Patroclus aware that his death is (on Dodds's interpretation) due to more than one cause, each of which would have been sufficient on its own to bring about his death. In fact Lesky has shown that Dodds is wrong to describe Patroclus' death as overdetermined.[12] The point is that the contributions of Apollo and Hector to Patroclus' death are not thought of as independent inputs, each of which would have been sufficient on its own to kill Patroclus. The gods work with (sometimes through) men: the term 'overdetermination' misses the essential unity of such action. I am not concerned here, however, with the question whether Dodds has correctly characterized the aetiology of Patroclus' death, but with the general principle that, contrary to what the lexical method supposes, it is quite possible (and indeed

[9] Böhme's comment: '... nicht mehrere Seelenteile treten nebeneinander, sondern was vorher als Anrede des Ich an den *thumos* beschrieben wurde, wird nun, wo Odysseus die Verantwortung für die ausgesprochenen Befürchtungen von sich abwälzen will, für ein Selbstgespräch seines *thumos* ausgegeben' ((n. 5), 80). And note that the soliloquy is closed with the words: ἧος ὁ ταῦθ' ὥρμαινε κατὰ φρένα καὶ κατὰ θυμόν ('While he was pondering these things in his heart and spirit', 411). Here the soliloquy is represented as having been conducted by Odysseus *in* his *thumos* (and *phrēn*).

[10] Further criticisms of the lexical method—different from mine—are to be found in H. Lloyd-Jones, *The Justice of Zeus* (2nd edn., Berkeley, 1983), *passim*.

[11] *The Greeks and the Irrational* (Berkeley, 1951), 7.

[12] A. Lesky, *Göttliche und menschliche Motivation im homerischen Epos* (SB Heidelberg 1961. 4 = Ch. 5, this vol.). On Lesky see further § III below.

entirely normal) for an individual or culture to dispose of a concept for which it possesses no name.

It would be a corollary of the assumption behind the lexical method that a linguistic community could never *discover* that it had all along been working, implicitly, with some concept and proceed to baptize it; rather, whenever a community coined a new term, the concept which that term denoted would simultaneously spring into existence as an *invention* of the linguistic advance. But that seems implausible. To take an example from another area of mindedness, I might describe someone as 'switched off'. The term I here use is an artefact of the industrial age, but does that mean that no one was ever switched off *before* the industrial age? Surely not: the term 'switched off' denotes—in a new way—a mental state which was around, and known to be around, long before the invention of the relevant kind of machine—namely the state of being inattentive. It *presents* the state of being inattentive in a special way by noticing an analogy between the human mind and inanimate machines. To capture the distinction between what is and what is not invented when such a term is brought into the language, we need to employ a Fregean framework which distinguishes between a referring device, which may be a proper name or a concept-expression, the referent of such a device, which may be an object or a concept, and the mode of presentation of the object or concept. The point may then be expressed as follows: it is possible for a community to invent a referring device for a referent which was there all along to be identified. It is clear that the mode of presentation must be ranged with what gets invented in this transaction rather than with what is already in place in the world: 'switched off' presents the state of being inattentive in a new mode.[13]

To forestall a potential line of objection, it should be noted that not everything which falls on the conceptual side of the thing/concept divide can be absorbed into the mode of presentation. That would lead to an extreme and unsustainable nominalism committed to a world of *Dinge an sich*. The state of being inattentive, or switched off, must have a conceptual component which is utterly in the world; and similarly

---

[13] For an elucidation of the Fregean framework employed here, see esp. G. Evans, *The Varieties of Reference* (Oxford, 1982), ch. 1, along with J. McDowell, 'On the Sense and Reference of a Proper Name', *Mind* 86 (1977), 159–85; D. Wiggins, 'The Sense and Reference of Predicates', in C. Wright (ed.), *Frege: Tradition and Influence* (Oxford, 1984), 126–43.

for the concept of the self. That component can present itself under different modes (and must, whenever it presents itself, do so under *some* mode), just as a thing can be referred to in different ways (and must, whenever it is referred to, be referred to in *some* way). It would be incoherent here either to suppose that the mind could peep behind the mode of presentation (conceived as *obstructing* view of the object) and observe the things and concepts in themselves, or to suppose at the other extreme that the object/concept and mode of presentation are so intimately connected with each other that the former must be individuated in terms of the latter. The difficult, but correct, position is that the relation is sufficiently intimate that the mode of presentation does indeed *present* (not obstruct) the object or concept (which cannot be presented in *no* way), but not so intimate that different presentations of the same object or concept are ruled out.

In certain of their uses, words like *noos* and *thumos* present the concept of the self. They do so under their own, detectably different, modes.[14] That Homer now has no word which corresponds to our word 'self' does not deprive him of the *concept* of selfhood, since what is presented by these words in the contexts which concern us (such as: 'he spoke to his *thumos*') is precisely the integrated, unitary item which the word 'self' also (and always as opposed to sometimes) refers to. The semantic *difference* between 'self' and *thumos* (in its relevant usage) must accordingly be located in the different *modes* under which these terms present the same *concept* (namely selfhood); in other words, the difference is a linguistic and not an ontological difference. Homer's world contains selves.

It would be a different kind of mistake to suppose that, because classical Greek thought did not possess the concept of will in its post-Kantian sense, it therefore did not have the concepts of intention or decision. These latter concepts can be captured by a vocabulary which is cognitivist and not volitional in character, simply because the cognitive need not be—and was not—conceived of as motivationally

---

[14] See here A. Schmitt, *Selbständigkeit und Abhängigkeit menschlichen Handelns bei Homer* (Abh. Mainz, 1990.5), 174–228 (note esp. n. 577). Schmitt argues that, although both *noos* and *thumos* comprise cognitive and volitional elements (see further below in this section), the characteristic activity of the latter is 'more subjective' (p. 212) than that of the former, in the sense that the *thumos* thinks in a restricted way (cf. p. 224), and is given to emotionally driven distortion of the facts, whereas the *noos* takes a more emotionally detached view of the overall moral significance of the agent's situation and options.

inert.[15] Aristotle's model of practical wisdom is set up in terms of the concepts *aisthēsis, nous,* and *orexis* (*Nicomachean Ethics* 1139[a]17–18), but the noetic and orectic elements are not logically independent of one another: there is no *gap* to be felt between an agent's proper perception of the morally relevant facts of a situation, in the context of an overall desire for *eudaimonia* or *eupraxia*—itself constituted by a distinctive way of seeing his life—and his decision to act appropriately. The impulse, intention or decision so to act is, on Aristotle's picture, *constituted* by the cognitive dispositions of the agent: so that a man who, confronted with a certain morally significant situation, did not decide to act in the morally appropriate way, would just not be *seeing* the relevant facts, or at any rate not seeing them in the right way. The volitional does not contribute an input over and above the cognitive, properly taken. We are tempted to think of willing as logically independent of seeing; Aristotle thought of willing as a special way of seeing.[16]

III

The second more precise version of the general thesis which I shall discuss is the claim, already mentioned, that Homeric heroes do not make proper decisions because their decisions are made for them, either by gods, or by forces internal to the agents themselves. My treatment of the former of these categories—those decisions which are allegedly made by gods—can be brief, since it has been conclusively demonstrated by several writers, and is now widely accepted, that the intervention of a god in a decision-making process does not derogate from the individual's autonomy or responsibility

---

[15] See here again Schmitt (n. 14), ibid., and V. Cessi, *Erkennen und Handeln in der Theorie des Tragischen bei Aristoteles* (Frankfurt/Main, 1987), *passim,* esp. the discussion of relevant Aristotelian passages, e.g. *DA* 414[b]1–6 at pp. 137 ff.; note also one of her main conclusions (p. 248): 'Für Aristoteles ist Wahrnehmen ein unterscheidender, aktiver und spontan werdender Erkenntnisakt, aus dem durch Betätigung des auf ihm beruhenden Vorstellungsvermögens unmittelbar ein Streben (*orexis*) zur Handlung entspringt.'
[16] On this topic in general see most helpfully A. Dihle, *The Theory of the Will in Classical Antiquity* (Berkeley, 1982), ch. 2, although Dihle is in my view unduly pessimistic about the competence of a purely cognitivist system of thought to construct a life-like theory of action. For relevant Homeric examples, see Fränkel (n. 1), 90–1.

for his action.[17] Athene intervenes to try to prevent Achilles from killing Agamemnon (*Iliad* I. 188 ff.), but she does not force him into line: 'I have come,' she tells him (I. 207 ff.), 'to check your anger, if you will listen (αἴ κε πίθηαι)'. She offers him a threefold recompense for his loss if he heeds her, and finishes: 'Do you restrain your hand; obey us.' Achilles replies that he ought to obey her, because it is better to do so. There is no compulsion in this: Achilles could disobey if he wished, but chooses not to; Aegisthus does disobey the gods although he is warned by Hermes of the consequences (*Odyssey* I. 32–43); and Odysseus decides not to take the advice proffered him by Leucothea (*Odyssey* 5. 333 ff.).

There are two points to be made here. One is that, as these examples show, divine interventions can stop short of annexing the individual's autonomy: the god puts some options before the individual, gives advice, but leaves the final decision to that individual. But it would be unsatisfactory to rest the case for the autonomy of Homer's creatures on such incidents, if only because such a strategy would implicitly concede to Snell that where agents' decisions are represented as divinely prompted, those agents are not genuinely responsible for their actions.[18] But that cannot be right. Agamemnon blames Zeus for the onset of *atē* which led him to slight Achilles (*Iliad* 19. 86 ff.), but he nevertheless makes amends to Achilles: he does not regard the fact that he was overcome by *atē* as diminishing his responsibility. Earlier, he blamed himself: with 19. 137 compare 9. 115–19. Ajax says of Achilles in the embassy scene of Book 9: 'Achilles has made wild the great-hearted *thumos* in his breast' (628–9), but shortly after adds, 'The gods have placed in your breast an implacable and evil *thumos*' (636–7), and then, 'Do you make your *thumos* gentle' (639), so apparently interweaving motifs of divine and human responsibility for the state of Achilles' *thumos*. As is familiar, Lesky has characterized such episodes in terms of 'double motivation'; but this characterization needs to be treated with caution. It is misleading if it is taken to suggest that divine and human impulses are equal (if interdependent) partners in the genesis of human action. Rather, the divine input is presented as consciously matched to an antecedently constituted human motivational array.

---

[17] See esp. Dodds (n. 11), ch. 1; Lesky (n. 12); E. Wüst, 'Von den Anfängen des Problems der Willensfreiheit', *RM* 101 (1958), 75–91; H. Schwabl, 'Zur Selbständigkeit des Menschen bei Homer', *WS* 67 (1954), 46–64.   [18] So Erbse (n. 1), 11 ff.

Hence such divine intervention cannot remove responsibility, because it prompts an agent to do what he might well, or perhaps even certainly would, have done anyway. The replications and supplementations of human motivation on the divine plane are deployed by Homer to subserve, not subvert, human autonomy.[19]

So much for the role of the gods. It has also been claimed by both Snell and Voigt that even when Homeric agents act independently of gods, they are at the mercy of forces which deprive them of that full degree of autonomy which we require of genuine agency. There is a basic, and rather surprising, confusion here between reasons and causes. Of course if Homeric agents were determined to action by irrational causes—passions, drives, and so on—then it would be the case that they did not possess a genuine power of agency. Sometimes Homeric agents—like any agents—are so determined to action, and I shall consider some of these cases in the next section. But it is obviously not *in general* true that Homeric agents are driven to action by passions operating in a crudely causal way on them; quite often they choose courses of action, in a thoroughly self-controlled way, for reasons. Odysseus makes just such a reasoned choice in the passage from *Iliad* 11 quoted above.

The mistake which Snell[20] and Voigt[21] make at this point is to claim that even such selections of courses of action for reasons are not genuine choices, on the ground that the reasons in turn

---

[19] An interesting early defence of the thesis that divine intervention in Homer does not detract from human freedom is afforded by Plutarch, *Coriolanus* 32. On this topic see in general Schmitt, 'Athenes Umgang mit den Menschen bei Homer', *Die alten Sprachen im Unterricht* 29 (1982), 6–23, and (n. 14) *passim*, esp. 36–46, 72–114. Schmitt rightly notes that although the gods in Homer do externalize internal motivations, they do not *merely* do so. For example, while Athene's words to Achilles give him a plan of action most appropriate to his situation—a better method of avenging himself than killing Agamemnon—she represents more than his own deliberations, for she acts out of concern not just for him, but also for Agamemnon (1. 196), a complex motivation which could hardly be credited to Achilles himself.

[20] *Aischylos* (n. 1), and elsewhere in opp. citt. (n. 1).

[21] (n. 3), 41. Here Voigt suggests that Homer's frequent use of such formulae as δοάσσατο κέρδιον εἶναι indicates that the agent is not really *choosing* the course of action which seems better. But the distinction is spurious, as I argue in the text. (Cf. also E. Harrison, 'Notes on Homeric Psychology', *Phoenix* 14 (1960), 63–80, at p. 79: 'Here the poet naturally uses a formula which focuses attention on the content of the decision. We know already *who* is involved on each occasion: all we wish to be told at this point is *what* he decides to do.') Voigt also claims (loc. cit.) that the description of the better course of action as *kerdion* removes it from the moral domain. But the line between the moral and the non-moral is not so easily drawn. A counter-example

determine the choice of action.[22] But action which is chosen for reasons is the only genuine sort of action we know. There is no suggestion here that reasons mechanically determine action—that is not a convincing model of human agency—but equally there is no *gap* between the reasons for an action and the action, in the sense that the reasons *and nothing else* rationalize (i.e. make rational sense of) the action. Action which is chosen for no reason at all—action on an existentialist model—is simply not recognizable as anything falling under the title of genuine self-conscious agency: it looks much more like movement occasioned by brute irrational impulse. There cannot be many examples of such action in ancient literature; even if there were any (I shall discuss one possible claimant below, section v), it would be strange to elevate them to the status of the only genuine type of action. Of course that is not what Snell wants: in his view the plays of Aeschylus contain many cases of genuine agency, and Aeschylus' agents do not conduct themselves in an existentialist void. They perform actions for reasons; but so do Homer's agents. What is the difference?

In his discussion of the passage quoted above from *Iliad* 11, Voigt suggests[23] that it is wrong to speak here of a genuine decision on Odysseus' part, because he does not really think of the reason which he settles on as *his own*; he simply remembers the norm which guides men of his social position, and acts accordingly. There are two points which need to be made here. The first is that *no* case of reasoned decision-making is going to be good enough for Voigt, because all such cases simply do involve an agent confronting himself with reasons which appeal to him because they answer to generally applicable norms of conduct of which he approves. An agent falls

---

to the claim is raised by Voigt himself (p. 44): at *Il.* 16. 652 Zeus decides that it would be *kerdion* to spare Patroclus for a little longer before he is slain by Hector. There is no gain (in Voigt's sense) in this for Zeus: his deliberation and decision relate to what he *ought* to do. Consider too Hector's deliberations at *Il.* 22. 99 ff. In outline Hector says: it would have been *kerdion* if I had followed Polydamas' advice (103), but since I did not do so, it is now *kerdion* to face Achilles in single combat (108). A moral 'ought' must be implicit in the second *kerdion* (Hector later replaces it by *belteron*, 129); so that it is senseless to deny it to the first *kerdion*. Only someone who thought that prudential considerations always *excluded* moral considerations could fail to see this. But a course of action may be moral precisely because it is prudent.

[22] To that extent their position is an existentialist rather than a Kantian one (cf. here Gill, *Personality in Greek Epic, Tragedy, and Philosophy* (Oxford, 1996), 46). This point is brought out by Schmitt (n. 14), esp. 28–35.

[23] (n. 3), 87 ff. Cf. Snell, *Ges. Schr.* (n. 1), 21.

back on reasons which have a certain objective status, in the sense
that they would, he must believe, appeal to any comparable agent
similarly circumstanced. In acting on the basis of those reasons, he
thereby makes them his own.[24]

Odysseus rests on the principle that as an *agathos* he ought not
to retreat. He could question whether he wants to be an *agathos*,[25]
but were he to do so, and then act against the principles proper to an
agathos, he would again have to do so *for reasons*—reasons which
would lay claim to having objective status in the above sense. One
set of reasons can only be questioned on the basis of another set of
reasons: you cannot escape from reasons as the basis of any rational action you hope to perform, and in so far as your action is
rational, your reasons for it must enjoy this objective status. Even if
Homeric agents were only capable of reasoning within stereotypical
categories—a charge levelled by Voigt—that would not go to show

---

[24] Hence the following can be seen to rest on confusion: 'Wenn... der Mensch
Homers unter dem Zwang der Konventionen handelt, entscheidet er sich nicht,
sondern er fügt sich der Notwendigkeit (in Snells Terminologie: "er reagiert"). Er kann
das bereitwillig, ja gern oder auch ungern tun, aber in allen Fällen wird ihm das Ziel
des Handelns vorgeschrieben. Deshalb kann auch ein bereitwilliges Gehorchen nicht
als freie Entscheidung gelten; denn zu dieser gehört nicht nur der Wille (bzw. die
Bereitwilligkeit), sondern auch das eigenständige Denken. Nur wenn der Verstand
unbehindert tätig sein kann, vollzieht sich eine Entscheidung in Freiheit. [...]
Selbstverständlich kann sich das Denken eine ihm fremde Konzeption aus Überzeugung
zu eigen machen. Dann aber sind es *seine* Gründe und *seine* Konsequenzen. Von
Gehorsam kann in diesem Fall schlechterdings nicht mehr gesprochen werden.
Man wird zugeben müssen, daß solche Fälle bei Homer nicht belegt sind' (Erbse
(n. 1), 9). But Homer's text is alive with decisions made by agents on the basis
of norms of which they approve; and their approval of these norms is just what
makes those decisions *their* decisions (so talk of 'necessity' here is out of place:
see n. 45 below). What does Erbse suppose renders such impulses cases of mere
'bereitwilliges Gehorchen', as distinct from 'freie Entscheidung'? A free decision can
only be made on the basis of reasons of which one approves, and it would be
viciously regressive to suppose that one freely chooses all reasons on the basis of
which one acts: at a certain point one must rest on reasons which one does not
choose, but which one recognizes as basic and authoritative. Obedience to norms
of which one approves thus coincides with, and does not stand in opposition to, any
self-legislation worth the name. (Only the existentialist agent seems to satisfy
Erbse's demand for 'eigenständiges Denken', and that by virtue of acting for no
reason at all.) On this topic in general see D. Cairns, *Aidōs* (Oxford, 1993),
Introduction and ch. 1, esp. 79–83, 139–46; B. Williams, *Shame and Necessity*
(Berkeley, 1993), esp. ch. 4.

[25] *Contra* Voigt, ibid. (cf. Snell, *Szenen* (n. 1), 18), who claims that such a revolt
would not be open to a Homeric agent. But to question the standards of conduct in
which he has been brought up, and which his social position demands of him, is
precisely what Achilles does in his speech to the embassy at *Il.* 9. 397 ff.

that they are not genuine agents. It would just show that they are genuine agents of a rather mundane sort. An agent's reasons may be thin and stereotypical, or they may be rich and interesting, but they cannot be radically *individual*, at least not if the agent is rational. A rational agent must choose reasons which would appeal to any other rational agent similarly circumstanced (the Kantian principle of universalizability). Aeschylean agents are no better off than Homer's agents in this respect.[26]

In fact Homer's agents are capable of reasoning which is not stereotypical; this is the second point.[27] Compare with Odysseus' deliberations the deliberations of Menelaus in the seventeenth book of the *Iliad* (91–105). Menelaus is defending Patroclus' body, and like Odysseus he is faced with the onset of superior numbers of Trojans: he has to decide whether to hold his ground or retreat. Menelaus considers the argument which swayed Odysseus—that it would be cowardly to retreat—expressing the point in terms of the *aidōs* he would feel, and the *nemesis* he would incur, if he retreated. But he wonders whether respecting his feeling of *aidōs* is worth the cost of being surrounded by the enemy. At this point the decisive consideration occurs to him: since Hector is fighting 'from a god', there is no shame in giving way before him. Finally he resolves to seek out Ajax: if the two of them could resist Hector—divinely aided though he be—and rescue Patroclus' body, that would be the best of a bad situation.

There is no reason why we should not acknowledge that Menelaus is aware here of a truth which Euripides' Phaedra was to make explicit (*Hippolytus* 385–7)—that there is bad *aidōs* as well as good *aidōs*.[28] Bad *aidōs* would in this situation amount to falling back on the rule of thumb that *agathoi* do not retreat. But Menelaus does not give way to the temptation to reason in this instinctive manner;

[26] Cf. Lloyd-Jones (n. 10), 240: '... all the time in ordinary life we automatically act in accordance with principles whose observance, by what Aristotle calls *ethismos*, has become a matter of habit; this does not mean that if called upon to justify those principles we would prove unable to do so.' Lloyd-Jones could have written this last clause as: 'this does not mean that such action is not genuine action, performed by the agent as a matter of his autonomous and self-conscious choice.' What Lloyd-Jones wrote is equivalent to my formulation, since the type of action alluded to in my formulation is the very type of action we can be called upon to justify.

[27] Cf. Gill (n. 22), 70–1.

[28] For an elucidation of the distinction as it applies to Phaedra, see Barrett's commentary ad loc.

he realizes that *aidōs* is not the morally relevant category in his situation. Here and now the morally relevant fact is that if he stood his ground he would be cut off and surrounded (94–5). Normally only a coward would think like that, but the crucial difference here is that Hector is fighting with divine assistance: only fools fight with gods (98–9); the Danaans are well aware of this, and will consequently withhold their indignation from him (100–1). Menelaus achieves a moral sophistication and insight in advance of acting such as Phaedra is only able to attain after she has (disastrously) acted.[29]

Menelaus in effect uses one moral norm (only fools fight the gods) to discount the course of action recommended by another norm (only cowards retreat); the sophistication of his reasoning derives from the fact that, to a man of Menelaus' standing and temperament, the second of these norms carries considerable weight. It is no small achievement that he is able to withstand its allure.[30] Let me stress once again—since it is so easy to go wrong here—that the fact that Menelaus counteracts one norm with *another norm* does not rob his decision of autonomy. *All* rational action operates within a context of norms of conduct. (The norms may not always be exhaustively codifiable—a point stressed by Aristotle: *Nicomachean Ethics* 2. 2.) But the fact that action is principled—and so in a certain sense not individualistic—does not derogate from the autonomy or self-consciousness of the agent who so acts. On the contrary, action which is *not principled*—in the sense of not resting on principles which, if formulated, could enjoy general appeal—is not recognizable as genuinely rational action (simply: action) at all.

---

[29] Compare Odysseus' deliberation in Polyphemus' cave (*Od.* 9. 295–306). He is initially tempted to stab Polyphemus—as one would expect of any hero in his circumstance—but he is restrained by a second *thumos* (303) which suggests a more intelligent policy. And, as with Menelaus, second thoughts are best. Contrast Phaedra, for whom second thoughts (*Hipp.* 436) are worse. Again, the fact that Odysseus' deliberation is described in terms of lobbying *thumoi* does not impugn the unitary status of his self. Rather, it is a vivid way of conveying the fact that ideas just do *occur* to one (out of nowhere, as it seems). But they occur to *one*, i.e. to the unitary, acting self. Homer can represent decisions which, as it seems, simply 'happen' to one as owing to the intervention of a god (e.g. Phoenix's decision not to murder his father, *Il.* 9. 458 ff.). There is nothing especially primitive in this: it is one way of portraying a type of process which is not perspicuous to the agent himself.

[30] Not surprisingly, Voigt (n. 3), 92 ff. cannot accommodate the sophistication and intelligence of Menelaus' reasoning; he has to suggest—surely implausibly—that Menelaus does select a cowardly course of action.

Here again the lexical method shows its deficiencies. The fact that Homeric decisions are never labelled as such[31]—they are never signalled by such verbs as *hairein* and *haireisthai*—does nothing to impugn their status as decisions. One of the most important crises in the *Iliad* is Achilles' decision to return to the fighting, thereby bringing upon himself a short but glorious life. I shall not trace the working out of this decision, since this has been admirably done by Schadewaldt.[32] Again, the absence of an explicit linguistic flag cannot render the decision which Achilles quite evidently makes in any sense unreal or not genuine. The crucial point comes in the eighteenth book, when Achilles tells his mother that he has resolved to take revenge on Hector for Patroclus' death. If you do, she says, you will not live long, since your death stands waiting behind Hector's death. Then let me die forthwith, replies Achilles—αὐτίκα τεθναίην (98)—since I could not save my friend. How can one seriously deny that τεθναίην *contains* Achilles' decision? In willing, with full awareness, its necessary consequence, Achilles thereby makes the decision.

IV

Animals clearly make choices in some sense—a dog might choose to go for the bone over here rather than the stick over there—but there nevertheless seems to be something to the denial that they make *genuine* decisions: at least, they do not seem to make decisions in full self-awareness of what they are doing. Descartes surely had a point with his 'agitur, non agit'. One reason which might be suggested why animals cannot make genuine decisions is that they do not possess the concept of a decision; they do not possess that concept because they do not possess a language. Roughly, they cannot think because they cannot talk.[33] As far as sheer decision-making is concerned, I have argued that the fact that Homeric heroes do not

---

[31] Voigt (n. 3), 17–18.

[32] 'Die Entscheidung des Achilleus', in *Von Homers Welt und Werk* (4th edn., Stuttgart, 1965), 234–67.

[33] For this general line, see L. Wittgenstein, *Philosophische Untersuchungen*, e.g. § 1. 650, 'Wir sagen, der Hund fürchtet, sein Herr werde ihn schlagen; aber nicht: er fürchte, sein Herr werde ihn morgen schlagen. Warum nicht?' The dog would need to be able to *talk* about tomorrow to be able to *think* about it. See also some of the papers of Donald Davidson collected in his *Inquiries into Truth and Interpretation* (Oxford, 1984), especially the paper entitled 'Thought and Talk'.

conceive of their decisions *as such* does nothing to impugn the status of those decisions as genuine decisions. But why then cannot dogs make genuine decisions? It must make a difference here that dogs have no language at all, whereas Homeric heroes have a sufficiently rich vocabulary—and, in particular, mental vocabulary—for mindedness to be in place. Gaps at the linguistic level being exceptional, and very few in number, they do not make for gaps at the ontological level. It is easy to underestimate how much is presupposed by the lifelike portrayal of a human being. When all of that structure and detail is in place, the sheer absence of a few lexical items is not necessarily going to have repercussions at the ontological level. The creation can in one sense break free of its creator: it may possess power and capacities for which it has no name (it has no name for them because the creator has no name for them). The absence of a name or two here and there, in the context of command of a coherent language, may be too small a deficiency to undermine the completeness of the mental ontology available to such a creature.

The picture emerging is obviously a slightly complicated one: although the difference between a dog and a Homeric hero is very great, it does not seem to be incommensurably great. That is perhaps what one would expect.[34] But without exploring the differences along the very general line just mentioned—difference in point of possession or otherwise of a whole language—I think there is a major distinction to be made at the level of decision-making itself. An animal cannot *reflect* on its decisions, whereas a human being can. Do Homeric heroes reflect on their decisions? The case of Achilles in dialogue with his mother after the death of Patroclus springs to mind at once, but rather than tackle the question absolutely literally, and so perhaps question-beggingly, I want now to examine the third way in which Snell renders his denial of full self-consciousness to Homeric heroes precise. Homeric heroes do not make decisions reflectively, Snell says, because they are not capable of *akrasia*.[35] The guiding idea is this: only an agent who is sometimes capable of being at the

---

[34] Since the difference between a dog and *any* human being is not incommensurably great. After all, a dog *can* fear that his master will beat him (that is already a significant achievement, denied to lower animals), even if he cannot fear that his master will beat him tomorrow.

[35] *Ges. Schr.* (n. 1), 59. Cf. Fränkel (n. 1), 87, for the suggestion that Hamlet represents a type inaccessible to Homer. Hamlet's *akrasia* is marked not by the impact of a desire to act in a way contrary to what, all things considered, has been judged to

mercy of forces, and who at these times knows and regrets that this is happening to him, is capable of making genuine decisions, in the sense of decisions which are not the outcome of a simple inter-action of forces. I think this is a powerful idea. Waiving the Socratic strategy of denying the existence of *akrasia*—surely an unsatisfying way out of the philosophical problems which the phenomenon undoubtedly raises—there is something appealing in the thought that if you are not *always* to be a helpless victim of drives and pas-sions, you must *sometimes* be (or be capable of being) just such a victim, while being simultaneously aware that that is what you are. Only an agent for whom incontinence (and, equally, continence) is a possibility can achieve the distance from his drives and passions requisite to assure him that he is something over and above those forces. To be able to observe the conflict of its desires is, on this attractive line, integral to the ability of a self to think of itself as a unitary item, forced to choose among—and hence not constituted by—the array of disparate desires clamouring for its attention.[36]

Snell denies that Homer's creatures are capable of *akrasia*; in contradistinction, Euripidean heroines such as Phaedra and Medea are said to be capable of it. But consider Helen at *Iliad* 3. 383 ff. Aphrodite has rescued Paris from death at the hands of Menelaus in single combat, and has placed him, bathed in fragrance, in his bridal chamber. Then she comes to Helen, who has been watching the combat from the walls of Troy. She disguises herself as an old woman, and tries to persuade Helen to go to Paris; but Helen sees through the disguise, and refuses: it would be *nemessēton*; let the goddess go to Paris herself, even forsake the way of the Olympians and marry him, since she cares for him so much. Aphrodite waxes wroth, and threatens to hate Helen as much as she now passionately loves her. Helen is cowed, and follows the goddess in silence to the chamber. There Paris is waiting for her. At first Helen chides him, saying he ought to have stayed on the battlefield and fallen to

---

be best, but rather by the *absence* of a desire to realize in action the preferred practical judgement. This type is not only inaccessible to Homer, but to classical thought in general, which would not have been able to make sense of an agent who has preponderating reasons for action, but nevertheless does not act; or indeed of an agent—such as Camus's Stranger—who has no appropriate reason for action, but nevertheless acts.

[36] Aristotle also makes the point that animals are not capable of *akrasia*, although his reason is that they are not capable of forming universal concepts (*NE* 1147^{b}4–6).

Menelaus, who is a better man than he is. Go now, she bids him, and re-enter the fray. But no, she continues, bethinking herself, do not go after all, for you might be killed. Paris stays, and they make love, while on the plain Menelaus searches in vain for his vanished foe.

This seems to be a case of akratic action. Helen really knows the truth: that Paris ought to fight Menelaus to the finish, even if he is killed. That she knows this is shown by her first reply to Aphrodite and her initial words to Paris himself. This knowledge also emerges in the self-conscious way she weaves the Trojan War and all its suffering, undertaken for her sake, into her web (3. 125–8); and in her feelings of self-disgust: she tells Priam she wishes she had died on that day she followed Paris to Troy, calling herself a slut (180); to Aphrodite she calls herself hateful (140), and to Hector a terrible, evil-intriguing bitch (6. 344). And yet she gives way to her disastrous passion, which in her later words to Hector she ascribes to the gods (6. 344 ff.), just as Priam ascribes the responsibility for the war not to her, but to the gods (3. 164–5). That Helen's passion is represented by the goddess Aphrodite[37] should not of course deter us from ascribing it fully to Helen herself: that is, as I have observed, a fundamental parameter of Homeric interpretation. In any case, we have in the present scene a double instance of *akrasia*: Helen first resists Aphrodite, then succumbs; first chides Paris, then again succumbs. It is clear that the two acts of succumbing are doublets: one operates on a partly divine plane, the other on a purely human plane. But as far as Helen's psychology is concerned, the same process is going on each time.

Aristotle insisted (*Nicomachean Ethics* 7. 3) that the akratic agent is in a sense aware of how he should act, and in a sense not, like a man asleep or drunk;[38] or, one might add, like someone overcome by a god (a passion) and forced to act accordingly. The akratic agent, on Aristotle's model, is in full possession of the major premiss of the relevant practical syllogism, but his perception of the situation is in

---

[37] She represents, as Voigt correctly observes ((n. 3), 67), Helen's 'Wesen und Vergangenheit'.

[38] Aristotle's model of *akrasia* is a cognitivist one: the failure is characterized as one of knowledge rather than of will. Democritus' treatment of *akrasia* is also strongly cognitivist (B53, 53a); Theognis (631) and Euripides (*Med.* 1078–80, *Hipp.* 373–87) give less explicitly cognitivist descriptions, but their characterizations are not couched in anything like the terms of a modern notion of the will. Again, I do not see any disadvantage in the cognitivist approach: its critics (e.g. Dihle (n. 16)) have difficulty expressing exactly *what*, other than a piece of terminology, it misses out.

some way damaged by the impact of a desire, so that he in some sense fails to see the situation straight.[39] I abstract somewhat from the precise details of Aristotle's account, which is riddled with difficulty, both textual and argumentational. But the general outline of the account is clear, and it seems fair to abstract sufficiently far to say that the akratic man's *knowledge* of what he should do (interlocking with his pursuit, in general, of *eudaimonia*) remains intact at the moment of weakness, while some aspect of his *perception* of the situation (in particular, his perception of the fact that this is a situation to which his overall knowledge is relevant) becomes dulled.[40] This surely fits Helen's case. She knows what Paris should do, and initially tells him to return to battle, even if that means his death; but she loves him and does not want to see him killed, so giving way to her desire she contradicts her command and bids him stay, *lest* he be killed. Aristotle remarks that the akratic man may, like a man asleep or drunk, come round from his *akrasia*. And that is exactly what happens to Helen: when we next hear of her, she is trying to persuade Paris to return to the fighting (6. 377–8).

Two further passages in the *Iliad* illustrate cases of *akrasia*: Achilles' reply to Ajax at 9. 644–55, and Hector's flight at 22. 136–7. After Ajax's plea to Achilles to return to the fighting, Achilles tells Ajax, in effect, that he is right, but that anger prevents him, Achilles, from acceding to the plea. But we note that Achilles no longer threatens to leave Troy the next day; instead he will stay, but not consider returning to the front before Hector is fighting around

---

[39] See here J. McDowell, 'Virtue and Reason', *Monist* 62 (1979), 331–50; D. Wiggins, 'Weakness of Will, Commensurability, and the Objects of Deliberation and Desire', repr. in Rorty (n. 4), 241–65; Cessi (n. 15), 228 ff.

[40] This is not quite how Aristotle presents the matter. He locates the impact of the desire at the minor premiss—rather than at the mental putting together of major and minor premisses—but this conflates *akrasia* with the sort of mistake with which *NE* 3. 1 deals, and is anyway implausible. He cannot locate the impact at the conclusion (*contra* A. Kenny, *Aristotle's Theory of the Will* (London, 1979), 161–2), since for Aristotle (in keeping with Greek cognitivism) there is no logical gap between conclusion and action (*NE* 1147^{a}25–31, *De Motu* 701^{a}8–25). Wiggins ((n. 39), 249–50) suggests that unless the gap is present, no room is left for syllogisms to compete with one another, and so for the akratic man to struggle. But the akratic man struggles—one might so put it—to *draw* the conclusion. Desire, backing the worse syllogism, interferes with his ability to hold on to the combination of major and minor premiss of the better syllogism. The syllogisms themselves are in conflict not in the sense that their conclusions actually do, in psychological reality, compete with each other—since not both conclusions are reached—but in the sense that they logically generate incompatible conclusions.

the huts and burning the ships. Achilles knows that his withdrawal
from the combat is now unjustified: Agamemnon has offered due
amends and he should accept them. But he is prevented from acting
on this knowledge by a passion which arises uncontrollably in his
heart, disabling his reason. Anger as a basis of akratic action is a
well-recognized phenomenon, and is given thorough treatment by
Aristotle (*Nicomachean Ethics* 7. 6), who points to four extenuating
features of such *akrasia*, three of which are exemplified by Achilles.
First, Aristotle writes, such *akrasia* is based on reason (*logos*) rather
than desire (*epithumia*). Achilles makes it clear that there is a reason
for his anger: it arises every time he recalls how he was slighted, and
treated as though he were a *metanastēs* (refugee) without honour.
Second, Aristotle says that anger is a natural emotion—that
obviously applies all the more to a Homeric hero, for whom anger is
the sanction of his honour. Third, it is an open, guileless emotion.
Achilles exemplifies this in the honest and straightforward way he
speaks to the embassy. Fourth, it is not pleasurable to the angry man,
but pains him. This does not apply to Achilles, who later describes
the sensation of anger as sweeter than flowing honey in the breast.
(It is in any case unclear that Aristotle is right about his fourth mark
of anger-based *akrasia*.)

Finally, when Hector faces Achilles he is overcome by fear and
turns on his heels. Again, this is a straightforward case of *akrasia*.
Hector really knows that he should go to meet Achilles: nothing else
can save him from the charge, which he fears may be levelled at him,
of having wantonly destroyed his people. But in keeping with the
cognitivist model of akratic action, Hector cannot keep hold of the
knowledge. He has to remind himself twice of his present duty (22.
108–10, 129–30), and in between these reminders he engages in a
long reflection on the possibility of trying to negotiate with Achilles.
But he really knows that negotiation would be useless, that his
reflections are pointless: the long protasis (111–21) in which he
dwells on the terms he might offer Achilles is given no apodosis.
Instead, he recalls himself to his senses. "—Ἀλλὰ τίη μοι ταῦτα
φίλος διελέξατο θυμός;" he asks (122): 'But why has my heart
spoken to me thus? If I went up to him unarmed, he would slay me
just as I am, like a woman. Now there is no way to whisper to him
from a tree or a rock like a maid and a youth, as a maid and a youth
whisper to one another. No, I must fight him, and we shall see
to which of us Zeus grants the victory.' In the whole of Hector's

soliloquy he is constantly trying to hold on to the knowledge that he must stand and face Achilles, that there is no alternative, but the knowledge is all the time slipping from him. Hector has the knowledge in one way, and in another way he does not have it (cf. *Nicomachean Ethics* 1147^{a}11–14): before the trembling seizes his limbs, he has already fallen victim to *akrasia*. He dies as a man before his body dies.[41]

V

There is surely no essential difference between the Homeric cases of *akrasia* I have described and those to be found in the plays of Euripides. Euripidean heroes possess greater powers of self-analysis; but the phenomenon which they analyse is already firmly in place in the Homeric mind. On all three counts which I have examined, Homeric decision-making stands up as a fully self-conscious, autonomous activity: the progress from Homer to the tragedians does not show a development in the area of grasp of the concept of a self. But there is, as I conceded at the beginning, *some* sort of difference between decisions made by heroes in Homer and those made by heroes in tragedy. What is it? I can only offer, in closing, some very general hints as to where I believe one should look for these differences.

The tragedians are morally more complex than Homer: more, and more difficult, factors influence the decisions of their heroes. Decision-making becomes something which is inherently difficult, and itself tragic, if its consequences are unavoidably bad however one decides. The psychology of *amēchania* emerges as a topic of increasing interest through lyric poetry to tragedy.[42] The initial moves in this

[41] It may of course be the case, as Walter Nicolai points out to me (and see his 'Wirkungsabsichten des Iliasdichters' in G. Kurz, D. Müller, and W. Nicolai (edd.), *Gnomosyne, Festchrift für Walter Marg* (Munich, 1981), 99), that Hector's reflections at 22. 111–21 hit on a policy—handing back Helen and making financial reparations—which it would have been politically intelligent to pursue; and again that his flight represents the continuation of a course of action—avoidance of combat with Achilles—which has until this point justified itself as the most practical way of defending Troy (cf. Gill (n. 22), 82 ff.). But what is decisive for Hector's *akrasia* is not what *is* the case, but what he *thinks* is the case; and his judgement, whether right or wrong, is that neither negotiation nor avoidance of combat is here and now morally possible for him. Hence his flight is an act of moral weakness.

[42] See e.g. Sappho 102, 130 L–P, Archilochus 13, 128 West, with Snell, *Szenen* (n. 1), ch. 2.

trend are already discernible in the *Odyssey*, being exemplified in Penelope's anxieties over Telemachus (4. 787 ff.), or Odysseus' uncertainty whether to punish the faithless maidservants (an uncertainty itself masking a deeper hesitation to confront the suitors on his own: 20. 1 ff.). But the cases of *amēchania* which the *Odyssey* presents lie far from tragedy. And while Achilles' decision in the *Iliad* to avenge his friend is to be sure tragic, it is so in a much simpler sense than Agamemnon's in the Hymn to Zeus, or than that of Pelasgus or Orestes. Achilles has no difficulty reaching his decision: he faces no insoluble moral dilemma with disaster threatening him on either side of the choice. All that is required of him is courage, and that is a virtue which he can unproblematically supply. The Aeschylean heroes I have mentioned, on the other hand, face dilemmas with moral demands on either side which are so compelling that the dilemmas are, even if not actually insoluble, as good as insoluble for the agents concerned. To solve them requires thought which, Pelasgus says, can go as deep as a diver: not into the soul, as Snell avers—that is not the area of search, for there is nothing to be found there—but into the *issue*, so as to make the right decision for (in Pelasgus' case) the city and the suppliants.

The soul is not the right area of search because the difficulty in a moral dilemma is a difficulty in the world and not in the self: Agamemnon balances the *objective* demands made on him by the behest of Artemis, his duty to the army, and his natural tie to his daughter. Pelasgus tries to ascertain from the suppliants whether the sons of Aegyptus have an *objective* legal claim on them. The maidens fail to satisfy him on this point, and instead threaten the city with an appalling pollution. That settles the matter for Pelasgus, who has to take the risk of future disaster in order, here and now, to avert the desecration of Zeus' altar. Orestes at the moment of crisis asks Pylades what he should do, and adds μητέρ᾽ αἰδεσθῶ κτανεῖν;— 'Should I scruple to kill my mother?' There is nothing irreducibly individual about the horror of matricide which lies behind his words: anyone in his position ought to experience the same feeling of recoil.

But there is a sense in which if a dilemma is simply insoluble then it is not tragic. That is the view implicit in Euripides' treatment of Agamemnon's dilemma in his *Iphigeneia in Aulis*. Agamemnon cannot decide what to do: there is really no means of deciding (the tension is resolved by Iphigeneia's decision) and, in Euripides' treatment, no feeling of tragedy in respect of the decision-making process itself. Agamemnon is in the position of the existentialist agent:[43] the world offers up no preponderating reason for action, the options are perfectly balanced, and so in a certain sense it does not matter what he does. Euripides shows that when *amēchania* is pushed to its limit it can actually inhibit the tragic response.

The agent who finds himself in the dilemma of Euripides' Agamemnon is not in a position of special self-awareness or autonomy: far from it. In the absence of any guidance from the side of the world, such a self is perforce thrown back on its own resources. But then a self *has* no resources of its own: it stands in permanent need of something which can only be supplied by the world—namely reasons for action, reasons which speak satisfyingly and compellingly for the courses of action to which they are keyed. The self which finds itself located in a world which does not tell it clearly and unambiguously what it must do is a poor and forlorn object, since it is not possible to conjure guidance into a world which otherwise affords none. Such a manoeuvre is no more than a shallow trick, and no respectable theory of knowledge can give it credence.[44] Euripides' Agamemnon might well envy the lot of his Homeric counterpart: for Homer's agents live in a world which repeatedly and generously serves them up preponderating reasons for action. So far from enslaving or doing away with the agent, such a world—this is the paradox of freedom—can alone set him free.[45]

---

[43] As Snell brings out in his discussion of the play in *Aischylos* (n. 1).

[44] I mean to oppose the positions taken up by Wiggins in his 'Truth, Invention and the Meaning of Life', *PBA* (1976), 331–78, and Williams in his *Ethics and the Limits of Philosophy* (London, 1985). Their respective recipes for bridging the gulf between unforthcoming world and beleaguered self—invention, confidence—only succeed in making terribly clear how unbridgeable the gulf is. If your decision is not constrained, then to the extent that it is not constrained it will be (*contra* Wiggins, 373) arbitrary. Equally, if you are not certain, it is no use pretending that you are.

[45] The paradox consists in this: when we reflect philosophically on the prerequisites for freedom, we are inclined to think that the agent must be confronted with a range of incommensurable possible courses of action, among which he is unconstrainedly free to choose, without prejudice to his rationality; but when we reflect on our actual practice, actions which are selected for preponderating reasons (actions which are *better* than their alternatives would have been) are our central cases of free, rational action. See here again Schmitt (n. 14), 213–14.

Postscript (2001). While this chapter was in proof, I learned of Viviana Cessi's tragic death. Frau Cessi's book (n. 15) on knowledge and action in Aristotle's theory of tragedy is a study of remarkable depth and power, and her untimely death is a sad loss to humane letters.

5

Divine and Human Causation in Homeric Epic

ALBIN LESKY

I

Even the most careless reader of the Homeric poems recalls numerous passages in which human behaviour is caused by the intervention of a deity. Particularly frequent in the *Iliad* are verses in which a god gives a warrior courage (*menos, tharsos*) above the norm, or else puts a stop to his frenzy, so that he turns to flight. The modes of divine operation extend from physical engagement by striking with the staff (*Iliad* 13. 59) through inspiration (ἐμπνεύειν, e.g. *Iliad* 19. 159)—a notion next door to magic—to the simple sending or inciting (ἐμβάλλειν, ἐνιέναι, ὀρνύναι, ὀτρύνειν, etc.) found in the expressions most frequently used, which say nothing about the method of transmission. The basis is experience without reflection: the warrior feels himself at one moment filled with irresistible courage, at another frustrated by fear, but in neither case does he understand the reasons. E. R. Dodds, in his famous book,[1] gives an excellent discussion of the irrational nature of this *menos* complex. There are fewer passages representing divine intervention in other mental processes. In the Embassy to Achilles Phoenix recounts how passionate indignation very nearly made him a parricide, ἀλλά τις ἀθανάτων παῦσεν χόλον ('but one of the immortals stopped his anger', 9. 459, transmitted only in Plutarch). Inhibiting thoughts of universal condemnation for such a deed are interpreted as intervention by a god. The case is not without significance for the possible ways of interpreting Homer, but as regards the present investigation it is important to note that it is in no way

[1] *The Greeks and the Irrational* (Berkeley and Los Angeles, 1951), 8–10.

typical. When Iris puts in Helen's heart sweet longing for her earlier life (Iliad 3. 139), she does that in a wholly natural way through the words that, disguised as Laodice, she speaks to her.

The most extensive group is a third, also discussed by Dodds, which might be called the atē group. The lines in which Agamemnon himself speaks of his blindness, or others do so, will be important for us later on; for the moment it is enough to notice a considerable difference between the two epics. In numerous places in the Iliad the gods' interference in human mental processes carries negative connotations. If someone behaves in a manner that cannot be rationally understood, it is said that a god has 'removed his phrenes', that is to say robbed him of his thinking part. A well-known example is Glaucus' exchange of armour with Diomedes.[2] This expression denotes essentially what we mean by saying that the perpetrator of an action must have been 'out of his mind'. The gods provoke the same outcome when they 'utterly destroy' or 'damage' a person's phrenes.[3] Such a conception is not entirely foreign to the Odyssey. When Odysseus invents his narrative of nocturnal enterprise before Troy, he relates that he had unaccountably set out without his cloak: 'a daimōn deluded me', παρὰ μ' ἤπαφε δαίμων (14. 488). Whereas in the Iliad it is the gods (all of them or particular named gods) who confuse men's thoughts, here it is the daimōn that is said to have blinded Odysseus, obviously for the lack of concreteness in the word. However, in the Odyssey the gods' usual mode of operation is the positive counterpart to their engendering of confusion in the Iliad. They do not take away the capacity to think, but supply useful thoughts at the appropriate time. When Odysseus is saved by the notion of swimming along the cliffs of Scheria until he finds a quiet bay, it came to him from Athena (5. 437). The phrase ἐπιφροσύνην δῶκε, 'gave him the idea', sounds like a complement of ἐκ φρένας εἵλετο, 'removed his wits', in Iliad 18. 311—I choose this example because there too it is Athena who is conceived as acting. It is also Athena from whom Odysseus expects the impetus to clear the armour from the hall (16. 282: ἐνὶ φρεσὶ θῆσιν, 'shall put it in my mind', another complement to removal of the phrenes); it is she too who, this time standing beside him, encourages him to test the suitors (17. 360) and gives Penelope the idea of showing herself in the

---

[2] Il. 6. 236; see too 9. 377, 18. 311, 19. 137.
[3] Il. 7.360, 12. 234, 17. 724.

men's hall (18. 158). Nor is it on a par with the Iliadic passages that
she should permit the suitors to continue indulging their insolence,
in order to feed anew her hero's angry pain (18. 346, 20. 284).
Once—it makes no difference that it is in one of his lying narratives—
Odysseus expressly says that Zeus, in a critical situation, put the
saving, if not exactly heroic, notion in his *phrenes* (14. 273).

Expression and conception are other than in the *Iliad*. It would be
imprudent to draw far-reaching conclusions from this fact about the
different intellectual attitudes of the two poems, but it deserves to be
noted none the less.

The scope of this inquiry is delimited by a range of passages in
which a person thinks a matter over for himself, or else acts in a
particular way without reflection, but also without divine intervention. That there are such cases is a well-established fact; only a few
examples can be given here. The stock example is Odysseus' soliloquy
in *Iliad* 11. 404–10.[4] The fact that Odysseus himself deliberates and
himself decides cannot be burked by explaining that, bound by the
code of nobility, he has no alternative but to hold his ground, for
some of the same formulae are used at 17. 90–105 when Menelaus
deliberates in a very similar situation, but with the opposite result: he
retreats in search of help, and leaves Patroclus' body unprotected.
Here too a human being is alone; he even contemplates the possi-
bility of fighting against a god ($\pi\rho\grave{o}s$ $\delta\alpha\acute{\iota}\mu o\nu a$, 98, 104), which in
favourable circumstances he does not regard as hopeless.

Only a passing reference need be made to the formula 'and thus
to him as he thought did it seem more advantageous' ($\mathring{\omega}\delta\epsilon$ $\delta\acute{\epsilon}/\mathring{\omega}s$
$\mathring{a}\rho a$ $o\acute{\iota}$ $\varphi\rho o\nu\acute{\epsilon}o\nu\tau\iota$ $\delta o\acute{a}\sigma\sigma a\tau o$ $\kappa\acute{\epsilon}\rho\delta\iota o\nu$ $\epsilon\mathring{\iota}\nu a\iota$).[5] It is found in both
Iliad and *Odyssey*, and always introduces a form of conduct that
results from purely human deliberation. We should note the possibility of switching between so to speak synonymous conceptions.
At *Odyssey* 22. 333–9 Phemius deliberates whether he should run
away or fling himself at Odysseus' feet; he takes the decision, as
our formula shows, entirely by himself. Odysseus, in his lying tale
to Eumaeus, is in a comparable situation (14. 266–80), but here

---

[4] Dodds (n. 1), 20 n. 31: 'a reasoned decision taken after consideration of possible
alternatives'.

[5] *Il.* 13. 458, 14. 23, 16. 652 (here it is Zeus who deliberates, in the same way as a
human being); *Od.* 5. 474, 6. 145 (good observations by H. Schwabl, 'Zur
Selbständigkeit des Menschen bei Homer', *WS* 67 (1954), 46–64 at 51), 15. 204,
18. 93, 22. 338, 24. 239.

the decision comes by way of a thought supplied to the man in distress by Zeus himself.

Perhaps more important than description of such individual cases is to observe that decisive factors of the actions are humanly determined throughout. At the beginning and the end of the course of events surrounding Achilles there is divine intervention in plenty; but at the point where he must decide Patroclus' fate and with it his own, he stands alone. In the grand structure of our *Iliad* (however it may have come into being), it is the Embassy to Achilles that determines the main characters' destiny. The path for him to return with full honour is prepared with entreaties and presents. The grand triptych of speeches goes to his heart with increasing power. To the shortest and most effective, that of Ajax, he himself replies (644–8): 'Everything you have said is agreeable to me, but my heart swells with rage when I think of how Atreus' son has treated me.' Insight into what is right does not yet allow the wrathful Achilles to leap over the wall behind which his anger has imprisoned him; all subsequent troubles have their origin here. What is played out before our eyes has only one stage, the soul of Achilles, who has knowledge and yet can do no otherwise than as his rage compels him. Not a word of the gods' being involved! Significance therefore also attached to the manner in which Phoenix (515–23) speaks of Achilles' wrath as something for which he alone is responsible: previously he could not be blamed for his anger,[6] but now it is time to renounce it. In the sequel too Achilles acts entirely on his own decisions and stimuli, when he dispatches Patroclus in his own armour and when, after the latter's death, he lays aside his anger as something with which he has no more to do. Even the unqualified urge for revenge that makes him refuse quarter to Lycaon and dishonour Hector's corpse arises from his own nature and nothing else. Only later do the gods intervene.

And what of Hector, who in the course of the battles repeatedly receives impulses from the gods and at times appears as a downright tool of the highest amongst them? His rejection of Polydamas' warnings is his blindness and his undoing, but he is in a situation decreed by Zeus, which does not save him from paying for it with his own life. But in his great hour and tragic end he is once more entirely alone. His speech to his spirit, *thumos* (22. 98) is a true soliloquy; the

---

[6] Verse 523 resumes 515–18 according to a well-known form of composition.

form of address already borders on the formulaic. The reflection that his honour debars him from retreat behind the protecting walls and that no mercy may be expected from Achilles is as much his as the decision to withstand his terrible opponent.[7] That nevertheless he then runs away shows only that the heroic world of Homer is populated by genuine human beings. That is why it is immortal.

Perhaps the independence that Homeric man preserves, for all the close connections between his world and the gods, is most clearly demonstrated when he rebels against a deity whose power he knows and feels. Helen does so in that unforgettable scene at the end of *Iliad* 3, in which she sees through the goddess's disguise and in wild revolt refuses to go to Paris' bed. The failure of her attempt, the transformation of the goddess of charm into a dangerously threatening demonic figure, and Helen's silence and abashed compliance, do not affect the point. What makes the impact here is the human being who opposes a deity in order to assert her own interest.

But does not a passage in the proem of the *Iliad* represent from the outset everything that happens in this epic as the result of the highest god's will? The words 'and Zeus' plan was fulfilled', Διὸς δ' ἐτελείετο βουλή, have been much discussed ever since the Alexandrians. Among the various proposals, assertion of a superordinate divine omnipotence is excluded by the linguistic usage of the poem. A specific plan must be intended; on that Wolfgang Kullmann is right, though I cannot accept his attempts to link this plan with the opening of the *Cypria*, in which Zeus plans to free the earth from overpopulation by means of a war.[8] Rather I agree with Von der Mühll[9] and others that the words can be taken only as a parenthetical addition to what precedes: the Achaeans' fearful losses, which began when Achilles in his wrath withdrew from the fighting, formed part of Zeus' plan, that very plan which he developed to please Thetis and revealed, as Schadewaldt showed in his *Iliasstudien*, in ever stronger manifestations. But this eliminates the possibility of interpreting the action of the *Iliad* in all its details as governed by Zeus pure and simple. The words say no more than that it was Zeus' plan to inflict severe damage on the Achaeans. Within

---

[7] Cf. J. H. Finley Jr., *Pindar and Aeschylus* (Cambridge, Mass., 1955), 186.

[8] *Philologus* 99 (1955), 167–92; 100 (1956), 132–3; *Die Quellen der Ilias* (*Hermes* Einzelschriften 14; Wiesbaden, 1960), 47 n. 2, 210.

[9] *Kritisches Hypomnema zur Ilias* (Basle, 1952), 13–14.

this framework the particular interventions of gods and the independent actions of human beings have their place.

It is worth dwelling on this proem for a moment, since it clearly illustrates the problems that concern us. Its dynamic movement merits admiration. The first word, μῆνιν, 'wrath', is a powerful announcement of the central theme that permits it to create a grandly articulated composition out of the confusion of battle. The wrath of Achilles is seen together with its fearful consequences, which are described as the working-out of the god's plan. After this mighty beginning the proem traverses the course of events backwards step by step, till it has reached the appropriate point for transition to self-contained narrative. In the dreadful slaughter lies the fulfilment of Zeus' plan, which in turn was caused by Achilles' wrath. Thus the divine intervention followed on the action of the human individual, which was rooted in his own nature. Now the chain of cause and effect is traced back further. How did the quarrel come about that led to the fateful wrath? A god, the son of Zeus and Leto, set Atreus' son and Achilles upon each other. The meaning of the somewhat indeterminate 'put together', ξυνέηκε, is revealed in the sequel: Apollo inflicted the plague on the camp, and that, as we shall later discover, set the kings at loggerheads. There is a kind of chiasmus: here the divine intervention comes first, the human strife is its consequence. The next question is the cause of Apollo's wrath. That was Agamemnon's treatment of his priest Chryses. There now comes a change of direction: the narrative begins and leads us into a way back, an ἄνω ὁδός, through the stages of the action so powerfully delineated in the proem, but now in their chronological sequence. What matters for us, however, is that the final *aition* is not an overarching plan of Zeus' but the unconsidered act of a human being who performs it not under the influence of a god, but rather in resistance to one: 'it did not please Atreus' son Agamemnon in his heart', οὐκ Ἀτρείδῃ Ἀγαμέμνονι ἥνδανε θυμῷ. Even the terms in which at 111–15 Agamemnon speaks of what has happened show that it was brought about solely and entirely by his personal will. Far be it from me to infer from this finding a privileging of human causation, but the case seems important for a true appreciation of the full range of epic possibilities.[10]

---

[10] Hermann Fränkel writes (*Early Greek Poetry and Philosophy*, trans. Moses Hadas and James Willis (Oxford, 1975), 64): 'According to Homeric belief all initiative is

Since in comparing human and divine causation we eliminate a quantity that repeatedly plays its part in epic, let me at least cite one example to show that it sometimes adds a further complication to these problems. At *Iliad* 5. 671–3 Odysseus deliberates whether to pursue the wounded Sarpedon or turn against the mass of the Lycians. As in some other cases,[11] a divinity intervenes in human deliberation and brings about a decision: at 674–6 Athena is said to have turned Odysseus' courage against the Lycians. But she acts not directly, but through Odysseus; and beyond her a third level is revealed when it is said not to have been fated, μόρσιμον, for Odysseus that he should kill Zeus' son. Thus the Athena who exercises an effect on Odysseus turns out to be the executant of a decree to which she too is subject. The passage shows how many layers of agency must be considered when the concept of fate is involved. In those portions of the poems which concern us that is not usually the case, so that for our purposes we may ignore the much-discussed problem of the relation between fate and personal gods. In general I agree with Martin Nilsson[12] and many other modern scholars that there were two originally coexisting sets of conceptions that subsequently came of necessity into conflict with each other.

II

I turn now to passages hitherto unjustly neglected in discussion of these questions, in which logical separation of the factors is difficult, sometimes even impossible. I begin with the introduction to the final *aristeia* vouchsafed Patroclus before his death. Gisela Strasburger, in her study of the lesser warriors in the *Iliad*,[13] calls 16. 684–91 difficult. It is precisely what we find surprising here that leads us to the heart of the problem. Patroclus incites horses and charioteer to pursue the fleeing Trojans and Lycians. Here the poet very carefully describes the point at which Patroclus, like Hector and Achilles, falls victim to disaster, since he does not know moderation and has not the wit to obey a timely warning. Homer calls him a fool and speaks

reserved for the gods'; but he rightly stresses in n. 1 that this does not fit the proem of the *Il.*, 'for the chain of causes and effects begins before Apollo's intervention'.

[11] e.g. *Il.* 1. 194, 8. 169, 10. 507.
[12] *Geschichte der griechischen Religion* I (3rd edn., Munich, 1967), 364–5.
[13] Diss. Frankfurt (1957), 57 n. 1.

of his delusion. Had he heeded the warning word of Peleus' son, he would have escaped the grim fate of death.

So far the action has evolved from Patroclus' thought and will, in short from inside him; we too should describe it in the same terms. But in the very next verse (688) Zeus comes into play, and now what happens to Patroclus is described as the outcome of his plan. His mind is always mightier than men. In this case he has removed all obstacles to the *thumos* in Patroclus' breast. What is meant by saying that Zeus' *noos* is stronger than human beings? We have not been told that Patroclus deliberated and hesitated at the recollection of his friend's warning; even before Zeus was mentioned, he was on the high road to destruction in the fullness of his infatuation. Gisela Strasburger drew the right conclusion from these lines: Patroclus' infatuation is the will of Zeus. What takes place within the man and what the god wills and brings to pass are united in a way that defies any rational partition but, in my opinion, represents an essential trait of the Homeric world-picture.

The reader might object that this conception of the passage is a modern interpretation, and require testimonies that put such an interaction of human and divine causation beyond all doubt. These are not lacking.

I have already expressed the view that the Embassy is the decisive portion of the *Iliad*, understood as an *Achilleis*; above all Achilles' answer to the last of the three ambassadors' speeches seemed important for its admission of his inner processes. I shall now look back at his dialogue with Phoenix and the previous one with Odysseus, which in accordance with a Homeric technique explained by Schadewaldt does not bring about any advance towards reconciliation, but rather a further setback, since Achilles threatens to depart. The poetry of the nations has few such scenes to show: on the one side the man who hates hypocrisy like the gates of hell (9. 312), on the other the experienced diplomat, he too a nobleman, but from another world. There is no escaping the shrillness of the dissonance. Now Phoenix must loosen the soil. He employs childhood reminiscences and paraenesis by allegory and exemplum. After shooting all his bolts, he can venture on the decisive appeal (9. 600–1):

ἀλλὰ σὺ μή μοι ταῦτα νόει φρεσί, μηδέ σε δαίμων
ἐνταῦθα τρέψειε, φίλος.

But do not, I beg you, harbour such thoughts in your mind, and may no *daimōn* turn you that way, my friend.

It is significant that Richmond Lattimore translates these lines:

Listen then; do not have such a thought in your mind; let not the spirit within you turn you that way, dear friend.[14]

The modern translator finds the dual causality unfamiliar and attempts to eliminate it by making the *daimōn* another power operating inside the human being. That is of course un-Homeric, for the *daimōn* operates from outside the human being's internal *phrenes*, from the divine world. To be sure these realms are usually felt in Homer as complementary, not as fundamentally opposed (though Apollo's words at *Iliad* 5. 440–2 ought not to be forgotten), but for that very reason there is no attempt to harmonize them by projecting everything into the human being's inner life. Modern perplexity at this passage is also betrayed in W. H. D. Rouse's attempt to render *daimōn* by 'fortune': 'let not fortune turn you into that path'.[15]

To interpret the passage correctly we must bear in mind that the sequence μή . . . μηδέ does not introduce alternatives, but closely cohering terms that belong together and complement each other. Among several examples[16] I choose that nearest to our passage, 9. 522–3. To Achilles have come the best and dearest to him of the Achaeans: τῶν μὴ σύ γε μῦθον ἐλέγξῃς μηδὲ πόδας ('do not put to shame their speech or their journey' [lit. 'feet']).

No linguistic commentary is required by a second passage, which belongs in our context and demonstrates an inseparable connection between divine and human causation. After the ambassadors' return the Achaeans are deeply depressed; a cheerful word is needed to revive their spirits. It is uttered by Diomedes: they should leave Achilles in his pride and not anxiously await his return to the ranks of the warriors (702–3):

$$τότε δ' αὖτε μαχήσεται, ὁππότε κέν μιν$$
$$θυμὸς ἐνὶ στήθεσσιν ἀνώγῃ καὶ θεὸς ὄρσῃ.$$

---

[14] *The Iliad of Homer* (Chicago, 1951).

[15] *The Iliad* (London, 1938; New York, 1950).

[16] *Il.* 1. 550, 19. 306, 21. 99, 22. 345, 23. 443, 24. 218–19; *Od.* 2. 230–1 = 5. 8–9, 5. 160–1, 11. 339–40, 16. 457–9, 17. 46–7, 23. 213. There is a different nuance in such cases as *Il.* 6. 57–9, *Od.* 24. 174, where μηδέ is intensifying; but here too there is an amplification of the thought, not an alternative.

He will fight again when the *thumos* in his breast commands him and a god incites him.

We may note in passing that in regard to the menacing notion of Achilles' departure for home there is reference to the *daimón*, whereas for his desired return to the war the driving force is the *theos*. This is one of the passages in which a nuance seems observable. In any case the clear and straightforward utterance in this line leaves no doubt that a human being's internal stimuli and divine intervention merge in the same action, which is motivated in both spheres.

Closest to these passages is a line spoken by Odysseus to Eurycleia (*Odyssey* 19. 485) and Penelope to Odysseus (*Odyssey* 23. 260);

$$\mathrm{\mathring{a}\lambda\lambda' \; \mathring{\epsilon}\pi\epsilon\mathgrave{\iota} \; \mathring{\epsilon}\varphi\rho\acute{a}\sigma\theta\eta\varsigma \; \kappa\alpha\acute{\iota} \; \tau o\iota \; \theta\epsilon\grave{o}\varsigma \; \mathring{\epsilon}\mu\beta\alpha\lambda\epsilon \; \theta\upsilon\mu\tilde{\omega}}$$

But now that you have bethought yourself and a god has put it in your *thumos*.

To render *kaí* by 'since' would be completely to miss the Homeric way of seeing things. The two parts of this utterance denote a whole, or if you will two sides of a whole. This collaboration between human being and deity is expressed somewhat differently at *Iliad* 15. 403, where Patroclus, before attempting to get Achilles to intervene, says to Eurypylus: 'who knows whether by speaking to him I may not σὺν δαίμονι ('with a *daimōn*') have an effect upon his *thumos*?' Similarly Telemachus at *Odyssey* 2. 372 consoles Eurycleia by saying that his resolution to sail in search of news is made οὔ τοι ἄνευ θεοῦ (not without a god). Odysseus too devises death for the suitors σὺν Ἀθήνῃ ('with Athena'; *Odyssey* 19. 2, 52). We are not so very far from German *mit Gott* ('with God', i.e. 'with God's help'); that is to say, the phenomenon we have observed in Homer is not divided by an unbridgeable gulf from our own possibilities of speech and thought, since we too dispense often enough with a strict logical division between the two spheres.

A veritable model for a series of similar cases is provided by *Odyssey* 13. 121, where the poet says that the gifts brought by Odysseus to Ithaca were given him by the Phaeacians διὰ μεγάθυμον Ἀθήνην (on account of Athena of the mighty *thumos*). That the goddess took an active part in no way annuls the gesture of noble generosity carried out by the Phaeacians.

This dual causation is as it were reflected in reverse when the human being takes note both of the gods' command and a fellow

human being's distress. Thus at *Iliad* 24. 503–4 Priam bids Achilles
have respect for the gods and take pity on him for the thought of his
own father. There is an exact correspondence at *Odyssey* 14. 389
when Eumaeus tells Odysseus he will show him kindness Δία ξένιον
δείσας αὐτόν τ᾽ ἐλεαίρων (fearing Zeus of the Stranger and pitying
you yourself).

Hermann Fränkel made the important observation that for
Homeric man body and soul are not distinguished as they are for us:
'Arms are as much an organ of the man himself, rather than of his
body, as *thymos* (the organ of excitement) is an organ of the man,
himself, rather than of his soul. The whole man is equally alive in all
his parts.'[17] It goes together with this that expressions concerning
the dual origin of an event, such as we have found in a psychological
context, return in exactly the same way for the strength and the
warriors and the effect of their weapons. Intermediate is *Iliad* 15. 636
ὣς τότ᾽ Ἀχαιοί | θεσπεσίως ἐφόβηθεν ὑφ᾽ Ἕκτορι καὶ Διὶ
πατρί (so then the Achaeans were wondrously put to panic by
Hector and father Zeus). This refers both to the physical fact of flight
and to the feeling of terror that caused it. Similar is the account of
Tydeus, who challenged the Cadmeans θυμὸν ἔχων ὃν κάρτερον
(5. 806: 'having his own mighty *thumos*'), but is helped to victory by
Athena. Here the impulse comes from within, but the deity plays a
part in the outcome.

Against these passages with a partial distinction, there stand a
number of others in which we are simply told that So-and-so prevailed together with a deity or was laid low by his opponent and a
god.[18] Some examples express this paratactically, 'man and god'.
Diomedes says at *Iliad* 6. 228 that there are Trojans enough for him
to kill, ὅν κε θεός γε πόρῃ καὶ ποσσὶ κιχείω (whomever a god
shall provide and I can catch). At *Iliad* 16. 103 Ajax is beset by the
noos of Zeus and the excellent Trojans. *Iliad* 20. 192, Achilles captured Lyrnessos with Athena and Father Zeus, has the same implication and recalls the *mit Gott* type discussed above. Nothing is said
in these passages about the nature of the divine assistance; but at
Iliad 20. 94–6 the narrative is more specific: Aeneas nearly fell by the
hands of Achilles and Athena; the goddess went before Achilles to

---

[17] (n. 10), 77.
[18] Examples in W. Kullmann, *Das Wirken der Götter in der Ilias* (Berlin, 1956),
108, including the important verse *Il.* 9. 702.

help him and incited him to kill the Trojans and Leleges. This is a halfway house to places where we see God and man physically collaborating: Patroclus is brought down by Apollo, Euphorbus, and Hector; Achilles will be slain by Paris and Apollo (*Iliad* 22. 359–60). Fighting apart, there is a remarkable passage in the simile *Iliad* 5. 499–502: men winnow grain and Demeter separates corn from chaff in the blowing wind. Her activity here comes very close to the essence of the notorious particular deities of the Romans, who are considered to perform a specific action.

In another not uncommon way of speaking, which might be called hypotactic, the god achieves his purpose through human activity. Here too we may observe variations. When Alcathous falls, we read τὸν τόθ᾽ ὑπ᾽ Ἰδομενῆι Ποσειδάων ἐδάμασσεν (*Iliad* 13. 434; 'him then Poseidon slew by Idomeneus'). Poseidon uses Idomeneus like a tool, but plays a part himself: he dazzles Alcathous and binds his limbs, so that he stands immobile like a pillar or a tree.[19] We may compare *Iliad* 22. 444–6, where Andromache, preparing the bath for Hector, does not yet know that Athena has overcome him by the hands of Achilles. The goddess was of a surety not idle in the process: in the guise of Deiphobus she entices Hector into combat and as a busy helper she gives Achilles back his lance after the first throw. But when at *Iliad* 16. 543 we read of Sarpedon τὸν δ᾽ ὑπὸ Πατρόκλῳ δάμασ᾽ ἔγχεϊ χάλκεος Ἄρης (him brazen Ares slew by Patroclus with the spear), and then return to the battle scene leading up to his death, we find no trace of divine intervention, but (if the expression be permissible for so gruesome an event) everything passes off quite naturally. Without being fully formulaic, the verse comes close to 'He was killed by Patroclus in battle.' We may cite as parallels *Iliad* 3. 352, 6. 368, 15. 613–14. The *Odyssey* has little occasion to speak thus; but this mode of expression is attested at 18. 155.

I have reserved for separate discussion a highly characteristic example from the *Iliad*, since it can take us a step further. Before the decisive duel Achilles calls out to Hector: 'There, is no escape left; Pallas Athena is about to slay you by my lance' (22. 270–1). This certainly does not mean that the gods can make a weapon especially effective or direct a missile to its target; the line says no more than σὺν Ἀθήνῃ at *Iliad* 20. 192, *Odyssey* 19. 2. Things are somewhat

[19] On the scene see Wolf H. Friedrich, *Verwundung und Tod in der Ilias; Homerische Darstellungsweisen* (Abh. Ak. Gött, Phil.-hist. Kl., 3rd ser., 38; Göttingen, 1956), 17.

different in Diomedes' *aristeia*, though he is also assisted by the goddess. His boldest exploit is the attack on Ares; it is here that Athena has most to do. She diverts the god's lance from Diomedes and when he thrusts she takes a hand and reinforces him; note the vivid ἐπέρεισε (gave added thrust) in *Iliad* 5. 856. True, here a man is fighting against a god, which is impossible without such reinforcement, but the scene has a very important parallel. The zenith of Hector's victorious career, and the nadir of the Achaeans' fortunes, is his attack on Protesilaus' ship. Not surprisingly, the poet lays great stress on it. When Hector charges the ship, the god gives assistance from behind: τὸν δὲ Ζεὺς ὦσεν ὄπισθεν | χειρὶ μάλα μεγάλῃ (15. 694–5; 'and Zeus propelled him from behind with his most mighty hand'). After all that has been said, we shall not agree with Nilsson in asserting that the poet here has plainly gone off the rails.[20] Gods can help in very drastic ways; besides, Zeus does much the same as Athena did in the *Diomedeia*. The verb ἐπέρεισε could be said of him as well. Whether the poet intended us to see Zeus in the flesh and physically feel the pressure of his mighty hand, or the frequent formula of the helping god is simply given additional emphasis, cannot now be determined; but far from a derailment, I see here a case in which the collaboration of man and god is laid before us to observe directly: Ἕκτωρ ἴθυσε ἀντίος ἀΐξας . . . Ζεὺς ὦσεν (Hector made straight for [the ship], rushing towards it . . . Zeus propelled).

Essentially the same is another kind of reinforcement, when Achilles at *Iliad* 18. 217–18 utters his fearful cries to scare the Trojans, but Athena also shouts from a distance and considerably increases the effect. Such divine support is there and not there in a moment: in 228 it is Achilles alone who cries out three times. Somewhat different, more of a merging, at bottom a united action by two parties is the simultaneous shouting by Eris and Agamemnon at the beginning of *Iliad* 11.[21]

Having shown earlier that this collaboration and mutuality between man and god is no less present in the physical sphere than in the mental (not that they are fundamentally distinct in Homer), we may now cite examples in which such reinforcement takes place in the latter sphere. In *Iliad* 8 the Achaeans need to be summoned to energetic resistance in a dangerous situation; Hera puts that thought into Agamemnon's mind αὐτῷ ποιπνύσαντι (8. 219: 'himself

---

[20] (n. 12), I. 370.   [21] Impressively interpreted by Fränkel (n. 10), 64–5.

having laboured'). Again: in Nestor's narrative Athena gives the Pylians the alarm: οὐδ' ἀέκοντα Πύλον κάτα λαὸν ἄγειρεν | ἀλλὰ μάλ' ἐσσυμένους πολεμίζειν (11. 716–17: 'and all over Pylos she roused the people, not unwilling, but hastening to the fray'). In *Odyssey* 1 Athena builds up Telemachus in every way she can. She gives him *menos* and *tharsos* and causes him to think of his father μᾶλλον ἔτ' ἢ τὸ πάροιθεν (322: 'even more than before'). Here, then, it is not a new impulse that originates with the deity, but something already present is increased by divine intervention. Human action is not simultaneously a god's, but the one strengthens the other, which would attain its end without such intervention.

Such reinforcement is occasionally found in larger contexts. In the assembly of elders in *Iliad* 2 Agamemnon announces that he will test the army by inviting it to flee; the leaders ought then to hold the masses back with timely words (75). The event is thus adequately prepared and would need no further causation for us to understand it. But when what Agamemnon has foreseen takes place, we are told a different story (155–6): 'Then would the Achaeans' return have been achieved in despite of fate, had not Hera addressed Athena.' Now it is the gods who operate and set Odysseus in motion. One and the same action is thus both prepared by human beings and furthered by divine reinforcement.

We have on several occasions been able to distinguish between immediate and tangible intervention by the deity and cases at least well on the way to a general formula for divine collaboration. Undoubtedly the greatest caution is needed in attempting to deduce patterns of evolution, but we may venture to suggest that the ancient and original element is the belief in the direct interference of gods who appear in person, stand by their protégés in battle, and can safeguard and advance a hero's life in the way the metopes at Olympia show for Heracles and Athena. The goddess, helping the strong man carry the vault of heaven with an easy movement of her hand, also affords a marvellous illustration of several epic scenes. That the conceptions interpreted here have a long history is evident from the wealth of variants in Homer. It is very probable that such a very ancient belief has its roots in the Mycenaean beginnings of heroic song. This may be supported by the consideration that in the *Iliad* and above all in the *Odyssey* by far the most prominent helper of heroes in their exploits is Athena, from whose function as warrior house-goddess of the Mycenaean palace this role is a natural

development. The Athena who in *Odyssey* 7. 81 enters the strong
house of Erechtheus will also have shared strife and danger with her
castellan. Nilsson has demonstrated the transition from the Mycenaean goddess of the palace to the Athena of epic with admirable
clarity.[22]

Furthermore it must have been very early that the belief developed, which is deeply embedded in the Greek gods' essence, that the
whole world is full of their activity, and that something may be
perceived or recognized in everything that happens, be it in nature or
human action and suffering.

In the course of these remarks, divergent interpretations have
already needed comment. First of all, it has become clear that I
strongly disagree with Nilsson's statement, still to be found in the
third edition of his *Geschichte der griechischen Religion*:[23] 'The divine
apparatus is a poetic construct that is worked to death.' I concur with
Hans Schwabl's protest,[24] and find the truth to be stated on the
closing pages of Bruno Snell's chapter 'The Olympian Gods'.[25]
Likewise it goes without saying that I regard as a monstrosity the
assertion of so outstanding a scholar as Paul Mazon: 'the truth is that
there was never a poem less religious than the *Iliad*'.[26] But that is not
the end of my disagreements. Dodds, in his famous book,[27] discusses
Iliad 9. 702–3, the passage on which I have laid so much stress, and
explains the double causation as 'over-determination'. In his most
recent and no less important work on the *Oresteia* he holds that such
over-determination is to be found in Homer. I agree with Schwabl
that that is not a sufficient account of this and other passages,[28] but
am unwilling to speak with Kullmann of a pre-established harmony
between divine will and human action.[29] Even if we chose to indulge
in the terminology of another age, it would hardly convey the fusion
of the two, as indeed Kullmann shows elsewhere in his book that he
understands full well.

On relating the above material to modern notions, we may discern
some definite gradations. Divine intervention added to human
action, gods who come to their heroes' aid, are notions that we can

---

[22] (n. 12), I. 345.   [23] Ibid. 371.   [24] (n. 5), 46.

[25] *The Discovery of the Mind*, trans. T. G. Rosenmeyer (Oxford, 1953), 40–2.

[26] *Introduction à l'Iliade* (Paris, 1948), 294.

[27] (n. 1), 16; cf. 'Morals and Politics in the *Oresteia*', PCPS 186 (1960), 27 = *The
Ancient Concept of Progress* (Oxford, 1973), 56–7.

[28] (n. 5), 57.   [29] (n. 18), 107.

more or less replicate. But that one and the same action, such as Achilles' departure for home or return to the fray can be brought about in equal but unlike ways by the human being and the god, is a unified conception that defies analysis with our logical tools. Such a range of ideas, all yet presupposing that all human life is filled with the divine, may be encountered in Homer with regard to a closely related topic, the bestowing of gifts on human beings by the gods. At bottom the passages about *menos* are relevant here: the god gives the ecstatic battle-rage, but it is the man who then performs the unheard-of deed.

In this world, it is taken for granted that men receive special abilities from the gods. We encounter expressions that indicate direct teaching by the god of the person so endowed. Artemis herself ($a\dot{v}\tau\dot{\eta}$) taught Scamandrius how to shoot every kind of game (*Iliad* 5. 51–2), an experienced carpenter owes his art to Athena's instructions ($\dot{v}\pi o\theta\eta\mu o\sigma\dot{v}\nu\eta\sigma\iota\nu$: *Iliad* 15. 411–12), Antilochus learnt many skills of horsemanship from Zeus and Poseidon because they were fond of him (*Iliad* 23. 306–8); and it absolutely goes without saying that the singer has his gifts of enchantment from the deity (*Odyssey* 8. 64, 481, 498). But in this context there is a passage in which the joint operation of the human and the divine cannot be simply analysed into the roles of giver and receiver. When Phemius begs for his life after the slaughter of the suitors, he appeals to the sacrality and dignity of the singer (*Odyssey* 22. 347–8):

αὐτοδίδακτος δ' εἰμί, θεὸς δέ μοι ἐν φρεσὶν οἴμας
παντοίας ἐνέφυσεν·

I am self-taught, a god implanted manifold paths of song in my mind.

Dodds's explanation is that Phemius 'has not memorised the lays of other minstrels, but is a creative poet who relies on the hexameter phrases welling up spontaneously as he needs them out of some unknown and uncontrollable depth'.[30] He may be right, and is certainly so when he declares: 'The two parts of his statement are not felt as contradictory.' We may go further: what Phemius feels welling up from the depth of his being as he sings is at the same time the gift of the god. Both parts of the statement belong to the same whole.

---

[30] (n. 1), 10. I afterwards discovered that Kurt Latte, 'Hesiods Dichterweihe', *Antike und Abendland* 2 (1946), 154 = *Kleine Schriften* (Munich, 1968), 63 gave the same

We meet the same fusion again at *Odyssey* 8. 44–5 in respect of Demodocus:

$$τῷ γάρ ῥα θεὸς περὶ δῶκεν ἀοιδήν$$
$$τέρπειν, ὅππη θυμὸς ἐποτρύνῃσιν ἀείδειν.$$

For the god has granted him song in abundance, to give delight howsoever his *thumos* stirs him to sing.

That is, he sings under the impulse of his *thumos* and on the basis of endowment given by the god. Both mean the same thing. A similar two-part expression occurs at *Iliad* 5. 53: Scamandrius is killed by Menelaus' spear; Artemis patroness of arrows availed him nothing, nothing his skill in archery.

At this point we must ask what the poet means us to imagine when he says that carpenters, archers, charioteers, and singers are taught by a god, and occasionally adds that the god himself (αὐτός) was the teacher. Should we in every case posit a procedure like that described in Pindar's *Thirteenth Olympian*, in which Athena, by instructions in a dream and the gift of a bridle, bestows on Bellerophon the ability to tame Pegasus?[31] Should we, in Antilochus' case, suppose that Zeus and Poseidon in person took the trouble to impart special aptitudes in driving a team to him? Or have these expressions already become formulae, meaning no more than that the divine masters show themselves 'somehow' in an exceptional skill?[32] We are on dangerous ground here and must unreservedly admit that solid knowledge is denied us. Nevertheless the assumption of an empty phrase is no less questionable than the assertion that behind every one of these expressions is a circumstantial story, not told here, of personal instruction of a human being by a deity. Perhaps the right answer—and an essential fact for Homer—is this. There is a fully live belief that a god, if it so pleases him, may give direct instruction to a mortal; on the other hand this notion is so

explanation, and also saw the wider context: 'Every instance of intellectual spontaneity appears in this age in a double aspect: it represents something inside one, but at the same time is the effect of a divine power that imparts it to the human being.'

[31] See Nikolaos Yalouris, 'Athena als Herrin der Pferde', *MH* 7 (1950), 19–101.

[32] Moderns can speak the same way. Ernst Penzoldt in his splendid novel *Die Powenzbande*, 68: 'these two young misses seemed to have been personally instructed by a Loving God in the most delightful passion'.

familiar and so loosely defined that a mortal with special gifts may be said without more ado to have been instructed by a deity. The speaker need not have a specific deity in mind in every case; that does not make the phrase an empty formula.

If this explanation is on the right lines, there is a solution to what for our logic is a blatant contradiction in Homer. At *Iliad* 15. 440–1 Ajax exhorts Teucer to take a hand: 'What have you done with your swift and deadly arrows, and the bow that Phoebus Apollo gave you?' There is no hint of such a tale as Virgil implies behind his tale of the endowing of Iapyx (*Aeneid* 12. 392–4). The passage can hardly be understood otherwise than those previously discussed, in which a human being is instructed by a deity. Something that in itself would be perfectly conceivable has simply become an expression for a special talent or a special weapon. Now in *Iliad* 2. 827 we hear that Apollo himself (αὐτός) gave his bow to Pandarus too. Later on (*Iliad* 4. 105–11), where we must have as clear a picture as possible of the weapon that will send the fateful arrow, we are told something different. Pandarus himself had shot the ibex from whose horns he had had a skilled craftsman make his bow. The size of the horns, the activity of the artisan as he carves and polishes, are described in detail. We appear compelled to register a contradiction; sure enough, Denys Page cited our passage among the discrepancies that in his view separated the Trojan catalogue in Book 2 from the rest of the *Iliad*.[33] But if we interpret the bestowing of the bow on Pandarus in the same way as that on Teucer and set both within the framework expounded here, then for the Homeric way of looking at things and speaking of them there is no contradiction.[34]

III

Between the free action of human beings and exclusive causation by the gods we have traversed a wide field in which the two spheres meet, intersect, and in several cases fully coincide. Only here is it true that, as Cedric H. Whitman elegantly puts it, 'There were few places

---

[33] *History and the Homeric Iliad* (Sather Classical Lectures, 31; Berkeley and Los Angeles, 1959), 140.
[34] In this I agree with Kullmann (n. 18), 58, who likewise denies there is a contradiction.

indeed where an ancient Greek could look and fail to see, not the work of God, but a god; and this is why everything in the *Iliad* happens twice, once on earth, and once in the timeless world of deity.'[35] However, we have been careful not to neglect the wealth of variations of which Homer is capable: to the cases in which divine and human are fully fused are opposed others in which the two stand apart, or the one may take the other's place. It is with these that we shall be concerned in what follows.

I have already remarked that when a deity confers assistance on human activity, whether physically or through an unexplained influence, there is automatically a certain distinction between the two spheres. In this connection we may quote a striking passage in *Iliad* 20, where a great hero's dependence on the gods is slightly qualified. Aeneas complains that Achilles always has one of the gods at his side to ward off harm, but then adds καὶ δ' ἄλλως τοῦ γ' ἰθὺ βέλος πέτετ(αι) (and apart from that his javelin always flies straight). Even without divine help, relying purely on himself, a mighty hero can achieve much.

A remarkable interplay between the divine gift and the performance left to the human being is demonstrated by Peleus' warning to Achilles as he sets off for war (*Iliad* 9. 254-6): 'My son, victorious strength Athena and Hera will give you, if they so wish, but do you μεγαλήτορα θυμόν | ἴσχειν ἐν στήθεσσι (restrain the great-hearted *thumos* in your breast).' The one is dependent on divine pleasure, the other the human being is expected to perform by his own effort.

At bottom, the gods themselves respect this sphere of human freedom. Occasionally they express it with the utmost urbanity by adding the phrase αἴ κε πίθηαι (provided you agree) to their warning or advice.[36] Athena uses it when she subdues Achilles' fury in his quarrel with Agamemnon (*Iliad* 1. 207); Poseidon when he advises the hero in a tight spot (*Iliad* 21. 293). It exactly matches human conversation (*Iliad* 23. 82, Patroclus' *eidōlon* speaking); Athena too uses it to Telemachus when in human form (*Odyssey* 1. 279). Certainly it is extremely ill advised to set at naught a warning, however courteously expressed, from the mouth of a god. Achilles

---

[35] *Homer and the Heroic Tradition* (Cambridge, Mass., 1958), 248.
[36] See Schwabl (n. 5), 49–50, who convincingly refutes the notion of conventional politeness.

says so himself *(Iliad* I. 216–17), in correct recognition: ὡς γὰρ ἄμεινον (it is better thus). But the possibility of disobeying a god's warning, of hardening the heart against a god's advice is demonstrated by Aegisthus' road to perdition. I shall have more to say on the proem of the *Odyssey* below.

Noteworthy, and consistent with my observations above on the different modes of divine intervention in the *Iliad* and the *Odyssey*, is the more frequent and sharper distinction of the two spheres in the later poem. At the beginning of Book 3 Telemachus confesses his young man's bashfulness about approaching the venerable old man, and Mentor-Athena reassures him (26–7): ἄλλα μὲν αὐτὸς ἐνὶ φρεσὶ σῇσι νοήσεις, | ἄλλα δὲ καὶ δαίμων ὑποθήσεται (some things [to say] you will think of yourself in your own mind, others a *daimōn* will suggest to you). The Iliadic passage discussed above (20. 99) is a step on the road to such a distinction, but there is hardly a genuine parallel for it in the older poem. We also know cases in the *Iliad* where a god's intervention puts a stop to human deliberations and brings about a decision. In the *Odyssey* this seems on one occasion to take place in reverse. In Book 1 Athena has shown Telemachus a way out of his troubles; at the end of the book we see him restlessly considering all night the words of his adviser, of whose nature he is aware (323). In this context, too, belong words spoken in Sparta by Helen, once more the noble glory of Menelaus' house: the Trojan women wept loudly when Odysseus killed many men on his successive spying mission, but she rejoiced ἐπεὶ ἤδη μοι κραδίη τέτραπτο νέεσθαι | ἂψ οἰκόνδ(ε) (4. 260–1; 'because already my heart was turned to going back home again'). In Helen's inner being, then, a change had taken place, which she describes thus: ἄτην δὲ μετέστενον, ἣν Ἀφροδίτη | δῶχ', ὅτε μ' ἤγαγε κεῖσε φίλης ἀπὸ πατρίδος αἴης (and I wept for regret at the infatuation that Aphrodite gave me, when she conveyed me there from my own fatherland). The passage is highly important for the possibilities of dividing the emphasis between the two spheres. Helen claims her change of affection to home and husband, and in consequence her affirmation of her present life, entirely for herself: 'my heart turned'. Her previous conduct was Aphrodite's doing; she had sent Ate upon her and set her upon the fateful path. We should not be prejudiced by false notions of Homeric primitivity into missing the refinement of this distinction, but the very fact of its possibility is important for our purpose. It is rather different, and comparable with such Iliadic

passages as the Diapeira (the Testing of the Army in Book 2),
when one and the same action is presented first as performed by a
human being, and then as having been caused by a god. In *Odyssey*
19 Penelope tells the beggar of her resolution, her own resolution,
to let her fate be decided the next day by the trial of the bow, but at
the beginning of Book 21 we are told that Athena puts it in
her mind to arrange the contest. This study would have been
written in vain if a follower of the analytical school were to posit a
contradiction.

Human and divine action are strikingly distinguished at one place
in the Nekuia (*Odyssey* 11. 272–3): Epikaste, albeit unwittingly, did a
fearsome deed by marrying her son, but the gods made it known
among men.

Ever since Werner Jaeger's important article,[37] particular attention has been paid to the proem of the *Odyssey*. It cannot be ignored
in our context either, for in it Zeus emphatically dissociates himself
and the world of the gods from the activity of men. If we may call
Zeus' speech a theodicy, it is only so in part; to that extent Nilsson's
objection is valid.[38] With all clarity Zeus indicates (34–5) that he is
speaking of those sufferings that individuals have to endure above
their fated measure ($\dot{\upsilon}\pi\grave{\epsilon}\rho$ $\mu\acute{o}\rho o\nu$) because their actions too have
been 'above measure', such as Aegisthus' adultery and murder. In
such cases of excess, the gods may also appear as admonishers. In
principle, Hermes' role in warning Aegisthus is not entirely different
from Athena's warning in *Iliad* 1 to Achilles, who in drawing his
sword against Agamemnon is about to act 'above measure'. The
difference in nature and worth of the persons warned governs the
difference in outcome. But within each individual's measure there
remains a wide scope for god and man to collaborate in success and
failure. It is absolutely not my intention to devalue the importance of
recognizing that Zeus' speech in the proem of the *Odyssey* sounds
new notes of reflection on divine governance and human fate, and
therefore occupies a significant place in the development of Greek
thought. However, I have attempted to show that it is not a revolution, but that the notion already attested in the *Iliad* of a thing's
happening $\dot{\upsilon}\pi\grave{\epsilon}\rho$ $\mu\acute{o}\rho o\nu$ (2. 155 $\dot{\upsilon}\pi\acute{\epsilon}\rho\mu o\rho a$, 20. 30, 21. 517) or $\dot{\upsilon}\pi\grave{\epsilon}\rho$
$a\hat{\imath}\sigma a\nu$ (16. 780, 17. 321) has been applied to the sphere of religion

---

[37] 'Solons Eunomie', SB Berlin 1926, 69–85 = *Scripta Minora* (Rome, 1960), I.
315–37.   [38] (n. 12), I. 363.

and ethics. That is not in total contradiction to the other conceptions examined here.

Naturally, the division between human and divine causation is most clearly seen when someone asks whether this or that event was caused by a man or a god. Here the *Odyssey* offers a whole series of examples. A good illustration is 9. 339, where Odysseus relates that the Cyclops, in the night before the crucial event, had driven all his beasts into the cave ἤ τι ὀϊσάμενος ἢ καὶ θεὸς ὣς ἐκέλευεν (either having had an idea or indeed [because] a god had bidden him so do).

Similar are 4. 712–13, 7. 263, 14. 178–9, 16. 356, of which the second passage merits additional remark on account of its charming point. Whereas Odysseus only speculates whether Calypso has received a message from Zeus or has let him go from her own change of heart, the listener knows that the former was true and that Calypso did not mention it because she wished the beloved man to take for a generous action (5. 190–1) what was really enforced obedience to a command of the supreme god. With incomparable facility and refinement the poet draws attention to these complexities when at 5. 195–6 he makes Odysseus sit on the same chair from which the gods' messenger had arisen a short while earlier.[39]

---

[39] Such refinements are characteristic of the poet of the *Od*. Of this kind is his taste for ironical play when gods appear in human form. The game is played at especial length in Book 3. Athena receives the golden cup from Nestor (40) and is now required to pour a libation to Poseidon and pray to him. When she obediently does so and very nicely prays first for Nestor's lineage and asks a blessing on the Pylians, she yet does not omit to beg success for her own enterprise, in which Odysseus is concerned—from her angry uncle, of all possible gods to pray to. It is also charming to see her, disguised as Mentor, utter the somewhat blasphemous remark to Telemachus that Nestor's ill wish for the suitors could not be fulfilled οὐδ' εἰ θεοὶ ὣς ἐθέλοιεν (3. 228; 'not even if the gods wished it so'), when Nestor has just held up Athena's help as the decisive factor for success! The goddess also takes care not to miss the opportunity, when she calls for the evening libation, of mentioning not only Poseidon but also the other gods, and therefore herself amongst them (3. 333). That is at any rate the first draft for Callimachus' Apollo, who swears by himself (fr. 114. 5); see Rudolf Kassel, *RM* 101 (1958), 235. For Athena cf. too 2. 433, 3. 135, 13. 121. From the *Il*. we may cite 17. 561–2: encouraged by Athena in the guise of Phoenix, Menelaus replies: 'My dear Phoenix, if only Athena would give me strength and help me!' But here the point is less ironical effect than Menelaus' piety and his close relation to his divine protectress, who indeed heartily rejoices at it (17. 567–8). This is no more than a first step towards what the *Od*. is happy to present at length.

In human dealings too the poet knows how to make the most of ironical moments, of which Odysseus in his beggar's guise affords plenty. Thus at 17. 201–2 he fully emphasizes the ironic situation by juxtaposing the contrasting words 'master' and 'beggar': ὁ δ' ἐς πόλιν ἦγεν ἄνακτα | πτωχῷ λευγαλέῳ ἐναλίγκιον (and to the city he led his master, who resembled a wretched beggar). How refined too is the

Also close to these passages is 2. 216–17, where Telemachus on his exploratory mission awaits either a mortal's report or a rumour originating with Zeus. Here, too, belongs the question Nestor puts to him at 3. 214–15 and Odysseus at 16. 95–6, whether he submits to the suitors by choice or because the men of the village hate him in obedience to the voice of a god?

Hermann Fränkel has given a sensitive interpretation of *Odyssey* 4. 712 and 7. 263, using them to show that the *Odyssey* occasionally makes a distinction that would not have occurred to the older age.[40] Such a definite statement requires at least one passage of the *Iliad* to be late, namely 6. 438–9, where Andromache speaks of a threatened sector of the wall that the Achaeans have already tried to storm three times:

ἦ πού τίς σφιν ἔνισπε θεοπροπίων ἐῢ εἰδώς,
ἦ νυ καὶ αὐτῶν θυμὸς ἐποτρύνει καὶ ἀνώγει.

Either someone well versed in divination has informed them, or their own *thumos* stirs and impels them.

That is not exactly the same as in the Odyssean passages, but here too the two spheres of causation are distinguished with the utmost clarity. And since in the Homilia or Conversation Scene I believe I hear the poet of the *Iliad* himself, here again I conclude as I did before in a similar case, that the *Odyssey* does not innovate outright but so powerfully develops hints already present in the *Iliad* that the two poems' difference in outlook cannot be mistaken.

Fränkel has forcefully separated the people of the *Odyssey* from those of the *Iliad*;[41] perhaps too forcefully, when he says that they begin to insulate themselves by their restraint and cunning from the outside world.[42] We must always consider how much of the difference is imposed by the plot itself and its general ambience. From this point of view—be it noted in passing—we must reconsider the question whether the greater role of moral themes in the *Odyssey* is the result of a (remarkably rapid) development or the difference

---

beggar's compliment to Penelope when he describes Odysseus' gleaming cloak (probably her own handiwork) and relates (19. 235) that women cast their expert gaze upon it. That this gaze was also directed at the wearer is a thought that the modern reader can scarcely suppress, but perhaps only because he has read his Ovid.

[40] (n. 10), 90.   [41] Ibid. 85–6.

[42] Schwabl (n. 5), 62, also raises objections to this formulation.

of setting or indeed the different personalities of the poets.[43] My disagreements with Fränkel are confined to nuances; I do not in the least wish to deny that he has made and disclosed important observations. The differences between the two epics that we have been able to observe are entirely in accordance with his findings.

I should not wish to suggest, however, that the worlds of the *Odyssey* and *Iliad* were divided by a wide gulf. If such gaps seem to appear (and their depth is sometimes exaggerated), there are enough footbridges and even road-bridges across them linking the two poems. Neither in the *Odyssey* nor in the *Iliad* does everything happen twice, as Whitman supposes for the latter, once on earth and once in the world of deity; but both have cases where this is so, and the *Odyssey* even has a particularly impressive one that embraces an important segment of the plot. Wolfgang Schadewaldt uncovered an essential factor in the poet's conception of the world when he showed how significant sequences of events may equally well originate in the world of the gods as in that of men.[44] Odysseus' return is a prime example: it begins as a decision of the gods, but then becomes the free choice of the man Odysseus. (Its significance does not depend on analytical inferences not drawn here.) Schadewaldt's demonstration that this constituent feature of the *Odyssey* is consistent with the *Iliad* is fully in line with my own position.

People in Homer may be governed in their actions by the gods, but their causation may also, as we have seen, be divided between the two spheres. We touch on a question of the greatest importance for Homeric thought, and indeed for Greek thought in general, when we attempt to determine the measure of responsibility in such cases that remains with the human being. My very first examples show that the divine impetus to an action or a god's collaboration with the human being does not reduce the latter's responsibility in the slightest. There is hardly anywhere where the fusion of divine and human is so clearly seen as in places where the man, for all that a god has intervened, must yet bear full responsibility.

---

[43] See e.g. Karl Reinhardt, 'Tradition und Geist im homerischen Epos', *Studium Generale* 4 (1951), 334–9 =*Tradition und Geist* (Göttingen, 1960), 5–15; his attempt to explain the differences by the individual characters of the poets is well worth considering. For first steps towards discussion in greater depth see to Pierre Chantraine, 'Le Divin et les dieux chez Homère', *Entretiens Hardt* 1 ([1952] 1954), 47–94, esp. p. 81.   [44] 'Der Prolog der Odyssee', *HSCP* 63 (1958), 23.

In the Embassy Scene Ajax says of Achilles, in his discontented speech, ἄγριον ἐν στήθεσσι θέτο μεγαλήτορα θυμόν (9. 629: 'he has made his great-hearted *thumos* wild in his breast'). A moment later he expresses exactly the same thought in the words σοὶ δ' ἄλληκτόν τε κακόν τε | θυμὸν ἐνὶ στήθεσσι θεοὶ θέσαν (9. 636–7: 'the gods have put an unrelenting and evil *thumos* in your breast'). After all that has been said here, we can no longer be surprised at the twofold aspect of one and the same thing, but it is instructive that the second passage is followed by εἵνεκα κούρης οἴης (for the sake of a girl and nothing more). It would be a complete misunderstanding to refer the reproach contained in these words to the gods, who cause such trouble for the sake of a mere girl. The full weight of the reproach lands on Achilles, and is fully compatible in the world of the *Iliad* with a phrase recognizing divine influence on the hero's attitude. At *Iliad* 3. 64 Paris relates his character to the delightful gifts of Aphrodite, but that in no way contradicts his admission immediately beforehand to Hector: 'Duly and not unduly have you reproached me.'[45] Nor does it help Idomeneus in any way at *Iliad* 13. 222–7 that he denies all blame on the warriors' part for their unfavourable situation and ascribes everything to the overbearing power of Kronos' son; Poseidon, in the guise of Thoas, replies with a threat against cowards and a call to battle.

In the *Odyssey* Penelope, awakened by Eurycleia from a refreshing sleep, dismisses the joyful news of Odysseus' triumph as a delusion (23. 11–14): 'Mother, the gods have made you mad; they can make the intelligent person stupid and the stupid intelligent. Certainly they have done harm to you; you used to have a head on your shoulders.' But that does not absolve Eurycleia from responsibility for ruining the queen's sleep, for Penelope continues: 'If another of my maids had come to wake me with this news I should have sent her away in anger; but you shall be protected by your years.'

The Iliadic depiction of Helen has tragic features. As little as it can ever be proved, one is unwilling to suppress the notion that her definitive portrait is due to none other than Homer himself; the Helen of the *Odyssey* has far less sharply drawn contours. The scene of Hector's visit to Paris and Helen in Book 6 is full of the subtlest traits; here we detect in Helen's words the sinister light in which she is viewed in the poem (6. 354–8). 'Sit down, brother-in-law, for you are

---

[45] Whitman (n. 35), 229 takes the same view.

weighed down with weariness and travail'

εἵνεκ' ἐμεῖο κυνὸς καὶ Ἀλεξάνδρου ἕνεκ' ἄτης,
οἷσιν ἐπὶ Ζεὺς θῆκε κακὸν μόρον, ὡς καὶ ὀπίσσω
ἀνθρώποισι πελώμεθ' ἀοίδιμοι ἐσσομένοισιν.

for my sake, bitch that I am, and because of Alexander's mad action; on us
Zeus has laid an evil destiny, so that even in future ages we shall be a subject of
song for men to come.

An evil destiny from Zeus has befallen Helen and made her a sad song
for future generations; but at the same time she feels and bears the
full responsibility for what has happened, so that she applies to
herself the highly insulting word 'bitch'. This, in ring composition,
resumes the even stronger self-condemnation at the start of her
speech κυνὸς κακομηχάνου ὀκρυοέσσης (6. 344: 'bitch whose evil
conduct chills the blood'), in which the first adjective emphasizes and
reinforces the fact that the action was hers.

The standpoints so closely connected here may also be separated.
A fine example of the poet's humanity appears in Priam's address to
Helen at the beginning of the Review from the Wall. He kindly invites
her to sit next to him (Iliad 3. 164):

οὔ τί μοι αἴτιός ἐσσί, θεοί νύ μοι αἴτιοί εἰσί

I do not blame you, I blame the gods.

If a human being finds it useful, the gods can be to blame for
everything; Odysseus takes the same line in the Nekuia when he tries
to talk Ajax out of his injured feelings (Odyssey 11. 555). But Helen
here takes a different view of herself and adopts one of the two
possible standpoints in no less isolation than Priam the other (3. 173–
5): 'Would I had chosen grim death when I followed your son here,
leaving my bedroom and kindred and the son begotten far off and my
delightful agemates.'

From this exchange of aspects—one finds oneself imagining the
same coin with first this face shown and then that—it also becomes
possible to understand how Agamemnon's atē is represented in the
Iliad.

In the great Reconciliation Scene in Book 19 Agamemnon
speaks of the infatuated state in which he took action against
Achilles (137):

ἀλλ' ἐπεὶ ἀασάμην καί μευ φρένας ἐξέλετο Ζεύς

But since I acted under Ate and Zeus took away my wits . . .

These words form part of a wide-ranging speech by Agamemnon in his own defence, which lays all the blame on the gods. First (87) he identifies Zeus, Moira, and the Erinys as the hostile powers that put destructive Ate in his mind. Next he allegorizes her in a manner looking forward to Hesiod, and cites an instance from the story of Heracles to show that Zeus, so to speak the Agamemnon of Olympus, is not proof against the evil Ate. All this to emphasize his assertion, 'it is not I who am guilty' (86: ἐγὼ δ' οὐκ αἴτιός εἰμί).

Bruno Snell opposed the Homeric man, who can say 'It was not I who did that, but a god led me to it', to the Aeschylean Orestes, who simply obeyed Apollo's orders in killing his mother, but must none the less bear the consequences of his action as if it were only his own.[46] I think this antithesis needs to be considered, and modified, at some length.

It must in any case be recognized that no one, not even Agamemnon himself, thinks that Zeus, Moira, Erinys, his allegorized Ate, and his Heracles exemplum can in the least change his personal responsibility and dispense him (say) from giving generous compensation.

But Agamemnon has already spoken earlier on about his error. Comparison of the two passages yields an at first astonishing result. We are in Book 9: the Embassy is being prepared. In the council preceding its dispatch, Nestor, after a respectful preamble, refers to Agamemnon's offence against Achilles in very direct terms; 'You, Agamemnon, did not refrain from grievously injuring Achilles, yielding to your great-hearted *thumos*' (109–10: σῷ μεγαλήτορι θυμῷ εἴξας). It was his *thumos*, then, a power that broke free inside him, that dragged Agamemnon to his ill-fated action. And the king does not attempt to contradict Nestor's assertion, but confirms it in a line that begins exactly like that in Book 19, but ends with a significant difference (9. 119).

ἀλλ' ἐπεὶ ἀασάμην φρεσὶ λευγαλέῃσι πιθήσας

But since I acted under Ate, obeying my baneful wits . . .

Incidentally, if we recall Nestor's words, we shall see how little *thumos* and *phrenes* are demarcated by firm definitions. In any case, both cases describe events within Agamemnon that led to his fateful

---

[46] *Der Aufbau der Sprache* (Hamburg, 1952), 197.

behaviour. The tone is very different from that in Book 19, where Agamemnon repudiates guilt as resting entirely with the gods.

It is interesting to examine various attempts that have been made to reconcile Agamemnon's two statements. In the age when analysis was the panacea, it naturally took little trouble to assign the lines to two different poets. Wilamowitz saw the matter accordingly: in the Embassy Agamemnon admitted his guilt, whereas the later poet of the Reconciliation Scene let him clutch at an excuse.[47] By contrast, Hermann Gundert sought to explain matters by psychological development on Agamemnon's part: the previous day he had admitted a purely personal failure, but later he recognized that he had been smitten by Zeus.[48] Gundert may have introduced too much psychology, but he seems to have come very close to the truth. I do not mean that Agamemnon exhibits two completely different psychological states in succession; such a portrayal could hardly exist in the world of Homeric epic. Rather, I should like to repeat my image of the two faces of one coin. We have to do with those two aspects of an action which, as we have realized in the course of our investigation, on the one hand belong very closely together, indeed form a unity, on the other change places with each other and can even be played off against each other. Which face of things Agamemnon sees and displays to other people depends—here I agree with Gundert—on his situation at the time. In the Embassy he is in the deepest depression. He is now ready to abandon the whole enterprise in earnest (in contrast to the pretence in Book 2). Everything has gone wrong, and the falling-out with Achilles is to blame. In such a downcast state he is ready to swallow all reproaches and even to concur with them. The Agamemnon of Book 19 is once again the king conscious of his dignity. He is no longer prepared to wear sackcloth and ashes, he takes his stand on his subjection to a power the gods sent against him and that not even gods are equal to. Two aspects of one and the same fact. If Agamemnon adopts them one after the other, that is in the end no different from when Priam and Helen in the Review from the Wall, from their respective points of view, distinguish what the Helen of Book 6 sees as a unity of divine and human causation.

[47] *Der Glaube der Hellenen* (Berlin, 1931–2), II. 117.
[48] 'Charakter und Schicksal homerischer Helden', *Neue Jahrbücher für Antike und deutsche Bildung* 3 (1940), 229.

What we have repeatedly observed is not a theological or psychological system, but rather the interplay of notions of which there are numerous variations, but only within a strictly limited framework. Understanding this seems to me of no small importance from the world-view of Homeric poetry.

This interpretation of Agamemnon's behaviour may be confirmed by a similar change of standpoint in Achilles. In Book 16, where he is forced to recognize that he can no longer be governed by his wrath, he gives powerful vent to it for one last time. In all his bitter words about Agamemnon's action (52–9) no god appears, nothing that might remotely excuse the man Agamemnon. In Book 19, however, where with a grand gesture Achilles lay aside his wrath as something that has lost all point, he courteously agrees with Agamemnon (270–4): Zeus, what havoc you wreak amongst men! It was Zeus who incited Atreus' son. Only Zeus did it, since he wanted so many killed. But the two standpoints are united in Achilles' answer to Odysseus in the Embassy scene. There (9. 367–76) he speaks, deeply embittered, of Agamemnon's action and the personal guilt he has incurred; but in line 377 follow the words: 'for designing Zeus took away his wits' (ἐκ γάρ εὑ φρένας εἵλετο μητίετα Ζεύς). Nor does atē in Achilles' complaint to his mother (1. 412) in any way denote the elimination of personal guilt, which is not overlooked before the generous courtesy of the Reconciliation Scene.[49]

We have now reached the point where we can judge things in the *Iliad* that of necessity cause difficulty for modern sensibilities: Pandarus' bowshot and its context. Hermann Fränkel has made excellent comments on this topic and convincingly demonstrated its significance 'in the artistic structure of the *Iliad*'—how splendid that he has the courage to speak of an artistic structure![50] With this bowshot the divine will corrects the course of events, which had been thrust out of the prescribed path by the conclusion of the treaty. At the same time, the shot means a renewal within the *Iliad* of the guilt that Troy had already incurred before the war by Paris' crime. But it is precisely as Trojan guilt that Pandarus' bowshot is relevant to

---

[49] Dodds (n. 1), 3 denies that in Book 19 Achilles politely accepts a fiction, since in Book 1 he has already spoken of Agamemnon's *atē*. That is right to the extent that Achilles certainly does not confirm a mere fiction out of courtesy, but endorses one possible way of viewing the matter; however, I hope I have shown that the tone of the two scenes is very different.   [50] Fränkel (n. 10), 66.

our discussion. That it is so understood within the poem is clearly expressed. In the Trojan assembly Antenor refers to the disturbing fact that they would now have to fight after openly breaking their oaths (Iliad 7. 351–2), and on the other side Diomedes exclaims that even a fool must now perceive that ruin awaits Troy (7. 401–2). But we know full well how this bowshot of Pandarus' came about. Zeus has bowed to Hera's will that Troy shall be destroyed and sent Athena, who was already burning to do something of the kind, down to earth to restart the fighting. She approaches Pandarus and persuades him to discharge the bowshot; it is relevant to our theme that none the less he is called 'mindless' (4. 104: ἄφρων). Thus the Trojans' guilt resides in an action by one of their number that from beginning to end was planned and brought about by the gods. Nevertheless, they have to endure the consequences of perjury till the very last. The modern reader has no way out to look for a compromise, but must accept the full weight of what Homer says in so many words. In this world the deed counts as such, the fact, the event that has been revealed to be a dis-ordering in the ordering of the world. Again, Fränkel has strongly emphasized the focus on the pure fact in his portrait of Homeric man.[51] It is very closely connected with the evaluation of the action as a pure effect. It is highly significant when in the Nekuia it is said that Epikaste 'committed a great crime in the ignorance of her mind' (Odyssey 11. 272: μέγα ἔργον ἔρεξεν ἀϊδρείῃσι νόοιο). Her complete subjective innocence counts for nothing; attention is confined to the objective fact of her action. In Homer's world Pandarus' bowshot is to be evaluated in exactly the same way: granted that the archer was a tool of the gods, that does not diminish his guilt and that of the Trojans, who will have to pay for it in full.

Can one fail to recognize the line leading from here into later Greek thought? Oedipus too has acted ἀϊδρείῃσι νόοιο and yet is punished for his μέγα ἔργον with full severity. That he executes this punishment himself is indeed the difference that makes him great. But in its essentials tragic guilt, by no means necessarily subjective guilt,[52]

---

[51] Ibid. 82–3. Goethe's adoption here too of Greek thinking is well brought out by Rudolf Pfeiffer, 'Goethe und der griechische Geist', Deutsche Vierteljahrsschrift für Literaturwissenschaft und Geistesgeschichte 12 (1934), 298 = Ausgewählte Schriften (Munich, 1960), 249.

[52] Valuable discussion in Kurt von Fritz, 'Tragische Schuld und poetische Gerechtigkeit in der Tragödie', Studium Generale, 8 (1955), 194–237, esp. 219.

is shaped by those traits of the Homeric world picture that I have
sought to draw.

IV

Ludwig Curtius once spoke of the merging of god and man as a
peculiarly Greek supposition that constantly recurred in new variations throughout Greek art.[53] It is not quite the same as what I have
been trying to prove for Homer, but both sprang from the same soil.

I declined earlier to speak of over-determination for the dual
causation of human action by man and god; nor do I think the
concept of pre-established harmony appropriate to the case. Rather, I
believe that Homeric poetry, through that form of myth which is
reserved to it alone, expresses a primal phenomenon of human
perception familiar for us too: for every one of us has more than once
in his life had the feeling that this or that action for which he must
answer does not entirely pertain to him, that 'something came over
him' and he cannot understand how it could have 'occurred' to him.
We therefore have not far to go in our search for an explanation of
the Homeric notions and may be wary of any attempt to explain
them by theories of development. I am thus reluctant to believe that
the poet of the *Iliad* played down older popular conceptions of purely
divine causation in favour of human initiative,[54] and cannot regard
the notorious 'divine apparatus' as a secondary accident. Rather, I
suggest that Walter Nestle hit the nail on the head when he described
Achilles' change of heart in *Iliad* 24 as 'a component of overall
reality, divine and human'.[55]

Goethe understood such 'overall reality' with his never-failing
immediacy in matters Greek. In his dramatic fragment *Prometheus*
(100–13) Prometheus addresses Minerva:[56]

> And you are to my spirit
> What it is to itself;
> From the very beginning

---

[53] 'Zur Interpretation griechischer Bildwerke', *Universitas* 3 (1948), 366.
[54] As posited by Kullmann (n. 18), 77.
[55] 'Odyssee-Interpretationen I', *Hermes* 77 (1942), 61.
[56] Pfeiffer (n. 51), 287 = 239, pointed to the Homeric material in this poem, albeit
accompanied by a psychological tone foreign to the Greeks; he also considered
Pandora 992–5 in this connection.

My words have been heaven's light to me!
Always, as if my soul were speaking to herself,
Opened herself to me,
And harmonies born with her
Rang out in her of themselves.
Those were your words.
Thus I myself was not self,
And a deity spoke,
When I imagined I spoke;
And when I imagined a god spoke,
I spoke myself.

For all that we spoke of a primal human phenomenon, its manifestation in Homer is individual both in nature and in breadth of effect. It would require a special investigation to show how the Homeric conception of collaborating divine and human forces continued to have multiple effects in later times; both the modification and the preservation of the original would deserve attention. At various points in this chapter I have attempted to show that modifications already exist in the *Odyssey*. There the gods are likelier to intervene in human thought by putting an idea into the mind, and the two spheres are more often separated by an 'either/or'; the special features of Zeus' speech in the proem also had to be brought out, though without separating this passage as a whole from the contexts under investigation. Since the *Odyssey* is the later of the two epics, it is an obvious course to posit exceptions; but we must also always bear in mind the difference of poet and of the background in which the poems are set. In this connection we have already touched on the question whether the 'higher morality' of the *Odyssey* on which stress is so often laid is simply the result of a development over a short space of time, or should be brought into relation with the personality of the poet, his theme, and the views of the social groups he addresses.[57]

For an example we may consider Odysseus' statements in the *Odyssey* that man is dependent and frail. Once again we have a view already found in other contexts, that human beings are subject to the gods is asserted often enough in the *Iliad*. We need only recall the jars out of which Zeus allots ill and good according to his pleasure (*Iliad* 24. 527–32). But in the *Odyssey* human frailty is spoken of in

[57] The problem is occasionally noted in Chantraine (n. 43), e.g. 75, 79, 81.

Albin Lesky

other tones, subtly distanced from the heroic world. It is after all a cowherd, Philoetius, who calls Zeus the most baleful of the gods, since he allows human beings, whom he himself has called into existence, to fall into want and misery (*Odyssey* 20. 201–3). And Odysseus in beggar's guise addresses Amphinomus in words that resemble those of Zeus at *Iliad* 17. 446–7 but are now spoken at a different intensity (*Odyssey* 18. 130–1):[58] there is nothing more wretched among all the creatures on earth than man, who has no option but to endure the lot assigned to him. Here already we have a clear expression of that helplessness (*amēchaniē*) whose importance in the world of lyric has been so impressively demonstrated by Rudolf Pfeiffer.[59] Furthermore, our passage already presents the ebb and flow of fortune (ῥυσμός) against which according to Archilochus (fragment 128. 7 West) man must stand firm. The ideas we have just found in the *Odyssey* are taken further in a passage of the hymn to Pythian Apollo, which once more demonstrates the pairing of standpoints. The Muses sing in alternation with the Musagete of the immortal gifts of the gods and the sufferings of human beings (191–3):

> ὅσ' ἔχοντες ὑπ' ἀθανάτοισι θεοῖσι
> ζώουσ' ἀφραδέες καὶ ἀμήχανοι, οὐδὲ δύνανται
> εὑρέμεναι θανάτοιό τ' ἄκος καὶ γήραος ἄλκαρ.

having all which under the immortal gods they live without intelligence and without resource, nor can they find a cure for death and a defence against old age.

Endurance and suffering is the lot of mortals, but at the same time it is their own *aphradiē*, their own want of intelligence, for which they must pay.

---

[58] On the warning to Amphinomus see Walter Nestle, 'Odyssee-Interpretationen II', *Hermes*, 77 (1942), 113–27, esp. 116.
[59] 'Gottheit und Individuum in der Lyrik', *Philologus* 84 (1929), 137–52 = *Ausgewählte Schriften* (n. 51), 42–54.

6

Affronts and Quarrels in the Iliad

DOUGLAS L. CAIRNS

This chapter deals with both the usage and meaning of key terms, and with the wider significance of the contexts in which they are used, in that order; in the first part, I use evidence from the *Odyssey* as well as the *Iliad*, but the title of the chapter is justified by the fact that the actual quarrels I consider in the second part are from the *Iliad*. It will be obvious that the first section has as its target the theories of A. W. H. Adkins. This is not 'flogging a dead horse', but recognition (*a*) of the importance of Adkins's work in setting the agenda for his successors and (*b*) of the enduring persuasiveness of many of his theories, even among those who would claim to repudiate them. Adkins, moreover, has been attacked, but not decisively refuted; in fact, he often comes off best in exchanges with his opponents.[1] I therefore make no apologies for engaging first with the Adkinsian approach, before moving on to consider the evidence from an alternative perspective. In doing so I shall argue both that Adkins's argument does not stand up in its own terms and that an approach

---

[1] See the exchange of views between Gagarin, Lloyd-Jones, and Adkins in *CP* 82 (1987). Gagarin's paper demonstrates both the direct influence of Adkins and the extent to which the assumptions behind Adkins's thesis are shared even by some who seek to modify it. Recently, both N. Yamagata, *Homeric Morality* (Leiden, 1994), and G. Zanker, *The Heart of Achilles* (Ann Arbor, 1994), have seen their work as challenging Adkins's account of Homeric ethics, but neither quite gets to the heart of the issues involved. More successful in subjecting the whole Adkinsian enterprise to rigorous scrutiny are B. Williams, *Shame and Necessity* (Berkeley, 1993), and C. Gill, *Personality in Greek Epic, Tragedy, and Philosophy* (Oxford, 1996). On Adkins, his antecedents, and his influence, see R. B. Louden, 'Introduction', in R. B. Louden and P. Schollmeier (edd.), *The Greeks and Us: Essays in Honor of A. W. H. Adkins* (Chicago, 1996), 1–16; for an earlier survey of responses to Adkins on Homer, see C. J. Rowe, 'The Nature of Homeric Morality' in C. A. Rubino and C. W. Shelmerdine (edd.), *Approaches to Homer* (Austin, 1983), 248–75. Adkins's own final contribution to the debate (*Comp.* 694–713) is a disappointingly bald restatement of his original thesis, which takes no account of his opponents' views.

such as his is unhelpful in making sense of the totality of the Homeric evidence.

Adkins is famous for his insistence that 'we are all Kantians now',[2] and the core of his most important work, *Merit and Responsibility*, is the claim that Greek thought of all periods from Homer to Aristotle failed to arrive at a satisfactory (Kantian) notion of moral responsibility, a failure which he locates in the Greeks' relative lack of interest in the purity of the will as opposed to success, efficacy, and the desirability of outcomes in their ethical evaluation of persons and their actions. Alongside this Kantian orientation, however, Adkins also reveals the influence of more recent moral philosophy, especially the concentration on the function and use of moral language characteristic of English philosophers in the middle years of the twentieth century.[3] Adkins's edifice is constructed on the basis of a positive distinction, which he traces back to the Homeric poems, between competitive and co-operative values.[4] This distinction is mirrored in another, between strong and weak terms of approval and disapproval, the strong being those which operate in the competitive sphere alone. A further element is supplied by a close attention to the reference of words of disapproval to agents or patients; this distinction is particularly relevant to the theme of this chapter, because, in the context of the affront, it subsumes those between co-operative and competitive spheres, weak and strong terms: if a term 'discredits' (Adkins's word) agents alone, it will decry a co-operative failure, whereas if its reference is to the patient, the recipient of the affront, then it highlights a competitive failure to defend oneself.

With these categories in mind we shall now examine certain terms crucial to Adkins's thesis which are also important for our understanding of attitudes to affronts and quarrels.

First *aischos*. The basic sense of this term is 'ugliness' (it continues to be used of physical ugliness long after *aischunē* has become regular in the transferred sense of 'disgrace'),[5] and in this sense, *aischos* can refer to a state of affairs, as in *Odyssey* 18. 220–5, where Penelope (225) tells Telemachus that he will suffer *aischos* and *lōbē* (disfigurement) among men for allowing a guest under his

---

[2] *Merit and Responsibility* (Oxford, 1960), 2.
[3] See the refs. to C. L. Stevenson and R. M. Hare at *Comp.* 695; cf. (n. 2), 38.
[4] For this distinction, and those discussed below, see Adkins (n. 2), ch. 3.
[5] *Aischunē* occurs first at Thgn. 1272; for the classical, physical sense of *aischos*, see (e.g.) Pl. *Symp.* 201a10.

protection to be 'disfigured' (ἀεικισθήμεναι, 222). Here *aischos* is a
state of affairs resulting from an affront, and it reflects badly on one
whose honour is associated with the patient of the affront.[6] In the
plural, *aischea* can refer to the affront itself, both verbal and non-
verbal, and to taunts which draw attention to the 'ugliness' of
another's situation. As a verbal affront, or as a taunt, *aischea* thus
refers to comments on the (alleged or supposed) *aischos* of another,
remarks which are intended to inflict, cause, or compound the
'ugliness' in which the recipient is implicated.[7] So *aischea*, 'insults',
cannot be considered in isolation from *aischos*, the condition in
which the affront may leave (and is intended to leave) its recipient:
aischos is both the aim and the frequent result of *aischea*, insults may
in fact constitute the ugliness, and the ugliness itself may call forth
further *aischea*.

So far, we have seen no reference to the discredit of agents in the
use of these terms; an affront is clearly intended to diminish the
honour of its patient, and, as Penelope warns Telemachus, dishonour, *aischos*, may well be its result. In *Odyssey* 1. 227–9, however,
Athena comments on the excessive *hubris* of the suitors (227,
ὑβρίζοντες ὑπερφιάλως): any sensible onlooker would experience
nemesis upon witnessing the many *aischea* taking place before him.
According to Adkins the precise reference of *aischea* is to the discredit of Telemachus;[8] *aischea* can only (and indeed must) be *aischron* (disgraceful) for their recipient. This, however, is clearly
wrong; the reference of *aischea* is to the suitors' affronts, so to their
attempts to dishonour another, but this attempt rebounds on them.
Athena is masquerading as a guest in Telemachus' house, and it is
incredible that she should describe a situation in terms designed to
draw attention to her host's disgrace.[9] Rather her designation of the
suitors' acts as *aischea* belongs with her description of their conduct
as *hubris* (illegitimate assertion of one's own claim to honour at the
expense of others);[10] it is to this that *aischea* refers, the illegitimacy

---

[6] Cf. *Il.* 13. 622.

[7] e.g. the *aischea* about Paris which so disturb his brother (*Il.* 6. 524), and to
which his wife wishes he would pay attention (6. 351). Cf. 3. 242, *Od.* 19. 373.

[8] Adkins (n. 2), 42.

[9] See A. A. Long, 'Morals and Values in Homer', *JHS* 90 (1970), 130–1.

[10] On *hubris* and dishonour, see N. R. E. Fisher, *Hybris: A Study in the Values of
Honour and Shame in Ancient Greece* (Warminster, 1992), with D. L. Cairns, 'Hybris,
Dishonour, and Thinking Big', *JHS* 116 (1996), 1–32.

being highlighted by the reference to the universal indignation (*nemesis*) which such actions excite. Since this is so, it is clear that an affront designated *aischea* can be ugly for its agent rather than for its patient, and that the connotation of 'ugliness' in the word can be used to draw attention to this fact.[11] It is not that behaviour which discredits Telemachus is somehow incidentally seen as discreditable for the suitors by means of the application of terms such as *hubris* and *nemesis*; on the contrary, conduct intended or likely to create *aischos* for its recipient can, in fact, constitute *aischos* for its perpetrator.

Next, 'ugly words'.[12] In this phrase the adjective *aischros* is glossed by Hesychius as 'capable of bringing disgrace' (τοῖς αἰσχύνην ἐνεγκεῖν δυναμένοις), an explanation obviously intended to forestall the assumption (natural for users of Greek in later centuries) that the adjective conveys disapproval of the manner of the address. This clearly is not the purpose of the phrase, and Hesychius is entirely right to describe 'ugly words' as those which are potentially *aischron* for their recipient. Yet this observation gives us no warrant to assume that the adjective itself refers inevitably to the actual discredit of patients. The primary reference of the adjective, I suggest, is not to the dishonour of patients, but to the fact of the affront itself; αἰσχρὰ ἔπη, I should say, means 'words that constitute an *aischos*' in much the same way as ὀνείδεια ἔπη means 'words that constitute an *oneidos* (reproach)'.[13] But to back this up I have to turn to the usage of the adverb *aischrōs*, and to the wider values exhibited in Iliadic quarrels.

Aischrōs occurs only twice in the poems, once in each.[14] Once again, the word occurs in the context of an affront; in both cases it

---

[11] So Long (n. 9), 131, comparing *Od.* 2. 85–6 (Antinous complains that Telemachus' charges are calculated to *aischunein* the suitors); cf. below, n. 27. One might also compare *Od.* 11. 433: by her extreme disloyalty to her husband Clytemnestra has inflicted *aischos* on her entire sex; she has inflicted dishonour on her husband, but she is herself dishonoured in the eyes of society. This observation, however, does not conflict with Adkins's thesis, for he allows that co-operative failure may be disgraceful for women, while denying that it can be so for men (n. 2: 36–7, 45); but in fact the possibility he allows in the case of women also extends to men, and the relevant value-terms can behave identically in the context of both male and female values.

[12] Αἰσχροῖς ἐπέεσσιν, *Il.* 3. 38, 6. 325, 13. 768, ἔπεσσ' αἰσχροῖσιν, 24. 238.

[13] See *Il.* 1. 519, 2. 277, 16. 628, 21. 480, *Od.* 18. 326; cf. *Il.* 22. 497 (ὀνειδείοισιν); also *Il.* 21. 393, 471 (ὀνείδειον μῦθον).

[14] *Il.* 23. 473, *Od.* 18. 321.

is the act of addressing another that is performed 'in an ugly manner'. Again, this focal reference to the affront entails a reference to the attempt to dishonour or humiliate, to place the recipient of the affront in a humiliating position or category. But even a brief look at the two passages reveals that the patient is not inevitably discredited. In *Odyssey* 18. 321 the words delivered *aischrōs* are directed at the disguised Odysseus by the unfaithful maidservant, Melantho. While it is certainly humiliating for Odysseus to have to endure such abuse from an inferior, it can hardly be that we are not also supposed to disapprove of Melantho's behaviour; ill-treatment of guests and abuse of one's master, even if he is incognito, scarcely constitute the sort of conduct commended by the *Odyssey*. Let it be clear, to be addressed *aischrōs* is to be placed in a situation which is potentially *aischron* for oneself, one which one may even oneself regard as *aischron*, but still *aischros* does not *mean* 'discreditable for the patient', and the mere use of a form of *aischros* does not entail that the recipient of an affront is inevitably dishonoured. Instead, I suggest two possibilities: (*a*) that there is a focal reference in such locutions to the occurrence of an affront; and (*b*) that the aesthetic aspect of the adjective and adverb may characterize the situation in a more general way.

To pursue this approach further, we need to look at the other passage in which the adverb occurs, which provides a convenient bridge from consideration of the behaviour of lexical items to examination of wider contexts. In the quarrel in *Iliad* 23 between the lesser Ajax and Idomeneus the former addresses the latter *aischrōs* (473), and Idomeneus clearly resents the affront, returning Ajax's insults in kind (482–7). Crucially, however, the quarrel is quickly brought to an end by Achilles (492–4), who comments on the 'inappropriateness' of the quarrel itself (οὐδὲ ἔοικε, 493). This inappropriateness, moreover, is such that disapproval of it is presented as a universal response, one which rests on values which even the participants in the quarrel share (καὶ δ' ἄλλῳ νεμεσᾶτον, ὅτις τοιαῦτά γε ῥέζοι, 'The pair of you would also feel *nemesis* at anyone else who acted in this way', 494).

Thus the quarrel itself is condemned under the same quasi-aesthetic standards as obtain in any use of the adjective *aischros*; quarrels do not look nice, and even if this distaste for quarrels is not actually part of the sense of the adverb *aischrōs* and the adjective *aischrōs* in such contexts (as I think), it is perfectly clear from this passage that the very fact of participation in a quarrel renders both parties open to criticism. As represented by Achilles, neither party stands to gain honour by pursuing the quarrel, neither is dishonoured by backing down, and, on the contrary, it is continuation of the quarrel itself which would, on the grounds of its unseemliness, meet with general disapproval.

The use of *nemesis* in this passage is of the utmost importance; first, there is the implication that Achilles' response is itself *nemesis*, a response, he claims, the opposing parties would share if they could step back from their emotional involvement in the situation and see themselves as they see others. Note, then, that Achilles' *nemesis* is impartial; he is neither victim of the affront nor partisan of either of the actors. This is an important fact about *nemesis*: it need not signify the response of the victim of an affront, but can express the reaction of the disinterested bystander, who represents the values of society as a whole.[15] Moreover, as the present passage makes clear, these values are capable of universalization: Ajax and Idomeneus would resent such behaviour in another, and therefore should recognize that they are in breach of universal standards personally endorsed by themselves. *Nemesis* is often used in locutions which make the same appeal to universal standards,[16] and one of the standards on which *nemesis* may be based holds that quarrels, violence, and excess are to be avoided.[17]

---

[15] See J.-C. Riedinger, 'Les Deux *Aidōs* chez Homère', *Rev. Phil.* 54 (1980), 70–5, 76. *Nemesis*, the central 'negative reactive attitude' in Homeric social and ethical discourse, thus covers both 'resentment' and its 'sympathetic or vicarious or disinterested or generalized' analogue, indignation: see P. F. Strawson, 'Freedom and Resentment', in *Freedom and Resentment and Other Essays* (London, 1974), 1–25, esp. 14. Strawson's account of 'reactive attitudes' is important in Gill's interpretation of *aidōs* and *nemesis* in Homer; see Gill (n. 1), 64–5 and chs. 1–2 *passim*.

[16] See *Od.* 6. 286, 15. 69–71 ('I too would feel *nemesis*'); with the present passage (*Il.* 23. 494, 'You too would feel *nemesis*') cf. 6. 329–30 ('You too would fight, fall out with anyone else who did such things'). On the significance of these passages, cf. M. W. Dickie, '*Dikē* as a Moral Term in Homer and Hesiod', *CP* 73 (1978), 94; I. M. Hohendahl-Zoetelief, *Manners in the Homeric Epic* (Leiden, 1980), 11–13; cf. D. L. Cairns, 'Mixing with Men and Nausicaa's *Nemesis*', *CQ* 40 (1990), 263–6, and Williams (n. 1), 83. *Od.* 1. 228–9 (discussed above) is also relevant, since there *nemesis* is described as the likely reaction of *any* sensible witness. *Nemesis*-verbs too, can be reflexive, and so denote one's own reaction to a (potential) breach of *aidōs* in oneself (*Il.* 16. 544, 17. 254, *Od.* 4. 158–9, etc.); the relevance of this to Democritus' ἑωυτὸν αἰδεῖσθαι (the verb *aideomai* used reflexively) is noted by J. F. Procopé, 'Democritus on Politics and the Care of the Soul', *CQ* 39 (1989), 323.

[17] e.g. *nemesis* is the reaction of the other gods to a god who becomes involved in human strife (*Il.* 5. 757, 872), because this involvement indicates over-eagerness to

That quarrels of this sort are unseemly and occasion for *nemesis* implies a lack of *aidōs* in their participants, for *aidōs* is an emotion which both rejects the unseemly (in which case the verb, *aideomai*, is typically followed, in Homer, by an infinitive) and forestalls the *nemesis* of others, both those who are the direct recipients of one's actions ('respect') and those who are their witnesses ('shame').[18] One very important and fundamental area in which *aidōs* is operative is that of *philotēs*. One's *philoi* enjoy a special claim to *timē* (honour) to which one's *aidōs* responds, and any failure to accord such *aidōs* is regarded as disreputable, and so liable to the *nemesis* of others.[19] Accordingly, *aidōs* often inhibits affronts and quarrels between *philoi*.[20] *Philotēs*, of course, can exist where there is no blood tie; in particular, the prominent members of the opposing armies at Troy are each other's *philoi*,[21] and this tie of *philotēs*

quarrel. Similarly, the expression πρὶν δ' οὔ τι νεμεσσητὸν κεχολῶσθαι ('thus far, no one could blame your anger', *Il.* 9. 523, *Od.* 22. 59), indicates that there are occasions when anger at an affront is *nemessēton*. Cf. Riedinger (n. 15), 72 (and 72–5 *passim* on the particular reference of *nemesis* to violent and quarrelsome behaviour). On the avoidance of strife and the importance of reconciliation in Homeric society, cf. K. Raaflaub in *Comp.* 632.

[18] *Aidōs* is thus the 'self-reactive' attitude, focusing one's demands on oneself vis-à-vis others, which is correlated with *nemesis* and its demands on others for oneself and on others for others: see Strawson (n. 15), 15. On the two uses of the verb *aideomai* with a (personal) accusative in Homer, see Riedinger (n. 15), 62–79; also D. L. Cairns, *Aidōs: The Psychology and Ethics of Honour and Shame in Ancient Greek Literature* (Oxford, 1993), 2–4. Among other treatments of *aidōs* in Homer, see esp. C. E. von Erffa, *Aidōs und verwandte Begriffe in ihrer Entwicklung von Homer bis Demokrit* (Philologus Suppl. 30. 2, 1937); J. M. Redfield, *Nature and Culture in the Iliad* (Chicago, 1975), 113–19; for an Adkinsian perspective, see M. Scott, 'Aidōs and Nemesis in the Works of Homer, and their Relevance to Social or Co-operative Values', *Acta Classica* 23 (1980), 1–14.

[19] The connection between *aidōs* and *philotēs* is fundamental, already apparent in the frequent combination of *aidoios* and *philos*. The links between *timē*, *philotēs*, and *aidōs* are well brought out by Riedinger, 'Rémarques sur la *timē* chez Homère', *REG* 89 (1976), 244–64, and id. (n. 15); cf. E. Benveniste, *Indo-European Language and Society* (Eng. trans. London, 1973), 277–8. See further Cairns (n. 18), 87–119. For *nemesis* at failure to show *aidōs* for one's *philoi* see (e.g.) *Il.* 17. 91–5, *Od.* 2. 136–7 (the *nemesis* Telemachus fears here is that which his *aidōs* forestalls at 20. 343).

[20] See *Il.* 21. 468 (Apollo and Poseidon), *Od.* 6. 329–30 (Athena and Poseidon).

[21] For copious evidence, see H. J. Kakridis, *La Notion de l' amitié et de l'hospitalité chez Homère* (Thessaloniki, 1963), 56–8 and *passim*; cf. H. van Wees, *Status Warriors: War, Violence and Society in Homer and History* (Amsterdam, 1992), 48, 337 n. 80; id. in *Comp.* 670–1; cf. the testimony of Aristotle at *EN* 1159^{b}27–9, 1160^{a}16–17 that *sustratiōtai* (fellow soldiers) are by definition *philoi*, and contrast D. Konstan, *Friendship in the Classical World* (Cambridge, 1997), 31–3. Accordingly, the statement of Adkins ('"Friendship" and "Self-Sufficiency" in Homer and Aristotle', *CQ* 13 (1963),

demands that they acknowledge each other's honour on a reciprocal basis.[22]

The force of such *aidōs* in defusing quarrels within the group is demonstrated in a passage of *Iliad* 4. Agamemnon abuses (νείκεσσεν, 368) Diomedes, accusing him of slacking and comparing him unfavourably with his father. Diomedes himself does not immediately respond, but his companion Sthenelus does, and clearly regards Agamemnon's remarks as an affront, apparently ready to commit his honour to wiping out the insult. Diomedes' response, however, is totally different. 'Out of *aidōs* for the rebuke of the reverend king' (αἰδεσθεὶς βασιλῆος ἐνιπὴν αἰδοίοιο, 402), he refrains from making any reply at all, and after Sthenelus has spoken, he explains why he feels no *nemesis* (413): he realizes (412–18) that Agamemnon is attempting to encourage the Achaeans, and accepts his right to do so; for, as he points out, both the glory of success and the sorrow of failure rest with him. Diomedes, then, feels no *nemesis* at remarks which another has taken as an affront because he can understand why they were made; he makes allowance for Agamemnon's aims, but his aims are not separable from his status as a superior king, itself inseparable from the pressures and responsibilities which that status entails. So Diomedes refuses to commit his honour because he accepts his place as a member of a group of *philoi* in which some enjoy more status than others. (If he later gets his own back when a suitable occasion arises (9. 33 ff.), this does not detract from the reflective nature of his response in Book 4.)

If Diomedes' response is the ideal, this does not mean that a response such as that of Sthenelus is not likely. Rather it is sometimes accepted as normal that *nemesis* (on the part of the recipient or his partisans) will follow remarks which can be construed as insulting.[23]

---

37) that 'Diomedes is far more closely bound to a Lycian who is his *philos* [a reference to *Il.* 6. 119–236] than to a Greek who is not, even during the Trojan War', requires the important qualification that, unless an active state of enmity exists between Diomedes and another of the Achaeans, all members of the Achaean army are his *philoi*.

[22] See the remarks of Ajax to Achilles in *Il.* 9, esp. 630–1: we honoured you with our *philotēs*; 640–2: we are your *philoi* and your guests, so show *aidōs* for us and for the obligations which exist between us. Cf. Gill (n. 1), 193–5.

[23] See e.g. *Il.* 10. 114–15: Nestor foresees *nemesis* on the part of Agamemnon should he charge Menelaus with dereliction of duty; cf. 129–30, where Nestor's denial that anyone will feel *nemesis* at Menelaus' orders in the present instance presupposes that brusque commands might otherwise be taken as insults. Cf. the frequent

Clearly, whether one takes offence (feels *nemesis*) or overrides one's *nemesis* with *aidōs* will depend on the seriousness of the affront, the status of the parties, and the character of the individual, but everything we have seen so far suggests that the ideal in every case is compromise rather than resentment, so that to regard oneself as affronted without good cause is deprecated.

Now to the quarrel that stands at the heart of the *Iliad*: in *Iliad* 1 the high emotional involvement of the parties which leads them to commit their honour and the abnormal situation in which a god inspires the return of a legitimate mark of honour combine to make the dispute difficult to resolve, but the normal values still apply, as Nestor's attempt to calm the two makes clear. He deprecates the fact that a quarrel is occurring at all (254–8), expresses the opinion that compromise is the better course (274), and urges each to consider the legitimate claim to *timē* of the other (275–84: Briseis is a *geras*, a legitimate acknowledgement of Achilles' *timē* as a warrior, mentioned by Nestor in 283–4, while Agamemnon is a superior *basileus*). These points have been made before,[24] and they could not be clearer. Nestor's disapproval of Agamemnon's part in the quarrel is conciliatory, and therefore muted, but his is an evaluation of the situation which resurfaces repeatedly until the quarrel is resolved, an evaluation which adumbrates a universal feeling of *nemesis* at Agamemnon's breach of *aidōs*.[25] Nestor's remarks on Agamemnon's failure to

precaution, μή νεμέσα ('do not feel *nemesis*': *Il.* 10. 145, 15. 115, 16. 22, *Od.* 23. 213); see Hohendahl-Zoetelief (n. 16), 22–4.

[24] See H. Lloyd-Jones, *The Justice of Zeus* (Berkeley, 1971), 12–13; cf. M. Schofield, 'Euboulia in the *Iliad*', *CQ* 36 (1986), 28 [= this vol., p. 255]; also Long (n. 9), 127, Riedinger (n. 19), 260–1, (n. 15), 73–4. To claim, as do Adkins, (n. 2), 37–8, 'Homeric Values and Homeric Society', *JHS* 91 (1971), 8–9, and M. M. Mackenzie, *Plato on Punishment* (Berkeley, 1981), 72–5, that Nestor advances only prudential arguments, is to misrepresent the situation (as Schofield points out). For additional discussion, largely centring on Adkins's interpretation of the phrase ἀγαθός περ ἐών (*agathos* though you be) in 275, see also K. J. Dover, 'The Portrayal of Moral Evaluation in Greek Poetry', *JHS* 103 (1983), 37–8, M. Gagarin, 'Morality in Homer', *CP* 82 (1987), 285–7, 303–5.

[25] See 9. 104–11 (Nestor; note the similarity to Thersites' criticism in 2. 239–40), 13. 107–15 (Poseidon, implying criticism among the Achaeans), 14. 49–51 (Agamemnon himself on the Achaeans' resentment), 19. 85–6 (Agamemnon refers to the Achaeans' frequent criticism), 181–3 (Odysseus, echoing Agamemnon's recognition of his own fault at 2. 375–8) with Riedinger (n. 15), 73–4, and O. Taplin, 'Agamemnon's Role in the *Iliad*', in C. B. R. Pelling (ed.), *Characterization and Individuality in Greek Literature* (Oxford, 1990), 74. It must be stressed that, given the ethics of reciprocity which dominate the *Iliad*, Agamemnon's admission that he

respect the *timē* of another therefore identify the same phenomenon
as do Achilles' charges of *anaideiē* (149, 158) and *hubris* (203, 214)
while Achilles, for his part, is reminded of the kind of response, the
aidōs for a superior which might override *nemesis* at an affront,
which is manifested by Diomedes in Book 4. So the ideals are quite
clear: quarrels are to be avoided, out of consideration for the *timē* of
others. In default of the achievement of this ideal, however, there is
more sympathy for Achilles than for Agamemnon, in so far as
retaliation for an affront is regarded more indulgently than its
initiation. This is why Phoenix can say (9. 523) with justification that
Achilles' anger against Agamemnon has, up to that point, not been
nemessēton (occasion for *nemesis*). Yet the very implication of that
phrase, with its pointed πρίν (previously, i.e. until now), is precisely
that there comes a point at which even understandable retaliation
becomes illegitimate; at every stage resolution of conflict is the ideal,
and prolongation of a quarrel after honourable compromise has
become possible is occasion for *nemesis* in the same way as is pro-
vocation of a quarrel in the first place or an excessive tendency to
regard oneself as affronted.

The major upshot of all this is that, behind the ideal that quarrels
are to be avoided, lies a notion of legitimacy in one's title to honour. If
such a thing exists, then clearly not all attempts to dishonour will
meet with the validation of those who matter, i.e. the generality of
'other people'. In any affront, the patient may feel himself dishonoured, but honour depends not exclusively on oneself, but also on
popular opinion, on the audience, and the audience may side with

initiated the quarrel is an admission of fault, not merely of error. Agamemnon thus
admits 'negative reciprocity' (taking with no intention to return; see M. Sahlins, *Stone
Age Economics* (London, 1974), 195); NB his threats simply to seize another's prize at
1. 137, 324; and see J. G. Howie, 'The *Iliad* as Exemplum', in Ø. Anderson, M. Dickie
(edd.), *Homer's World* (Bergen, 1995), 149–50; cf. A. Teffeteller, "Αὐτὸς ἀπούρας:
Iliad 1. 356", *CQ* 40 (1990), 16–20. Similarly, his attempt at compensation involves
making good this (acknowledged) fault and restoring reciprocity, not merely
propitiating an angry individual whose services he has found to be indispensable.
See Gill (n. 1), 144. This is not to deny that there may also be in Agamemnon's
extravagant offer of compensation an attempt to demonstrate his superiority to
Achilles, as is claimed by W. Donlan, 'Duelling with Gifts in the *Iliad*: As the Audience
Saw It', *Colby Quarterly* 29 (1993), 155–72. For an excellent interpretation of the
quarrel between Achilles and Agamemnon in the light of the 'rules' of reciprocal
exchange, see L. Muellner, *The Anger of Achilles* (Ithaca, NY, 1996), 96–116; on
Homeric reciprocity in general, cf. W. Donlan, 'Reciprocities in Homer', *CW* 75. 3
(1982), 137–75, and C. Gill, N. Postlethwaite, and R. Seaford (edd.), *Reciprocity in
Ancient Greece* (Oxford, 1998), esp. 51–104.

either party, with neither, or may reserve judgement, depending on the circumstances. *Timē* is awarded by the group as a whole, and the group will not award *timē* for an action which it does not regard as valuable (and clearly, society will not regard infringement of its own norms as valuable).[26] Accordingly, when the view is expressed that 'anyone' would experience *nemesis* at *aischea*, it is impossible that this should be compatible with that recognition of the success of the agent and failure of the patient which is required if the one is to win *timē* and the other to be dishonoured. An audience which regards one's conduct as *nemessēton* cannot with consistency reward that conduct with *timē*, and the general attitude is that to attempt to increase one's honour at the expense of another member of the group is occasion for *nemesis*.[27]

This idea of a legitimate title to honour entails a concept of fairness in the recognition of others' rights or entitlements.[28] This means that it is by no means misplaced to talk about a concept of 'justice' in this context, and so Lloyd-Jones is right to suggest that such a concept is operative in Nestor's remarks in *Iliad* 1.[29] What needs to be stressed is that this concept of justice is part of the code of honour, not in any way extraneous to or supervenient upon it. This idea of 'justice in

[26] The importance of the community in awarding *timē* is well stressed by Van Wees (n. 21), 61–165 *passim*.

[27] The failure to see that terms of disapproval, such as *aischron*, cannot be considered without the closest reference to the concept of *nemesis* (and that *aischron* etc. must therefore also be related to *aidōs*, in the sense that any action inhibited by *aidōs* must be regarded by the agent as *aischron*), is one of the greatest weaknesses of Adkins's approach, a weakness which lies in a surprising unwillingness to consider Homeric values as a whole.

[28] The notion of legitimacy in one's title to honour also explains why it is that the victims of an affront tend to draw attention to the fact, to appeal to the impartial judgement of witnesses, and to complain at the conduct of the perpetrator (see Riedinger (n. 15), 76); the indignation of Menelaus at the disfiguring (*aischunein*) of his *aretē* (excellence) by Antilochus (*Il.* 23. 570–85) and of Antinous at what he regards as unjust criticism on the part of Telemachus (criticism which he feels is capable of bringing disgrace on (*aischunein*) himself and his fellow suitors, *Od.* 2. 85–6; cf. above, n. 11) illustrates an appeal to a standard which categorizes certain forms of affront as illegitimate; cf. *Il.* 13. 622–3. Note that, in *Il.* 23, Antilochus, when he cools down, is immediately impressed by the force of Menelaus' (strikingly 'legalistic') arguments; when his judgement is no longer clouded by emotional involvement and the excitement of his apparent success, therefore, he accepts that Menelaus' appeal to impartial standards of fairness is justified, that in his youthful impetuosity he had failed to observe the norms of accepted conduct; cf. A. Schmitt, *Selbständigkeit und Abhängigkeit menschlichen Handelns bei Homer* (Abh. Mainz, 1990.5), 207–11.

[29] Lloyd-Jones (n. 24), 13; cf. Schofield (n. 24), 28 [= this vol., p. 254].

honour' is not separable from that of justice *simpliciter*; no *dikē*-word occurs in Nestor's evaluation of the quarrel in *Iliad* 1, but at 19. 181 Odysseus describes Agamemnon's conduct towards Achilles as a failure to be *dikaios*, and this clearly focuses on the same failure to accord honour where honour is due as is identified by Nestor. Similarly, in Hesiod, Tyrtaeus, Theognis, etc. *dikē* frequently subsumes the requirement that legitimate claims to honour be recognized.[30] This application of *dikē* may also be traced in classical literature (e.g. Odysseus' recognition and validation of Ajax's *timē* in Sophocles' *Ajax* is presented in terms of the *dikē* which recognizes the right to honour),[31] and lies behind those elements of Athenian law which demonstrate that that society takes considerable care to prevent illegitimate acts of dishonour among its members (witness the laws against seduction, an offence against the honour of the woman's *kurios*, and against *hubris*, a concept which has a fundamental reference to dishonour).[32] Thus even though there is no mention of *dikē* in most of the passages of the *Iliad* discussed above, still those passages do exemplify the requirement that legitimate claims to honour be recognized, which later Greeks describe quite regularly in terms of *dikē*. The relevant 'rights' may well be conferred on the basis of one's power or abilities, or of one's participation in some specific group or relationship, but, as legitimate expectations backed up by the social sanction of disapproval, they are clearly the pre- or proto-legal forerunners of the kind of rights which may be established by statutory law,[33] and the concept of *timē* contributes to this implicit concept of rights in much the same way as it does in

[30] See Hes. *Op.* 191, 213–18, 238, 327–34 (discussed in Cairns (n. 18), 152–6), Tyrt. 12. 37–42 West (Cairns (n. 18), 163), Thgn. 27–30, 292 (Cairns (n. 18), 172). The views of M. Gagarin (*'Dikē* in the *Works and Days', CP* 68 (1973), 81–94, and *'Dikē* in Archaic Greek Thought', *CP* 69 (1974), 186–97) that *dikē* refers, exclusively in Hesiod and usually in the Archaic poets, to aspects of the legal process, and that the entitlements involved in the process of *dikē* are exclusively economic, are frequently disproved by the evidence. Cf. D. B. Claus, 'Defining Moral Terms in *Works and Days', TAPA* 107 (1977), 73–84, Dickie (n. 16). (Gagarin tacitly modifies his former account of *dikē* in Hesiod in his *Early Greek Law* (Berkeley, 1986), 46–9, especially 49.)

[31] See *Aj.* 1332–45, and cf. R. P. Winnington-Ingram, *Sophocles: An Interpretation* (Cambridge, 1980), 66. I discuss this point more fully in (n. 18), 238–40. For a different view, see G. Zanker, 'Sophocles' *Ajax* and the Heroic Values of the *Iliad', CQ* 42 (1992), 20–5, and cf. n. 38 below.

[32] See Fisher (n. 10), 62–8, 493–500.

[33] That *aidōs*, the emotion which recognizes legitimate claims to *timē* in others, implies a sense of obligation which may be regarded as a precursor to a juridical mode

Classical Athens, where *timē* regularly denotes the basic level of entitlement under the law that is enjoyed by all citizens alike.

These observations entail the rejection of several of the most cherished and widely held assumptions about the nature of Homeric society:

1. The model of the 'zero-sum' game—the idea that honour is a commodity which passes inevitably from one side to the other in affront—is not applicable; if I commit an act by which I intend to dishonour you, and am myself dishonoured by doing so, then there is no simple exchange of honour; to dishonour another is not always to win honour for oneself.[34] The importance of the audience of 'other people' in validating or refusing to validate a claim to honour in itself renders the zero-sum view untenable. This is underlined by the existence of a term, *hubris*, which specifically denotes illegitimate dishonouring of another person; the honour of the illegitimately dishonoured does not pass to the agent of the affront. Nor need honour be won at the expense of another member of the group: at *Odyssey* 1. 95 it is Athena's purpose that Telemachus should win *kleos* on his journey to Pylos and Sparta; in the episodes which follow, this acquisition of *kleos* involves his general growth in heroic stature and the recognition accorded him by the important people he meets, not just the amassing of guest-gifts, and there is no one who suffers a loss corresponding to Telemachus' gain.[35] Where, however, individual A commits his honour to the achievement of a specific goal, then clearly achievement of the same goal by individual B will mean that B will win honour and A will lose. This is why Achilles' remarks to Patroclus at *Iliad* 16. 83–90, to the effect that success for Patroclus against the Trojans would diminish Achilles' honour, seem to bear out the zero-sum view. The germ of truth in that view is that honour is typically a matter of comparison: to claim too much for

---

of thought is the position of L. Gernet, 'Law and Prelaw in Ancient Greece', in *The Anthropology of Ancient Greece* (Eng. trans. Baltimore, 1981), 147–9.

[34] For the 'zero-sum' view, see A. W. H. Adkins, 'Honour and Punishment in the Homeric Poems', *BICS* (1960), 31, A. W. Gouldner, *Enter Plato* (London, 1965), 49–51, Redfield (n. 18), 33, Mackenzie (n. 24), 75, L. B. Carter, *The Quiet Athenian* (Oxford, 1986), 5–6. The zero-sum model belongs with a view of honour as a commodity invested in scarce material goods; that such a model is inapplicable to Homer is demonstrated by Van Wees (n. 21), 69–77 and 349 n. 30.

[35] Cf. Redfield (n. 18), 33–4; contrast S. D. Goldhill, *The Poet's Voice* (Cambridge, 1991), 70.

oneself is to undervalue others, and people typically see others' prestige as reflecting on their own; but the element of comparison may also be manifested in co-operation, as we see in the way that *aidōs* encompasses a sense of one's own honour relative to that of others.[36] The fundamental flaw of the zero-sum model, however, is that it is incompatible with the requirement that honour in Homer be seen in terms of reciprocity, for reciprocity as a general strategy can only get off the ground where it is possible for the exchange of goods and services involved to be non-zero-sum in nature.[37]

2. No sharp dichotomy exists between competitive and co-operative values. The code of honour is inclusive, and the protectiveness of one's own honour which promotes self-assertion also entails a sensitivity to the vulnerability of one's honour at the point at which self-assertion, by violating the claims of others, becomes dishonourable for oneself.[38] This inclusiveness we saw in the usage of *aischos* and *aischea* (since my *aischea* intended to dishonour you may in fact be ugly for me), and it is also apparent in the usage of *aideomai*, which signifies concern both for one's own and for others' honour.[39]

3. Honour is typically associated with shame, and the two concepts are indeed correlative. Homeric society, moreover, is one which

[36] See Cairns (n. 10), 32.

[37] This is the lesson of the game-theory approach to human co-operation exemplified in R. Axelrod, *The Evolution of Co-operation* (Harmondsworth, 1984); for this approach in a classical context, cf. W. Burkert, *Creation of the Sacred* (Cambridge, Mass., 1996), 138–55; Axelrod's model is forced to support a relativist study of Classical Athenian society by G. Herman, 'Reciprocity, Altruism, and the Prisoner's Dilemma: The Special Case of Classical Athens' in Gill *et al.* (n. 25), 199–226; for further elucidation (and due emphasis on reciprocity as an evolutionarily stable strategy), see R. Dawkins, *The Selfish Gene* (2nd edn., Oxford, 1989), 202–33, R. Wright, *The Moral Animal* (London, 1995), 189–209 (esp. 193–7 on 'non-zero-sumness'), M. Ridley, *The Origins of Virtue* (London, 1996), 53–66.

[38] My position should thus be distinguished from that of G. Zanker, who has frequently argued that the competitive impulse of honour may often in fact promote co-operation; this is certainly true, but since it is wrong to regard honour in Homer (or in Greek society generally) as an intrinsically competitive notion, the role of honour in co-operation is much wider than Zanker suggests. See Zanker (n. 1), 1–45; (n. 31); and cf. id., 'Loyalty in the *Iliad*', *PLLS* 6 (1990), 211–27. The assumption that 'honour' is essentially competitive also underpins the article of M. Finkelberg, '*Timē* and *Aretē* in Homer', *CQ* 48 (1998), 14–28.

[39] This last point is well brought out by Riedinger (n. 15); cf. Williams (n. 1), 83. On the inclusivity of the Homeric code of honour, see also id. (n. 19), and Schofield (n. 24), esp. 17–18 [=this vol., pp. 238–9]. On the collapse of the competitive/co-operative antithesis, cf. Rowe (n. 1), 254–61.

is thoroughly permeated by profound attachment to standards of the honourable. But this does not make that society a 'shame-culture', for a shame-culture is one in which fear of the external sanction of disapproval takes the place of concern for the intrinsic character of one's actions,[40] and we have seen that Homeric characters are capable of explicit recognition that the values under which they live are universalizable and capable of being personally endorsed by individual members of society. If I can point out that any impartial individual would feel *nemesis* at a certain course of action, if I can argue that you too would feel *nemesis* were another to act as you do, if I can feel *nemesis* at my own conduct or reject conduct because it is of the sort at which I should feel *nemesis*, then I acknowledge that individuals can endorse, appropriate, and *internalize* the values of their society, and so it is wrong to suggest that Homeric man simply conforms to external standards out of fear of punishment or disgrace.[41]

Examination of the terms used to refer to affronts and quarrels, then, must take place in the context of a wider and more sensitive interpretation of the dynamics of the narrative situation and of the normative categories and relationships within which the participants operate. The term *aischron* is only one of several which convey similar, quasi-aesthetic disapproval; the expression of such disapproval must be placed in the general context of society's repertoire of negative reactive attitudes, most prominently *nemesis*; and the operation of *nemesis* must be studied in the context of its relation to the complex of attitudes and relationships centred on the Homeric concept of honour. Properly carried out, study of critical episodes of affront and quarrel can alert us to features of Homeric values which are absolutely fundamental to an appreciation of the ethical infrastructure of the *Iliad*.

---

[40] For this basic premiss of the shame-culture/guilt-culture antithesis in the work of Margaret Mead, Ruth Benedict, and others, see Cairns (n. 18), 27–47; cf. and contrast Williams (n. 1), 75–102 *passim*; also Gill (n. 1), 66–7. For general criticism of the cultural determinism of Mead and other followers of Franz Boas, see D. Freeman, *Margaret Mead and Samoa: The Making and Unmaking of an Anthropological Myth* (Canberra, 1983); cf. M. Carrithers, *Why Humans Have Cultures* (Oxford, 1992), *passim*, esp. 1–33; Ridley (n. 36), *passim*, esp. 256–9.

[41] Cf. Dickie (n. 16), 94–5; Williams (n. 1), 81–4; Gill (n. 1), 66, 75, 80–5.

The reflexive pair, *aidōs* and *nemesis*,[42] are the crucial ethical attitudes underpinning the reciprocal relationships of honour which structure social interaction in Homer. The former measures one's own claim to honour against the expectations and the claims of others, and the latter responds to perceived infringements of one's own or others' claims; in covering a range of reactions from sensitivity regarding public exposure to shame over breaches of personally endorsed standards, from resentment to indignation, the usage of these terms recognizes no absolute (Kantian) antithesis between moral and non-moral (prudential) judgements. None the less, Homeric characters are capable of drawing distinctions which correspond to a more pragmatic and less austere version of this categorization: Achilles believes it worthwhile to point out that Ajax and Idomeneus are themselves falling short of the standards they would wish to see observed by others.[43] To be sure, the forms of universalization and impartiality observed in the Homeric poems are rooted in the ethics of reciprocity which operate in the context of specific relationships and communities: to recognize that one's expectations of others must be matched by one's expectations of oneself is simply to accept the dynamics of reciprocity in more general terms; similarly, to extend one's other-concern to an outsider in recognition of an (actually or potentially) shared predicament (as does Achilles to Priam in *Iliad* 24), is to apply the generalized reciprocity which obtains within specific relationships at another level.[44]

[42] Redfield (n. 18), 115; Williams (n. 1), 80.

[43] J. Annas, *The Morality of Happiness* (Oxford, 1993), 73, 121–4, similarly notes that later Greek ethical theory, while relying on no absolute antithesis of the moral and the prudential, remains capable of distinguishing between moral and non-moral motives.

[44] See Gill (n. 1), 341–2, id., 'Altruism or Reciprocity in Greek Philosophy?' in Gill *et al.* (n. 25), 312–13; cf. K. J. Dover, *Greek Popular Morality in the Time of Plato and Aristotle* (Oxford, 1974), 269–72; Rutherford, this vol., Ch. 8, § V [=*JHS* 1982, 158–60] H. van Wees, 'Reciprocity in Anthropological Theory', in Gill *et al.* (n. 25), 22. Discussion of the Achilles–Priam scene in *Il.* 24 must also take Priam's supplication into account, for supplication is (at least in part) a mechanism for extending reciprocity beyond pre-existing relationships: see J. Gould, 'Hiketeia', *JHS* 93 (1973), 74–103. On all this, contrast G. Zanker, 'Beyond Reciprocity: The Akhilleus-Priam Scene in *Iliad* 24', in Gill *et al.* (n. 25), 72–92 (who sees Achilles' response to Priam as a form of altruism which transcends [sic] reciprocity). Contrast also N. Postlethwaite's view ('Akhilleus and Agamemnon: Generalized Reciprocity', ibid. 93–104) that the form of reciprocity most immediately relevant in the Achilles–Priam scene is that involved in Achilles' attempt to outdo Agamemnon in conspicuous generosity.

Homeric universalization and impartiality should therefore not be confused with their much more abstract Kantian counterparts.[45] Yet it is wrong to grant Kantians a monopoly in these terms, and I believe that we should recognize in the ethics of the *Iliad* important points of contact with the everyday categories of modern, non-Kantian moral discourse.

[45] See B. Williams, *Ethics and the Limits of Philosophy* (London, 1985), 60, 82–5, 92, 115, on more and less defensible versions of universalization. On impartiality, see J. Elster, *Alchemies of the Mind: Rationality and the Emotions* (Cambridge, 1999), 339: impartiality is not to be identified with any single conception of justice, but is 'a necessary feature of any view that wants to be taken seriously as a conception of justice'.

7

Euboulia *in the* Iliad

MALCOLM SCHOFIELD

INTRODUCTION

The word *euboulia*, which means *excellence in counsel or sound judgement*, occurs in only three places in the authentic writings of Plato. The sophist Protagoras makes *euboulia* the focus of his whole enterprise (*Protagoras* 318e–319a):

What I teach a person is good judgement about his own affairs—how best he may manage his own household; and about the affairs of the city—how he may be most able to handle the business of the city both in action and in speech.

Thrasymachus, too, thinks well of *euboulia*. Invited by Socrates to call injustice *kakoētheia* (vicious disposition—he has just identified justice as 'an altogether noble good nature (*euētheia*)', i.e. as simple-mindedness), he declines the sophistry and says (*Republic* 348d): 'No, I call it good judgement.' But Plato finds little occasion to introduce the concept in developing his own ethical and political philosophy. The one place where he mentions *euboulia* is in his defence of the thesis that his ideal city possesses the four cardinal virtues. He begins with wisdom, and justifies the ascription of wisdom to the city on the ground that it has *euboulia* (*Republic* 428b)—which he goes on to identify with the knowledge required by the guardians: 'with this a person does not deliberate on behalf of any of the elements in the city, but for the whole city itself—how it may best have dealings with itself and with the other cities' (428c–d). It is normally rather dangerous to draw an inference from the absence or rarity of a word to the absence or rarity of the idea expressed by the word. But in the present instance we need have no qualms in doing so. Having assimilated *euboulia* (which was equated with political skill in the *Protagoras* (319a)) to guardianship, Plato can abandon any further enquiry into the arts of good judgement and counsel and concentrate instead on guardianship. The ideal city is constructed as it is precisely to avoid the need for politics and its arts. What the guardians are required to know is how to keep the class structure intact ('how the city may best have dealings with itself')—and that involves keeping the education system going, lying well and truly about the basis of the class system, and maintaining a firm grip on the breeding arrangements. These administrative skills are ultimately grounded in the knowledge of the principles of stability, order, and harmony which comes from the study of mathematics and dialectic. They have little in common with the arts of persuasion or the political judgement needed in an actual Greek state.

I begin this chapter with these reflections on Plato because I suspect his motivated neglect (or rather, Utopian hijacking) of *euboulia* does much to explain its neglect by the most influential writers on early Greek intellectual history. What Plato is interested in is justice and moral excellence and the question of the unity or complexity of the human mind: these are the topics that preoccupy (for example) Snell and Dodds and Adkins.[1] But Protagoras was not the only figure in early Greek literature and thought who found it important to ponder *euboulia*. The qualities needed by a good politician or king or counsellor are explored by Thucydides, by the tragedians, and, to begin at the beginning, by Homer—to name only the most important. Nor is it in the least surprising that they should be. It is a commonplace that the *polis* was not only the Greeks' distinctive form of community but the indispensable cradle of those unique and extraordinary intellectual and artistic developments of the late Archaic and Classical periods which have shaped western civilization. How could the creators of such an intensely political and powerfully creative institution not have reflected on the intellectual as well as the moral virtues required of a statesman or adviser? That tradition of reflection began with Homer. Yet on the whole Homeric scholars do not appear to be much interested in the *euboulia* of the Homeric hero. Here they differ from the ancient Greeks themselves, who as is well known regarded Homer not only as their greatest poet but as a teacher, a fount of wisdom on all the topics touched on or

---

[1] B. Snell, *The Discovery of the Mind* (Eng. trans., Oxford, 1953); E. R. Dodds, *The Greeks and the Irrational* (Berkeley, 1951); A. W. H. Adkins, *Merit and Responsibility* (Oxford, 1960).

adumbrated in his poems. This is as true of kingship and *euboulia*
as any other subject, as witness the very title of Philodemus' fragmentary treatise *On the Good King according to Homer*, a work in
which the names of Nestor and Odysseus evidently figured frequently
as paradigms of *phronēsis*, practical understanding (col. XI 22 ff.),
and in which the importance of *sunhedria* (assemblies) and *euboulia*
apparently occupied a whole section of its own (col. XIII 22–XIV).[2] Is
kingship strictly speaking or ideally absolute? Or should kings be
subject to their advisers? Dio Chrysostom appeals to Homer's treatment of Agamemnon as relying on Nestor and the council of elders to
support the latter alternative (*Oration* 56). Should old men engage in
public affairs? Certainly, answers Plutarch in his essay on the subject; and he supports his argument that the old are superior in
counsel, foresight, *logos*, good sense, prudent thought, soundness,
and experience by Homeric texts, and above all by the example of
Nestor, of whom Agamemnon said (*Iliad* 2. 372): 'Would that I
had ten such advisers among the Achaeans' (see especially *Moralia*
788–90, 795).

In work of recent years I have discovered only one substantial
treatment of *euboulia* in Homer: a brilliant, trenchant and provo-
catively dismissive passage of a few close-packed pages in Sir Moses
Finley's *The World of Odysseus*.[3] Finley's view of *boulē* (counsel,
judgement) in Homer is diametrically opposed to that of a Dio or a
Plutarch. It is not just that where Dio expatiates on Agamemnon's
submissiveness to Nestor and the elders, Finley lays stress on the fact
that the Homeric king was free to ignore the expressions of sentiment
voiced in council or assembly and go his own way, although at the
risk of revolt;[4] or that where for Plutarch Nestor was 'the prototype
of the wisdom of old age, the voice of experience', for Finley he 'was
not that at all', but simply a storehouse of heroic exempla useful not
for clarifying men's minds but for bolstering their morale.[5] The heart
of the matter is that on Finley's interpretation of Homer's system of
values, there is no room for *euboulia*, or more accurately for anything Thucydides or Aristotle would have recognized as genuine
euboulia, at all.

[2] See O. Murray, 'Philodemus on the Good King according to Homer', *JRS* 55
(1965), 161–82.
[3] References are to the second revised edition published by Penguin Books
(Harmondsworth, 1979).   [4] Finley (n. 3), 80–2.
[5] (n. 3), 114–15.

In what follows I shall first present a survey of the evidence in the text of the *Iliad* that prima facie tells against Finley's account, which I then go on to report and discuss. The rest of the chapter will develop an alternative analysis of the themes he introduces. I make no apology for approaching the subject *via* a book that is now over thirty years old. Perhaps the very authority of *The World of Odysseus* has helped to create an impression that *euboulia* not only has little weight in the Homeric scheme of values but is not even worth investigation. I am sure Finley hoped rather to provoke curiosity and argument.

It will already have been becoming apparent that I come to Homer as a student of Greek intellectual history and political theory, not as a Homeric scholar. In my patchy reading of the secondary literature the work I have found much the most helpful and stimulating in exploring Homeric *euboulia* is James Redfield's 'long, subtle and complex' book *Nature and Culture in the Iliad*.[6] Indeed, anyone familiar with the method and main theses of that work could probably construct the argument of this chapter for himself. At the same time, I must acknowledge a more general debt to some recent studies of the quality of human rationality in early Greece, notably books by G. E. R. Lloyd, G. S. Kirk, and—on *mētis*—M. Detienne and J.-P. Vernant.[7] *Mētis*, cunning intelligence, is not identical with *euboulia*: it has roughly the same relationship to it as *deinotēs*, cleverness, has to *phronēsis* in Aristotle's plotting of the intellectual virtues.[8] But it is an essential ingredient of the *euboulia* of a Nestor or an Odysseus, and consequently the present essay should be read as complementary to chapters 1 and 10 (especially) of *Cunning Intelligence*.[9]

---

[6] J. M. Redfield, *Nature and Culture in the Iliad: The Tragedy of Hector* (Chicago, 1975), so described by Finley (n. 3), 184.

[7] G. E. R. Lloyd, *Magic, Reason, and Experience* (Cambridge, 1979); G. S. Kirk, *The Nature of Greek Myths* (London, 1974), ch. 12; M. Detienne and J.-P. Vernant, *Cunning Intelligence in Greek Culture and Society* (Hassocks, 1978).

[8] So Detienne and Vernant (n. 7), 316–17.

[9] I have restricted my attention to the *Iliad*, principally because it is much richer in councils and assemblies than the *Odyssey*, but also because I want to avoid the complications raised by the problem of whether the poet of the *Od.* is different from the poet of the *Il.* —for if they are different (as the arguments of G. S. Kirk, *The Songs of Homer* (Cambridge, 1962) and more recently J. Griffin, *Homer* (Oxford, 1980) persuade me), then it may be prudent method not to assume that the social and intellectual worlds of the two poems are the same. I have tried to avoid begging questions about the poetics and compositional techniques of Homer, and about the extent to which we are justified in seeing the *Il.* as a monument of tragic architecture, every detail controlled by a conception of the whole.

SOME EVIDENCE

The *Iliad* is full of assemblies (*agorai*) and councils (*boulai*), in heaven, in Troy, and above all in the Greek camp before Troy. To rehearse them all would be tedious and needless for our purposes; let it suffice simply to recall six Greek parleys particularly notable for their length or their weight in the development of the poem. First of these, of course, in position and in significance is the assembly to which Achilles summons the host at the beginning of Book 1 (53 ff.), for it is the forum in which his great quarrel with Agamemnon takes place. It is followed by a council and then a further assembly in Book 2: at the council Agamemnon reports his dream and explains to the Achaean chieftains his plan to stir the Greeks to battle again; when that plan fails disastrously, Odysseus and Nestor address Agamemnon before the assembled forces and advise him and them on what to do next. Third, and a direct sequel to the assembly of Book 1, is the assembly of Book 9, followed by a council, at which the Argives look for remedies for their worsening position and Nestor prevails upon Agamemnon to send an embassy to Achilles—which in turn engages in a massive parley with the sulking hero. Immediately afterwards, in Book 10, the nocturnal prowlings of the Greek leaders culminate in the council that results in the Doloneia. Book 14 begins with an informal council at the point in the story when Greek fortunes are at their lowest ebb; as in Book 9, so here once again Agamemnon is dissuaded from returning home (or more strictly from making as if to do so). Finally, balancing the assembly of Book 1 is the further assembly called by Achilles at the opening of Book 19, at which Agamemnon and Achilles are reconciled and Achilles is restrained from taking immediate revenge for Patroclus. All these discussions and debates have this at least in common: they are not mere episodes, relaxations from the real action of the poem; they are its motive forces, of greater intrinsic interest, and generating more tension, than most of the passages which retail the actual fighting. Assemblies and councils have a similar structural and dynamic function in much heroic poetry.[10] For example, the plot of *The Song of Roland* is launched and in part shaped by the sequence of deliberations which begin the poem: Marsilion's council at Saragossa,

---

[10] The assembly or council theme in Yugoslav oral epic is studied by A. B. Lord in *The Singer of Tales* (Cambridge, Mass., 1960), 68–81.

Blancandrin's embassy to Charlemagne, and then—at much greater length—'that council which came to such sore grief', when Roland and Ganelon quarrel at Charlemagne's court.

The prominence of councils and assemblies, and in general parleys, in the *Iliad* reflects the fact that life, and in particular life at the front, is a difficult practical business, demanding intelligence and judgement as well as prowess. And since parleys are needed to cope with that business, it comes as no surprise to find *euboulia* recognized as a pre-eminent virtue of the Homeric chieftain.[11]

Excellence in counsel is often coupled with prowess in fighting as one of the two chief ways in which a man may outshine his peers. Nestor, attempting to reconcile Achilles and Agamemnon, describes them flatteringly to their faces as excelling the Danaans equally in counsel and in fighting (1. 258). He employs a similar technique with Diomedes (9. 53–4), when in response to a stirring speech made by him he establishes the tone and something of the direction of his reply with the words: 'Son of Tydeus, you are exceedingly valiant in war, and in counsel you are the best among all your contemporaries.' Odysseus likewise employs the same contrast in upbraiding the plebeian loudmouths of Book 2 with the charge (200–2): 'My good man, sit still and listen to the words of others who are better than you, whereas you are a weakling, not fit for war, of no account either in war or in counsel.' He himself, on the other hand, earns extravagant admiration for his beating of Thersites, and provokes in the common soldier the following words (2. 272–4): 'Heavens, Odysseus has in truth performed fine deeds countless in number, initiating good counsels and preparing for war, but now is this deed the best by far that he has done among the Argives.' Here the opposition is less sharp: preparations for war have as much if not more in common with counsels as with war itself; and Odysseus' initiatives in counsel and preparation are implicitly reckoned

---

[11] As Lloyd says (n. 7: 59), 'There can be few societies that do not, in some degree, prize skill in speaking, and the variety of contexts in which it may be displayed is very great. Apart from in the arts of the poet or story-teller and of the seer or prophet, eloquence may be exhibited in a number of more or less formalised situations, including eulogies of the powerful and contests of abuse such as the song duels reported from the Eskimos.' And he continues: 'Good speaking and good judgement—and the two are often not sharply distinguished—need to be shown wherever groups of individuals meet to discuss matters of consequence concerning the running of the society, its day-to-day life and internal affairs and its relations with its neighbours.'

themselves as notable deeds. Indeed, what these lines reflect is the
fact that ability in fighting and excellence in counsel are not so much
opposed as interdependent qualities. Let it not be thought that the
coupling of *euboulia* and prowess is confined to contexts in which
Nestor and Odysseus, Homer's paradigms of *euboulia*, figure. We find
Helenus urging Aeneas and Hector to make a stand and rally the
Trojan host 'since on you above all of the Trojans and Lycians the
burden of toil lies, because in every enterprise you are best both at
fighting and at thinking' (6. 77–9). And we are told that when
Achilles sat in wrath by the swift-plying ships 'he never went into the
assembly which brings glory to a man nor ever into the war' (1. 490–
1), although it was abstinence from war and the war-cry that caused
him pangs of longing. Again, Peleus sent Phoenix with Achilles to
the war to teach him 'to be a speaker of words and a doer of deeds',[12]
because he 'did not yet understand equal war nor assemblies where
men win pre-eminence' (9. 438–43). Nor does Achilles reject the
notion that excellence requires a man to perform superbly in counsel
as well as in battle, although he admits that that is not the sphere in
which he himself is pre-eminent (18. 105–6). In his reply to Odysseus'
attempt in the embassy to persuade him to relent he couches his
refusal in these words: 'I will not join in considering counsels with
him, nor yet deeds' (9. 374).

The idea that a hero will ideally be distinguished in both wisdom
and valour is one the *Iliad* shares with other heroic poetry.[13]
Blancandrin is introduced as 'for valour a mighty knight withal, and
fit of wit for to counsel his lord' (*Roland*, 25–6); Marsilion buttresses
the resolve of the traitor Ganelon with a speech which begins: 'You
are both bold and wise' (ibid. 648); and as the armies are marshalled
for the final battle the poet exclaims (ibid. 3172–5):

> A noble sight is the Emir this day:
> White is his beard as any flower on spray,
> He is in council a man discreet and sage,
> And in the battle stubborn and undismayed.

---

[12] The scholia almost invariably comment on the two virtues of thought and
action or soul an body they take Homer to be commending in these passages. In the
present case an especially interesting inference from 9. 442–3 is drawn by schol. b:
'and thereby he shows that *euboulia* is better than all [sc. speeches and actions]'
(καὶ ὅτι δὲ πάντων [sc. μύθων τε καὶ ἔργων] κρείττων ἡ εὐβουλία δηλοῖ
διὰ τούτου).

[13] For some passages in the *Od.*, Hesiod, and Pindar similar to those collected
above in the *Il.* see e.g. W. G. Thalmann, *Conventions of Form and Thought in Early*

We find the same conception in *Beowulf*: 'Then Wulfgar spoke; the warlike spirit of this Wendel prince, his wisdom in judgement, were known to many' (vv. 348–50). And Ashhere, 'the hero that Hrothgar loved better than any on earth among his retinue' (vv. 1296–7), was not only 'a strong warrior, noted in battle' (vv. 1298–9), but 'my closest counsellor, keeper of my thoughts' (v. 1325). Finally, in his farewell to Beowulf Hrothgar praises the wisdom of his parting words, although of course it has hitherto been his exploits as a fighter that have mattered: 'You are rich in strength and ripe of mind, you wise in your utterance' (vv. 1844–5); and he declares him therefore fit to be king of the Sea-Geats should need arise.

The importance Homer and his protagonists assign to *euboulia* is also reflected in the titles they are given. They are, of course, *aristēes* and *hērōes*, heroes and exponents of excellence, *basilēes*, kings or princes, ἡγήτορες ἠδὲ μέδοντες, leaders and rulers of men.[14] But equally they are *boulēphoroi*, counsellors, and *gerontes*, elders, so called not (at least on the Greek side) with much regard to their age but because they are the men 'for whom it is fitting to advise counsels' (10. 146–7). Much of their deliberation is naturally about military tactics and strategy—at its broadest the question 'whether to flee or to fight' (10. 147; this is the topic of the debates in Books 2, 10, and 14, and initially in Book 9 also), although that question is as complex as life itself, for it involves considerations about the value of the campaign and its objective, about honour and shame, promises and comradeship, and about the will of Zeus. In Book 1, however, the counsel Nestor offers is designed not to propound the solution to a military problem, but to settle a quarrel; and in Book 9 his object is to persuade Agamemnon to eat one half of the humble pie whose other half is offered to Achilles by the embassy. All these exercises in deliberation fall within the general responsibility of a counsellor as it is defined in the words of the dream in Book 2 (24–5): 'A man who is a counsellor must not sleep all night, when peoples are entrusted to him and he has so many cares'; or again in those of the real Nestor to Agamemnon in Book 9

Greek Epic Poetry (Baltimore, 1984), 182 and n. 46. Cf. F. Solmsen, 'The "Gift" of Speech in Homer and Hesiod', *TAPA* 85 (1954), 1–15.

[14] But this phrase already carries a hint of *euboulia*, for, of course, the verb *medō* seems to imply 'organize in a thinking way'. Cf. e.g. P. Chantraine, *Dictionnaire étymologique de la langue grecque* (Paris, 1968), s.v.

(96–102; cf. 2. 204–6):

Most noble son of Atreus, Agamemnon king of men, in you will I cease, from you I will begin, because you are king of many peoples and Zeus has entrusted to you sceptre and *themistes*,[15] so that you may deliberate for them. Therefore you above all men must speak and listen, and bring things about for another too, when his heart bids him speak for good; and on you will depend whatever he begins.[16]

It is perhaps tempting to think of Agamemnon just as a weak and indecisive military commander. But Homer is at pains to make us aware that his office is greater than the man and larger than generalship (1. 277–81): 'Do not think, son of Peleus,' says Nestor, 'to quarrel with a king, might against might, since no equal honour is the lot of a sceptred king, to whom Zeus has given glory. Even if you are valiant, and a goddess mother bore you, yet he is better, since he is king over more men.' His and Odysseus' references particularly to the king's responsibility for administering the customary laws (*themistes*, 2. 206, 9. 99) take us unobtrusively but emphatically from any purely military conception of Agamemnon's position to the Hesiodic notion of one upon whom 'all the people look as he determines *themistes* with straight decisions (*dikai*); and he by his unerring speech swiftly and skilfully calms a great quarrel; for this is why kings are judged wise, because they accomplish restitution easily for people wronged in their dealings, soothing them with gentle words' (*Theogony* 84–90).

The World of Odysseus takes a different view of Homeric kingship (p. 97): 'The king gave military leadership and protection, and he gave little else, despite some hints of royal justice (and injustice) scattered through the *Odyssey*.' The texts to which we have just referred show that 'royal justice' is a concept known to the *Iliad* too. It might perhaps be argued that since Book 9 is under suspicion of belonging to the latest stratum in the composition of the

---

[15] *Themistes* needs explanation rather than translation. Hugh Lloyd-Jones thinks the best definition of *themis* is 'declaration of a divine command or of a command advised by a god' (*The Justice of Zeus* (Berkeley, 1971), 116 n. 23). *Themistes* are thought by the Greeks to come from god, but to the armchair anthropological observer they appear as 'customs, usages, principles of justice' (ibid. 6). As Finley puts it well (n. 3: 78 n.): '*Themis* is untranslatable. A gift of the gods and a mark of civilized existence, sometimes it means right custom, proper procedure, social order, and sometimes merely the will of the gods (as revealed by an omen, for example) with little of the idea of right.'

[16] For an interesting comment on the hymnic character of 97 and its significance see Thalmann (n. 13), 140–2.

Iliad, 9. 95–102 cannot safely be exploited as evidence of the poem's general conception of kingship. And perhaps Odysseus' similar words at 2. 204–6 (which include the famous dictum: 'To have many rulers is not good: let there be one ruler, one king') will likewise be thought too exceptional to be pressed into evidence. But Lloyd-Jones notes a couple of more matter-of-fact passages which attest the king's role in upholding something like justice: 'the Achaean chiefs "protect the *themistes* that come from Zeus" (1. 238), as Sarpedon protects Lycia "by his judgements and his strength" (16. 542)'.[17]

I take it that something must be conceded to Finley: however much or little is made of these texts, there is no denying that the exercise of *euboulia* in justice is something only occasionally mentioned, not presented or explored, in the *Iliad*. But Finley is not entitled to infer very much from this. The *Iliad* is about war, not the life of the communities governed by the warriors. So one would not expect to see them at work administering the *themistes*. Yet it is scarcely conceivable that, if a Homeric king was (unlike Telemachus) firmly in control of the community he governed, he would not be called upon (or take it upon himself) to settle disputes according to the *themistes*—however real or imaginary the Homeric world is taken to be. Finley takes a simile of the *Odyssey* (19. 107–14) which connects the just rule of a god-fearing king with agricultural prosperity to be an anachronism, introducing a carefully controlled contemporary note foreign to the politically more primitive world of Odysseus (p. 97). Let us suppose that he is right about that passage, and that something similar may be true of the description of city and rural life on the shield of Achilles in the *Iliad* (18. 483–608).[18] We can agree to leave such arguably anachronistic passages as these out of the argument for present purposes. What concerns us is something much simpler: the bare idea of kings using good judgement in the dispensation of justice. It is hard to believe that *this* idea is tied to the contemporary eighth-century world, and not perfectly at home in the world inhabited by Agamemnon, Nestor, and the rest.

So far our evidence shows simply that *euboulia* is regarded as a pre-eminent excellence of kings and heroes. Other passages must be cited to show the quality of their (and Homer's) attachment to it.

[17] Lloyd-Jones (n. 15), 6–7.
[18] So e.g. G. S. Kirk, *Homer and the Oral Tradition* (Cambridge, 1976), 11–12; *contra* O. Taplin, 'The Shield of Achilles within the *Iliad*', *G&R* 27 (1980), 1–21 [= this vol., Ch. 11].

When you love or esteem a thing, you are apt to dwell on its salient features in your conversation. Just so does Homer have his heroes talk about counsel and the assembly. Here, for example, is Nestor endeavouring to bring home to the Greeks the seriousness of the commitments which underpin their assembly before Troy, and which should govern its conduct (2. 337–43):

Heavens, you are in truth conducting your assembly like children—childish children, who have no care for deeds of war. What will become of our covenants and oaths? The counsels and plans of men might as well be in the fire, and the pure drink-offerings and the right hands of fellowship in which we trusted. For vainly we are struggling with each other in our words, nor can we find any expedient at all, for all our long stay here.

The assembly can be an effective and constructive forum of debate, a *proper* assembly, only if its participants remember the bonds of mutual loyalty, undertaken for a common purpose, which constitute their assembly as an assembly of consenting adults. Those bonds—oaths, covenants, pledges—exercise the force they do because they are the deeply expressive signs which men use quite generally (not just for military purposes) to declare that they have knit themselves together. Here, next, is Agamemnon on the etiquette of the assembly (19. 78–82), in an attempt to win sympathy for the excuses he is about to offer: 'Danaan heroes, companions of Ares, friends: it is good to listen to him who stands, nor is it seemly to interrupt; for that would be hard even for a skilled man. In a loud uproar of men how could one hear or speak? Even a penetrating speaker is damaged.' And here is the Trojan Antenor celebrating the different qualities of Menelaus and Odysseus as speakers (3. 209–24):

But when they mingled among the assembled Trojans, while people stood Menelaus was the more conspicuous with his broad shoulders, but when both were sitting Odysseus was the more impressive. And when they were weaving words and counsels before everyone, then Menelaus spoke fluently, a few words only, but very penetratingly, for he was not wordy nor off target; he was in fact the younger. But when Odysseus of many wiles rose up, he stood still, and he looked down, fixing his eyes on the ground, and he did not move his staff either backwards or forwards, but he held it stiff, like a man of no understanding: you would have said he was full of rage and just senseless. Yet when he released his great voice from his chest, and words like snowflakes in winter, then no other mortal could contend with Odysseus. Then we were not so astonished as we looked upon Odysseus' bearing.

Like so many passages exemplifying *euboulia* in the Homeric heroes, this famous text was later in antiquity used to argue Homer's interest in questions of political and rhetorical theory: Menelaus was seen as the first exponent of the plain, Odysseus of the grand style (cf. e.g. Cicero, *Brutus* 40 and 50; Quintilian, *Institutio oratoria* 12. 10. 64; Aulus Gellius 6. 14. 7; and other texts collected in L. Radermacher, *Artium Scriptores* (Vienna, 1951), pp. 6 ff.). Finally, here are two passages concerned with *boulē* itself, both the more eloquent because of the circumstances in which they were uttered. As he embarks on his nocturnal reconnaissance Diomedes asks for a companion, and gives celebrated utterance to the maxim that two heads are better than one (10. 224–6): 'When two go together one sees before the other how advantage may come about; on his own, even if he perceives something, his wit is shorter and his scheme fragile.' Then at the end of the poem, when the ghost of Patroclus visits Achilles he speaks these haunting words (23. 75–9): 'Give me your hand, I pray lamenting. For I shall not come again from Hades, since you have given me my dues in the funeral pyre. We shall not sit, living men apart from our dear comrades, giving and taking counsels: the hateful fate has swallowed me which was my lot from when I was born.' Both texts are about companionship, the one appropriate to a nocturnal mission of great danger, the other full of aching nostalgia for pleasures that can never more be enjoyed—pleasures of shared *boulē* that are represented as the essence of friendship.

THE HEROIC CODE

The culture of the world portrayed in the *Iliad* is a warrior culture, and (says Finley)

the main theme of a warrior culture is constructed on two notes—prowess and honour. The one is the hero's essential attribute, the other his essential aim. Every value, every judgement, every action, all skills and talents have the function of either defining honour or realising it . . . The heroic code [of the Homeric poems] was complete and unambiguous, so much so that neither the poet nor his characters ever had occasion to debate it . . . The basic values of the society were given, predetermined, and so were a man's place in the society and the privileges and duties that followed from his status. They were not subject to analysis or debate, and the other issues left only the narrowest margin for the exercise of what we should call judgement (as distinct from

work skills, including knowledge of the tactics of armed combat). . . . The
significant fact is that never in either the *Iliad* or the *Odyssey* is there a
rational discussion, a sustained, disciplined consideration of circumstances
and their implications, of possible courses of action, their advantages and
disadvantages ((n. 3) 113–15).[19]

Finley anticipates a number of lines of objection to the claims he
puts forward, and in particular to his denial that there is rational
discussion in the Homeric poems. I mention three of the chief points
he makes. First, he argues that most speeches at most Homeric
councils and assemblies aim to persuade by threat, by warning, by
encouragement; in short, by emotional appeal, not by reasoned
reflection upon experience or analysis of alternative possibilities.
Second, he discounts the idea that Nestor and Odysseus are paradigms of wisdom: Nestor's *forte* lies in 'bolstering morale' or
'soothing overheated tempers', Odysseus (in the *Odyssey*) is a clever
liar; neither practises the rationality or controlled rational behaviour
prerequisite for wisdom. Third, he pours cold water on the sort of
evidence for a high valuation of intelligence and good judgement in
Homer which was presented in the previous section of this chapter.
We must not 'be misled by the numerous formulas which, in one or
another variant, speak of a man of counsel. For us counsel is deliberation; wise counsel, deliberation based on knowledge, experience,
rational analysis, judgement. But counsel for Homer pointed less to
the reasons than to the decision itself, and hence to the power of
authority' ((n. 3) 115).

---

[19] Finley concedes that 'there are lengthy arguments, as between Achilles and
Agamemnon, or between Telemachus and the suitors'. But these, he claims, 'are
quarrels, not discussions, in which each side seeks to overpower the other by threats,
and to win over the assembled multitude by emotional appeal, by harangue, and by
warning' (n. 3: 114). The implication, I take it, is that the quarrel of *Il.* 1 does not
involve the conflict of different *principles*, but only a collision between Ach.'s and
Ag.'s quests for one and the same goal: honour. This account has some attractions.
But it runs into difficulty as soon as one enquires: what are we to say about the critic
who asks himself 'Is Ach. or Ag. right?' The critic could not avoid describing and
assessing the quarrel in terms of conflicting reasons—reasons actually offered or
capable of being offered in justification or censure of the protagonists' behaviour. How
else could he be a critic? It cannot be denied that the critic appears often enough in
the *Il.*: Nestor in 1. 254–84 and 9. 103–13 is only the earliest of his incarnations. The
main thesis I am going to argue in this section of the chapter could be put as a point
about the protagonist and the critic: Finley's conception of the heroic code is informed
exclusively by the protagonist's viewpoint; a more adequate account will need to
accommodate the critic's viewpoint too, not least because the protagonist is expected
to exercise the *euboulia* of the critic.

I shall examine these latter arguments in due course. It is Finley's fundamental characterization of the heroic code and the consequences he draws from it that require first attention. I have two observations to make, which both bear on the relation between *euboulia* and the heroic code. The first is in a way a development of some of the things Finley says, but it has a problematic consequence which constitutes my second point.

Peleus sent Phoenix with Achilles to Troy because he 'did not yet understand equal war nor assemblies where men win pre-eminence' (9. 440–1). If we try to accommodate Peleus' thinking within the heroic code as defined by Finley, we are surely bound to extend the notion of prowess beyond that of martial performance on the battlefield. Peleus recognizes a prowess in counsel and its expression in oratory. So, too, do the warriors of the *Iliad*. Consider Diomedes' speech at the beginning of Book 9 (31–49). Agamemnon has called an assembly, and in despair has urged the Achaeans to flee and return home, on the ground that it is now clear that it is not the will of Zeus that they should take Troy. In his reply Diomedes calls Agamemnon a fool and a coward, and tells him he can go home if he likes, but the rest of the Achaeans will stay until they sack Troy—or if they too go home he and Sthenelus will take it single-handed. Then Homer reports the response: 'So he spoke, and all the sons of the Achaeans shouted aloud, in admiration at the words of horse-taming Diomedes' (50–1). His crude emotional appeal (Finley's general view of the Homeric harangue is palpably right in this instance) is followed by a vastly more subtle exercise in counsel from Nestor. But the crucial point for the present is that Diomedes' speech is in its own way as much a feat of prowess as one of his exploits on the battlefield; and it wins him an immediate reward of honour or glory in the applause of the host (and in a tactful compliment from Nestor). Similar applause greets other speeches in the *Iliad*—as, for example, when after disposing of Thersites Odysseus rallies the Greeks at the beginning of Book 2 in a masterly oratorical performance, the culmination of what has been called his *aristeia* (2. 333–5):

So he spoke, and the Argives gave a great shout, and all around the ships echoed terribly to the voice of the Achaeans as they praised the words of god-like Odysseus.

The prowess which earns glory, then, may be displayed in speech as well as in action. This is an obvious enough point, yet it is

surprising how little attention is drawn to it in most accounts of the
heroic code in Homer. The reason for the omission is clear enough:
the greatest and the most tragic displays of prowess in the *Iliad* are
unquestionably the deeds of Diomedes, Patroclus, Hector, and
Achilles on the battlefield.[20] But a good two-thirds of the *Iliad* is
direct discourse; and Homer surely expects us to revel, as the
Achaeans do, in the splendid style of the counsels, pleas, threats and
taunts of the chief heroes—much of what is glorious about them is
crystallized in the guile or arrogance or nobility of their talk.

It is a virtue of Finley's treatment of heroism that all this is
implicitly recognized in it. If 'all skills and talents have the function
of . . . realising [honour]',[21] then the ultimate goal of good counsel or
a fine exhortation or taunt is to win honour for the speaker. Hence
part at least of the explanation of the emotive character of much of
the talk in Homeric councils and assemblies: honour inspires
passion, for it matters enormously and is a precarious possession;
therefore when a speaker knows that his speech is regarded as a test
of his mettle, the speech will often betray or exploit passion and
emotion before any other quality.

It may be thought that there is something paradoxical in the idea
that the goal of counsel is honour for the counsellor: surely the object
of giving counsel is to help solve a practical problem? If there were
a difficulty, it would be one that faced any view of life which—unlike
modern deontological or utilitarian philosophies—made the attainment or exercise of virtue the chief object of human existence, as do
(for example) Plato, Aristotle, and the Stoics. Such a conception of
life is not, in fact, necessarily paradoxical. This can be seen from
consideration of one area of life where many people would still
subscribe to the view that virtue or excellence is or should be the
object of the exercise, viz. sport. In sport we play to win, but the
game's the thing—that is, the exercise of our skills and talents it calls
forth, and the enjoyment this gives us and perhaps onlookers, too.
A distinction effectively forged by the Stoics is useful here.[22] The

---

[20] The *Il.*'s imaginative sympathies, like the *Song of Roland*'s, are with the rash
young men who are the focus of the narrative and whose rashness sustains it. But the
heroic ethic is not entirely geared to their point of view: it demands an old head on
young shoulders. Probably it would only occur to someone middle-aged to write a
paper on a poem about youth pointing this out.

[21] Finley (n. 3), 113.

[22] I am following Gisela Striker's fascinating paper on Antipater's subtle defence of
the coherence of Stoic ethics against Academic criticism: see 'Antipater, or the Art of

intended result of playing football is winning: the *goal* is to display and enjoy the display of one's footballing skills. The prime object in playing is to achieve the goal, for it matters more than the intended result. Indeed, there would be no point to winning if playing were not intrinsically worthwhile.

The intelligibility of this common attitude to sport illuminates not only Stoic ethics but Homeric *euboulia*. A heroic counsellor aims to solve the problem in hand. A successful solution is the intended result of his advice. But in so far as he and others see his counsel as a display of prowess, its real goal is something else: the honour accorded to someone who exhibits the appropriate excellences in his advice—pre-eminently spirit and (I would maintain against Finley) wisdom. His solution may be ignored, as for example in Nestor's attempt to reconcile Achilles and Agamemnon in Book I of the *Iliad*. The failure does little to detract from the esteem Nestor wins from every reader (as presumably from the assembled Greeks) for his splendidly sensible intervention. The world of the *Iliad* has sometimes been called a 'results culture', in the belief that for the Homeric hero what matters much more than anything else is success or failure in his enterprises. But the keynote of the heroic code, as Finley says, is honour or glory. And (as we shall see further presently) achieving honour is compatible with a certain amount of failure. Indeed, recent writers such as Redfield and Griffin have done much to show how the peculiar magnificence of Achilles consists in his pursuit of glory at the same time as he recognizes the ultimate futility of all human endeavours. To resume the analogy of sport: Homeric heroes are risk-takers, more like competitive amateurs than professionals; if glory were a simple function of success, they would be more prudent—all Olivers, no Rolands.

I have been arguing that giving counsel is for the Homeric hero a form of prowess: that is its place in the heroic code as defined by Finley; and so interpreted it can be expected to be an emotional affair often enough. Thus far the argument is compatible with *The World of Odysseus*. Now we come to a difficulty. If *euboulia* is a form of prowess comparable in significance only with martial valour, the

Living', in M. Schofield and G. Striker (edd.), *The Norms of Nature* (Cambridge, 1986). There is, of course, a more general affinity between the views of life characteristic of Stoicism and the *Il.*, noted e.g. by Griffin (n. 9). 40, despite the massive difference between the optimism of Cleanthes' *Hymn to Zeus* 1–6 (*SVF* I. 537) and the pessimism of *Il.* 17. 446–7, the Homeric model for lines 4–5 of Cleanthes' poem.

prospect opens of conflict between the values which constitute the code, despite Finley's claim that it is complete and unambiguous. The warrior may find his heroically impulsive pursuit of martial glory opposed by his heroic good judgement.

This possibility would presumably be disallowed by Finley, for a reason reported at the beginning of this section: for the Homeric hero an excellent performance in the assembly does not (according to Finley) involve exercise of the judgement which might oppose martial heroism, but the sort of rhetoric which would encourage it. There *is* a consideration, Finley concedes,[23] which is sometimes raised against the heroic course of action: prudence. But prudence is not a heroic virtue. Its promptings do not indicate conflict of values *within* the framework of the heroic code. Without challenging the code head on, it introduces a point of view *external to it*. It is significant that its personification in the *Iliad* is not the great hero Nestor, but the Trojan Polydamas. Both Nestor and Polydamas offer counsel: Nestor's is 'emotional and psychological', heroically pre-occupied with honour and glory; Polydamas unheroically urges caution.

Here we see Finley making a further application of the dichotomy between emotion, honour, and the heroic, on the one hand, and reason, prudence, and the non-heroic or unheroic on the other. My contention is that the *Iliad* works with a more complex conception of the heroic than this. Why and how could be argued in a number of different ways. I restrict myself to considerations derived from examination of *euboulia*.

Euboulia is itself a many-faceted virtue. A good counsellor must be able to work both on the reason and on the emotions, if only because all deliberative oratory must appeal directly or indirectly to passions and desires, but in all except the crudest cases by presenting considerations—that is, reasons—of one sort or another to the audience. He must have the gift of persuading his audience a lot more often than not, but at the same time he must usually be right. He must concentrate on what is to be done now, but this will involve drawing on past experience and thinking about the future. Heroic *euboulia* does, therefore, sometimes appear in the guise Finley has identified: sometimes Homer holds up a Nestor for admiration because he succeeds in stirring men to bravery by appeal principally

----

[23] Finley (n. 3), 115–16.

to their sense of honour (e.g. 7. 123–74)—that is what his *euboulia* here consists in. On other occasions, however, the considerations it urges upon the mind are more numerous and various than honour: prudence, pity, justice, and a sense of propriety.[24] It is often intent on being reasonable. And what then makes a counsellor admirable may not be the success and spirit of his persuasion (he perhaps fails) but his good judgement and his courage and eloquence in expressing it.

I have suggested that a commitment to *euboulia* already imports into the heroic code the possibility of a conflict of values. Here is the argument for this thesis: the hero's esteem for *euboulia* (as I shall show) commits him to listening to reason. Listening to reason is not treated as if it were to be defined simply in terms of the pursuit of honour; i.e. it is not decided in advance that the only considerations which count as reasonable are those that favour the course of honour. Nor could it very well be defined in such terms. For being reasonable must imply being ready to give weight to any considerations which deserve to be given weight. And how can anyone tell which these are until he has thought about them? It is a crucial assumption of and about rationality that one cannot: that there is or may be more to discover about oneself and the world than one yet knows.[25] The hero committed to *euboulia*, then, has to reckon with the fact that he may find himself having to take seriously claims upon him other than honour and perhaps opposed to honour. Esteem for *euboulia* thus introduces an open-endedness into the heroic code, which accordingly lacks the high degree of determinacy ascribed to it by Finley.

The hero's moral universe undergoes further complication if what *euboulia* presents him with on a given occasion is a reasonable appeal to justice or pity or propriety or prudence which actually does conflict with the dictates of honour—so that he cannot simultaneously act prudently or justly etc. *and* do what his sense of honour demands. The difficulties can best be explored by asking: are justice, prudence, pity, propriety—the claims which *euboulia* typically introduces—themselves intrinsically heroic qualities?

[24] On propriety see A. A. Long, 'Morals and Values in Homer', *JHS* 90 (1970), 129–39.
[25] Cf. Heraclitus B 18 DK (no. 210 in G. S. Kirk, J. E. Raven, and M. Schofield, *The Presocratic Philosophers* (Cambridge, 1983)): ἐὰν μὴ ἔλπηται ἀνέλπιστον οὐκ ἐξευρήσει, ἀνεξερεύνητον ἐὸν καὶ ἄπορον (If one does not expect the unexpected one will not find it out, since it is not to be searched out, and is difficult to compass).

One might argue: No. For heroism is to be seen as defined by honour; a quality only counts as heroic if and when it helps to realize honour. But justice, prudence, and the rest exert the pull they do on us independently: it is not true that they can register with us only when they also represent the claim of honour. On this view of the question, it is no longer just the heroic code which supplies the hero with a guide to conduct. In so far as he is attentive to the thoroughly heroic excellence of *euboulia*, he is obliged on occasion to attach serious importance to non-heroic considerations; and it cannot be assumed that he will always decide in favour of the course of honour. A hero may swallow his pride and decide to let caution or pity for his dependants (for example) govern his behaviour. It is conceivable that the excellence of the judgement which leads him to do so will earn him honour, but the factors which figure in his judgement range beyond honour.

One might, however, construe the heroic code more liberally, and argue that such qualities as justice and prudence are best accorded a place within it. There are two distinct grounds on which this strategy might be defended. First, justice at least is more intimately connected with honour than we have so far allowed. It may sometimes consist in giving honour where honour is due, as we shall see when examining Nestor's intervention in the quarrel of Book I. In such a case a concern for justice *is* a concern for honour, although an altruistic concern which may (and on this occasion does) conflict with naked egoistical pursuit of glory. This possibility of conflict shows that, if there is reason to treat justice as a properly heroic value, there is at the same time reason to judge that considerations of honour may themselves point in different directions, and so yield the hero no unambiguous guide to conduct. (A hero might, of course, decide to dissolve the ambiguity by adopting an ordering principle: always prefer the immediate claims of your own honour to any other consideration. But he would thereby be effectively abandoning any respect for *euboulia*, which heroes are supposed to value. So the ordering principle, attractive though it is to a Hector or an Achilles, should not be regarded as something built into the heroic code itself.) Second, even if (by contrast) prudence, for example, is not a matter of honour, it is certainly a value recognized as having claims on the hero; so why deny it a place in the heroic code? There is surely some advantage in identifying the code as the whole system of values which govern the hero's behaviour, and which he shares with others

(such as his wife and other dependants) who may attach more
weight to prudence and less to honour than he does himself. If we
take this view of the code, then honour will still have to have the
dominant position in it—if it is to count as a *heroic* code. But once
again, there could be no presumption that the claims of honour
ought always to silence those of other values which find a place in
the code.

Finley claimed that 'the heroic code was complete and unambiguous' ((n. 3), 113). I have argued that, if narrowly defined in terms of
honour, it is far from complete; but if it is more liberally construed, it
is plainly not unambiguous. The argument (whose conclusion is not
new) has confined itself to consideration of what follows from the
pre-eminent status of *euboulia* as a heroic virtue. It has made
some assumptions about *euboulia*, particularly its rationality and
the scope of its concerns, which must now be justified. Therefore
I turn to some detailed case studies of Polydamas, Nestor, and the rest
as counsellors.[26]

HECTOR AND POLYDAMAS

A great hero often has a close companion: Achilles has Patroclus,
Gilgamesh has Enkidu, Roland has Oliver. The companion is himself
a hero of stature, but he lacks the consummate arrogance and
heedlessness of danger that mark the greatest heroes. He has a
compensating excellence in which he outshines them—wisdom:

> Roland is fierce and Oliver is wise
> And both for valour may bear away the prize.
>
> (Roland, 1093–4)

His function is to act as the voice of wisdom in his friend's ear,
sometimes to be heeded, but ultimately to be disregarded with consequences simultaneously disastrous and supremely glorious.

It may be that the epic tradition on which Homer draws knew of
a Trojan warrior called Polydamas son of Panthous. But there is

---

[26] It will now be apparent that on my account the Homeric ideal of the hero
prefigures the Aristotelian *phronimos*. I have said and shall say nothing about
Aristotle's conception of *euboulia* (for which see *EN* 6. 9 ($1142^{a}32-^{b}33$); cf. (on
deliberative oratory) *Rhet.* I. 4–6). But in a sense the whole paper is an Aristotelian
reading of the *Iliad*.

every reason to suppose that as Hector's companion or adviser he is entirely Homer's creation[27]—a colourless and artificial creation, it must be confessed. As two excellent discussions by Reinhardt and Redfield[28] bring out, Polydamas achieves no individuality. He has no interesting associations or history, no distinctive personality, no memorable acts of valour to his credit. 'He exists in the *Iliad* only on the Great Day of Battle'; and his existence is entirely functional. He is in the poem solely to perform 'as Hector's *alter ego*' almost as a projection of prudent misgivings on Hector's part about his own impulsiveness: 'He was Hector's companion, and they were born on a single night—but the one was far superior in words, the other with the spear' (18. 251–2).

There is no doubt about Polydamas' heroic stature. His father is one of Priam's counsellors (3. 146), and he is presumably a brother of the Euphorbus (probably no less a Homeric creation)[29] who wounds Patroclus. He is given enough in the way of martial exploits, including at one point a boast over a fallen adversary (14. 453–7), to establish his credentials as a leading Trojan warrior.[30] Nor is there doubt about what his excellence as a counsellor consists in. He is

---

[27] But the argument of this section does not depend on the truth of this claim.

[28] K. Reinhardt, *Die Ilias und ihr Dichter* (Göttingen, 1961), 272–7; Redfield (n. 6), 143–53. The quotations that follow are from p. 143 of Redfield's discussion.

[29] This is the suggestion of S. Farron in his interesting article on Hector's mediocrity as a warrior, 'The Character of Hector in the *Iliad*', *Acta Classica* 21 (1978), 39–57 at 49 n. 35: 'It is possible that the reason why Euphorbus . . . is killed soon after he performs his great deed [sc. of wounding Patroclus] is that he did not originally exist in the tradition but was introduced precisely in order to diminish Hector's accomplishments. Since there were no traditional stories about him, he was eliminated after he had served his purpose.'

[30] At 12. 211–15 Polydamas says (according to the *textus receptus*): 'Hector, always you rebuke me in assemblies, although my counsel is good—since it is not in the least seemly for one of the people ($\delta\hat{\eta}\mu o\nu$ $\dot{\epsilon}\acute{o}\nu\tau a$) to speak beside the mark, neither in council nor in war, but always to increase your power. But now once again I will speak out as seems to me best.' On the grounds that Polydamas is a noble, not a commoner, T. W. Allen (CR 20 (1906), 5) proposed to emend $\delta\hat{\eta}\mu o\nu$ to $\delta\acute{\eta}\mu o\nu$, from $\delta\acute{\eta}\mu\omega\nu$ (otherwise not attested), and meaning 'knowing', 'prudent'. This was a desperate remedy for the real problem that Pol. seems to refer to himself as a commoner if $\delta\hat{\eta}\mu o\nu$ is read. I think the solution (which was suggested to me by James Diggle) is to take his words as bitterly sarcastic: 'since . . . power' represents the attitude to himself that Pol. takes to underlie Hector's rebukes—Pol. is as good as a commoner, whose job if he speaks at all is to support Hec.'s cause with appropriate deference, not to say anything 'beside the mark', i.e. anything independent which might not be in line with Hec.'s own view. Redfield (n. 6: 144) avoids the difficulty by translating the received text differently: 'Since it suits you not at all that our speeches differ among the folk.' But I cannot see how to get that out of the Greek.

adept at sizing up a military situation and its tactical possibilities, and then presenting a sensible assessment of their advantages and disadvantages (particularly the disadvantages) in support of his preferred solution. Thus the Trojans halt in their advance at the ditch planted with stakes outside the Greek camp. Polydamas advises that they proceed on foot: it would be difficult to drive chariots through the stakes; opposite is the wall of the camp; there is no room for charioteers to manoeuvre and fight; and if they did get through but then had to withdraw, the rush back into the ditch would be disastrous (12. 61–79). After a period of great Trojan success the two Ajaxes and the Locrian archers put them in some disarray, and Polydamas foresees a disorderly retreat by the generality of the Trojans. He points out to Hector that, although the battle still rages about him, the other Trojans have either withdrawn from the fighting or continue isolated from each other and against superior numbers. What is needed is a tactical withdrawal by Hector so that he can convene a council of war which can then make a decision on a concerted attack or (as Polydamas hints is more prudent) a general withdrawal (13. 726–47). When Achilles at last returns to the field, the Trojans are panic-stricken, and meet in assembly at the end of the day before even taking supper. Polydamas advises an immediate withdrawal to the city. If they stay, Achilles will wreak havoc on the morrow. But if they make use of the night and retire, they will have the physical protection of the fortifications of the city and the tactical advantage of a nocturnal council. Achilles may attack the city, but if so he will fail and return to the ships in frustration (18. 254–83). Polydamas' talk is all of advantage and safety and never of honour. As he puts it himself in some lines critical of Hector (13. 727–34):

Hector, you do not know how to listen to persuasion. Because God has given you feats of war, in counsel too you want to excel others in knowledge. But you will not be able to succeed in everything at once yourself. God gives one man feats of war, but in the heart of another far-seeing Zeus places a good understanding, and from him many men get advantage and he saves many, and he himself knows it very well.

Polydamas represents it as a fault in Hector that he rejects good advice (cf. 12. 211–12) and good advisers, and charges him with something like megalomania (12. 214). This is Homer's assessment, too. In an earlier interchange, when Polydamas' interpretation of an omen is not to Hector's liking (12. 195–250), the rights and wrongs of the argument are by no means clear.[31] But when it comes to the assembly that meets after Achilles' return to the fray, the poet introduces Polydamas as 'wise Polydamas', who 'alone saw before and after', and he stresses his good intent and his superiority to Hector in speech (18. 249–53). After Hector rejects his advice, Homer comments (18. 310–13):

So Hector spoke and the Trojans applauded—fools, for Pallas Athene took away their wits. They gave assent to Hector although his plan was bad, but no one praised Polydamas, who devised good counsel.[32]

And in due course Hector reproaches himself for ignoring him: 'I have destroyed the host by my recklessness' (22. 104). As *euboulia* in a hero is regarded as an excellence, so folly is reckoned a weakness.

Why should Hector's disdain of Polydamas' counsel count as folly? It can only be because he has wilfully ignored something he could and should have taken account of: the likelihood of a Trojan reverse, with the loss of many men, if he remained in the field. Does this show that heroes value very highly something other than honour: the avoidance of heavy profitless losses? Certainly Polydamas would see it that way, to judge from the way he expresses himself in the speech quoted above (13. 727–34). Life and security are things he evidently treats as valuable in themselves, as does (for example) Priam when he pleads with Hector not to attempt single combat with Achilles (22. 56–9):

No, come within the wall, my child, so that you may save the men and women of Troy, and not give great glory to the son of Peleus but yourself be bereft of dear life.

But does Hector share their concern for life and safety? When he wails 'I have destroyed the host by my recklessness', what he really

[31] See Reinhardt (n. 28), 273–5, followed by H. Erbse, 'Ettore nell' Iliade', *SCO* 27 (1978), 13–34, at 19–20.
[32] Erbse (n. 31), 20–2 ingeniously argues that Hector is *not* criticized for misjudgement: he has well-founded tactical and strategic reasons, presented in his reply to Polydamas (18. 285–309), for rejecting his advice; he merely labours under the forgivable ignorance of the divine plan for Troy. Erbse then (p. 23) explains 22. 104 away as a sort of representation of what Hec. fears will be the Trojan view of his generalship. This perversely alters the natural meaning of both 18. 310–13 and 22. 104. Certainly Hec. has a military rationale for the course he advocates at 18. 285–309: it is just not a very sensible one in the immediate circumstances. Redfield (n. 6: 152–3) has a much better balanced treatment of the issue.

regrets, it might be said, is his own dishonour: folly is a matter for reproach; and losing men is losing face. But, of course, losing men could not be a matter of losing face unless human life was regarded as precious in itself. Finley himself stresses the hero's love of life ((n.3), 113): 'The Homeric heroes loved life fiercely, as they did and felt everything with passion, and no less martyr-like characters could be imagined; but even life must surrender to honour.'

The logical structure of Hector's pursuit of honour is much better expressed by the idea that other values must *surrender* to honour than by Finley's other formulation, which says that they *define* or *realize* it. Like the heroic esteem for *euboulia*, it can be illuminated by comparison with the Stoic conception of virtue as explicated by Antipater. Hector fights to defend the walls of Troy because they are what stand between the Greeks and the things the Trojans value in and for themselves—children, wives, kin, and a settled and independent way of life. The fact that these are at stake helps to give depth and point to the conflict between the armies, as Homer makes us aware when he takes us behind the city walls. It is what endows the role and character of Hector with a greater density than is found in those of the principal Greek heroes. To revert to our earlier terminology, we may say that the life and safety of Troy is the *intended result* of his military exploits. And it is precisely when Hector bears in mind that the war is waged with an overall intention that he listens to Polydamas and his prudent tactical advice: prudence is sometimes necessary if the Trojans are to achieve their objective. Life, safety, prudence are all, then, concerns that Hector must acknowledge if he is to fight the *Trojan* war at all. But his overriding *goal* is the achievement of glory (e.g. 6. 441–6) or (near the bitter end) the avoidance of further dishonour (22. 99 ff.); and for this he is prepared to surrender his own life and the lives of all he holds most dear. From the point of view of honour, the defence of Troy merely provides the occasion or material for display of valour, just as for the Stoic conforming with nature by selecting the things that are natural for men to do or have simply provides the forum in which virtue can be practised.

At one point (12. 243) Hector famously says: 'One omen is best, to fight back for the fatherland.' For want of the distinction between goal and intended result both Finley and Erbse, one of his most thoughtful critics, are led astray in their treatment of this line. Finley, rightly convinced that honour is Hector's overriding goal, wrongly thinks himself forced to the false conclusion that patriotic sentiment is non-heroic and at odds with the whole course of Hector's behaviour.[33] Erbse is no less rightly persuaded that 12. 243 expresses something at the core of Hector's heroic idea—viz. the intention with which he fights. Just as wrongly, he feels he must therefore explain away passages such as 6. 441–6 or 22. 99 ff. where Hector plainly sets his own quest for honour and glory above concern for his family or his city.[34]

Critics of Stoic ethics, ancient and modern, have always found their theory of the goal of life schizophrenic. How can it be both preferable to have a family life and be in good health ('primary natural things') and yet ultimately these do not matter *at all*? Is not the preference that of one creature, an embodied animal with affections, and the indifference that of another, a purely rational being?[35] There is a similar tension in the *Iliad* between the keenness of the hero's appetite for life and concern for those he protects, and his ultimate rejection of anything but honour. It is because *euboulia* typically makes the success of an enterprise its focus that the great heroes, intent only (when it comes to the crunch) on their own glory, are deficient in it—and so programmed, contrary to all their desires, for imperfection.

Is it, as Redfield holds, the heroic ethic itself which drives Hector and Achilles to this self-destructively exclusive preoccupation with nothing but honour?[36] Or is Griffin right to object that the cause is rather (in Achilles' case) too passionate emotion or (in Hector's) strategic misjudgement: faults of individual psychology recognizable as such from the standpoint of the heroic ethic itself?[37] We are now in a position to see that these are not genuine alternatives. The heroic code gives a high ranking to *euboulia*, and hence (if for no other reason) ample scope for criticism of Achilles and Hector. But a value system which gives honour the structural position of a goal distinct

---

[33] Finley (n. 3), 116–17. For discussion of patriotism in Homer see e.g. P. A. L. Greenhalgh, 'Patriotism in the Homeric World', *Historia* 21 (1972), 528–37; S. Scully, 'The Polis in Homer: A Definition and Interpretation', *Ramus* 10 (1981), 1–34. Patriotism is possible without the state, which, as Finley rightly holds, is what the Homeric *polis* is not (for criteria of statehood see W. G. Runciman, 'Origins of States: The Case of Archaic Greece', *Comp. Stud. in Soc. and Hist.* 24 (1982), 351–77).

[34] Erbse (n. 31), 23–4, 29–32.

[35] See e.g. A. A. Long, *Hellenistic Philosophy* (London, 1974), 189–99.

[36] See esp. ch. 3, 'The Hero', of Redfield (n. 6).

[37] J. Griffin, *Homer on Life and Death* (Oxford, 1980), 74 n. 46, 145–6 with n. 6.

from the intended results of action clearly has a dynamism of its own. Any goal that is intrinsically desirable exercises an attractive force; where it is a goal whose attainment matters much more than the intended results of actions undertaken for its sake (as honour is in the heroic scheme of things), any other consideration (e.g. safety or prudence) must tend to pale into insignificance. So we must agree with Griffin when (in a passage I take to be incompatible with his criticism of Redfield) he says:[38] 'The hero is trapped by the logic of his heroism.' He *need* not be trapped, if like Odysseus he remains heroically attentive to the demands of *euboulia*; but if he is trapped, we can hold the logic—or, as I should prefer to say, the dynamism— of his heroism responsible.

This general heroic predicament is fully worked out by Homer only in Hector's case. He succeeds in making it a particularly stark instance of the predicament by the pains he takes to establish Hector's very identity as a function of his attachment to his family (e.g. 6. 405–39) and his city (e.g. 6. 403, 22. 410–11). The choice Hector has to make between his honour and the protection of Troy and his kinsfolk is so painful precisely because he is essentially their protector, but yet he is him and not them. Homer prepares us for it by the sequence of encounters with Polydamas, which is sustained through several books (12, 13, 18) and almost constitutes a script of the plot of Hector's downfall. It culminates in the great deliberative monologue of 22. 98–131, in which the poet has him rehearse in internal debate his mostly vanished or vanishing options.[39] The external struggle with Polydamas and the interior argument in Hector's own mind are alike symbolic of the dynamic tension within the heroic ethic. Their contrivance to my mind supports both the currently popular reading of the *Iliad* as a tragedy and more parti- cularly Redfield's interpretation of it as an exploration of 'the lim- itations and self-contradictions' of the heroic ethic.[40] Hector could have been brought to his final defeat by Achilles without committing a lapse of judgement. Homer not only gives him a fatal lapse. He designs a schematic dramatization of the lapse as the outcome of a struggle between thought and impulse, or again between the hero

[38] Griffin (n. 9), 43.
[39] For discussion of this speech see B. C. Fenik, 'Stylization and Variety: Four Monologues in the *Iliad*', in Fenik (ed.), *Tradition and Invention* (Leiden, 1978); and R. W. Sharples, '"But why has my spirit spoken with me thus?" Homeric Decision-Making', *G&R* 30 (1983), 1–7.   [40] Redfield (n. 6), 85.

and his kin and community (represented, of course, not only by
Polydamas but much more memorably by Andromache in Book 6
and by Priam and Hecuba in Book 22). If telling a story can (as
Redfield proposes) constitute an enquiry, it is (*inter alia*) the presence
of this sort of thematic schematism that will have to establish it
as such.

THE GREEKS IN COUNCIL

The Greek assembly in Book 1 famously degenerates into a quarrel.
The council of gods at the beginning of Book 20 is summoned not for
discussion or debate but to receive the issue of an instruction. But
sometimes there is a difficult practical problem to be solved, and the
point of a council is to find the best answer by means of rational
discussion. Just such a discussion occurs at the beginning of Book 14.

At a very low point in Greek fortunes Nestor decides after internal
debate not to return to the fray but to seek out Agamemnon. He
meets him as he goes back to the battlefield from the ships in the
company of Odysseus and Diomedes. All three are wounded and sick
at heart, and the sight of Nestor coming away from the fighting
makes them fear the worst. A discussion ensues. There are six contributions to it:

1. *Agamemnon*, addressing Nestor, sums up the state of the battle—
   or rather (and characteristically) of his own fears about it: he is
   apprehensive that Hector will succeed in carrying out his threat of
   burning the ships, and that the Greeks for their part are as angry
   with him as Achilles is and have no wish to fight by the ships.
2. *Nestor* in his report on the fighting confirms that the Greeks are
   being routed. He proposes that they consider what to do 'if wit
   may achieve anything'. He offers no plan of his own, but advises
   that the heroes not return to the battle since they are wounded.
3. *Agamemnon* makes (again characteristically) a rather ambiguous
   proposal that has defeatism written all over it. He suggests that
   since their defences have failed and the gods appear to be against
   them, the Greeks should take the first steps towards putting all
   their ships to sea.
4. *Odysseus* upbraids Agamemnon, obviously taking his suggestion
   to be a thinly veiled move to abandon the campaign against Troy
   altogether. He argues that his plan is not appropriate for a proud

and grimly determined army such as theirs, which is not prepared to abandon the attempt on Troy now when it has already cost them so much. He condemns Agamemnon's talk as defeatist. And he points out that the outcome of his counsel would be likely to be that the Greeks will panic completely and allow the Trojans to destroy them.

5. *Agamemnon* accepts the rebuke and acknowledges that Odysseus has captured the mood of the army. He invites 'a better plan than this'.

6. *Diomedes* takes up the invitation with apologies for his boldness as a young man in doing so. After attempting to prove his fitness to speak by citing the valour of his father and grandfather, he advises that they return to the battle—but only to encourage the fainthearted, not to fight themselves, since they are wounded.

And that is what they agree to do.
Finley said ((n. 3), 114):

The significant fact is that never in either the *Iliad* or the *Odyssey* is there a rational discussion, a sustained, disciplined consideration of circumstances and their implications, of possible courses of action, their advantages and disadvantages.

The council in Book 14 shows that Finley's fact is not a fact. An assessment is made of the military situation and accepted by all parties to the discussion. Its crucial components are three: (*a*) the Trojans are routing the Greeks; (*b*) the Greek ships are threatened; (*c*) the Greek leaders are wounded. Two main alternative courses of action—returning to battle and saving the ships by other means— are considered. In thinking about them each speaker at least implicitly takes (*a*), (*b*), and (*c*) into account. In view of (*c*) in particular, Nestor counsels against the return of the leaders to battle. In line with this Agamemnon proposes a solution to (*b*) that will avoid it. Odysseus insists that this alternative will not do: it is cowardly and it will involve both immediate defeat and the abandonment of the campaign. Diomedes concludes that they must after all adopt the first alternative of a return to the battle. They can cope with (*c*), which Nestor had adduced against this option, by encouraging the others, not fighting themselves.

Thus the advantages and disadvantages of the two alternatives are thoroughly explored. Diomedes, it is true, has little to say in favour of

his proposal, but then he only needs to point out how it can be made
to avoid the disadvantage Nestor had drawn attention to—given that
Agamemnon's proposal has been rejected. Every speaker offers
reasonable counsel; and counsel is what *boulē* is in this context
(14. 102), not (as Finley claims) decision, for it is Agamemnon's
defeatist plan (*mētis*, v. 107) that gets called *boulē*. In most cases the
counsel is supported by explicit reasoning: most notably and elabo-
rately by Odysseus, least so by Diomedes. This fits Diomedes' role and
character as the youngest and least experienced of those conferring.
It does not detract from the rationality and effectiveness of his
solution. What Diomedes *does* present arguments for is his right to be
heard. These consist in an appeal to the prowess of his family: 'it is
one's stature in the warrior community that confers the expectation
of being listened to with respect'.[41] But his counsel is accepted not
because it comes from the doughtiest fighter, but because it appears
the best way out of the difficulty.

The rationality of the discussion is not compromised by the emotion the heroes evince in its course. Without Agamemnon's fears and
the spirit and determination of Odysseus there would be no argument, and Agamemnon loses it because the course he proposes is
seen as cowardly, not just counterproductive. The charge of cowardice, however, is tactfully left only half explicit, nor is it meant
to settle matters on its own. It forms part of a disciplined and
reasoned case.

How much should be made of this passage? It has to be admitted
that the council it describes is unusual among the parleys of the *Iliad*
in its sustained and single-minded concentration on the rational
solution of a problem. That does not mean that it can be dismissed
as untypical. It has a significance that makes it much more than
one episode among others; and the roles taken in the discussion
by the different Greek leaders are so thoroughly in character
that some general inference about *euboulia* may legitimately be
drawn.

The main Greek councils and assemblies in the *Iliad* all have
important dramatic functions, but functions of different sorts. Those
in 1 and 19, for example, are indispensable to the plot, needed to
begin and end the great quarrel. The whole of Book 2, as has often

[41] A. W. H. Adkins, 'Values, Goals, and Emotions in the *Iliad*', *CP* 77 (1982),
292–326, at 298.

been remarked, is irrelevant to the development of the plot; the point of the council and assembly in 2 is accordingly quite different—to reveal the characters of Agamemnon, Nestor, and Odysseus and to show the effect of the long war on the Greeks. The council in 14 is no more needed in the plot than that in 2. Had Agamemnon, Odysseus, and Diomedes not met Nestor at all, but returned without any parley to the battlefield, the ensuing sequence of events could have remained the same. I suggest that their council has a symbolic and a paradigmatic function.[42] It marks the desperation of the Greek cause at this point in the battle. At the same time it indicates the way great heroes in military command will behave in a crisis. A crisis must be met not with panic but with courage, and not merely courage but careful thought. So Homer presents the Greek leaders in rational discussion. Rational discussion is not just something that happens on this occasion, we must infer. It may not actually occur all that frequently in the narrative of the poem. But it is a heroic ideal in an epic about the heroic ideal.

That is to say, the conduct of the discussion as a whole constitutes an ideal. Agamemnon's part in it is characteristically disastrous. His counsel is governed by fear and anxiety: mostly for the army, but also for his own standing with the Greeks. A proper concern for his troops is an elementary requirement in a commander, but Agamemnon is too close to panic. His positive proposal is plainly incompetent, for the reasons exposed by Odysseus. He accepts Odysseus' rebuke graciously, but the self-knowledge revealed by his request that someone 'may speak a better plan than this' (14. 107) does not restore faith in his fitness to be commander. The comparison of words and behaviour is instructive: Odysseus' and Diomedes' act of returning to the battlefield is matched by the conviction of their speeches; Agamemnon, too, had been returning, but his words show his indecision and lack of resolve. All this is typical of the dominant strain in Agamemnon's character and behaviour throughout the *Iliad*. Homer says to us in this episode not merely: this is how Agamemnon behaved, but: this is what Agamemnon is like.

Two aspects of the portrayal are of particular interest to us. The first is that the focus of this passage, like most of the more memorable scenes in which Agamemnon figures, is his performance as a commander, not his prowess as fighter. It might be felt that, although the

---

[42] Cf. in general Griffin (n. 37), ch. 1.

ideal hero is a speaker of words as well as a doer of deeds (9. 443), when it comes to presenting his major heroes the poet of the *Iliad* puts all the emphasis, on martial prowess. This is perhaps true of Ajax: but he is the exception who proves the rule, as a brief look at the other major Greek heroes will confirm. In Agamemnon's case it is his shortcomings as a deviser of counsel and as a decision-maker which preoccupy Homer and the reader. If Agamemnon is no good, that is because he is no good at *boulē*. This brings me to the second point. The reason for Homer's emphasis here is obviously that in a supreme military commander it is *euboulia*, understood as ability in tactics, strategy, and the power to persuade, not warrior prowess, that counts most. Agamemnon is therefore quite properly more concerned with the ultimate fate of the campaign and the need not to sustain heavy losses than with leading a glorious charge into the fray or scoring personal triumphs in combat. His predicament illustrates from another angle the same point of tension within the heroic code as emerged in considering Hector. Both see that it may be more prudent to accept defeat. The difference is that Agamemnon has less spirit but more regard for his responsibility to exercise *euboulia* than Hector. He knows that returning home empty-handed will bring dishonour (2. 115, 9. 22), although he tries to pretend that 'there is no impropriety in fleeing from evil' (14. 80). Now the place of *euboulia* in the heroic code is such that its deliverances cannot properly be ignored or rejected as cowardly: if reason matters, then it matters. Accordingly Odysseus' main complaint against Agamemnon in 14 is that his plan is a bad plan, not informed by *euboulia*.

Odysseus' main scenes in the *Iliad*, like Agamemnon's, are mostly ones in which he figures as a counsellor and speaker. Unlike Agamemnon he excels in this sphere. As he himself puts it at 19. 216–19:

Achilles son of Peleus, best by far of the Achaeans, you are mightier than me and not a little better with the spear, but I can far surpass you in thought, since I was born first and know more things.

Finley, presumably thinking of the Odysseus of the *Odyssey*, dismisses him as a liar,[43] although I prefer Kirk's judgement that 'with few exceptions he is represented as behaving extremely

---

[43] Finley (n. 3), 115.

rationally, indeed as initiating complex processes of analysis and decision-making that would do credit to Bertrand Russell himself'.[44] In the *Iliad* he stands out among the heroes of both sides for his skill as a public speaker, which is harnessed to loyalty, good judgement (although like all the Greeks he misjudges Achilles in Book 9), and grim determination.

Two passages are worth recalling. After Agamemnon's catastrophic address to the army at the beginning of Book 2 Odysseus saves the day with a whole series of interventions: first exhortations to individual chieftains and men, then his popular attack on Thersites, and finally a long and cleverly judged speech, balancing Agamemnon's inept performance, to the army as a whole. It begins with an attempt to shame the Greeks for breaking their promises to Agamemnon and wailing like women and children; then it concedes that there is a lot to wail about; there follows a reminder, in rivetingly vivid detail, of the portent of snake and sparrows they witnessed at Aulis, and of Calchas' interpretation—that in the tenth year of siege Troy will fall. The triumphant conclusion is that the Greeks are now on the brink of that success. The whole is a splendid example of the preacher's art: sin is condemned, the sinner pitied, a miracle retailed and salvation promised—on the preacher's terms.

No less admirable is Odysseus' handling of Achilles in Book 19. Achilles has been rather offhand in his reply to Agamemnon's offer of recompense and has proposed an immediate return to battle. Odysseus responds with a firm speech which puts him tactfully in his place while assuring him of the sympathy of the other Greek leaders in his great quarrel. An immediate return to battle is out of the question (the men must eat). Now is the time rather for Agamemnon to give his gifts, and swear on oath. And he tells Agamemnon to his face to behave with more justice in future. When Achilles persists with his proposal, Odysseus resists again, and with the authority of experience lays it down that in war death cannot merit a fast. His restraint is as heroic as Achilles' desire for war, not least because he takes risks in arguing with him, as in a different way he took a risk in the Doloneia of Book 10. Here, too, he succeeds.

In Odysseus' oratory there is not so much of the rational analysis which marks Polydamas' advice to Hector. But what he

[44] Kirk (n. 7), 288.

says is always reasoned and reasonable, although it exploits emotion, too.

Redfield supplies a convenient summary of a well-known Homeric contrast:[45]

In Homeric society a distinction is made between the young man and the mature man, a distinction correlated with the distinction between council and battle as arenas of excellence and with the contrast between the word and the deed. Excellence in both speech and combat are required of the perfect hero (9. 433; cf. lines 510–16), but speech develops later in life (9. 53–61). In a culture where physical strength and beauty are so important, old age can only be hateful—*stugeros, lugros, oloos*—but there are certain partially compensating advantages. The young man's mind is hasty, and his wits are slight (23. 590). The elder 'knows more' (13. 355, 21. 440); there is an authority which belongs to age (1. 259, 9. 160–1).

Among the Greek counsellors of the *Iliad* Nestor has a special place as the eldest and Diomedes as the youngest.

Finley has some harsh things to say about Nestor. In his talk Nestor never aimed 'at selecting the course of action' nor did he formulate anything that could properly 'be called a significant and reasoned' suggestion—except once, when at 7. 323–43 he proposed the building of the defensive wall before the Greek camp ((n.3) 114–15). This is a puzzling claim. Nestor influences policy decisively by his advice on several other occasions. For example, he is responsible for the division of the army into tribes and phratries (2. 360–8); he engineers the sending of the embassy to Achilles (9. 96–113); he conceives of the plan of a nocturnal reconnoitre which results in the capture of Dolon (10. 204–17). All these schemes are recommended by Nestor on reasonable grounds, and all are treated as significant by the poet. Although only the episode of the embassy is important within the overall development of the *Iliad*, each of them shapes the rest of the book in which it occurs. Nor should it be forgotten that it is Nestor's appeal to Patroclus (11. 655–803) which is directly responsible for his return to the battlefield (16. 20 ff.) and so indirectly for Achilles' own reappearance. As Dio Chrysostom points out (56. 9), so dominant is Nestor in formulation of tactics and strategy that when Zeus wishes to deceive Agamemnon by the dream, the dream adroitly adopts the form of the old man,

---

[45] Redfield (n. 6), 110–11.

rightly confident that Agamemnon will then find its message irresistible.[46]

We are sometimes prone to think of Nestor merely as a boastful and garrulous old man, overly fond of autobiographical anecdote (as above all, perhaps, in his enormously long speech at 11. 656–803). This view of him was apparently current in antiquity also, for Dio devotes one of his discourses to an examination of the question whether in his speech of mediation in Book 1 Nestor's appeal to his own experience is simply bragging (*Oration* 57). For what he tells Achilles and Agamemnon is that the men of his youth were better men than they, but never made light of Nestor: they summoned him to be with them, they understood his counsels, they obeyed his words (1. 259–73). Dio's evaluation of this passage of reminiscence is clearly correct. Nestor, he says, perceives that Achilles and Agamemnon are misbehaving because of their arrogance. By his reference to the men of old he intends to shock them into humility as one might prick or squeeze a swelling. His reference to himself is designed to convince them that he is the doctor to whom they must turn if they are to be cured. It is, as Norman Austin puts it,[47] 'a strong appeal for a

---

[46] It is strange that, of all Nestor's exercises in counsel, his advice to build the wall should meet with Finley's special approval. As Kirk says (n. 9: 219), 'Nestor's original suggestion of building the wall was cursory and odd, and was associated with the proposal that the burnt bones of the Achaean dead should be collected for carrying back to their children after the war.' Kirk's new commentary on *Il.* 1–4 (*Il. Comm.* 1) is particularly good value on Nestor. See e.g. his notes on 1. 247–91, 2. 20–1, 2. 76–83, 2. 336–68, 4. 291–309.

[47] N. Austin, 'The Function of Digressions in the *Iliad*', in J. Wright (ed.), *Essays on the Iliad* (Bloomington, Ind., 1978), 70–84, at 75. This essay has many helpful things to say about Nestor's digressions, esp. the one at 11. 656 ff. Austin suggests (79) that 'where the drama is most intense the digressions are the longest and the details the fullest', and that 'the length of the anecdote is in direct proportion to the necessity for persuasion at the moment' (he thinks particularly of the story of Meleager in Book 9 and Nestor's story in Book 11, and argues that they 'mark the most desperate stages in the deteriorating [military] situation'). The first of these propositions seems to me simply false: the *drama* is much more intense in the quarrel in Book 1 than it is in Book 11 at least. Austin concedes (83) that 'the digressions do not create suspense in the modern sense' although they do occur at dramatic moments. He claims, however, that prolix as they are they do represent 'a *concentration* of tension' (my italics). I think this is a false trail. As Austin himself shows, the very long anecdotes of Books 9 and 11 are designed to stop Achilles and Patroclus from concentrating on themselves and the present to the exclusion of all else, by diverting their attention to remoter times and places. The point is to induce a sense of perspective on the present which may shift their attitudes. Austin's final sentence reads (84): 'It [the Iliadic digression] brings time to a standstill and locks our attention unremittingly on the celebration of the present moment.' For 'present' read 'past'. Pat Easterling suggests to me that we

hearing', just like Diomedes' in 14. 110–27. It says to Achilles and Agamemnon: recognize a tried and tested moral authority which has a greater claim on your attention than the demands of your immediate selves.

No speech of Nestor has been more discussed in recent years than this intervention of his in the great quarrel. It is worth a little more attention in the present context, since it illuminates the nature of his *euboulia* and also some of the complexities of the heroic code that we have been exploring. The speech falls into three parts. Nestor begins by observing that the rift and its likely consequences can bring joy only to the Trojans (254–8). Then he asks the two heroes to accept the counsel he has to offer, and (as we have noted) cites at some length some of the experience which entitles him to have his advice heeded (259–74). Finally he presents his proposals, briefly and trenchantly: Agamemnon should let Achilles keep Briseis— because the girl was given to him as a mark of honour; Achilles must not quarrel with a king—because Zeus gives special honour and glory to a king; and Agamemnon must desist from his anger with Achilles—because Achilles is the bulwark of the Achaeans (275–84).

There is nothing notably emotional about Nestor's appeal. He is trying to cool the temperature, not raise it. All his proposals are eminently reasonable; and they are all explicitly supported by rea-sons—reasons that appeal not to the emotions but to cool con-sideration of the claims of justice and prudence. It is sometimes implied that Nestor only puts real weight on his prudential argu-ments.[48] Indeed M. M. Mackenzie goes so far as to claim that he *has* only prudential arguments—ignoring the reason Nestor gives Agamemnon for returning Briseis, and redrafting the reason he offers Achilles for not quarrelling with Agamemnon (he should 'admit Agamemnon's superiority, since by his action he is jeopardizing the Greek position at Troy').[49] It is as if Nestor's case were complete by

should compare e.g. the account of how Odysseus got his scar (*Od.* 19. 383–466): a very long digression 'poised between the moments when Eurycleia recognizes the scar (vv. 392–3) and when she reacts to the recognition (vv. 467–75)'. She would 'emphasise the significance or weight given to any episode which is *embellished*, whether by elaborate descriptions or by speeches' rather than notions like tension or suspense.

[48] This seems to be Adkins's view (n. 41), 292–326, at 299 and 325.

[49] M. M. Mackenzie, *Plato on Punishment* (Berkeley and Los Angeles, 1981), 73–4.

v. 257. Hugh Lloyd-Jones had made the appropriate reply:[50]

This speech of Nestor's may contain no mention of an abstract notion of justice, but justice is what Nestor is aiming at; he wishes to settle the dispute by persuading each participant to accord to the other his proper *timē*.

Achilles and Agamemnon are invited to think not just of themselves and their own honour, but of the other man's point of view, and what *his* position or situation entitles *him* to expect. This sort of thinking is certainly given weight by Odysseus, for he concludes his first speech in the reconciliation scene with an explicit directive to Agamemnon about just behaviour (19. 181–3):

You, son of Atreus, will have to be juster in the future in other cases too. For there is no shame for a king in making amends to a man if he was the one first to create trouble.

What must motivate the denial that Nestor has any or any significant concern with justice in his speech in Book 1 is, I think, a more fundamental conviction about the Homeric hero: that the hero is so predominantly concerned with his own honour and well-being that there would be little or no point in Nestor's appealing to anything but prudential considerations. To this the short answer can only be: but he does, so there must be. There is one very obvious reason why there has to be: if honour matters so much, then it also matters a great deal that every hero should recognize the honour due to every other hero.

One might attempt to support the idea that there cannot be by adducing in evidence Adkins's thesis that Nestor has no *moral* vocabulary powerful enough to trump considerations of what is due to a hero expressed in terms of his claims as an *agathos*. I take it, however, that this thesis is by now thoroughly discredited. Let us consider, as Adkins did, what Nestor says to Agamemnon at 1. 275: 'Do not, *agathos* though you be, take the girl from him.' On this Adkins commented:[51]

That is to say, an *agathos* might well do this without ceasing to be an *agathos*, and indeed derives a claim to do it from the fact that he is an *agathos*; but in this case Nestor is begging Agamemnon not to do it.

Long has pointed out that this badly distorts Nestor's plea. Nestor supports it with an argument: the Greeks gave Briseis to Achilles as

[50] Lloyd-Jones (n. 15), 13.   [51] Adkins (n. 1), 37.

a prize. His words seem to have an implication quite the opposite of
that suggested by Adkins: your being an *agathos* gives you no claim
on the girl, and certainly none to override Achilles' claim, which
derives from the fact that she was given to him by the army.[52] So
interpreted they throw no clear light on the question of whether
Nestor does or does not have available in the heroic vocabulary an
evaluative expression stronger than *agathos*. But in a recent article of
great clarity and magisterial common sense Sir Kenneth Dover has
shown that that question is in any case an obscure and inappropriate
one.[53] What matters at least as much as the words a speaker chooses
is what he is using them to achieve. In the present instance Nestor is
trying to *persuade* a powerful prince to be *reasonable* and in consequence to change course. To tell a man publicly and in the
strongest terms available that he is in the wrong is generally not the
most effective way of persuading him to see reason. The strong
language of moral denunciation is just inappropriate. Of course,
Nestor's more tactful plea fails. This is certainly because of the
strength of something—not language, however, but Agamemnon's
care at that moment for his own honour, which outweighs any
regard for justice or for the likely consequences of his behaviour. He
is propelled by the dynamic of the heroic code, but not inevitably
propelled:[54] sometimes *euboulia* prevails, with Agamemnon as with
most other heroes. (The whole plot of the *Iliad* turns on the fact—
bitterly regretted—that he loses his wits (9. 377) or that his mind
becomes infatuated (9. 119, 19. 88). There could be no stronger
testimony to the importance of *euboulia* in the heroic scheme of
things.)

   Tact is the hallmark of Nestor's *euboulia*.[55] This is evident in the
first few lines of his speech in Book 1, when he describes Achilles and
Agamemnon as 'surpassing the Danaans both in counsel and at
fighting' (1. 258). Because this is transparently untrue (neither is
much good at counsel), Finley thought we must retranslate *boulē*
as 'power of decision' to make it true.[56] But the retranslation will not
work in most other contexts. It is better to leave *boulē* to mean
'counsel' and to recognize a tactful insincerity, designed to coax the
quarrelling princes into exercising such *euboulia* as they possess.

---

[52] Long (n. 24), 127.
[53] 'The Portrayal of Moral Evaluation in Greek Poetry', *JHS* 103 (1983), 35–48.
[54] See Redfield (n. 6), 94–8, on Ag.'s behaviour in the quarrel.
[55] Cf. Lloyd-Jones (n. 15), 14.   [56] Finley (n. 3), 115.

Much of Nestor's advice is intended to bolster Agamemnon's authority, even when (as here) it opposes his will. Thus at the beginning of Book 2 he lends decisive support to Agamemnon's plan with the highly ambiguous argument that the dream would be reckoned deception were it not the dream of him who boasts to be best of the Achaeans (2. 76–83). This is ingenious as well as tactful, like his counsels at the beginning of Book 9. Diomedes has opposed Agamemnon's speech urging a return home with a robust charge of cowardice that catches the popular mood. Nestor seizes his opportunity. He compliments Diomedes on his prudent counsel, with just enough condescension to suggest that, although the inexperienced young man may have settled one issue, much remains to be discussed—and Agamemnon is the man to preside over the further deliberations. When these are held, he softens the harsh message he has to deliver to Agamemnon with the most eloquent account of the pre-eminence and authority of the king to be found in the *Iliad* (9. 52–78, 96–113).

Nestor calls Diomedes 'exceedingly valiant in war and the best in counsel of all your contemporaries' (9. 54). Diomedes is after Odysseus the most perfect hero of the *Iliad*, and he is so because in him *euboulia* (albeit a raw *euboulia*) and warrior prowess are better balanced than in anyone else but him.[57] Griffin observes how 'the poet shows us Diomede making no immediate protest when unjustly and publicly criticised by [Agamemnon] in Book 4, and then asserting himself, firmly but calmly, in Book 9 . . . The Diomede scene is evidently present in order to form a contrast with the behaviour of Achilles . . . If Achilles were like Diomede, there would be no *Iliad* at all.'[58] It is consequently important for Homer to present Diomedes excelling in counsel as well as on the field of battle. His counsel is the opposite of Nestor's: forthright and uncomplicated. And as

[57] But Kirk (in the course of an interesting discussion of the Teichoskopia, where Odysseus is treated as *the* great Greek hero) finds Od.'s character 'complex and contradictory' (*Il. Comm.* I. 287). This assessment of the Iliadic Odysseus is amplified in R. B. Rutherford, 'The Philosophy of the *Odyssey*', *JHS* 106 (1986), 145–62, a rich article which explores *euboulia* in the *Od*.

[58] Griffin (n. 37), 74. The incident also recalls an earlier occasion (7. 379–402) when of all of the Greek leaders it is again only Diomedes who has the spirit to offer decisively defiant advice in a difficult situation. A passage which forms another interesting contrast with the behaviour of Ag. in Book 1 is 8. 130–71, where Diomedes, like Ag., is inclined on grounds of honour to reject Nestor's advice despite acknowledging its soundness, but unlike Ag. is saved (from attempting single combat with Hector) by a sign from Zeus.

C. A. Querbach suggests in a recent study, its characteristic virtues are often reinforced by deliberate juxtaposition with speeches by Nestor, as in the incident in Book 9 just described or in the scene from Book 14 recalled at the beginning of this section.[59] 'Forthright' need not imply 'unthinking'; and (for example) the boldness of Diomedes' enterprise in the Doloneia of Book 10 is complemented by his shrewdness in inviting a companion to join in the spying mission (10. 220–6).

By his own account (18. 106) and that of others (11. 786–9, 19. 216–19) Achilles is inferior to others in counsel and the assembly,[60] although he handles the quarrels and complications of the funeral games with great judgement. Does his stature as the greatest hero of the *Iliad* indicate that excellence in thought and speech is a virtue only of the second rank? There are many ways of resisting this simplistic conclusion. One is to note that Achilles' first and decisive action in the epic (1. 54) is an example of *euboulia*: he summons an assembly to tackle the problem of the plague.[61] Another is to reflect on some sentences of Redfield which sum up much recent thought about Achilles:[62]

Achilles is an outsize figure. He is stronger, swifter, braver, than the other heroes, and his anger also is larger than any they could feel. And Achilles is a hero with exceptional powers of intellect and speech; he has an unique capacity to generalise his immediate experience and state it in universal terms.

Such intensity and indeed alienation of thought and feeling do not well equip him for argument with the likes of Odysseus in the assembly. They show how Achilles transcends heroic *euboulia* just as he transcends other heroic attitudes. But they confirm that the Homeric hero is heroic in mind as well as in action.

[59] C. A. Querbach, 'Conflicts between Young and Old in Homer's *Iliad*', in S. Bertman (ed.), *The Conflict of Generations in Ancient Greece and Rome* (Amsterdam, 1976).

[60] But the scholiast thinks he can infer from 9. 374 that Achilles was not merely practised in the martial arts but also βουλεύειν ἄριστος: so schol. bT ad loc.

[61] I owe this point to Pat Easterling, who further observes that he is the first person to talk about *themistes* (1. 237–9). The character of Ach.'s entry into the action is balanced by the stress Homer lays on his withdrawal as being from 'the assembly which brings men glory' at 1. 490. As schol. bT says of 1. 490–1: 'Homer knows the two virtues of men, action and speech. But he gives preference to speech.' (Here at least, we might add in qualification.)   [62] Redfield (n. 6), 17.

CONCLUSION

The World of Odysseus represents an enterprise in many ways very different from the studies by Snell, Dodds, and others in the tradition of *Geistesgeschichte*. But in its treatment of the heroic code and of the scope it leaves for choice and reason it shares with them a certain primitivist tendency. There is no question that the social world represented in the *Iliad* or the *Odyssey* is simpler in organization than the society of (for example) Classical Athens. Nor should it be disputed that its relative simplicity of structure determines and is reflected in simpler and less analytical ways of talking and thinking about most other things, including human nature: no council in the *Iliad* is or could be as sophisticated as the debate on Mytilene in Thucydides 3. But it is a further step again (this I call the primitivist step) to hold not only (what I have conceded) that reason has a narrower scope and is less self-conscious and self-critical in the Homeric world, but also that the Homeric hero is not really rational at all—because there is no social or ethical room for him to use reason except as the instrument of his passions. In this chapter I have tried to show why we should resist this primitivist move, which I take to be as misconceived as most other versions of primitivism. My arguments have been derived from the *Iliad* itself. But they express a more general conviction that the circumstances of human life are and always will have been too complex, and the intelligence of humans too various, for the primitivist picture to be credible.[63]

[63] I owe thanks to many friends and colleagues who have encouraged me to work out these ideas for publication. I am esp. grateful to Cynthia Farrar and Robin Osborne, who gave me the opportunity to present a first version to their *polis* seminar in Cambridge, and to Fred Rosen, whose 1983 *polis* conference at the LSE heard a later draft. For comments on the penultimate draft I am indebted to Pat Easterling, Geoffrey Kirk, Geoffrey Lloyd, and Michael Reeve. I alone, of course, am responsible for the final outcome.

8

Tragic Form and Feeling in the Iliad

R. B. RUTHERFORD

ἰοὺ ἰού τὰ πάντ' ἂν ἐξήκοι σαφῆ
Alas, alas. All now is clear.

(Sophocles, *Oedipus Tyrannus* 1182)

These hours of backward clearness come to all men and women, once at least, when they read the past in the light of the present, with the reasons of things, like unobserved finger-posts, protruding where they never saw them before. The journey behind them is mapped out, and figured with its false steps, its wrong observations, all its infatuated, deluded geography.

(Henry James, *The Bostonians*, ch. 39)[1]

I

This chapter is intended to contribute to the study of both Homer and Greek tragedy, and more particularly to the study of the influence of the epic upon the later poets. The current revival of interest among scholars writing in English in the poetic qualities of the Homeric poems must be welcomed by all who care for the continuing survival and propagation of Classical literature.[2] The renewed emphasis on

---

[1] I owe this parallel to Dr M. Winterbottom, whose teaching has enhanced my understanding of Homer as of other authors with whom his name is more usually associated. I have also been much helped by comments on this chapter by Dr O. Taplin, and by many discussions of Homer with Dr E. Kearns. Finally, I thank Professor P. Easterling and the late C. W. Macleod, for valuable criticisms and advice, and the latter for constant stimulus over a longer period. I offer this chapter as a tribute to his memory.

[2] See esp. J. Griffin, *Homer on Life and Death* (Oxford, 1980) and the articles which preceded this outstanding study; and now C. W. Macleod, *Homer: Iliad XXIV* (Cambridge, 1982). Adam Parry, in his introduction to Milman Parry, *The Making of Homeric Verse* (Oxford, 1971), pp. L–LIX, had already pointed the way: cf. Macleod, *Notes & Queries* 21 (1974), 318–19.

the validity of literary criticism as applied to presumably oral texts may encourage a more positive appreciation of the subtlety of Homeric narrative techniques, and of the coherent plan which unifies each poem. The aim of this chapter is to focus attention on a number of elements in Greek tragedy which are already present in Homer, and especially on the way in which these poets exploit the theme of knowledge—knowledge of one's future, knowledge of one's circumstances, knowledge of oneself. Recent scholarship on tragedy has paid much more attention to literary criticism in general and to poetic irony in particular: these insights can also illuminate the epic. Conversely, the renewed interest in Homer's structural and thematic complexity should also enrich the study of the tragedians, his true heirs.[3]

I begin and end with Homer, in the belief that this is where the greater need for serious literary criticism still lies; and on the whole I restrict my attention to the *Iliad*, not because there are no connections between the *Odyssey* and tragedy in terms of plot and technique, but because these links are for the most part of a different kind. The *Odyssey* finds its closest affinity with Euripides, who for related reasons figures less prominently in this chapter than his two predecessors.[4] The kind of play that Euripides makes with knowledge and ignorance of identity is very Odyssean in quality; but there is correspondingly less focus, at least in the majority of his *oeuvre*, on the Iliadic themes of self-knowledge and understanding of the divine plan. The present chapter is not, however, intended as an exhaustive treatment of those themes, even if that were possible, but is meant to stimulate further and broader discussion.

In *Iliad* 18, Achilles learns of the death of Patroclus, and immediately realizes his own responsibility and his past errors. His impetuous demand that Zeus show him honour by punishing the Greek army has been fulfilled, but with bitter and ironic consequences for himself. (See 1. 407–12, 505–10; 18. 73–84.) In the scene in which this news reaches him we see the meaning of this reversal, which is to lead to his own death, presented symbolically: thus Achilles grovels on the

---

[3] For ancient statements of the debt which the tragedians owed to Homer, see Pl. *Resp.* 10, 595c, Arist. *Poet.* 4, 1448^{b}38–9, 8, 1451^{a}22–30, 23, 1459^{a}29–34; also A. Gudeman (ed.), *Aristoteles Peri Poetikes* (Berlin, 1934), on *Poet.* 3, 1448^{a}6; Aesch. *ap.* Athen. 7, 347e; *Vita Soph.* 20; Ps.-Plut. *de vita et poesi Hom.* 213; Radt, *TGF* IV T 115–16; N. J. Richardson, *CQ* 30 (1980), 270.

[4] For related contrasts see Arist. *Poet.* 24, 1459^{b}10–16; Ps.-Long. 9. 15, 29. 2 with D. A. Russell's nn. (*'Longinus': On the Sublime* (Oxford, 1964)) ad loc.

earth, defiles his face with dust and dirt, lies outstretched like a dead man (18. 22–7), and is mourned by the slave-girls and by the nymphs who attend on Thetis (23–31, 35–69).[5] But this scene is more than simply passionate and plangent: for despite his frenzied grief, Achilles' speeches here and throughout the rest of the poem are pervaded by a terrible rationality, not unlike the speech in which Oedipus endeavours to explain why he blinded himself (Sophocles, *Oedipus Tyrannus* 1369 ff.). Achilles both recognizes his responsibility and accepts the consequences. It is in part this clear-sightedness that makes him a heroic figure. Whereas formerly, ignorant of the details of his fate, he wished to evade it (9. 316–20, 401–16), he now learns of the imminence of his death and accepts it (18. 95 ff.).[6] Homer makes it plain that Achilles' doom is of his own choosing, and also that the death of Patroclus was his own responsibility; for Achilles failed to remember a divine warning (18. 6–14, discussed further in section IV below). This misjudgement undermines Achilles' former self-confidence and egoism: it also transforms his earlier desire for either life or honour (9. 413, 415) into a longing for revenge and a prayer for death (18. 90–3, 98–106).[7]

This scene is a crucial turning-point in the poem, not least because of the divine background; for the gods have not only foreseen and prophesied Achilles' error of judgement, but have also made its enormity painfully clear to him. All Achilles' hopes, expectations, and assumptions have been deceived. This situation, above all the powerful moment of revelation, is tragic not only in the emotions it expresses, but in its thematic significance: for the gulf between human deliberation and divine foreknowledge is a constant theme in Greek tragedy as in Homer. 'The desires of Zeus are hard to track; in darkness and shadow the paths of his thought move to their goal, undiscernible', sings the chorus of Aeschylus' *Suppliants* (87–90). 'Nothing that is of the divine is clear to mortal sight', laments Megara in Euripides' *Heracles* (62). 'In our vainglory we think ourselves wiser than the gods', says Theseus with stern disapproval (Euripides, *Suppliants* 217–18).[8] Earlier in the *Iliad* the Greek

---

[5] On this episode see further K. Reinhardt, *Die Ilias und ihr Dichter* (Göttingen, 1961), 348–73.   [6] Cf. Macleod, *Iliad* XXIV (n. 2), 23–8.

[7] On death-wishes in tragedy, see C. Collard (ed.), *Euripides: Supplices* (Groningen, 1975), on 86.   [8] See further Collard ad loc. and on 504–5.

embassy supplicated Achilles like a god (see 9. 158–9, 496–501; cf. 155, 297, 301–3). But man is not a god, as Achilles is to learn and as tragedy teaches. Above all, Achilles is bound by mortality; and the same gods who honoured him and raised him up will ultimately bring about his end.[9]

Achilles, then, in many respects foreshadows the heroes of tragedy, and in particular those of Sophocles' plays—in his defiant resolution, his impatience with consolation, his longing to die and so to remove the shame and guilt of his actions.[10] Typical of tragedy also is his indifference to others' advice or their willingness to help: this is powerfully captured in the way that Antilochus sits helplessly by him, weeping but unable to help (18. 32 ff.).[11] Finally, Achilles is the archetypal tragic figure in his inability, for all his power and greatness, to dictate or influence the course of future events: for even when he seems most in control, his own plans and prestige form part of a wider picture which he can see only in details. And even in the later books of the poem, as his knowledge and understanding of events increase, so too does his helplessness.

Thus the *peripeteia* of the *Iliad*, like that of the *Oedipus Tyrannus*, depends on a change in the hero's knowledge of his position, a change that confirms and explains past foreknowledge. This new knowledge also reveals the extent and the catastrophic consequences of past ignorance and error. The pathos of such a situation emerges from the actual construction of the narrative, ἐξ αὐτῆς τῆς συστάσεως τῶν πραγμάτων, ὅπερ ἐστὶ πρότερον καὶ ποιητοῦ ἀμείνονος ('from the actual structure of events, the thing which is more important and is the work of a superior poet',

---

[9] Another aspect of Achilles' human limitations is brought out in the Theomachy. Here his defiance of the gods is perilous, and for all his greatness he will be punished: he himself recalls this at 21. 275 ff., and the gods, especially Scamander, resent his brutality (21. 136, 147, 214, 217–21, 306, 314–15). This stands in contrast with the prudence of Diomedes in the earlier theomachy: Diomedes remembers the warning he has received (5. 815–24) from Athene, and observes the limits laid upon him (see 5. 121 ff., 443–4, 606, 815–24; 6. 129–41 is not therefore inconsistent). See further Ø. Andersen, *Die Diomedesgestalt in der Ilias*, SO Supp. 25 (1975), ch. IV; and on theomachoi in tragedy J. C. Kamerbeek, *Mnemos.* 1 (1948), 271–83.

[10] In general, see B. M. W. Knox, *The Heroic Temper* (Berkeley and Los Angeles. 1964), chs. 1–2, esp. pp. 50–2.

[11] Antilochus' fear that Achilles will kill himself (18. 34) also finds echoes in tragedy, e.g. Soph. *Aj.* 326–7, 583–8, Eur. *Med.* 37, and the whole final scene of the *Heracles* (see G. W. Bond (ed.), *Euripides: Heracles* (Oxford, 1981) on 1248; W. B. Stanford (ed.), *Sophocles: Ajax* (London, 1963), appendix E).

Aristotle, *Poetics* 14, 1453ᵇ2).[12] The author exploits the knowledge
and expectations of his audience, and as his work advances he
brings out further the connection of cause and effect, the sombre
inevitability of choice and consequence. This tragic pattern is
already present in the *Iliad*—more diffusely presented, as the epic
form made natural, but in no way less sophisticated or less profound.[13] The object of this chapter is to develop some of these
comparisons between Homer and his successors, and to comment,
albeit selectively, on the tragic and compassionate outlook that
these structural devices serve to communicate.

II

In Chapters 14 and 16 of the *Poetics* Aristotle discusses the different
categories of *anagnōrisis* (recognition), and the closely related ideas
of *agnoia* (ignorance) and *hamartia* (error). At 14, 1453ᵇ27 ff. he sets
out the possibilities for the agents involved: either (1) they can be
εἰδότας καὶ γιγνώσκοντας (conscious and aware) concerning
what they are doing and whom they are damaging, as is the case
with Medea in Euripides; or (2) they can commit the deed
ἀγνοοῦντας . . . εἶθ' ὕστερον ἀναγνωρίσαι τὴν φιλίαν, ὥσπερ ὁ
Σοφοκλέους Οἰδίπους (in ignorance . . . and then subsequently
recognize the relationship, like Oedipus in Sophocles); or (3) they
may through their ignorance intend to do τι τῶν ἀνηκέστων (one
of the incurable acts) and then ἀναγνωρίσαι πρὶν ποιῆσαι
('recognize the other before committing the act', as happens in
Euripides *Ion, IT, Cresphontes, Helle*).

  From his examples and his references to *philia*, it is plain that
Aristotle considered *anagnōrisis* to be a matter of the characters
knowing each other's identities, and especially being aware of their
familial relationships (cf. 14, 1453ᵇ20 ff.).[14] This again is something
that he traces back to the epic, finding its ancestry in the recog-
nition-scenes in the second half of the *Odyssey* (referred to at 16,
1454ᵇ25 ff.). While this conception is central to the plays he cites,
above all the *OT*, it can be viewed rather as a sub-class of a

---

  [12] Cf. B. Vickers, *Towards Greek Tragedy* (London, 1973), 62.
  [13] *Contra* J. M. Bremer, *Hamartia* (Amsterdam, 1969), 99, 'in a more or less
rudimentary form in Homer'.
  [14] Cf. B. M. W. Knox, *Word and Action* (Baltimore, 1979), 21–2.

broader and more significant kind of recognition, which I should
prefer to call 'realization'. This is not in fact discussed by Aristotle,
although it seems to be allowed for in the general definition of
anagnōrisis given in *Poetics* 11, 1452ª29 ff., which is also the
passage that makes clearest the connection with human ignorance. The relevant lines run as follows:

ἀναγνώρισις δέ, ὥσπερ καὶ τοὔνομα σημαίνει, ἐξ ἀγνοίας εἰς
γνῶσιν μεταβολή, ἢ εἰς φιλίαν ἢ εἰς ἔχθραν, τῶν πρὸς εὐτυχίαν ἢ
δυστυχίαν ὡρισμένων· καλλίστη δὲ ἀναγνώρισις, ὅταν ἅμα
περιπετείᾳ γένηται, οἷον ἔχει ἡ ἐν τῷ Οἰδίποδι. εἰσὶν μὲν οὖν καὶ
ἄλλαι ἀναγνωρίσεις· καὶ γὰρ πρὸς ἄψυχα καὶ τὰ τυχόντα †ἐστὶν
ὥσπερ εἴρηται συμβαίνει† καὶ εἰ πέπραγέ τις ἢ μὴ πέπραγεν ἔστιν
ἀναγνωρίσαι.[15]

'Recognition', as the name indicates, is a change from ignorance into
knowledge, either into a friendly state or one of enmity, involving matters
which are related to prosperity or misfortune. The best type of recognition is
when it coincides with reversal, as happens with the one in the *Oedipus*.
There are also other sorts of recognition; as has been stated, such things can
occur with inanimate and incidental things as well, and one can recognize
whether one has or has not done something.

Aristotle goes on to say that the most powerful kind of recognition *is*
that involving blood-relationship, but he clearly recognizes that other
possibilities exist, notably the discovery 'whether one has done
something', a no less apt description of what happens at the climax of
the *OT*. Indeed, for all the power and terror which the story of Oedipus'
incest and parricide possesses (cf. *Poetics* 14, 1453ᵇ1–7), its full pathos
is brought out just as much by the way in which Oedipus' power
and wisdom, his supreme energy, his faith in himself and his own
mentality, are the very things which lead him to ruin and despair, and
which in the end prove useless to him. The *anagnōrisis* of Oedipus
entails the acquisition of fresh knowledge which changes his
whole perspective: the final piece of the jigsaw is in place, and forces
him to see the true state of affairs, to apprehend the magnitude of his
error.[16]

---

[15] For helpful observations on this passage and its context, see G. F. Else, *Aristotle's
Poetics: The Argument* (Cambridge, Mass., 1957), 342–55.

[16] For 'error' and 'flaw' in the *OT* and elsewhere, see esp. T. C. W. Stinton, *CQ* 25
(1975), 221–54 [= Stinton, *Collected Papers on Greek Tragedy* (Oxford, 1990), 143–85],
and the discussion in subsequent issues. For the Homeric background see Bremer
(n. 13), 99–111, who somewhat overemphasizes the element of divine *control*.

The key moment, at which Oedipus does see the truth and feels his
world collapsing around him, comes with the line (1182) which is set
at the head of this chapter. All has now emerged *clearly* (σαφῆ): he
sees his error,[17] even later when he is blind, and this contrasts with
his earlier failure to understand and see his situation (esp. 412–19).
This sequence provides the clearest example in tragedy of a conception which we can discern also in the play most closely akin to
OT, namely *Trachiniae*. Here too the fate of Heracles is foretold by
prophecy but misunderstood; then at the end of the play the truth is
seen in the light of new information, but it is seen too late. Again the
critical moment is recognized in the words of the suffering hero: at
Trachiniae 1145, when Hyllus informs him that the agent of his death
was the supposed love-potion made from the centaur's blood,
Heracles cries:

οἴμοι, φρονῶ δὴ ξυμφορᾶς ἵν᾽ ἕσταμεν.

Alas, I understand now in what ill fortune I stand.

Shortly afterwards he explains: he was forewarned (1159 πρόφαντον)
that he would die by the hand of no living creature (1162–5):

ὅδ᾽ οὖν ὁ θὴρ Κένταυρος, ὡς τὸ θεῖον ἦν
πρόφαντον, οὕτω ζῶντά μ᾽ ἔκτεινεν θανών.
φανῶ δ᾽ ἐγὼ τούτοισι συμβαίνοντ᾽ ἴσα
μαντεῖα καινά, τοῖς πάλαι ξυνήγορα.

So this beast, the Centaur, though dead has slain me while I was living, as
the divine prediction said. And now I shall reveal fresh prophecies which
are the same and in accord with the others, in harmony with the words of
earlier times.

Heracles had also been told by the oracles of Dodona that after a fixed
time, which is now elapsed, all his labours would be over. Now the
interpretation of this too is clear:

τὸ δ᾽ ἦν ἄρ᾽ οὐδὲν ἄλλο πλὴν θανεῖν ἐμέ.

This meant nothing else than that I was to die. (1172)

ταῦτ᾽ οὖν ἐπειδὴ λαμπρὰ συμβαίνει, τέκνον

Now, since all this is now clearly coming about, my son . . . (1174)

---

[17] Cf. R. G. A. Buxton, *JHS* 100 (1980), 22–37; also a forthcoming study by David
Seale, as Mrs Easterling informs me. [D. Seale, *Vision and Stagecraft in Sophocles*
(London 1982).]

Here λαμπρά is like σαφῆ in the parallel passage of *OT*. In both
cases the imperfection of human knowledge and judgement allows a
man to believe he has reason for confidence and hope, only to find
that he has in reality only seen a part of the picture. Absolute
knowledge belongs only to the gods, and although in tragedy, as in
the work of Herodotus,[18] the gods may grant us occasional fragments of information, man's very humanity leads him to mis-
understand and to judge amiss. Yet the poet in part shares the
knowledge of the gods, and permits the audience to anticipate the
hero's realization.

In this respect *Trachiniae* differs, however, from *OT*, since the
ambiguity about the actual content of the oracles is preserved
throughout much of the play,[19] and this means that the audience's
foreknowledge is not so certain, whereas the true irony of Oedipus'
situation is established and exploited by the poet from the beginning.
Further, the action of *Trachiniae* allots error and death to Deianira as
well as Heracles. In her case this error is the product of purely human
reasoning and impulse, and regretted when she realizes the consequences. The position of Deianira is analogous to that of Heracles
only in that she sees the truth too late:

$$\text{ὁρῶ δέ μ' ἔργον δεινὸν ἐξειργασμένην.}$$

I see that I have committed a terrible deed. (706)

$$\text{ὧν ἐγὼ μεθύστερον,}$$
$$\text{ὅτ' οὐκέτ' ἀρκεῖ, τὴν μάθησιν ἄρνυμαι.}$$

Of this I gain knowledge too late, when there is no help in it. (710–11)

Thus she appreciates that her reasoning powers (cf. 590 ff., answered
by 668–9) have in fact been clouded by her hopes, hopes that
sprang from the all-too-natural weakness of human love, which she
had recognized as present in herself before she ever laid her plans

---

[18] For a comparison of oracle-types in Herodotus and Greek tragedy, see
B. M. W. Knox, *Oedipus at Thebes* (Yale, 1957), 33–47. For examples of ironic twist
and unexpected fulfilment, see Hdt. 1. 53. 2, 66. 2–4, 3. 64. 4 (cf. Shakespeare, *2
Henry IV* iv. v *ad fin.*), 6. 76. 1 and 80; also J. Fontenrose, *The Delphic Oracle*
(Berkeley and Los Angeles, 1978), 58–70, 80, 96–100. On Herodotus and Sophocles
see now A. J. Podlecki, in *Greece and the Eastern Mediterranean*, FS F. Schachermeyer,
ed. K. H. Kinzl (Berlin, 1977), 248–9.

[19] See W. Kranz, *Studien zur antiken Literatur und ihrem Fortwirken* (Heidelberg,
1967), 285 ff.; M. D. Reeve, *GRBS* 11 (1970), 283 ff.

(438 ff., esp. 444).[20] But there is nothing supernatural in her sudden, guilty horror: rather, her experience and that of Heracles represent two elements in a tragic plot, which in the other play are united in the figure and fate of Oedipus, at once the victim of divine admonition and human weakness.

Hyllus, the son of Heracles and Deianira, provides another element. In his ignorance he denounces Deianira as a treacherous murderess, and in her guilty awareness of what she has done she is unable to answer him. Thus she finds herself alienated from both husband and son (see esp. 790–3, 807–9), and departs in silence, having nothing further to live for. In due course Hyllus learns how he has misjudged her, and experiences the agony of knowing that it was his cruelty that drove her to suicide (932–5):

> ἰδὼν δ' ὁ παῖς ᾤμωξεν· ἔγνω γὰρ τάλας
> τοὔργον κατ' ὀργὴν ὡς ἐφάψειεν τόδε,
> <u>ὄψ' ἐκδιδαχθεὶς</u> τῶν κατ' οἶκον οὕνεκα
> ἄκουσα πρὸς τοῦ θηρὸς ἔρξειεν τάδε.

When he saw this the boy uttered a wail, for he knew, poor wretch, that he had accused her of a crime in anger; he *learned too late* from those in the house that she had done all this involuntarily, on account of the centaur.

The pattern of 'late learning' in the two dramas has been commented on by a number of critics,[21] but it does not seem to have been realized quite how prevalent it is, and how integrally related to themes which have generally received much more attention, such as the power and knowledge of the gods, above all when contrasted with the limitations and failures of human insight and action. These themes are

---

[20] Line 444 is sensitively defended by T. C. W. Stinton, *JHS* 96 (1976) 135–6 [= *Collected Papers* (n. 16), 219–21].

[21] See esp. C. H. Whitman, *Sophocles: A Study in Heroic Humanism* (Cambridge, Mass., 1951), ch. 6, and p. 265 n. 4, citing Soph. *Ant.* (quoted in text), and also Aesch. *Ag.* 1425, Pind. *Pyth.* 5. 28 ff., Eur. *Or.* 99, Aeschin. 3. 157. Add Eur. *Alc.* 940 (with Dale's comm. (*Euripides: Alcestis* (Oxford, 1954), p. XXII); *Hipp.* 1401 (and the whole situation of Theseus at the time of Artemis's relevation); *Ba.* 1120–1, 1285, 1296, 1345; perhaps Aesch. *Septem* 655, 709–11. See also A. D. Nock, *Essays on Religion and the Ancient World* (Oxford, 1972), 538; M. L. West (ed.), *Hesiod: Works and Days* (Oxford, 1978), on *Op.* 86–7, adding Hom. *Od.* 8. 564–71 with 13. 125–87 (esp. 169, 172–3); 9. 507 ff., 18. 124–57. The non-tragic nature of the *Od.* (cf F. Jacoby, *Kl. Philol. Schriften* (Berlin, 1961), I. 107–39) means that the *opsimathia* pattern is attached to unsympathetic characters (Aegisthus, the Cyclops, the suitors), not to the successful hero, whom the prophecies favour. (The fate of the Phaeacians is an interesting exception.) In the *Il.*, compare 2. 325, 330 (the Greeks *will* sack Troy).

central to much that is greatest and most influential in Greek literature and thought; and already in the *Iliad* they are united in the
tragic pattern of human *opsimathia* (late learning).

The *Antigone* provides us with a further example. There Creon is
warned by wiser men: by the chorus his views are doubted or cor-
rected from an early stage (perhaps 213; further 278–9, 724–5, 770),
but it is only after the representative of the gods, Tiresias, has spoken
that they also make their feelings plain (1091–4, 1098; cf. 509). In
the end Creon yields, accepting the chorus's plea for *euboulia* ('good
judgement', 1098), and realizing that he is forced to obey (1105–6).
But his change of mind comes too late, and he finds that he has
destroyed not only the offender but his son and his wife. Like Oedipus
he accepts the responsibility for his own misjudgements and mis-
takes. The language of his speech at this point is rich in the voca-
bulary of rational thought: 1261 ἰὼ | φρενῶν δυσφρόνων
ἁμαρτήματα (alas for the errors of my ill-judged judgement); 1265
ὤμοι ἐμῶν ἄνολβα βουλευμάτων (o woe for the miseries my
decisions have brought about); 1268–9 ἔθανες, ἀπελύθης | ἐμαῖς
οὐδὲ σαῖσι δυσβουλίαις (You have perished, you have been cut off,
through my own folly, not yours). The chorus grimly says to him
(1270): οἴμ᾽ ὡς ἔοικας ὀψὲ τὴν δίκην ἰδεῖν (Ah, you seem to have
seen justice, too late). And Creon replies (1271): οἴμοι | ἔχω μαθὼν
δείλαιος (Alas, poor wretch that I am, I have learned). Thus
the stress Creon himself laid on τῶν ἀρίστων . . . βουλευμάτων
('the best decisions', 179) as essential for any statesman finds its
ironic reversal: and the deeper but still incomplete vision of the
chorus reflecting on the powers and wonder of mankind (332 ff.)[22] is
qualified and yet also confirmed. Human wisdom has been shown as
imperfect and two-edged (365–70, cf. 1347–53); and one thing from

A related conception, that of πάθει μάθος (learning through suffering) has received
much more attention: cf. E. R. Dodds, *The Ancient Concept of Progress* (Oxford, 1973),
59–62; West on Hes. *Op.* 218; Headlam–Thomson (*The Oresteia of Aeschylus* (2nd
edn., Amsterdam, 1966)) on Aesch. *Eum.* 520–1, who point out that this idea is in
turn linked with the precept γνῶθι σεαυτόν (know thyself). Such self-knowledge
involves above all consciousness of the gulf between god and man: see *Il.* 5. 440–2,
16. 705–9, 24. 525–6, etc.; *Od.* 18. 129–42; also N. J. Richardson (ed.), *The Homeric
Hymn to Demeter* (Oxford, 1974) on *h. Cer.* 147–3.

[22] For an interesting though occasionally fanciful analysis of this ode see C. P. Segal,
Arion 3 (1964), 46–66 = *Sophocles*, ed. T. Woodard (Englewood Cliffs, NJ, 1966),
62–85. For further connections with 5th-cent. thought see Knox (n. 18), 107 ff.,
E. A. Havelock, *The Liberal Temper in Greek Politics* (London 1957), 66 ff.

which no mortal, neither Antigone nor Creon, can find a remedy or an escape is the irreversible force of death.[23]

III

Not only oracles but prophetic dreams function in this manner in the tragedians. Again, this is a legacy of Homer.[24] In the *Odyssey* in particular, the dreams which Athene grants to Penelope offer both hope and cause for unease. Dreams may deceive, as Penelope explains (19. 560–9) and as we know from the second book of the *Iliad*; and like oracular pronouncements they can be misinterpreted and may provoke illogical, though very human, reactions. A famous and much-debated instance is the dream Penelope narrates at 19. 535–53, in which she grieved at the slaughter of her geese.[25] Her failure to interpret the omen, recognizing the eagle as Odysseus, surely prefigures her doubts and hesitation in Book 23, and this is consistent with Penelope's disillusioned hopelessness, the fruit of many disappointments. The theme of omens misunderstood or ignored, which is constantly exploited in the *Odyssey*, is thus adapted to the special case of Penelope, with particularly poignant and sympathetic force.[26] (Compare Euripides, *IT* 42–58, where Iphigenia interprets an optimistic dream pessimistically.)

In Aeschylus' *Persae* and *Choephori*, and in Sophocles' *Electra*, the dreams which disturb the rest of the Persian queen and of Clytemnestra are prophetic, and function in a way parallel to the Delphic warning which is given to Oedipus: while the foreknowledge

[23] For related themes in Sophocles see the passages collected by J. C. Opstelten, *Sophocles and Greek Pessimism* (Amsterdam, 1952), 124–5. For the futility of human intelligence and insight as a recurrent theme in Euripides' plays see Dodds (n. 21), 80–9; also Opstelten 132 (very unselective). For the general prevalence of this theme in 5th-cent. literature see C. W. Macleod, *PCPS* 25 (1979), 53–60 [= Macleod, *Collected Essays* (Oxford, 1983), 124–31].

[24] See esp. E. R. Dodds, *The Greeks and the Irrational* (Berkeley and Los Angeles, 1951), 102–11; also W. S. Messor, *The Dream in Homer and Greek Tragedy* (New York, 1918).

[25] Cf. G. Méautis, *Paideia* 15 (1960), 81–6.

[26] In general on omens in the *Odyssey* see A. J. Podlecki, *G&R* 14 (1967), 12–23. For Herodotean parallels involving dreams misunderstood or ignored see 1. 34. 2 with 45. 2, 107–8, 209–10. 1, 3. 124. 1–2, 125. 4, 5. 55–6, 6. 107, 7. 12–19. Omens ignored: Hdt. 1. 59. 2, 7. 37. 3, 57. 1–2, etc. The wise adviser: H. Bischoff, *Der Warner bei Herodot* (Diss. Marburg, 1932); R. Lattimore, *CP* 34 (1939), 24–35.

is terrible, no advice or aid is given which might enable the human recipient to escape. But it is striking that the fulfilment is also presented, as it were, intellectually: the Queen, who in the earlier part of the play is ignorant of the very location of Athens (231), and more significantly about its form of government (241–2), advances in understanding as she does in dismay and suffering. We may also note the close verbal resemblance between her reaction to the messenger's grim catalogue of disaster and the moments of horrified insight quoted from the Sophoclean plays in the previous section. She cries (518–19):

ὦ νυκτὸς ὄψις ἐμφανὴς ἐνυπνίων,
ὡς κάρτα μοι σαφῶς ἐδήλωσας κακά.

o manifest vision of my nightly dreams, how very clearly you revealed to me my misfortunes.

All is only too clear, too late. This suggests a touch of dramatic irony in her earlier narration of the dream: never has she seen a dream so *clear* (179 ἐναργές), but the full meaning and force of the vision is not apparent to her until the later scene. With this comprehension comes realization of the wider significance, of the divine hand at work (472–3); this also stands in contrast with Xerxes' ignorance (361, 373, 454). Whereas the queen had previously had to question the chorus about Athens and Greece, she now pronounces with authority: this is Xerxes' bitter, but righteous, punishment (473–7). In this she is the true wife of Darius, who subsequently confirms the supernatural interpretation of events. She speaks with heightened dignity in disaster; it is she who proposes the summoning of Darius' ghost, and she addresses him as an equal: the two royal figures remorselessly fill the gaps in each other's knowledge.

For Darius too recognizes the Persian downfall as the fulfilment of a supernatural warning, in this case oracular (740–50; 800–4). The warnings he passed on to his son were not sufficient (783); they were based, moreover, on insufficient consciousness of the danger on Darius' part: φεῦ ταχεῖα ('oh no, so swift. . .', 739) and ἐγώ . . . ηὔχουν ('I hoped', 740–1) emphasize that he had thought the disaster might still be postponed for many generations (cf. Herodotus I. 13. 2 with 91: another case of warnings forgotten). Yet the intensity of the tragedy lies in the very fact of the warnings—their obscurity before, their terrible clarity and inevitability when seen in their fulfilment. Nor are the gods to blame, who have been both just and consistent: for Xerxes, as for Sophocles' Creon, the personal responsibility is inescapable.[27]

Again, in the *Choephori*, Aeschylus lays powerful stress on the dream of Clytemnestra, who like Atossa attempts to avert it by prayer and sacrifice. It is referred to at an early stage (32 ff.), described to Orestes (523 ff.), and explained by him (540 ff.). This is important because the dream, if true and truly interpreted (cf. 542, 551), provides confirmation of the divine mandate, commanding and assuring the success of Orestes' mission; it serves a similar function to the taking of omens. Later, the dream is referred to again at the climax of the play, as Orestes confronts Clytemnestra. Here again, to understand the dream's interpretation is to see the hopelessness of her position (*Choephori* 928–9):

> Κλ.   οἲ 'γώ, τεκοῦσα τόνδ' ὄφιν ἐθρεψάμην.
> Ὀρ.   ἦ κάρτα μάντις οὑξ ὀνειράτων φόβος.[28]

Clyt. Woe is me, I bore and nurtured this snake.
Or. Yes, your fear on account of your dreams was indeed prophetic.

A somewhat similar stroke introduces this scene, as the slave cries out, 'I tell you, the dead are killing the living' (886), to which Clytemnestra replies with a flash of near-despair (887–8):

> οἲ 'γώ [cf. 928], ξυνῆκα τοὔπος ἐξ αἰνιγμάτων.
> δόλοις ὀλούμεθ' ὥσπερ οὖν ἐκτείναμεν.

Ah woe is me, I understand your meaning from this riddle. By guile we slew, and so too we shall be slain.

No oracle is involved here, but the riddling phrase of the slave creates a comparable effect, allowing Clytemnestra to interpret it with her characteristic speed and acumen. Yet her defiance, and her dialectical skill, prove useless in the ensuing scene (in contrast with her verbal and physical victory in the corresponding exchange in the *Agamemnon*, 931 ff.[29]). And the slave's words voice a more significant truth concerning the vengeance of the dead and the anger

---

[27] In general on the theology of the *Persae* see R. P. Winnington-Ingram, *JHS* 93 (1973), 210–19 [revised as *Studies in Aeschylus* (Cambridge, 1983), 1–15].

[28] I strongly doubt Page's reattribution of 929 to Clytemnestra, and less certainly question the likelihood of Macleod's proposal *apud* O. Taplin, *The Stagecraft of Aeschylus* (Oxford, 1977), 356 n. 2.   [29] Cf. Taplin (n. 28), 356–7.

of the nether gods: the ambiguous, riddling syntax gives his line the quality of an omen, for riddles and oracles are akin.[30] Clytemnestra's response shows her realization of the central truth of the trilogy, the law of retribution: but as with Agamemnon and Orestes, the full realization comes only with the event.[31]

The richest source in Aeschylus' work of such intellectual and prophetic imagery is the *Agamemnon* itself: indeed, the whole *Oresteia* may from one point of view be studied in terms of the degree of insight and foresight which its different characters possess.[32] The language of prophecy and premonition runs through the choruses;[33] the prophet Calchas has warned them of disasters past and to come; the prophetess Cassandra speaks with an authority that confirms and deepens their greatest fears. The choral odes present a conflict between the speakers' compulsion to seek explanation, to understand the chain of events preceding the return and downfall of Agamemnon, and their human reluctance to contemplate the possible outcome (esp. 248–55). It is in the latter spirit that they withdraw their acceptance of the news that Troy has fallen (475–87). This clash of feelings reaches its highest intensity in the ode that follows Agamemnon's entry into the palace: here the language of foreknowledge is very prominent (977 τερασκόπου (omen-reading), 978 μαντιπολεῖ (plays the prophet), 981 δυσκρίτων (hard to interpret), 989 αὐτόμαρτυς (its own witness), 991 αὐτοδίδακτος (self-taught), 992, 999 ἐλπίδος ('hope' or 'anticipation'), 995 ματᾴζει (vainly foresee); also 997 τελεσφόροις ∼ 1000 τελεσφόρον (accomplishing), cf. *Choephori* 541 on Clytemnestra's dream). Here it serves to heighten our sense of the chorus's terror as they wait poised between doubt and certainty about events within

---

[30] Cf. West (n. 21) on Hes. *Op.* 202.

[31] The 'riddle' passage is imitated by Sophocles at *El.* 1476–81 (as the repetition of ξυνῆκα τοὔπος makes certain). There the victim is Aegisthus, and when he recognizes Orestes' identity, the latter taunts him as a *mantis* (prophet) who has failed until that moment (1481). But Aegisthus, like Polymestor in Eur. *Hec.* 1257–84, achieves a kind of status at the end as a prophet of future evils (*El.* 1497–8; cf. n. 38), which Orestes' bluster cannot simply brush aside (1499 ἐγώ σοι μάντις εἰμὶ τῶνδ' ἄκρος (I am a prophet of this for you), says Orestes, deliberately refusing to look further). This scene thus carries heavy implications of reprisals for the victors, however hazily defined. Different again is the prophetic role of Cassandra in Eur. *Tro.* 353–461. [32] See Dodds, loc. cit. (n. 21); Taplin (n. 28), 327–9, 356–7.

[33] See further B. Alexanderson, *Eranos* 67 (1969), 1–23; W. C. Scott, *Phoenix* 23 (1969), 336–46; D. Sansone, *Aeschylean Metaphors for Intellectual Activity*, Hermes Einzelschr. 35 (1975), ch. 3.

the house. These events Cassandra, the true *mantis*, will shortly
unveil in their full and terrible significance. Her insight is that of
divine dispensation: where the chorus guess and fear, she truly knows.
Yet the subsequent scene shows not only the difficulty she finds in
conveying her insight to others and convincing them (1074–5,
1077–8, 1105–6, 1112–13, 1119 ff., 1130 ff.) but their reluctance to
accept it even when they do understand (1162 ff., 1173 ff.). The
chorus shrink from the dark prophecy that she finally makes explicit
(1247, and her subsequent replies). Moreover, Cassandra's knowledge of his own fate gives her neither protection nor consolation (cf.
sections IV–V below on Achilles' similar foreknowledge); nor does it
enable her to help Agamemnon or the chorus. Such knowledge
brings its possessor neither nobility nor fame (despite the chorus's
hopes, 1302, 1304), but only a clearer insight into the tragedy of
humanity—its infinite blindness and insignificance in contrast with
the supreme and inescapable power of the gods (*Agamemnon* 1322–
30; 1485–8, where the chorus too have come to share in Cassandra's
despairing fatalism).

ἰὼ βρότεια πράγματα ('Alas for the fortunes of humanity',
1327). Cassandra's words sum up a view of the world which derives
from Homer, and which is prominent also in the pessimism of
Archaic lyric. Man is ephemeral and wretched; above all, he cannot
know his future, and so can never guarantee the security of his
happiness or his expectations.[34] But the proper response to this is
not simply despair, but pity (*Agamemnon* 1321 (the chorus); 1330
(Cassandra))—pity that recognizes the community of human suffering, pity that is founded in knowledge of one's limitations and
which is granted to those who share them with oneself.[35] The tragedy of Cassandra is that pity is all that she can give, to her father
and brothers and her people as to Agamemnon, who has destroyed
them. So also for Achilles the understanding which allows him to
pity his enemy comes too late; and his own death, the place and
authors of which are known to him, can no longer be altered or
postponed, but only awaited.

---

[34] H. Fränkel, *TAPA* 77 (1946), 131–45 and *Early Greek Poetry and Philosophy*
(Oxford, 1975), index p. 530, provides a valuable collection of material. This also
figures as a central theme in Griffin (n. 2), esp. ch. 6 (more fully *CQ* 28 (1978), 1–22).
[35] Cf. section V below.

IV

Without having exhausted either the examples of this motif in tragedy or the significance of those presented above, we may now look back to the more large-scale, more intricate use of the same pattern in the *Iliad*. Here the central figure in the pattern is of course Achilles; but it is also important to define the similarities and differences between his actions and reactions, and those of both Patroclus and Hector.[36]

The poet's great design makes the death of Patroclus lead inevitably to the death of Hector, and the slaying of Hector by Achilles in turn precipitates Achilles' own death (cf. 18. 96 αὐτίκα γάρ τοι ἔπειτα μεθ᾽ Ἕκτορα πότμος ἑτοῖμος, 'for straight away after Hector is your death waiting'). The moment of each hero's supreme triumph makes his destruction inevitable. This sequence is emphasized by the parallels between the death-scenes of Patroclus and Hector.[37] Both fall before a superior warrior; Patroclus and Hector have both overstepped the limits of their strength and fortune; and in both cases the final execution is assisted by a divine champion who aids the victor. Thus Apollo helps bring about the doom of Patroclus, Athene that of Hector. Moreover, both Patroclus and Hector have a moment of prophetic power before the end comes:[38] Patroclus warns Hector that Achilles will destroy him, and Hector foretells Achilles' death beneath the arrows of Paris, who in his turn will be aided by Apollo (16. 853–4; 22. 358–60). This divine intervention is far from rendering the human agents insignificant or devoid of interest; rather, the divine support reflects and in a sense symbolizes the superiority of the victor. What Patroclus, Hector, and Achilles achieve on the battlefield in no way misrepresents their individual

[36] Griffin (n. 2), 43–4, 163, makes important points in this connection, but his remarks are very brief. See further the excellent essay by W. Schadewaldt, *Von Homers Welt und Werk* (4th edn., Stuttgart, 1965) 240–67; and on Hector, H. Erbse, *Ausgewählte Schriften* (Berlin and New York, 1979) 1–18 = *Kyklos*, FS R. Keydell (Berlin, 1978), 1–19.

[37] Parallels and connections may also be seen between the deaths of these heroes and that of Sarpedon in Book 16: for interesting remarks on the significance of these, and on Sarpedon and his 'code' (12. 310–28) as a foil to the lonelier and more tragic fates of Patroclus, Hector and Achilles, see M. Mueller, *Mosaic* 3 (1970). 86–103 = *Essays on the Iliad*, ed. J. Wright (Bloomington, Ind., 1978), 105–23.

[38] On the last words of dying men as prophetic, see also Pl. *Ap.* 39c; Virg. *Aen.* 4. 614 ff., 10. 739–41; *Genesis* 48–9; Shakespeare, *Richard II* II. II. 31 ff.; A. S. Pease (ed.), *M. Tulli Ciceronis De divinatione* (Urbana, Ill., 1920–3), on Cic. *Div.* I 63–4.

heroic stature and prowess.[39] The divine background, however, provides a higher significance and, by granting us a broader vision of the events than the participants possess themselves, achieves a truly tragic irony.

On a larger scale than these individual moments of foresight, the deaths of all three heroes are foretold and foreshadowed throughout the poem.[40] In particular, the poet grants his audience progressive revelations by means of the episodes in which Zeus prophesies subsequent events. These prophecies are full enough to give the listeners an outline of what is to come, and so allow them to savour the grim pattern of irony and reversal of fortune as it unfolds. On the other hand, the details are not sketched in, and some important episodes are not predicted, so that this device does not prevent Homer from utilizing the equally vital techniques of surprise and suspense.[41]

As Zeus had promised in 1. 547–8, he tells Hera first when he chooses to divulge his plans. First, in 8. 470–83 he prophesies the rout of the Achaeans, Patroclus' entry into battle, and his death, but nothing further. Second, in 15. 49–77, he predicts the events of Books 16–22, especially the *aristeia* (period of triumph in battle) of Hector, the appearance of Patroclus, the slaying of Sarpedon, the death of Patroclus and the revenge of Achilles—but *not* the later relenting of Achilles and the restoration of Hector's corpse. He also foretells the failure of the Trojan forces after the fall of Hector, and the ultimate sack of Troy (15. 69–71; cf. 22. 410 ff.;[42] also 4. 1–103). Irrespective, therefore, of whether the *Iliad* involves major mythological innovation,[43] we can be certain that from these passages the audience knows what is to happen to both Patroclus and Hector, and responds with appropriate pity and anticipation at 11. 604 (the poet on Patroclus): ἔκμολεν ἶσος Ἄρηϊ, κακοῦ δ' ἄρα οἱ πέλεν ἀρχή (he came forth, a

[39] Further, A. Lesky, *Göttliche und menschliche Motivation im homerischen Epos*, SB Heidelberg 1961. 4, esp. pp. 22–44 [= this vol., Ch. 5].

[40] For a useful collection of passages see G. E. Duckworth, *Foreshadowing and Suspense in the Epics of Homer, Apollonius and Virgil* (Princeton, 1933), 38–9, 53–5, 60–1, 71, 92, *et passim*. More briefly, C. H. Moore, *HSCP* 32 (1921), 109–16.

[41] Compare the method of Euripidean prologues, and of Homer's own proems (cf. B. A. van Groningen, *Mededelingen der Koninklijke Nederlandse Akademie van Wetenschappen, Afd. Letterkunde* 9. 8 (1946); and on proemia in general, Richardson (n. 21), on *h. Cer.* 1–3, R. G. Austin (ed.), *P. Vergili Maronis Aeneidos liber primus* (Oxford, 1971), on 1. 1–11, and bibliographies there).

[42] On the significance of this passage see Griffin (n. 2), 1; and compare Priam's speech at 22. 59–76.

[43] For bibliography of this 'neo-analyst' school of criticism, see A. Heubeck, in B. Fenik (ed.), *Homer: Tradition and Invention* (Leiden, 1978), 9 n. 27.

match for Ares, and that was the beginning of his doom).[44] This effect is sustained and heightened by the further comments of the narrator, and those of Zeus himself, as the action of the subsequent books is played out. Patroclus, Hector, and Achilles are all presented as being, in their different ways, blind, overconfident, and doomed.

A selection of the most important passages will show better than any paraphrase how Homer, with divine impartiality,[45] achieves the effect described.

15. 610–14 (which must be read in the light of the preceding forecast by the narrator at 592–604):

> αὐτὸς γάρ οἱ ἀπ' αἰθέρος ἦεν ἀμύντωρ
> Ζεύς, ὅς μιν πλεόνεσσι μετ' ἀνδράσι μοῦνον ἐόντα
> τίμα καὶ κύδαινε. μινυνθάδιος γάρ ἔμελλεν
> ἔσσεσθ'· ἤδη γάρ οἱ ἐπόρνυε μόρσιμον ἦμαρ
> Παλλὰς Ἀθηναίη ὑπὸ Πηλεΐδαο βίηφιν.

For Zeus was his helper from heaven, Zeus who brought him honour and glory, a single man among many men; for he was to be short-lived. Already Pallas Athena was preparing his day of doom before the might of the son of Peleus.

16. 46–7:

> ὣς φάτο λισσόμενος [sc. Patroclus] μέγα νήπιος·[46] ἦ γάρ ἔμελλεν
> οἷ αὐτῷ θάνατόν τε κακὸν καὶ κῆρα λιτέσθαι.

Thus he spoke in entreaty, great fool that he was. For he was ready to beg cruel death and destruction for himself.

(Compare 16. 236–8, 249–56: Zeus will not grant the whole of Achilles' prayer; 16. 644–55: Zeus ponders ἀμφὶ φόνῳ Πατρόκλου (regarding Patroclus' death) when to bring it about, but the actual fact that he is to die is not in question.)

16. 684–8:

> Πάτροκλος δ' ἵπποισι καὶ Αὐτομέδοντι κελεύσας
> Τρῶας καὶ Λυκίους μετεκίαθε, καὶ μέγ' ἀάσθη
> νήπιος· εἰ δέ ἔπος Πηληϊάδαο φύλαξεν,
> ἦ τ' ἂν ὑπέφυγε κῆρα κακὴν μέλανος θανάτοιο.
> ἀλλ' αἰεί τε Διὸς κρείσσων νόος ἠέ περ ἀνδρῶν.

Patroclus went on in pursuit of the Trojans and Lycians, calling out orders to his horses and to Automedon—foolish man. If he had heeded the words of

---

[44] Cf. Griffin (n. 2), 85.   [45] Cf. J. T. Kakridis, *Homer Revisited* (Lund, 1971), 64.
[46] On Homer's use of this word see Bremer (n. 13), 101 n. 9.

Peleus' son, he would have escaped the hard doom of dark death. But always the mind of Zeus is more powerful than that of men.

16. 692–3:

> ἔνθα τίνα πρῶτον, τίνα δ' ὕστατον ἐξενάριξας,
> Πατρόκλεις, ὅτε δή σε θεοὶ θάνατόνδε κάλεσσαν;

Whom first, whom last, did you slay at that time, Patroclus, while the gods called you on to your death?

16. 796–800:

> πάρος γε μὲν οὐ θέμις ἦεν
> ἱππόκομον πήληκα μιαίνεσθαι κονίῃσιν,
> ἀλλ' ἀνδρὸς θείοιο κάρη χαρίεν τε μέτωπον
> ῥύετ' Ἀχιλλῆος· τότε δὲ Ζεὺς Ἕκτορι δῶκεν
> ᾗ κεφαλῇ φορέειν, σχεδόθεν δέ οἱ ἦεν ὄλεθρος.[47]

Before this time it was wrong for the horse-hair-plumed helm to be defiled by the dust; instead it protected the head and the graceful brow of a godlike man, Achilles. But at that hour Zeus granted it to Hector to wear upon his head, and doom was near at hand for him.

(This motif—that Hector's moment of glory also seals and signifies his own doom—is developed shortly afterwards, in 17. 183–97, in which Hector dons the armour taken from Patroclus' corpse—which is, of course, the armour of Achilles: cf. 17. 186, etc.)[48]

17. 194–7:

> ὁ δ' ἄμβροτα τεύχεα δῦνε
> Πηλεΐδεω Ἀχιλῆος, ἅ οἱ θεοὶ Οὐρανίωνες
> πατρὶ φίλῳ ἔπορον· ὁ δ' ἄρα ᾧ παιδὶ ὄπασσε
> γηράς· ἀλλ' οὐχ υἱὸς ἐν ἔντεσι πατρὸς ἐγήρα.

He donned the immortal armour of Achilles son of Peleus, which the gods who live in heaven gave to Achilles' father; and he gave it to his son when he grew old; but the son did not grow old in his father's armour.

---

[47] The close verbal connection with 22. 403–4 (Zeus permits the defilement of Hector's body) is another link between the two scenes.

[48] See esp. 17. 202–3 (quoted in text), 448–50, 472–3, ἀτὰρ τά γε τεύχε' ἔχει κορυθαίολος Ἕκτωρ (repeated from 17. 122; cf. 18. 21), 18. 131–2, 188, 197. The repetitions and emphasis on the physical possession of the armour by Hector make the object symbolically significant. Part of the point of Book 18 is that Hector's triumph in acquiring Achilles' old armour is negated by the acquisition of new and greater armour. And in 22. 322–7 it is a weakness in the plundered armour that proves Hector's undoing (for Virgilian imitation, see Aen. 10. 496 ff., 503–5, 12. 941–4). For such significant objects see Griffin (n. 2), ch. 1 (he does not discuss this example). Again the Homeric technique is inherited by Greek tragedy: see O. Taplin, Greek Tragedy in Action (London, 1978), ch. 6. An obvious parallel is the bow of Philoctetes.

Thus even when the drama of Hector and Patroclus is at the centre of the stage, we are not allowed to forget that Achilles' doom is interwoven with theirs, and equally pitiable. Hector has no reason to feel pride or pleasure in the armour and his victory; and when Achilles' victory over Hector finally comes, he too will have little reason to rejoice.[49] Indeed, the fulfilment of his vengeance gives Achilles as little satisfaction as the fulfilment of his prayer to Zeus in the first book: for the latter brings about Patroclus' death, the former Achilles' own.

Like the poet himself, Zeus contemplates the action on earth with foreknowledge and compassion, above all at 17. 198 ff., when he speaks of Hector thus (201–8):

> ἆ δείλ᾽, οὐδέ τί τοι θάνατος καταθύμιός ἐστιν,
> ὃς δή τοι σχεδὸν εἶσι· σὺ δ᾽ ἄμβροτα τεύχεα δύνεις
> ἀνδρὸς ἀριστῆος . . .
>   ἀτάρ τοι νῦν γε μέγα κράτος ἐγγυαλίξω,
> τῶν ποινὴν ὅ τοι οὔ τι μάχης ἐκ νοστήσαντι
> δέξεται Ἀνδρομάχη κλυτὰ τεύχεα Πηλείωνος.

'Poor wretch, death is not at all in your thoughts, though it stands near you. But you are putting on the immortal armour of a man of supreme prowess. . . . but I shall now endow you with great strength, as recompense, for never will Andromache take from you the glorious arms of Peleus' son on your return from battle.'

We may see here an echo and reversal of Hector's prayer in Book 6 (476–81). Not only will Andromache never see their son returning proudly with captured armour, but she will never see Hector himself thus again.

While Patroclus lies dead on the plain, the concentration of the Greek army and of Homer's audience is repeatedly directed to the questions 'When will Achilles hear? What will he do?' (see esp. 17. 105, 121, 641, 654, 691, 701, 709). But as yet Achilles sits in untroubled calm by his ships, and his total ignorance of what has happened is powerfully brought out by the following passage, set in the centre of a long series of scenes entirely devoted to the fighting over Patroclus'

---

[49] The *kleos* (glory) gained from his victory does not seem to me to alter this picture, for even glory no longer means anything to Achilles. (18. 121 is belied by his final attitude in Book 24: note esp. his indifferent tone at 139–40, and the deep disillusionment expressed in 540–2. See further Griffin (n. 2), 98–101.) This is another way in which the mood and reactions of Achilles during his first wrath (see 19. 315–43) are echoed in more tragic circumstances in the final books of the poem.

body (17. 400–11):

> τοῖον Ζεὺς ἐπὶ Πατρόκλῳ ἀνδρῶν τε καὶ ἵππων
> ἤματι τῷ ἐτάνυσσε κακὸν πόνον· οὐδ᾽ ἄρα πώ τι
> ᾔδεε Πάτροκλον τεθνηότα δῖος Ἀχιλλεύς·
> πολλὸν γάρ ῥ᾽ ἀπάνευθε νεῶν μάρναντο θοάων,
> τείχει ὕπο Τρώων· τό μιν οὔ ποτε ἔλπετο θυμῷ
>
> . . . .
>
> τεθνάμεν, ἀλλὰ ζωὸν ἐνιχριμφθέντα πύλῃσιν
> ἂψ ἀπονοστήσειν, ἐπεὶ οὐδὲ τὸ ἔλπετο πάμπαν,
> ἐκπέρσειν πτολίεθρον ἄνευ ἔθεν, οὐδὲ σὺν αὐτῷ·
> δὴ τότε γ᾽ οὔ οἱ ἔειπε κακὸν τόσον ὅσσον ἐτύχθη
> μήτηρ, ὅττι ῥά οἱ πολὺ φίλτατος ὤλεθ᾽ ἑταῖρος.

Such was the terrible struggle of men and horses that Zeus spread out on that day over Patroclus. But godlike Achilles as yet had no knowledge at all of Patroclus' death. For they were fighting far away from the speedy ships, beneath the city wall of the Trojans. He never supposed that he was dead, but expected that living he would skirt the city gates and return once more; for he did not at all suppose that he would sack the town without him, nor even with him. . . . At that time indeed his mother did not tell him so great a misfortune had befallen, that the comrade dearest to him by far had perished.

All Achilles' careful warnings to Patroclus have been frustrated, and as yet he does not even know it.

The irony here is enhanced by the way in which the wishes of Achilles finally prove self-defeating. His actions ever since the first book have brought about this disastrous conclusion. In that book Zeus promised him *timē* through the rout and humiliation of the Greeks, as well as massive compensation for his mistreatment (1. 493–530). As the promise of Zeus, this unfailingly comes true, but in a manner very different from anything Achilles had expected (cf. 17. 405, 407 ἔλπετο above).

The parallelism between scenes in Books 1 and 18 serves to show this more clearly. In both books Achilles is filled with anger and grief; in both, Thetis comes from the sea to speak to him and offer comfort; in both, she first addresses him with the words (1. 362–3, 18. 73–4):

> "τέκνον, τί κλαίεις; τί δέ σε φρένας ἵκετο πένθος;
> ἐξαύδα, μὴ κεῦθε."

'My son, why are you weeping? What grief has come upon your heart? Speak out, do not hide it.'

But however passionate the anger of Achilles in Book 1, its pettiness becomes evident in retrospect, when it is replaced by the terrible agony and furious hatred that consumes Achilles when he learns of Patroclus' death. Nevertheless, for all his hatred of Hector, the supreme horror of the situation of Achilles lies in his recognition that he himself has destroyed his beloved friend, by accepting his plea in Book 16 and allowing him to enter the battle when he, Achilles, would not be there to protect him.

Achilles therefore does not rebuke his mother or cry curses on Zeus; he admits that his former wish has been fulfilled:[50]

'τὰ μὲν δή τοι τετέλεσται
ἐκ Διός, ὡς ἄρα δὴ πρίν γ' εὔχεο χεῖρας ἀνασχών.'

'Those things have truly been accomplished by Zeus, the very same that you begged for before, holding your hands up in prayer.' (18. 74—Thetis)

'μῆτερ ἐμή, τὰ μὲν ἄρ μοι Ὀλύμπιος ἐξετέλεσσεν·
ἀλλὰ τί μοι τῶν ἦδος, ἐπεὶ φίλος ὤλεθ' ἑταῖρος,
Πάτροκλος, τὸν ἐγὼ περὶ πάντων τῖον ἑταίρων,
ἶσον ἐμῇ κεφαλῇ τὸν ἀπώλεσα,[51] . . .'

'Mother mine, yes, the Olympian has indeed accomplished this for me. But what pleasure can I feel in this, when my dear friend is dead, Patroclus, whom I honoured beyond all my friends, on a par with my own life. I have destroyed him . . .' (18. 79—Achilles)

Again, later in the same book Achilles, as he weeps over the corpse of Patroclus, is forced to admit that his hopes of a safe homecoming for them both were empty fantasies (18. 328):

ἀλλ' οὐ Ζεὺς ἄνδρεσσι νοήματα πάντα τελευτᾷ.

But Zeus does not bring all men's expectations to fulfilment.[52]

---

[50] Again there are verbal echoes, through the significant use of τελεῖν (to accomplish) and cognates: 18. 74 τετέλεσται (have been accomplished) and 79 ἐξετέλεσσεν (has accomplished) should be related not only to 18. 4 τὰ φρονέοντ' ἀνὰ θυμὸν ἃ δὴ τετελεσμένα ἦεν (pondering in his heart what had come to pass), but also to 1. 523 ἐμοὶ δέ κε ταῦτα μελήσεται, ὄφρα τελέσσω (these matters will be my concern, so that I may accomplish them) and 526–7 οὐ γὰρ ἐμὸν παλινάγρετον οὐδ' ἀπατηλὸν | οὐδ' ἀτελεύτητον, ὅ τί . . . κατανεύσω (for that which I assent to with a nod of my head cannot be taken back, it is devoid of deception, and it does not fail of accomplishment. Cf. the title Ζεὺς τέλειος ('Zeus the accomplisher'; see E. Fraenkel (ed.), *Aeschylus: Agamemnon* (Oxford, 1950), on *Ag.* 973–4).

[51] On the force of this word see most recently Griffin (n. 2), 163 n. 41, who is more cautious than I would be about finding the meaning 'destroyed' present.

[52] For other formulations of this theme, see *Od.* 5. 103–4, Hes. *Op.* 105 οὕτως οὐ τί πῃ ἔστι Διὸς νόον ἐξαλέασθαι (thus in no way is it possible to evade the mind

As in the Sophoclean examples, human advice and divine fore-warning are insufficient guides: a man of superior ability, intelligence and merit, one of τῶν ἐν μεγάλῃ δόξῃ ὄντων καὶ εὐτυχίᾳ, οἷον Οἰδίπους (those who are held in high repute and enjoy good fortune, like Oedipus), in Aristotelian terms (*Poetics* 13, 1453ᵃ10),[53] can still go wrong through ignorance of the whole truth, μήτε διὰ κακίαν καὶ μοχθηρίαν . . . ἀλλὰ δι' ἁμαρτίαν τινά (not through wickedness or baseness . . . but because of some mistake) (ibid. 8–10, cf. 15–16).

Achilles' mistake is all the more poignant because his mother had been able to tell him so much, and yet it was not enough: it was still possible for him to overlook the crucial warning that she did once give, that the best of the Myrmidons would be killed by the Trojans during his lifetime (see 18. 9–11).[54] This passage establishes a further significant parallelism between the cases of Patroclus, Hector, and Achilles. Each receives a warning on both the divine and the human level. In Patroclus' case the warning comes first from Achilles (16. 87–96; cf. 684–98); and later, at the height of his *aristeia* he receives a command from Apollo to give up his vain attempt to storm Troy (16. 705–11). At this he falls back, but does not withdraw from the field, and so in the end he faces defeat. Hector is warned by Iris

---

of Zeus), 483 ff., *Theog.* 613, Semonides 1. 1 ff. West, Theognis 141–2, Solon 13. 63 ff. West, id. 17 West, Heraclitus B 78, Pind. fr. 61 Maehler, Aesch. *Supp.* 92 ff., 1057, *Ag.* 1487–8, Eur. *Or.* 1545–6, *Hel.* 1137–43 and R. Kannicht (ed.), *Euripides: Helena* (Heidelberg, 1969), ad loc.

[53] On the other hand, ὁ μήτε ἀρετῇ διαφέρων καὶ δικαιοσύνῃ ('the man who is not exceptional in excellence or just dealing', 13, 1453ᵃ8) does not seem an altogether suitable description of Achilles, and it might be said that Aristotle here overstates his point. It is not necessary to deny that a tragic hero can be superior in such qualities, as in birth and fortune, only to insist that he should possess also the human weaknesses that make him akin to ourselves (cf. nn. 60–1, 71–2). This is the case with Achilles as with Oedipus.

[54] There is a difficulty in reconciling 18. 9–11 with 17. 404–11: cf. W. Leaf (ed.), *Homer: The Iliad* II (London, 1888), on 17. 408, 'The discrepancy of course arises from difference of authorship, and we need not try to remove it by excision of lines'; contrast Reinhardt (n. 5), 373–4. Homer's words do not seem to make a contradiction inevitable. Thetis had told Achilles many things, including, perhaps, the content of 17. 406–7? Cf. 16. 91 ff.: 97–100 (Achilles' strange prayer) seem to imply that he does know that the Greeks will sack Troy without him and Patroclus, but he wishes that the reverse could be true: cf. 18. 329–32; 19. 328–33. But Thetis does *not* tell him *now* (on the force of δὴ τότε see Leaf ad loc.) that Patroclus *has* fallen (not 'will fall'). But the passage is difficult, and perhaps deliberately made unclear, on any account. Others may prefer to have recourse to *Tychoismus* (R. D. Dawe, *PCPS* 9 (1963), 21–62): so e.g. M. M. Willcock, *A Companion to Homer's Iliad* (Chicago and London, 1976) on 9. 410, 16. 50–1, 17. 408. See also Schol. Did. 18. 10–11, for a different approach.

that Zeus' favour will give him victory until the sun sets that day
(11. 193-4, 208-9, recalled at 17. 441-55); and just after the fateful
appearance of Achilles on the rampart, ready to re-enter the battle,
the sun does set (18. 239-42). But Hector in the moment of glory
cannot accept that he has reached the limit of his good fortune.
He insists on remaining on the plain that night and eagerly awaits the
renewed fighting next day, even though the voice of human reason,
in the person of Polydamas,[55] reinforces the divine warning (18. 243-
313, esp. 250-2, 293-5, 305-6). Polydamas is in the right, as the
poet's comment points out with ominous severity (18. 310-13), and
as Hector will later realize (22. 99-107). Finally there is the case of
Achilles himself. Here the embassy-book seems to provide a warning
on the human level, especially through the paradigm of Meleager and
the fable of the Litai and Ate. The Greeks feel that in some sense
Achilles is going too far, wanting too much (see esp. 9. 510-12, 523,
598-602, 628-38), and Phoenix especially voices their uneasy suspicion that he may have to suffer for this, even though he does not
suspect the form which Achilles' downfall will in fact take.[56] On the
divine level, Achilles is warned by Thetis but misunderstands or
forgets (above). In each case the pattern is clear: success and glory are
promised, but with qualification; the hero ignores the warning or
misses its point; and the glory which he sought turns into disaster.

No less important than the resemblances between the main
characters are their differences. Again these may usefully be formulated in terms of knowledge, and particularly self-knowledge. It is
noteworthy that Patroclus' death comes upon him wholly as a
surprise: filled with the fervour of battle, he is struck down from
behind by Apollo, whereupon Euphorbus and Hector finish the job
(16. 786-842). Even in defeat he is defiant and contemptuous: he
answers taunt with taunt (16. 844-54), blames the gods for his
downfall, and declares that even if twenty Hectors had faced him, he
could have prevailed (847-8). Apart from his prophecy of Hector's
death, he betrays no understanding of the wider scheme of Zeus, nor
indeed any appreciation of the impact that his death will have upon

[55] Homer's treatment of Hector and Polydamas is well expounded by J. M. Redfield,
Nature and Culture in the Iliad (Chicago and London, 1975), 136-53; see also Erbse
(n. 36), 5-6, 8-10.
[56] On the integrity of Book 9 and the place of Phoenix's speech in the structure of
the book and of the epic, see esp. D. Motzkus, *Untersuchungen zum 9. Buch der Ilias
unter besonderer Berücksichtigung der Phoinixgestalt* (Hamburg, 1964), 37-46. See
also Reinhardt (n. 5), 212-42.

Achilles. Above all he sees no further than Hector's death; he shows no knowledge of Achilles' own.

Hector's reaction reveals his characteristic and increasing over-confidence.[57] Here and later his hope is that his success will continue and that he may even be a match for Achilles himself (16. 860–1, 18. 305–9, 20. 366–72, 434–7). But his ambition is shown to be delusion by the comments of Zeus and of the poet himself, even in this very scene (16. 799–800; cf. 17. 198 ff., quoted above). In the end, Hector, put to flight by Achilles the next day, is forced to acknowledge his error and to confess that Polydamas was right (22. 99–107). Even then, however, a trace of hope that he might still win out flares up in his heart (22. 130; also 256–9, 279–80, 285–8). Only when his ally Deiphobus proves to be the treacherous Athene does he recognize that he is doomed, and steel himself for his final hopeless attack, with words that again echo the death-scene of Patroclus (22. 297; cf. 16. 693):

$$\mathring{\omega} \; \pi \acute{o} \pi o \iota, \; \mathring{\eta} \; \mu \acute{a} \lambda a \; \delta \acute{\eta} \; \mu \epsilon \; \theta \epsilon o \grave{\iota} \; \theta \acute{a} \nu a \tau \acute{o} \nu \delta \epsilon \; \kappa \acute{a} \lambda \epsilon \sigma \sigma a \nu.$$

Alas, surely the gods did indeed call me to my death.

It fits the pattern suggested here that in Book 16 the formula is used by the narrator, in Book 22 by Hector himself. This reflects the different degrees of insight or awareness which Patroclus and Hector possess at the moment of death. Hector now understands what he had failed to see before and what Patroclus never saw, that the gods supported him before for a purpose, but with that purpose achieved, they will do so no longer; and so, as Hector acknowledges, $\nu \hat{\upsilon} \nu \; a \mathring{\upsilon} \tau \acute{e} \; \mu \epsilon \; \mu o \hat{\iota} \rho a \; \kappa \iota \chi \acute{a} \nu \epsilon \iota$ ('now my doom comes upon me', 22. 303; cf. 203–4, 212–13). This speech of Hector's goes beyond even his earlier speech before the walls (22. 99 ff.) in showing him rid of his illusions. At the last, he recognizes that his own calculations and hopes were bound to fail.

The case of Achilles is more complex again. Like Hector, he sees that he has been deceived and destroyed by the very favour of heaven. Like Hector, but unlike Patroclus, he recognizes also his own responsibility for what has befallen him and those he cares for. Like Hector, he is warned of his imminent death; but unlike him, he chooses the course that will lead to his death with open eyes and

---

[57] Cf. Redfield, loc. cit. (n. 55), esp. 145, 150; Willcock (n. 54), on 12. 237–8, 13. 823.

without self-deception.[58] Achilles and Hector are opposites in many ways: Achilles the invader, Hector the defender; Achilles son of a goddess, Hector all too human; Achilles a man apart, all but indifferent to concubine and child (19. 56–63, 326–7), Hector a man who fights to protect his beloved family and city; Achilles a lone fighter, Hector leader of a community and its allies.[59] But this does not mean that Achilles is devoid of human illusion and weakness, or that he has nothing to learn after he has made his final choice of death (18. 90–1, 98–100, and esp. 115–16 = 22. 365–6). Earlier in the poem it is the humiliation of Agamemnon that is all-important to him; later, the punishment of Hector. Neither of these vindictive ends can be permitted to stand as the final expression of the character of Achilles or of the poet's tragic yet compassionate vision.

The association of Patroclus and Hector, stressed by the parallel death-scenes, is one of the means by which the poet shows the gods bringing death and sorrow indiscriminately to both sides. But even this fundamental aspect of the poem is subordinate to a greater theme. Not only the audience, but Achilles himself, comes to see Patroclus and Hector as equals in death; and in them, Achilles also sees himself. Through his suffering and the increased insight that his experience brings, he transcends the values of the Greek army, preoccupied with winning a victory that he will never see. The supreme moment in the last book of the *Iliad* comes when Achilles finds it in himself to respond to the equal suffering in his enemy Priam, the father of Patroclus' killer, and understands that despite the enmity between them, he and Priam have more in common than he can ever again have with his fellow-Greeks. Community of suffering leads to a fuller realization of their kinship, not by blood or nationality, but as two human beings, the victims of the common fate of man, grief and death.[60]

---

[58] See esp. Schadewaldt (n. 36), 257, 263–4; also Griffin (n. 2), 163, who concisely collects and sums up the relevant passages.

[59] Cf. (with rather different emphasis) Redfield (n. 55), 108–13, 119–27. On the individualism of Achilles see also Knox, loc. cit. (n. 10); J. Griffin, *JHS* 97 (1977), 43–4 [= this vol., pp. 374–5]; Macleod, *Iliad* xxiv (n. 2), 23–8.

[60] R. Northrop Frye, *Anatomy of Criticism* (Princeton, 1957), 319 comments: 'It is hardly possible to overestimate the importance for western literature of the *Iliad's* demonstration that the fall of an enemy, no less than of a friend or leader, is tragic and not comic.' See further Vickers (n. 12), ch. 2; K. J. Dover, *Greek Popular Morality* (Oxford, 1974), 268–72; F. Martinazzoli, *Sapphica et Vergilia* (Bari, 1958), a work known to me only from J. G. Griffith's review in *CR* 9 (1959), 285.

V

This mutual understanding and pity (*sumpatheia, homoiopatheia*) is another theme which, inherited from Homer, animates much that is greatest and most moving in Greek tragedy. It is natural, and right, that a man should recognize his own weakness and vulnerability, and that seeing such qualities in another he should understand the bond of humanity which cuts across more temporary or man-made distinctions. Thus in the *Ajax* Odysseus in a famous speech declines to gloat over his humiliated adversary, because he must acknowledge that he too may come to such a state (*Ajax* 124–6, cf. 1365–7). Theseus sees the similarity between the aged Oedipus' experiences and his own (*OC* 560–8; cf. Virgil, *Aeneid* 1. 628–30, 8. 333–6). Hecuba begs the merciless victor Odysseus to show magnanimity to the defeated side, for he should not assume that he will always be successful (Euripides, *Hecuba* 282–5, cf. 340; also *Supplices* 549–57)—very much the same grounds on which the more enlightened Cyrus, in Herodotus' account, spares the vanquished Croesus (Herodotus 1. 86. 6):[61]

καὶ τὸν Κῦρον ἀκούσαντα τῶν ἑρμηνέων τὰ Κροῖσος εἶπε, μεταγνόντα τε καὶ ἐννώσαντα ὅτι καὶ αὐτὸς ἄνθρωπος ἐὼν ἄλλον ἄνθρωπον, γενόμενον ἑωυτοῦ εὐδαιμονίῃ οὐκ ἐλάσσω, ζῶντα πυρὶ διδοίη, πρός τε τούτοισι δείσαντα τὴν τίσιν καὶ ἐπιλεξάμενον ὡς οὐδὲν εἴη τῶν ἐν ἀνθρώποισι ἀσφαλέως ἔχον, κελεύειν σβεννύναι τὴν ταχίστην τὸ καιόμενον πῦρ.

When Cyrus heard from the interpreters what Croesus had said, changing his mind and reflecting that he, who was himself merely a man, was casting another man into fire while still alive, and a man who had been his own equal in good fortune, and also fearing retribution and reasoning to himself

---

[61] Further, note esp. *Od.* 8. 485–531, where Odysseus, expecting to enjoy Demodocus' song of his own glorious deeds at Troy, finds himself weeping tears of *pity* (531: the preceding simile associates the victor Odysseus with the sufferings of the victims, as does the repetition in 530–1: τῆς δ᾽ ἐλεεινοτάτῳ ἄχεϊ φθινύθουσι παρειαί· | ὡς Ὀδυσσεὺς ἐλεεινὸν ὑπ᾽ ὀφρύσι δάκρυον εἶβεν ('her cheeks are wasted with *most piteous* grief; so too Odysseus shed a *piteous* tear beneath his eyelids'). See also Soph. *Trach.* 303–6, *Phil.* 500–6. Thuc. 5. 90; perhaps Hdt. 6. 21 οἰκήϊα κακά ('their own misfortunes'), but the exact sense is disputed, see R. W. Macan, *Herodotus: The Fourth, Fifth, and Sixth Books* (London, 1895), ad loc. The Homeric–tragic ethic of *homoiopatheia* should be contrasted with the principle 'do good to your friends and harm to your enemies', for which see J. F. Kells (ed.), *Sophocles: Electra* (Cambridge, 1973), 8; Dover (n. 60), 180–4; Knox (n. 14), 127–8, 152–3 (= *HSCP* 65 (1961), 3–5, 29–30).

that there was nothing secure in human life, he gave orders to extinguish the blazing fire as speedily as possible.

As often, Homeric practice anticipates the schematizing of rhetorical theory:[62] thus Aristotle insists that a misfortune that is to arouse pity must be such that the pitier (in *Iliad* 24 Achilles) can suppose that he, or someone dear to him (Peleus) might suffer in the same way (*Rhetoric* 2. 8, 1385^{b}13 ff.; cf. *Rhetorica ad Alexandrum* 1444^{a}12–14).

It can hardly be overemphasized that in Homer, as in tragedy, the poignancy and urgency of the appeal to pity lie in the ease with which the entreaty is often ignored. It has been observed that no human supplication represented in the action of the *Iliad* proves successful before Priam's to Achilles.[63] Indeed, Agamemnon's injunction in 6. 55–60 to slaughter all the people of Troy, even the unborn babe in the womb, prepares us for the ever-mounting tide of brutality and destruction[64] which is to culminate in the bloodthirsty vengeance of Achilles, sustained with horrifying effect throughout Books 20–22. Again, the fears of Priam (22. 60–79), the laments of the Trojans,[65] and above all Andromache's prophecy of the fate of Astyanax (24. 734–9), remind us that the victors will have no mercy. Consequently, the actions of Achilles in Book 24 break out of a pattern, emphasizing his uniqueness in a new way. His magnanimity is isolated, and in a sense futile, for it changes nothing in the situation of Priam and Troy, or of Achilles himself; but it would be wrong to see it as any less admirable or precious for that reason.

---

[62] On Homeric rhetoric see L. Radermacher, *Artium Scriptores*, SB Wien 226. 3 (Vienna, 1951), 1–10; G. Kennedy, *AJP* 78 (1957), 26 ff.; K. J. Dover, *Lysias and the Corpus Lysiacum* (Berkeley and Los Angeles, 1968), 175–81. On pity in rhetorical theory, with useful references to Homeric precedent, see E. B. Stevens, *AJP* 65 (1944), 1–25; add that Arist. *Rhet.* 2.8, 1385^{b}27, though more intellectualized (cf. Eur. *Hcld.* 458–60, fr. 407), corresponds to *Il.* 24. 157–8 = 186–7.

[63] J. Gould, *JHS* 93 (1973), 80–2. Further, Macleod, *Iliad* xxiv (n. 2), 15–22.

[64] Cf C. Segal, *The Theme of the Mutilation of the Corpse in the Iliad*, *Mnemos.* Suppl. 17 (1971), 18, 72–3.

[65] For the significance of ritual lamentation, tearing of clothes, etc., see Griffin (n. 2), 2–3 (for tragic parallels to the motif discussed there see Collard (n. 7) on Eur. *Supp.* 990 ff.); Vickers (n. 12), 87–96; M. Alexiou, *The Ritual Lament in Greek Tradition* (Cambridge, 1974) *passim*, esp. chs. 1–2, 6, 8; also her index, s.vv. 'self-mutilation', 'laceration', etc. In both subject-matter and form the tragic *kommos* (ritual lament) is influenced by *Il.* 22. 437–515, 24. 718–76 (though for a contrast of the genres, see Macleod (n. 2), on 24. 721–2). For this aspect of tragedy see H. D. Broadhead (ed.), *Aeschylus: Persae* (Cambridge, 1960), appendix 4; Collard on Eur. *Supp.* 1114–64.

The scene in which Priam supplicates Achilles is so familiar that only a few specific comments will be required in order to show its importance for the themes of this chapter. In the *Iliad* as a whole Achilles is seen to suffer two great wraths, one against Agamemnon, the other against Hector and all associated with him. The first fades into insignificance when the second has begun. The dispute between Achilles and Agamemnon is formally brought to a conclusion in Book 19, but there Achilles is consumed by such frantic eagerness to take the field against Hector that he barely takes any notice of the proceedings. In particular he ignores the exhortations to eat in order to strengthen himself (esp. 19. 205–14, 305–8). Here the abstinence of Achilles, his indifference to human needs,[66] reinforces his doomed isolation. Similarly in the fighting which follows, he does battle alone, dedicated to his revenge. None but he must be the slayer of Hector (22. 205–7). But in Book 24, with the truer reconciliation and the suppression of his second and greater anger, he himself urges food on the grief-stricken Priam, as Odysseus and others had tried to do before in his own case (24. 601–20).[67]

In Priam Achilles sees his own father Peleus,[68] and he realizes the other side to the killing of Hector—not just revenge and punishment, but the agony of a parent's grief and the certain doom of a whole people. And by analogy, he sees that Hector is to Priam as he himself is to his lonely father Peleus (see esp. 24. 486–92, 503–4, 534–43). Further, the grief of Achilles for Patroclus corresponds to that of Priam, and all the Trojans, for the lost Hector. But the chain of destruction is not ended; for at the end of the poem both Achilles and

---

[66] For grief-stricken *asitia* (fasting) see Griffin (n. 2), 15–17, and add *Od.* 4. 788, *h. Cer.* 47 ff. and Richardson (n. 21), ad loc., Soph. *Aj.* 324, Eur. *Med.* 24, *Hipp.* 135 ff., 277, *Supp.* 1105–6, *Or.* 39–41, 189.

[67] Thus the arguments at 19. 155 ff., 178–80, 216 ff., 302 ff., correspond to Achilles' speeches to Priam at 24. 522–4, 549–51, 599–620; Achilles' statement of his own supreme misfortune in 19. 315–37 corresponds to Priam's at 24. 486–506; Achilles' refusal to bathe (23. 38–47) is like Priam remaining uncleansed of the dung in which he grovelled after Hector's death (22. 414, 24. 162–5); Achilles cannot sleep (24. 3–13; cf. 23. 62–7, where he sleeps only to dream of Patroclus), and Priam has not closed his eyes since Hector's death (24. 635–42). Note also the bitter injunction οὐδέ μιν ἀνστήσεις ('you will not raise him up again', 24. 551, cf 756; Soph. *El.* 137 ff., is an instance of this motif in tragedy).

[68] Compare the way in which Deianira comes to see both the similarity (Soph. *Trach.* 465, cf. 25) and the differences between herself and her rival Iole (303–6, 441–8).

Troy must be resigned to the inevitable. The events presented in the *Iliad* itself have determined the destruction of both.

The suffering of Achilles and the sympathy he feels for Priam make themselves manifest in generalization, for in both Homer and tragedy the individual struggles to see himself in a context, and so to make some coherent sense of his misery;[69] which is to say, again, that it is part of human nature to seek to understand the course of events even when they are beyond human understanding. Homeric epic differs from drama in presenting more fully and impartially the actual decisions and motivations of the gods, which may be weighed and assessed against the imperfect guesses of the human participants. But with due allowance for poetic elaboration (in the imagery of the two jars), Achilles' account of the state of man is borne out by the preceding action, whereas his earlier guesses, like those of Agamemnon, Hector, and the rest, were not. Consequently the utterance of Achilles, especially in such a scene and with such a companion, possesses much more significance and power.

Part of that significance lies in the consolatory force of the generalization: it is not Priam alone who has suffered (525 ff., answering 505).[70] But this is cold comfort at best, as both Achilles and Homer know. We should rather see Achilles as trying to instil in both Priam and himself a greater degree of objectivity and realism. Again suffering brings a fuller kind of understanding, if in the midst of it the two men can make themselves look beyond the individual's sorrow, beyond even the combined sorrow of two opponents and two sides,[71]

---

[69] For instance, Hyllus' speech at the end of *Trach.* (lines 1257–78 are incredibly rejected by Dawe: no supporting argument in his *Studies on the Text of Sophocles* III (Leiden, 1978)). Eur. *Tro.* 1240–5 is another good example, and one with evident Homeric background: cf. *Il.* 3. 125–8, 6. 355–8, *Od.* 1. 346–59, 8. 577–80, 24. 196–202; Griffin (n. 2), 97–102; W. Marg, *Homer über die Dichtung* (2nd edn., Münster, 1971); Macleod, *Iliad* XXIV (n. 2), 1–8, and his paper 'Homer on Poetry and the Poetry of Homer', to be published in his *Collected Essays* [(n. 23), 1–15 = this vol., Ch. 9]. This passage of *Troades* refutes the contention of Taplin (n. 28), 133 and of D. Bain, *Actors and Audience* (Oxford, 1977), 208 ff., that no case of theatrical self-reference can be found in Greek tragedy. Hecuba's utterance here is in fact very close to the passage of *Julius Caesar* cited by Bain 209 n. 1. (Tangentially relevant to this question: Bond (n. 11), on Eur. *Her.* 1021–2.)

[70] Cf. *Od.* 1. 353–5; R. Kassel, *Untersuchungen zur griechischen und römischen Konsolationsliteratur*, Zetemata 18 (Munich, 1958), 54–5. The uselessness of grieving over an inevitable loss is 'consolatio pervulgata quidem illa maxime' (Cic. *Fam.* 5. 16. 2).

[71] On the absence of partisanship or of any kind of 'panhellenism' in the *Il.* see Kakridis (n. 45), 54 ff.; also C. S. Lewis, *A Preface to Paradise Lost* (London, 1942),

and can contemplate these particular griefs in the light of the true condition of all humanity.[72]

At the end of the poem there is no more room for illusion: both Achilles and Priam finally know. But as often in literature as in life, that knowledge, and even the moment of mutual understanding and sympathy that follows from it, is powerless to alter the course of subsequent events. The imperfect knowledge of mankind can never hope to outwit the gods, just as mortal success can never surpass or outlast their eternal joys.

ADDITIONAL NOTE (2000)

The preliminary remarks on the state of Homeric studies are inevitably now very dated. I need not give an account of the developments in Homeric criticism since 1982, and can instead refer to my comments in *Homer* (*G&R* New Surveys in the Classics 26, 1996), which also contains my most recent thoughts on the *Iliad* in general.

ch. 5. In tragedy, the message of Aeschylus' *Persae* is not aimed at barbarians alone: see e.g. Broadhead (n. 65), pp. xv–xviii, xxi, xxviii–xxix; H. D. F. Kitto, *Poiesis* (Berkeley and Los Angeles, 1966), 74–106. In Eur. *IA* I take it that the character and behaviour of the participants is meant to undermine the not-so-high ideals expressed by Agamemnon and picked up by Iphigenia (*contra* D. J. Conacher, *Euripidean Drama* (Toronto, 1967), 261–4, with further bibliography). Note also the portrayal of the Trojan captives in *Hec.*, *Tro.*, *Andr.* A striking line, which epitomizes Euripides' realistic, and Homeric, stand on this is *Tro.* 764: (Andromache speaks) ὦ βάρβαρ' ἐξευρόντες Ἕλληνες κακά (You Greeks, devisers of barbarian atrocities!). Here as elsewhere (n. 61) Homer anticipates the best elements of 5th-cent. ethics: cf. Antiph. Soph. B 44b DK; Eur. *Phaeth.* 163 and J. Diggle (ed.), *Euripides: Phaethon* (Cambridge, 1970), ad loc. Contrast the facile arrogance of popular opinion about *barbaroi*: e.g. Isoc. 4. 131, 15. 293, and even Arist. *Pol.* 7. 7. 1327^{b}20 ff. Further, Dover (n. 60), 83 ff., 279–83; F. W. Walbank, *Phoenix* 5 (1951), 41–60 [= Walbank, *Selected Papers* (Cambridge, 1985), 1–19].

[72] Priam and Achilles are paradigms of humanity; which is not to deny that they are also vividly imagined and fully rounded characters. For individuals in tragedy as *exempla* of the human condition, see esp. Aesch. *Ag.* 1331–42, Soph. *OT* 1186–96, *Ant.* 1155–71; also H. Friis Johansen, *General Reflection in Tragic Rhesis* (Copenhagen, 1959), ch. 8. Such archetypal figures are fit subject-matter for poetry that is concerned with something broader than the narrative of an individual or a single historical sequence of events. Cf. Arist. *Poet.* 9, 1451^{a}36–^{b}11; perhaps Thuc. 1 22, 4? Further, F. W. Walbank, *Historia* 9 (1960), 216–34 [= *Selected Papers* (n. 71), 224–41]; G. E. M. de Ste Croix, in B. Levick (ed.), *The Ancient Historian and his Materials*, Studies presented to C. E. Stevens (Farnborough, 1975), 51–2 [= A. O. Rorty (ed.), *Essays on Aristotle's Poetics* (Princeton, 1992), 27–9].

The general argument of the chapter still seems to me sound (for some other work along comparable lines see *BICS* 38 (1991–3), 41 n. 11 = this volume, Ch. 3, n. 11), though if I were to restate the position now I would make less use of Aristotle's model. More serious is the fact that in section IV, whereas Hector's and Patroclus' blunders are relatively clear, I was not entirely plain or consistent in my account of Achilles' 'error': is the crucial point his rejection of the embassy in Book 9, or the failure to remember Thetis' warning until he mentions it at the opening of Book 18? If we must choose, I would now opt unhesitatingly for the scene in Book 9 (cf. *Homer, G&R* op. cit. 49–52). But it may be that it is misguided to speak of one crucial error rather than an accelerating path towards disaster and ultimately self-destruction.

There are two other major criticisms I would now make. The first concerns the title, and the use of the word 'form' on occasion elsewhere (e.g. n. 65). Obviously, this was not intended to imply that Homeric epic bears any similarity to tragedy in metre or even broader structural units. 'Form' means rather certain characteristic plot-patterns or sequences of events, such as the warning ignored and then remembered too late: what Aristotle meant by the σύστασις τῶν πραγμάτων (structure of the events). But since I was also concerned to point out various parallel motifs and other aspects of the shared subject-matter of epic and tragedy, the term is evidently used too freely, and the alliteration is achieved at the expense of precision.

The other criticism would be that both epic and tragedy are treated in a way which I now see as culpably unhistorical. Both genres are seen as conveying a kind of pessimistic wisdom which is essentially the same, though expressed in different styles (and the last section extends the comparison into other genres such as historiography). Obviously the notion that tragic wisdom, or truths about the human condition, are the same in Homer's day as in Sophocles', let alone the twenty-first century, runs counter to the historical relativism which dominates most modern scholarship in literary studies and beyond. It is now commonplace that values, social attitudes, behaviour patterns are in important ways culturally conditioned and vary from one period and one society to another. While this doctrine can sometimes be exaggerated (for instance, it remains the case that human beings still universally die, and generally mourn their dead, particularly family and friends, though the different ways of doing so demand attention), I would find it impossible today to write as though these views did not exist or did not matter. As is well known, students of tragedy have now rebelled against the older approach which emphasized the 'timeless wisdom' of the dramatists, and the works of the great tragedians are more often studied as the product of Athenian democratic society and in relation to that society's values and ideology (see e.g. J. Winkler and F. Zeitlin (edd.), *Nothing to do with Dionysus?* (Princeton, 1980), and C. B. R. Pelling (ed.), *Greek Tragedy and the Historian* (Oxford, 1997); for criticism of this approach see J. Griffin, *CQ* 48 (1998), 39–61, and the reply by R. Seaford in *CQ* 50 (2000), 30–44). Homeric epic, so hard to localize in place and time, is less easily anchored in its social and historical context, but important work has been done here too: see e.g. K. Raaflaub, in *The Ancient Greek City-State*, ed. M. H. Hansen (Copenhagen, 1993), 41–105. In particular I have learned much from the bold and stimulating work of R. Seaford, *Reciprocity and Ritual: Homer and Tragedy in the Developing City-State* (Oxford, 1994): see esp. his ch. 5. Seaford persuasively argues that the differences between Homer and tragedy are more significant than the similarities (cf. Seaford, *TAPA* 119 (1989), 88 ff.), and that they partly arise from the fact that Attic tragedy is the product of the *polis* and its rituals. To the extent that my chapter neglected the gulf between Homer and tragedy in order to stress the continuity of mythical and emotional preoccupations, it is undoubtedly one-sided; but the continuity, as the ancient critics recognized, is a real one. (See also J. Herington, *Poetry into Drama* (Berkeley and Los Angeles, 1985), 133–6, 213–16.)

On the last section of the chapter many further references could be added: I confine myself to two of general relevance, which move beyond the genres discussed: Aristotle, *Nicomachean Ethics* 9. 11 on friendship in adversity, and J. Hornblower, *Hieronymus of Cardia* (Oxford, 1982), 104–6, on compassionate conquerors in ancient historiography.

Finally, a few details: 1. S. Goldhill, *The Poet's Voice* (Cambridge, 1991) 91 n. 69 rightly points out that my n. 49 goes too far in saying that after Book 18 glory no longer means anything to Achilles, and quotes against this statement 22. 207.

2. D. Bain, 'Some Reflections on the Illusion in Greek Tragedy', *BICS* 34 (1987), 1–14 at p. 10 fairly objects to my claim about the *Troades* passage cited in n. 69: the speech in question refers to song, not drama, and the dramatic illusion is bent but not broken. I would

accept this correction, though the climate has changed so much that I would now be more concerned, like Bain, to slow and impose more discipline on the frenzied quest for metatextual references. For a recent discussion with bibliography see O. Taplin and P. Wilson, *PCPS* 39 (1993), 169–80, though I have several reservations about this paper.

3. In section 1 or elsewhere I should have cited the fragment of Aeschylus' *Myrmidons* (fr. 139 Radt = 62 Lloyd-Jones), in which it is plausibly conjectured that Achilles is lamenting after the death of Patroclus, referring to his own folly and comparing himself to the eagle slain by an arrow sped by his own feather (cf. K. Reinhardt, *Sophocles* (Eng. trans., Oxford, 1979) 4: 'the meaning of the whole *Iliad* is there *in parvo*').

9

Homer on Poetry and
the Poetry of Homer

C. W. MACLEOD

'We pedants know better.'[1] These leaden and ironic words form part of A. E. Housman's attempt to show that textual scholarship and literary criticism are two very different, or even incompatible, skills. The immediate issue was Matthew Arnold's translation of *Iliad* 24, line 506. As it happens, Housman was wrong on that point, and Arnold right; and this should give us pause over the larger question. In fact the spring of scholarship cannot and has not run on uncontaminated by the scum and garbage of criticism. So in 1981 we can expect more and more scholars, for good or ill, to consider Homer as a poet rather than a *corpus vile* of lays or motifs or formulae. Now it would not be surprising if, as a serious poet, Homer reflected on the nature and purpose of his work; and such reflections have indeed left their mark upon it. They make too a proper basis for the study of his poetry; for just as scholars have, as best they can, to learn to be critics, so critics have to learn what the poets they read can teach them about poetry. There have been good discussions of Homer's poetics in recent years; and what I have to say owes much to them. If I venture to return to the topic, it is because I believe that there are still worthwhile conclusions to be drawn from it about Homer's poetry. In particular, I shall consider one question which is a challenge to any who think of the *Iliad* as a significant whole, that is whether Book 24 is its true ending and a fitting conclusion.

In this chapter I shall refer almost more often to the *Odyssey* than to the *Iliad*. This calls for a word of explanation. For myself, I am content to believe that the author of both was the same man; and I do

---

[1] 'Introductory Lecture' (1892) in *Selected Prose*, ed. J. Carter (Cambridge, 1961), 15. I have limited documentation to a minimum; for further references, see my commentary on *Iliad* 24 (Cambridge, 1982), esp. pp. 1–8.

not think there is any real evidence to tell against that assumption. But it is hardly possible to prove it either. What is clear, however, is that the *Iliad* and *Odyssey*, despite their many differences, are both epic poems; and this is more than a matter of outward form. Both are slices of life from the age of heroes; both are principally concerned with suffering (cf. *algea* in *Iliad* 1.2, *Odyssey* 1.4); and in both a divine dispensation, which extends beyond the limits of its narrative, unfolds throughout the poem. There are also points where they are significantly related. I shall touch briefly now on one of them since it partly concerns *Iliad* 24; another, from *Odyssey* 8, will be handled later.

In *Odyssey* 11 Odysseus meets and converses with Achilles in the underworld. He consoles his companion by contrasting their destinies: Achilles is 'most blessed' because he was honoured in his lifetime by the Greeks 'like a god', and now rules among the dead, whereas he himself is suffering continually and still in search of his homeland. The whole *Iliad* is the tale of how the honour due to Achilles was first denied and then, with tragic consequences, restored to him; and his coming death, the price he has to pay for winning glory, haunts the whole poem. Achilles, in reply to Odysseus, rejects this comfort, but asks after his father Peleus and his son Neoptolemus: for Peleus, he fears that men now 'dishonour' him and wishes that he himself were alive to protect him, as he protected the Greeks at Troy. This recalls *Iliad* 24 (488-9, 540-2), where Priam imagines Peleus harassed by his neighbours and Achilles regrets that because he is fighting at Troy he cannot tend his father's old age; much the same motif occurs in *Iliad* 19 (321-5) in a passage where his thoughts also turn to Neoptolemus. Odysseus then goes on to tell Achilles about his son. In council, Neoptolemus distinguished himself at Troy, but the primacy went to Nestor and Odysseus, as it does in the *Iliad*: in Book 1, when Achilles yields to Nestor, and in Book 19, when he has to give in to Odysseus' insistence that the army eat before fighting. But in battle Neoptolemus, again like his father, was supreme. This gives some solace to Achilles, whose shade strides off 'rejoicing because I told him that his son had excelled' (540).

In this passage the life and destiny of Achilles—the dominant subject of the *Iliad*—is reworked. No amount of honour can compensate for the emptiness of death; yet an early death was what Achilles chose, to avenge Patroclus and redeem his own name. At the same time, the honour which his son and image wins brings him joy. The tension between the horror of death and the demand for glory is the tragedy of the whole *Iliad*; it finds expression in Achilles' mouth here, as it does more painfully and bitterly in *Iliad* 9. The tragedy is heightened by the contrast with the fate of Odysseus: though he suffers more and longer than Achilles, he survives to save his family from 'dishonour', the depredations of the suitors; and though his sufferings will last beyond the end of the poem, the culmination of the *Odyssey* is not like what the end of the *Iliad* so emphatically envisages, the death of its hero and the destruction of a city, but the return of Odysseus, the reunion of the wife with the husband, and the restoration of the home and kingdom to their master.

If, then, the *Odyssey* is the same sort of poem as the *Iliad*, and if it refashions and reconsiders the central theme of the *Iliad*, we may expect its reflections on poetry to be relevant to the earlier work.

There is another matter on which a few preliminary words are called for. There are two poets in the *Odyssey*, Phemius and Demodocus, but it is not only the places where they are concerned or where poetry is mentioned that are relevant to understanding Homer's notion of his art. When Odysseus relates his adventures truly to the Phaeacians or falsely to Eumaeus, when Helen, Menelaus, and Nestor recall their experiences at Troy or afterwards, they are to all intents and purposes poets. Their tales are one element in the poem as a whole, and they concern events which either belong to the stock of epic narrative or else deliberately simulate it; and the tellers perform, like poets, to a company of banqueters after dinner. Moreover, the reactions they evoke are the same as those which poets evoke.

These reactions in their turn pose a further problem. More than once in the *Odyssey* we read of characters responding to poems which tell of their own life or the lives of their nearest and dearest. Now the Greeks were well aware that tragic poetry is necessarily, in Gorgias' words (*Helen* 9) 'the fortunes and misfortunes of *other* lives and persons'. This recognition is neatly expressed in the story of Phrynichus (Herodotus 6. 21), who, after producing a tragedy on the capture of Miletus by the Persians, was heavily fined by the Athenians and had any future production of his play banned because he had 'reminded them of their own troubles'. What Phrynichus did

was to infringe the laws of tragedy, and so also those of the city.
Again, Aristotle in the *Rhetoric* notes that when overcome with
horror we cannot feel pity (1385^b32-3); and such horror, he
observes, recalling another story from Herodotus (3. 14), is likely to
be caused by the suffering of those closest to us (1386^a18-24). If,
then, so sharp a line is drawn between feelings about our own and
about others' woes, can the reactions of people involved in the events
narrated suggest what reactions poetry would normally be taken to
elicit? The answer, I think, is 'yes'. The responses of the people
concerned are distinguished from other responses; so we can see
them for what they are. But they also cannot but affect our own
responses; because they are there in the poem they come to form part
of the hearer's reaction to it. Further, if some measure of detachment
is needed for tragedy to have its effect, so too, obviously, is some
measure of involvement. To quote Gorgias again, what the poet's
account of others' destinies calls forth is 'a feeling of our own' ($\H{\iota}\delta\iota\acute{o}\nu$
$\tau\iota\ \pi\acute{a}\theta\eta\mu\alpha$); and Aristotle's discussion makes it plain in a number of
ways how the pitier must feel the pitied and his fate to be close to
himself and his own. Indeed, Homer's narrative, by indicating
diverse reactions among the audience or within single hearers, forms
a subtle account of the complex manner in which poetry works on
the heart and mind.

Let us now consider, then, the 'poetics' of Homer: first some
notions concerning poetry, and then some passages in which we can
see poetry at work, manifesting what it is conceived to be and
achieving what it is thought to do.

When the Greek envoys arrive at Achilles' tent in *Iliad* 9, they
find him, now that he is no longer himself winning glory in battle,
singing 'the stories of famous men' (189 $\kappa\lambda\acute{e}a$ $\grave{a}\nu\delta\rho\grave{\omega}\nu$); the same
phrase is used of Demodocus' theme in *Odyssey* 8. 73–4, 'a tale
whose fame was then reaching the sky': it is the story of a quarrel
like that of *Iliad* 1. And Odysseus in *Odyssey* 9 (19–20) announces
his identity thus: 'I am Odysseus, son of Laertes, who am known to
all men for my wiles and whose fame reaches the sky'; this is the
introduction to four books' worth of his own adventures. The name
of the poet Phemius is clearly a *nom parlant* (from *phēmē*, 'report'):
and he, like Demodocus, retails stories which they help to diffuse
and whose characters thus acquire renown. If a tale brings fame
it must be believed; and the stories told in the *Iliad* and *Odyssey*
are clearly all supposed to be true (with the obvious exception

of Odysseus' false accounts of his past in the latter half of the
Odyssey). And the heroic tales are true not merely for the char-
acters in the poem, but for the poet and his public. The Catalogue of
Ships in Book 2 begins:

Tell me, now, Muses, who have your home on Olympus—for you are gods,
you are present and know everything, while we only hear a rumour and
know nothing—who were the leaders and princes of the Greeks...

The same opening line—ἔσπετε νῦν μοι Μοῦσαι, Ὀλύμπια
δώματ' ἔχουσαι—recurs three times to introduce a particular item
of narrative: who first encountered Agamemnon (11. 218), who was
the first of the Greeks to slaughter Trojans after Poseidon had turned
the tide of battle (14. 508), and how the fire first fell on the Greek
ships (16. 112). The huge amount of narrative detail in the *Iliad* is
offered not as tradition or invention, but as information. Indeed, the
poet is distinguished from other *raconteurs* precisely by his veracity.
Alcinous comments on Odysseus' stories in *Odyssey* 11 (363–8):

Odysseus, to judge by the look of you, you are not a deceiver like the many
men scattered over the earth who compose false tales such that one cannot
even see [that they are false]: no, your speech is fine, your wits good, and you
tell your story cunningly (ἐπισταμένως), like a poet, your own sufferings
and those of all the Greeks.

It is striking that the poetic quality of Odysseus'—or of Homer's—
narrative is not, as might seem natural to us or to later Greeks, a
reason for suspecting it, but for thinking it true: it is the liar, not the
poet, who can pass off a false tale for a true one. The word 'cunningly' (ἐπισταμένως), like 'well' (κατὰ κόσμον) in Odysseus'
praise of Demodocus (8. 489; cf. 14. 363 for the use of the term),
refers to the truth rather than the artistry of what is told, or at least
not to the artistry in isolation from the truth. So too the Sirens, who
(like the Muses) in Homer represent the charms of poetry, know
everything that happened at Troy and that happens on earth (12.
189–91): they fascinate not merely because their voices are beautiful,
but because they possess the knowledge typical of the poet in the
highest possible degree. Elsewhere in the *Odyssey* there are references to wanderers who tell stories that they know will please their
hearers in the hope of a reward (14. 124; 23. 216), and Odysseus
himself fabricates stories for reasons of his own. No doubt the poet
stood out, with pride, among all kinds of inferior story-tellers because
his subject-matter was history, great events truly commemorated.

This claim of veracity is not easy for us to understand; but it cannot be dismissed as mere convention. For Homer took the Muses seriously, as one can see from the story of Thamyris (*Iliad* 2. 594–600). He boasted that he would win a song contest even if the Muses were his opponents; as a punishment for his presumption they mutilated him and removed his power of song. This story in its immediate context is a quite gratuitous addition; where it does belong is with the invocation to the Muses a hundred lines earlier. It reminds us that they are truly goddesses and celebrates their power, as the Greeks often do by showing how they punish those who offend them. But what then do they mean to the poet?

To us it might seem possible that Homer could believe all he sang to be true if it were all tradition; but we can see from the proem to the Catalogue of Ships that Homer was quite able to entertain doubts about the truth of the tradition: 'We only hear a rumour, we know nothing.' This is in effect the same observation as Hesiod's when he says that Muses told him 'We can retail many falsehoods which look like truths' (*Theogony* 27). Homer, it seems, would deny that a false song was inspired by the Muses: Hesiod, on the other hand, extends to them the notion familiar to the Greeks, including Homer, that the gods are prone to deceive; but both are admitting that singers can lie. So Homer's Muses cannot be simply equated with 'the tradition'. It is also hard to imagine that of all the detail in the Homeric poems—particularly the *Iliad* with its mass of minor fighters and combats—nothing was invented by the poet himself. But what the scholar naturally dissects the poet no less naturally feels to be a single whole. Tradition and invention are part of the same thing, the gift of song (*aoidē*); and when the poet sings he simply creates, his business is not to sift the various factors which enable him to do so: in Hesiod's language, the Muses teach him song (cf. *Theogony* 22). Thus Phemius says (*Odyssey* 22. 347–8): 'I am self-taught and the god put all kinds of theme into my mind.' He does not mention any human teacher or tradition which has supplied him with either matter or techniques, though there must have been such; nor does he distinguish his own contribution from the god's. Eskimo and Kirghiz minstrels too, we are told,[2] speak of their poems as purely 'given', whether

---

[2] R. Finnegan, *Oral Poetry* (Cambridge, 1977), 193; *An Anthology of Oral Poetry* (London, 1978), 226–7.

from within or from god; and yet they are produced by hard work with recognizable formal conventions which have to be learnt. Likewise in Homer there is no sign of any attempt to separate tradition from originality, or technique from inspiration. The singer, then, takes what he sings to be true in so far as he is sure of being inspired.

The Muses' work is not confined to supplying information. This is how Odysseus comments on the song of Demodocus in *Odyssey* 8 (487–9):

Demodocus, I praise you above all men. Either the Muse, daughter of Zeus, or Apollo must have taught you. For you sing so well ($\kappa\alpha\tau\grave{\alpha}$ $\kappa\acute{o}\sigma\mu o\nu$) of the fate of the Greeks, all that they did and endured and toiled, as if you had been there yourself ($\acute{\omega}s$ $\alpha\mathring{v}\tau\grave{o}s$ $\pi\alpha\rho\epsilon\acute{\omega}\nu$) or heard it from one who was.

What makes Demodocus' poem good is not only its truth but its authenticity: it is as if it were an eyewitness account because it makes the events come alive in the hearer's imagination; and since Odysseus actually was 'present', he is in a particularly good position to vouch for his judgement. And this is the gift of the Muses: 'as if you had been there' recalls the address to the goddesses in *Iliad* 2, 'You are there' ($\pi\acute{\alpha}\rho\epsilon\sigma\tau\epsilon$). For Democritus (B 18, 21 DK), Homer and other poets were able to produce 'beautiful' (*kala*) poems because they were divinely inspired; for Pindar (*Olympian* 1. 29–32), the poet is able to persuade his hearers that what is incredible is true because of the 'charm' (*charis*) of his words. But for Homer beauty and truth are inseparably linked, and both given by the Muses, in the quality of authenticity. In later times this vividness—*enargeia*, in the language of literary criticism—was often thought proper to history. Thus Plutarch finds it in both Xenophon and Thucydides; or Duris criticizes Ephorus and Theopompus for falling short of the events they describe because they lacked 'attractiveness' (*hēdonē*) and 'vividness' (*mimēsis*) and 'were concerned only to give a bare record' ($\alpha\mathring{v}\tau o\hat{v}$ $\delta\grave{\epsilon}$ $\tau o\hat{v}$ $\gamma\rho\acute{\alpha}\phi\epsilon\iota\nu$ $\mu\acute{o}\nu o\nu$ $\mathring{\epsilon}\pi\epsilon\mu\epsilon\lambda\acute{\eta}\theta\eta\sigma\alpha\nu$).[3] Since both epic and history deal with what really happened, it is their business to be, as well as truthful, realistic.

So it is that poetry not merely informs, but pleases: *hēdonē* and *mimēsis* are connected, as in Duris, and the pleasure springs not only from the acquisition of knowledge, but from participation. The word

---

[3] Cf. F. W. Walbank, *Historia* 9 (1960), 216–34.

terpein (delight) regularly describes the effect of poetry in Homer (*Iliad* 1. 474; 9. 189; *Odyssey* 1. 347, 422; 8. 91, 368, 429, 542; 12. 188; 17. 385, 606; 18. 304); and Phemius, whose name is as we saw an eloquent one, has also the 'speaking' patronymic, Terpiades (22. 330). This pleasure is sometimes called by an intenser term, 'enchantment' (*thelgein*). Thus Eumaeus describes the effect of Odysseus' tale (17. 518–21):

As when people gaze at a singer whom the gods have taught to sing tales men love to hear, and they are eager to listen to him when he sings: just so did he bewitch me . . .

or when Odysseus addresses the Phaeacians it is said (11. 333–4 = 13. 1–2):

Thus he spoke, and they were all silent; they were held enchanted in the shadowy hall.

The Sirens represent this power of enchantment in an extreme and dangerous form.

Similar language is commonly used in later Greek authors to denote what poetry or oratory can do to their audience; but in Homer there is perhaps a special force in this notion of poetry as a form of magic. For Homeric poetry embodies a paradox and a mystery, in that it gives pleasure though its subject is always painful: the stuff of epic is in Odysseus' words 'all that the Achaeans did and endured and toiled'. The proem to the *Iliad* itself makes this abundantly clear. There is no word here of honour and glory, only of human passion, death, and degradation, with behind it all the will of an all-powerful god:

Sing, goddess, of the anger of Achilles, Peleus' son, that ruinous anger which caused ten thousand sorrows for the Greeks and sent many mighty souls down to Hades, making their bodies a prey for dogs and a meal for birds; and the plan of Zeus was accomplished . . .

Certainly the *Iliad* tells of heroes whose chief concern is to win renown in battle and it celebrates their strength and courage; but they are also men who suffer far from their homes and families and who face death in every moment. Horror and weariness of war, expressed in the regular epithets for it (δακρυόεντα, στονόεντα, πολύδακρυν, etc.), pervade the whole poem: they are vividly present already in the mouths of Achilles and Agamemnon in Book 1, or in the king's speech and the army's response to it in Book 2. This strain

in the *Iliad* is summed up by Nestor's words to Telemachus in
Odyssey 3 (103–14):

My friend, since you remind me of the sorrow we, the irresistible sons of the
Achaeans, endured in that country, all we suffered in our ships wandering
over the murky sea in search of plunder wherever Achilles led us, and all
the fighting round the city of king Priam; there, in time, all our best men
were killed. There lies warlike Ajax, there Achilles, there Patroclus, peerless
counsellor, and there my own dear son, strong and noble, Antilochus, a swift
runner and a brave fighter. And many other troubles we endured besides:
what mortal man could tell them all?

And where there is most glory, doom is most present: the greatest
victors of the poem—Patroclus, Hector, and Achilles—all not only
take precious lives, but are fated to lose their own soon afterwards, as
Homer reminds us in their moments of triumph. In short, as the
scholion on the first line of the poem succinctly puts it: 'he invented a
tragic proem for a series of tragedies.' Homer, 'the pathfinder of
tragedy', as Plato called him, is also the first to point to the paradox of
tragedy, often discussed after him, that it gives pleasure by representing what is grim and sad.

There are, moreover, hints in Homer about how this is possible. It
is partly because the hearer is detached from what he hears: as
Eumaeus says to Odysseus (15. 399–401): 'Let us take pleasure in
each other's grim woes as we recall them; for a man who has suffered
and wandered much takes pleasure even in sorrows when they are
past.' Likewise, Penelope in Book 23 (306–9) can take pleasure in the
tale of Odysseus' labours and sufferings now that it is all over. The
distance from the events which time gives to the agents corresponds
to the distance that separates the hearer from another's experience.
Such detachment, as I indicated before, is a condition of a proper
response to tragedy. But this negative condition demands a positive
complement; and what this is is shown by another remark of
Eumaeus' to Odysseus (14. 361–2): 'Poor stranger (ἆ δειλὲ ξείνων)
truly you moved my heart (θυμὸν ὄρινας) as you recounted all this,
your many sufferings and wanderings.' (This is the same story that
Eumaeus describes as 'enchanting' him in Book 17.) The pleasure
consists in the stirring of the emotions; and the emotion concerned is
above all pity: θυμὸν ὀρίνειν, 'move his heart', is what Priam aims
to do and does to Achilles in *Iliad* 24 (467); and ἆ δειλέ are the
words which begin his reply to the old man's appeal (518). Pity is

identified by Aristotle in the *Poetics* as an emotion proper to tragedy; and what tragedy brings about is not, as Plato saw it in *Republic* 10, the satisfaction of starved feeling—still less in Aristotle's unhappy and all-too-successful term, a catharsis—but a warm response to a fellow man. The truth or realism of poetry makes it possible for the hearers to react as Eumaeus does to what he believes is a true story. This is a fact which fascinated and appalled Augustine in the *Confessions* (3. 2); and, as he saw, such pity is a pleasure, although its object is suffering, because it draws on 'the spring of fellow-feeling' (*vena amicitiae*).

But now it is time to examine in more breadth some of the episodes which represent Homer's conception of poetry, and in particular the performances of Demodocus in *Odyssey* 8.

The first song of the Phaeacian singer (72–82) tells of a quarrel between Odysseus and Achilles. The dispute caused Agamemnon to rejoice, because of a prophecy Apollo had given him at Delphi just before the expedition left for Troy. What the god foretold must have been that Troy would fall soon after 'the best of the Achaeans' (79) had quarrelled. What Agamemnon did not know was that it was his own quarrel with Achilles ten years later which was meant. As Odysseus hears this tale, he secretly weeps and groans, while the Phaeacians are delighted by it (83–92). Here, then, are two important motifs from the *Iliad*: the quarrel of the two 'best men among the Greeks' as the beginning of a series of troubles (Book 1), and the deception by a god of the Greek leader (Book 2)—or, more broadly, men's unwitting fulfilment of a divinely determined train of events: *Odyssey* 8. 81–2, 'the beginning of troubles for Trojans and Greeks was surging on through the plan of Zeus', echoes *Iliad* 1. 2–5, 'ten thousand sufferings for the Greeks. . . and the plan of Zeus was achieved'. (A similar set of motifs begins Nestor's tale of the Greeks' return home in *Odyssey* 3: there are quarrels among the Greek leaders (136, 161) caused by the gods, the angry Athena, or Zeus, Agamemnon fails to understand the goddess's intentions (143–6), and Zeus plans woe for the army (152, 160), which then comes about.) Here too is the proper response of the audience: they are to be pleased like the Phaeacians, but also moved; for Odysseus' tears reveal what a participant, and so also a fully sympathetic hearer of the *Odyssey*, would feel about such a tale.

The second song of Demodocus (266–366) is in lighter vein. It is a story of the gods, whose doings, as we see throughout Homer, are as much the poet's business—and as much part of his exceptional knowledge—as men's: likewise Phemius' repertoire in *Odyssey* 1. 338 is ἔργ' ἀνδρῶν τε θεῶν τε (the deeds of men and gods). This time Demodocus tells of the adultery of Aphrodite with Ares, and of how Hephaestus took his revenge and received his compensation, against a varied background of sententious disapproval and rumbustious humour on the part of the other gods. The theme of the song fits firmly into the *Odyssey*: the unfaithful wife on Olympus contrasts with Penelope, the faithful wife on earth, and the offended divine husband, like the offended human husband, employs guile to inflict a well-deserved punishment on the wrongdoers. The punishment for the man is a grisly death, whereas the gods are only made to look foolish: Hermes can even cheerfully envy Ares, for all his bonds, and Aphrodite finally goes off to be bathed and cosseted by the Graces at home in Cyprus. But that the divine action should echo in tones of fun what is deeply serious among men is also typical of the *Iliad*: perhaps the most striking example is the quarrel of Zeus with Hera which follows Agamemnon's with Achilles in Book 1. The gods' dispute returns to laughter (500)—it is not worth spoiling the pleasures of the banquet for men; but the human beings' ends in increased resentment and brings 'ten thousand sufferings'. Moreover, the story of Ares and Aphrodite is a close relative to the deception of Zeus in *Iliad* 14. Both gods and men feel sexual passion. But the loves of Zeus and Hera are pure pleasure: soft grasses grow spontaneously to cushion their embraces and a golden, dew-dripping cloud covers them around. Hera succeeds in deceiving Zeus; but the consequence is that he reasserts his authority the more firmly (though without violence), and in the mean time the Greeks have enjoyed some remission. Very different is the parallel scene in Book 3 (cf. especially 3. 441–6 with 14. 313–28) where Paris carries an embittered and reluctant Helen off to bed. Though this action in itself has no serious consequences, the narrative is shaped so as to recall that a lover's infatuation, and the goddess of love's favour for him, were the cause of the whole war; and though Helen regrets what she did, she cannot now, if she ever could, resist the will of Aphrodite: she sees through the goddess's deceit (399, 405), but remains none the less her pawn. In love, then, as in other things, the ease and gaiety of the Olympians sets in relief the compulsions and the painfulness of mortal existence: the two worlds in Demodocus are a poetic contrast, as throughout the *Iliad*. But the gods' doings can also in themselves amuse and refresh the audience: this time both the Phaeacians and Odysseus are delighted by the song (367–9).

The third song of Demodocus completes and culminates the series: it deals with the end of the Trojan War as the first one did with the beginning; similarly in the *Iliad*, though the events which make up the main narrative are confined to a matter of days, the cause and the beginning of the war are recalled and the destruction of Troy constantly envisaged. This time Odysseus solicits a tale from the poet about what he openly names as one of his own triumphs, the Trojan horse (492–9). Demodocus complies, following the story through to the sack of the city and giving prominence to Odysseus' part in it (499–520). One might have expected that, having heard himself duly represented as an epic hero, Odysseus would rejoice in this performance too: here, if anywhere, poetry is the κλέα ἀνδρῶν, the celebration of great men and their deeds. But in fact his reaction is to weep, as he did after the bard's first song:

Thus sang the famous singer; and Odysseus' heart was melted. Tears dropped from his eyes and wetted his cheeks. As a woman weeps, falling to clasp her husband who has fallen in defence of his city and his people, to keep off the pitiless day of doom from his town and his children: seeing him in his death throes, she clings to him, shrilly wailing; but the enemy, striking her back and shoulders from behind with their spears, lead her off to slavery, to have toil and groaning; and her cheeks melt with most pitiable grief—just so did Odysseus drop down pitiable tears from his eyes. (521–31)

The simile is shaped so as to bring out the workings of pity in Odysseus' mind: he weeps *like* a woman whose husband has died in defence of his city and who is taken into captivity—like Andromache, in effect—because her suffering, through the poet's art, has become his own. Homer in his characteristic manner—narrative and simile—expresses the same thought as Gorgias later did with antithesis and assonance: 'as words tell of the fortunes and misfortunes of other men and lives, the soul feels a feeling all its own' (*Helen* 9). And just as Demodocus creates involvement, at the same time he exploits detachment: Odysseus can feel what he does because the passage of time allows him to look afresh at his own heroic achievements. So the song which was to glorify the hero is felt by the hero himself as a moving record of the pain and sorrow he helped to cause.

The first time that Odysseus had wept Alcinous had tactfully relieved and concealed his guest's sorrow by starting the games (94–103). This time, however, he cannot forbear to discover who the stranger is and what causes his tears (577–80):

Tell me why you are weeping and groaning in your heart as you hear of the fate of the Greeks and Troy. But it was the gods who brought it about: they spun destruction for those men, so that future generations might have a song.

With these words, the Phaeacian king, who is not involved in the events concerned, tries to console Odysseus. They recall the words which Helen, a participant, speaks with chagrin in the *Iliad* (6. 357–8):

for whom [sc. Paris and herself] Zeus made an unhappy destiny, so that we might be a theme for song in future generations.

This is a striking and significant contrast to the episode in Book 3 where Helen is weaving a tapestry of the battles she herself has caused (125–8): there she is detached enough to be the artist of her own fateful deeds. But here the perspective is different and complementary. For those who live out what poets retail, the suffering which is the stuff of poetry is merely bitter experience; and yet it is proper that men should have poetry to enjoy. Moreover, to listen to poetry is not only to find pleasure; it can also be to understand that suffering belongs to all men, and so too to learn to live with our own. In *Odyssey* 1 Penelope asks Phemius to stop singing of the return of the Greeks from Troy because that stirs up her longing for Odysseus:

Phemius, you know many other tales of men and gods that poets sing which can charm and soothe ($\beta\rho o\tau\hat{\omega}\nu\ \theta\epsilon\lambda\kappa\tau\acute{\eta}\rho\iota\alpha$)... (337–8)

For her, poetry should be like Helen's drug in *Odyssey* 4 (219–34): if poetry 'enchants', it also kills pain; and a similar notion of its purpose finds expression in Hesiod (*Theogony* 55, 92–8). In *Odyssey* 4 Helen administers her potion in order that her family and guests may then appreciate stories about Odysseus without being overcome by grief. In Book 1 the poetry seems again to deal with a subject which is too close and too painful to the hearers; but Telemachus answers his mother (353–5):

Let your heart endure and listen. Odysseus was not the only one who lost his homecoming at Troy: many other men were undone too.

The story of Odysseus' labours is in the last analysis a typically human story; and in the *Odyssey* itself the homecomings of the other Greeks are included, and compared and contrasted with the hero's.

Telemachus' words correspond closely to a fragment of the Attic comedian Timocles (*CAF* II. 453 = Athenaeus 223 B) which says that tragedy is useful because it teaches us that someone has always suffered worse than ourselves; and Polybius makes a similar claim for history (I. I. 2). Thus poetry can give a kind of comfort which is more than a 'drug' because it represents truth—not merely historical truth, but the realities of life; and because of its artistic realism it can convey with peculiar force the essential message of ancient consolations: *non tibi hoc soli* and *humana humane ferenda* (Cicero, *Tusculans*, 3. 79, 34).

I have tried to indicate as I went along a number of ways in which Homer on poetry illuminates the poetry of Homer, and especially the *Iliad* as a whole. Let me now conclude by turning in particular to *Iliad* 24. I shall take as headings three of the major themes of Homer's poetics: (1) glory, (2) pity, and (3) consolation.

   I. Book 24, no less than the rest of the *Iliad*, is the celebration of famous deeds. But here the glory is not that of the warrior. Achilles wins praise and renown by accepting Priam's supplication and gifts and by renouncing his furious vengeance on Hector's body. As Zeus puts it to Thetis (108–19):

The gods are urging Hermes to steal the body. But I mean to attach this glory [*kudos*] to Achilles . . . Tell him the gods are angry with him, and I above all, because in his madness he has not released Hector's corpse . . . and I will send Iris to Priam to make him go and ransom his son . . . bringing gifts to mollify Achilles' heart.

And thus the hero wins an honour which is profoundly different from the honour he demanded in Book 1 and obtained in the rest of the poem. This is brought out very sharply by the contrast with Book 1. There Thetis goes from Achilles to Zeus and persuades the god to give Achilles honour by bringing destruction to his companions: here Thetis goes to Achilles from Zeus and persuades him to win honour himself by showing mercy to an enemy. Priam too wins renown. He bears 'what no other man on earth has ever borne, to reach to my mouth the hands of my son's killer' (505–6). 'Endure' (*tlēnai*) is what, in Homer, heroes characteristically do in war (*Iliad* 3. 157; 11. 317; 23. 607), as Nestor movingly observes in the passage I quoted from *Odyssey* 3; Priam finally appears as the supreme example of such endurance. This is what evokes the wonder of

Achilles and his companions when he enters (480–4). His heroic
status is also brought out by the parallel with Hector in Book 22.
Both men go out 'alone' (22. 39; 24. 148 = 177, 203, 519) to meet
Achilles; and Hecuba tries to prevent both their departures. But
whereas Hector succumbs to him in battle, Priam persuades him as a
suppliant; and where Hector failed in begging him to let his body be
ransomed, Priam succeeds. So it is that Achilles and Priam, after
eating together, sit wondering at each other (628–32); for they are
equally godlike men and epic heroes, extraordinary in their nobility
as in their grief.

  Thus *Iliad* 24 continues, but also transforms, the κλέα ἀνδρῶν.
The glory here is won not by inflicting or accepting a pitiless death,
but by evoking or offering pity; and Achilles, like Odysseus during
Demodocus' last song, is so overcome by pity that he shows himself
quite indifferent to his own fame and prowess: 'I do not care for
Peleus' old age, since I sit idly here, far from my homeland, bringing
grief to you and your children' (540–2). There are greater values in
the *Iliad* than fame; and these emerge most magnificently at the end
of the poem. This leads us on to the second heading.

  2. The centre of Book 24 is the scene where Priam moves Achilles
to compassion and the two men weep together sharing their griefs,
for Peleus and Patroclus, and for Hector. By comparing himself to
Peleus, Priam the orator does what the poet is doing throughout. The
bulk of the *Iliad* is concerned with men who behave pitilessly, and
Book 24 with men who inspire and feel pity. But it would be a gross
mistake to conclude that the spirit of Book 24 was therefore different
from that of the rest of the poem. For both kinds of action, in contrasting but complementary ways, arouse compassion in the poet's
audience. What happens in Book 24 is that the pity implicit in all the
battle scenes takes explicit form in the narrative. The sufferings of
bereaved parents are in fact sometimes mentioned where heroes die,
for example in 5. 152–7:

He [Diomede] went after Xanthus and Thoon, sons of Phaenops, both precious
children; for he was consumed by grim old age and begot no other son to put
over his inheritance. Then Diomede killed them . . . and left groaning and grim
sorrow to their father, who never welcomed them home alive from the war;
and executors divided the inheritance among themselves.

In Book 24 two such parents, Priam and Peleus, hold the stage, and
the pathos of many passing references is massed into one great scene.

Likewise, two features of war as Homer describes it in the *Iliad* are that supplication on the battlefield is always rejected and that warriors who die there can expect to receive no burial. These are facts which are meant to evoke pity and horror. They are not the mere routine of battle, because we know from the *Iliad* itself that lives *can* be spared and that burial *can* be allowed in war. In Book 24 the same concern for mercy and for burial finds expression in an episode where mercy *is* shown and burial *is* conceded.

3. Priam and Achilles do not only share their tears; they also see their destinies as part of a common human lot. Without that recognition there could be no pity; it is also the basis of consolation. Achilles helps Priam to live with the loss of his son by showing him that trouble comes to all men, and has come to Peleus no less than to Priam: *non tibi hoc soli* and *humana humane ferenda*. Just as pity becomes overt in Book 24, so does consolation: the characters are described as feeling and seeing and thinking what the audience are meant to throughout. And without the seeing and thinking, the pity would be mere sentiment, and the poetry mere enchantment; as it is, *Iliad* 24 embodies a conception of poetry like Telemachus'—as a vehicle of truth. The truth in question is that human life, whatever else it may contain, includes shared suffering and inevitable death, and that human destinies are the gift of gods who do not always work with human notions of justice. This is also the heart of Homeric and Archaic Greek morality. As Odysseus says to Amphinomus (*Odyssey* 18. 130–42):

There is nothing feebler than man of all the things that breathe and walk on the earth. He never thinks he will fall into trouble when the gods give him prosperity and vigour; but when the blessed gods bring sorrows, then he bears them too, reluctantly, with an enduring heart . . . So let no man be a wrongdoer; let him keep the gods' gifts quietly, whatever they give him.

It is this sense of common weakness and suffering which gives men a reason to treat each other with respect. It also gives them a reason to pity each other, as Cyrus pities Croesus in Herodotus (1. 86) when he sees that 'he, a man, was about to burn alive another man who had been no less fortunate than himself', or as Odysseus pities Ajax in Sophocles (*Ajax* 122–4): 'I pity him, for I see that we living men are nothing but phantoms or a bodiless shadow.' Such understanding is, in fact, the cognitive and rational element in compassion.

Schopenhauer[4] was surely right to see this as a truer origin and a
sounder basis of morality than Kant's categorical imperative; and so
Horace (*Epistles* I. 2) or Matthew Arnold were also right to seek
edification in Homer, because the poet's work is, if not didactic in
form, profoundly ethical in spirit.

APPENDIX

I owe the story which follows to Peter Levi: he had it from an
anthropologist who had worked in the Mani and heard it from the
grandson of the murdered man. It illustrates powerfully and economically some of my main themes. It also shows the vitality of the
Homeric notion of poetry.

A girl in the deep Mani was married in another village; her husband was shot
in a quarrel, and she decided to come home. (So far her own family had no
obligation of vengeance.) On the way she had to pass through the murderer's
village, and there she was mocked. When she got home she told no one this,
for fear of causing more bloodshed. But her youngest brother, who was close
to her, saw she was upset beyond what was explained; he drew her outside
and discovered why.

He then went off and hid in a tree near the tower of the mocker's family.
There he waited days until the mocker sat opposite the window he commanded, playing with his young son. He shot the man dead in his chair. He
escaped by passing through the centre of that village while the villagers were
out looking for him. After many adventures he got away to Athens, where he
joined the bodyguard of the Duchess of Piacenza, whose town house was high
up on Penteli. (Since he was now in exile there was no obligation on anyone
in the Mani to pursue him further.) Most of his life passed in Attica.

One night he was caught out in the countryside in a thunderstorm, and
took refuge in a police station. In Greece the police do not serve in their own
area, and these policemen happened to come from the Mani. They gave him
food and drink, and they sang songs of their own region. Someone sang the
epic or ballad or lay of his own adventure. He wept when he heard it. They
asked who he was and he told them. His return home was arranged. He was
formally reconciled with the last inheritor of the obligation to vengeance,
the child who had been on the murdered man's knee, and who was now
full-grown.

---

[4] *Die Welt als Wille und Vorstellung*, I. 4. 67.

A 'Beautiful Death' and the Disfigured Corpse in Homeric Epic

JEAN-PIERRE VERNANT

He whom the god loves dies young.

(Menander)

Beneath the walls of Troy that have watched him flee in desperation before Achilles, Hector now stands still. He knows he is about to die. Athena has tricked him; all the gods have abandoned him. Fate (*moira*) has already laid its hand on him. Even though it is no longer in his power to conquer and survive, he must still fulfil the demands that warrior status makes on him and his peers: he must transform his death into eternal glory, change the fate of all creatures subject to demise into a blessing that is his alone and whose lustre will be his forever. 'No, I do not intend to die without a struggle and without glory (*akleiōs*), or without some great deed whose fame will live on among men to come (ἐσσομένοισι πυθέσθαι)' (*Iliad* 22. 304–5; cf. 22. 110).

The *Iliad* calls *aneres* (*andres*) those men who are in the fullness of their masculine nature, both male and courageous, who have a particular way of dying in battle, at the acme of their lives. As if it were an initiation, such a death endows the warrior with the set of qualities, honours, and values for which the elite, the *aristoi*, compete throughout their lives. This 'beautiful death', this *kalos thanatos*, to use the term employed in Athenian funeral orations,[1]

---

[1] The present chapter owes a great deal to Nicole Loraux, *L'Invention d'Athènes: Histoire de l'oraison funèbre dans la 'cité classique'* (Paris and The Hague, 1981), trans. A. Sheridan under the title *The Invention of Athens* (Cambridge, Mass., 1986), which analyses the theme of beautiful death in the Athenian funeral oration. Loraux has published several articles on the same topic: 'Marathon ou l'histoire idéologique', *REA* 75 (1983), 13–42; 'Socrate, contre-poison de l'oraison funèbre', *AC* 43 (1974),

is like a photographic developer that reveals in the person of the
fallen warrior the eminent quality of the *anēr agathos*, the man of
virtue and valour.[2] It guarantees unassailable renown to the man
who has given his life for his refusal to be dishonoured in battle, or to
be shamed as a coward. A beautiful death is also a glorious death
(*eukleēs thanatos*). For all time to come, it elevates the fallen warrior
to a state of glory; and the lustre of this celebrity, this *kleos*, that
henceforth surrounds his name and person is the ultimate accolade
that represents his greatest accomplishment, the winning of *aretē*.
Through a beautiful death, excellence no longer has to be continually measured against someone else or to be tested in combat.
Rather, excellence is actualized all at once and forever after in the
deed that puts an end to the hero's life.

This is the meaning of the fate of Achilles, whose character is
both exemplary and ambiguous, embodying not only the demands
but also the contradictions of the heroic ideal. If Achilles seems to
push the logic of honour to an extreme—to absurdity—it is because
he somehow places himself above the standard rules of the game. As
he himself explains, since his birth he has been offered two destinies
to carry him to where all human existence finds its limit, two destinies that are mutually exclusive (*Iliad* 9. 410 ff.). He can have
either the warrior's imperishable glory (*kleos aphthiton*) but a short
life, or a long life in his own home without any renown whatsoever.
Achilles did not even have to make the choice; he found himself
always leaning towards the short life. Dedicated from the outset—
one might say by nature[3]—to a beautiful death, he goes through life
as if he were already suffused with the aura of the posthumous glory
that was always his goal. That is why he finds it impossible, in
applying the code of honour, to negotiate, to compromise, to yield to
circumstances or power relations; craven settlements are, of course,
out of the question, but he cannot make even the necessary

112–211; '*Hebe et Andreia*: Deux versions de la mort du combattant athénien', *Anc.
Soc.* 6 (1975), 1–31; 'La "Belle Mort" Spartiate', *Ktèma* 2 (1977), 105–20.

[2] For Homer's use of *agathos* as an absolute, without any qualification, see *Il.* 21.
280 and the comments of W. J. Verdenius, 'Tyrtaeus 6–7 D: A Commentary',
Mnemos. 22 (1969), 338.

[3] As early as Book 1, Achilles declares, 'Since, my mother, you bore me to be a man
with a short life, therefore Zeus of the loud thunder on Olympus should grant me
honour at least'; like an echo, Thetis replies: 'indeed your lifetime is to be short, of no
length. Now it has befallen that your life must be brief and bitter beyond all men's'
(*Il.* 1. 352–4 and 416–18; see also *Il.* 19. 329, 421).

adjustments without which the system can no longer function. For Achilles every insult is equally intolerable and unforgivable, no matter where it comes from and however high above him the agent's position on the social scale. Any apology, any honourable offer of compensation (no matter how satisfying to his pride it might seem from its size and public nature) remains empty and ineffective. Like a crime of treason, an insult to Achilles can only be repaid, in his eyes, with the complete and utter humiliation of the guilty party. Such an extreme sense of honour makes Achilles a marginal figure, isolated in the lofty solitude of his wrath. The other Greeks criticize this excess as aberrant, an instance of Error personified, of *Atē* (*Iliad* 9. 510–12). Agamemnon accuses him of pushing the spirit of competition to the point that he has to be first always, everywhere, and in everything, and that as a result he can think of nothing but rivalry, dispute, and combat (*Iliad* 1. 288, 177). Nestor reproaches him for his conduct in its disregard of the customary order of precedence, in that he goes so far as to contend with a king to whom Zeus has given not only the sceptre, power, and command but also the right to the highest honours (*Iliad* 1. 278). Odysseus, Phoenix, Ajax, and even Patroclus deplore his intractable hardness, his ferocious resentment, and his savage and inhuman heart that is deaf to pity, and as oblivious to the pleas of his friends as it is to the apologies and reparations that ought to satisfy him. Could Achilles then be immune to *aidōs*? *Aidōs* is the feeling of reserve and restraint that functions like a brake in both upward and downward directions to maintain equilibrium in situations in which differences in status or disparities in strength make open, equal competition impossible. It is also the respectful fear that keeps a safe distance between the weakest and the strongest. In making explicit the inferiority of one of the actors, *aidōs* puts him at the discretion of the other, so that, disarmed by this submissiveness, the stronger might take the initiative in establishing friendly relations (*philia*) by according the one who puts himself under the other's protection the share of honour that is due to him. But conversely, *aidōs* is also the renunciation by the stronger of violence and aggression towards the weaker who is at the other's mercy and therefore is no longer a rival. Now it is the reconciliation between the injured party and the one who has agreed to abase himself by an offer of compensation, and thus publicly to acknowledge the honour (*timē*) he had first insulted. Finally, *aidōs* is the relinquishing of vengeance and the restoration of amity between two groups when, after a murder, the blood price representing the *timē* of the victim has been agreed on and paid in full to his kin.[4]

At an assembly of the gods, Apollo too accuses Achilles of having lost all sense of pity, and thereby of disregarding *aidōs* (*Iliad* 24. 44).

None the less, the weight of such evidence is not primarily psychological in nature. It has less to do with Achilles' character than with the ambiguities of his position, the equivocation of his role within the value system of the epic tradition. Achilles' attitude and behaviour contain a paradox that is disturbing so long as one concentrates on individual psychology. Achilles is completely convinced of his superiority in the realm of warfare, and this occupies the highest position on the scale of qualities that make for excellence in his eyes as well as those of his companions in battle. Moreover, there is no Greek, no Trojan, who does not share Achilles' belief and does not recognize him as the undisputed exemplar of martial *aretē* (*Iliad* 2. 768–9).[5] Although his self-confidence is supported by unanimous agreement among others, it hardly guarantees safety and security; it is yoked instead to an edgy irritability and a profound obsession with humiliation.

To be sure Agamemnon's taking Briseis away is an insult that strikes Achilles at his most sensitive point. It strips him of his *geras*, the special portion awarded him from the communal booty. A *geras* is an extraordinary privilege granted under exceptional circumstances; it acknowledges superiority, either in rank or in status (as for Agamemnon) or in valour and daring (as for Achilles). Over and above any material advantage, a *geras* has value as a mark of prestige and a consecration of a social supremacy: everyone gets a share, determined by lot, but the élite and only the élite receive a *geras* in addition. Confiscating Achilles' *geras*, then, somehow denies his pre-eminence in battle, the very heroic quality that everyone concedes to him. The other soldiers maintain silence— admittedly tinged with disapproval—in the face of the king's misconduct, and it makes them accomplices with him in the crime for which they will have to pay the price. None the less, Achilles'

---

[4] Ajax contrasts Achilles' inflexible spirit with the softer temper of those who accept a blood price (*poinē*) and a settlement (*aidesis*).

[5] At *Il.* 2. 768–9, the poet himself presents Achilles' superiority as an objective truth.

reaction displays a number of troubling characteristics. Agamemnon
is not trying to insult him personally, and never, even at the hottest
point of the argument, does he denigrate Achilles' outstanding
martial prowess. Achilles demands that Agamemnon give up his
own prize, Chryseis, for the sake of the common good; in order to rid
the Greek camp of the plague, the girl must be returned to her father,
who is a priest of Apollo. Agamemnon is willing to do so, on the
condition that he receive a *geras* in return, so that he, the king,
might not be the only one who has to live without his portion of
honour (*Iliad* 1. 118–19). If it means that he will have to get the *geras*
of one of his companions—be it Ajax, Odysseus, or Achilles—no
matter, although he predicts that the other will be furious (*Iliad* 1.
138–9; cf. 145–6). It is at this point that Achilles explodes, and his
wrath reveals the real split that divides the two men. Achilles sees no
common ground between the *timē* inherent in kingly status, the kind
of *timē* Nestor extols as coming from Zeus (*Iliad* 1. 278–9), and the
kind the warrior gains by his ceaseless toil 'in the front rank' where
danger is omnipresent. So far as he can see, in this war that belongs
primarily to Agamemnon and his brother, Agamemnon constantly
leaves it to others to give their lives in the heart of the fray; lagging
back (ὄπισθε μένων) in the shelter of the camp (*Iliad* 9. 332; cf. 1.
227–9), near the ships, he is not a man to join his noble companions
in an ambush, nor does he offer himself as a combatant in a duel to
the death. 'All that,' Achilles tells Agamemnon, 'seems like death to
you (τὸ δέ τοι κῆρ εἴδεται εἶναι)' (*Iliad* 1. 228).[6] For all that he is
the kingliest (*basileutatos*) among the lords, he has not crossed the
boundary that separates ordinary men from the truly heroic. The
latter, by accepting from the beginning the fact that life is short,
devote themselves completely and single-mindedly to war, adventure, glory, and death. For the man who adopts Achilles' chivalric
perspective, it is one's own life itself that is at stake, in every test of
honour (*Iliad* 9. 322). Since a reversal means that one has lost once
and for all, that one has lost life itself, success must carry value with
it at a level that surpasses, and is not measurable by, normal distinctions and awards. The logic of heroic honour is one of all or
nothing, and it operates outside of and beyond hierarchies of rank. If
Achilles is not recognized as supreme and in a way unique, he feels
himself reduced to nothing. Without meeting any overt resistance,

---

[6] Diomedes makes the same assessment of Agamemnon at *Il.* 9. 30–50.

he declares himself ἄριστος Ἀχαιῶν, the best of the Greeks, and
he boasts that in the past he has carried the burden of the war and in
the future will be the only defence against the Trojan onslaught.
Therefore he can present himself not only as dishonoured, *atimos*,
due to the insult he has suffered (*Iliad* 1. 171, 356), but also—if he lets
it pass without comment—as the feeblest coward, a less than
nothing (*outidanos*), a homeless and worthless drifter, a kind of non-
person (*Iliad* 9. 648). Between the perpetual glory that is his destiny
and the lowest degree of contempt there is no intermediate level
where Achilles can find a place. Every affront to his dignity brings
him from the heights to the depths, because what is being challenged
through him is a set of values that must be accepted without reser-
vation or equivocation if it is not to be wholly diminished. To insult
Achilles is to put the coward and the champion in the same category
and to give them, as he says, the same *timē* (*Iliad* 9. 319). Heroic
action is thus stripped of its function as an absolute criterion, a
touchstone that shows what a man is worth.

It is for this reason that Odysseus, Phoenix, and Ajax fail in the
mission entrusted to them to soften Achilles' resolve and persuade
him to give up his anger. Although they use the same words, Achilles
does not speak the same language as the envoys sent to fetch him.
Agamemnon has come to his senses, and on his behalf the ambassadors offer all that a king can give and more in such circumstances:
first, Briseis herself whom he is ready to give back, just as she was
when she was taken, along with an oath that Agamemnon has not
slept with her; tripods, gold, pitchers, horses, female slaves and
concubines; finally, whichever of Agamemnon's own daughters
Achilles might choose as a wife, along with a lavish dowry and, to go
with this marriage that would make Achilles his son-in-law, the rule
over seven cities in his kingdom. Achilles refuses. If he were to
accept, he would put himself on the same ground as his enemy. Such
goods are adjuncts to the *timē* of the king and signs both of his power
over others and the privileges attached to his rank. To accept the
king's offer would be an admission that the sheer quantity of his
possessions counterbalances true valour, such as Achilles alone
brings to the Achaean army. In all that they symbolize, the gifts are
hateful (*Iliad* 9. 378). Their very abundance seems to express contempt for the warrior, whose participation in battle does not put at
risk his sheep or oxen, tripods or gold, but his very life, his fragile
psuchē (*Iliad* 9. 322). Agamemnon's treasure, like all the riches the

world covets, consists of things that can always be acquired, exchanged, recovered if they are lost, or obtained in one way or another. The price the warrior pays to attain virtue is of a completely different order: 'A man's life cannot come back again, it cannot be lifted nor captured again by force, once it has crossed the teeth's barrier' (*Iliad* 9. 408–9). It is his life—his very identity, in its heroic form—that Achilles has put at the service of the army. And it is his life that Agamemnon has insulted in treating the hero the way he did. For Achilles, no wealth, no mark of honour, no social distinction could take precedence over a *psuchē* that nothing in the world can match (οὐ γὰρ ἐμοὶ ψυχῆς ἀντάξιον, 9. 401); by risking his life fearlessly in all the battles that Agamemnon shuns like death, Achilles has already dedicated himself to glory inspired by action.

After Odysseus speaks, old Phoenix argues that if Achilles accepts the reparations, as is customary and correct, and returns to battle, the Achaeans 'will honour [him] like a god'; but if he refuses, they will never give him the same respect (οὐκέθ' ὁμῶς τιμῆς ἔσεαι), even if he comes back later and saves them from the misery of war (*Iliad* 9. 605). It is a wasted effort. By now Achilles sees a sharp division between two kinds of glory, two kinds of honour. The one is ordinary *timē*: public esteem, ready to extol him, to reward him with a literal king's ransom, if and only if he yields. The other is extra-ordinary *timē*: the eternal glory that is his destiny if he remains the same as he has always been. For the first time, Achilles openly rejects the Achaeans' praise, which he had once sought more than anything else. He tells Phoenix that he now has as little need of this latter *timē* (οὔ τί με ταύτης χρεὼ τιμῆς, *Iliad* 9. 607–8) as he does of Agamemnon and his offer—they mean as much to him as a splinter of wood (*Iliad* 9. 378). He is concerned only with the honour in the destiny controlled by Zeus (Διὸς αἶσα *Iliad* 9. 608),[7] the early death (*ōkumoros*, *Iliad* 1. 417; 18. 95) that his mother had foretold: 'Now it has befallen that your life must be brief and bitter beyond all men's. To a bad destiny (*aisa*) I bore you in my chambers' (*Iliad* 1. 417–18). Once it has been accepted, however, an early death has its corollary in immortal glory, of which the epic hero sings.

Achilles' refusal highlights the tension between ordinary honour, the societal approval necessary for self-definition, and the much greater demands of heroic honour, in which one still needs to be

---

[7] φρονέω δὲ τετιμῆσθαι Διὸς αἴσῃ.

recognized, but now as set apart on another level, to be famed 'among men to come'. This tension appears in outline at those points where the two types of honour are so closely linked as to seem almost blended.

This is the case in Book 12 when Sarpedon exhorts Glaucus to take the lead among the Lycians in attacking the wall the Greeks have built (*Iliad* 12. 310–28). Why, he asks, are we honoured in Lycia with all the privileges and honours of a king? Why do men treat us as if we were gods? Is it not because we feel obliged always to stand in the Lycians' first line of battle (Λυκίοισι μέτα πρώτοισιν) so that all the Lycian warriors can say, 'Indeed they are not without glory (*akleees*) these kings of our Lycia . . . since they fight in the forefront' (*Iliad* 12. 318–21)? Just as Achilles is a son of Thetis, Sarpedon is a son of Zeus; among the Trojan warriors, in his courage and his prowess in battle, he is like a lion whose gnawing hunger drives him, heedless of danger, after his prey. He does not care that the flock is in an enclosed pasture, guarded by herdsmen armed with pikes and accompanied by dogs. Once he is on the attack, nothing will turn him away. There are only two possible endings: either he will snatch his victim, against and despite all odds, or he will be struck by a spear and fall (*Iliad* 12. 305–6). The same spirit makes Sarpedon ready to attack the Greeks' barricade, behind which death awaits him. Without hesitation he leaps over the parapet and plunges into the fray. When he sees his companions flee before Patroclus, who is wearing Achilles' armour and is in a murderous fury, he rebukes them; he calls out his intention to go into single combat with the man we know is destined to kill him (*Iliad* 16. 433–4). Sarpedon meets him in order to 'know' him, to find out what he is, that is, to use a fight to the death to determine his 'worth' as a warrior (*Iliad* 16. 423–4).[8] Leaving aside the love Zeus feels for him and the special treatment accorded by the gods to his corpse, Sarpedon's attitude makes him resemble Achilles; both of them belong to the same sphere of heroic existence, and they share a radical definition of honour.

None the less, if we believe Sarpedon's words, there seems to be a direct correspondence between the status of a king and the excellence of a warrior, between the *timē* due to the former and the *kleos*

---

[8] The phrase is ὄφρα δαείω | ὅς τις ὅδε κρατέει. Hector displays the same attitude towards Diomedes at *Il.* 8. 532 and 535; at *Il.* 3. 53, Hector urges Paris to confront Menelaus 'to learn what sort of man he is'.

sought by the latter. To fight in the front line, as Achilles and Sarpedon do, underlies and justifies their royal privileges; it could be said that to be a king, one must behave like a hero, and to be a hero, one must be born a king. Such an optimistic vision joins together the diverse factors of social prominence and personal virtue; it also reflects the ambiguity of Homeric terminology, in which, according to their context, the same words—*agathos, esthlos, aretē,* and *timē*—can denote high birth, wealth, success, martial courage, and fame. There is no clear distinction among the concepts.[9]

Still, in Sarpedon's own speech we find a trace of the fissure that, in Achilles' case, brutally separates heroic life—with its hopes, its demands, its peculiar ideals—from ordinary life controlled by a social code of honour. First Sarpedon lists the advantages granted a king, such as comfort, good land, good wine, renown, and a place of honour, and he says that they are like the price men pay for the benefits wrought by the king's exceptional valour on the battlefield. Sarpedon, however, then adds a comment that lays bare the true nature of heroic activity and thus undercuts the previous statement: 'Supposing that you and I, escaping this battle, would be able to live on forever, ageless, immortal, so neither would I myself go on fighting in the foremost nor would I urge you into the fighting where men win glory. But now, seeing that the spirits of death stand close about us in their thousands, no man can turn aside nor escape them, let us go on and win glory for ourselves or yield it to others' (*Iliad* 12. 322–8).[10] Hence it is neither material advantage, nor primacy of place, nor the tokens of honour that can propel a man to stake his *psuchē* in the pitiless combat where glory is won. If it were only a matter of getting the goods one enjoys during life and loses with its end, there would not be a single warrior, Sarpedon claims, who would not bolt at the moment when, while enjoying life, he would have to risk losing everything along with it. The real meaning of heroic activity lies elsewhere. It has nothing to do with practical calculation or with the need for social prestige. Rather, it is in a way metaphysical. The gods have so arranged it that the human

---

[9] On this point, see the classic studies of A. W. H. Adkins; e.g. *Moral Values and Political Behaviour in Ancient Greece* (London, 1972), 12–16.

[10] The same theme appears in Callinus fr. 1. 8–13 West; also Pind. *Ol.* 1. 82–4: 'Since we must die, why sit in the shade and uselessly pass a hidden old age, far from all beauty?' Cf. Lys. 2. 78.

condition is not only mortal but also, like all earthly life after its youthful efflorescence, subject to the debilitating effects of age. Heroic striving has its roots in the will to escape ageing and death, however 'inevitable' they may be, and leave them both behind. Death is overcome when it is made welcome instead of merely being experienced, and when it makes life a perpetual gamble and endows it with exemplary value so that men will praise it as a model of 'imperishable glory'. When the hero gives up a long life in favour of an early death, whatever he loses in honours paid to his living person he more than regains a hundredfold with the glory that will suffuse his memory for all time to come. Archaic Greek culture is one in which everyone lives in terms of others, under the eyes and in the esteem of others, where the basis of a personality is confirmed by the extent to which its reputation is known; in such a context, real death lies in amnesia, silence, demeaning obscurity, the absence of fame.[11] By contrast, real existence—for the living or the dead—comes from being recognized, valued, and honoured. Above all, it comes from being glorified as the central figure in a song of praise, a story that endlessly tells and retells a destiny admired by all. In this sense, the hero, by the fame he has acquired in pledging his life to battle, inscribes his reality as an individual subject on the collective memory of the group; the death that has given his biography its conclusion has also given it permanence. Through the public arena of those exploits in which he was wholly engaged, he continues, beyond the reach of death, to be present in the community of the living. Converted into legend and linked with others like it, his personality forms the skein of a tradition that each generation must learn and make its own in order to enter fully into social and cultural existence.

Heroic honour goes far beyond ordinary esteem, the relative and ephemeral marks of rank; in its quest for the absolute condition of *kleos aphthiton* (imperishable glory), it assumes the existence of a tradition of oral poetry, which serves as a repository of shared culture and as societal memory for the group. In what we have come to call the 'Homeric world', heroic honour and epic poetry are inseparable. There is no *kleos* except that which is sung, and—except for the praise of the gods—sung poetry has no purpose other than to recall

---

[11] See Marcel Detienne, *Les Maîtres de vérité dans la Grèce archaïque* (Paris, 1967), 20–6.

the great deeds, κλέα ἀνδρῶν, performed by the heroes of ages past. Epic poetry preserves such deeds in memory by making them more vivid than the audience's small quotidian lives.[12] A short life, a feat of arms, a beautiful death: all these have meaning only to the extent that they are contained and celebrated in a song and thereby confirm the hero as *aoidimos*, worthy of being sung. The literary transformation by epic endows the hero with the status, the fullness of existence, and the permanence that alone can justify the extreme demands of the heroic ideal and the sacrifices it entails. When an honour is required that surpasses honour, it has a 'literary' dimension. This is not to say that heroic honour is only a stylistic convention and the hero only a fiction. The glorification of a 'beautiful death' in Sparta and Athens during the high classical period shows that the heroic ideal retained its importance and its effect on behaviour, even in historical contexts as far removed from the Homeric world as the city-state. Still, in order for heroic honour to stay alive at the heart of a society and put its stamp on the whole system of values, poetry has to be more than a pastime. Poetry must continue to play a role in education and upbringing; it serves to transmit, to teach, and to make manifest within each individual the alloy of knowledge, beliefs, attitudes, and values that make up a culture. Only epic poetry has the importance and power to confer on the hero's quest for deathless glory both institutional solidity and societal approval, without which the quest would be merely a subjective fantasy. We might be surprised to find a yearning for an afterlife that was reduced, as we might think, to 'literary' immortality; if so, we would be misunderstanding the differences that separate the Archaic Greek individual and society from our own. There is structural relation between the ancient personality—exteriorized, grafted onto public opinion—and epic poetry, that functions as *paideia* in its glorification of exemplary heroes and their will to live on in 'imperishable glory'. The modern personality—an interiorized ego, unique, apart—has the same, structural relation with its 'purely' literary genres, like the novel, the autobiography, or the private diary, which preserve the hope of living on as a special immortal spirit.

---

[12] Hes. *Theog.* 99–101; see Detienne (n. 11), 21–3. I owe a great deal to the fine book by James Redfield, *Nature and Culture in the Iliad: The Tragedy of Hector* (Chicago, 1975), esp. 30 ff.

Of all the characters depicted in the *Iliad*, Achilles is the only one who is shown actually performing poetic song.[13] When the envoys sent by Agamemnon arrive at the Myrmidons' camp, Achilles is in his tent. Accompanying himself on the cithara, he is singing for himself and for Patroclus, seated across from him. What does Achilles take pleasure in when he sings under such circumstances? The very subject that the *aoidoi*, with Homer prime among them, sing in poems like the *Iliad*: 'He sings of the deeds of heroes' (*Iliad* 9. 189). Achilles is the model of the heroic warrior; in choosing a short life and deathless glory, he embodies an ideal of honour so elevated that, in its name he will reject both the gifts of the king and the *timē* of his own companions in arms. He is the one the great epic shows, at this critical moment in his career, singing about the exploits of heroes. What a literary tactic, what an image *en abîme*![14] But the lesson of the episode is clear: Achilles' great deeds are glorified by Homer in the *Iliad*, yet to exist fully in the eyes of the hero who longs to perform them, they must be reflected and preserved in a song that exalts their fame. As a heroic character, Achilles exists to himself only in the mirror of the song that reflects his own image. The song also reflects, in the form of *klea*, the exploits to which he has chosen to sacrifice his life so that he will forever after be the Achilles sung by Homer in the *Iliad* and by all the Greeks to come.

To pass by death is also to escape the process of ageing. For the Greeks death and old age go together (Mimnermus fragment 2. 5–7 West). Growing old means that one must watch the fabric of life gradually becoming frayed, damaged, torn by the same power of destruction, the *kēr*, that leads to death. ἥβης ἄνθος, says Homer. It has been shown that this formula, taken up and developed by the elegiac and lyric poets, directly inspired the funerary epitaphs that extol the warriors who are taken in 'the flower of youth', that is, dying in combat.[15] Just as a flower fades, so do the qualities that make life worth while: once vigour, beauty, grace, and agility have

---

[13] See Pierre Vidal-Naquet, 'L'*Iliade* sans travesti', preface to Paul Mazon's translation of the *Iliad* (Paris, 1975), 32.

[14] For a similar action in the *Od.* with a different meaning, see Françoise Frontisi-Ducroux, 'Homère et le temps retrouvé', *Critique* 348 (May 1976), 542. A parallel to Achilles' song about heroic activity is Helen's depiction of it in weaving, *Il*. 3. 125–8 (cf. 6. 357–8, her conviction that she and Paris will become a theme of song).

[15] See Loraux, '*Hebe*' (n. 1). She writes: 'When it celebrates the *aretē* of a warrior, every verse epitaph tends to use epic formulae, of which ἀγλαὸν ἥβην ὤλεσαν is only one instance among many in the *dēmosion sēma*' (24). Regarding the use of the

shed their glow on a person during his 'shining youth' (*aglaos hēbē*), they do not stay fixed and firm but soon wither and then vanish. The flower of age—when one enjoys the full maturity of one's life's strength—is the burgeoning growth of springtime, of which the old man, in the winter of his life, before even descending to his grave, already feels himself deprived.[16] That is the meaning of the myth of Tithonus: what good is it to have immortality if one is not protected from ageing? More shrewdly, Sarpedon tells Glaucus of his dream of eluding both old age and death, of being *agēraos* as well as *athanatos* (*Iliad* 12. 323; cf. 8. 539). Then and only then could it be said of the warrior's exploit that the game is not worth the effort. Poor Tithonus, daily sinking deeper into senility in the heavenly sanctuary where Eos had to leave him, is no more than a specter of a living man, an animated corpse; his endless ageing dooms him to an illusion of existence that death has completely destroyed from within.[17]

To fall on the battlefield saves the warrior from such inexorable decay, such deterioration of all the virtues that comprise masculine *aretē*. Heroic death seizes the fighter when he is at his *akmē*, a fully adult man (*anēr*), completely intact in the integrity of a vital power still untouched by any decrepitude. He will haunt the memory of men to come, in whose eyes his death has secured him in the lustre of ideal youth. Thus the *kleos aphthiton* the hero gains through his early death also opens to him the path to eternal youth. Just as Heracles has to endure the pyre on Mount Oeta in order to marry Hebe— and thereby be confirmed as *agēraos* (Hesiod, *Theogony* 955)— it is a 'beautiful death' that makes the warrior altogether *athanatos* and *agēraos*. In the imperishable glory conferred on him by the song

formula 'he/they lost his/their shining youth' to denote death on the battlefield, she notes: 'Such continuity between the aristocratic epitaph, praising an individual, and the collective, democratic epitaph of the *dēmosion sēma* deserves close attention, because it suggests the persistence of a specific representation of the dead man as young' (20).

[16] On the association of youthful military prowess and springtime, see Loraux, '*Hebe*' (n. 1), 9–12; she refers to Pericles' funeral oration (doubtless the *epitaphios* for those who died at Samos), wherein the Athenian statesman compares the youth, whom death in battle has stolen from the city, with springtime which has faded from the year. Cf. Arist. *Rhet.* 1. 7, 1365ᵃ31–3, 10, 1411ᵃ1–4.

[17] See *h. Ven.* 1. 218–38; also Mimn. fr. 4 West: 'For Tithonus [Zeus] decreed a deathless evil, old age, which is still worse than a horrible death.' The phrase 'deathless evil' involves a play on words, *kakon aphthiton*, that recalls and contrasts with *kleos aphthiton*. The young warrior who dies gets imperishable glory; the old man, alive forever, gets imperishable misery.

about his deeds, he becomes immune to ageing in the same way that, as much as it is humanly possible, he escapes the destruction of death.

This theme of the warrior's guaranteeing himself perpetual youth at the moment he accepts death in battle can also be found again with various modulation, in the rhetoric of the Athenian funeral oration. But, as Nicole Loraux has observed, its origins must be sought in epic; the Athenians do use it at public funerals to praise those who by their civic spirit have given their lives during the year on behalf of their city. When the theme is so used, it is a projection onto the figure of the hoplite—citizen-soldier, adult, and father of a family—of the heroic image of the warrior of epic who is, above all, a young man. Within Homeric society, the contrast between *kouroi* and *gerontes* is not simply a matter of age, and the *gerontes* are not all 'aged' in our sense of the term. None the less, there *is* a sharp distinction between two spheres of activity and competence. Warfare privileges physical strength and valiant ardour, while planning requires speaking ability and prudence. Between the bold adventurer ($\pi\rho\eta\kappa\tau\grave{\eta}\rho$ $\check{\epsilon}\rho\gamma\omega\nu$) and the eloquent adviser ($\mu\acute{\upsilon}\theta\omega\nu$ $\dot{\rho}\eta\tau\acute{\eta}\rho$), the difference is principally one of age (*Iliad* 9. 52–61; 11. 786–9). The wisdom of the *gerōn* counterbalances the impetuousness of the young men, designated by the term *hoplōteroi*, which defines youth by its ability to bear arms (*Iliad* 3. 108–10). If the 'deep-voiced speaker' from Pylos, old Nestor, offers copious wise advice, and his experience in combat appears more in the form of comments than in exploits, it is because age is weighing him down and he is no longer a *kouros* (*Iliad* 4.321).[18] Advising and speaking (*boulē, muthoi*) are the province and privilege of the *gerontes*; the younger men (*neōteroi*) have the task of spear-work and asserting themselves in their own strength.[19] Hence we find the formula, repeated like a refrain, that punctuates most of Nestor's lengthy orations to his troops. Whether giving them instructions or encouraging them in a struggle in which he will play only a marginal role, he says, 'Ah, if only I were young again, if only my strength were what it was ($\epsilon\check{\iota}\theta'$ $\grave{\omega}s$ $\mathring{\eta}\beta\acute{\omega}o\iota\mu\iota$ $\beta\acute{\iota}\eta$ $\delta\acute{\epsilon}$ $\mu o\iota$ $\check{\epsilon}\mu\pi\epsilon\delta os$ $\epsilon\check{\iota}\eta$)' (*Iliad* 7. 157).[20] Nestor regrets the loss of his

---

[18] He says, 'If I was a young man then, old age has taken me now' (*Il.* 4. 321).

[19] *Il.* 4. 322–5; cf. 3. 149–51; in Troy the *dēmogerontes* sit in council, because 'for them age has put an end to warfare, but they are excellent speakers'.

[20] Cf. also 11. 670; 23. 629; and 4. 313–15, where Agamemnon tells Nestor, 'Aged sir, if only, as the spirit is in your bosom, so might your knees be also and the strength

martial prowess along with his vanished youth. In this context, *Hēbē* is less a precisely defined age group than the time of life when one feels oneself in a state of superiority, when success and acclaim (*kudos*) seem to follow you naturally, seem linked to your undertakings (*erikudēs hēbē; Iliad* 11. 225)—more prosaically, when you are in full possession of your powers: physical power, above all, but also suppleness of the body, flexibility, steadiness in the legs, and swiftness in movement (*Iliad* 11. 669; 13. 512–15; 23. 627–8). To possess *hēbē* is to combine all the qualities that make a full-fledged warrior. Idomeneus is a formidable fighter but already greying (*mesaipolios*, 13. 361), and when he admits his fear before Aeneas' onslaught, he calls to his companions for help and explains, 'He has the flower of youth, which is the greatest *kratos* (καὶ δ' ἔχει ἥβης ἄνθος, ὅ τε κράτος ἐστὶ μέγιστον)' (*Iliad* 13. 484). Valiant as he is, Idomeneus feels the burden of age: 'no longer in an outrush could his limbs stay steady beneath him (οὐ γὰρ ἔτ' ἔμπεδα γυῖα) either to dash in after his spear, or to get clear again' (*Iliad* 13. 512–13). As Emile Benveniste has shown, *kratos* does not merely denote physical strength, like *biē* or *ischus*, but the superiority that enables a warrior to dominate his opponent, to prevail against him and vanquish him in combat. In this sense, the warrior's *aristeia* is to some extent included in *hēbē*, and we can understand more clearly how the heroic point of view conjoins the warrior's death with youth. Just as ordinary honour is paralleled by heroic honour, ordinary youth—merely a question of age—has a counterpart in heroic youth, which is radiant in combat and finds its fulfilment in death on the battlefield. Here we can quote Nicole Loraux, who has understood and expressed the point superbly:

Homeric epic gives two very different versions of the death of the *kouros*. This is not surprising: while youth is a pure quality for the hero, it is a prosaic physical fact for those whom the gods have less favoured. Although the death of young soldiers is a frequent occurrence in the *Iliad*, it is not always touchingly glorious . . . In some cases youth is only one characteristic among others, which does not distinguish one death from among the vast and ultimately unimportant number of victims. In other words, youth as a quality does not inform the warrior's last moments, and he dies manfully but without any special glory. For the hero, by contrast, death takes place under

stay steady within you.' In the same way, at 8. 103, Diomedes says, 'your strength is broken, and bitter age is on you'.

the sign of *hēbē*; even if youth had not been specifically attributed to the warrior, he possesses it at the exact moment he loses it; *hēbē* is the last word, for both Patroclus and Hector, whose 'spirit flies to Hades, mourning its fate, leaving behind strength and youth' (λιποῦσ᾽ ἀνδροτῆτα καὶ ἥβην, *Iliad* 16. 857, 22. 363). In fact this mention of a youth that is lost and mourned, but also exalted, is denied to all the other combatants; *hēbē* becomes a type of charisma, reserved for the heroic elite—for Achilles' most valiant opponent and for the man who was not just Achilles' friend but his double.[21]

The *hēbē* that Patroclus and Hector lose along with their lives is one they possessed more fully than other *kouroi*, though the latter might have been younger. It is this same *hēbē* that Achilles guarantees for himself in perpetuity by choosing a short life and an early, heroic death. While the warrior is alive, his youth appears primarily in vigour (*biē*), strength (*kratos*), and endurance (*alkē*); when he has become a weak, lifeless corpse, the glow of his youth persists in the extraordinary beauty of his body. In Homer the word *sōma* means precisely a body from which life has fled, the husk or shell of a once-living being. So long as the body is alive, it is seen as a system of organs and limbs animated by their individual impulses; it is a locus for the meeting, and occasional conflict, of impulses or competing forces. At death, when the body is deserted by these, it acquires its formal unity. After being the subject of and medium for various actions, more or less spontaneous, it has become wholly an object for others. Above all, it is an object of contemplation, a visual spectacle, and therefore a focus for care, mourning, and funeral rites.[22] During the course of a battle, a warrior may have seemed to become a menace, a terror, or comfort, occasioning panic or flight, or inspiring courage and attack. Lying on the battlefield, however, he is exposed as a simple figure with identifiable attributes: this is truly Patroclus, and this Hector, but reduced to their external appearance, to the unique look of their bodies that enables others to recognize them. For the living man, of course, an imposing presence, grace, and beauty have their place as elements of personality, but for the warrior in action, such attributes are eclipsed by those highlighted by battle. What shines from the body of the hero is less the charming glow

[21] Loraux, 'Hebe' (n. 1), 22–3.
[22] On this point, see the remarks of J.-P. Vernant in *Problèmes de la personne*, ed. I. Meyerson (Paris, 1973), and Redfield (n. 12), 178 ff.

of youth (*chariestatē hēbē*)[23] than the sheen of the bronze he is
wearing, the flash of his sword and breastplate, the glitter of his
eyes, the radiance of the ardour that fires him (*Iliad* 19. 365–6,
375–7, 381, 398). When Achilles reappears on the battlefield after
his long absence, stark terror seizes the Trojans as they see him
'shining in his armour' (*Iliad* 20. 46). Beside the Scaean gates
Priam groans aloud, batters his head, pleads with Hector to return
to the shelter of the walls. Priam has just been the first to see
Achilles: 'He swept along the flat land in full shining, like that star
which comes on in the autumn and whose conspicuous brightness
far outshines the stars that are numbered in the night's darkening,
the star they give the name of Orion's Dog, which is the brightest
among the stars and yet is wrought as a sign of evil and brings on
fever for unfortunate mortals. Such was the flare of the bronze that
girt his chest in his running' (*Iliad* 22. 25–32). When Hector
himself catches sight of Achilles, on whom the bronze shines 'like
flaming fire or the rising sun', he too is terrified; he turns and
takes flight (*Iliad* 22. 134–7). The active, terrifying radiance of the
live warrior must be differentiated from the remarkable beauty of
his corpse, preserved in a youthfulness that age can no longer
mar. Hector's *psuchē* has scarcely left his body, 'losing its strength
and its youth', before Achilles strips the armour from the torso.
The Achaeans rush together in order to see the enemy who, more
than any other, had done them harm, and in order to aim more
blows at his body. As they approach the hero, now no more than
a *sōma*, an empty and inert cadaver, 'they marvel at Hector's size
and at his admirable beauty (οἳ καὶ θηήσαντο φυὴν καὶ εἶδος
ἀγητὸν Ἕκτορος)' (*Iliad* 22. 370–1).[24] We might be surprised at
this reaction if old Priam had not already illuminated the
difference between the pitiable and frightful death of an old man

---

[23] *Il.* 24. 348: the subject is Hermes, who has disguised himself as a young prince
whose beard has just begun to grow. At 3. 44–5, Paris' beauty (*kalon eidos*) is no
disguise, for he has neither strength nor courage (cf. 3. 39, 55, 392). At 21. 108,
Achilles tells Lycaon, who is pleading for his life, 'I too, as you see, am handsome and
tall (καὶ ἐγὼ καλός τε μέγας τε)', but this means that Lycaon's death is
imminent. Beautiful as Achilles may be, death hangs over his head too; the day is
near when his life will be taken in battle. This is not Achilles in the fury of action, but
the hero seeing himself under the sign of death. On Agamemnon's beauty, 'kingly'
rather than soldierly, cf. 3. 169–70.

[24] Cf. *Od.* 24. 44: when Achilles has died, his 'beautiful body' is washed in warm
water; also Eur. *Supp.* 783: the sight of the dead Argive soldiers is beautiful—*kalon
theama*—though bitter.

and the beautiful death of a warrior cut down in his prime. 'For a young man all is decorous (πάντ᾽ ἐπέοικεν) when he is cut down in battle and torn with the sharp bronze, and lies there dead, and though dead still all that shows about him is beautiful (πάντα καλά)' (Iliad 22. 71–3).

In Priam's mind, the description of the young warrior, beautiful in his death, hardly supplies a motive for Hector to go up against Achilles; rather it should force Hector to take pity on the horrible death that awaits an old man like Priam if, deprived of his son's assistance, he should die on the sword or the spear of his enemies. The repulsive picture painted by the aged king strikingly explains how unnatural and scandalous it is when a warrior's death, a 'red' death, befalls an old man; the latter's dignity calls for an end that is tranquil, almost solemn, surrounded by the quiet of his home and family. The blood, the wounds, and the grime on the corpse of a young hero recall his courage and enhance his beauty with masculine strength, but on an old man—grey-headed, grey-bearded, withered—their ugliness becomes almost obscene. Priam envisions himself not merely dead at his own gates, but dismembered and torn by dogs, not just any dogs but his own dogs, raised and fed by him in his palace, who will revert to savagery and make him their prey, and after feasting on his flesh and gnawing his genitals, will stretch out, sated, in the entryway they so recently guarded. 'When an old man is dead and down, and the dogs mutilate the grey head and the grey beard and the parts that are secret, this, for all sad mortality, is the sight most pitiful' (Iliad 22. 74–6). Priam is describing a world turned upside down, with all its values reversed, bestiality installed at the centre of the domestic hearth, and an old man's dignity turned into an object of derision in its ugliness and shame, with everything human that belonged to his body destroyed. A bloody death is beautiful and glorious when it strikes the hero in the fullness of youth; it raises him above the human condition and saves him from common death by conferring sublime lustre on his demise. The same kind of death, for an old man, drops him beneath the level of humanity and changes his end from a shared fate into a horrible monstrosity.

In one of the surviving fragments of his poetry, Tyrtaeus imitates this passage of the Iliad, using some of the same formulas.[25] The

---

[25] In addition to the commentary by Carlo Prato on this fr. (see his edn. of Tyrtaeus (Rome, 1968), 93–102), see C. R. Dawson, 'Spoudaiogeloion: Random Thoughts on Occasional Poems', YCS 19 (1966), 50–8; Verdenius (n. 2), 337–55.

differences that often appear both in the details and in the overall picture derive from the Spartan context: the hoplite in the phalanx, fighting shoulder to shoulder and shield to shield, is no longer the champion of Homeric epic. His duty is to stand fast without leaving his position, not to distinguish himself in individual combat. To ensure that 'dying is a fine thing ($\tau\epsilon\theta\nu\acute{\alpha}\mu\epsilon\nu\alpha\iota$ $\gamma\grave{\alpha}\rho$ $\kappa\alpha\lambda\acute{o}\nu$) when one has fallen in the front rank, a man full of heart' (fragment 10. 1–2 West), it must occur in defence of the fatherland. Only then does the dead man's glory remain forever and only then is the hero immortal (*athanatos*) even though he has gone beneath the earth (fragment 12. 31–2 West). Thus there is no longer so radical a breach as there was between heroic honour and honour plain and simple; at Sparta there is no incompatibility between long life and martial valour, between glory (as Achilles defines it) and old age. If the soldiers who are able to stand fast in the line also have the good fortune to return home safe and sound, they share for the rest of their lives in the same honour and glory as those who fell. When they grow old, their excellence deserves the respect of the whole city (fragment 12. 39–42 West).

Sparta thereby uses the prestige of the epic warrior's achievement and of heroic honour as a means of competition and social advancement. From the *agōgē* on, there is something like a codified rule of glory and shame; judging by military accomplishments, the city apportions and assigns praise or blame, respect or contempt, marks of esteem or of abasement, condemning the 'tremblers' (*tresantes*) to the humiliating insults of women and to censure and dishonour ($\ddot{o}\nu\epsilon\iota\delta o_{\varsigma}$ $\kappa\alpha\grave{\iota}$ $\grave{\alpha}\tau\iota\mu\acute{\iota}\eta$) in the community at large (cf. Herodotus 7. 231).

For Tyrtaeus, moreover, 'the man who is older (*palaioteros*) and more revered (*geraios*)', whose death is contrasted with that of a youth (*neos*), is not the miserable dotard described by Priam to arouse Hector's pity, but a brave hoplite; this old man courageously fought and died 'in the front rank', the place in the phalanx normally occupied by the *neoi*. We could think that his sacrifice only deserves to be extolled even further. On the contrary, if fragment 10 was claiming that it was fine (*kalon*) to die in the first rank, this same death becomes despicable for the older man who falls ahead of the *neoi*. In the 'ugliness' decried by the word *aischron* there is a hint of 'moral' disapproval: the horror of the scene serves to exhort the *neoi* not to yield their place in the forefront to men older than they. The

whole context, however, with its contrast between beautiful and
ugly and the 'spectacular' quality of the entire description, reveals
the persistence of an 'aesthetic' vision—in the broadest sense of the
term—of heroic death in its close attachment to *hēbē*.

Indeed it is an ugly thing when an old man, fallen in the front rank, lies before
the young men, with his white head and grey beard, having breathed out his
brave strength into the dust, clutching his bloody genitals—a horror for the
eyes and shameful to see (αἰσχρὰ τά γ' ὀφθαλμοῖς καὶ νεμεσητὸν ἰδεῖν)
in his nakedness. For the young men all is proper (νέοισι δὲ πάντ'
ἐπέοικεν) when they are in the brilliant flowering of their youth, an object of
admiration for men (ἀνδράσι μὲν θηητὸς ἰδεῖν) and desire for women
(ἐρατὸς δὲ γυναιξί) in life (ζωὸς ἐών), and beautiful in death in the first
rank (καλὸς δ' ἐν προμάχοισι πεσών). (Fragment 10. 21–30 West)

It seems true, then, as Dawson suggests, that there is a double
dimension to beauty, just as there is to honour and youth. At the end
of his discussion of Tyrtaeus, Dawson concludes, 'Sensuous beauty
may come in life, but true beauty comes in heroic death.'[26] Beauty in
heroic death—this is certainly the source of the rule ascribed to
Lycurgus, according to which Spartan warriors allow their hair to
grow long and flowing, without cutting it, and give it special care on
the eve of battle. The hair on a man's head is like the flower of his
vitality, the foliage of his age. Hair shows the age of the person whose
head it adorns; at the same time, it is a part of the body that has a
growth and a life of its own—when cut it grows back, it preserves
itself without decaying—so that it can represent the individual. One
can offer a clipping of one's hair as if it were a gift of one's self. Just as
the old man is identifiable by his white head and beard, *hēbē* too is
marked by the first appearance of a downy beard and by an adult's
haircut.[27] There is a well-known connection between *kouros* and
keirō, 'to cut one's hair'; more generally, the great phases in a person's life, changes in status, are highlighted by the cutting and
offering of a lock of hair, or sometimes even by cutting all of it off, as
in the case of a new bride at Sparta. In the *Iliad*, the companions of
Patroclus, including Achilles himself, cut off their hair over the
corpse of their dead friend before consigning him to the pyre. They

---

[26] Dawson (n. 25), 57.
[27] Cf. Aesch. *Ag.* 79–81: 'The very old walk a three-footed way by the time their
foliage is withered.'

cover the whole body with their hair, as if they were clothing it for its last journey with their own youthful, manly vitality: 'his corpse completely covered with hair that they cut from their heads and then placed on him' (*Iliad* 23. 135–6).[28]

His companions adorn the dead man with that which most embodies their nature as fierce warriors, while his wife (if he has one) or his mother (as in Hector's case, for example) offer the precious garments they have woven for him; thus they connect him, even in the hereafter, with that female realm to which he was linked by being a son or a husband. When Xenophon explains the wearing of long hair as a way of making the Spartan soldiers look 'taller, nobler, and more terrifying' (*Constitution of the Spartans* 11. 3),[29] he does not contradict the criterion of beauty this custom confers on them; he only emphasizes that it is not a matter of any kind of attractiveness, like Paris' sensuous beauty or feminine loveliness, but of the beauty unique to a warrior. It is this latter kind, no doubt, that was sought by Homer's warriors, those the epic calls 'long-haired Achaeans (κάρη κομόωντες Ἀχαιοί)'.[30]

Herodotus offers us a revealing episode (7. 208–9). Before testing the resistance of the Spartan squadron guarding Thermopylae, Xerxes sends a Persian horseman to spy on them. On his return, the spy reports that he saw the Spartans exercising in the palaestra and combing out their long hair. The king, astonished, summons the exiled Spartan ruler Demaratus and asks him for an explanation. 'It is a Spartan custom,' Demaratus says, 'that when their men are about to risk their lives, they groom their hair.' Victory or death was the law at Sparta, and at Thermopylae the choice was reduced to one of its terms: to die well. On the eve of a battle in which life is at stake, it is one and the same thing to impress the enemy with a 'tall, noble, terrifying' appearance and to prepare to die on the battlefield, to leave a beautiful corpse, in its youth, like that of Hector admired by the Greeks.[31]

---

[28] For Achilles' own hair, cf. 23. 144–51; cf. Andromache's laments for her husband Hector (*Il.* 22. 508–14).

[29] Cf. Loraux, 'La "Belle Mort"' (n. 1), 105–20.

[30] *Il.* 2. 443, 472; 18. 359; 3. 43. The last passage is particularly telling, for the 'long-haired' Achaeans justly laugh at the youthful beauty of Paris, who, far from being a brave warrior, has no courage, strength, or tenacity.

[31] Cf. Plut. *Lyc.* 22. 1: long hair will make the handsome more noble, and the ugly more terrifying.

If the youth and beauty of the fallen hero's body reflect the shining glory for which he sacrificed his life, the mistreatment of an enemy's corpse takes on a new meaning. Charles Segal and James Redfield have emphasized the importance in the *Iliad* of the theme of the mutilation of the corpse: in the course of the poem it steadily increases in force until it culminates in the deranged fury of the abuse Achilles inflicts on Hector's corpse. There can be no doubt that the poet is using this motif to convey the ambiguities of heroic warfare. When battles become more heated, chivalrous combat—with its rules, its code, its prohibitions—is transformed into savage struggle, in which the bestiality that lurks in violence comes to the surface in all the participants. It is no longer enough to triumph in a lawful duel, to confirm one's own *aretē* over another's; with the opponent dead, one attacks his corpse, as a predator does its prey. Since the victor cannot fulfil the formulaic wish to devour the body raw, he dismembers and consumes through the mediation of dogs and birds. Thus the epic hero is doubly threatened with the loss of his humanity; if the hero dies, his body might be given over to the beasts, not in a beautiful death, but in that nightmarish horror described by Priam; if the hero kills and then mutilates the corpse, he risks a descent into that very savagery Priam ascribed to his dogs. All this is true enough, but we must ask whether the link is not even tighter, between the heroic ideal and the mutilation of the corpse: does not the hero's beautiful death, which grants him eternal glory, have as its necessary corollary, its sinister obverse, the disfigurement and debasement of the dead opponent's body, so as to deny him access to the memory of men to come? If, in the heroic point of view, staying alive means little compared with dying well, the same perspective shows that what is most important is not to kill one's enemy but to deprive him of a beautiful death.

Aikia (Homeric *aeikeiē*), the action of *aikizein*, of disgracing or doing outrage to the corpse appears, even on the linguistic level,[32] as the negation of that propriety ($\pi \acute{\alpha} \nu \tau$' $\acute{\epsilon} \pi \acute{\epsilon} o \iota \kappa \epsilon \nu$) that Homer and Tyrtaeus attribute to the body of the *neos* exposed on the field of battle, and the replacement of *panta kala* by *aischron*. *Aikizein* is also

---

[32] Cf. Louis Gernet, *Recherches sur le développement de la pensée juridique et morale en Grèce* (Paris, 1917), 211. The terms contain, with an alpha privative, the root -*weik*, which marks concurrence, conformity, resemblance.

aischunein, 'make ugly', 'debase'.[33] It involves obliterating from the body of the dead warrior those marks of manly youth and beauty that are manifested there like visible signs of glory. In place of the beautiful death of the hero suffused with *hēbē*, the effort is made to substitute the vision of the frightful doom that haunts old Priam's thoughts: a body stripped of all youth, all beauty, all masculinity (that is the meaning of the strange allusion, in both Tyrtaeus and Homer, to the genitals devoured or held blood-soaked in the hand), and finally of all humanity. Why such relentlessness against what Apollo calls inert clay (κωφὴ γαῖα, *Iliad* 24. 54)? Why the desire to ferret out the person from an enemy's corpse whose *psuchē* has already fled and is now only an empty husk? Why, unless the person remains connected to this dead body and to that which its appearance, its *eidos*, represents? For the hero to attain *kleos aphthiton*, it is essential that his name and exploits be known by men to come, that they persist in memory. The first condition is that they be celebrated in a song that will never perish; the second is that his corpse have received its portion of honour (γέρας θανόντων, *Iliad* 16. 457, 675), that he not have been deprived of the *timē* that is owed to him and that will let him enter into the farthest reaches of death, bringing him to a new state, to the social status of death, all the while remaining a bearer of life's values, of youth, of beauty that the body incarnates and which, on him, have been consecrated by heroic death.

What does it mean to enter into the furthest reaches of death? The fatal blow that strikes the hero liberates his *psuchē*, which flees the limbs, leaving behind its strength and youth. Yet for all that, it has not passed through the gates of death. Death is not a simple demise, a privation of life; it is a transformation of which the corpse is both the instrument and the object, a transmutation of the subject that functions in and through the body. Funerary rites actualize this change of condition; at their conclusion, the individual has left the realm of the living, in the same way as his cremated body has vanished into the hereafter, and as his *psuchē* has reached the shores of Hades, never to return. The individual has disappeared then from the fabric of social relations in which his existence was a strand. In this respect, he is henceforth an absence, a void, but he continues to exist on another plane, in a form of being that is released from the attrition of time and destruction. The hero survives in the permanence of his

---

[33] Cf. *Il.* 22. 75, which can be compared to 22. 336; also 18. 24, 27; 24. 418.

name and the lustre of his renown, both of which remain present not only in the memory of those who knew him when he was alive, but for all men in ages to come. This inscription in societal memory takes two interdependent and parallel forms. The hero is committed to memory, memorized, in the field of epic song which, to celebrate his immortal glory, is placed under the sign of Memory, making itself memory by making him memorable. The hero is also commemorated in the *mnēma*, the memorial constituted at the end of the funeral rites by the construction of a tomb and the raising of a *sēma*, serving like epic to evoke for men to come (ἐσσομένοισι) a glory that is now certain not to perish.[34] Its very fixity and stability contrast the grave marker with the fleeting, transitory nature of the values that graced the human body during life. 'It remains without moving, changeless (*empedon*), once it has been placed over the tomb of a man or a woman who has died' (*Iliad* 17. 432–5). *Empedos* means 'intact' or 'immutable'; if the qualities that comprise a warrior's *aristeia*—ardour (*menos*), might (*biē*), the limbs (*guia*)—had this character of *empedos*,[35] the warrior hero would be immune to old age. He would not have to lose his youth and beauty in a heroic death in order to acquire them definitively in the world beyond. In its own way, by the immutability of its material and shape, and by the continuity of its presence, the *mnēma* conveys the paradox of the values of life, youth, and beauty, which one can ensure for oneself only by losing them, which become eternal possessions only when one ceases to be.

The treatment of the corpse in the funerary ritual derives from a paradox of the same kind. First it is beautified; it is washed with warm water to cleanse it of soil and stain; its wounds are effaced with an unguent; the skin, rubbed with oil, takes on a special sheen; perfumed and adorned with precious materials, the corpse is then laid out on a litter to be viewed and mourned by the dead man's near and dear ones (*Iliad* 18. 346–53; *Odyssey* 24. 44–6). In the Homeric tradition, the corpse is then burned on a pyre whose flames consume all that is made of flesh and blood, that is, everything both edible and

[34] The same formula to describe the *sēma* (καὶ ἐσσομένοισι πυθέσθαι) appears at *Od.* 11. 76 and *Il.* 22. 305; at *Od.* 4. 584, Menelaus orders the erection of a tomb for Agamemnon, 'so that his glory (*kleos*) might remain forever', and at *Il.* 7. 91, Hector believes that the tomb of an enemy he has beaten will remind future generations of his triumph, so that his *kleos* will not die.
[35] For the use of *empedos* with *menos*, see *Il.* 5. 254; with *biē*, 4. 314; with *guia*, 23. 627.

subject to decay and thus attached to that ephemeral kind of existence where life and death are inextricably mingled. All that remains is the 'white bones', incorruptible and not entirely burned to ash; these are easy to distinguish from the ashes of the pyre so they may be collected and deposited in a tomb. If we compare sacrificial ritual with funerary practices, we can say that 'the fire's part' is reversed: the flames of the funerary pyre consume that which the sacrifice preserves to be consumed by men. The victim's flesh, laden with fat, is the share of 'mortal men' who dine on it, since they must eat in order to subsist, obeying the exigencies of a perishable being that must be nourished indefinitely if it is not to be extinguished. The 'white bones' of the sacrificed animal, inedible and incorruptible— inedible because incorruptible—are burned on the altar as the share of the immortal gods who receive them in the form of fragrant smoke. In funeral rites, these same white bones remain under the earth as the trace—extended by the burial mound, the *sēma*, the stele—that is left behind by the person of the deceased; in his absence, it is the form in which he remains, present to the world of the living. The fire of the funerary pyre, by contrast, consumes and sends into the realm of the invisible, along with the perishable flesh and blood, a person's entire physical appearance and the attributes that can be seen on the body: stature, beauty, youth, individuality, glamour, flowing hair. These corporeal aspects incarnate values that are at once aesthetic, religious, social, and personal, and define the status of a singular individual in the eyes of the group. These values in turn are all the more precious for being so fragile and newly in bloom, as the life that made them flower immediately withers them. The visible form of the body, such as is displayed when it is laid out for viewing at the beginning of the funeral rites, can only be saved from corruption by disappearing into the invisible. If the beauty, youth, and masculinity of the corpse are to be definitively his and are to be attached to the figure of the deceased, they require that the body have stopped being a living hero.

This finality of funerary practices is most clearly revealed precisely where they are missing and especially where they are ritually negated in the procedures of outrage visited on the enemy corpse. In its attempt to deprive the enemy of access to the status of a glorious death his heroic end had earned for him, his mistreatment, by the nature of the cruelty it inflicts, allows us better to understand the means that funerary rites normally use to immortalize the warrior in his beautiful death.

One kind of cruelty consists in defiling the bloody corpse with dust and in tearing his flesh, so that the enemy will lose his individual appearance, his clear set of features, his colour and glamour; he loses his distinct form along with his human aspect, so that he becomes unrecognizable. When Achilles begins to abuse Hector, he ties the corpse to his chariot to tear off its skin,[36] by letting it—especially the head and the hair—drag on the ground in the dust: 'A cloud of dust rose where Hector was dragged, his dark hair was falling about him, and all that head that was once so handsome (πάρος χαρίεν) was tumbled in the dust' (Iliad 22. 401–3). By dirtying and disfiguring the corpse, instead of purifying and anointing it, aeikeiē seeks to destroy the individuality of a body that was the source of the charm of youth and life. Achilles wants Hector to be like Sarpedon: 'No longer could a man, even a knowing one, have made out the godlike Sarpedon, since he was piled from head to ends of feet under a mass of weapons, the blood and the dust' (Iliad 16. 638–40). The reduction of the body to a formless mass, indistinguishable now from the ground on which it lies, not only eradicates the dead man's unique appearance; such treatment also eliminates the difference between lifeless matter and a living creature. Thus the corpse is no longer the visible aspect of the person but the inert clod of which Apollo spoke. Earth and dust defile the body because their contact pollutes it, inasmuch as they belong to a realm that is the opposite of life. During the process of mourning, at the point when the relatives of the dead man bring him closer to life by making one last reflection of life glow on his corpse, they in turn draw closer to the deceased by simulating their own entry into the formless world of death; they inflict on their own bodies a kind of fictive outrage by defiling themselves and tearing their hair, by rolling in the dust, by smearing their faces with ashes. Achilles does the same when he learns of Patroclus' death: 'He befouls his charming face (χαρίεν δ' ᾔσχυνε πρόσωπον)' (Iliad 18. 24) just as he defiles the fair face of Hector in the dust.

There is another type of aeikeiē: the body is dismembered, hacked up, torn into pieces; the head, arms, hands, and legs are removed, chopped up piece by piece (μελεϊστὶ ταμεῖν, Iliad 24. 409).[37] Ajax,

---

[36] Il. 24. 21 and 23. 187; both passages contain the verb apodruptō (flay, lacerate).

[37] We shall pass over the problems of maschalismos, for which one should consult E. Rohde, Psyche: The Cult of Souls and Belief in Immortality among the Greeks, 8th. edn., trans. W. B. Hillis (New York, 1925), Appendix 2, 582–6; these problems occupy another level of analysis which will be the subject of a future study.

in fury, cuts the head of Imbrios from his delicate neck and hurls it like a ball (*sphairēdon*) to roll in the dust (*Iliad* 13. 202–5). Hector would like to impale Patroclus' head on a stake after having severed it from his neck (*Iliad* 18. 176–7). Agamemnon kills Hippolochus and then 'cuts off his hands and severs his neck with his sword, and rolls him like a piece of wood (ὄλμον ὣς) through the crowd' (*Iliad* 11. 146–7). A head like a ball, a torso like a log: in losing its formal unity, the human body is reduced to the condition of a thing along with its disfigurement. In *Pythian* 4, Pindar says, 'If someone were to strip the branches from a great oak with a sharp-edged axe and defile its astounding beauty' (4. 263–4). It is precisely such beauty that astonishes the Greeks when they look on the dead Hector, and that is the target of the outrage directed at the corpse, an attack on the integrity of the human body.

The dismemberment of the corpse, whose remains are scattered here and there, culminates in the practice described in the first verses of the *Iliad* and recalled throughout the poem: leaving the body as food for dogs, birds, and fish. This outrage carries horror to its height. The body is torn to pieces and devoured raw instead of being consigned to the fire that, in burning it, restores it to wholeness in the world beyond. The hero whose body is surrendered to the voracity of wild animals is excluded from death while also having fallen from the human condition. He cannot pass through the gates of Hades, for he has not had his 'share of fire'; he has no place of burial, no mound or *sēma*, no location for his body that would mark for his society the site where he is to be found; there he would continue his relations with his country, his lineage, his descendants, or even simply with the chance passers-by. Excluded from death, he is equally banished from human memory. Moreover, to hand someone over to wild animals does not mean only to deprive him of the status of a dead man by preventing his funeral. It is also to dissolve him into confusion and return him to chaos, utter non-humanity. In the belly of the beasts that have devoured him, he becomes the flesh and blood of wild animals, and there is no longer the slightest appearance or trace of humanity: he is no longer in any way a person.

There is one last kind of outrage. Free rein is given to the powers of corruption that are at work in the bodies of mortal creatures; the corpse, deprived of burial, is left to decompose and rot on its own, eaten by the worms and the flies that have entered into his open wounds. When Achilles is preparing to re-enter combat, he worries out loud to his mother. What will happen to Patroclus' body while the battle lasts? 'I am sadly afraid, during this time, for the warlike son of Menoetius that flies might get into the wounds beaten by bronze in his body and breed worms in them, and these make foul the body, seeing that the life is killed in him, and that all his flesh may be rotted' (*Iliad* 19. 23–7).[38]

The body abandoned to decomposition is the complete reversal, or inversion, of a beautiful death. At one extreme is the youthful and manly beauty of the warrior whose body inspires amazement, envy, and admiration, even among his enemies; at the other is that which surpasses ugliness, the monstrousness of a being become worse than nothing, of a form that has sunk into the unspeakable. On one side is the imperishable glory that raises the hero above the common fate by making his name and individual appearance endure in human memory. On the other side is an infamy more terrible than the oblivion and silence reserved for the ordinary dead, that indistinct cohort of the deceased normally dispatched to Hades where they merge into the mass of those who, unlike the 'glorious heroes', are called the 'nameless', the *nōnumnoi*.[39] The mutilated corpse shares neither in the silence that surrounds the ordinary dead nor in the song praising the heroic dead. Neither living, because it has been killed, nor dead, because it has been deprived of funeral rites; as a scrap of matter lost on the edge of existence, it represents that which can neither be celebrated nor forgotten—the horror of the indescribable, absolutely unspeakable, which cuts you off altogether from the living, the dead, and the self.

Achilles, the glorious warrior, the fighter for heroic honour, exerts all his energy in dishonouring the corpse of the Trojan champion, who was his opposite number in the enemy camp and who, by killing Patroclus, killed someone like Achilles' other self. The man of imperishable glory plans to doom his rival to the most extreme kinds of disgrace. He will not succeed. There is much talk in the *Iliad* of dead warriors surrendered to dogs and birds. But whenever threats of disfigurement are specified and abuse is committed, it involves a warrior whose body is ultimately saved. The horror of the disfigured corpse is evoked for Sarpedon, Patroclus, and Hector—that is, for the

---

[38] Cf. also *Il.* 22. 509 and 24. 414–15.

[39] Hes. *Op.* 154; Aesch. *Pers.* 1003; cf. J.-P. Vernant, *Mythe et pensée chez les Grecs: Etudes de psychologie historique* (10th edn., Paris, 1985), 35, 68–9.

three characters who share with Achilles the quality of a hero. In
these three cases, the allusion to disfigurement leads, by a contrastive
effect, to an emphasis on the beauty of a heroic death, which, in spite
of everything, brings the dead man his tribute of immortal glory.
When Sarpedon falls to Patroclus' spear, it is his valour and courage
that induce the Achaeans to lay hold of him to abuse his corpse (*Iliad*
16. 545, 559). In the ensuing fracas, Sarpedon is already unrecognizable, covered as he is from head to foot with blood and dust. Zeus
dispatches Apollo to wipe off the black blood, to wash him in the
river's running water, to anoint him with ambrosia, to dress him in
splendid garments, and to hand him over to Sleep and Death, who
are to transfer him to Lycia. There his brothers and parents will bury
him in a tomb, under a stele, 'for this is the honour due to the dead
(τὸ γὰρ γέρας ἐστὶ θανόντων)' (*Iliad* 16. 667–75).

To counter Achilles' anxiety about the possibility that Patroclus'
body may rot, eaten by worms, Thetis replies: 'Even if he lies here for
a full year, his flesh will remain always intact (*empedos*) or even
better than before (ἢ καὶ ἀρείων)' (*Iliad* 19. 33). Supporting her
words with deeds, the goddess infuses ambrosia and rosy nectar into
Patroclus' nostrils, so his flesh may remain intact (*empedos*, *Iliad* 19.
38–9). During the whole time Achilles is relentlessly abusing Hector's
corpse, dragging it in the dust, giving it over to the feasting of dogs.
Aphrodite drives the animals away from the dead man night and
day. 'She anoints him with divine oil, fragrant of roses, fearing that
Achilles would tear off his skin by dragging him' (*Iliad* 23. 186–7).
For his part, Apollo brings a dark mist from the heavens. 'He did not
want the heat of the sun to dry the skin too quickly around the
muscles and the limbs' (*Iliad* 23. 190–1; 24. 20–1). 'Too quickly'
means before the body is returned to Priam and undergoes the
funeral rites that will send it into the hereafter intact, in the integrity
of his beauty, *eumorphos*, as Aeschylus says in the *Agamemnon*
about the bodies of the Greeks buried under the walls of Troy.[40] As he
is making his way towards Achilles' tent, Priam meets Hermes,
disguised as a young horseman. Priam asks him if his son has already
been cut to pieces and thrown to the dogs. Hermes replies:

Aged sir, neither have any dogs eaten him, nor have the birds, but he lies yet
beside the ship of Achilles at the shelters, and as he was (*keinos*); now here is

---

[40] The fallen Greeks rest *eumorphoi* in Trojan soil—so *Ag.* 454, which recalls the
eumorphoi kolossoi (beautiful statues) of 416.

the twelfth dawn he has lain there, nor does his flesh decay nor do worms feed on him. . . . It is true, Achilles drags him at random around his beloved companion's tomb . . . yet he cannot mutilate him (οὐδέ μιν αἰσχύνει). You yourself can see (θηοῖό κεν αὐτός) when you go there how fresh with dew (ἐερσήεις) he lies, and the blood is all washed from him, nor is there any corruption (οὐδέ ποθι μιαρός). So it is that the blessed immortals care for your son, though he is nothing but a dead man; because in their hearts they loved him. (*Iliad* 24. 411–24)

In all three cases the scenario is about the same. The gods miraculously save the hero from the shame of abuse that—by disfiguring, denaturing, his body until it is no longer recognizable as his own, or even as a human body, or even as a body at all—would reduce him to a state of non-being. To preserve him as he was (*keinos*) when death took him on the battlefield, the gods perform the human rituals of cleansing and beautification but use divine unguents: these elixirs of immortality preserve 'intact', despite all the abuse, that youth and beauty, which can only fade on the body of a living man, but which death in battle fixes forever on the hero's form, just as a stele remains erect forever to mark a tomb.

Epic uses the theme of the disfigurement of the corpse to underscore the exceptional position and status of heroic honour, of a beautiful death, of imperishable glory: they far surpass ordinary honour, death, and renown. In that agonistic culture, one proves one's worth only against another's, on top of and to the detriment of a rival. As a result, the heroic qualities imply their opposite, a radical form of dishonour, as far beneath the norm as heroism is above it: an absolute annihilation, a definitive and total disgrace.

With the constant allusions to bodies devoured by dogs or rotting in the sun, the story uses the theme of the mutilated corpse to outline the place where the double inversion of the beautiful death occurs. In the case of the hero, however, this vision of a person reduced to nothing, plunged into horror, is rejected at the very moment it is described. War, hatred, and destructive violence cannot prevail against those who are inspired by the heroic definition of honour and are pledged to a short life. From the moment a great deed has been accomplished, its truth cannot tarnish; it becomes the raw material of epic. How could the body of the hero have been disfigured and his memory eradicated? His fame lives in memory forever, and it inspires the direct vision of the past that is the privilege of the epic poet. Nothing can spoil a beautiful death: its aura stems from and continues to shine through the diffusion of epic language, which speaks of glory and thus makes it real forever after. The beauty of *kalos thanatos* does not differ from that of the song, which in celebrating such beauty transforms itself into deathless memory in the unbroken chain of generations.

II

The Shield of Achilles within the Iliad

OLIVER TAPLIN

I

Why is the shield of Achilles, instrument of war in a poem of war, covered with scenes of delightful peace, of agriculture, festival, song, and dance? I shall try to approach an answer to this question by looking at the scenes on the shield in relation to the rest of Homer, I mean the *Iliad* and *Odyssey*.[1]

The 130-line set-piece comes as the calm before the storm at a turning point in the epic. The long central day of battle, which dawned with the first line of Book 11, has just ended (18. 239–41). Achilles has without a second thought determined to return to the battlefield even though he knows his death is bound to follow (18. 78–126, esp. 95–8). Hector has made the no less lethal decision to stay outside the city and fight, though he on the contrary does not realize that it seals his fate (18. 243–314).[2]

This is the shield that Achilles will carry through the massacre of Books 20 and 21 and which will avert Hector's last throw (22. 290–1; cf. 313–14). It is the defiant front presented to the foe by the most terrible killer in the *Iliad*. What would the audience have expected the poet to put on the shield of such a warrior? Consider first the

---

[1] Little in this chapter is new, though much may be unfamiliar to those brought up on the kind of Homeric studies which have prevailed in Britain and America for some half a century now. I have been especially helped by three essays on the shield: W. Schadewaldt, *Von Homers Welt und Werk* (4th edn., Stuttgart, 1965), 352–74 (first publ. 1938), K. Reinhardt, *Die Ilias und ihr Dichter* (Göttingen, 1961), 401–11 (first publ. 1956), and W. Marg, *Homer über die Dichtung* (1st edn., Münster, 1957, 2nd edn., 1971). Their influence has been pervasive and I shall not try to single out every concurrence. For a list of those renegades who have taken the shield seriously in English see n. 30 below. I am indebted to Colin Macleod and Malcolm Willcock for some helpful suggestions and corrections.

[2] For the contrasts between these two crucial decisions to fight see Schadewaldt's superb essay, 'Die Entscheidung des Achilleus', in (n. 1), 234–67.

shield which Agamemnon takes up before his gruesome *aristeia*:[3]

And he took up the man-enclosing elaborate stark shield, a thing of splendour. There were ten circles of bronze upon it, and set about it were twenty knobs of tin, pale-shining, and in the very centre another knob of dark cobalt. And circled in the midst of all was the blank-eyed face of the Gorgon with her stare of horror, and Fear was inscribed on it, and Terror. (11. 32–7)

The demons are designed to inspire terror in the enemy. Compare also the aegis of Zeus donned by Athena (5. 736–42: Panic, Strife, and their crew surround the Gorgon's head), and the baldrick which Odysseus sees on the ghost of Heracles at *Odyssey* 11. 609 ff., covered with beasts and carnage. 'May he who artfully designed them. . . never again do any designing,' comments Odysseus. Looking outside Homer (and leaving aside the shield of Aeneas in *Aeneid* 8), the ready comparison is the description in lines 141–317 of the fragment of epic narrative usually known as the *Shield of Heracles* and associated (undeservedly) with the name of Hesiod.[4] This too is a shield made by Hephaestus for a great fighter, and it is moreover obviously under the influence of the shield in the *Iliad*. Yet it is dominated by terror and slaughter. Here is a typical extract: 'By them stood Darkness of Death, mournful and fearful, pale, shrivelled, shrunk with hunger, swollen kneed. Long nails tipped her hands, and she dribbled at the nose, and from her cheeks blood dripped down to the ground. She stood leering hideously, and much dust sodden with tears lay upon her shoulders' ([Hesiod] *Aspis* 264–70, trans. Evelyn-White).

So the joys of civilization and fertility on our shield are peculiar. Why all this and not the usual horrors? The question is reinforced by the representations of Achilles' shield in later visual art, which do not try to reproduce Homer's scenes but simply show the Gorgon and other standard devices.[5] More tellingly, Euripides actually protests

[3] See J. Armstrong's excellent article on arming scenes, *AJP* 79 (1958), 337 ff., esp. 344–5. All the translations are Lattimore's, with slight alterations where necessary.

[4] The useful introduction and commentary by C. F. Russo (*Hesiodi Scutum* (2nd edn., Florence, 1965)), esp. 29–35, date the poem to the 6th cent. Anyone who has read the *Shield of Heracles* can hardly continue to believe that the *Il.* and *Od.* were merely typical products of a tradition in which the author submerged his individual genius. I am not sure why Jasper Griffin does not make more use of this third-rate cyclic-type blustering in his excellent article, 'The Epic Cycle and the Uniqueness of Homer', *JHS* 97 (1977), 39 ff. [= this vol., Ch. 12].

[5] See the useful pamphlet on the shield of Achilles by K. Fittschen in the series *Archaeologica Homerica*: Kap. N, Bildkunst, Teil 1 (Göttingen, 1973), esp. 2; and cf. the plates on pp. 93–109 and 181–3 of K. Friis Johansen, *The Iliad in Early Greek Art* (Copenhagen, 1967).

against the Iliadic shield. The chorus of his *Electra* (442–86) make it clear that they are singing of the celebrated shield (κλεινᾶς, 455); but it is designed to terrify the Trojans (456–7). In the centre it has the sun and constellations, as in Homer, but they are there to panic Hector (468–9), and round the edge skims Perseus with the Gorgon's head (458 ff., a motif from the *Shield of Heracles*). A more recent poet, reacting like Euripides to a brutal and all-consuming war, has also reforged the Homeric shield to suit its fell recipient. W. H. Auden's fine poem 'The Shield of Achilles' begins[6]

> She looked over his shoulder
>   For vines and olive trees,
> Marble well-governed cities
>   And ships upon untamed seas,
> But there on the shining metal
>   His hands had put instead
> An artificial wilderness
>   And a sky like lead.

Three times Thetis looks to see the scenes which she expects because she knows them—or rather we know them—from Homer, and each time she is presented with a scene from a world of militaristic and totalitarian inhumanity. At the end even the child is corrupted and knows no better:

> A ragged urchin, aimless and alone,
>   Loitered about that vacancy, a bird
> Flew up to safety from his well-aimed stone:
>   That girls are raped, that two boys knife a third,
>   Were axioms to him, who'd never heard
> Of any world where promises were kept,
> Or one could weep because another wept.
>   The thin-lipped armourer,
>   Hephaestos, hobbled away,
>   Thetis of the shining breasts
>   Cried out in dismay
>   At what the god had wrought
>   To please her son, the strong
>   Iron-hearted man-slaying Achilles
>   Who would not live long.[7]

[6] First publ. in *Poetry* for Oct. 1952. I can find no external reason to think that the poem was written earlier than 1952.

[7] 'Who would not live long': ōkumoros, minunthadios. The motif is introduced in Book 1 (352, 416–17) and recurs throughout: see Schadewaldt (n. 1), 260–1.

It appears that Auden sees Achilles as the prototype of the Aryan superman and makes his shield prefigure accordingly. In the same way Euripides presents the events of his *Electra* as the aftermath of the inhumanity of Agamemnon and his chiefs of staff.

Why, then, does Homer fill his shield with scenes which he repeatedly insists are beautiful and with people who delight in their innocent activities? My question does not seem to have concerned English-speaking critics in our times: at least, I cannot find it raised in any of the standard books on Homer, by which I mean the ten or so books by Lord, Bowra, Page, Finley, and Kirk.[8] I can, however, offer three explanations which would be in keeping with the attitudes to be found in these books. One would be that the shield is based on some actual artefact, perhaps some heirloom fossilized by the oral tradition (this is the standard explanation of, for instance, the boar's-tusk helmet at 10. 257 ff.). This must be mistaken.[9] Nothing really like this shield has ever been found nor ever will be, no more than the exemplars of Hephaestus' automata at 18. 417 ff. That is the whole point: the shield—like those golden gynaikoids—is a wonder of divine craftsmanship unlike anything known in our age. The decoration of the shield is derived from poetic invention not from history.

Next it might be answered that the shield affords relief from the protracted battle narratives. It is orthodox to claim this as a function of Homeric similes (though most similes are in fact placed to intensify rather than relieve). It is true that the shield takes us far from the Trojan war, but that is hardly enough to explain its detail. After all, the rest of Books 18 and 19 are relief from battle scenes.[10] We are still left with the question, why this particular sort of relief?

Third, the explanation which is, I suspect, most in keeping with the dominant school of what might be called 'primitive oral poetics', namely that the oral poet has simply wandered on from one thing to another as the improvisatory Muse has taken him. Once

---

'Iron-hearted': the metaphor is rare in the *Iliad*, but is used by Hector of Achilles as he dies at 22. 357 (otherwise only of Priam at 24. 205, 521). 'Man-slaying': is it not likely that Auden derived the epithet from the phrase χεῖρας ἐπ' ἀνδροφόνους at 18. 317? The only other times the epithet is used of hands are also about Achilles: 23. 18 and 24. 479—the latter at the greatest moment of the entire *Il*. I shall return to the subject of Auden and *Il*. 24 at the end.

[8] For the less orthodox scholars see n. 30 below.

[9] See Fittschen (n. 5), *passim*. For a bibliography of such views see Fittschen, 4–5.

[10] 18. 148–238 is the only fighting between 18. 1 and 20. 156 ff.

he had decided to elaborate the shield at appropriate length for its maker and recipient he has added and added inorganically. The reason why I think this would be the orthodox account is that the standard view of the elaborated similes is that after starting off from a point of comparison they develop paratactically at the poet's pleasure. 'The poet follows his fancy and develops the picture without much care for his reason for using it.'[11] According to this view the poet would have settled on the subject-matter of the shield, not because it was relevant—or come to that irrelevant—to the *Iliad* as a whole, but because that is what happened to come into his mind as he went along. I can only ask anyone who reckons this is obviously the right answer to bear with me while I look at an alternative. But I am more likely to make headway with someone who finds it hard to believe that a poet who worked in that way could have so consistently commanded the attention, indeed adulation, of our civilization.

II

My starting-point is that the shield is not the only place in Homer where we encounter peace and prosperity and people delighting in their lives. I shall survey the shield scene by scene relating each to similar pictures elsewhere, and looking for similarities of tone and feeling as well as of subject-matter. There will be three main sources. First, the settled societies of the *Odyssey*; that is, Nestor's Pylos and Menelaus' Sparta, visited by Telemachus in Books 3 and 4 and showing him, and us, a proper re-established *oikos* to contrast with Ithaca and Mycenae; and even more the Phaeacia of Alcinous which serves for Odysseus as the transition and model between the remote disordered worlds of his wanderings and his disrupted home. Indeed the description of the palace of Alcinous at *Odyssey* 7. 81 ff.,

[11] Quoted from C. M. Bowra, *Tradition and Design in the Iliad* (Oxford, 1930), 126. I have found the most thoroughgoing and readable assertion of the paratactic approach in the article by J. A. Notopoulos, *TAPA* 80 (1949), 1 ff. The notion has been adapted and updated by G. S. Kirk under the term 'cumulation', particularly in his paper, 'Verse-Structure and Sentence-Structure', in *Homer and the Oral Tradition* (Cambridge, 1976), 146 ff., esp. 167 ff. (1st publ. in *YCS* 20 (1966), 73 ff.). Note this on p. 171: 'Arming scenes, descriptions of pieces of armour, developed similes, the description of minor figures and their genealogy whether or not in a catalogue—these are the typical *loci* for cumulation.'

especially the gardens (112–33), is the set-piece closest of all to the shield of Achilles. Second, there is the peacetime world of many of the similes, especially in the *Iliad*. And lastly Troy, at least Troy were it not for the war, as it was in the days of peace before the Achaeans came.

When these three elements are put together we arrive at an easy hedonistic existence spent in feasting with the pastimes of conversation, song and dance, making love—in fact a life such as the gods lead. This is the life that humans aspire to, even if they only achieve it in brief snatches. ('We live in unhappiness, but the gods themselves have no sorrows', *Iliad* 24. 526.) Witness Menelaus' odd homily on satiety at *Iliad* 13. 620–39: he contrasts war with life's pleasures, 'sleep and love-making, the sweetness of song and the stately dancing' (636–7, ὕπνου καὶ φιλότητος | μολπῆς τε γλυκερῆς καὶ ἀμύμονος ὀρχηθμοῖο). Thus when at last Odysseus' house is cleared of the suitors there are celebrations:

> First they went and washed, and put their tunics upon them, and the women arrayed themselves in their finery, while the inspired singer took up his hollowed lyre and stirred within them the impulse for the sweetness of song and the stately dancing. Now the great house resounded aloud to the thud of their footsteps, as the men celebrated there, and the fair girdled women.
> (*Odyssey* 23. 141–7)

But the Homeric good life is most memorably summed up by Alcinous' couplet on the pursuits of the blessed Phaeacians (*Odyssey* 8. 248–9):

> αἰεὶ δ' ἡμῖν δαίς τε φίλη κίθαρίς τε χοροί τε
> εἵματά τ' ἐξημοιβά λοετρά τε θερμὰ καὶ εὐναί.

Always the feast is dear to us, and the lyre and dances
and changes of clothing and hot baths and beds.

The precise plan of the shield is not made so clear by the poem that it is beyond doubt; and we should bear in mind Lessing's point that we are told of the making of the shield not given a map of the finished product.[12] It is not even clear that the shield is to be envisaged as decorated with five concentric circles. Moreover it is not likely that

---

[12] Lessing, *Laocoon*, chs. 17–19. This point has been stressed by H. A. Gaertner, 'Beobachtungen zum Schild des Achilleus', in H. Görgemanns and E. A. Schmidt (edd.), *Studien zum antiken Epos* (Meisenheim/Glan, 1976), 46 ff.

our text is exactly as it left Homer; some lines have probably been
added and possibly others have been omitted (see further below). The
divisions and arrangement which I shall adopt are widely accepted
and make, I think, a coherent whole; but they are not essential to my
argument.

The First (Inmost) Circle (483–9): The Earth, Heavens, and Sea[13]

After the first all-inclusive line it is only the heavens which are given
any detail. It is enough for now to remark that the sun, moon, and
constellations are the cosmic constants and the markers of the passage of time, reflected in Homer by recurrent formulae whatever the
human vicissitudes they may accompany.

The Second Circle: City Life

The two cities are clearly set out as a pair—see 490–1, 509. Each in
turn provides two scenes.

(a) The City at Peace, (i) 491–6: Marriage Celebrations. Of all the
pleasant occasions of civil life, especially in a highly kin-conscious
world, a wedding might be singled out as the most unifying and
optimistic. It is also a time for every one to indulge in the 'good life'.
Compare with the shield the wedding celebrations for Hermione
which greet Telemachus on his arrival at Sparta (*Odyssey* 4. 15–19):

> So these neighbours and townsmen of glorious Menelaus
> were at their feasting all about the great house with the high roof,
> and taking their ease, and among them stepped an inspired singer
> playing his lyre, while among the dancers two acrobats
> led the measure of song and dance revolving among them.

And at such times thoughts turn in due course to bed. We have in
fact most of the delights enumerated by Alcinous.

The accomplishments of singing and dancing, which are of course
useless and even despised in time of war,[14] epitomize the pleasures of

---

[13] It would undoubtedly make most sense if line 483 ('land, heaven, sea') were a
summary of the entire shield, and 484–9 the details of the first circle, showing only
the heavens; this is maintained by Fittschen (n. 5), 10. But there are difficulties, above
all the construction of 484; this interpretation is impossible without emendation.

[14] Cf. in various circumstances the rebukes and taunts at *Il.* 3. 54, 15. 508, 16. 617,
16. 745–50, 24. 261.

peace. The Phaeacians are, as appropriate, especially good at dancing (see *Odyssey* 8. 250–65). The wives at their doors represent
'home' no less tellingly. The marital home is what the Achaeans
have had to leave behind. 'Nine years have gone by, and the timbers
of our ships have rotted away and the cables are broken, and far
away our wives and our young children are sitting within our halls
and wait for us' (*Iliad* 2. 134–7). And the meeting of Hector and
Andromache in Troy suggests poignantly what might be if it were
not disrupted by war.[15]

(ii) 497–508: The Law Case. There has been much discussion of the
precise legal problem and procedure here.[16] What matters for present
purposes is that we have the stable justice of a civilized city. *Dikē*
(508) is used here in a sense similar to that in the famous 'Hesiodic'
simile at 16. 384 ff. Here is no vendetta or the perilous exile which
Homer and his audience associated with a murderer in the age of
heroes. We have, rather, arbitrators, speeches on both sides, and
considered judgements.

The sceptre (505) is the symbol of a well-ordered hierarchy
(though within the *Iliad* it has been somewhat mishandled in the
first two books). Note also the well-shaped or polished stones that the
elders sit on (ἐπὶ ξεστοῖσι λίθοις, 504). This is the epithet used to
describe the masonry of the marvellous palace of Priam (6. 242 ff.),
and even of the palace of Zeus (20. 11); but compare above all the
council-stones of well-ordered Pylos where Nestor sits and Neleus sat
before him. 'Nestor went outside and took his seat upon the polished
stones which were there in place for him in front of the towering
doorway, white stones, with a shine on them that glistened' (*Odyssey*
3. 406–8; cf. also Scheria at *Odyssey* 8. 6–7).

(b) The City at War, (i) 509–19: The Siege. We do not have to seek far
for parallels to this scene. Here—somewhat altered, for we are
dealing with a subtle poet not a crude emblematist—here we have
the *Iliad* and its belligerent deities.[17] On the shield there are *two*

---

[15] Those who are inclined to fall for the stuff about women and wives in M. I. Finley,
The World of Odysseus (2nd edn., London, 1977), 126 ff., should read *Il.* 6 as an
antidote. They might also take note of *Od.* 6. 180–5 (overlooked by Finley).
[16] See notably H. Hommel in P. Steinmetz (ed.), *Politeia und Res Publica* (FS
R. Stark, Palingenesia 4, Wiesbaden, 1969), 11 ff., and Ø. Andersen, *SO* 51 (1976),
5 ff., esp. 11–16.   [17] Cf. Andersen (n. 16), 9.

besieging armies (their relation to each other is obscure), but like
the Achaeans they are not agreed among themselves. The besieged
are making a foray, not to drive the invaders back and burn their
ships, but to make an ambush for provisions. Yet we are unmistak-
ably put in mind of Troy by the old men, women, and children on
the walls (rather than in their doorways or in the *agora* as in the
city at peace). Closest of all probably are Hector's instructions at
8. 518–22:

> Let the boys who are in their first youth and the grey-browed elders
> take stations on the god-founded bastions that circle the city;
> and as for the women, have our wives, each one in her own house,
> kindle a great fire; let there be a watch kept steadily
> lest a sudden attack get into the town when the fighters have left it.

But we think also of Helen with Priam and the chattering elders on the
walls above the Scaean gates (3. 146 ff.), and of Priam watching and
pleading with his son (21. 526 ff., 22. 25 ff.). We remember that Hector
did not find Andromache and the child at home, but on the Great
Tower (6. 386 ff.); and that is where she rushes maenad-like when
she hears of Hector's death (22. 462; cf. 447). The city on the shield
stands for every threatened homeland: within the *Iliad* Troy is such
a city.

(ii) 520–34: The Ambush of the Herd. This violent devastation of the
pastoral world takes us away from Troy itself to the countryside of
the Troad and the neighbouring cities, which, as we are often
reminded, the Achaeans, and above all Achilles, have been looting
for nine years. Compare the seven brothers of Andromache, sons of
Eetion king of Thebe: 'Achilles slaughtered all of them as they were
tending their white sheep and their lumbering oxen' (6. 423–4). He
was kinder to Isus and Antiphus, sons of Priam: 'Achilles had caught
these two at the knees of Ida and bound them in pliant willows
as they watched by their sheep, and released them for ransom'
(11. 105–6).[18] The pathos of the ruthless warrior cutting down

---

[18] Achilles had once come upon Aeneas herding on the slopes of Ida, but Aeneas
ran and escaped (20. 187 ff.). Ach. would often spare the Trojans he captured, like
Lycaon whom he caught in Priam's garden cutting fig branches to make a chariot
rail; but the death of Patroclus changes all that.

the innocent pastoral world is quintessentially Homeric, and is wonderfully conveyed here by the two herdsmen. One moment they are going along with the flock 'playing happily on pipes, and they took no thought of treachery' (526), the next they lie killed.[19]

(iii) 535–40: The Ensuing Mêlée. Here we have the kind of scene which might have been expected on a shield, monstrous ghouls fighting over the dying and the dead. And, indeed, four of the six lines (535–8) also occur on the *Shield of Heracles* (156–9). This primitive conception of battle is not typical of the *Iliad*. On this and other good grounds Solmsen has condemned lines 535–40 as an interpolation (or 'plus-verses') derived from the *Shield of Heracles*.[20] We can see exactly the same phenomenon a little later, though this time the plus-verses never became canonical. In *P. Berol.* 9774 (first century BC) after line 608 at the end of the shield are four more verses describing a harbour full of fishes: the lines are almost the same as *Shield of Heracles*, 207–13.[21]

The Third Circle: Rural Life

There follows a series of scenes of people going about agricultural tasks. Seeing that the first three clearly represent spring, summer, and autumn, I take it that 573 ff. shows winter.[22]

(a) 541–9: Spring. Note the emphasis on the fertility of the soil: it is a dark, deep tilth, and enough for many ploughmen. For pictures of ploughing in similes see 10. 351 ff., 13. 703 ff. (also *Odyssey* 13. 31 ff.). The cup of wine at the end of each furlong is a civilized touch. Hecuba offered wine to Hector in Book 6 (258 ff.); but bloody war is not the time for such ceremony and relief (6. 264–8).

---

[19] On pathos in the *Il.* see the exceptionally perceptive and well-argued article by J. Griffin, *CQ* 26 (1976), 161 ff.

[20] F. Solmsen, *Hermes* 93 (1965), 1–6. Further points against 535–8 are added by J. M. Lynn-George, *Hermes* 106 (1978), 396–405; Lynn-George defends 539–40 as Homeric, but unconvincingly to my mind. On the primitive notion of *kēres* (fates, death-spirits) see J. M. Redfield, *Nature and Culture in the Iliad* (Chicago, 1975), 184–5.

[21] For full details see S. West, *The Ptolemaic Papyri of Homer* (Cologne, 1967), 132–6.

[22] It is often said that the division of the year into *four* seasons is not to be found before Alcman (fr. 20 PMGF). But all four of Alcman's seasons—ἔαρ, θέρος, ὀπώρη, and χεῖμα—are to be found in Hom.

(b) 550–6: *Summer.* We also find reapers in a striking simile:

> And the men, like two lines of reapers who, facing each other,
> drive their course all down the field of wheat or barley
> for a man blessed in substance, and the cut swathes drop showering,
> so Trojans and Achaeans driving in against one another
> cut men down . . .

$$(\text{11. 67–9})$$

On the shield the children helping, their arms full of golden swathes, is the kind of touch for which Homer used to be justly famous. The harvest is hot, hungry work, and for the scene to be complete there has to be a good meal of meat being prepared, beneath, of course, thick leafy shade—ὑπὸ δρυΐ (558).[23]

But the most telling figure of all in this vignette is the lord with his sceptre standing by, silently joyful. This is his *temenos* (550), an especially desirable estate granted to him, the kind of privilege which any great *basileus* might hope to return to after the war, the kind which Achilles might have had if he had chosen long life instead of glorious death.[24] This is the life which Odysseus is striving to win back to in the *Odyssey*, and he gives a memorable account of it (19. 109–14):

> As of some king, a fine man and god-fearing,
> who, ruling as lord over many powerful people,
> upholds the way of good government, and the black earth yields him
> barley and wheat, his trees are heavy with fruit, his sheepflocks
> continue to bear young, the sea gives him fish, because of
> his good leadership, and his people prosper under him.

The prosperity and good government go hand in hand.

(c) 561–7: *Autumn.* The grape harvest with its heavy fruit and promise of next year's wine inspires song and dance (on which see above). The pickers are 'young girls and young men, in all their light-hearted innocence' (παρθενικαὶ (δὲ) καὶ ἠΐθεοι ἀταλὰ φρονέοντες, 567). Elsewhere in the *Iliad* only the infant Astyanax is graced with this quality (ἀταλάφρονα, 6. 400). But these boys and

---

[23] Kirk (n. 11), 12, asserts that the king is going to eat all the roast beef while the workers will have barley mash. I cannot see any reason for preferring this to the interpretation well argued for by W. Leaf (*The Iliad* II (1st edn., London, 1888), ad loc.): the heralds have performed the slaughter and jointing; the women are actually cooking it, and this involves sprinkling the meat with barley, exactly as at *Od.* 14. 77.

[24] Cf. Gaertner (n. 12), 61–3. For some examples of such *temenē* in the *Il.* cf. 6. 194 (Bellerophon), 9. 576 (Meleager), 12. 313 (Glaucus and Sarpedon), 20. 184 (Aeneas).

girls on the shield are older, and there is another passage where that age of ingenuous first love is most poignantly evoked: as his death approaches Hector realizes that it is no good trying to talk gently to Achilles 'talking love like a young man and a young girl, in the way a young man and a young maiden talk love together' (22. 127–8). The phrase conjures up a world of youth and delight which could not be further from the confrontation of Achilles and Hector.[25]

(d) 573–89: Winter. The cattle are kept in the midden-yard ($\kappa\acute{o}\pi\rho o\nu$, 575) during the winter nights; but as the herdsmen set off for the water meadows we seem to be entering another pastoral idyll. The lions break in on this as though to prevent the world of the shield from being too perfect. We are, of course, in the realm of the similes still, in fact we are bound to be reminded by this of the similes. In the peacetime agricultural world man's worst enemy is the lion, not other men.

(I must confess that I am not clear how the last three lines, 587–9, fit in. The scene is different from all the others, not only because much briefer, but also because it contains no human figures. Yet it is clearly marked off from the scene of the winter herding and the lions. The lines may be interpolated: see Leaf ad loc.)

The Fourth Circle (590–606): The Dance

It appears that the dance goes all the way round without subdivision. Although they sometimes move in lines (602) the emphasis is put on the circular dance by the one simile within the *ekphrasis*, the potter testing his wheel. The length and unity of this scene make it appear the climax of the whole shield.[26] As in the scene of the vintage we see $\mathring{\eta}\mathring{\iota}\theta\epsilon o\iota$ $\kappa\alpha\mathring{\iota}$ $\pi\alpha\rho\theta\acute{\epsilon}\nu o\iota$ ('youths and girls', 593) but in several respects this section forms a 'ring' with the wedding scene at the beginning. As before there is singing and dancing, and again the onlookers delight in the festive spectacle. There are in addition a pair of

---

[25] Who is to say that it is pure coincidence that the unusual verb $\grave{o}\alpha\rho\acute{\iota}\zeta\epsilon\iota\nu$ also occurs at 6. 516 used of the conversation of Hector and Andromache? See the good remarks of E. T. Owen, *The Story of the Iliad* (Toronto, 1946, repr. Ann Arbor, 1966), 121–2; cf. C. P. Segal, *The Theme of the Mutilation of the Corpse in the Iliad (Mnemos.* Suppl. 17, Leiden, 1971), 36.

[26] J. T. Kakridis has produced comparative material which confirms that the main scene of an 'imagined ecphrasis' should come last: see *Homer Revisited* (Lund, 1971), 108 ff., esp. 123 (1st publ. in *WS* 76 (1963), 7 ff.). Gaertner (n. 12: 53 n. 18) argues that the king's *temenos* is the climactic scene of the shield, but he does not refute Kakridis.

tumblers, and, if we are prepared to import a line from the otherwise identical formulae at *Odyssey* 4. 17–19 (quoted above), we would have a poet, the one and only *aoidos* to appear in the *Iliad*. We might feel that the shield would not be complete without him.[27]

Homer dwells on the clothing and appearance of the young men and women (595–8):

> These wore, the maidens long light robes, but the men wore tunics
> of finespun work and shining softly, touched with olive oil.
> (τῶν δ' αἱ μὲν λεπτὰς ὀθόνας ἔχον, οἱ δὲ χιτῶνας
> εἵατ' ἐϋννήτους, ἦκα στίλβοντες ἐλαίῳ.)
> And the girls wore fair garlands on their heads, while the young men
> carried golden knives that hung from sword-belts of silver.

Fine clothing is, one might say, the hallmark of a prosperous civilized society in Homer, and its making and care the distinction of its women. Alcinous singled out changes of clothing as a delight of the Phaeacians, and fine weaving is stressed in the utopian picture of his palace (*Odyssey* 7. 105–11). And it is, of course, in order to wash the clothing of Alcinous' household that Nausicaa goes to the shore (*Odyssey* 6. 13–112). Her unmarried brothers, for instance, are always wanting newly laundered clothes when they go dancing (64–5).

In the *Iliad* this kind of raiment comes almost exclusively from two places—Troy and Olympus. When Diomedes wounds Aphrodite his spear rips 'through the immortal robe that the very Graces had woven for her carefully' (5. 338; cf. 5. 315, and the veil of Artemis at 21. 507). Athene, more used to battle, takes off her 'elaborate robe which she herself had wrought with her hands' patience' (5. 735 = 8. 386). And of course when Hera prepares herself to seduce Zeus she has an especially seductive toilette (14. 169 ff., esp. 171–81).

Turning to Troy, the fine quality of Helen's dress in Book 3 is reiterated,[28] and when Aphrodite fetches her to Paris she

---

[27] Most editors since Wolf have included the line and believed that it was wrongly ejected by Aristarchus. This rests on a long stretch of fictional pedantry in Athenaeus Book 4 (180a–181c). But all the experts on Aristarchus are quite clear that Athenaeus cannot have got his facts right—perhaps he did not try to. For full bibliography see H. Erbse (ed.), *Scholia Graeca in Homeri Iliadem* IV (Berlin, 1975), 509. The case for the line must stand or fall without Athenaeus.

[28] 141, ἀργεννῇσι ὀθόνῃσιν; 385, νεκταρέου ἑανοῦ; 419, ἑανῷ ἀργῆτι φαεινῷ. 3. 385 surely gives extra point to Athena's taunt at 5. 421–5; but at the time in Book 3 Aphrodite's treatment of Helen is no joke.

says (391–4):

> He is in his chamber now, in the bed with its circled pattern,
> shining in his raiment and beauty (κάλλεΐ τε στίλβων, καὶ εἵμασιν).
> You would not think he came from fighting a man,
> but was going rather to a dance or rested from dancing lately.

In Book 6 Hecuba goes to the palace treasure-chamber to find a robe to dedicate to Athene (289–95).

> There lay the elaborately wrought robes, the work of Sidonian
> women, whom Alexandros himself, the god-like, had brought home
> from the land of Sidon, crossing the wide sea, on that journey
> when he brought back also gloriously descended Helen.
> Hecuba lifted out one and took it as a gift to Athena,
> that which was the loveliest in design and the largest,
> and shone like a star. It lay beneath the others.

That offering fails, of course, and its inevitable failure is woven into its guilty history. But it is that same treasure-chamber which Priam goes to in Book 24 to fetch the ransom for Achilles (228–31):

> He lifted back the fair covering of his clothes-chest
> and from inside took out twelve robes surpassingly lovely
> and twelve mantles to be worn single, as many blankets,
> as many great white cloaks, also the same number of tunics (χιτῶνας).

This supplication succeeds, and Achilles carefully leaves for wrapping the corpse of Hector 'two great cloaks and a fine-spun tunic' (δύο φάρε' ἐΰννητόν τε χιτῶνα, 580; cf. 588). The fine clothing of Troy, and above all of the household of Priam, is dispersed as ransom or used for wrapping corpses—and what is left is due to be looted or burned.

So the washing-troughs in Book 22 are no gratuitous detail (let alone a quaint record of real-life hydrography). Three times Hector is pursued by Achilles round the walls of Troy, past the springs of Scamander, the river of Troy (22. 153–6):

> Beside these in this place, and close to them, are the washing-hollows
> of stone, and magnificent, where the wives of the Trojans and their lovely
> daughters washed the clothes to shining, in the old days
> when there was peace, before the coming of the sons of the Achaeans.

So Hector's heroism and his death are closely associated with the place that epitomizes the former prosperity and delight of Troy, Troy which once Hector falls is doomed to burn. The motif is continued in

Andromache's lament at the end of the book. She mourns Hector's corpse (22. 510–13):

... naked, though in your house there is clothing laid up
that is fine-textured (λεπτά) and pleasant, wrought by the hands of women.
But all of these I will burn up in the fire's blazing,
no use to you, since you will never be laid away in them.[29]

But she is wrong. Achilles himself has the corpse of Hector wrapped in the fine raiment of Troy (24. 588–90). And at the very end of the epic the ashes of Hector are buried in a casket 'wrapped about with soft robes of purple' (24. 796).

The dance on the shield of Achilles shows, then, how fine raiment *should* be put to use, how it was used at Troy in the old days before the Achaeans came: the rest of the *Iliad* shows the uses they have to put it to in wartime.

The Fifth (Outmost) Circle (606–7): Ocean

He made on it the great strength of the Ocean River
which ran around the uttermost rim of the shield's strong structure.

The inmost circle showed the heavens which are above the earth, the outmost the stream of Ocean which runs round the earth. The shield presents, that is, a kind of microcosm or epitome of the world. I hope by now that this is clear: it would, I believe, have been clear to the original audience from the first line (483),

ἐν μὲν γαῖαν ἔτευξ᾽, ἐν δ᾽ οὐρανόν, ἐν δὲ θάλασσαν . . .

III

The shield is a microcosm. This elementary observation is a commonplace, indeed the starting-point, for critics like Schadewaldt and Reinhardt; but it is not to be found in the standard handbooks read in England, only in some less orthodox works of the kind that students are often warned off.[30] The shield is a microcosm; but that does not

---

[29] See Schadewaldt's brilliant essay on the death of Hector, (n. 1), 268 ff., esp. 331–2; also Segal (n. 25), 46–7.

[30] Pride of place must go to Owen (n. 25), 186–9. This admirable book is directed to students rather than research scholars, but that does not explain the unjust neglect of it. I suspect that it has been axiomatic that any Homeric study which does not take account of oral composition must be totally valueless; I see no justification for this

mean it includes in miniature every single thing to be found in the world—that would be impossible, and is not in any case the way that poetry and art work. They select and emphasize in order to impart meaning. The shield omits, for instance, poverty and misery; it omits trade and seafaring; it does not figure religion or cult, and it does not figure mythology or named heroes and places. The omissions might prove instructive, but I wish to concentrate on what is there.

I hope I have shown that on the whole the scenes are those of prosperous settled societies at peace, representing the Homeric picture of the good life. But the shield is a microcosm, not a utopia, and death and destruction are also there, though in inverse proportion to the rest of the *Iliad*. Rural life is invaded by the lions, and one of the two cities is surrounded by armies and carnage. I argued that the city and its besiegers are meant to put us in mind of Troy and the Achaeans, in fact of the rest of the *Iliad*. What I now wish to suggest is that the city on the shield puts the *Iliad* itself into perspective; it puts war and prowess into perspective within the world as a whole. On the shield the *Iliad* takes up, so to speak, one half of one of the five circles. It is as though Homer has allowed us temporarily to stand back from the poem and see it in its place—like a 'detail' from the reproduction of a painting—within a larger landscape, a landscape which is usually blotted from sight by the all-consuming narrative in the foreground. This interpretation is close to that of Schadewaldt (n. 1, esp. 368), and of Owen in *The Story of the Iliad* (186–9).

He lifts our eyes from their concentration upon the battlefield to the contemplation of other scenes which remind us of the fullness and variety of life; it is a breathing-space in the battle, in which we have time to look around us and remember that this is only an incident in the busy world of human activities, that though Troy may fall and Achilles' life be wrecked, the world goes on as before; and in that remembrance there is at the same time relief of emotional tension and yet a heightening of expectation through the holding back of the long-awaited crisis, and also a deepening of the poignancy of the tragedy by seeing it thus against the large indifferent background of the wider life of the world. (Owen, 187–8)

attitude. Other works in English which say things worth saying about the shield of Ach. are J. T. Sheppard, *The Pattern of the Iliad* (London, 1922), 1–10, esp. 8, C. H. Whitman, *Homer and the Heroic Tradition* (Cambridge, Mass., 1958), 205–6, G. A. Duethorn, *Achilles' Shield and the Structure of the Iliad* (Amhurst, 1962), C. R. Beye, *The Iliad, the Odyssey, and the Epic Tradition* (Garden City, 1966), 143–4, Redfield (n. 20), 187–8. I find K. J. Atchity, *Homer's Iliad, The Shield of Memory* (Carbondale, 1978) disappointingly diffuse and fanciful.

But I hear the protest that this kind of interpretation is the product of sentimental pacifism and is contradicted by the whole spirit of the *Iliad*. The *Iliad*, it is claimed, is a poem of heroic war; it glorifies war and glorifies those who kill most successfully. 'The *Iliad* is saturated in blood, a fact which cannot be hidden or argued away, twist the evidence as we may in a vain attempt to fit archaic Greek values to a more gentle code of ethics. The poet and his audience lingered lovingly over every act of slaughter' (Finley (n. 15), 118). But not even Professor Finley can believe that this is the only attitude to be found in Homer. We do not have to go to the 'unheroic' Hesiod to find 'One kind of Strife fosters evil war and battle, being cruel: her no man loves'.[31] Odysseus himself speaks of 'the wars, and throwing spears with polished hafts, and the arrows, gloomy things, which to other men are terrible' (*Odyssey* 14. 225–6), and Menelaus sitting at home in Sparta among the spoils of Troy laments (*Odyssey* 4. 97–9),

> I wish I lived in my house with only a third part of all
> these goods, and that the men were alive who died in those days
> in wide Troy land far away from horse-pasturing Argos.

But our standard authorities feel that such attitudes are alien to the heroic ethos and to Homer proper. They write them off as later, anachronistic, and incongruous. Take, for instance, Finley (n. 15), on the good king at *Odyssey* 19. 107 ff. (quoted above): 'Everything that Homer tells us demonstrates that here he permitted a contemporary note to enter, carefully restricting it, however, to a harmless simile and thus avoiding any possible contradiction in the narrative itself.' The professor of History abhors 'contradiction', and he sifts the poem for the history and discards the contemporary or anachronistic accretions. For a historian this may be legitimate method, but it has also been applied by a professor of Literature. This same strategy is even more fully worked out for the *Iliad* by G. S. Kirk in his essay 'Homer: The Meaning of an Oral Tradition'.[32] He implies (11–12) that the unwarlike tone of the similes and the shield of Achilles are foreign and somehow inessential: 'These intrusions are morally and aesthetically permissible; they do not break the heroic mood that must predominate before Troy because they are formally enclosed in similes or in a digression about armour.' But he is well

[31] *Op.* 14–15; see M. L. West's n. (*Hesiod: Works and Days* (Oxford, 1978)) on 15.
[32] (n. 11), 1 ff. (1st publ. 1972); cf. also pp. 50–2 (1st publ. 1968).

aware that such attitudes are not only found on the shield and in the similes. On p. 11 he nips through the greatest scenes in the *Iliad*— Hector and Andromache, Achilles' rejection of the embassy, Priam and Achilles ('more unnerving'[33])—and concludes 'what is happening here is that the *subsequent poetical tradition* [K.'s italics] has allowed these occasional flashes of humanity to illuminate the severer architecture of the heroic soul'. The metaphors are rather obscure, but presumably the 'heroic soul' is what the *Iliad* is really about and 'heroic soul' is free from all contaminations of 'humanity'. These authorities, then, see anything that is not really 'heroic' and does not glorify war as 'subsequent' and detachable.

Chronologically speaking these divisions might be right, but as literary criticism they are invalid. Within a work of literature tensions, even contradictions, are inseparable parts of a complex whole. The strategy of Professors Finley and Kirk is in fact left over from the good old days of the multi-layered analysts: in these days of 'the monumental poet' we cannot split Homer into consistent layers so easily. I shall try to maintain that the shield of Achilles is much more than just 'a digression about armour' by looking at other ways in which in the *Iliad* war is set against a larger world view, other elements which confirm and give context to the striking effect created by the shield. It is, I suggest, as though there lay behind the *Iliad* the whole world of peace and ordinary life, but only glimpsed occasionally through gaps or windows in the martial canvas which fills the foreground.

This other world is seen most directly in Troy itself, since the Trojans still have to live in the setting of their former prosperity and joy. Troy as it was, as it might be were it not for the war, is envisaged most clearly in the scenes of Book 6—the palace of Priam, its treasure-chamber, the whole scene between Hector and Andromache. But the peacetime Troy is glimpsed, subliminally almost, throughout the poem in the formulaic epithets: the city is spacious, well built,

---

[33] 'Achilles' temporary compassion for Priam . . . is more unnerving . . . but then Achilles sees his own father in Priam, and in any case he rapidly suppresses the unheroic emotion and threatens a renewal of anger, the proper heroic reaction to an enemy.' This is not the place to explain why I take this to be a fundamental misconstruction of Book 24 and of the whole *Iliad*. It will have to serve for now to observe that what lines 560–70 do is to show what an *effort* of willpower it is for Ach. to overcome the 'proper heroic reaction'; but the whole point is that, unlike Ag. in Book 1, he succeeds. The lines do not mark the end of his compassion but its continuation (see esp. 633–4, 671–2).

with fertile lands; it has fine horses and lovely women. The motif of
the former wealth of Troy and of its royal house runs right
through,[34] and it reaches its fulfilment, like so many of the motifs of
the *Iliad*, in the scene between Achilles and Priam (24. 543–8):

> And you, old sir, we are told that you prospered once . . .
> . . . of all these you were lord once in your wealth and your children.
> But now the Uranian gods have brought me, an affliction upon you,
> for ever there is fighting about your city, and men killed.

We also glimpse the world that the Achaeans and the Trojan allies
have left behind, the world they hope to win back to when the war is
over (cf. the *Odyssey*). Again and again we are given fleeting glances
of wives and families, native rivers, fertile estates, and beautiful
treasures. They have left these to go to war, and many shall never
return. These lost delights are evoked above all to emphasize the
pathos of slaughter. Such passages are discussed in an essay of great
insight by Jasper Griffin (see n. 19):

> But in the *Iliad* the lesser heroes are shown in all the pathos of their death,
> the change from the brightness of life to a dark and meaningless existence,
> the grief of their friends and families; but the style preserves the poem from
> sentimentality on the one hand and sadism on the other. Stripped of the sort
> of passages here discussed, it would lose not merely an ornament, but a vital
> part of its nature. (p. 186)

Third, there are the similes. Many are drawn, of course, from the
world of peace, of rural life, from the everyday life of ordinary people,
the audience. What has to be further appreciated is that some of the
simile-pictures derive their power from an actual *contrast* with the
world of war which they are compared to.[35] What this contrast does
is to oblige the audience to reconsider the context through the
comparison, to look at it again in the light of the difference as well as
the similarity. I hope to make the point simply by four illustrations.
The tranquillity of the snowscape at 12. 278–86, spanning from
mountain-top across the lowlands and out to sea, muffling all
disturbance, throws us back with all the more shock into the din

---

[34] See notably 2. 796–7; 18. 288 ff.; 9. 403, τὸ πρὶν ἐπ' εἰρήνης, πρὶν ἐλθεῖν
υἷας Ἀχαιῶν = 22. 156 (see above).

[35] Only some similes, not all. I consider it a great mistake to try to isolate a single
function for all Homeric similes: on the contrary Hom. seems to expect his audience to
be alert to a wide variety. Far from providing relaxation the similes are especially
taxing because of the very unpredictability of the relation of each to its context.

and violence of the Trojan attack on the wall. When the fire of Hephaestus sweeps through the vegetation on the banks of Scamander and even the fish are tortured, it is likened to a breeze that dries a newly irrigated plot and so delights the gardener (21. 346–7). Agamemnon's wound hurts like a woman's labour pains (11. 269–72), and when Gorgythion is killed his head droops like a poppy-head heavy with seed (8. 306–7). Again and again pain and destruction and violent death are compared to fertile agriculture, creative craftsmanship, useful objects and tasks, scenes of peace and innocent delight. I quote the conclusion of a valuable article by D. H. Porter:[36]

> The grimness and bloodiness of the battlefield are inevitably rendered darker and more tragic by the constant brief glimpses we get in the similes of a world where milk flows, flowers and crops grow in the fields, shepherds tend their flocks, and small children play. Conversely, these momentary glimpses of the world of peace are made more idyllic and poignant by the panorama of violence and destruction which surround them.

The similes thus let us—indeed make us—look through the war to the peace that lies behind it, to the peace that the warriors have abandoned and which many of them will never know again. The similes make us see war as wasteful and destructive, the blight of peace and pleasure. And this is, I suggest, what the shield of Achilles does, but on a far larger scale. *It makes us think about war and see it in relation to peace.* Achilles has just made the decision which will lead to Hector's death and then to his own; Hector has just made the decision which will lead to his death and then to the sack of Troy. At this point we are made to contemplate the life that Achilles has renounced and the civilization that Troy will never regain. The two finest things in the *Iliad*—Achilles and Troy—will never again enjoy the existence portrayed on the shield: that is the price of war and of heroic glory. The shield of Achilles brings home the loss, the cost of the events of the *Iliad*.

I trust I do not seem to be maintaining that the *Iliad* is an anti-war epic, a pacifist tract—that would be almost as much of a distortion as the opposite extreme which I am attacking. The *Iliad* does not

[36] See in general Porter's excellent article, 'Violent Juxtaposition in the Similes of the *Iliad*', *CJ* 68 (1972), 11–21 (the quotation is from p. 19); also Redfield (n. 20), 186 ff. On the Ag. simile see also C. Moulton, *Similes in the Homeric Poems* (Göttingen, 1977), 98–9; on Gorgythion, M. Silk, *Interaction in Poetic Imagery* (Cambridge, 1974), 5.

explicitly condemn war nor does it try to sweeten it: indeed its equity
is essential to its greatness. It presents both sides, victory and defeat,
the destroyer and the destroyed; and it does not judge between them.
The gain and the loss are put side by side without prejudice. In terms
of quantity, of course, much more of the poem is taken up with war
and killing, but the glimpses of peace and loss stand out all the more
by contrast, as a simile stands out in a battle-scene, or the shield of
Achilles in the poem as a whole.

The *Iliad* is a poem of war in which valiant heroes win glory in battle
and prove their worth by killing the enemy. The poem is the product of a
tradition of martial epic, songs of the κλέα ἀνδρῶν; and it does not
deny—let alone condemn—the fundamental premiss of its own tradition, that mighty deeds of battle are fit matter for the immortality of
song. Many early Greek epics may have consisted solely of narrative of
the glorious exploits of Greek warriors,[37] but the *Iliad* is much, much
more than that. The poem itself is the primary and incontrovertible
source for what Homer regards as important, and it outweighs any
amount of comparative material from other cultures or of synthesized
versions of the 'Heroic World'. Homer shows what is important by
conferring on it the immortality of song. Consider, after all, what it is
that wins the major characters their immortality in the poem as it is.
Hector may win glory by his victories in battle during the central books,
but he is remembered above all for his scene with Andromache and for
his failure and death in battle defending his fatherland.[38] Achilles is not
immortalized for his massacre of Trojans in Books 20 and 21 so much as
for his impending death before his time, for his rejection of the embassy
in Book 9, and for his treatment of Priam.[39] Certainly some of the lesser
heroes win their place in the poem for their deeds in battle, but there are
others who are immortalized for what they do and say off the field, not
only Thersites, Paris, or Nestor, but Helen, Hecuba, and Priam. In fact,
to cut a long story short, the great figures of the *Iliad* are great not
because of the outstanding slaughter they inflict, but because of the
quality of their suffering and the way that they bear it.

---

[37] It is clear that the construction of battle narratives was highly traditional. This is
one of many important points which receive interesting confirmation in B. Fenik,
Typical Battle Scenes in the Iliad (Wiesbaden, 1968). The tradition was evidently
chauvinistically pro-Greek: on Hom.'s departure from this see the fine essay, "ἀεὶ
φιλέλλην ὁ ποιητής?" in Kakridis (n. 26), 54 ff. (1st publ. in *WS* 69 (1956), 26 ff.).

[38] See the brief but telling remarks by Griffin (n. 19), 186–7.

[39] NB esp. 24. 110, spoken by Zeus to Thetis, αὐτὰρ ἐγὼ τόδε κῦδος Ἀχιλλῆϊ
προτιάπτω (but I put this glory (*kudos*) on Achilles). The *kudos* is to pity Priam and
accept the ransom, thus proving correct Zeus' estimate of him in 24. 157–8 rather
than Apollo's in 24. 39 ff.

The *Iliad* owes its tragic greatness to Homer's ability to appreciate and sympathize with *both* aspects of heroic war. He shows how for every victory there is a defeat, how for every triumphant killing there is another human killed. Glorious deeds are done, mighty prowess displayed: at the same time fine cities are burned, fathers lose their sons, women lose their families and freedom. This is implicit in Achilles' own decision:

> Now I must win excellent glory,
> and drive someone of the women of Troy, or some deep-girdled
> Dardanian woman, lifting up to her soft cheeks both hands
> to wipe away the close bursts of tears in her lamentation,
> and learn that I stayed too long out of the fighting
>
> (18. 121–5)

—and explicit in his words to Priam in Book 24. He does not look after his old father Peleus 'since far from the land of my fathers I sit here in Troy, and bring nothing but sorrow to you and your children' (24. 541–2). Homer gives victory and prowess their due recognition, but he never loses sight of the human cost, of the waste of what might have flourished and brought joy. Human beings protect their dependants and win glory, and thus war is important: human beings also suffer and endure, and war is a great cause of this.

The scope of Homer's sympathy has perhaps never been more deeply expressed than in Simone Weil's essay, *The Iliad, or The Poem of Force*.[40] It was not written for scholars and is not argued in the academic mode: it none the less conveys a fundamental understanding of the *Iliad*. A single quotation will have to serve:

And yet such an accumulation of violences would be cold without that accent of incurable bitterness which continually makes itself felt, although often indicated only by a single word, sometimes only by a play of verse, by a run over line. It is this which makes the *Iliad* a unique poem, this bitterness, issuing from its tenderness, and which extends, as the light of the sun, equally over all men. Never does the tone of the poem cease to be impregnated by this bitterness, nor does it ever descend to the level of a complaint. . . Nothing precious is despised, whether or not destined to perish. The destitution and misery of all men is shown without dissimulation or disdain . . . and whatever is destroyed is regretted.

---

[40] Originally in *Cahiers du sud* 1940–1, and reprinted in *La Source grecque* (Paris, 1952); translated into Eng. as a pamphlet by M. McCarthy (New York, 1945, repr. 1967), and in the collection *Intimations of Christianity among the Ancient Greeks* (London, 1957) by E. C. Geissbuhler.

The person who found this dimension in the *Iliad* was not some complacent pedant, but a young woman who renounced pacifism in 1939 and died in 1943, consumed by regret for man's inhumanity to man.

Simone Weil understood the *Iliad* more fully than W. H. Auden. Auden was disturbed that the great poem of war should include the shield of Achilles, and insisted that art must present war in all its brutal inhumanity without such loopholes. But the *Iliad* is not only a poem of war, it is also a poem of peace. It is a tragic poem, and in it war prevails over peace—but that has been the tragic history of so much of mankind.

The extent of Auden's partiality is brought out by his ragged urchin 'who'd never heard of any world where promises were kept, | or one could weep because another wept'. Let me end by quoting in full the passage which in many ways the whole *Iliad* has been leading up to. Priam has come to the tent of Achilles, and ends his plea for the ransom of Hector:

'Honour then the gods, Achilles, and take pity on me
remembering your father, yet I am still more pitiful;
I have gone through what no other mortal on earth has gone through;
I put my lips to the hands of the man who has killed my children.'
So he spoke, and stirred in the other a passion of grieving
for his own father. He took the old man's hand and pushed him
gently away, and the two remembered, as Priam sat huddled
at the feet of Achilles and wept close for manslaughtering Hector
and Achilles wept now for his own father, now again
for Patroclus. The sound of their mourning moved in the house. Then
when great Achilles had taken full satisfaction in sorrow
and the passion of it had gone from his mind and body, thereafter
he rose from his chair, and took the old man by the hand, and set him
on his feet again, in pity for the grey head and the grey beard,
and spoke to him and addressed him in winged words: 'Ah, unlucky,
surely you have had much evil to endure in your spirit.
How could you dare to come alone to the ships of the Achaeans
and before my eyes, when I am one who have killed in such numbers
such brave sons of yours? The heart in you is iron. Come, then,
and sit down upon this chair, and you and I will even let
our sorrows lie still in the heart for all our grieving. There is not
any advantage to be won from grim lamentation.
Such is the way the gods spun life for unfortunate mortals,
that we live in unhappiness, but the gods themselves have no sorrows.'

(24. 503–26)

12

The Epic Cycle and the
Uniqueness of Homer

JASPER GRIFFIN

Daß die Griechen selbst die anderen homerischen Epen früh ver-
kommen lassen konnten, kann ich ihnen auch heute nicht vergeben.

(Wilamowitz)[1]

Es ist kein qualitativer Unterschied zwischen Ὁμηρικὸν *und*
κυκλικόν.

(Wilamowitz)[2]

The Homeric poems are the subject of such a flood of print that a
definite justification is needed by one who adds to it. Especially perhaps is this so if the Epic Cycle is to be involved; 'enough and too
much has been written about the Epic Cycle', said T. W. Allen in
1908.[3] My argument will be that the Cycle has still not been fully
exploited as a source to show, by comparison and contrast, the
particular character and style of the two great epics, particularly the
Iliad. With the domination of Homeric scholarship in English by
formulaic studies on the one hand and archaeology on the other,
the poems themselves have perhaps been less discussed than might
have been expected, and the uniqueness of the Homeric style and
picture of the world has not been fully brought out. Most treatments
of the Cycle[4] have been concerned to assert or to deny that it

---

I am greatly indebted for advice to Professor Hugh Lloyd-Jones.

[1] *Erinnerungen* (Leipzig, 1928), 58.

[2] *Homerische Untersuchungen* (Berlin, 1884), 375.   [3] *CQ* 2 (1908), 64.

[4] Here cited from vol. v of the OCT of Homer, ed. T. W. Allen (2nd edn., 1912),
sometimes needing to be supplemented by E. Bethe, *Homer: Dichtung und Sage* II. 2
(2nd edn., Leipzig, 1929), a fuller collection and discussion of the fragments.
[The standard editions are now those of A. Bernabé, *Poetarum Epicorum Graecorum*

contained poems or incidents earlier than the surviving epics,[5] a question which will not be raised here. Most recent writers on Homer have more or less ignored the Cycle; even Hermann Fränkel, the first part of whose book *Dichtung und Philosophie des frühen Griechentums* is perhaps the most illuminating single work to have appeared on Homer in the twentieth century,[6] does not discuss it, although it could have been made to support many of his arguments. No inferences are based on it, for example, in Wace and Stubbings, *Companion to Homer*, nor by Sir Maurice Bowra in his posthumous *Homer*. 'My remarks are restricted to the two epics,' says J. B. Hainsworth in his short account;[7] and G. S. Kirk, who does refer to the style of the fragments, does so summarily and without quotation. Yet after all the Cycle was a large body of early Greek heroic poetry, composed at a time not too far removed from that of the great epics,[8] and at least passing as being in the same manner. We have some 120 lines quoted in the original, and a good deal of information about the content of the poems. If it proves possible to draw from this material any clear contrast with the *Iliad*, it may be felt that this will bring out the individuality of the latter even more strikingly than does the epic poetry, currently more often invoked, of the ancient Hittites or the modern Yugoslavs.[9]

It is at once evident that the Cycle contained a number of things to which the *Iliad*, and to a lesser extent the *Odyssey* also, was

Testimonia et Fragmenta (Leipzig, 1987) and M. Davies, *Epicorum Graecorum Fragmenta* (Göttingen, 1988).]

[5] The attempts by Pestalozzi, Schadewaldt, Kullmann, and others to show that various passages in the *Il.* are derived from episodes in the Cyclic poems for which we have evidence seem to me not to have produced a single satisfactory example: see the sceptical discussion by A. Dihle, *Homer-Probleme* (Opladen, 1970), ch. 1. That is not to say that other, earlier, poems on such themes did not influence the *Il.* and the *Od.*

[6] 2nd edn., Munich, 1972, Eng. trans. *Early Greek Poetry and Philosophy* (Oxford, 1975). 'Eine jeweils rechtzeitige Konsultation des fränkelschen Buches würde wohl überhaupt manche Seite gelehrter Literatur ungeschrieben lassen' (Dihle (n. 5), 15 n. 13).

[7] J. B. Hainsworth, *Homer*. G&R New Surveys in the Classics 3 (Oxford, 1969), 3.

[8] It is not really possible to date these lost poems. If, as we are told (Paus. 9. 9. 5), Callinus ascribed the *Thebais* to Homer, that implies a very early date for that poem; A. Severyns, *Le Cycle épique dans l'école d'Aristarque* (Liège, 1928), 313, puts the *Aethiopis* as early as the 8th cent. But forms like Ἰλιακοῖο and αἰδοῖ in the *Cypria* point to a considerably later date; Wilamowitz (n. 2), 367, J. Wackernagel, *Sprachliche Untersuchungen zu Homer* (Göttingen, 1916), 182. Probably A. Lesky (*Geschichte der griechischen Literatur* (3rd edn., Berne, 1971), 104) is right to put the composition of the Cyclic epics in general in the late 7th cent.

[9] Interesting material and reservations on this: F. Dirlmeier, *Das serbokroatische Heldenlied und Homer*, SB Heidelberg 1971. 1.

inhospitable. Some of these are assembled by D. B. Monro in *JHS* 5 (1884), 1 ff.,[10] and by Rzach in his valuable article 'Kyklos' in *RE* XI. 2823-35. The fantastic, the miraculous, and the romantic, all exceeded in the Cycle the austere limits to which the *Iliad* confines them.[11] Under the heading of the fantastic we may list: the fabulous eye-sight of Lynceus (*Cypria* fragment XI), who could survey the whole Peloponnese at one glance and descry Castor and Polydeuces hiding in a hollow tree; the snow-white Cycnus (*Cypria*) and the black Memnon (*Aethiopis*), both slain by Achilles; the valuable daughters of Anius, Oeno, Spermo, and Elais (Wine-girl, Seed-girl, Oil-girl), who could produce at will the commodities of which they were eponymous, and who fed the Achaeans at Troy for nine years (*Cypria* fragment XX); the transformations of Nemesis and Zeus, she fleeing his advances through a chain of metamorphoses, he pursuing in the same manner and possessing her, it seems, in the form of a bird[12] (*Cypria* fragment VII). Closely akin is the notion of certain people or things possessing magical powers, so that Troy could not fall unless the Palladium were removed (*Iliou Persis* fragment I), or Philoctetes and his bow and arrows were brought to Troy (*Ilias Parva*); while the wound of Telephus could be cured only by the weapon which made it (*Cypria*). We observe by contrast that in the *Iliad* there is no hint of any talisman for Troy, not even in connection with Rhesus and his horses in the eccentric Book 10; the entry of Odysseus into Troy reported at *Odyssey* 4. 242 ff. was apparently motivated only by the purely 'natural' motive of killing and plundering the enemy.

The *Iliad* is notably more cautious with the fantastic. Aristotle[13] pointed out that Homer puts many things into the mouths of his characters, when he himself does not wish to vouch for their truth, most notably in the stories told by Odysseus in the *Odyssey* and Glaucus' reminiscences of Bellerophon in *Iliad* 6. Such exotic types as Amazons and Ethiops are in Homer kept to transient and distant

[10] It is a pity that Monro rather played down this aspect of the matter in his Appendix on 'Homer and the Cyclic Poets' in his edn. of the *Od.*, vol. II (Oxford, 1901), 340-84; pp. 352-3 contain a little on it.

[11] V. Magnien, 'La Discrétion homérique', *REG* 37 (1924), 141-63, e.g. p. 142: 'Il a évité de décrire les êtres trop différents de . . . cette humanité idéale qu'est la divinité.'

[12] A goose, not a swan, according to W. Luppe, *Philologus* 118 (1974), 193 ff.

[13] Fragment 163 Rose [= 387 Gigon] = schol. T in *Il.* 19. 108; see also schol. T in *Il.* 20. 234. Another application of the distinction: what the poet says himself must be self-consistent, but what his characters are made to say need not (Eustath. 640. 50; Porphyry, *Quaest. ad Hom. Il.* p. 99. 22 ff. Schrader).

allusions,[14] in contrast with the *Aethiopis*, central characters in which were Memnon the Ethiop and Penthesilea the Amazon. It has been shown[15] that behind the *Iliad* and known to it is the story that the armour of Achilles was impenetrable (the original reason why it must be knocked off Patroclus in *Iliad* 16 by Apollo before he can be killed); but the *Iliad* has suppressed this, which would place the wearer of the armour in a position incompatible with the serious concern of the poem with death. The *Iliad* prefers to say, with pregnant irony, only that it is 'not easy' for mortal men to break the works of gods, 20. 265. An un-killable warrior in the *Iliad* is an absurdity, and the uniqueness of the armour is its beauty alone. Invulnerability, too, is un-Homeric; but it seems that Ajax was invulnerable in the *Aethiopis*.[16] Other sources ascribed invulnerability also to Achilles,[17] and also such swiftness at running that he could catch deer (Pindar *Nem.* 3. 51), while his leap ashore from his ship at Troy was so mighty that it produced a fountain (Antimachus fragment 84 Wyss), but in the *Iliad* we have only the formulaic expression πόδας ὠκὺς Ἀχιλλεύς (swift-footed Achilles), and when he pursues Hector in Book 22 no miraculous speed allows him to catch him up. Superhuman fleetness of foot, like the superhuman vision of Lynceus, is not allowed in the Homeric vision of the world.[18] Like the story that in childhood Achilles was fed on the raw entrails of wild beasts,[19] these bizarre features are not tolerated in Homer, where real humanity is insisted upon for all characters, and as far as possible the tutorship of Achilles by Chiron the centaur is suppressed in favour of the man Phoenix. It is of interest here that in the Argonaut story, which as we know from *Odyssey* 12. 69–72 was very early the subject of epic (Ἀργὼ πᾶσι μέλουσα (The Argo, which interests everyone), with Hera as Jason's helping deity), such special endowments were characteristic: Lynceus' eye-sight, the two Boreads

---

[14] Amazons: *Il.* 3. 189 (a reminiscence of Priam), 6. 196 (family history of Glaucus). Ethiops: *Il.* 1. 423, 23. 206 (gods go off to see them); *Od.* 4. 84 (a reminiscence of Menelaus).

[15] P. J. Kakridis, 'Achilles' Rüstung', *Hermes* 89 (1961), 288–97.

[16] See Severyns (n. 8), 328.

[17] Discussed judiciously by E. Drerup, *Das Homerproblem in der Gegenwart* (Würzburg, 1921), 231 n. 3, who thinks the motif pre-Homeric.

[18] On *Il.* 20. 226 ff. see below, at n. 24.

[19] D. S. Robertson, 'The Food of Achilles', *CR* 54 (1940), 177–80. The transformation by Homer of the wholly superhuman heroes of older belief is eloquently described by P. Von der Mühll, *Der große Aias* (Basle, 1930), 40 ff. As he puts it, 'Heroen sind die Helden Homers in einem neuen, menschlicheren Sinn.'

who could fly, Orpheus with supernatural music, etc.; the ship, too, could talk.[20] This confirms that it was the *Iliad* which was exceptional in this respect.

The episode of Anius' daughters combines the fantastic with a pedantic desire to work out problems implicit in the *Iliad*. It answers the question how the Achaeans solved the problem of supplies in a ten-year siege, as fragments XVIII and XIX of the *Cypria* attempt to explain how Chryseis was captured by the Achaeans when her city of Chryse was not (she was on a visit to Thebe at the time). Revealingly, Thucydides tried to answer the same question. His solution is rational (I. II): difficulty of supplies made the Achaeans take a small force to Troy, and even of that force part was always away foraging for food—and so the war lasted ten years. The solution of the *Cypria* is magical, in a way alien to Homer, for whom of course the problem of commissariat is not interesting, except for the good wine which Jason's son sent them from Lesbos, 7. 467.

The transformations of Nemesis no doubt derive from the better-known story of the transformations of Thetis,[21] to whom as a sea-nymph this mutability was more appropriate (cf. Proteus in Menelaus' story in *Odyssey* 4). The question of Thetis' relationship with Peleus was an ancient difficulty,[22] for although the *Iliad* ignores the story that Peleus wrestled with her, held her fast through her metamorphoses, and so won her, but that as soon as she could she escaped back into the sea, yet she says (18. 434) that she was reluctant to marry a man, and when Achilles calls her, it is from the sea that she comes; while Peleus apparently lives alone. The natural inference is that the poet of the *Iliad* is familiar with the story but has suppressed it[23]—preferring unexplained mystery to the monstrousness of

---

[20] R. Carpenter, *Folk Tale, Fiction, and Saga in the Homeric Epics* (Berkeley, 1946), 143–4; R. Roux, *Le Problème des Argonautes* (Paris, 1949), esp. ch. 4, 'Les Figures Argonautiques'. Among the Argonauts both Iphiclus and Euphemus were gifted with fabulous speed at running.

[21] So Lesky in *RE* XIX. 298, s.v. 'Peleus'. On the mythical pattern of shape-changers and their defeat, see now M. Detienne and J.-P. Vernant, *Les Ruses de l'intelligence* (Paris, 1974), esp. 107ff. [Eng. trans. *Cunning Intelligence in Greek Literature and Society* (Hassocks, 1978)].

[22] e.g. schol. bT in *Il.* I. 396: ἄξιον δὲ καὶ τοῦτο παρασήμηνασθαι, ὅτι καθ' Ὅμηρον οὐ νεογνὸν κατέλιπεν Ἀχιλλέα ἡ Θέτις (It is also worth mentioning in passing that according to Homer Thetis did not leave Achilles behind as an infant); schol. on 18. 434, καὶ ἔτλην ἀνέρος εὐνὴν | πολλὰ μάλ' οὐκ ἐθέλουσα (and much against my will I endured the bed of a man). Aristarchus denied that Homer knew this story, invented by οἱ νεώτεροι (later poets).   [23] So Lesky (n. 21).

metamorphosis and the ascription to Thetis of an un-human Nixie character. It is thus all the more striking that in the *Cypria* the motif was fully developed in connection with an amour of Zeus. This allows another contrast with the *Iliad*: when Zeus tells Hera of the ladies who have aroused his passion, 14. 315 ff., there is no suggestion that he came to Europa as a bull, or to Danae in a shower of gold. Periclymenus, Nestor's brother, was a shape-changer (Hesiod fragment 33 M–W), but there is no hint of that when the *Odyssey* names him, 11. 286, nor when Nestor tells how his brothers were slain by Heracles, *Iliad* 11. 692. The cyclic *Titanomachia*, fragment VIII, told the story of Cronos possessing Philyra in stallion-form and so begetting Chiron the centaur, but when the *Iliad* speaks of the fabulous horse Arion we hear only that he 'was of divine birth' (ἐκ θεόφιν γένος ἦεν, 23. 347), not that he was begotten by Poseidon in the form of a stallion. The passage in Book 20 which tells of Boreas impregnating the mares of Erichthonius ἵππῳ ἐεισάμενος (in the form of a stallion) is in all probability a late Attic interpolation, and in any case is much less striking of a wind than of a great god.[24]

That this love of the fantastic was not restricted to the Trojan epics only is clear from the fact that *Epigonoi* fragment II dealt with the uncatchable Teumesian fox. When pursued by the hound of Cephalus, which nothing could escape, it produced a logical puzzle resolved only when Zeus turned both animals to stone. Uncatchable foxes and inescapable hounds are of course as alien to Homer as impenetrable armour or invulnerable flesh.

The Cycle also admits miracles of a sort which Homer does not,[25] in relation to the most basic conditions of human life. In the *Nostoi* fragment VI Medea magically rejuvenated old Aeson:

αὐτίκα δ᾽ Αἴσονα θῆκε φίλον κόρον ἡβώοντα
γῆρας ἀποξύσασα ἰδυίῃσι πραπίδεσσι.

---

[24] Winds in the form of horses: Call. fr. 110. 54 Pf.; H. Lloyd-Jones in *CQ* 7 (1957), 24 [= *Academic Papers: Greek, Epic, Lyric, and Tragedy* (Oxford, 1990), 383–5]. Erichthonius in *Il.* 20 an Attic interpolation: so A. Fick, *Die homerische Ilias* (Göttingen, 1886); W. Leaf, *The Iliad* II (London, 1888), ad loc.; E. Heitsch, *Aphrodite-hymnus, Aeneas und Homer* (Hypomnemata 15, Göttingen, 1965), 124–35. The counter-argument of H. Erbse, *RM* 110 (1967), 24, that Erichthonius may have entered Attica from this passage, seems unlikely for many reasons, not least his importance in the ancient initiation-festival of the Arrephoria; cf. W. Burkert in *Hermes* 94 (1966), 1–25. *Il.* 16. 150 is rather different; see Leaf ad loc.

[25] Fränkel (n. 6), 71–2 (Eng. trans.).

Straightaway she made Aeson a dear and vigorous youth
stripping off old age by her cunning wits.

These execrable lines (what is the significance of φίλον κόρον?)
derive from *Iliad* 9. 445, where Phoenix says to Achilles, 'I should
not leave you, φίλον τέκος' ('dear child', the source, I suppose, of
the un-Homeric φίλον κόρον)

> οὐδ' εἴ κέν μοι ὑποσταίη θεὸς αὐτὸς
> γῆρας ἀποξύσας θήσειν νέον ἡβώοντα.

not even if the god himself were to promise
to strip off my old age and make me a vigorous young man.

In the *Iliad* of course this is an impossible condition, just as it is when
Nestor says, as he so often does say, εἴθ' ὡς ἡβώοιμι ... (would that I
were as young as when ...). The *Odyssey* is a little less unrelenting:
old Laertes prays to Athena and is granted one powerful cast of his
spear, 24. 520, the goddess breathing power into him. So in the
Odyssey we find a remarkable but not unthinkable event (exaggerated into a miracle for Iolaus by Euripides, *Heraclidae* 843 ff.), but
in the Cycle a piece of magic.

Even more, in the accommodating world of the Cycle death itself
can be evaded. In the *Iliad* no rule is more ineluctable than that
expounded by Patroclus' ghost, 23. 69 ff.: the dead do not return.
Even Heracles could not evade death: *Iliad* 18. 117 οὐδὲ γὰρ
οὐδὲ βίη Ἡρακλῆος φύγε κῆρα, | ὅς περ φίλτατος ἔσκε Διὶ
Κρονίωνι ἄνακτι (for not even mighty Heracles escaped death, even
though he was most dear to Lord Zeus, son of Cronus). Hector the
favourite of Zeus and Sarpedon his son must die; they can receive no
more than the honours of burial. Achilles himself is under the
shadow of death, and that fact is vital for the *Iliad*, especially its latter
books. Schadewaldt points out that it is essential for the conversation between Achilles and Priam in Book 24,[26] which without that
background would produce an entirely different and far less tragic
effect; also the conduct of Achilles in a scene like that with Lycaon in
21 would be unbearable were it not that he must himself soon die,
and that he knows it. Even in the less austere *Odyssey*, where by his
own account Menelaus is exempted from death 'because he has
Helen and is son-in-law of Zeus', 4. 561, Achilles is really dead, and

---

[26] W. Schadewaldt, *Von Homers Welt und Werk* (4th edn., Stuttgart, 1965), 261.

bitterly does he deplore his lot, 11. 488 ff. But in the Cycle these things were managed more sympathetically. Unlike Sarpedon and Hector, Memnon in the *Aethiopis* was given immortality by Zeus after being killed by Achilles, and Achilles himself was taken by his mother to the White Island.[27] Again: in the *Iliad* the Dioscuri are dead and buried, 3. 243, which allows the poet an unmatched moment of pathos;[28] but in the *Cypria* Zeus gave them 'immortality on alternate days' (p. 103. 16). In the same poem, Iphigenia was taken to the Taurian land and made immortal by Artemis (p. 104. 19). In the *Telegony*, when Odysseus' son Telegonus has unwittingly killed his father, he is married to Penelope and Telemachus to Circe, who made them all immortal (p. 109. 26), a resolution rightly called by Severyns 'ce dénouement à la fois romanesque et ridicule'.[29] Even in the sombre *Thebaid* Athena was in the act of bringing immortality to the wounded Tydeus when his conduct made her change her mind.[30] The significance of this difference is great. For the *Iliad*, human life is defined by the double inevitability of age and death; for the gods, men's opposite, immortality and eternal youth are inseparable.[31] Men must die: in youth they must fight, and if they are not slain they live on only to be old and helpless. The gods remain forever young—αὐτοὶ δέ τ᾽ ἀκηδέες εἰσίν (they themselves are without care) says Achilles of them without bitterness, 24. 526. This is what makes the *Iliad* both true and tragic, and the very different procedure of the Cycle indicates profoundly different attitudes to the fundamental nature of human life and death, and consequently to human heroism and the relation of men to the gods.

The attitude towards women and children is also different. Homer is sparing in ascribing offspring to his characters, and also has no penchant for romantic scenes between men and women. For Homer, Helen has only one child, her daughter Hermione by Menelaus; she

[27] Bethe (n. 4), 248, denies that the translation of Achilles comes from the *Aethiopis*. His grounds are insufficient: could the poem have allowed Eos to get for her son what Thetis could not get for her incomparable Achilles?

[28] See A. Parry in *YCS* 20 (1966), 197 ff. It comes as a shock to find that the scholiasts thought the passage 'added nothing to the poetry', schol. b in 3. 236.

[29] A. Severyns, *Recherches sur la Chrestomathie de Proclos* (Paris, 1938), 11. 90.

[30] Schol. Gen. in *Il.* 5. 126: ἡ ἱστορία παρὰ τοῖς κυκλικοῖς (the story is found in the Cyclic poets). Not in Allen; cf. E. Bethe, *Thebanische Heldenlieder* (Leipzig, 1891), 76, Severyns (n. 8), 219.

[31] The word *agērōs* (ageless) occurs nine times in the epics and four times in the *Hymns*, always with the word *athanatos* (immortal). On Homer and death see now Griffin, *CQ* 26 (1976), 186.

has no children by Paris (*Odyssey* 4. 12–14).

Ἑλένη δὲ θεοὶ γόνον οὐκέτ᾽ ἔφαινον
ἐπεὶ δὴ τὸ πρῶτον ἐγείνατο παῖδ᾽ ἐρατεινήν,
Ἑρμιόνην, ἣ εἶδος ἔχε χρυσῆς Ἀφροδίτης.

The gods granted Helen no more offspring
once she had borne a lovely daughter,
Hermione, who had the beauty of golden Aphrodite.

But the *Cypria*, fragment IX, gave her a son by Paris, Aganus by name, as well as a son Pleisthenes by Menelaus: οἱ νεώτεροι (later poets) gave her other sons by both husbands.[32] In the same way the *Telegony* gave Odysseus a son, Telegonus, by Calypso, and a second son by Penelope, Arcesilaus (the poem had a strong Cyrenean colouring), and a son Polypoetes by Callidice the Thesprotian princess. We recall that the Hesiodic poems made him by Circe father of Agrius and Latinus, and by Calypso of Nausinous and Nausithous (*Theogony* 1011 ff.). The hint at *Odyssey* 3. 404 led 'Hesiod' to give Telemachus a son by Nestor's daughter Polycaste (fragment 221 M–W); Hellanicus, *FGH* 4 F 156, wrote of a union between Telemachus and Nausicae, which Jacoby ad loc. thinks must already have been in the *Nostoi*.

The difference is again not trivial. In the *Iliad* the relationship of Paris and Helen is contrasted with that of Hector and Andromache: the wrong and the right way for husband and wife to live together.[33] The virtue of Hector and the devotion of Andromache contrast with Paris' frivolity and Helen's contempt; especially *Iliad* 3. 428 ff., 6. 349 ff., and the final scene of Book 6. It is part of such a conception that Andromache should have a child and Helen should not. The union of Helen and Paris is not a real marriage, and the presence of a child would destroy its clearly depicted atmosphere of hedonism and guilt. We have only to imagine the impact of the presence of a baby on the scene at the end of *Iliad* 3, and of the absence of Astyanax from the end of Book 6. All this is thrown away by the Cycle in its indiscriminate passion for elaboration, just as the contrast between Helen's rightful husband Menelaus and her adultery with Paris, so

[32] For names see schol. A in *Il.* 3. 175 as well as *Cypria* fr. IX, and *RE* VII. 2830. 48 ff., s.v. 'Helene' (Pfuhl).

[33] e.g. schol. in *Il.* 6. 492: ἔστι δὲ ἤδη σκοπεῖν διάφορα Ἀλεξάνδρου καὶ Ἕκτορος, κτλ. (It is possible to observe the different characters of Alexandros and Hector ... ').

clear in the *Iliad*, is blurred when the *Ilias Parva* makes her marry
Deiphobus after Paris' death. As for Odysseus, the *Odyssey* makes
effective use of the evil fortune by which in each generation of his
house only one son was born, 16. 117 ff.: Telemachus, like Odysseus,
is alone in the world. The Cyclic conception of a world liberally
populated by half-brothers is as different as it is inferior. Again all the
outlines are blurred, and the contrast between Odysseus' dreamlike
liaisons with distant goddesses and his real *gamos* (marriage) with
Penelope is lost. And the cynical misconduct of Odysseus in the
Telegony, in marrying a Thesprotian princess when there is apparently nothing to stop him going home to Penelope, brings out by
contrast the sacrifice and renunciation which he made for her sake in
the *Odyssey*.

The surplus children have brought us already to the proliferation
of intrigues and episodes of romance. Homer's treatment of Nausicae,
touching and perfect in its inconclusiveness, must be developed into
a regular love-affair; so must an incidental reference to Telemachus
being bathed by Nestor's daughter. Far more was it inevitable that
Achilles, the most glamorous of heroes, should be given a sex-life
richer than the Homeric poems allow him. In the *Iliad* Achilles is
always an isolated figure.[34] The only woman important to him is his
goddess mother, and as for poor Briseis, who had hoped he would
marry her (19. 297), he can say only that it would have been better if
she had died before she occasioned his quarrel with Agamemnon
(19. 59). Although he claims to 'love' her (9. 342), it is clear that he is
anything but romantic about her; she is a possession among others
(9. 664), and at the end of the poem his mother is recommending
intercourse with a 'woman' to cheer him up (24. 130). He has a son,
Neoptolemus, who is being brought up on Scyros, 'if he is still alive'
(19. 327).[35] The mother is not named, and in view of 9. 668, where
we learn that Achilles captured steep Scyros and took women from it
as booty, it seems that she is to be thought of, if thought of at all, as a
captive. The scholiasts indeed reject with indignation the tale of
Achilles hidden there among women, and insist that for Homer he

---

[34] He is eloquently contrasted with Siegfried in this respect by E. Rohde, *Der
griechische Roman* (4th edn., Wiesbaden, 1914), 4.
[35] This line and the attitude it implies shocked the Alexandrians: schol. A ad loc.,
καὶ ταῦτα μηδὲ πόρρω τῆς Σκύρου κειμένης (and this even though Scyros is
not far away). As usual they resorted to deletion.

went to Scyros as a hero, to conquer.[36] Naturally this did not satisfy
the romantic creators of the Cycle, and in the *Cypria* (fragment 13. 2
in Bethe: not in Allen: from the Scholia Didymi, regrettably not
included by Erbse in his edition of the Scholia on the *Iliad*), Achilles
ἐν ταῖς παρθένοις συνδιατρίβων ἔφθειρε Δηιδάμειαν τὴν
Λυκομήδους, ἥτις ἐξ αὐτοῦ ἐγέννησε Πύρρον (while spending
time among the maidens seduced Deidameia, daughter of Lycomedes,
who bore Pyrrhus by him). That is, the *Cypria* told the story not as a
'heroic' one of conquest but as a romantic intrigue.

Then Iphigenia had to be fetched to Aulis for sacrifice, 'on the
pretext of a marriage with Achilles' (*Cypria*, p. 104. 17). Homer of
course is altogether silent about Iphigenia, the great epics relishing
neither human sacrifice[37] nor killing within the family, whence the
silence in the *Odyssey* about the way in which Clytemnestra died.[38]
A link between Achilles and Helen was naturally too tempting not to
be forged. Hesiod, fragment 204. 87 ff. M–W, explains that she would
have married him in the first place, had he not been too young, while
late sources make them live together after death on the White
Island, cf. *RE* VII, s.v. 'Helene', 2828. 14 ff; the *Cypria* went on

---

[36] Schol. T in 9. 668: the story of his concealment among women is an invention
of the *neōteroi*, ὁ δὲ ποιητὴς ἡρωικῶς πανοπλίαν αὐτὸν ἐνδύσας εἰς τὴν
Σκῦρον ἀπεβίβασεν οὐ παρθένων ἀλλὰ ἀνδρῶν διαπραξόμενον ἔργα
(whereas the poet, dressing him heroically in a panoply, puts him on Scyros to
perform men's deeds, not those of girls). So too Eustath. 1956. 18.

[37] G. Murray, *The Rise of the Greek Epic* (4th edn., New York, 1960), 130–40.

[38] Schol. A in *Il.* 9. 456, ὡς μηδὲ ἄκοντας ἀδικεῖν γονεῖς, διὸ οὐδὲ περὶ τοῦ
φόνου τῆς Κλυταιμήστρας φησίν (so that people should not even against their
will wrong their parents, which is why [the poet] does not mention the murder of
Clytemnestra either); schol. in *Od.* 15. 248 on the matricide of Alcmaeon. It was
surely perverse of Bethe (n. 4: 268) to argue from this silence that in the *Nostoi* she
perhaps committed suicide. The *Od.* even pushes this tendency so far as implicitly
to deny that Oedipus had children by his mother, 11. 271–4: μητέρα τ' Οἰδιπόδαο
ἴδον καλὴν Ἐπικάστην, | ἣ μέγα ἔργον ἔρεξεν ἀιδρείῃσι νόοιο, | γημαμένη
ᾧ υἱεῖ· ὁ δ' ὃν πατέρ' ἐξεναρίξας | γῆμεν· ἄφαρ δ' ἀνάπυστα θεοὶ θέσαν
ἀνθρώποισιν (I saw the mother of Oedipus, fair Epicaste, who did a terrible thing in
the ignorance of her mind, by marrying her own son; he married her after killing his
own father, but forthwith the gods made all known to men). It was pointed out in
antiquity (Paus. 9. 5. 10) that the word ἄφαρ (forthwith) seems to rule out the
production of children. This is the more striking as it has been shown by L. Deubner,
Oedipusprobleme, Abh. Preuss. Ak. Wiss. 1942. 4, 34 ff., that this passage of the *Od.* is
based on the version of the cyclic *Oedipodeia*, in which Oedipus had by her two sons,
Phrastor and Laonytus. Deubner argues that ἄφαρ need not rule out an interval of a
year, time enough for twins to be born, cf. *Od.* 2. 93, 2. 167, and *h. Cer.* 452; I guess
that the poet wished to gloss over the incestuous offspring, and so used a phrase
which suggested that there was none.

(p. 105. 7) to tell how Achilles 'desired to see Helen, and Aphrodite and Thetis brought them together;[39] thereafter Achilles restrained the Achaeans when they rushed to sail home.'[40] Here we have the re-using and transformation of an Iliadic motif. The mutiny of *Iliad* 2 and its suppression by Odysseus has been given a romantic and un-Homeric motivation; the army must stay at Troy because Achilles has seen the beauty of Helen. One sees how akin these later epics are to the romantic novel, and is perhaps irreverently reminded of the Duke of Buckingham in *The Three Musketeers*, making war between France and England because of his love for the French queen.

The next lady in the story is the Amazon Penthesileia. Scholars have disagreed on the question whether in the *Aethiopis* Achilles was represented as loving her, at or after the moment when he slew her; most have agreed with Rohde[41] that in an early epic so perverse a motif is impossible. But it seems clear from Proclus' summary at least that Thersites taunted Achilles with this feeling, and consequently that even if it did not happen in the epic, it was not simply unthinkable—rather as Achilles at *Iliad* 1. 225 calls Agamemnon οἰνοβαρές (drunkard); of course we never in the epic see a hero drunk, but the idea was not therefore one which could not enter a heroic head. Achilles behaved with chivalry towards her corpse and killed Thersites for abusing it.

After Achilles' death Polyxena was sacrificed at his tomb (*Iliou Persis*). Here too the motivation is hard to discern beneath the rank growth of mythological exuberance (cf. the article 'Polyxena' by Wüst in *RE* xxi 1840 ff.).[42] Later sources colour the episode with a sinister eroticism: Achilles claimed in death the woman he had desired in life. Probably this was not developed in the Cyclic poem, but we observe the repeated pattern of Achilles being brought

[39] Bethe (n. 4), 243 'cannot bring himself to accept this romantic story as part of a heroic epic'. It is rather depressing to see how subjectively scholars behave in this matter. Wilamowitz (*Kleine Schriften* iv (Berlin, 1962), 364, and v. 2 (Berlin, 1937), 77) thought Laius' rape of Chrysippus and invention of homosexual love was told in the Theban epics; Deubner (n. 38: 5) denies this on the ground that such a subject is 'einem alten Epos alles andere als angemessen'. As for Achilles and Helen, it is by no means the only romantic story in the Cycle, and doubtless Rzach (*RE* xi. 2391. 4–10) and Severyns (n. 8: 304) are right to accept it.

[40] For Bethe (n. 4), 243 the evidence that Achilles restrained them is of course a 'kaum verständliche Notiz', as on his anti-romantic assumptions it is bound to be.

[41] (n. 34), 110 n. 2 (not quite in agreement with what he said on p. 46: 'eine romantische Sehnsucht'). Bethe emphatically rejects it for the *Aethiopis*.

[42] In his view she was originally 'a valkyrie', 1844. 29.

into connection with the killing of a young woman—Iphigenia, Penthesileia, Polyxena. In the *Iliad* he slew twelve Trojan youths at the pyre of Patroclus, 23. 175,[43] his motive being revenge (σέθεν κταμένοιο χολωθείς (in anger at your killing), 18. 337); this is exceeded and made more exciting by the slaughter of a princess. In the *Iliad* women are not killed, but men are slain and women are enslaved. The Cycle was different. Apart from Achilles and the series of his deadly encounters with women, a famous scene in the *Ilias Parva* (fragment XVII) told how Menelaus drew his sword to kill Helen but was overcome by her beauty and spared her. The scene must have been striking (Rzach calls it 'ein Glanzpunkt des Epos'[44]), and again it has the same character: the perverse attraction of the sword drawn against a beautiful woman, and the romantic resolution of the incident. The *Iliad* never talks of killing Helen but rather of 'avenging her cares and groans' τείσασθαι Ἑλένης ὁρμήματά τε στοναχάς τε,[45] while the *Odyssey* depicts her, once returned to hearth and husband, as dignified and indeed commanding. Her activities in Troy at the time of its fall are left by the *Odyssey* deeply ambiguous,[46] but she is far above explicit criticism, let alone physical chastisement. The conception of the hero in the *Iliad* is both more heroic—the

---

[43] I do not think the phrase κακὰ δὲ φρεσὶ μήδετο ἔργα (he plotted evil deeds in his mind) is intended to express explicit condemnation of this act, a view which goes back to antiquity (schol. AT ad loc.: ὥσπερ ἀγανακτῶν ὁ ποιητής φησι· κακὰ δὲ φρεσὶ μήδετο ἔργα, 'as though distressed, the poet says, "he plotted evil deeds in his mind") and is still popular; for refs. cf. C. P. Segal, *The Theme of the Mutilation of the Corpse in the Iliad* (Leiden, 1971), 13. Contra cf. S. E. Bassett, *TAPA* 64 (1933), 41–65; and such passages as *Il.* 7. 478 (παννύχιος δέ σφιν κακὰ μήδετο μητίετα Ζεύς, 'all night long wise Zeus plotted evil for them'), and *Od.* 8. 273 (Hephaestus plans the net to catch Ares and Aphrodite): βῆ ῥ' ἴμεν ἐς χαλκεῶνα, κακὰ φρεσὶ βυσσοδομεύων (he set off for the smithy, brooding evil in the depth of his soul). In both cases the phrase means 'evil *for the victim*'. The same disagreement over the ἀεικέα ἔργα (unseemly deeds) to which Achilles subjected Hector's corpse, 22. 395; cf. Bassett, p. 44.

[44] (n. 39), 2417. 42. He goes on to call it 'almost romantic', 2419. 46; the 'almost' seems to be a bow to the convention among scholars that nothing really romantic is to be allowed to have appeared in the Cycle.

[45] As the AT scholia on *Il.* 2. 356 rightly say, ὡς αὐτῆς ἀκουσίως παρὰ τοῖς πολεμίοις οὔσης, ἵν' ἀξιοχρέως ἦ βοηθεῖσθαι (implying that her presence among the enemy is involuntary, in order that she should be worthy of rescue).

[46] Well handled by P. Cauer, *NJbb* 3 (1900), 608; more detailed psychological explanations are given by A. Maniet, *AC* 16 (1947), 37–46; R. Schmiel, *TAPA* 103 (1972), 463–72. Against such psychological elaboration of what Homer does not say about his characters, J. T. Kakridis, *Homer Revisited* (Lund, 1971), 14–15, and, on Helen, his paper 'Dichterische Gestalten und wirkliche Menschen bei Homer', in K. Gaiser (ed.), *Das Altertum und jedes neue Gute* (FS Schadewaldt, Stuttgart, 1970), 51–64.

warrior does not war on women—and also no doubt more realistic.
As in the classical period, it would have been felt as a waste to put
perfectly good women to the sword. In the Cycle both heroism and
realism are rejected in favour of an over-heated taste for sadistically
coloured scenes; more striking, even more perverse effects are once
again what is desired.

The *Iliad* is also distinguished by the consistency with which it
excludes low human types and motives.[47] Thersites alone contrasts
starkly with the heroes; like homosexual love, traitors and cowards
are stylized out of existence. Paris is *alkimos* (brave), although at
times he does not exert himself, *Iliad* 6. 521, and when a hero does
not fight the assumption is that the reason will be heroic resentment:
Iliad 6. 326 Paris;[48] *Iliad* 13. 460 Aeneas—as well as Achilles himself
and Meleager in Book 9. By contrast, in the Cycle great heroes would
do anything to avoid military service. Amphiaraus' wife had to be
bribed to make him go to Thebes, Achilles was hidden among
women, and Odysseus pretended to be mad (*Cypria*, p. 103. 25).
Unmasked by the clever Palamedes, Odysseus had his revenge,
murdering him with Diomede's help by drowning him while he was
fishing (*Cypria* fragment XXI). It is hard to imagine a scene more alien
to Homer. Fishing is itself unheroic in Homer, and it was often
pointed out in antiquity that his heroes exist exclusively on roast
beef, evidently because it was the heroic dish *par excellence*,[49] while
fish are eaten by Odysseus' men only when in desperate straits
($\H{\epsilon}\tau\epsilon\iota\rho\epsilon$ $\delta\H{\epsilon}$ $\gamma\alpha\sigma\tau\H{\epsilon}\rho\alpha$ $\lambda\iota\mu\H{o}s$). Nor can a great hero in Homer meet so
inglorious a death as drowning, which both Achilles in the *Iliad*, 21.
281, and Odysseus in the *Odyssey*, 5. 312, call $\lambda\epsilon\upsilon\gamma\H{\alpha}\lambda\epsilon os$ $\theta\H{\alpha}\nu\alpha\tau os$
(a miserable death) and contrast bitterly with a proper heroic death
in action. The end of the Locrian Aias, *Odyssey* 4. 499 ff., is clearly
exceptional, as he is directly slain by a god, and that after he had
succeeded in reaching land; and his is the 'contemptible end of a
boastful hero' (Merry and Riddell ad loc.). But most un-Homeric of all
is the treacherous murder of an ally for selfish reasons. The *Odyssey*
does not even mention the attack by Ajax in his madness on the
Achaean leaders, *Odyssey* 11. 549–50., which was told in the *Ilias*

---

[47] The point is made by K. Reinhardt, *Tradition und Geist* (Göttingen, 1960), 10.

[48] The speculations based on this by E. Heitsch, 'Der Zorn des Paris', in E. Fries
(ed.), *Festschr. J. Klein* (Göttingen, 1967), 216–47, consequently seem to me unreal.

[49] Iliadic diet is discussed at length in Athenaeus 8–11, 25; cf. also e.g. schol. A in
Il. 16. 407, 747.

Parva, but speaks of the contest for the armour of Achilles simply as having cost the life of Ajax. The murder of Palamedes led in the Cycle to his father Nauplius avenging himself on the Greek fleet by luring it on to the rocks (*Nostoi*); this is alien to Homer, who does not mention Palamedes and ascribes the Achaeans' disastrous homecoming to the anger of Athena alone (*Odyssey* 1. 327). Treachery and revenge on one's friends are alike excluded by the noble ethos of the *Iliad*.

It seems highly likely that the Cycle contained another incident of treachery. Hesychius and others, *Ilias Parva* fragment 9. 2 Bethe (not visible in Allen), tell us of the proverbial expression Διομήδειος ἀνάγκη (Diomede's constraint), of which several explanations were current, that ὁ τὴν μικρὰν ᾿Ιλιάδα ⟨γράψας⟩ φησὶν ἐπὶ τῆς τοῦ Παλλαδίου κλοπῆς γενέσθαι (the author of the *Ilias Parva* says that it gets its name from the theft of the Palladium). The story to which this must refer is that as they returned from Troy, having stolen the Palladium on a night expedition, Odysseus tried to kill Diomede who was walking in front of him, but that Diomede seeing the shadow of his drawn sword in the moonlight forced him to go in front, tying his hands and driving him with his sword. Bethe indeed rejects this story as incredible for the Cycle ('unmöglich kann die kleine Ilias so erzählt haben ... ganz und gar unglaublich ... ' p. 255), but he must admit that if we do not accept the story then the connection of the proverb with the poem is inexplicable ('die Hauptsache muß fortgefallen sein', he pleads). The parallel of the treacherous killing of Palamedes perhaps obliges us to accept this story, too, especially when we recall that the epic *Alcmaeonis*, fragment 1, told of the murder of Phocus by his half-brothers Peleus and Telamon.

On the Trojan side, Helenus when captured by the Greeks tells them what they must do to destroy his own city (*Ilias Parva* p. 106. 24).

The absence of individual villains in the *Iliad* (for even the shot of Pandarus at Menelaus in breach of the truce, although it will ensure the fall of Troy as a punishment, is regarded by his enemies as 'glorious for him' (but a grievous blow for them), τῷ μὲν κλεός, ἄμμι δὲ πένθος, *Iliad* 4. 197) is accompanied by the treatment of the Trojan enemy as being in no way monstrous or hateful. Homer ensures that the Achaeans regularly have the best of it,[50] and the

---

[50] M. H. van der Valk, 'Homer's Nationalistic Attitude', *AC* 22 (1953), 5 ff.; Kakridis (n. 46), 54 ff. The question is much canvassed in the ancient commentaries, e.g. schol. bT in *Il*. 8. 78, 274, 487; Eustath. 237. 27, 370. 15.

Trojans have certain characteristic defects, especially recklessness, over-confidence, and frivolity;[51] but only in the *Doloneia* are they cowardly and abject, and that is one of the many ways in which that Book differs from the rest of the *Iliad*.[52] In the Theban epics, by contrast, the Seven seem to have been presented as monsters.[53] The blasphemer Capaneus, blasted by Zeus with the thunder-bolt, and the savage Tydeus, from whom Athena turned away in disgust as he gnawed the skull of his dead enemy[54]—such persons are in the *Iliad* unthinkable, just like the family feuds and disasters of the house of Laius and the story of Amphiaraus, his treacherous wife and his avenging son, all of which bring into the centre of the stage horrors which the Homeric poems keep as far as possible out of sight. The saucy Sthenelus, Capaneus' son, who says 'We are better men than our fathers' and is silenced by Diomede (*Iliad* 4. 405) shows the modest limits within which the *Iliad* confines blasphemy; nor does Zeus in that poem blast men with his bolt, as he blasted Capaneus and as in the *Cypria* he blasted Idas (Bethe, *RE* v. 1115. 10–21, s.v. 'Dioskuren'), but on the contrary he sends it only as a sign and a warning[55]—another way in which the *Iliad* is more urbane and less violent than other early epics.

The heroes of the *Iliad* are not puritans, but they are never shown revelling in the pleasures of the table. Like sex,[56] eating and drinking are expressed with scrupulous decency; heroes eat only roast beef, and the formulae employed emphasize anything rather than actual

---

[51] Paris, Dolon, and Hector are all θρασύδειλοι (rash but cowardly), schol. in *Il.* 3. 19; Trojans are boasters, schol. in *Il.* 17. 186. Cf. W.-H. Friedrich, *Verwundung und Tod in der Ilias* (Göttingen, 1956), 20 ff.

[52] Well brought out by Reinhardt (n. 47), 9. See also F. Klingner, *Hermes* 75 (1940), 346 = *Studien zur griechischen und römischen Literatur* (Zürich, 1964), 17.

[53] See Reinhardt (n. 47), 14–15.

[54] Significantly, both Achilles (*Il.* 22. 346) and Hecuba (*Il.* 24. 212) express the wish to feast on the enemy's flesh, but this cannot actually happen. Cf. also 4. 35.

[55] Pointed out by M. P. Nilsson, *Opuscula Selecta* (Lund, 1951), I. 359. In *Il.* 8, and only in that Book, Zeus goes so far as to cast his warning bolts 'among the Achaeans' or before Diomede's chariot, 8. 76, 133.

[56] Wackernagel (n. 8), 224 ff.; in antiquity, e.g. schol. T in *Il.* 9. 134 (θαυμασίως φύσεως νόμῳ τὴν αἰσχρὰν λέξιν ἐκάλυψε, τὰ τῆς συμπλοκῆς ταπεινὰ καὶ ἀνθρώπινα τιμιωτάταις προσηγορίαις ἐπισκιάζων, 'he has concealed the vulgar expression admirably by means of a law of nature, cloaking the low and human aspects of intercourse in most dignified terms'), and Hes. fr. 208 M–W, where the delicate brevity with which Homer describes Anteia's attempt to seduce Bellerophon is contrasted with the prurient fullness of the Hesiodic account of the attempt by Acastus' wife upon the virtue of Peleus.

ingestion. 'They stretched out their hands to the food which lay ready; and when they had put off their desire for food and drink, then...'[57] The feast is δαὶς ἐίση, 'evenly shared', a moral not a physical quality. Even the most explicit passage, of which Schmid–Stählin[58] observe that its frank praise of the table 'falls somewhat outside the spirit of Homer', puts the emphasis at least as much on listening to a singer as on enjoying the food (*Odyssey* 9. 5–12).

> οὐ γὰρ ἐγώ γέ τί φημι τέλος χαριέστερον εἶναι
> ἢ ὅτ᾽ ἐυφροσύνη μὲν ἔχῃ κατὰ δῆμον ἅπαντα,
> δαιτύμονες δ᾽ ἀνὰ δώματ᾽ ἀκουάζωνται ἀοιδοῦ
> ἥμενοι ἐξειῆς, παρὰ δὲ πλήθωσι τράπεζαι
> σίτου καὶ κρειῶν, μέθυ δ᾽ ἐκ κρατῆρος ἀφύσσων
> οἰνοχόος φορέῃσι καὶ ἐγχείῃ δεπάεσσιν·
> τοῦτό τί μοι κάλλιστον ἐνὶ φρεσὶν εἴδεται εἶναι.

For I say that there is no fulfilment more delightful than when good cheer prevails throughout the community, and the banqueters, sitting in their rows throughout the halls, listen to a bard, and beside them the tables are full of bread and meat, and drawing wine from the mixing-bowl the wine-pourer brings it and pours it in the cups. This seems to my mind to be the finest thing.

Still more is this true of wine; the heroes are careful with it, and we do not see them the worse for drink. Revealingly un-Homeric is the extra line quoted by Dioscurides at *Iliad* 9. 119a, where Agamemnon says:

> 119 ἀλλ᾽ ἐπεὶ ἀασάμην φρεσὶ λευγαλέῃσι πιθήσας,
> 119a ἢ οἴνῳ μεθύων, ἤ μ᾽ ἔβλαψαν θεοὶ αὐτοί,
> 120 ἄψ ἐθέλω ἀρέσαι...

But since I was deluded and trusted my baneful wits, either because I was drunk on wine, or the gods themselves impaired me, I am willing to make amends...

Uncharacteristically, Wilamowitz[59] hesitated and admitted uncertainty whether the verse was Homeric; but in these severe poems

---

[57] It is wrong of C. M. Bowra, *Heroic Poetry* (London, 1952), 198, to call such accounts of feasts 'perfunctory'. See rather Fränkel (n. 6), 28–9 (Eng. trans.).

[58] W. Schmid, O. Stählin, *Geschichte der griechischen Literatur* (Munich, 1929), I. I. 178.

[59] *Die Ilias und Homer* (Berlin, 1916), 66 n. 2. Rightly Van der Valk, *Researches on the Text and Scholia of the Iliad* (Leiden, 1964), II. 486, calls this 'incredible'.

only characters like the Cyclops (*Odyssey* 9) or the centaur Eurytion (*Odyssey* 21. 295) can really be drunk. It is out of keeping with all this for Menelaus to be told, as he was in the *Cypria* fragment XIII, that wine exists to cheer up the gloomy:

οἶνόν τοι Μενέλαε θεοὶ ποιήσαν ἄριστον
θνητοῖς ἀνθρώποισιν ἀποσκεδάσαι μελεδῶνας,

Menelaus, know that the gods made wine the best thing for men to scatter their cares with,

just as the praise given by Hesiod to the Aeacidae, fragment 206 M–W, that they were 'as fond of fighting as of their dinner', πολέμῳ κεχαρηότες ἠύτε δαιτί, presents a greatly coarsened version of the Homeric warrior, ἀκόρητος ἀύτης (insatiable for the shout of battle).[60] Homeric heroes do not revel in their dinner.

These differences, especially those concerning the basic human issues of age and death, are naturally accompanied by differences in the conception of the gods. We have already seen the importance attached to particular images (Palladium), and the occurrence of human sacrifice (Iphigeneia). Another striking example is provided by fragment v of the *Titanomachia*:

μέσσοισιν δ' ὠρχεῖτο πατὴρ ἀνδρῶν τε θεῶν τε.

The father of gods and men danced in their midst.

It is likely[61] that the occasion was the first day of Zeus' rule of the world, after the defeat of the Titans. In the *Iliad* no god dances. In the *Homeric Hymn to Apollo*, 188–206, only the younger gods dance while Zeus delights his mighty heart looking on, but in the *Iliad* 1. 603 with the other gods he listens to the music of Apollo and the song of the Muses. Imagination fails to see the Zeus of the *Iliad* dancing.

We have already mentioned the metamorphoses of Zeus and Nemesis. It can be added that the central importance of a being like Nemesis, a transparent personification, is also un-Homeric; in

In antiquity, when the commentators were looking for a reason why, at *Il.* 14, 75, Agamemnon disgracefully proposed flight, it did not occur to them to mention drink.

[60] On the eccentric passage *Il.* 13. 613 ff., where the Trojans are blamed for this quality, normally a virtue, see B. Fenik, *Typical Battle Scenes in the Iliad* (*Hermes* Einzelschr. 21, Wiesbaden, 1968), 147, and schol. bT in *Il.* 16. 617: a virtue turned into a reproach in the mouth of a taunting enemy.

[61] So W. Kranz in *Studi Castiglioni* I (1960), 481.

the *Iliad* such figures as Eris, Deimos, and Phobos simply underline what is visibly happening on the human level, while Atē and the Litai are expounded at length only in reported speech (9. 502 ff.; 19. 91 ff.). Nemesis appears as a goddess not in Homer but in Hesiod (*Theogony* 223, *Erga* 200). Welcker thought[62] that the un-Homeric conception of Helen as child of Nemesis had a depth of thought behind it, and made Helen's sin 'a breach of law which brought ruin with it', as in the *Agamemnon* of Aeschylus, but I cannot share this flattering view, nor do I find, as he did, an impressive irony in the idea of Nemesis herself trying to evade Zeus. The pun Νέμεσις—νέμεσις (*Cypria* fragment VII) does not add to the impression of seriousness in the passage.

In the Cycle, but not in Homer, homicides need to be purified; in the *Aethiopis* Achilles after killing Thersites had to sail to Lesbos where he sacrificed to Apollo, Artemis, and Leto, and was purified (καθαίρεται) by Odysseus. The ancients[63] were aware that this was un-Homeric; what we have in the *Aethiopis* is presumably the influence of Delphi.[64]

Highly characteristic of the Cycle was the great number of oracles and prophecies it contained. W. Kullmann[65] lists 17 recorded in our sources and rightly infers that such a number must have given the Cycle a strongly deterministic character. Perhaps in accordance with this was the development in the *Cypria* of the Iliadic idea of the 'will of Zeus', Διὸς δ' ἐτελείετο βουλή. The prologue to *Iliad* I uses this phrase in such a way as to apply both to the events of the poem as a whole, and also in particular, if pressed, to the plan which Zeus devises with Thetis. Eustathius well observes, 20. 5, that in the prologue Homer glorifies his own poem by promising that it will contain μυρία καὶ ἡρωικά (countless heroic things), ἐνταῦθα δὲ κορωνίδα τινὰ ἐπιτιθεὶς αὐξήσεως ἐπάγει "Διὸς δ' ἐτελείετο βουλή", ὡς μὴ ἂν τῆς τοῦ Ἀχίλλεως μήνιδος τοιαῦτα δυνησομένης, εἰ μὴ θεία τις ἦν βουλή: 'and then he adds a crowning piece of glorification by adding "and the will of Zeus

[62] F. G. Welcker, *Der epische Cyclus* (2nd edn., Bonn, 1865), II. 159.
[63] Schol. T in *Il.* 11. 690: παρ' Ὁμήρῳ οὐκ οἴδαμεν φονέα καθαιρόμενον ἀλλὰ ἀντιτίνοντα ἢ φυγαδευόμενον (in Homer purification of the homicide is unknown; rather he pays compensation or goes into exile).
[64] e.g. Lesky (n. 8), 104.
[65] W. Kullmann, *Die Quellen der Ilias* (*Hermes* Einzelschr. 14, Wiesbaden, 1960), 221.

was fulfilled", suggesting that the anger of Achilles could not have done all this without some divine will.' But the Cyclic poet felt the need to spell out fully the effective Homeric hint, and so the story was told of Zeus planning to reduce the over-population of the world by means of the Trojan war. The idea is of a distressing thinness and flatness, dissolving the *Iliad*'s imposing opaqueness to an all too perspicuous 'rationality'; the whole story is thus made predetermined, and a sort of unity is imposed upon it, of a rather superficial sort.

My purpose in this enquiry has not been the arid one of disparaging lost poems, but rather to use them to illuminate the great epics we have. The tendency of much recent work on Homer has been to suggest that all epics have much the same qualities, and even that out of a well-organized formulaic technique a poem like the *Iliad* was more or less bound to appear; sometimes it seems that its appearance is envisaged as almost spontaneous. The Cyclic epics show how remote this is from the truth. Beneath a superficial similarity the style was very different, and so were the attitudes and assumptions embodied in the poems. Wilamowitz[66] was right to point out that cyclic material has got into the two epics, but overstated his case when he said that the *Iliad* itself was 'nothing but a κυκλικὸν ποίημα' (Cyclic poem), and that there was no distinction between Homeric and Cyclic. Such a distinction did exist, and was due to the exceptional genius which went into the creation of the two Homeric epics, especially the *Iliad*. The strict, radical, and consistently heroic interpretation of the world presented by the *Iliad* made it quite different from the Cycle, still content with monsters, miracles, metamorphoses, and an un-tragic attitude towards mortality, all seasoned with exoticism and romance, and composed in a flatter, looser, less dramatic style. The contrast helps to bring out the greatness and the uniqueness of that achievement.

[66] (n. 2), 373 ff.

13

Past and Future in the Iliad

WOLFGANG KULLMANN

I

Homer had no such abstract notion of time as appears in the intellectual development of later Greece and modern times. For him the word *chronos* means 'duration', not a specific time or indeed 'time'.[1] Nowhere in the *Iliad* is anything like 'time' the subject of a clause. At best the word 'day' (*ēmar*) may be regarded as the equivalent of our concept 'time'. Instead of 'at the time when' we often find 'on the day when...' ($\mathring{\eta}\mu\alpha\tau\iota\ \tau\hat{\omega}$, $\H{o}\tau\epsilon$...).[2] The 'day' may also on occasion be the subject of a clause and possess a definite affective value: 'the day will come when...' ($\H{\epsilon}\sigma\sigma\epsilon\tau\alpha\iota\ \mathring{\eta}\mu\alpha\rho$, $\H{o}\tau$᾽ $\H{\alpha}\nu$...). Normally, however, past and future events are reported directly, with no allusion to the time of their occurrence other than the verbal form. Naturally the epic knows specific indications of time in days and years.

Yet Homer's general failure to conceptualize the notion of time abstractly does not mean that he lacked awareness for the time-relations of events in his epic.[3] Rather, the following discussions, which do not aim at a linguistic or intellectual solution to the problem of time, are intended to show that the poet was particularly concerned to rescue the present actions he portrays from the isolation that the epic narrative form threatens to impose on them, and to stress the relations between the concrete past and future events beyond the poem and the present events treated within it.

[1] Fundamental for Homer's conception of time in general is H. Fränkel, 'Die Zeitauffassung in der frühgriechischen Literatur', *Wege und Formen frühgriechischen Denkens* (4th edn., Munich, 1960), 17–22.; cf. also M. Treu, *Von Homer zur Lyrik* (Zetemata 12; Munich, 1955), 123–35.   [2] See Fränkel (n. 1), 5–6.
[3] So Fränkel (n. 1), 2–3 seems wrongly to suppose; he takes no notice of the important references to past and future in the speeches.

That past and present play such a great part in the *Iliad* is in a sense due to its dramatic composition, which we must therefore examine next.

II

Dramatic composition is one of the *Iliad*'s most striking features, as has been constantly re-emphasized. Aristotle had declared in its praise that only one or two tragedies could be made out of the *Iliad*—and the *Odyssey*—but plenty out of the *Cypria* and eight (or 'more than eight'[4]) out of the *Little Iliad* (*Poetics* 1459^{b}2–7); he appears to regard the form of the Iliad as to a certain extent anticipating that of tragedy, which he seems to have taken for the high point of poetry. The dramatic character of the *Iliad* is manifested above all in the concentration on a single theme, rooted in the psychological sphere, that holds the whole poem together: the Wrath of Achilles. At first the hero's wrath is directed against Agamemnon, who has robbed him of Briseis, then, when Patroclus, attempting to ward off an Achaean defeat, meets death at Hector's hands, against Hector. Only when Hector has been slain, his corpse insulted and ransomed by Priam, and Achilles has been reunited with Briseis, is that wrath at an end.[5] That a long epic such as the *Iliad* should concentrate on the treatment of a single motif like this stands out amongst all the early Greek epics that we know. A motif that viewed from other epics seems possible only as the subject of an episode becomes in the *Iliad* the theme sustaining the whole poem. As in drama the narrated time is thus extraordinarily compressed. The plot of the *Iliad* gives the impression, for all the episodes that prolong it, that, as with drama, one has before one a particular—artistically self-contained—segment of a larger whole, the whole of the Trojan War. Aristotle saw something of the sort when he recognized Homer's genius precisely in eschewing as his theme the organic unity—achievable as it was in itself—of the Trojan War, in order to discipline his poetry by confinement to a 'part' (*Poetics* 1459^{a}30–7).[6]

---

[4] See the app. crit. ad loc. in R. Kassel's edition (Oxford, 1965).

[5] Cf. W. Schadewaldt, *Von Homers Welt und Werk* (4th edn., Stuttgart, 1965), 181–5, 332–50, esp. 340–9.

[6] On the *Poetics* passage and the related problems see K. Nickau, 'Epeisodion und Episode. Zu einem Begriff der aristotelischen Poetik', *MH* 23 (1966), 155–71.

On bringing the *Iliad* into comparison with the *Odyssey*, the only other early Greek epic still preserved, we observe the difference at once. While the *Iliad* lays the events of a mere few days before our eyes in dramatic concentration, the *Odyssey* narrates a far longer period of time. We hear of the individual stopping-points of Odysseus' wandering; the events of his return, and the slaughter of the suitors. Nevertheless the *Odyssey*—in part owing to the influence of the *Iliad*—is composed using individual dramatic elements. Some of the wanderings are presented in flashback through Odysseus' own narration.[7] Simultaneous but spatially separate actions are related one after the other in segmental fashion with artful changes of scene.[8] Nevertheless the chronological style of narration preponderates, but the episodes do not, as in the *Iliad*, cluster round the segments of a main episode running throughout the poem, even though the *Odyssey* is guaranteed its unity by being directed towards the goal of Odysseus' homecoming.

Even more different in composition from the *Iliad* are the cyclic epics narrating the events preceding or following the action of that poem. Although no more than summaries of these epics' contents and a few fragments have reached us, their overall narrative style is still to some extent recognizable. They relate, without dramatic artifice, a multitude of loosely connected happenings in exact chronological sequence;[9] thus the *Cypria* gives a fully detailed account of events from the origin of the Trojan War to the setting forth of the Trojan Alliance. In the *Nostoi*, which recounted the individual heroes' homecoming, as the *Odyssey* that of Odysseus, simultaneous events were also treated; but this problem clearly lacked dramatic function.[10]

We may surmise that this chronological narrative mode is not a simplification of the dramatic Iliadic mode, but that the latter developed from the former.[11] This is suggested first of all by the inherently greater complexity of dramatic composition,[12] and in

---

[7] On the retrospective technique of the *Od.* cf. B. Hellwig, *Raum und Zeit im homerischen Epos* (Spudasmata 2; Hildesheim, 1964), 49 ff.

[8] On this cf. U. Hölscher, *Untersuchungen zur Form der Odyssee. Szenenwechsel und gleichzeitige Handlungen* (*Hermes* Einzelschriften 6; Berlin, 1939).

[9] On this widespread form of epic cf. C. M. Bowra, *Heroic Poetry* (London, 1952), 359–60.

[10] Cf. Hölscher (n. 8), 76, who rightly emphasizes the difference from the *Od.*

[11] Cf. J. Th. Kakridis, *Homeric Researches* (Lund, 1949), 91–5.

[12] See too Kakridis (n. 11), loc. cit.

particular by the presupposition in the *Iliad*, excerpt that it is, of the chronological framework of the Trojan War. Especial importance, however, attaches to another feature of the *Iliad*: from beneath its surface, so to speak, we catch glimmerings of a chronological structure that covers the whole extent of the Trojan War.[13] Even if we completely disregard the *direct* allusions to *antehomerica* and *posthomerica*, i.e. stories preceding or following the subject of the *Iliad*, there are peculiar parallels to the events of the beginning and end of the war; moreover, the parallels with the former are concentrated in the early books of the *Iliad* and those with the latter mainly in the second half. In a certain sense our *Iliad* thus 'represents' the entire course of the war. Thus, to begin with the most striking case, the listing of the individual contingents of the Achaean army in Book 2 recalls the situation at Aulis. The fact that the enumeration takes place in a catalogue of *ships* makes the supposition unavoidable.

In Book 3 Paris is snatched away by Aphrodite from the duel with Menelaus, which was meant to decide the war and save both sides further fighting, and Helen is obliged to visit the fugitive in her chamber. The parallel with Paris' breach of his guestfriend Menelaus' trust and the abduction of Helen is obvious.[14] But it is not only the two chief moments of the prehistory, the abduction of Helen and Aulis, that have left their reflections in the *Iliad*, but other details too. At the initial landing in Troy, there was no doubt a similar report to that which the goddess Iris, in the guise of Priam's son Polites, gives the Trojans in 2. 786–806 of the Achaean army's approach. The arrangements made in Book 3 for the war to be decided by a duel between Menelaus and Paris correspond to the negotiations between an Achaean embassy and the Trojans before the fighting began. When Helen, in the same book, identifies the Achaean heroes for the Trojan elders in the ninth year of the war, the scene is related to the time when siege was first laid to the city, which would be far more appropriate for such a review. Even Agamemnon's muster of the army in Book 4 summons up associations with the start of the

[13] Cf. A. Heubeck, 'Zur inneren Form der Ilias', *Gymnasium* 65 (1958), 40–7; W. Kullmann, *Die Quellen der Ilias (Troischer Sagenkreis)* (*Hermes* Einzelschriften 14; Wiesbaden, 1960), 227–357 365–8. (with detailed references).

[14] On this relation cf. K. Reinhardt, 'Das Parisurteil' (1938), repr. in id., *Tradition und Geist*, ed. C. Becker (Göttingen, 1960), 30 [now translated in P. V. Jones and G. M. Wright, *Homer: German Scholarship in Translation* (Oxford, 1997), 170–91].

fighting. And just as in the *Iliad* past events are brought back to life, so those at the end of the war are reflected in it. The circumstances of Patroclus' death as related in Book 16 resemble those of Achilles' death so closely that the former appears to be a premonition of the latter.[15] The wretched Priam of Book 24, who has lost his son Hector, corresponds to the wretched Priam at the capture of Troy, who lives to see the ruin of his city and his house. Thus in a certain sense the events of the beginning and the end of the war are symbolically repeated in the *Iliad*.[16] That is to say, the mythical facts are transposed to situations comprehensible only in their light.

These observations naturally raise the question of the time-relation between the cyclical epics and the *Iliad*, since nearly all the events showing through in the latter were treated in the former; the question is all the more urgent for the *Iliad*'s many direct allusions to the myths in them.[17] But even without reference to their chronology it is clear that Homer's epic knowledge extends over the whole Trojan War and was in his view while he composed his own poem. By suggestive echoes of the entire course of the war he confers on the epic of Achilles' wrath the character of an *Iliad*, i.e. as a complete treatment of the Trojan War. The single episode of the wrath is split up into its different segments and interrupted by episodes recalling the beginning and end of the war. Compositionally there is still a glimpse of the episodic ordering of chronological epic.[18] At the same time this poetic technique brings out an inner relationship between the events of the *Iliad* and those of the beginning and end of the war. The power of the past and the future on the Iliadic present is especially prominent. A peculiar background quality is conferred on the

[15] On the multiplicity of associations see Schadewaldt (n. 5), 166–72; see too below, pp. 403–4.

[16] Cf. Kullmann (n. 13), 366–8, with further examples.

[17] Even if we assume that all the cyclic epics were *written down* only after the *Iliad*, it is likely that some or all of them, in whole or in part, merely fix oral epic already known to Homer, even if perhaps in a somewhat different form. To this extent one cannot, in the strict sense, speak of 'post-Homeric' composition; cf. Kullmann (n. 13), 360 ff. On the method and results of 'neo-analysis' in using the cyclic epic to find older motives that influenced the *Il.* see too W. Kullmann, 'Oral Poetry Theory and Neo-analysis in Homeric Research', *GRBS* 25 (1984), 307–23, repr. in id., *Homerische Motive: Beiträge zur Entstehung, Eigenart und Wirkung von Ilias und Odyssee* (Stuttgart, 1992), 140–55, and ibid. 67–99, 100–34.

[18] Since the objective measurement of time in the *Il.* is clearly evident, there is no temporal blending of the beginning and end of the war with the situation of the *Il.*; I cannot agree with Fränkel (n. 1), 3.

individual situations of the *Iliad* by the events they recall and the impending doom they portend. Dramatic composition, confined to the wrath motif with its tight time-limits yet preserving the structure of grand epic, immediately entails the uncovering of relations between the depicted present on the one hand and the past and future on the other. This effect is no mere accidental result of using a particular poetic technique; there is a poetic intention behind it.

However, the poet naturally does not merely suggest a relation of past and future to present in this indirect fashion, but expresses things past and future directly. For this too space is made available by the dramatic concentration on the Wrath. It is hence very striking that past and future are emphasized far more in the epic characters' direct speech than in narrative. The latter, moreover, leaves the epic time-plane more often in the representation of details than in the main questions.[19] For example, Homer's narrative never incorporates too obviously far-reaching decisions by the gods that determine the entire course of events, other than in the opening verses of the *Iliad*, which mention a comprehensive 'plan of Zeus'.[20] Instead past and future are reflected above all in the consciousness of men (and correspondingly of the gods), thus constituting the inner world of the mind,[21] marked by a complicated interlacing of past, present, and future.[22]

III

Our best course is to start from individual characters in the *Iliad*, since each displays a quite different relation to past and future. However, we can give only a selection here, and shall reserve the central characters of Hector and Achilles to the end.[23]

---

[19] See e.g. 6. 12–17, where the poet points to the tragedy of Axylus' death at the hands of Diomedes: he had hospitably assisted so many strangers in his house, but now found none to help him in his turn.

[20] Cf. W. Kullmann, 'Ein vorhomerisches Motiv im Iliasproömium', in *Homerische Motive* (n. 17), 11–35 (cf. ibid. 36–7, 107–8).

[21] On such 'change of direction' in grand narrations cf. E. Lämmert, *Bauformen des Erzählens* (8th edn., Stuttgart, 1991; 1st edn., 1955), 30–1.

[22] Cf. Husserl's analysis of consciousness in terms of retentions, protentions, and presentations; see W. Szilasi, *Einführung in die Phänomenologie Edmund Husserls* (Tübingen, 1959), 83–8.

[23] The Homeric gods must be left to one side; naturally their immortality makes a difference to these questions.

Particular interest attaches to *Helen*.[24] Myth makes her the specific cause of the Trojan War; she has a central place in the plot of the *Cypria*. In the *Iliad* she has no significance for the action, yet astonishingly plays a great part in the poem none the less. She is, so to speak, a symbol of the past and in a sense also of the fatal future. Had the poet been concerned only with representing events spanned by his narrative, he could have dispensed with her; her presence in itself demonstrates that he is concerned to set them in a broader timeframe.

When she appears on the wall of Troy to watch the duel between her former husband Menelaus and her current husband Paris, which is meant to decide the war, the assembled elders have in view her abduction and Paris' breach of trust. In their relatively naïve judgement of these events and their possible consequences, they express the opinion that they cannot be blamed for fighting so long over such a woman. Naturally this respect only partially conceals presentiment of the coming disaster. The elders urge the return of the disastrous Helen. Priam excuses her, speaking ambiguously of the gods' responsibility for the war. Helen herself, ashamed at the sight of the husband she has deserted, and filled with the deepest remorse, declares (*Iliad* 3. 173–5):

ὡς ὄφελεν θάνατός μοι ἁδεῖν κακὸς ὁππότε δεῦρο
υἱέϊ σῷ ἑπόμην, θάλαμον γνωτούς τε λιποῦσα
παῖδά τε τηλυγέτην καὶ ὁμηλικίην ἐρατεινήν.

Would I had chosen grim death when I followed your son here, leaving my bedroom and kindred and my late-born daughter and my delightful agemates.

But she knows her remorse is in vain. She perceives that her past decision cannot be reversed, though she cannot come to terms with the fact (176–7). For all her passionate rebellion against her fate, she feels the inevitability of the path once embarked on so intensely that her marriage to Menelaus, which existed in the past and which she now longs to recover, recedes for her, despite its very close, almost tangible proximity in space, into the furthest distance in time, even to the bounds of unreality: she points out Agamemnon to Priam and

---

[24] On what follows see Reinhardt (n. 14); also W. Kullmann, *Das Wirken der Götter in der Ilias* (Berlin, 1956), 114 n. 1.

says (180)

δαὴρ αὖτ᾽ ἐμός ἔσκε κυνώπιδος, εἴ ποτ᾽ ἔην γε.

and he was my brother-in-law, slut that I am, if indeed he ever was.

The distance in time from her life in Sparta is made even more vivid when Homer portrays her as missing her two brothers Castor and Polydeuces without knowing that they have already died in Sparta. Helen is finally compelled by Aphrodite to visit Paris, after his shameful rescue, in his bedroom. Aphrodite appears to her in the shape of a wool-spinning woman, her intimate from Sparta, who perhaps played a part at the time of Paris' visit. Helen recognizes her and interrogates her. But all is in vain. The attempt to free herself from the curse of past guilt has failed. Not even Helen's rebuke to Paris, an echo of her resistance, can change anything now. It changes at once into a warning against Menelaus, which carries with it an unspoken acknowledgement of present reality. Paris assures Helen he has never loved her so much, not even when they were first together after the flight from Sparta. They go to bed with each other again, and the futility of the attempt to wipe away the consequences of their past deed is now fully revealed. The past, so to speak, has repeated itself once more.

In Book 6, again, when she encounters Hector and Paris, Helen quarrels with her fate without being able to escape it. At first she expresses an even more extreme wish than in Book 3, that she had been snatched away by the wind on the day of her birth, but then makes her peace with her situation with the thought that the gods have decreed these troubles thus. Then she laments that it had to be the cowardly and dishonourable Paris who abducted her, but accepts that this fate too is ineluctable and foretells ill to come for Paris. Thus here too, in a psychological interpretation of the myth, we see how the present torments of the soul are rooted in the past. How monstrously heavy this burden of the past is for Helen also appears at the end of the poem, when she weeps over Hector's corpse; it would have been better if she had perished before Paris abducted her than to have lived in this manner away from her homeland for twenty years, even though she had never heard a bad or hurtful word from Hector. Once again Helen is depicted as a figure who cannot escape the power of past events and is a kind of symbol of the fate that her abduction has hung over Troy. Her position as the last of Hector's mourners indicates that the entire course of events befalling Troy,

Hector's death included, is the inescapable result of the past, of the abduction from Sparta.

If in Helen's case it is above all feelings of remorse, resistance, and finally of resignation to her fate that determine her attitude to past and future and match her part-voluntary, part-involuntary departure from Sparta, *Odysseus* knows how to obtain something positive from the past, without overlooking its power. A clear instance comes in Book 2, where he undertakes to strengthen the army's morale. He sympathizes with discontent after nine years of war, but nevertheless regards a return home as shameful. With a reference to Calchas' prophecy in Aulis he challenges the army to stand fast (301–4):

> εὖ γὰρ δὴ τόδε ἴδμεν ἐνὶ φρεσίν, ἐστὲ δὲ πάντες
> μάρτυροι, οὓς μὴ κῆρες ἔβαν θανάτοιο φέρουσαι·
> χθιζά τε καὶ πρωΐζ, ὅτ’ ἐς Αὐλίδα νῆες Ἀχαιῶν
> ἠγερέθοντο κακὰ Πριάμῳ καὶ Τρωσὶ φέρουσαι.

We all know full well in our hearts, and all of you are witnesses whom the Keres of death have not carried off: *it was yesterday or the day before*, when the ships of the Achaeans were gathered at Aulis bringing ills to Priam and the Trojans.

He then relates the miracle of the sparrows and Calchas' interpretation that the fighting would last ten years.

Odysseus thus, though fully cognizant of objective time (nine years), brings the past so close to the present that for him and his hearers it is like something that happened yesterday or the day before. From this proximity of favourable omens in the past he creates confidence for the future, which must bring prompt victory over the Trojans. We see how differently the past can be experienced. For Helen her marriage to Menelaus becomes infinitely distant, and she can say of Agamemnon: 'that is my former brother-in-law, if he ever was'. An event almost as far back took place for Odysseus 'yesterday or the day before',[25] and whereas in her case the sense of distance led to resignation, in his the sense of proximity leads to optimism. There is a similar picture of him in Book 9, where he wishes to talk Achilles

---

[25] Later parallels for this expression (χθιζά τε καὶ πρωΐζ’) in Treu (n. 1), 128; I cannot share Treu's opinion that χθιζά is not attested with reference to 'length of time and distance from today'. Linguistically the notion is unambiguous; but we must have an eye to the difference between objectively measuring time and subjectively experiencing it.

into returning to the fray by reminding him of his father Peleus'
instructions, and in Book 14, where he opposes Agamemnon's
suggestion of flight (83–9):

Ἀτρεΐδη ποῖόν σε ἔπος φύγεν ἕρκος ὀδόντων·
οὐλόμεν᾽, αἴθ᾽ ὤφελλες ἀεικελίου στρατοῦ ἄλλου
σημαίνειν, μὴ δ᾽ ἄμμιν ἀνασσέμεν, οἷσιν ἄρα Ζεὺς
ἐκ νεότητος ἔδωκε καὶ ἐς γῆρας τολυπεύειν
ἀργαλέους πολέμους, ὄφρα φθιόμεσθα ἕκαστος.
οὕτω δὴ μέμονας Τρώων πόλιν εὐρυάγυιαν
καλλείψειν, ἧς εἵνεκ᾽ ὀϊζύομεν κακὰ πολλά;

Atrides, what a word has escaped your fence of teeth! Wretched man, you
should be commander of some other army of dastards, not lord over us, for
whom Zeus decreed the endurance of laborious wars from youth to old age,
that we may each of us perish. Do you think you will thus abandon the
Trojans' city of broad streets, for which we suffer so many troubles?

In this speech, just as in Helen's, there is a sense that fate must
ineluctably run its course; but the idea has been made positive. A
destiny hangs over the entire generation that fights at Troy, whom
the poet on other occasions calls heroes or demigods, and who are
remote in time from his contemporaries; yet from recognizing this
destiny Odysseus draws the strength to see the war through to the
end. In a most unusual way an entire lifetime is seen as governed by
Zeus' specific plan, which aims at the destruction of mankind, but of
which one should make the best. Odysseus' disposition, like Helen's,
is represented in a manner that fits the facts recorded by tradition of
this hero, the trick of the wooden horse, the accomplishment of the
laborious return.[26]

A few words should be said here about *Nestor*,[27] who, like
Odysseus but even more so, appears in the *Iliad* as a bearer of
warnings. His portrayal is another mark of Homer's concern with
considering the present in the light of past and future. Nestor differs
from Odysseus in having more than the earlier history of the Trojan
War in view. That is not only the case in Book 1, where he refers to
his role as adviser in the battle of the Lapiths and Centaurs in
attempting to mediate between Achilles and Agamemnon, but also
in Book 7, where he relates his victory over the violent Ereuthalion,

---

[26] To be sure Odysseus' cunning has its brutal sides in legend, which are
suppressed in the *Il.* Cf. Kullmann (n. 13), 383, 385.

[27] On Nestor cf. Kullmann (n. 13), 95–7.; K. Reinhardt, *Die Ilias und ihr Dichter*
(Göttingen, 1961), 76–9.; on the motif of 'bygone generations' see Treu (n. 1), 28–35.

and especially in Book 11, where he gives a detailed account of his heroic deeds in the Pylians' war against the Eleans, in particular his battle against the Aktorione/Molione, before he reaches his warning and request to Patroclus to use his influence with Achilles. It is striking that these earlier events, which are reported as *exempla*, have a far more mythical character than the events of the *Iliad* and the Trojan War.[28] But it is not only the mythical character of that age that divides the people of the *Iliad* from it. More importantly, they no longer feel this remote past as relevant to their fate. Hence Nestor, who according to the poet saw three generations, protrudes like a relic from the distant past into the present, and it is highly significant that he perceives his youthful exploits as almost unreal. ὡς ἔον, εἴ ποτ' ἔον γε, 'So I was, if I ever was,' he says at 11. 762. Helen spoke similarly of her marriage to Menelaus, but in Nestor's mouth the words are completely without affect, almost objective. This shows that for Homer time does not extend in linear fashion as a continuum, but is articulated generation by generation in closed segments with their own characters.[29]

Agamemnon has yet another relation to past and future.[30] If Helen and Odysseus—and in a different way Nestor too—were distinguished by their very lively sense of what has been and is to come, Agamemnon is especially remarkable for his great uncertainty. It is already on display in Book 1, when Calchas at Achilles' instigation brings forward the capture of Chryseis as the reason why the Achaean army has been smitten with a plague.

> Μάντι κακῶν, οὐ πώ ποτέ μοι τὸ κρήγυον εἶπας·
> αἰεί τοι τὰ κάκ' ἐστι φίλα φρεσὶ μαντεύεσθαι,
> ἐσθλὸν δ' οὔτε τί πω εἶπας ἔπος οὔτ' ἐτέλεσσας.

Prophet of woe! You have never told me anything to my advantage; you always enjoy prophesying woe, but you have never said or fulfilled a good word yet.

So says Agamemnon at *Iliad* 1. 106–8. One may suspect that he has a highly specific prophecy of Calchas' in mind; at any rate we know from the myth that at Aulis, when the expedition was prevented by contrary winds from sailing to Troy, Calchas called

---

[28] On the representation of the mythical past in the *Il.* cf. Kullmann (n. 24), 94.
[29] On the Trojan War as the fatal time of a particular generation see besides 14. 85–7 also 12. 23.   [30] See also Kullmann (n. 13), 90–3.
[31] Cf. Kullmann (n. 13), 131–2; id. (n. 17), 111.

upon Agamemnon to sacrifice his daughter Iphigenia.[31] It is very
interesting that Agamemnon exaggerates his rebuke. Instead of 'on a
previous occasion too you did not' he says 'never yet' and 'always'.[32]
The single event is stripped of its singularity and generalized. It is
characteristic of Agamemnon that he draws the wrong conclusion
for his conduct, the cause of the entire quarrel with Achilles.

Lack of insight into the inevitability of the past is paralleled by
astonishing misjudgement of the future. Agamemnon's thinking
constantly revolves round the end of the war, but he completely
miscalculates. In Book 2, misled by a deceptive dream from Zeus, he
imagines that he can capture Troy without Achilles; in 9 and 14, by
contrast, he thinks the Trojans have won and is determined to
depart, being hindered only by Nestor's and Odysseus' interventions.
For such false appreciations the Homeric term is *atē*, 'infatuation',
which Agamemnon himself uses in his speech of reconciliation to
Achilles in 19. 86–136,[33] characterizing it in detail through an
aetiological myth.[34]

If we ask what caused the poet to depict Agamemnon in this
manner, we must surely think of the unhappy homecoming that
legend made await him after the war, or even the mutiny of the army
before Troy, which was probably also a feature of the ancient myth.
To the uncertainty of his life in the myth corresponds in the *Iliad* a
character marked by uncertainty and blindness.

On one occasion, nevertheless, Agamemnon does know how the
war will end: in Book 4, when his brother Menelaus has been hit by
Pandarus' treacherous shot, he exclaims (163–9):

> εὖ γὰρ ἐγὼ τόδε οἶδα κατὰ φρένα καὶ κατὰ θυμόν·
> ἔσσεται ἦμαρ ὅτ' ἄν ποτ' ὀλώλῃ Ἴλιος ἱρὴ
> καὶ Πρίαμος καὶ λαὸς ἐϋμμελίω Πριάμοιο,
> Ζεὺς δέ σφι Κρονίδης ὑψίζυγος αἰθέρι ναίων
> αὐτὸς ἐπισσείῃσιν ἐρεμνὴν αἰγίδα πᾶσι
> τῆσδ' ἀπάτης κοτέων· τὰ μὲν ἔσσεται οὐκ ἀτέλεστα.

---

[32] Exaggeration by 'always' occurs elsewhere in the *Il.*: at 1. 541 Hera uses it of
Zeus' stealth, in 3. 60 Paris says to Hector 'your heart is always as hard as an axe'.
Over the dead Patroclus Briseis exclaims. ὥς μοι δέχεται κακὸν ἐκ κακοῦ αἰεί,
'always one misfortune follows another for me' (19. 290). Cf. also the claim of never
having been so much in love made by Paris (3. 442, cf. p. 392) and Zeus (14. 315).

[33] The word is also used in the *Il.* with reference to Paris (for the abduction of
Helen), Achilles, and Patroclus.

[34] See Schadewaldt (n. 5), 339–40; id., *Hellas und Hesperien* (2nd edn., Zurich and
Stuttgart, 1970), I. 27 with n. 21.

For I know full well in my heart and my mind: the day will come when sacred Ilion shall be destroyed, and Priam, and the people of Priam of the good lance. Zeus son of Kronos, he that is seated aloft, who dwelleth in the aether, himself shall shake the shadowy aegis over them all, in wrath at this deceit; it shall not fail of effect.

Troy is destined to destruction: from now on that is certain not only from the abduction of Helen, but also from Pandarus' treachery. That the supreme commander of the Achaeans gives expression to this fact, having already made Paris' breach of trust the occasion for assembling the expedition against Troy, makes the present breach of trust appear to be the consequence of the first.

This combination of blindness as to his own future and occasional visionary foreboding of Troy's coming ills is also found in Hector, to whom we shall now turn; but in his case both attain the level of tragedy.

IV

In *Hector*[35] the part played by past and future in the consciousness of Iliadic characters becomes especially clear. It is very plain that he is not tied to any definite attitude to past and future.[36] He appears sometimes informed, sometimes ignorant; sometimes with knowledge, sometimes without it. His oscillation, as will be shown, is not subject to any straight-line development. But his presentations of past and future surprise modern readers with their intensity.

So far as the future is concerned, in Book 3 Hector believes the war will be decided by the duel between the chief opponents, Menelaus and Paris. In his conversation with his mother in Book 6, he wishes, obviously in response to his brother's disappearance from the duel, that Paris may die, since he regards him as Troy's great misfortune (281–5). When Andromache tries to restrain Hector from fighting outside the walls, pleads with him to take pity on their son, and reminds him of her own dreadful destiny, Hector replies that he entirely shares his wife's worries, but shies from the reproach of cowardice and, being noble, wishes to fight amongst the leaders. His

---

[35] On Hector, cf. especially W. Schadewaldt, *Iliasstudien* (Leipzig, 1938; 3rd edn., Darmstadt, 1966), 103–9; id. (n. 5), 207–33; id., 'Hektor in der Ilias', *WS* 69 (1956), 5–25 (repr. *Hellas und Hesperien* (n. 34), I. 21–38).

[36] Appropriately, he seems to play virtually no part in myth outside the *Il.*

attitude here is not based on repudiation in principle of his wife's position, but stems from an even more radical view of the future, shown by 447–9, which—for sure not without reason—are identical with those the listener has already heard Agamemnon say (4. 163–5): the day will come when sacred Ilion shall be destroyed . . . It is in the same cast of mind that Hector goes on to say that he would rather die than live to see Andromache enslaved. Husband and wife thus both fear catastrophe, but Andromache, who is even more strongly impressed by past events, sees less far into the future than Hector. Her despair is still combined with a last hope for the future, while Hector's decisiveness comes from the certainty of hopelessness, which makes any avoidance seem doomed in advance. His insight, however, lasts only for a moment. Even in respect of Astyanax he expresses more hopeful wishes, in his last words to his wife he leaves the future to fate, *aisa*, and again at the end of the book his conversation with Paris concerns the possibility for a victorious outcome to the war. In his challenge to a duel in Book 7 he regards the situation as undecided; in the course of the ensuing battles, misled by Iris' prophecy in Book 11, he even attains a highly questionable confidence in victory.[37] Not that this confidence is unbounded to begin with. His famous retort to Polydamas' admonition in 12. 243, εἷς οἰωνὸς ἄριστος ἀμύνεσθαι περὶ πάτρης (One omen alone is the best, to fight for one's fatherland), is not to be accounted blasphemy. If fighting for the fatherland is called the best oracle to follow, that means that Polydamas' warning may be correct as to Trojan lives, but must be rejected because it runs counter to the duty of defending the city. One should not pay over-anxious heed to augury, for there are things more important than the life that may be protected by the observation of such omens. Not till Book 13 does his delusion become blatant, when he describes himself as son of Zeus and again refuses, at least in part, to follow Polydamas' warning. However, hardly has the situation turned a little against the Trojans, he is in complete despair again and believes that Troy's end is at hand. In the battle for the ships in Book 15 he is presumptuously jubilant and again entirely intent on victory; he does not change this attitude even in Book 18, when Achilles already appears threateningly in view. Yet in Book 22, in his encounter with Achilles, he once more has the possibility of his imminent death in view.

---

[37] Cf. Reinhardt (n. 27), 179.

His view of the past is also inconsistent. At first he feels Paris'
action as a burden of doom (3. 40–2, 6. 281–5); even after the military
turn-round in Book 13 he immediately alludes to Helen's abduction,
but in the intoxication of victory in Book 15 he suddenly thinks he
can find the Achaeans in the wrong, claiming that they sailed to
Troy *against* the will of the gods, and that the Trojan elders were
wrong to hold him back from the battle against his will (720–5).
Similarly in Book 18, thinking of Troy's better days in the past, he
casts Polydamas' third warning to the winds. Only before the duel
with Achilles does he consider once again whether he can escape
death by making good the Trojans' original wrong, the abduction of
Helen.

Thus Hector's is not a straightforward development as Reinhardt
supposes ('first the man of vision. . .then the blind man').[38] If he
changes his outlook, that is, as the frequency of his fluctuations
shows, not the expression of individual character; rather it is forced
on him by the various situations. This changing way of relating past
and future to the present displays a general human characteristic.
Nevertheless, it is surprising that Hector even in (as it were) everyday
situations should think of the remote beginning and the still distant
end of the war, for instance in the dialogue with Andromache and in
Book 13, where he is affected, more contingently, by a military
situation that has become unfavourable.[39] Iliadic man is obviously
far more inclined than modern man to take the present for the result
of the past and a sign of the future and regard every present event as
belonging to a great complex of destinies whose beginning and end
are decisive.[40]

Similar behaviour may be observed in Hector's wife *Andromache*.
Even in her dialogue with Hector in Book 6 she describes to her
husband how Achilles in her absence killed her father and her seven
brothers in Hypoplakian Thebes; for that reason Hector should
stay in the citadel and not make his son an orphan and his wife
a widow. The experiences of the past lead her to fear woe for the
future.

---

[38] Reinhardt (n. 27), 273.

[39] Cf. too 15. 557–8, where one of the Trojan Melanippoi is admonished to fight by
the alternative 'death of the Achaeans or the fall of Troy'.

[40] Cf. 22. 116, where Hector speaks of the $\nu\epsilon\acute{\iota}\kappa\epsilon o\varsigma\ \dot{\alpha}\rho\chi\acute{\eta}$, 'beginning of strife'. The
concept of *archē*, 'beginning', also appears at 5. 63, where the ships that brought Paris
to the land of the Achaeans, are called *archekakoi*, 'beginners of evil'.

A particularly marked relationship to past and future is shown by her lament for the fallen Hector (22. 477–85):

> Ἕκτορ ἐγὼ δύστηνος· ἰῇ ἄρα γεινόμεθ' αἴσῃ
> ἀμφότεροι, σὺ μὲν ἐν Τροίῃ Πριάμου κατὰ δῶμα,
> αὐτὰρ ἐγὼ Θήβῃσιν ὑπὸ Πλάκῳ ὑληέσσῃ
> ἐν δόμῳ Ἠετίωνος, ὅ μ' ἔτρεφε τυτθὸν ἐοῦσαν
> δύσμορος αἰνόμορον· ὡς μὴ ὤφελλε τεκέσθαι.
> νῦν δὲ . . .
>
> . . . ἐμὲ στυγερῷ ἐνὶ πένθεϊ λείπεις
> χήρην ἐν μεγάροισι· πάϊς δ' ἔτι νήπιος αὕτως,
> ὃν τέκομεν σύ τ' ἐγώ τε δυσάμμοροι . . .

Hector, ill is my fortune: to a single fate, I see, were we both born, you in Troy in Priam's halls, I in Thebes under wooded Plakos in the house of Eetion, who brought me up when I was little, he ill-fated, me fated to woe: would he had never begotten me! As it is . . . you leave me in grievous lamentation, a widow in the palace: and our son is still a mere babe, whom you and I begot together.

She goes on to describe the fate in store for her and her son: even if he survives the war, he must always endure outrages. Hector's friends will only occasionally take pity on him, he will be unwelcome everywhere since his father is no longer alive, having once been the mainstay of Troy. Only after this dismal thought for the future does she turn her mind back to the present, to her husband's corpse and the impossibility of giving him a fitting funeral.

In this way Andromache, with a great impact, at once sets Hector's death in a great complex of destinies. She takes it as a symbol of her own fate ('to a single fate, *aisa*, were we both born') and that of her son. Her thoughts do not dwell on the present at all, but leap to and fro between birth and the extinction of the family. She experiences her husband's death as part of a destiny that incorporated her own fortune all along and now incorporates her son's.

The case is the same with the lament she sings when Priam returns from the Achaean camp with Hector's corpse (24. 725–45). Here too she first declares that he, dying so young, has made her a widow, that their son is still only a baby. She says she does not expect him to reach adulthood; before then the city will have been razed to the ground. Hector, her guardian, who defended the city itself and also protected the women and children who lived in it, is no more. The women will no doubt be carried away on the ships, herself amongst them. Her thoughts wander back to Astyanax, whom she addresses directly although he is not present. Either he will be compelled to follow her into slavery, or one of the Achaeans will throw him from the citadel from rancour and the desire for revenge, because Hector had killed his brother or father or son, for very many Achaeans had died at Hector's hands. Astyanax' father had not been gentle in fearsome fight. But the greatest grief will now be hers; he will nevermore be able to take his leave of her and say a wise word for her to remember.

Obviously Andromache here is even more pessimistic about the future, recalling Hector's fears in his speech in Book 6 and seeing her own and her son's fate against the background of Troy's fall, which in Book 22 she had still regarded as remote. Her speech thus fits squarely into the poetical conception of Book 24, where the same theme has already been heard in Priam's encounter with Achilles. Hector's death becomes, subjectively, a sign that Troy itself will fall, and in its fall her son will be enslaved or killed and she herself will become a slave. Again it is highly significant that Andromache thinks at once of the ultimate consequences, even though the fall of Troy is certainly not to be expected there and then. Neither from a direct statement by the poet nor in myth (if one allows the cyclic epics as evidence) is the fall of Troy linked directly to Hector's death.[41] Nevertheless as a consequence of this death Andromache subjectively experiences in advance what earlier epic must have objectively narrated about the destruction of Troy: the Achaeans will wreak a fearful vengeance, the women will be dragged off to the ships, and a child like Astyanax will either have to accompany them into slavery or be murdered in revenge.[42] The present is put under

[41] To be sure, at 6. 403 the poet explains the Trojans' name for Hector's son, Astyanax, 'Lord of the City', with the words 'for Hector alone was wont to protect Ilion'. But that does not point beyond the *Il*. into the future, as is shown by 22. 506–7, where Andromache takes up these words, slightly altered, even though here she still regards a favourable outcome as possible. In Book 24 the link (not necessarily to be understood as causal) between Hector's death and the fall of Troy is made, in pure subjectivity, by Andromache herself. On Hector as a possible invention of Homer's see e.g. H. Erbse, 'Über die sogenannte Aeneis im 20. Buch der Ilias', *RM* 110 (1967), 23. However, scholars are not agreed on the matter. Reinhardt (n. 27), 365 takes Hector for an ancient legendary figure, claiming that the motif of the 'contrasting brothers' is ancient. But this cannot be proved. It is also possible that Paris' character was blackened in the *Il*. for the stylized contrast with Hector (see Kullmann (n. 13), 43).

[42] It is problematic whether Homer knew Andromache's and her son's fate from earlier epic (cf. Kullmann (n. 13), 187, 353). I do not think it can be proved, although the *Little Iliad* described how Neoptolemus flung Astyanax off the citadel and led off Andromache as a slave (fr. 13 Bethe = 21 Bernabé = 20 Davies): Andromache

intensive questioning for any manifestations of Fate's or the gods'
will, and the conjectural future determines the understanding of the
present. The future is portrayed in such detail (as it was to some
extent in Book 22) that for Andromache it seems almost more real
than the present. The possibility of such a portrayal results once
more from the dramatic composition of the *Iliad*, which creates the
narrative space for facts of the story to be presented in the characters'
consciousness as reminiscences and presentiments.

V

Achilles[43] is distinguished from the other characters of the *Iliad* by
the obviously peculiar relation to past and future conferred on him
by being the son of a goddess. At several places we are surprised by
the inner freedom that he shows in relation to past events and the
future. When in Book 1 he speaks of his coming to Troy as a
volunteer, and in Book 9 he contemplates returning to Phthia and
there entering on his father's inheritance in peace, past and future do
not seem to be weighing him down. In Book 24, too, his dialogue
with Priam shows him contemplating his fate with massive calm. But
Achilles' semi-divine descent, the precondition of his freedom, brings
with it the special problems of his own fate. He must constantly live
in the consciousness imparted to him by Thetis that he is destined to
fame, but also to an early death. Nor does his greater insight into the
future preserve him from a final failure to recognize how this destiny
is realized and with what great suffering it is entwined. He is thus to
the highest degree deluded when he sends Patroclus against the
Trojans in his own armour. This is especially clear at the end of his

envisages his enslavement or killing by the brother, son, or father of someone killed
by Hector, which Neoptolemus is not. However, it should be borne in mind that
Andromache's thoughts arise entirely from her psychological situation, just like those
in Book 24 (which conflict with them), and that she is thinking of a revenge murder.
In the *Little Iliad* Neoptolemus appears not as an avenger, but as brutally continuing
his father's work. The *Il.* thus affords no evidence for an allusion to know myth, such
as we should have if (e.g.) Andromache had said the Achaeans, after killing the
father, would certainly continue their work by killing the son. It is probably the other
way round: the *Little Iliad* tried to attach itself to the *Il.* (so too W. Theiler, 'Ilias und
Odyssee in der Verflechtung ihres Entstehens', *MH* 19 (1962), 24 n. 109).

[43] On Achilles see too Kullmann (n. 13), 108 ff., Reinhardt (n. 27), 29 ff. *et passim*.

closing injunction to Patroclus (16. 97–100):[44]

αἲ γάρ, Ζεῦ τε πάτερ καὶ Ἀθηναίη καὶ Ἄπολλον,
μήτε τις οὖν Τρώων θάνατον φύγοι ὅσσοι ἔασι,
μήτε τις Ἀργείων, νῶϊν δ᾽ ἐκδῦμεν ὄλεθρον,
ὄφρ᾽ οἶοι Τροίης ἱερὰ κρήδεμνα λύωμεν.

Father Zeus and Athene and Apollo, would that neither could any of all the
Trojans escape death, nor any of the Achaeans, but we two could avoid
destruction, that we alone could breach Troy's sacred fortifications.

Achilles' divided feelings, his hatred for Agamemnon and his followers but also his hatred for Troy, blind him to the danger facing
Patroclus and attach themselves to an exceedingly unreal vision of
the future, on whose unreality his forgetting the brevity of his own
life bestows a particularly tragic irony. And in Book 16, as the poet
exceptionally states by way of narrative, Achilles knows nothing of
Patroclus' death.

Thus, even if Achilles often rises above the common measure of
human freedom, in the resolution of his destiny he must experience
the tragedy of mortals all the more strongly. This is manifest in the
great scene of lamentation for Patroclus in Book 18, in which, as was
seen some time ago,[45] both the details described by the poet and
Achilles' own words point forward most strongly to his impending
death. Just as for Andromache and Priam the recovery of Hector in
Book 24 anticipates the fall of Troy, Patroclus' death becomes here
a sign of Achilles' own demise. In his immediate linking of present
experiences with the remote past and the future he resembles the
other heroes. In his speech to Thetis at 79–94 he attempts to
understand the entire complex of destinies to which Patroclus' death
belongs. His loan of his armour to Patroclus and its capture by Hector
stir him to perceive the root of the entire evil, the marriage of the
goddess Thetis to the mortal Peleus, at which the arms were given
Peleus as a gift. He wishes that this marriage (and with it his birth)
had not taken place. As it is, Thetis will not be spared grief for his
death, which is a certainty and which he himself desires so long as he
has not overcome Hector. We see that Achilles does not begin by
foreseeing his death as following *logically* from that of Patroclus,

---

[44] Cf. Reinhardt (n. 27), 76.
[45] Cf. J. Th. Kakridis, Ἡ σκηνὴ τῶν Νηρηίδων εἰς τὸ Σ τῆς Ἰλιάδος,
Ἀθηνᾶ 42 (1930), 66 ff.; id. (n. 11), 65–75; H. Pestalozzi, *Die Achilleis als Quelle der
Ilias* (Erlenbach and Zurich, 1945), *passim*; Schadewaldt (n. 5), 166, 250, *et saepius*.

but associates them spontaneously. Thetis supplements Achilles' thoughts by stating once more that he has only a short time to live and that his destiny is waiting hard on the heels of Hector's. In his answer Achilles again expresses his wish to die, laments his error in not coming to the aid of Patroclus and his other comrades, and thereafter is entirely taken up with thoughts about his own future, which smother those about Patroclus. He wishes to receive death, he says, at such time as the gods shall bring it about, and before then win glory.

In the reconciliation with Agamemnon in Book 19 Achilles likewise goes behind the immediate outbreak of the quarrel to the true cause and wishes it undone: Briseis ought to have been killed on the day he destroyed the city of Lyrnessus; then his wrath would not have caused so many Achaeans to perish at enemy hands. Nothing so much as this constantly repeated wish to erase the past can demonstrate the monstrous burden that the past represents for the people of the *Iliad*.

In his address to the dead Patroclus (19. 315–37) Achilles distances himself even more from the present than he had on learning of his friend's death, and thinks beyond his own death to the uncertain position of his son and his father.

The closing books of the *Iliad* show an Achilles entirely resigned to his expectation of death: when he kills Hector (22. 365–6); in his dream of Patroclus (23. 103–7), which leads him to reflect on existence in Hades; in his prayer to his homeland river of Spercheios (23. 144–51); and finally in his encounter with Priam in Book 24. This last scene has an especial claim on our interest, since here Achilles illustrates the yoking of mankind between past and future with an allegory. In 518–51 he offers Priam consolation for Hector. The gods have determined that wretched mortals shall live in tribulation. Two jars stand in Zeus' palace, one full of bad gifts and one of good, and Zeus distributes either a mixture of gifts, or only bad ones. Thus the gods had given Peleus noble gifts from birth onwards: he was distinguished before all mortals in blessings, wealth, power, and an immortal wife. But even to him a deity had given misfortune, since he has no heir, but only a son who is destined to an early death; for he, Achilles, will not look after Peleus in his old age, sitting far from his homeland in Troy in order to harm Priam and his children. Priam too had once been blessed with wealth and sons, but the gods had decreed that he should suffer from the many battles and killings about the city. Therefore he should not weep for his son: he will undergo another misfortune himself before he can rouse him back to life.

In this speech, one of the high points of the *Iliad*, the constraint by the future characteristic of its world is for once presented in a universal form. The fates of Patroclus and Hector cause Achilles to focus intently on those awaiting Peleus (determined by his own death) and Priam, and on the underlying universal human law of tragic reversal, to which even those called happy are subject. Achilles speaks openly of his own death, and ends by discreetly hinting at the fall of Troy and Priam's death. If one adds Priam's speeches before the ransom and Andromache's at the return of the body, in the last book of the *Iliad* the entire tragic course of the war is reflected in the characters' words. We think of Achilles' death, the capture and sacking of the city, the murder of Priam, the enslavement or slaughter of the women and children, and the rape of Cassandra. However, the distinguishing feature of the poem's close is the human greatness to which Achilles and Priam finally attain, visible in their mutual wonderment (24. 629–32).

Inseparable in the myth from the fate of Troy is the character of *Priam*. Even for the heroes of the *Iliad* his destiny and Troy's are identical. They call Troy 'Priam's city', and the consequences of a particular action are measured by his probable reaction, by whether or not he will rejoice. Like Helen he is a character who confers *chronological depth*, especially in relation to the future. Past events, the abduction of Helen and Paris' breach of trust, he sees more as strokes of fate than as guilt on his son's or his people's part. Conversely he envies Agamemnon his good fortune and his power (3. 182–90). His fear of the future appears a little later (3. 304–9), when he announces his intention of returning to Troy before the decisive duel between Menelaus and Paris, since he cannot bear to watch the encounter, whose outcome is still uncertain. Fear is also expressed in his warning to Hector not to be drawn into fighting Achilles (22. 38–76). This speech is particularly interesting in that the vision of the future depicted solely to deter Hector attains such breadth and independence that in the end Priam himself takes it, and not the present, as the true reality. Bitterly he declares that he and his sons will die and his daughters be ravished, that the women's quarters will be ransacked and the little children slaughtered. His own dogs will tear him to pieces and lap his blood. This vision becomes so overpowering that in comparison with the fate in store for him he calls even that of the younger people fortunate, since their death in battle has nothing degrading or ugly about it; the admonitory intent is forgotten. This whole speech is psychologically comprehensible only by taking into account the extraordinary extent to which the characters of the *Iliad* are future-directed. The poet also knows how to capture the intensity of this relation to the future in an image. In 22. 410–11 he uses a comparison to describe how after Hector's death the sense of doom spread in Priam's entourage: the grief was as if beetling Troy were consumed by fire from the ground up. Even without express mention, this simile sets up an involuntary association with the actual burning of the city in the *Iliupersis* or sack of Troy that Homer undoubtedly knew from myth.[46] Priam is also fully aware of the coming destruction in Book 24 when he girds himself to ransom his son Hector. He wishes only to die before he sees the city ransacked and plundered with his own eyes (244–6). This certainty of forthcoming misfortune and this living in the future contrast with a sense that the past is unreal, so that even though his son's death is recent Priam can use the same expression as Helen and Nestor, 'if he ever was' (24. 426): εἴ ποτ᾽ ἔην γε. Thus the spell of the future reaches perhaps its climax in Priam's speeches.

VI

The parade of the major characters reveals that most of the simple basic ways in which human beings experience time, constantly readapted in Western literature, are already present in Homer. The past is affirmed (Odysseus, Nestor) or lamented (Helen, Achilles), the future seen either clearly (Helen, Odysseus, Priam) or falsely (Agamemnon), or people vary between recognition and failure to recognize (Hector, to a lesser extent Achilles). Often the past is distorted by emotion. Sometimes it appears at such a distance that its reality is called into question (Helen, Priam),[47] sometimes it is perceived so intently as to approach the present till it is only 'yesterday or the day before' (Odysseus).[48] Or a momentary irritation generalizes a single past event into 'always' (Agamemnon, Paris), or

---

[46] See Kullmann (n. 13), 155.
[47] See above, pp. 392, 405–6.
[48] See above, p. 393.

grief sees a particular misfortune as being in a sequence of lasting misfortune (Briseis), or the intensity of pleasure sweeps away the pleasure of the past with 'never so much' (Paris).[49] Finally regret at past blindness, or even simply despair at a particular situation, can evoke the wish to wipe out the past: 'if only this or that had (not) happened' (Helen, Achilles, cf. Hector)[50] or, more strongly, 'if only I had not been born' (Helen, Andromache, cf. Achilles).[51] Similarly emotion may distort the future, as when Achilles hopes to take Troy with Patroclus alone, or Hector longs for his brother's death.[52]

However, the perception of time in the *Iliad* also has its own peculiarities. Even this emotive depiction, in itself nothing unusual, points by its frequency and its often extreme form to the tragic feeling for life and time that is the special feature of human beings in the poem. In general they perceive the past as something burdensome that has determined in advance the direction that their destiny will take. On the other hand, anything that happens to them, however trivial, stirs them at once to thoughts about the future. Behind this is the religious sense that the controlling paths of their destiny have already been determined. And they seek signs by which these paths may be ascertained. Thus the present event is not experienced in the present and as a fact; it becomes a confirmation of something that has already announced itself in the past, and a sign of the future. Achilles, the son of a goddess, retains a relative freedom in the face of the immediate past and the immediate future, but feels all the more strongly that he is affected by complexes of fate lying further back, linked with his divine birth and descent; nor is he free from human fallibility.

In general human beings in Homer—naturally in accordance with individual perceptiveness, temperament, and character—allow their judgements of present and future to be directly imposed on them by the situation at each moment, which also explains their occasional inconsistency. Only in Helen have we a character who does not unresistingly accept the present made for her by her past fate, but fights against it. The vehemence with which she strives against the power of a past determination, only in the end to succumb, reminds us of similarly passionate characters in Racine.[53]

---

[49] See above, p. 396 with n. 32; p. 392.
[50] See above, pp. 392, 403, 399.
[51] See above, pp. 391, 400, 403.
[52] See above, pp. 403, 397.
[53] Cf. G. Poulet, *Études sur le temps humain* i (Paris, 1953), ch. 6, 'Notes sur le temps racinien', 104 ff. On Racine's manner—distantly comparable with Homer's—of

Much in Iliadic conceptions of time matches general Greek sentiment.[54] We recall the oracles and bird-omens widespread even
outside Homer in the Greek world (in Greek epic too), behind which
there is also the wish to see the present in the framework of far-
reaching lines of fate. In Homer this religious component is less
marked; but in him too this same cast of mind, but in a far more
sublimated and indeed spiritualized form, determines human beings'
consciousness of time.[55]

making past and future affect the action, e.g. in *Andromaque* and *Iphigénie*, cf. ibid.
109 ff.

[54] B. A. van Groningen, *In the Grip of the Past* (London, 1953), has given an
excellent demonstration in detail of the significance that the past had for the Greeks,
but his investigation still needs amplifying on the future side.

[55] A detailed study of the religious background of the Iliadic sense of time could not
be accommodated within the topic.

14

The Wrath of Thetis

LAURA M. SLATKIN

The first question to arise in any inquiry into the role of Thetis in the *Iliad* must be why a figure of evidently minor stature—whose appearances in the poem are few—serves such a crucial function in its plot. Why is it that the poem assigns to Thetis the awesome role of persuading Zeus to set in motion the events of the *Iliad*, to invert the inevitable course of the fall of Troy? An initial answer to this might be, because Achilles is her son, and this poem is his story; so that a methodologically more fruitful way of posing the question is, why has the *Iliad* taken as its hero the son of Thetis?

The *Iliad*'s presentation of Thetis is of a subsidiary deity who is characterized by helplessness and by impotent grief. Her presentation of herself is as the epitome of sorrow and vulnerability in the face of her son's mortality. Consider her lament to her Nereid sisters at 18. 54–62:

> Alas for my sorrow, alas for my wretched-best-childbearing,
> since I bore a child faultless and powerful,
> pre-eminent among heroes; and he grew like a young shoot,
> I nourished him like a tree on an orchard's slope,
> I sent him forth with the curved ships to Ilium
> to fight the Trojans. But never again shall I welcome him
> returning home to the house of Peleus.
> Still, while he lives and looks on the sunlight
> he grieves, and I, going to him, am all unable to help him.

But the *Iliad* shows us another side as well. In a key passage in Book 1 Achilles, in order to obtain from Zeus the favour that will determine the trajectory of the plot, invokes not Athena or Hera, those powerful, inveterate pro-Greeks, but his mother. He asks Thetis to make his request of Zeus, reminding her of how she saved Zeus when the other Olympians wished to bind him (1. 393–412):

> But you, if you are able to, protect your own son:
> going to Olympus, pray to Zeus, if in fact you ever
> aided the heart of Zeus by word or action.
> For I have often heard you in my father's halls
> avowing it, when you declared that from Kronos' son of the dark clouds
> you alone among the immortals warded off unseemly destruction
> at the time when the other Olympians wanted to bind him,
> Hera and Poseidon and Pallas Athena;
> but you went, goddess, and set him free from his bonds,
> quickly summoning the hundred-handed one to high Olympus,
> the one whom the gods call Briareos, but all men call
> Aegaeon—for he is greater in strength than his father—
> who, rejoicing in his glory, sat beside the son of Kronos.
> And the blessed gods feared him, and ceased binding Zeus.
> Reminding him of these things now sit beside him and take his knees,
> in the hope that he may somehow be willing to help the Trojans
> and the others—the Achaeans—to force against the ships' sterns and
>   around the sea
> as they are slaughtered, so that they may all benefit from their king,
> and so that the son of Atreus, wide-ruling Agamemnon, may realize
> his disastrous folly, that he did not honour the best of the Achaeans.

Here we see the *Iliad* alluding to aspects of Thetis' mythology which it does not elaborate and which do not overtly reflect the subject-matter of heroic poetry. Why does it do so? The question is twofold: why does it allude to Thetis' power, but why does its reference remain only an allusion? Why does it present us with an apparent contradiction: if the mother of Achilles is so helpless, why was she able to rescue Zeus; and if she rescued Zeus, why is she so helpless? Why does the *Iliad* remind us of Thetis' efficacious power in another context while it presents her to us in an attitude of lamenting and grieving without recourse?

This chapter will attempt to see the Homeric use of Thetis in the perspective of her mythology, and to make some suggestions about its value in helping us to read the *Iliad* as a whole. Our best initial index of comparison with the *Iliad*'s Thetis is afforded by Thetis' role in another epic treatment, the cyclic *Aethiopis*, where we are presented not only with Thetis and Achilles but with a strikingly similar relationship, namely that of the divine Dawn Eos and her son Memnon.

The heroic identity of Memnon, the Trojan ally, was established in the *Aethiopis*, whose now lost five books related his single combat against Achilles, among other events.[1] In the *Aethiopis*, the confrontation between Achilles and Memnon seems to have made use of the same narrative features that characterize the climactic duel of *Iliad* 22: the contest followed upon the death of Achilles' close friend at the hands of his chief Trojan adversary, and was preceded by Thetis' prophecy of the outcome. In the *Aethiopis* Achilles avenged the killing of Nestor's son Antilochus, whose death at the hands of Memnon is referred to at *Odyssey* 4. 187–8.

Memnon, although functioning in a role like Hector's, is a mirror image of Achilles as the *Iliad* represents him. The association of these two heroes, not principally as adversaries but as parallel figures, is reflected in the poetry of Pindar, who more than once describes Memnon in terms appropriate to Achilles in the *Iliad*—singularly so, as they are the terms Achilles uses of himself—calling him $M\acute{\epsilon}\mu\nu\nu\nu\sigma$ $o\mathring{v}\kappa\ \mathring{\alpha}\pi\sigma\nu\sigma\sigma\tau\acute{\eta}\sigma\alpha\nu\tau\sigma\varsigma$ (Memnon [who] did not return home).[2] Pre-eminent among his allies, bearing armour made by Hephaestus, Memnon is the child of a divine mother, Eos, and a mortal father, Tithonus. This last feature was apparently given emphasis by the narrative shape of the *Aethiopis*: the actual presence of the two goddesses Eos and Thetis on the field of battle, contrasting the mortal vulnerability of the opponents with their equal heritage from the mother's immortal line, may have generated the poem's narrative tension.[3] What the *Iliad* treats as a unique and isolating phenomenon, the *Aethiopis* developed along alternative traditional lines, giving prominence to the theme of mortal/immortal duality by doubling its embodiment, in the two heroes Memnon and Achilles.

Iconographic evidence supplements the version of the myth given by the *Aethiopis*. The symmetry of the two heroes is reflected in

[1] See Proclus' summary in Allen, *Homeri Opera* v. 106. For a discussion of the range of its contents, see A. Severyns, *Le Cycle épique dans l'école d'Aristarque* (Liège, 1928), 313–27; G. L. Huxley, *Greek Epic Poetry: From Eumelos to Panyassis* (London, 1969), 144–9. On the structure and style of the Cycle see W. Kullmann, *Die Quellen der Ilias* (*Hermes* Einzelschriften 14; Wiesbaden, 1960), 204–303, esp. 212–14.

[2] *Nem.* 6. 50. See also *Ol.* 2. 83 and *Nem.* 3. 63.

[3] To precisely what effect the *Aethiopis* used this traditional parallelism is of course a matter for speculation; in any case, as the iconographic evidence indicates (see below), the poem very likely transmitted this inherited confrontation without special innovation. W. Burkert writes 'When Achilles fights with Memnon, the two divine mothers, Thetis and Eos, rush to the scene—this was probably the subject of a pre-Iliad epic song,' *Greek Religion* (Cambridge, Mass., 1985), 121.

numerous examples of Archaic art. Vase-paintings, illustrating the *monomachia* (single combat) of Memnon and Achilles, significantly portray Eos and Thetis facing each other, each at her son's side.[4] The parallelism persists even in the outcome of the duel, although ultimately one hero will win and the other will lose. Vase-painting corroborates the existence, in the tradition also shared by the *Aethiopis*, of a *kērostasia* (weighing of fates) in which Hermes weighs the *kēres* of Memnon and Achilles in the presence of Eos and Thetis.[5] In the *Aethiopis*, the paired mothers are equated in their involvement in the struggle, each present to protect her son.[6]

The efforts of Thetis and Eos in the *Aethiopis* are essentially identical. In only one respect are Thetis and Eos distinguished in Proclus' summary of the *Aethiopis*. Unlike Eos, Thetis communicates to Achilles some foreknowledge about his adversary: τὰ κατὰ τὸν Μέμνονα προλέγει (she foretells the events concerning Memnon).[7] Eos requests of Zeus, and obtains, immortality for Memnon. Thetis does not actually ask Zeus for immortality for Achilles; but she

---

[4] In his important study *The Iliad in Early Greek Art* (Copenhagen, 1967), K. Friis Johansen, referring to 'a well-known type of picture that was very popular in early Greek art, a conventional monomachy framed by two standing female figures', points out that 'There can be no doubt that this type was originally invented for the fight between Achilles and Memnon in the presence of their mothers Thetis and Eos' (pp. 200–1). M. E. Clark and W. D. E. Coulson discuss the iconography of the *Aethiopis* and its adaptations in painting, as well as the poem's relation to the *Il.*, in 'Memnon and Sarpedon', *MH* 35 (1978), 65–73.

[5] On the iconography of this subject see E. Wüst, *RE* XXIII. 2 (1959), 1442; G. E. Lung, *Memnon. Archäologische Studien zur Aethiopis* (Bonn, 1912), 14–19; and the discussion in Friis Johansen (n. 4), 261. Also K. Schefold, *Myth and Legend in Early Greek Art* (London, 1966), 10. The weighing of the fates of Memnon and Achilles is not specifically mentioned by Proclus in his summary, although it provided the subject for Aeschylus' lost *Psychostasia*, as we learn from e.g. schol. A on 8. 70 and Eustathius on 8. 73 (699. 31). For views in support of its existence in the *Aethiopis* see Clark and Coulson (n. 4); B. C. Dietrich, 'The Judgment of Zeus', *RM* 107 (1964), 97–125, esp. 112–13; Severyns (n. 1), 318–19.

[6] See Schefold (n. 5), 45.

[7] In the reconstruction of the 'Memnonis' offered by neo-analytic research, Thetis here foretells Achilles' imminent death which is to follow upon his slaying of Memnon. According to this hypothesis, Thetis' prophetic warning here is the cause of Achilles' abstention from battle, which he will re-enter only after the death of his friend Antilochus. G. Schoeck, *Ilias und Aethiopis* (Zurich, 1961), 38–48 contributes the interesting observation that the *Iliad* makes reference to a prophecy from Thetis precisely at those junctures where the question of Achilles' return to battle arises, e.g. 11. 790–803, 16. 36–51. He argues that the *Iliad* in this way adverts to a 'Memnonis' prototype, in which Thetis' prophecy was the specific cause of Achilles' absence from battle; that is, Achilles absented himself from battle at his mother's request.

herself 'having snatched her son away from the pyre, transports him to the White Island'. Like Elysion, the White Island represents the refuge of immortality for heroes, where they live on once they have not avoided but—even better—transcended death.[8] The *Aethiopis*, then, emphasized the hero's divine heritage as a way of separating him from ordinary human existence, and his access to communication with the gods as a way of resolving the conflict between heroic stature and mortal limitation.

The tradition represented by the *Aethiopis* and by our iconographic examples thus posits an identity not only between Achilles and Memnon but between Thetis and Eos, based on their roles as immortal guardians and protectors of their mortal children. From a narrative standpoint this parallelism is more than an instance of the Cycle's fondness for repetition or doublets. The *Aethiopis* shows us not a recapitulation of a prior situation by a subsequent one, but a rendering of the mythological equation between the two figures as a simultaneous juxtaposition, a mirroring in which each reflects, and must assume the dimensions of, her counterpart.

The identity between the two mothers in the tradition transmitted by the *Aethiopis* and the vase-paintings reinforces the uniqueness of Thetis in the *Iliad*—the incomparable singularity of her position to which the poem explicitly calls attention at 18. 429–34:

> Hephaestus, is there anyone, of all the goddesses on Olympus
> who has endured so many baneful sorrows in her heart,
> as many as the griefs Zeus the son of Kronos has given me beyond all
> others? Of all the daughters of the sea he forced on me a mortal man
> Aeacus' son Peleus, and I endured the bed of a mortal man
> utterly unwilling though I was.

But if the *Iliad* treats Thetis' position as unparalleled, then an examination of its treatment in the light of the sources of the Thetis–Eos

---

[8] The use of the White Island motif, like that of Elysium at *Odyssey* 4. 563, is an acknowledgement of the religious and social phenomenon of the hero-cult, which is generally excluded from direct reference in Homeric epic. E. Rohde, in *Psyche. Seelencult und Unsterblichkeitsglaube der Griechen* (Freiburg, 1898), III. 371 [Eng. trans. London, 1925] calls Leuke a 'Sonderelysion' for Achilles. Rohde offers a discussion of the thematic equivalence of Leuke, Elysium, and the Isles of the Blessed at 365–78. On Elysium as a cult concept, see W. Burkert, 'Elysion', *Glotta* 39 (1961), 208–13, and T. Hadzisteliou-Price, 'Hero-Cult and Homer', *Historia* 22 (1973), 133–4. Examination of the diction (as transmitted by Proclus, at any rate) will show that the terms used for Thetis' actions are those used to describe cult-practice. See G. Nagy, 'Phaethon, Sappho's Phaon, and the White Rock of Leukas', *HSCP* 77 (1973), 137–77.

equation can serve as an introduction to the *Iliad*'s process of interpreting and selectively shaping its mythology, preserving for us
dimensions of Thetis that elucidate her role in the *Iliad* even when Eos
is not present to help evoke them.

Comparative evidence indicates the connection of several female
deities, notable in Greek and Indic mythologies, to the prototype of an
Indo-European Dawn Goddess, *Ausos.[9] The representatives of this
important Indo-European figure who most closely assume her
functions in their respective poetic traditions are Indic Usas and
Greek Eos. However, the shared attributes of these Greek and Indic
Dawn goddesses, which link them to their prototype, yield a still
more productive legacy in Greek epic, where they are inherited by
Aphrodite, among others.

In analysing the elements which Aphrodite and Eos share, and
which identify them (with Usas) as descendants of the Indo-European
Dawn Goddess,[10] we recognize motifs that are significant in the story
of Thetis. Chief among these is the association of the immortal
goddess with a mortal lover.[11] Like Usas in the Vedic hymns, Eos
unites with various lovers, among whom Tithonus is prominent in
epic; Aphrodite has union with several, notably Anchises; and Thetis
is joined to Peleus. Although the outcome of a love relationship
between immortal and mortal may be benign, the potential for
extraordinary pathos in such a story is clear.

Eos and her lovers serve as the model for goddess–mortal relationships[12] with their essential antithesis between the timelessness
of the goddess and the temporality of her lover. Eos and her lovers
are even cited by characters *within* epic as exemplary of such

---

[9] On the etymology of Attic Ἕως (= Ionic Ἠώς), see Pierre Chantraine, *Diction-naire étymologique de la langue grecque* (Paris, 1968), 394–5.

[10] The evidence for the Indo-European origins of these deities is presented in D. D. Boedeker, *Aphrodite's Entry into Greek Epic* (Leiden, 1974), whose subject is Greek epic's integration of Aphrodite's inherited features, through diction and theme, into its development of her character and role. See also the discussion in P. Friedrich, *The Meaning of Aphrodite* (Chicago, 1978), who considers that 'the Proto-Indo-European goddess of dawn was one of several main sources for the Greek Aphrodite' (p. 31).

[11] Boedeker (n. 10), 67 writes: 'The tradition of the mortal lover of the Dawn-goddess is an old one; in Greek epic it is surely the most obvious aspect of Eos' mythology. Comparative evidence from the *Rig-Veda* indicates that this feature of solar mythology dates back to common Indo-European, although in Greek myth it may have been amplified beyond its original importance.' See also C. P. Segal, 'The Homeric Hymn to Aphrodite: A Structuralist Approach', *CW* 67 (1974), 205–12.

[12] Boedeker (n. 10), 69.

relationships. Aphrodite herself tells Eos' story (*Homeric Hymn to Aphrodite* 218–38); Calypso knows it as well, even though, as the *Odyssey* points out, she lives very far away (*Odyssey* 5. 121); and both compare it to their own stories. The marriage of Thetis to Peleus exhibits the same antithetical pattern. Because Eos typifies such goddess–mortal relationships, Thetis is perceived synchronically as being connected with her, as in the *Aethiopis*, and thus shares dictional features associated with her; although Thetis cannot be shown definitively, as Eos has been, to be a direct descendant, or hypostasis, of the Indo-European Dawn Goddess. Their relationship is structurally homologous, rather than historical.

In Greek epic, the themes attached to the goddess and her mortal lover are recapitulated with much greater emphasis in the relationship between the goddess and her son, the offspring of her union with her mortal lover. Eos and Memnon, as an instance of this, reinforce the Eos–Thetis parallel. But in the case of Eos, the pattern of whose relationship with Tithonus is repeated in part with Memnon—as she requests and obtains his immortality—the erotic aspect of her mythology dominates. Thetis' erotic aspect, discernible (as we shall see) in the tradition followed by Pindar and Aeschylus, where both mortal and immortal partners woo her, is subordinated to her maternal aspect, as she appears in the *Iliad*.

Certain elements in the constellation of motifs common to the divinities sharing the mythology of the Dawn Goddess are preserved by the *Iliad*; others are significantly reworked. The motif of the goddess's protection of the mortal hero she loves is a central traditional feature shared by the immortal mothers (and lovers) who inherit, or are assimilated to, the mythology of the Dawn Goddess.[13] Its variations, apart from Eos and Thetis in the *Aethiopis*, include Calypso in the *Odyssey* and Aphrodite in the *Homeric Hymn to Aphrodite* as well as in the *Iliad*.[14] This tradition is well known to the

---

[13] In *Achilles, Patroclus and the Meaning of Philos* (Innsbruck, 1980), D. Sinos has shown in detail that the *kourotrophos* or nurturing function of the goddess, revealed in the diction of vegetal growth, as for example at *Il.* 18. 437–8, is apparent in the relationship in cult between the *kourotrophos* goddess and the *kouros*. The protection motif is a correlate of this function in myth. See also G. Nagy, *The Best of the Achaeans* (Baltimore, 1979), 174–210, as well as R. Merkelbach, 'KOROS', *ZPE* 8 (1971) 80 and P. Vidal-Naquet, 'Le Chasseur noir et l'origine de l'ephébie athénienne', *Annales ESC* 23 (1968), 947–9.

[14] On the related attributes of these goddesses, see Boedeker (n. 10), 64–84.

Iliad, where in two dramatic episodes Aphrodite acts to protect her favourites from imminent danger, snatching them away from battle at the crucial moment. In Book 3 she rescues Paris as he is about to be overpowered by Menelaus; in 5 it is Aeneas whom she saves from the onslaught of Diomedes. To snatch a hero from danger, to protect him from death, however, offers a paradox of which the *Iliad* and *Odyssey* are conscious: that preserving a hero from death means denying him a heroic life.

Thus Calypso, who compares her intention towards Odysseus with Eos' abduction of Orion,[15] wants by sequestering Odysseus to offer him immortality; but this would inevitably mean the loss of his goal, the impossibility of completing the travels, the denial of his identity. From a perspective that is intrinsic to the *Odyssey* as to the *Iliad*, it would mean the extinction of heroic subject-matter, the negation of epic. Calypso 'the concealer' uses persuasive arguments in her attempt to hide Odysseus from mortality; her ultimate failure measures the hero's commitment to his mortal existence. Aphrodite, on the other hand, is a successful concealer, shielding her favourites by hiding them, Paris in a cloud of mist and Aeneas in her flowing robe;[16] but while both escape destruction and survive the *Iliad*, their individual heroism, from an epic standpoint, has been permanently compromised.

Thetis, like Calypso and Aphrodite, is associated by the *Iliad* with impenetrable clouds, with veils, and with concealment. But the *Iliad* does not pursue the parallelism of this aspect of their mythology. Thetis never spirits Achilles away from danger, and she never tempts him with immortality. On the contrary, it is she who states the human limits of his choice. Repeatedly, the absoluteness of the *Iliad*'s rejection of the idea of immortality emerges from its treatment, in relation to Achilles, of this protection motif, which figures so importantly in the immortal goddess–mortal lover or son stories, and which has a pre-eminent place in Thetis' mythology.

Thetis acts on behalf of Achilles in the *Iliad* only after asserting repeatedly the knowledge that he must die, and finally, in 18, the certainty that it is to happen soon. It is only then, after establishing her awareness of Achilles' vulnerability, her understanding that he cannot be saved, that she makes her gesture towards protecting him.

---

[15] 5. 121–4.   [16] 3. 380–2 (Paris), 5. 314–15 (Aeneas).

She asks Hephaestus to create new armour for him, to replace the old armour worn by Patroclus and lost to Hector.

The *Iliad*'s treatment of the *hoplopoiia* (armour-making) is underscored by the evident existence of a similar scene in the *Aethiopis*, in which Memnon entered the battle wearing ἡφαιστότευκτον πανοπλίαν (a panoply fashioned by Hephaestus) prior to Eos' successful plea for his immortality. In the *Aethiopis*, apparently, Memnon's divine armour anticipated the successful intervention of divinity, and was emblematic of its redemptive patronage. It confirmed Memnon's special relationship with the gods which would make immortality possible for him.[17] In the *Iliad*, the supreme implement of protection made by Hephaestus at Thetis' request is the shield, which only Achilles can endure to look at when Thetis brings it to him. But it precisely does not fulfil, as it does for Memnon, the promise of ultimate divine preservation through the agency of his mother. The *Iliad*'s rejection of this outcome for Achilles, and hence for its conception of heroism, is expressly stated. Thetis prefaces her request of Hephaestus with a summary of the *Iliad* up to that point, and Hephaestus replies (18. 463–7):

> Take heart: do not let these things distress your thoughts.
> If only I were able to hide him away
> from grievous death, when dire fate overtakes him,
> as surely as there will be beautiful armour for him, such as
> anyone among many mortal men will marvel at, whoever sees it.

In other words, the *Iliad* uses this constellation of traditional elements—the divine armour, the protection motif—in order to violate conventional expectations of their potency, and it does so for the sake of the primacy of the theme of mortality, as Thetis' lament to the Nereids at 18. 54–62 explicitly and deliberately reminds us:

> Alas for my sorrow, alas for my wretched-best-childbearing,
> since I bore a child faultless and powerful,
> pre-eminent among heroes; and he grew like a young shoot.
> I nourished him like a tree on an orchard's slope,
> I sent him forth with the curved ships to Ilium
> to fight the Trojans. But never again shall I welcome him
> returning home to the house of Peleus.

---

[17] See J. Griffin, 'The Epic Cycle and the Uniqueness of Homer', *JHS* 97 (1977), 39–53, esp. 42–3, on immortality in the Cycle poems [= this vol., Ch. 12].

> Still, while he lives and looks on the sunlight
> he grieves, and I, going to him, am all unable to help him.

The semi-divine hero is inextricably associated with non-human perfection and scope, but instead of conceiving of him as elevated by this into the realm of divinity, the *Iliad*'s vision is of an exacting mortal aspect which exerts its levelling effect on the immortal affiliations and expectations of the hero. These retain their authenticity, but no longer their overriding authority as guarantors of immortal stature.

Thus, the *Iliad*'s rejection of the possibility of Achilles' salvation through Thetis results in its emphasis on her helpless status, which is put into relief as a radical contrast to her part in the tradition of divine protectresses—one might even say, her role as protectress *par excellence*. For the *Iliad*, in such provocative allusions as Achilles' speech at 1. 394–412, depicts Thetis as the efficacious protectress not of heroes but of gods.[18]

In the *Iliad*, Thetis has a present and, prospectively, a future defined by the mortal condition of her son, and as such she is known in her dependent attitude of sorrowing and caring. But the *Iliad* recognizes that she has a past as well, and in recalling it at crucial points suggests a source for her role that is far more important than initially appears.

How does the *Iliad* reveal a character's past? Typically, through the character's own reminiscences and reflections on his previous achievements or position. But Thetis never refers to any past that does not include her son. Instead, Hephaestus gives the only first-person account of Thetis' previous activities, anterior to the time-frame of the epic.

In Book 18, when Thetis arrives to request the new set of armour for Achilles, Hephaestus responds to the news of her presence with an account of how she had saved him after Hera had cast him out of Olympus.[19] In Book 6, there is another instance of Thetis preserving

---

[18] M. Lang, in C. A. Rubino and C. W. Shelmerdine (edd.), *Approaches to Homer* (Austin, 1983), 153–4, suggests that 'hurling out of heaven and rescues by Thetis seem to have been popular motifs', noting that Thetis 'made a speciality of rescue (witness her deliverance of Zeus in 1. 396 ff., and her rescue of Dionysus in 6. 130 ff.)'.

[19] 18. 394–405. That Eurynome, who otherwise does not figure in Homeric epic, is named here as a participant in the rescue of Hephaestus, may be explained by the particular context of Hephaestus' conversation with Charis. Elsewhere in Homer, Hephaestus is the husband of Aphrodite; but here Charis is his wife, as in the *Theog.*

a god from disaster which is, similarly, not related by her but in this case by Diomedes, who cites it as part of an example of how dangerous it is to fight with the gods. Diomedes describes how Lycurgus chased Dionysus with a cattle prod until Dionysus in terror leapt into the sea where he was sheltered by Thetis.[20]

Together with the episode described by Hephaestus in 18, this account associates Thetis in a divine past—uninvolved with human events—with a level of divine invulnerability extraordinary by Olympian standards. Where within the framework of the *Iliad* the ultimate recourse is to Zeus for protection,[21] here the poem seems to point to an alternative structure of cosmic relations, one which was neither overthrown by the Olympian order (in so far as Thetis, unlike, say, the Titans, still functions) nor upheld by it (in so far as no challenge to the Olympian order persists), but whose relation to it was otherwise resolved.

We do not have far to look for explicit confirmation of this in the poem. Thetis, the rescuer of Hephaestus and Dionysus, was first and foremost the rescuer of Zeus. The most general, but most potent, statement of her power in this regard is expressed by the formula $\lambda o \iota \gamma \grave{o} \nu$ $\mathring{a} \mu \hat{v} \nu a \iota$ (to ward off destruction).[22] The ability to $\lambda o \iota \gamma \grave{o} \nu$ $\mathring{a} \mu \hat{v} \nu a \iota$ (or $\mathring{a} \mu \acute{v} \nu \epsilon \iota \nu$) within the *Iliad* is shared exclusively by Achilles, Apollo, and Zeus: although others are put in a position to do so, and make the attempt, only these three have the power to 'ward off destruction', to be efficacious in restoring order to the world of the poem. Thetis alone, however, is credited with having had such power in the divine realm, for she alone was able to 'ward off destruction' from Zeus. She herself unbound Zeus, summoning the hundred-handed Briareos as a kind of guarantor or reminder of her power.[23] That Thetis saves Zeus from being bound deserves special attention. I wish to suggest that the motif of binding on Olympus, together with

(945–6), where he is married to one of the Charites (there specifically Aglaia; Homer uses simply the generic Charis). And at *Theog.* 907–9, Hesiod identifies the Charites as the daughters of Eurynome. The inclusion of Hesiodic Eurynome, therefore, is owed to the presence of her Hesiodic child. Moreover, the mention of Eurynome here, and perhaps even the presence of Charis, are motivated by what emerges, as I hope to show below, as the *theogonic* context of references to Thetis' power.

[20] 6. 123–37.

[21] As at 21. 505–13, where Artemis retreats to Zeus when attacked and struck by Hera.

[22] For a detailed discussion of the thematics of this formula, see Nagy (n. 13), 74–8.

[23] 1. 401–5, cited above.

the reference to Briareos, specifically evokes the succession myth and
the divine genealogy on which it is founded.

The motif of binding is central to the account of the succession
myth in the *Theogony*, recurring as one of the primary ways to assert
divine sovereignty over a potential or actual challenger. Ouranos
attempts to ensure his power over Briareos and his other children by
binding them; ultimately they are freed by Zeus, who in turn wants
their allegiance in his own bid for hegemony, and their willingness
to co-operate is based on their gratitude at being unbound. With the
aid of Briareos and his brothers, the Olympians, once they have
managed to overpower Kronos and the other Titans, bind them and
cast them beneath the earth.[24]

Binding is the ultimate penalty in the divine realm, where by
definition there is no death. It serves not to deprive an opponent of
existence, but to render him impotent.[25] Once bound, a god cannot
escape his bondage by himself, no matter how great his strength. In
this sense it is not finally an expression of physical strength
(although violence certainly enters into the Titanomachy) but of
what has been called 'terrible sovereignty'.[26]

The attempt to bind Zeus recounted at 1. 396–406 thus constitutes
a mutinous effort at supplanting him and imposing a new divine
regime—on the pattern of his own overthrowing of Kronos and the
Titans.[27] Thetis' act in rescuing Zeus is therefore nothing less than
supreme: an act that restores the cosmic equilibrium. Once having
loosed the bonds, she summons Briareos, not to perform, but simply
to sit beside Zeus as a reminder of Zeus' final mastery in the succession myth struggle. Briareos and his brothers, in Hesiod (as later
in Apollodorus) are never instigators but agents; Thetis' power to
summon the hundred-hander, the *hekatoncheir* here—beyond what
the insurgent gods are capable of—recalls Zeus' own successful use
of Briareos and his brothers. Not even a single one of Briareos' hands
needs to be laid on the mutinous gods here: they are overwhelmed

---

[24] *Theog.* 147–58, 501–2, 617–735.
[25] References to binding of gods in the *Iliad* include the account of the binding of
Ares by Otus and Ephialtes at 5. 385–91; of Hera by Zeus at 15. 19–20; Zeus' threat to
the other gods at 8. 17–27.
[26] On the metaphysical nature of binding, see M. Eliade, *Images and Symbols*, trans.
P. Mairet (New York, 1969), ch. 3, 'The "God Who Binds" and the Symbolism of
Knots', 92–124.
[27] On binding as an expression and instrument of sovereignty, see G. Dumezil,
Ouranos–Varuna: étude de mythologie comparée indo-européenne (Paris, 1934).

by the assertion of sovereignty implied by the presence of Briareos, rather than overpowered by him. In this sense, one can see Briareos' narrative function as a mirror of his dramatic function: as a reminder. The binding element in itself is a sufficient allusion to the succession myth, so that Briareos is included as a multiplication of the motif.

Linked to this cosmic act on the part of Thetis is the phrase ὁ γὰρ αὗτε βίην οὗ πατρὸς ἀμείνων (for he is greater in strength than his father)—a reference about which it has rightly been said that 'much remains obscure'.[28] Yet some light may be shed on the difficulties by reminding ourselves that the reference to 'the son who is greater than his father' is significant for Thetis in a crucial dimension of her mythology.

Pindar *Isthmian* 8, where Thetis' story is the ode's central myth, recounts that Zeus and Poseidon were rivals for the hand of Thetis, each wishing to be her husband, for love possessed them. But the gods decided not to bring about either marriage, once they had heard from Themis that Thetis was destined to bear a son who would be greater than his father. Therefore, Themis counselled, let Thetis marry a mortal instead, and see her son die in war. This divine prize should be given to Aeacus' son Peleus, the most reverent of men.[29] *Isthmian* 8 thus reveals Thetis as a figure of cosmic capacity, whose existence promises profound consequences for the gods. Not only does she generate strife between Zeus and Poseidon because of their love for her, but her potential for bearing a son greater than his father threatens the entire divine order.[30] Themis, the guardian of

---

[28] Kirk, *Il. Comm.* I. 95 on 403–4. See pp. 93–5 for a valuable discussion of I. 396–406.

[29] *Isthm.* 8. 29–38. C. M. Bowra, *Pindar* (Oxford, 1964), 88–9 writes: '[*Isthmian* 8] is concerned with the consequences of what will happen if Thetis marries either Zeus or Poseidon. If she does, says Themis, it is πεπρωμένον [fated] that her son will be stronger than either. Here everything turns on the meaning of πεπρωμένον. It is clear that it is not a decision of the gods on Olympus but something which is bound to happen unless they take avoiding action ... What Pindar means is that, the gods being what they are, such a union will inevitably bring forth a being stronger than they. The gods have their own nature, and this is a consequence of it.'

[30] The relationship of *Isthm.* 8 to the Aeschylean treatment of Thetis is considered more fully in the larger study of which this chapter forms a part [*The Power of Thetis* (Berkeley and Los Angeles, 1991), 74–6]. See the discussion in M. Griffith (ed.), *Aeschylus: Prometheus Bound* (Cambridge, 1983), 4–6, as well as that in G. Thomson (ed.), *Aeschylus: Prometheus Bound* (Cambridge, 1932), 21–2. In *PV* the focus on intergenerational succession emphasizes the absolute supremacy of Zeus, diminishing

social order,[31] tries to avert a catastrophic *neikos* (quarrel),[32] on the scale of previous intergenerational succession struggles; this is what Thetis has the power to engender.

While the danger to Zeus posed by the attempt of Hera, Athena, and Poseidon was averted by Thetis, therefore, she herself presented the greatest challenge of all to his supremacy, according to the myth as known to Pindar in *Isthmian* 8.[33] The phrase ὁ γὰρ αὖτε βίην οὗ πατρὸς ἀμείνων (for he is greater in strength than his father) used of Briareos at *Iliad* 1. 404 describes, in the tradition followed by Pindar, the position of Achilles and recalls his association with the theme of ongoing genealogy and generational strife.

Thetis' cosmic potential, enunciated by Pindar in *Isthmian* 8 is presented with remarkable clarity in a local context, in Laconia, where incidentally Pausanias tells us she was worshipped with utmost reverence in cult.[34] In Alcman's cosmogony (fragment 5 *PMGF*)[35] we learn that Laconian poetic traditions reflect the belief that Thetis was not simply a cosmic force, but *the* cosmic force: she not only has power in the sea, but is the generative principle in the

the importance of Poseidon in the courtship of Thetis and its consequences. Nevertheless, as Prof. Helen Bacon points out to me, *PV* 920–7 may well be an allusion to Poseidon's role in the pursuit of Thetis. See Griffith ad loc.

[31] On the role of Themis, cf. A. Köhnken, 'Gods and Descendants of Aiakos in Pindar's Eighth Isthmian Ode', *BICS* 22 (1975), 33 n. 19. Apollodorus 3. 13. 5 says that one version attributes to Themis, and another to Prometheus, the revelation of the secret that Thetis will bear a son greater than his father: τὸν ταύτης αὐτῷ γεννηθέντα οὐρανοῦ δυναστεύσειν (that the son born to him by her would be ruler of heaven).

[32] *Isthm.* 8. 47–9. Note Themis' role in the *Cypria* where *eris* also plays a crucial part. See Nagy (n. 13), 253–75 and 309–16 on the overlapping semantics of *eris* and *neikos* and their implications for traditional Greek poetry.

[33] It is necessary to proceed with the greatest caution when reading Pindar (or any later author) as evidence for traditions latent in Homeric poetry. Two considerations encourage the validity of doing so here. First, that Pindar has been shown to preserve highly archaic material reaching back even to an Indo-European provenance, as illustrated by E. Benveniste's discussion of *Pythian* 3, in 'La Doctrine médicale des Indo-Européens', *Revue de l'Histoire des Religions* 130 (1945), 5–12. Second, that as C. Greengard has demonstrated, *Isthm.* 8 'draws … heavily on the themes and movements of the *Iliad* tragedy', *The Structure of Pindar's Epinician Odes* (Amsterdam, 1980), 35. Her comprehensive analysis concludes that 'the diction itself of *I.* 8 is more than usually allusive to that of the *Iliad*' (36 n. 27). It seems reasonable to suppose that Pindar in *Isthm.* 8 draws on mythology present in the *Il.* in some form, and recoverable from it—even if deeply embedded and only allusively evident to us.

[34] Paus. 3. 14. 4–6.
[35] Originally edited by E. Lobel in *P. Oxy.* XXIV, no. 2390, fr. 2.

universe. Alcman seems to have presented Thetis as the primal, divine creative force, through whose agency *Poros* 'the way' and *Tekmōr* 'the sign' came into being.

Known to us only through a commentary, the cosmogony appears to have envisaged a sequence of creation in which at first only undifferentiated matter existed; then Thetis, the γένεσις παντῶν (source of all things) appeared, and generated Poros and Tekmor. Darkness existed as a third feature, later followed by day, moon, and stars. The point to stress here is that this cosmogony, with Thetis the creatrix as demiurge, involves not primarily the bringing into being of matter, but rather the discrimination of objects, the ordering of space, the illumination of darkness with light. It is therefore an intellectual rather than a physical creation.

This aspect of Alcman's poem has been discussed by M. Detienne and J.-P. Vernant, who argue convincingly for a close connection between Thetis and Metis.[36] In different versions of their mythology, Thetis and Metis have associations with bonds and binding; both are sea-powers; both shape-shifters; both loved by Zeus; both destined to bear a son greater than his father. Some scholars, like M. L. West, have seen the name of Thetis as defining her role.[37] Detienne and Vernant suggest that it is the power of metamorphosis as an attribute that disposes these goddesses of the sea to a crucial cosmological role: they 'contain' the potential shapes of everything created and creatable. Their emphasis on Thetis' connections with the sea includes the possibility of understanding Poros and Tekmor as navigational phenomena. Thus Thetis' role in the cosmogony is as a force against chaos, the principle *positively* corresponding to *negatively* defined limitless disorder.

The *Iliad*'s acknowledgement of Thetis' cosmic power, known to these traditions,[38] locates it in a past to which she herself does not

---

[36] M. Detienne and J.-P. Vernant, *Les Ruses de l'intelligence: la métis des Grecs* (Paris, 1974), 127–64 [Eng. trans. *Cunning Intelligence in Greek Culture and Society* (Hassocks, 1978)], which develops a number of ideas on this subject first presented in J.-P. Vernant, 'Thetis et le poème cosmogonique d'Alcman', *Hommages à Marie Delcourt*, Collection Latomus 114 (Brussels, 1970), 219–33.

[37] M. L. West, 'Three Presocratic Cosmologies', *CQ* 57 (1963), 154–7 and 'Alcman and Pythagoras', *CQ* 61 (1967), 1–7; see also *Early Greek Philosophy and the Orient* (Oxford, 1971), 206–8.

[38] It is important to stress that we obviously cannot assume a single common bearing on Thetis' mythology in Pindar, Alcman, Aeschylus, Apollodorus (or, for example, Herodotus, who records at 7. 191. 2 that the Persians sacrificed to Thetis at

refer. Her grief is her pre-eminent attribute in the poem. Her references
to herself, mentioned above, are uniquely to her sorrow over her son.
In contexts where we might expect allusions, like that in Achilles'
speech in 1, to her former power, she claims for herself only suffering
beyond that of all other Olympians. Thus, at 18. 429–31:

> Hephaestus, is there anyone, of all the goddesses on Olympus
> who has endured so many baneful sorrows in her heart,
> as many as the griefs Zeus the son of Kronos has given me beyond
> all others?

In what follows I will suggest the way in which the grief of
Thetis represents the link between her past and her present in the
Iliad.

In the *Iliad*, as G. Nagy has pointed out, *achos* (grief) is a constant
for Achilles, while his continuous grief involves shifting consequences for other people. Achilles' capacity to effect a *transfert du
mal*, through which his *achos* is passed on to the Achaeans and
ultimately to the Trojans, is part of the dynamic of his *mēnis*. As
Nagy puts it, 'the ἄχος [*achos*] of Achilles leads to the μῆνις [*mēnis*]
of Achilles leads to the ἄχος [*achos*] of the Achaeans'.[39]

Achilles is the only hero of whom the substantive *mēnis* is used in
Homer. In a detailed study of the semantics of *mēnis*, C. Watkins has
shown that 'μῆνις [*mēnis*] is on a wholly different level from the
other Homeric words for "wrath". The ominous, baneful character of
μῆνις [*mēnis*] is plain. It is a dangerous notion, which one must fear;
a sacral, "numinous" (θεῶν) notion, to be sure, but one of which
even the gods are concerned with ridding themselves.'[40] Moreover,
Watkins writes, 'The association of divine wrath with a mortal by
this very fact elevates that mortal outside the normal ambience of the
human condition toward the sphere of the divine.'[41]

Mēnis thus not only designates Achilles' power—divine in scope—
to exact vengeance by transforming events according to his will, but
it specifically associates Achilles with Apollo and Zeus, the two gods
whose *mēnis* is, in the case of each, explicitly identified and isolated

Cape Sepias); but at the same time we may usefully draw attention to these authors'
identification of Thetis as invested with vast cosmic power—an identification that
seems to stem from elsewhere than the *Il.*'s *overt* presentation of her.

[39] Nagy (n. 13), 80.
[40] C. Watkins, 'On *Mῆνις*', *Indo-European Studies* 3 (1977), 694–5.
[41] Watkins (n. 40), 690.

as propelling and controlling the events of the poem.[42] In addition, Zeus, Apollo, and—uniquely among mortals—Achilles can generate or remove *achos*.

When Apollo and Achilles are involved in removing *achos* from the Achaeans, they are said to ward off *loigos* (devastation). Apollo is appealed to by Chryses to remove the *loigos* with which the god has afflicted the Greek army.[43] Achilles is requested to λοιγὸν ἀμύνειν (ward off devastation), where, as in the case of Apollo, λοιγόν designates the plight into which he himself has cast the Achaeans: it is the term used to designate the Battle at the Ships.[44] In fact, the successful capacity to λοιγὸν ἀμύνειν (or ἀμῦναι) *within the framework* of the *Iliad* is restricted to the two figures of *mēnis*— Apollo and Achilles—who, like the third, Zeus, can both ward destruction away from the Greeks and bring it on them as well.

The single other possessor of the ability to λοιγὸν ἀμῦναι successfully is Thetis. We have examined the passage in Book 1 which identifies her as the rescuer of the divine regime; she alone was able to λοιγὸν ἀμῦναι for Zeus, to protect him from destruction. But if the power to λοιγὸν ἀμῦναι is bivalent—if the one who wields it can not only avert destruction but bring it on—then the threat posed by Thetis, who could λοιγὸν ἀμῦναι on a cosmic level, is potentially the greatest of all. For Thetis' *achos* is supreme among the gods of the *Iliad*: the *transfert du mal* she might effect would be on an equal scale. Remembering that for Achilles 'achos leads to *mēnis* leads to the *achos* of others', we may ask the question, why does the *Iliad* not predicate a *mēnis* of Thetis? The answer, I suggest, is that it does so— by allusion and digression integrating into its own narrative mythology that is not evidently appropriate to *kleos*-epic as a genre.

If we consider the grief that Thetis endures because of the imminent loss of her son (whose prospective death she already mourns in her *goos* (lament) at 18. 52–64), and her power to respond on a cosmic scale, we recognize elements that combine elsewhere in a context in which it is appropriate to show full-fledged divine *mēnis* in action, namely in the *Homeric Hymn to Demeter*. The *Hymn* is precisely about the consequences of *mēnis* that ensues from Demeter's grief over the loss of Kore.

---

[42] Zeus' *mēnis* is referred to at 5. 34; 13. 624; 15. 122. On the *mēnis* of Achilles and Apollo, see Nagy (n. 13), 69–83.   [43] 1. 456.   [44] 16. 32.

Much as Thetis' grief is evoked instantly when she hears Achilles' lament for Patroclus in Book 18, implicitly signalling his own death,[45] so *achos* seizes Demeter at the moment when she hears her daughter's cry as she is abducted into the underworld by Hades.[46] What follows is Demeter's wrath at the gods' complicity in the irrevocable violation of Persephone, and through her wrath both Olympians and mortals are bound to suffer disastrously. She isolates herself from the gods, prepares full-scale devastation, and finally brings the Olympians to their knees. Zeus is compelled to dissuade her, sending Iris with his appeal (*Hymn to Demeter* 318–23):

> She arrived at the town of fragrant Eleusis
> and found dark-robed Demeter in the temple
> and addressed her, speaking winged words:
> 'Demeter, Zeus the father, whose wisdom is unfailing, summons you
> to come among the tribes of the immortal gods.
> Come then, do not let my message from Zeus be unaccomplished.'

But Demeter's *mēnis* is too great: she does not comply, and Hermes must be sent to Hades so that Demeter may see her daughter. Hermes reports (347–51):

> Hades, dark-haired ruler of the perished,
> Zeus the father bids you bring illustrious Persephone
> out of Erebus to be among the gods, so that her mother,
> looking upon her, may cease from anger and dire wrath
> against the immortals.

Among a number of correspondences between Demeter and Thetis, there is an especially telling parallel in the κάλυμμα κυάνεον (dark cloak) Demeter puts on as she rushes out in search of Kore, which is subsequently reflected in her epithet *kuanopeplos* (dark-robed). *Kuanopeplos* is used to describe Demeter four times in the course of the *Hymn*, within a space of only slightly over one hundred lines,[47] characterizing her at the height of her ominous wrath, in the course of the gods' efforts to appease her.[48] The final instance of the epithet at 442 occurs after the reunion of Demeter and Kore, but *before* Zeus

---

[45] 18. 35–7: 'He cried out piercingly, and his regal mother heard him | as she sat in the depths of the sea beside her aged father, | and she cried in lament in turn.'

[46] *H. Dem.* 38–44, cited below.   [47] *H. Dem.* 319; 360; 374; 442.

[48] *Kuanopeplos* is glossed by a fuller description of the goddess's black garment at 181–3, when she has separated herself from the gods, specifically out of wrath (see n. 54 below).

has appeased Demeter's wrath, guaranteeing her *timai* (honours) and the return of her daughter for two-thirds of the year. Once Demeter has agreed to renounce her wrath, the epithet is not used again.

Demeter's dark aspect originates with the onset of her *achos*:

> The crests of the mountains and the depths of the sea echoed
> with her immortal voice, and her regal mother heard her.
> Instantly grief seized her heart, and she ripped
> the covering on her fragrant hair with her own hands,
> and around both shoulders she threw a dark cloak,
> and sped like a bird over land and sea,
> searching.

(Hymn to Demeter 38–44)

This image of Demeter covering herself with a dark shawl has been shown to signify her transformation from a passive state of grief to an active state of anger.[49] In contrast to the image of the black cloud which surrounds a dying warrior or a mourner, here the goddess's deliberate assumption of the dark garment betokens her dire spirit of retaliation, the realization of her imminent wrath.[50]

In this connection, the cult of Demeter Melaina at Phigalia in Arcadia deserves attention. Pausanias reports (8. 42. 1–4) that the Phigalians, by their own account, have given Demeter the *epiklēsis* Melaina because of her black clothing, which she put on for two reasons: first, out of anger at Poseidon for his intercourse with her,

---

[49] Full argumentation is given in an unpublished paper, 'Demeter and the Black Robe of Grief', by D. Petegorsky, who demonstrates the distinction between the dying warrior being covered by a dark cloud, in such phrases as νεφέλη δέ μιν ἀμφεκάλυψε | κυανέη ('a dark cloud enshrouded him', *Iliad* 20. 417–18) or μέλαν νέφος ἀμφεκάλυψεν ('a black cloud enshrouded him', 16. 350), and Demeter's assertive action in cloaking herself with her black garment. I am greatly indebted to him for making his important analysis available to me.

[50] Petegorsky (n. 49) compares Simonides (fr. 121 D) on the heroes of Thermopylae, who 'donned the dark cloud of death after conferring unquenchable fame on their dear fatherland' (1–2). To quote from his analysis: 'What is crucial in the poem is the change from a situation in which the cloud of death, as a force beyond their control, consumes the warriors, to one in which they have appropriated death by turning it into a voluntary act—they are not passively slain, rather they choose actively to die. The grammar reflects this change. The familiar dark covering phrase is transformed from one in which the dark agent is the subject of the verb of covering and the person who is to die is the object, into one in which the heroes have become the subjects and the cloud the object of the verb ἀμφιβάλλομαι. This is especially interesting in that the verb which is used of Demeter putting on the dark shawl is βάλλομαι, and it is said that she puts it on both (ἀμφοτέρων) shoulders' (23).

and second, out of grief over the abduction of Persephone. Two reasons—but her anger is the first. The Phigalians further explain that Zeus, having learned about Demeter's appearance (σχήματος ... ὡς εἶχε) and her *clothing* (ἐσθῆτα ἐνεδέδυτο ποίαν), sent the Moirai to persuade the goddess to put aside her anger (first) and to abate her grief (second). Moreover, in their worship of Demeter Melaina the Phigalians are said—by way of introduction to their cult—to agree with the Thelpusian account of Demeter's rape by Poseidon. This account, which the Phigalia passage begins by referring to, Pausanias records at 8. 25. 4–5 in order to explain why the goddess is worshipped by the Thelpusians as Demeter Erinus. After Poseidon forced himself on her as she was searching for her daughter, Demeter was enraged at what had happened, and was therefore given the *epiklēsis* Erinus because of her wrath (τοῦ μηνίματος μὲν ἔνεκα Ἐρινύς, 8. 25. 6). Demeter Erinus and Demeter Melaina are congruent references to the same story: the black-garbed goddess is a metonym of the wrathful, avenging goddess.

There is only one other dark *kalumma* in Homeric epic, and it belongs to Thetis. She wraps herself in it when in Book 24 Iris announces Zeus' request that she come to Olympus. Here the context is again, as in the *Hymn to Demeter*, one of *achos*.[51] Because of her *achos* Thetis all but refuses to join the other gods. Unlike Demeter in the *Hymn* she does respond to the summons; and yet, the dark cloak she then puts on expresses, as with Demeter, the active principle that her grief presupposes (24. 93–6):

> So she spoke and, radiant among goddesses, she took up
> her dark cloak, and there is no blacker garment than this.
> She set out, and before her swift, wind-stepping Iris led the way.

The very request from Zeus acknowledges that she and Achilles together have, like Demeter, brought Olympus to its knees. Her potential for retaliation is signalled explicitly: Zeus says, as she takes her place next to him (24. 104–5),

> You have come to Olympus, divine Thetis, although sorrowing
> with a grief beyond forgetting in your heart. And I myself know it.

Alaston, derived from *lanthanomai*, means, on the one hand, 'unforgettable'. The semantics of *alastōr* (avenging spirit) in tragedy,

---

[51] 24. 92, ἔχω δ' ἄχε' ἄκριτα θυμῷ (I have countless *achea* in my heart).

however, as well as the morphological parallel with *aphthiton*, indicate that it can also mean 'unforgetting'.[52] In this sense, the *penthos* of Thetis has the same ominous character as that of her son, whose final *penthos* over the death of Patroclus drives him to his devastating vengeance.

The image of the goddess taking up her κάλυμμα κυάνεον (dark cloak) may be seen, I suggest, as conveying the implicit threat of *mēnis*.[53] That Thetis wears a dark cloak 'than which there is no blacker garment' accords with her having a cosmic potential for revenge—bivalent as we have seen λοιγὸν ἀμῦναι to be—that is greater than any other.

Why then does the *Iliad* not refer overtly to the wrath of Thetis? Thetis, as observed earlier, never refers to her own power, in contexts where we would expect it, but to her own grief. That grief, however, is twofold. When she accounts for it most fully, to Hephaestus in 18, she separates the two aspects of it (18. 429–37):

Hephaestus, is there anyone, of all the goddesses on Olympus
who has endured so many baneful sorrows in her heart,
as many as the griefs Zeus the son of Kronos has given me beyond all others?
Of all the daughters of the sea he forced on me a mortal man
Aeacus' son Peleus, and I endured the bed of a mortal man
utterly unwilling though I was. And that one lies
in his halls, shattered by baneful old age. But now for me there are other
  sorrows:
since he gave me a son to bear and to raise,
pre-eminent among heroes, and he grew like a young shoot.

The primary cause of her suffering was being forced by Zeus the son of Kronos to submit against her will to marriage to a mortal. Thus the *Iliad* returns us to the crucial feature of Thetis' mythology, her role in the succession myth. She was forced to marry a mortal

---

[52] Among other examples from tragedy, see *Ag.* 1500–4. In *Comparative Studies in Greek and Indic Meter* (Cambridge, Mass., 1974), 256–61, G. Nagy discusses the traditional relationship of the complementary themes of *kleos* and *penthos* and the morphology of their epithets. See as well the analysis in Chantraine (n. 9), 554. Also the discussion of verse 911 in Wilamowitz's edition of Euripides' *Herakles* (Bad Homburg, 1959; reprint of the 1895 edn.), III. 202.

[53] M. Nagler has demonstrated the symbolic signification of clothing and gestures related to it in his discussion of Homeric *krēdemnon*, in *Spontaneity and Tradition: A Study in the Oral Art of Homer* (Berkeley, 1974), 27–63. See also S. Lowenstam, *The Death of Patroklos: A Study in Typology*, Beiträge zur klassischen Philologie 133 (Königstein, 1981) on the symbolic force of gesture in the *Il.*

because her potential for bearing a son greater than his father meant that marriage to Zeus or Poseidon would begin the entire world-order over again.

Here once more there is a striking parallel with the *Hymn to Demeter*, which stresses Demeter's anger not so much against Hades as against Zeus, who ordained the rape of Persephone by his brother. The poem is explicit on this point. Helios identifies Zeus as exclusively *aitios* (responsible) in the abduction of Persephone (75–9), upon hearing which Demeter is said to feel a 'more terrible' *achos* and to withdraw from the company of the gods out of rage at Zeus (90–4):

> and grief more terrible and savage entered her heart.
> Thereupon in anger at the son of Kronos of the black clouds,
> shunning the assembly of the gods and high Olympus
> she went to the cities and fertile fields of men,
> long disfiguring her appearance.

In the context of her wrathful isolation from the gods, as noted above, elaborate mention is made of her black garment.[54]

The implicit wrath of Thetis has an analogous source. Given that the tripartite division of the universe is shared between the three brothers—Zeus and Poseidon on the one hand, Hades on the other—we see that these two myths share in the first place a preoccupation with the imposition and preservation of the existing hierarchy of divine power. Both the *Hymn to Demeter* and Pindar's *Isthmian 8*, in treating Thetis' mythology, are equipped by the nature of their genres to emphasize this concern. Their other common element, namely grief over the confrontation with mortality, is what heroic epic uniquely elaborates.

The *Iliad* is about the condition of being human, and about heroic endeavour as its most encompassing expression. The *Iliad* insists at every opportunity on the irreducible fact of human mortality, and in

---

[54] See *h. Cer.* 181–3 and cf. n. 48. It is perhaps worth adding that in Homer the formula τετιημένος ἦτορ ('disturbed at heart', *h. Cer.* 181) when it is used to describe the gods, always denotes anger rather than sorrow; when Hera and Athena sit apart from Zeus and refuse to speak to him for preventing them from assisting the Achaeans, they are said to be φίλον τετιημέναι ἦτορ (disturbed at heart) at *Il.* 8. 437; and when Hephaestus discovered the adultery of Aphrodite and Ares, 'he set out for his house, disturbed in his dear heart; | and he stood in the doorway, and savage anger seized him' (*Od.* 8. 303–4). For a psychoanalytic perspective on the hymn's representation of Demeter's resistance to the patriarchal order, see M. Arthur, 'Politics and Pomegranates: An Interpretation of the Homeric Hymn to Demeter', *Arethusa* 10. 1 (Spring, 1977), 7–47.

order to do so it reworks traditional motifs, such as the protection motif, as suggested above. The values it asserts, its definition of heroism, emerge in the human, not the divine, sphere.

For this reason, it is more useful to ask, not why the *Iliad* omits specific mention of a *mēnis* of Thetis, but why it gives us so much evidence for one; and why at crucial points in the narrative it reminds its audience of the theogonic mythology of Thetis as cosmic force. This sort of question may be said to motivate an inquiry such as the present one, whose goal is to reinforce our awareness of how, and for what purposes, Homeric epic integrates diverse mythological material into its narrative, and of the ways in which it unifies such material thematically.

Thetis provides an intriguing example of the convergence of these dynamic processes, in that the way in which her mythology is resonant but subordinated corresponds to the Homeric insight that it literally underlies or forms the substratum of the heroism of Achilles. The intrinsic relation of parent to child, in which the parent's story becomes the child's story, is not banal here, but has special significance. The reality of Thetis' generative power has as its issue the fact of Achilles' mortality. In this sense *Isthmian* 8 is describing where the *Iliad* should begin.

It has been argued by C. Watkins that whereas the *Iliad* demands the resolution of a wrath (whose religious stature is established by its very diction) in its initial thematic statement, the formula which would express such a resolution is rigorously suppressed. Suffice it here to quote the conclusion to Watkins's detailed analysis:[55]

We have shown on the one hand the equivalence of $\mu\hat{\eta}\nu\iota\varsigma$ [*mēnis*] and $\chi\acute{o}\lambda o\varsigma$ [*cholos*] in the mouth of the one who says 'I', and the equivalence of $\mu\hat{\eta}\nu\iota\varsigma$ [*mēnis*] and $\mu\eta\nu\iota\theta\mu\acute{o}\varsigma$ [*mēnithmos*], for which the latter is the tabu substitute precisely in $\mu\eta\nu\iota\theta\mu\grave{o}\nu \kappa\alpha\tau\alpha\pi\alpha\upsilon\sigma\acute{e}\mu\epsilon\nu$ [to put an end to my wrath] 16. 62. We have shown on the other hand that $\mu\acute{e}\nu o\varsigma$ [*menos*] in the sense of 'anger, wrath' is an echo, a phonetic icon, of the forbidden word $\mu\hat{\eta}\nu\iota\varsigma$ [*mēnis*]. Everything then would indicate that the dramatic resolution of the *Iliad* as a whole, whose theme 'wrath' is announced from its very first word, is expressed by a formula 'put an end to one's wrath', *whose real verbal expression* $\pi\alpha\acute{\upsilon}\epsilon\iota\nu + \mu\hat{\eta}\nu\iota\nu$ *never surfaces*. It is a formula hidden behind the vocabulary tabu, a particular condition on the plane of the parole, of the message, of the one who is speaking and the one who is addressed.

[55] Watkins (n. 40), 703–4.

Similarly, what informs the human stature of Achilles is Thetis' cosmic, theogonic power, her role in the succession myth; and although the *Iliad* never reverts to it explicitly, it returns us to it repeatedly. For had Themis not intervened, Thetis would have borne the son greater than his father, and the entire chain of succession in heaven would have continued: Achilles would have been not the greatest of the heroes, but the ruler of the universe. The price of Zeus' hegemony is Achilles' death. This is the definitive instance of the potency of themes in Homeric epic which exert their influence on the subject-matter of the poems, yet which do not *surface* (in Watkins's term) because of the constraints of the genre; nevertheless, the poem reveals them, through evocative diction, through oblique reference, even through significant omission.

It is in this sense that we can understand what appears to be a revision of the prayer formula by Achilles through Thetis to Zeus in Book I. It has been shown that the typical arrangement of prayers, as represented in Archaic poetry, consists of the invocation of the god or goddess; the claim that the person praying is entitled to a favour in return—based on the premiss that this constitutes a formal communication of reciprocal obligations between god and hero.[56]

In directing his request for a favour from Zeus to Thetis, Achilles has translated his reminder of a 'past favour granted' into *her* past aid to Zeus. But he prefaces his request, and invokes his mother, by saying (1. 352–4):

> Mother, since you did bear me to be short-lived,
> surely high-thundering Olympian Zeus ought to
> grant me honour.

In other words, Achilles' favour to Zeus consists in his being *minunthadios* (short-lived), whereby Zeus' sovereignty is guaranteed.

To reiterate, the *Iliad* reminds us of Thetis' mythology, through allusions to her power and through emphasis on the reciprocity of *achos* that she and Achilles share—his Iliadic and hers meta-Iliadic— in order to assert the meaning of human life in relation to the entire

---

[56] I am paraphrasing here from the detailed discussion of the formal structure of Homeric prayers in Leonard C. Muellner, *The Meaning of Homeric EYXOMAI through its Formulas* (Innsbruck, 1976), 27–8. See also H. Meyer, *Hymnische Stilelemente in der frühgriechischen Dichtung* (Diss. Cologne, 1933), esp. 9–16; E. Norden, *Agnostos Theos* (Leipzig, 1913), 143–76; M. Lang, 'Reason and Purpose in Homeric Prayers', *CW* 68 (1975), 309–14.

cosmic structure, in order to show that cosmic equilibrium is bought at the cost of human mortality. The alternative would mean perpetual evolution, perpetual violent succession, perpetual disorder.

The tradition of Thetis' power whose eventual issue is in the figure of Achilles both enhances his stature and is subsumed in it. Thus it represents the ultimate example of thematic integration. As heroic epic is concerned with the deeds of men rather than the deeds of gods, with Achilles the moral hero, the wrath of Thetis—potent in another framework—becomes absorbed in the actual wrath of her son. Achilles' invocation, in Book 1, of Thetis' cosmic power that once rescued Zeus, must also evoke the power that once threatened to supplant him; and once again, as in *Isthmian* 8, its corollary is the death of Achilles in battle.

That Thetis' power to persuade Zeus to favour Achilles has a source that the poem sees as located in an anterior (or extra-Iliadic) tradition, is expressed not only in Achilles' speech in Book 1, but in a telling passage in Book 15. The result of Thetis' persuading Zeus to favour Achilles is the Trojans' success in bringing fire to the Achaean ships. In Book 15, at the final stage of the Trojans' advantage from the favour granted to Achilles before the death of Patroclus commits him to re-enter the fighting, the situation is described as follows (15. 592–9):

> But the Trojans like ravening lions
> charged at the ships, and were fulfilling the bidding of Zeus
> who continually roused great strength in them and beguiled the spirit
> of the Argives and denied them victory, but urged on the others.
> For Zeus' intention was to give victory to Hector,
> Priam's son, so that he might hurl on the curved ships
> blazing, unwearying fire, and accomplish entirely
> the extraordinary prayer of Thetis.

Significantly, Thetis' prayer is qualified by the Iliadic *hapax exaision*. It has been shown that the phrases ὑπὲρ μοῖραν and κατὰ μοῖραν (beyond/in accordance with destiny, *moira*) and by extension the equivalent phrases ὑπὲρ αἶσαν and κατὰ αἶσαν (beyond/in accordance with *aisa*) are used in Homeric epic self-referentially, to signify adherence to or contravention of the composition's own traditions.[57] We may therefore observe that the exercise of Thetis'

---

[57] Nagy (n. 13), 40: 'Within the conventions of epic composition, an incident that is untraditional would be ὑπὲρ μοῖραν "beyond destiny". For example, it would

power with its massive consequences for inverting the course of the Trojan War is *exaision*—neither according to, nor opposed to, Iliadic tradition, but *outside* it and requiring integration into it.

The *Hymn to Demeter* demands a sacral resolution in terms appropriate to Demeter's wrath. Heroic epic demands a human one, and the *Iliad* presents it in 24. Thetis must accept the mortal condition of Achilles, of which, as *Isthmian* 8 explains, she is the cause. This acceptance means the defusing of *mēnis*, leaving only *achos*. It is thus comprehensible thematically that Thetis should be the agent of Achilles' returning the body of Hector; of his acceptance not only of his mortality but of the universality of the conditions of human existence as he expounds them to Priam in 24.

As such Thetis is the instrument of his renunciation of *mēnis* in the poem. In a sense the submerged formula $\pi\alpha\acute{v}\epsilon\iota\nu + \mu\hat{\eta}\nu\iota\nu$ (to put an end to *mēnis*) is enacted twice, not only on the human and divine levels, but twice in time: in the 'long-time' eternality of the succession myth and in the time-span of the Iliadic plot. The intersection is the lifespan of Achilles. With this perspective we can see the *Iliad's* concern with the individual's experience of his mortal limitations and the existential choices they demand, but equally its concern with their metaphysical consequences in relation to the entire cosmic structure.

Through Thetis' agency, finally, the Plan of Zeus is kept from yielding to the Plan of Achilles. In Alcman's cosmogony, she is a force of order and orientation, establishing bearings and a goal in the presence of darkness and chaos. So, too, the order that the *Iliad* asserts is served by Thetis: once a threat to Olympian stability, she takes her place again as its protector.[58]

violate tradition to let Achilles kill Aeneas in *Iliad* xx, although the immediate situation in the narrative seems to make it inevitable; accordingly, Poseidon intervenes and saves Aeneas, telling him that his death at this point would be "beyond destiny" ($\acute{v}\pi\grave{\epsilon}\rho \ \mu o\hat{\iota}\rho\alpha\nu$: xx 336).'

[58] The study of Homeric mythology and oral style [n. 30], of which this chapter forms part, owes thanks to more people than can be acknowledged here; I have expressed my gratitude to them in that context. The present chapter, a version of which was first given as a talk at Princeton University in November 1979, has benefited from the illuminating criticisms of A. E. Johnson, and of J. H. Finley, Jr., G. Nagy, and R. Sacks, as well as from the valuable suggestions of H. Bacon, S. Bershtel, N. O. Brown, P. Easterling, D. Frame, A. Hayum, R. Janko, N. Loraux, R. Slatkin, F. Zeitlin, and of the editor and anonymous referees of *TAPA*.

15

Mythological Paradeigma in the Iliad

M. M. WILLCOCK

An inquiry[1] into the use of paradeigma in the *Iliad* must begin with Niobe. At 24. 602 Achilles introduces Niobe in order to encourage Priam to have some food. The dead body of the best of Priam's sons has now been placed on the wagon ready for its journey back to Troy. Achilles says (I paraphrase), 'Now let us eat. For even Niobe ate food, and she had lost *twelve* children. Apollo and Artemis killed them all; they lay nine days in their blood and there was no one to bury them, because Zeus had turned the people into stone. On the tenth day the gods buried them. But she managed to eat some food, when she was tired of weeping. And now among the mountains, although turned into stone, she still broods over her sorrows. But come, let us also eat. You can weep for your son again later' (24. 601–19).

Kakridis (n. 1), 96–105[2] explains Homer's use of the Niobe story. Niobe's situation as described is clearly very like Priam's, only more so. Priam has lost one child: Niobe lost all twelve; and yet Niobe ate

---

[1] The following books and articles will be referred to below: E. Bethe, 'Ilias und Meleager', *RM* 74 (1925), 1–12; P. Cauer, *Grundfragen der Homerkritik* (3rd edn., Leipzig, 1921–3); E. Drerup, *Homerische Poetik* I: *Das Homerproblem in der Gegenwart* (Würzburg, 1921); G. Finsler, *Homer* I (2nd edn., Leipzig, 1913); E. Howald, 'Meleager und Achill', *RM* 73 (1924), 402–25; J. T. Kakridis, *Homeric Researches* (Lund, 1949); M. C. van der Kolf, *RE* xv.1 (1931) s.v. Meleagros, 447–50; W. Kraus, 'Meleagros in der Ilias', *WS* 63 (1948), 8–21; A. B. Lord, *The Singer of Tales* (Cambridge, Mass., 1960); D. Mülder, *Die Ilias und ihre Quellen* (Berlin, 1910); M. Noé, *Phoinix, Ilias und Homer* (Leipzig, 1940), 54–89; R. Öhler, *Mythologische Exempla in der älteren griechischen Dichtung* (Diss. Basle, 1925); D. L. Page, *History and the Homeric Iliad* (Berkeley, 1959); C. Robert, *Die griechischen Heldensage* I (Berlin, 1920), 88–100; E. Sachs, 'Die Meleagererzählung in der Ilias', *Philologus* 88 (1933), 16–29; W. Schadewaldt, *Iliasstudien* (Leipzig, 1938, 2nd edn. 1943, repr. Darmstadt, 1966); P. Von der Mühll, *Kritisches Hypomnema zur Ilias* (Basle, 1952); U. von Wilamowitz-Moellendorff, *Die Ilias und Homer* (Berlin, 1916).

[2] Following Öhler (n. 1), 5–7 and Kakridis's own article in *RM* 79 (1930), 113–22.

food. *A fortiori* Priam should eat. What makes the story important and the starting-point for this discussion is the fact that it is more than improbable that there was any legend at all that Niobe had partaken of food after her children had been killed. The detail is irrelevant to the universal story that she was turned to stone, and it does not recur in any version after Homer (except where a late author, e.g. Lucian, *De luctu* 24, is actually quoting Homer). The situation is not that Homer has chosen a suitable mythological example as an encouragement to Priam—rather *he has invented it*. As Kakridis says (99), 'Niobe in Book 24 eats for the simple reason that Priam must eat. The genuine tradition knew nothing of a Niobe who "remembered to eat" either before or after Homer; it knew only of the mother who was petrified by grief for the loss of her children.'[3]

Hector has been lying in the dust unburied. Achilles says that the children of Niobe were left unburied, *because Zeus had turned the people into stone* (611),

$$\lambda\alpha o\grave{v}s \ \delta\grave{\epsilon} \ \lambda\acute{\iota}\theta ovs \ \pi o\acute{\iota}\eta\sigma\epsilon \ K\rho ov\acute{\iota}\omega v.$$

This is another bland invention by the poet. To get the parallel with Hector, he wants the children unburied; to get possible buriers out of the way, he turns the people into stone. He is using a fairly common motif,[4] but there appears to be a strong underlying reason for his choice of that motif here. Consciously or subconsciously he is affected by the fact that there is petrifaction in the story already. In the regular version Niobe is turned to stone; to explain the inactivity of the people, Homer has *them* turned to stone.[5]

---

[3] F. Wehrli, *RE* Suppl v (1931), 575, s.v. Leto, and W. Schadewaldt, SB Heidelberg 24 (1933/4), 3. 31 n. I agree that Niobe's eating is an invention of the poet of the *Iliad*.

[4] e.g. the Deucalion story ($\lambda\alpha\acute{o}s = \lambda\hat{\alpha}\alpha s$), and what Perseus did to Polydectes and his unfortunate companions. For Zeus acting in this way, cf. 2. 319 $\lambda\hat{\alpha}\alpha v \ \gamma\acute{\alpha}\rho \ \mu\iota v$ $\acute{\epsilon}\theta\eta\kappa\epsilon \ K\rho\acute{o}vov \ \pi\acute{\alpha}\ddot{\iota}s \ \grave{\alpha}\gamma\kappa v\lambda o\mu\acute{\eta}\tau\epsilon\omega$, 'for the son of crooked-counselling Cronus turned it to stone'.

[5] The petrifaction of Niobe does still occur in Homer's version as we have it, side by side with the petrifaction of the people. Beginning with the Alexandrian scholars many have considered these lines (614–17) interpolated. The strongest arguments against them are that they are inconsistent with the point of Achilles' story, and that they 'break the ring' (see nn. 6 and 7 below). Von der Mühll (n. 1: 385), however, argues that 614–17 are not wholly out of place. Niobe dries her tears and eats, but she will weep again later, just as Priam is told in line 619 that he will have the opportunity to weep later. Whether 614–17 are interpolated or not does not affect the fact of the transfer of the motif of petrifaction from Niobe to the people.

This interesting transfer of the motif of petrifaction in the
Niobe story seems to be closely parallel to something that is said by
Lord (n. 1: 97) about the Yugoslavian songs. Talking about association of themes in songs of a common type, he says, 'Habitual
association of themes, however, need not be merely linear, that is to
say, theme b always follows theme a, and theme c always follows
theme b. Sometimes the presence of theme a in a song calls forth the
presence of theme b somewhere in the song, but not necessarily in an
a–b relationship, not necessarily following one another immediately.
Where the association is linear, it is close to the logic of the narrative,
and the themes are generally of a kind that are included in a larger
complex. Where the association is not linear, it seems to me that we
are dealing with a force or "tension" that might be termed "submerged". The habit is hidden, but felt. It arises from the depths of the
tradition through the workings of the traditional processes to
inevitable expression.' In this way Lord describes the appearance of
certain regular themes in songs of a common type. It seems to me
that the same force is at work in the Niobe story; petrifaction is
associated with Niobe and therefore comes in as a motif, although in
an abnormal part of the story.

The form of the Niobe paradeigma is one of the best examples in
the *Iliad* of what is called ring-composition.[6] This is a stylistic
method common in digressions of all sorts in early Greek poetry,
particularly the Homeric poems. Basically, ring-composition simply
means that the digression repeats at its end the statement made at its
beginning. When, as often, it is used in a paradeigma, the system
becomes a five-part one; Nestle (n. 1) describes it as thesis—reason—
narrative—reason—thesis. This is perfectly exemplified by 24. 601,
602, 603–12, 613, 618[7]—(1) Let us eat. (2) For even Niobe ate.
(3) This was her story. (4) She ate. (5) Let us also eat.

Paradeigma may be defined as a myth introduced for exhortation
or consolation, 'You must do this, because X, who was in more or less
the same situation as you, and a more significant person, did it.'
The Niobe story shows that, in order to produce his parallel in the

[6] The term ring-composition seems to have originated with H. Fränkel (*Gött.
Nachr.* (1924), 97 n. 4). On its use particularly in paradeigma, see Öhler (n. 1), 7,
Fränkel, in his review of Öhler, *Gnomon* 3 (1927), 569, and W. Nestle in *Hermes* 77
(1942), 66 n. 3.
[7] For the scheme to be exact it helps to omit 614–17 as interpolated (n. 5 above). It
is, however, a question whether we ought to require mathematical exactness in a
matter like this.

paradeigma, the author of the *Iliad* is prepared to *invent the significant details of the myth*. This is a radical procedure. Can we see him doing the same elsewhere in the *Iliad*? I think we can; and indeed that this is a notable feature of his use of mythology. I offer seven examples, leaving to the end Meleager, the most important example of all.

1. 259–74. Achilles and Agamemnon are abusing each other. Nestor tries to calm them down. In an example, of ring-composition very like the Niobe story in 24, Nestor is made to say, 'Be guided by me. You are both younger than I am. I used to associate with better men than you, men like Pirithous, Dryas, Caeneus, Exadius, Polyphemus, and even Theseus.[8] Mighty as they were (they fought against the centaurs), they asked me to fight with them, and I did. And they listened to my advice. Therefore I ask you also to listen to my advice.'

Can we really assert that there was in pre-Homeric poetry some *Nestoris,[9] in which the hero went from Pylos to fight on the side of Pirithous and company in the far north? It is surely unlikely. Much more probably this is an *a fortiori* encouragement to Achilles and Agamemnon to listen to Nestor's words, with a mythological situation introduced for the purpose.[10]

1. 393–407. Achilles is asking his mother to go to Olympus and persuade Zeus to honour him by helping the Trojans. 'If you have ever helped Zeus by word or deed, go and ask this favour now.' And Achilles produces a mythological story which shows Thetis helping Zeus: 'Many times have I heard you boasting in my father's house[11] that you alone once saved Zeus when the other gods, Hera

---

[8] Theseus (line 265) may be an Athenian-inspired interpolation, as no doubt Aristarchus believed. Discussion and references in Von der Mühll (n. 1), 24 n. 29.

[9] It has sometimes been assumed that there was heroic poetry about Nestor which is extensively quoted from in the *Iliad*. Nestor has four long speeches in which he recounts the achievements of his youth: 1. 254–84 (the Lapiths); 7. 124–60 (Ereuthalion); 11. 656–803 (wars in the Peloponnese); 23. 626–50 (athletic successes). W. Leaf, *The Iliad, edited with English notes and introduction* 1 (1st edn., London, 1886), 239, wrote, 'We...see reasons for believing that a speech by Nestor about his youthful prowess offered a convenient opportunity for later interpolation.' But Leaf was an analyst. It seems rather that a speech by Nestor about his youthful prowess offered a convenient opportunity for the invention of the poet.

[10] Mülder (n. 1), 47 and Von der Mühll (n. 1), 24 n. 29 agree that Nestor's presence with the Lapiths is an impromptu poetic invention.

[11] For the beginning of the paradeigma cf. 21. 475–7. In that passage Apollo has just properly refused to fight against his uncle Poseidon. Artemis is annoyed and uses

and Poseidon and Athene, wished to bind him. You brought the hundred-handed giant whom the gods call Briareos, but men call him Aegaeon—because he is more powerful than his father—and the giant sat by Zeus and the gods were afraid. Remind him of that, and ask his help now.'

Zenodotus athetized 396–406, no doubt because of their mythological difficulties. Both ancient (the scholia) and modern commentators have had the greatest difficulty in explaining the various details of the story. The problems disappear if we accept that the whole thing may be sheer invention.[12] This is to some extent supported by the fact that Thetis does not repeat the story when she actually makes her appeal to Zeus later in the book.

Briareos, the hekatoncheir, is a typical supporter of Zeus and that is why he is brought into the story. He helps Zeus against the Titans in Hesiod (*Theogony* 734, 817).

The two lines which raise particular mythological difficulty (apart from the whole story) are 400 and 404. (*a*) Why (in 400) these three particular gods? Why should Hera, Poseidon, and Athene have wished to bind Zeus? The line has caused great offence and occasioned the most varied and imaginative explanations. The answer is a pregnant one. It is precisely because these are the three gods who support the Greeks in the *Iliad*, and who *would therefore most wish to prevent Zeus acceding to Thetis' request*, that they are made the opponents of Zeus in the invented myth.[13]

(*b*) In 404 Briareos/Aegaeon is stated to be more powerful than his father. I believe that this detail is an intrusion from the other story connecting Thetis with Zeus, the story found in the *Prometheus*

---

a paradeigma, 'Let me never again hear you boasting in my father's house, as you have in the past, that you are prepared to fight against Poseidon.' Aristarchus athetized those three lines on the ground that they contradict the character of Apollo and his previous behaviour. They do. And thus they betray the fact that they are sheer invention with no other basis than the needs of the moment. The poet uses the same method in the two passages: (1. 396–7) πολλάκι γάρ σεο πατρὸς ἐνὶ μεγάροισιν ἄκουσα εὐχομένης and (21. 475–6) μή σευ νῦν ἔτι πατρὸς ἐνὶ μεγάροισιν ἀκούσω εὐχομένου.

[12] Mülder (n. 1), 139, Von der Mühll (n. 1), 26 n. 35.

[13] The scholia, among many explanations, offer something like this, namely that these are the Achaean gods, mentioned by name in order to influence Zeus to listen to Thetis. J. Wackernagel, *Sprachliche Untersuchungen zu Homer* (Göttingen, 1916), 233, thinks 400 interpolated, but ascribes to the interpolator the motive that is here ascribed to the author, namely to mention the gods who would object to Thetis influencing Zeus.

Vinctus and in Pindar's Eighth *Isthmian*, namely that she was fated to bring forth a child who was *stronger than his father*.[14] If this is true, the intrusive detail is exactly parallel to the petrifaction of the people in the Niobe paradeigma—it is caused by what Lord calls 'the submerged force of a non-linear association'.

4. 370–400. Agamemnon tells a tale of Tydeus as an example to Tydeus' son Diomedes. The pattern is the usual one of a paradeigma: 'Why are you skulking here, Diomedes? Tydeus used not to skulk in battle.' Then comes a long story illustrating Tydeus' bravery, followed by, 'Such was Tydeus; but his son is not such a fighter as he was.' The example of Tydeus' prowess is in 384–98. When the army of the Seven against Thebes was approaching the city, they sent Tydeus forward as an ambassador. He proceeded to beat all the Thebans at athletics, which so annoyed them that they laid an ambush to kill him on the way back, fifty men led by two murderous-sounding leaders—Maeon son of Haemon and Polyphontes son of Autophonus. Tydeus killed them all except Maeon, whom he sent back to the city to give the news.

If it were possible to choose a lost work of Greek literature for recovery, the epic *Thebaid* would come high on a preference list. It would answer more questions about Homer than all the deciphering of Mycenaean tablets and excavating of tholos tombs. Without the *Thebaid* we cannot say for certain that the story given here by Homer did not occur in the legends of the Theban war. It looks in fact as if Tydeus' embassy to Thebes was a regular feature of the legend.[15] In that case the background to the paradeigma at least would be known to the hearers, just as the centaur-Lapith war existed in legend and made a background to Nestor's paradeigma in Book I.

The exploit of Tydeus on the other hand looks suspicious. It bears the marks of exaggeration; and the name of the second murderer at least is an invention. Polyphontes son of Autophonus the assassin bears a resemblance to Polyidus the seer (13. 663), Harmonides the carpenter (5. 59–60), and the list of Phaeacians in *Odyssey*

---

[14] J. van Leeuwen (ed.), *Homeri carmina: Ilias* I (Leiden, 1912), ad loc., and Von der Mühll (n. 1), 27 also think that 404 may be a reminiscence of that tale about Thetis' fated son.

[15] C. Robert, *Die griechische Heldensage* III. 1 (Berlin, 1921), 932, discusses this question.

8. 111–14.[16] Maeon son of Haemon has a Theban-sounding father and may be authentic; noticeably he is the only survivor.

The embassy of Tydeus is used for a paradeigma twice elsewhere in the *Iliad*. In 5. 800–13, Athene refers to Tydeus' deeds when he was actually at Thebes on his embassy. In 10. 284–91, Diomedes says that his father achieved marvellous deeds on the way back (289):

ἀτὰρ ἂψ ἀπιὼν μάλα μέρμερα μήσατο ἔργα.

It would certainly seem that the 'marvellous feats' refer to the ambush and its results as described in Book 4. If the details in Book 4 are invented, 10. 289 looks like an allusion by the poet to his own invented story.

Tydeus' embassy to Thebes was probably part of the Theban legend; the unsuccessful ambush on the way back may or may not have been. Polyphontes' name suggests invention.

5. 382–404. This is the famous consolation offered by Dione to her daughter Aphrodite when she has been wounded on the wrist by Diomedes. It is a list of gods who have been wounded by mortals, and a strange though effective list it is. As Öhler points out (n. 1: 41–2), the ring-composition type of paradeigma is used when it is a question of exhortation to a positive course of action; but for consolation the accumulation of examples underlines the point that is being made.

None of the incidents is known elsewhere. 'Bear up, my child,' says Dione; 'many gods have suffered at the hands of men. Ares suffered when Otus and Ephialtes bound him. He lay in bonds for thirteen months in a bronze jar. And Ares would have perished [!] there, had not Hermes got him out. Hera suffered when Heracles shot her in the breast with an arrow. Hades received an arrow in the shoulder from the same man—in Pylos, among the dead men. He went back to Olympus in pain, but was healed by Paeëon; for he was not subject to death.'

Just as there were legends of Thebes which are now lost, so there seem to have been lost legends of Heracles, including occasions when he fought against individual gods. Pindar has an equally difficult

---

[16] Polyphontes was taken over by later writers. Aeschylus makes him one of the Theban seven (*Sept.* 448); the mythographers give the name to the herald of Laius (Robert III. 1 (n. 15), 890 n. 2).

442

M. M. Willcock

allusion in *Olympian* 9. 28–35:

> ἀγαθοὶ δὲ καὶ σοφοὶ κατὰ δαίμον' ἄνδρες
> ἐγένοντ'· ἐπεὶ ἀντίον
> πῶς ἂν τριόδοντος Ἡρακλέης σκύταλον τίναξε χερσίν,
> ἁνίκ' ἀμφὶ Πύλον σταθεὶς ἤρειδε Ποσειδάν,
> ἤρειδεν δέ μιν ἀργυρέῳ τόξῳ πολεμίζων
> Φοῖβος, οὐδ' Ἀΐδας ἀκινήταν ἔχε ῥάβδον κτλ.

With the aid of god men have become warriors and poets: for how otherwise could Heracles have brandished his club against the trident, when Poseidon, standing about Pylos, pressed him hard, and Phoebus, fighting with silver bow, pressed him hard, nor did Hades hold his staff still (etc.).

No satisfying explanation has been found for Pindar's statements, and they cannot be tied in detail to Dione's.

The three stories given in the *Iliad* may be taken from pre-existing legend, but equally they may be simple invention. H. Fränkel gives his opinion that they are suspiciously obscure;[17] others deduce a Heracles epic for the latter two,[18] and this may perhaps be true. But Ares shut in a bronze jar by Otus and Ephialtes is certainly odd. Otus and Ephialtes were the typical opponents of the gods, just as Briareos was the typical helper of Zeus. And the statement that Ares would have perished creates the same impression of strangeness as Ares' own muddled alternatives in lines 885–7 of this same book:

> ἦ τέ κε δηρόν
> αὐτοῦ πήματ' ἔπασχον ἐν αἰνῇσιν νεκάδεσσιν,
> ἦ κε ζὼς ἀμενηνὸς ἔα χαλκοῖο τυπῇσι.

Indeed I would have suffered pain there for a long time among the dreadful corpses, or, still alive, I would have been incapacitated by the strokes of bronze.

On balance, I should join Fränkel in suspecting that all three stories are invented for the purpose of Dione's paradeigma.

7. 124–60. This is Nestor's speech when the Greek leaders are hesitating to accept Hector's challenge to a single combat. Nestor certainly refers to an old legend as the background of his paradeigma,

---

[17] *Dichtung und Philosophie des frühen Griechentums* (New York, 1951), 106 n. 10 = *Early Greek Poetry and Philosophy* (trans. M. Hadas and J. Willis, Oxford, 1975), 75 n. 14.

[18] Gilbert Murray, *The Rise of the Greek Epic* (3rd edn., Oxford, 1924), 180, Von der Mühll (n. 1), 97.

of Areïthoüs the mace-man and how Lycurgus killed him where the road was narrow and he had no room to swing his mace. Areïthoüs the mace-man's son is killed by Paris in lines 8–10 of this book. Perhaps also (but not necessarily) there was legendary authority for Nestor having killed an opponent called Ereuthalion, for he mentions the fact in 4. 319:

ὡς ἔμεν ὡς ὅτε δῖον 'Ερευθαλίωνα κατέκταν

to be as I was when I killed brilliant Ereuthalion.

Where it does seem probable that Homer is inventing is in the detail of the paradeigma itself. Areïthoüs and Lycurgus only come in as a background; Ereuthalion, we hear, had been Lycurgus' squire and had inherited from him the armour of Areïthoüs. But the story is full of difficulties of place and time.[19] Most obviously the chronology cannot be squared with lines 8–10. In Nestor's speech we are told that (*a*) Lycurgus killed Areïthoüs and took his armour; (*b*) when Lycurgus grew old, he gave the armour to Ereuthalion; (*c*) Ereuthalion had been killed by Nestor in his youth. In no way can this be made to fit a son of Areïthoüs fighting at Troy (line 8).

We are therefore suspicious of the setting of Nestor's paradeigma for a start. Then we find that the paradeigma itself is suspiciously close to the present circumstances. Ereuthalion challenged all the leaders of the Pylians to a single combat; they were afraid and held back; eventually Nestor came forward and of course killed Ereuthalion. The circumstances of the reminiscence seem to be adapted to Hector's challenge.

18. 394–405. Thetis has asked Hephaestus to make armour for her son. Hephaestus gives the reason why Thetis can claim his help. The reason as given seems at first sight a poor copy of the story of Zeus hurling Hephaestus from Olympus which is mentioned in 1. 590–4 ('From morn to noon he fell, from noon to dewy eve'). In Book 18 he says that he once fell a long way because his shameless mother wanted to hide him because he was lame. And Thetis and one of her sea-sisters looked after him for nine years.

But there is no need to speak of a copy of Book 1. Hurling out of Olympus appears as a relatively common theme in the *Iliad*. Apart from Hephaestus in Books 1 and 18, in 14. 258 Hypnus says that Zeus

---

[19] See Leaf's notes (n. 9) on 135 (133 in the 2nd edn.) and 149.

would have thrown him out on a previous occasion if he had not been prevented; in 15. 23 Zeus recollects hurling out an undefined number of gods; in 19. 130 Zeus threw Ate out of heaven. The motif is common, available to the poet to use as and where he wishes.

Hiding away and being looked after by Thetis in the sea are also a motif that occurs elsewhere; in 6. 136 Thetis sheltered the frightened Dionysus.[20]

Before we come to Meleager, the points that have emerged so far may be summarized:

A. The mythological example is commonly used in speeches in the *Iliad* when one character wishes to influence the actions of another. Usually it is a matter of exhortation or consolation. This is what is meant by a paradeigma.

B. The form in which the paradeigma appears is often what is called ring-composition. 'You should behave in this way. A famous mythological figure once did so. He was in the following situation (surprisingly parallel to yours). He behaved in this way. Therefore you should do the same.'

C. The parallelism between the mythological story and the immediate situation often seems to be the creation of the poet. Obviously mythology was not as fixed as we may have believed, and certainly as the Alexandrians believed. The scholia are useless on this subject. We have seen that the poet was free to invent details within an already existing framework of legend. The background (of Niobe and her children, the centaur-Lapith war, Tydeus' embassy to Thebes, Areïthoüs and his mace) was there in the legends before Homer. What he has invented is the detailed story necessary for the paradeigma.

D. Homeric invention is sometimes betrayed by some phrase which is irrational in the context, but whose provenance can be explained. Sometimes this phrase has been caused by a detail of another version of the story making its way by force into Homer's version, as in the petrifaction of the people in 24. 611 and the phrase 'better than his father' of Aegaeon in 1. 404. Sometimes a curious phrase simply reflects the carefree composition of Homer, as in the mention of the three Achaean gods in 1. 400, the name of the second murderer in 4. 395, and the statement in 5. 388 that Ares would have perished in his jar.

[20] Θέτις δ' (θ') ὑπεδέξατο κόλπῳ, 6. 136 and 18. 398.

E.   When Homer is inventing, he tends to use stock motifs. This leads us to Lord's extension of the Milman Parry theory of formulaic composition of oral epic poetry. Not only did the oral poet have a stock of formulas for regular use as occasion required; he also from his wide repertoire of heroic stories had a stock of motifs and themes, which naturally came in when the need of the moment called them forth.[21] The examples we have seen, where Homeric invention makes use of a theme recognizable to us from elsewhere, are Zeus turning the people to stone in 24. 611; Briareos as the supporter of Zeus in 1. 402–3; Otus and Ephialtes as the enemies of the gods in 5. 385; an unwanted deity thrown out of heaven in 18. 395, and protected in Thetis' bosom in 18. 398.[22]

With these five points in mind, let us turn to the paradeigma of paradeigmas, the story of Meleager in 9. 524–605.[23] Phoenix is asking Achilles to accept the rich compensation offered to him and to return to the fighting. He adduces the parallel of Meleager, who (so he says) once found himself in the same position as Achilles is in now. We shall take in turn (*a*) the beginning and end of the episode (524–8 and 597–605); (*b*) the background to the paradeigma (the origin of the war between the Curetes and the Aetolians, 529–49, and the digression on Meleager's wife's family, 557–64); (*c*) the paradeigma proper (550–6 and 565–99).

(*a*) The introduction is particularly interesting because 524–6 seem clearly to refer to pre-Homeric poetry and to state that anger themes were quite common:

οὕτω καὶ τῶν πρόσθεν ἐπευθόμεθα κλέα ἀνδρῶν
ἡρώων, ὅτε κέν τιν' ἐπιζάφελος χόλος ἵκοι·
δωρητοί τε πέλοντο παράρρητοί τ' ἐπέεσσιν.

'Such tales have we heard of the heroes of the past, when they were overtaken by violent anger; they were willing to accept compensation and to be won over by appeals.'

---

[21] A. B. Lord, 'Composition by Theme in Homer and Southslavic Epos', *TAPA* 82 (1951), 71–80; and ch. 4 of *The Singer of Tales* (n. 1).

[22] The pattern of points C, D, and E suggests a particular poet. The *Odyssey* does not offer comparable examples.

[23] The story of Meleager in the speech of Phoenix has been among the most discussed passages of the *Il.* during the twentieth century. The chronological order of the contributions to this discussion listed in n. 1 is: Finsler (1913), Robert (1920), Howald (1924), Bethe (1925), Van der Kolf (1931), Sachs (1933), Schadewaldt (1938), Noé (1940), Kraus (1948), Kakridis (1949), Von der Mühll (1952).

With that introduction, Phoenix starts on the story he has to tell: 'I remember this episode from long ago, and will tell it to you, my friends.'

The end is the typical end of a paradeigma, drawing the lesson afforded by the mythological situation to that of Achilles. To paraphrase: 'So Meleager finally saved the Aetolians, but he did it for nothing, because they did not give him the presents they had previously offered. Don't behave like him, my friend. Come while the gifts are on offer. If you enter the battle later without compensation, you will not receive so much credit, even though you are successful.' Phoenix says that Meleager did not come when asked, and so, although he came later, he did not get the offered gifts. Some modern scholars have tried to escape from the natural meaning of these words by seeing an allusion to Meleager's death; they say he died in the battle as soon as he had driven away the enemy, and so was in no position to receive the gifts.[24] That his death is referred to in line 572 we shall see; but the point of these lines at the end is perfectly clear—they are a further encouragement or warning to Achilles to come when asked, so that he may be sure of receiving the gifts. The implication of Meleager's death as a result of his return to the battle is not to be found in them. Far better for us to follow Kraus[25] and compare this sudden materialistic argument with the unexpected materialism of the poet's comment on the exchange of armour between Glaucus and Diomedes in 6. 234-6.

(b) The background to the war in which Meleager was involved is given in ring-composition form in 529-49. The narrative begins with the final result—the war between the Curetes and the Aetolians—and then describes how the previous events have led up to the war. Line 529's Κουρῆτές τε μάχοντο καὶ Αἰτωλοὶ μενεχάρμαι (The Curetes and the stalwart Aetolians were at war) is picked up again in 549, Κουρήτων τε μεσηγὺ καὶ Αἰτωλῶν μεγαθύμων (between the Curetes and the brave Aetolians). The story of Oeneus' omission of a sacrifice to Artemis, her sending the boar, the hunt, and the dispute about the spoils, is told swiftly, if clearly. The style is unlike Homer's usual narrative style, which is straightforward and unhurried. The compression of the narrative here has inspired the common

---

[24] Van der Kolf (n. 1), 448, Schadewaldt (n. 1), 141, Kakridis (n. 1), 13.
[25] Kraus (n. 1), 10.

modern comment that Homer is so allusive and concise that he must be abbreviating an already existing poem.[26]

The other piece of background information which we are given is a digression in 557–64 on the history of the parents of Cleopatra, Meleager's wife. This is a further example of ring-composition: 555–6, 'Angry with his mother, he lay by his wedded wife Cleopatra . . . ', is answered by 565–6, 'by her he lay brooding on his wrath, angered by the curses of his mother'. The central digression is most obscure and allusive, and seems like an abbreviation of a longer narrative. Indeed it has a Hesiodic flavour, like the short biographies which we can see in the fragments of the *Ehoeae* (*Catalogue of Women*).

It was mentioned above as a common comment that the Meleager story in Phoenix's speech is so allusive and concise that it is likely to be a summary of a previously existing version. The fact is that the conciseness and allusiveness are almost wholly confined to these two passages of background information. In Meleager's own story there is an obscurity in 550–2, but it will be argued that that is not caused by any previously existing poem; otherwise the narrative runs on perfectly clearly except for the extremely allusive κασιγνήτοιο φόνοιο (because of her brother's death) in 567. Nobody could possibly understand this reason for Althaea's curse on her son, if he did not already know the saga—that Meleager had killed his uncle, his mother's brother. It is a question of knowledge of the story, not of abbreviation of some particular poem.

(*c*) The central story of Meleager consists of (i) 550–6, his anger, which made him withdraw from the fighting; (ii) 565–72, the reason for his anger (his mother's curse); (iii) 573–99, the increasing danger of the city of Calydon, the successive appeals to Meleager to intervene, and his final return to the battle.

(i) 550–6. The situation is that of Achilles. 'So long as Meleager was in the battle, the Curetes had the worst of it and could not remain outside the walls of the city in spite of their numbers. But when Meleager was overtaken by anger (as happens even to reasonable people) then, angry with his mother Althaea, he lay beside his wedded wife, fair Cleopatra.'

[26] Finsler (n. 1), 39, Öhler (n. 1), 14, Van der Kolf (n. 1), 448, Kraus (n. 1), 14, G. S. Kirk, *The Songs of Homer* (Cambridge, 1962), 166.

ὄφρα μὲν οὖν Μελέαγρος ἀρηΐφιλος πολέμιζε,
τόφρα δὲ Κουρήτεσσι κακῶς ἦν, οὐδ᾽ ἐδύναντο
τείχεος ἔκτοσθεν μίμνειν πολέες περ ἐόντες. (550–3)

We should compare 9. 352–3:

ὄφρα δ᾽ ἐγώ μετ᾽ Ἀχαιοῖσιν πολέμιζον
οὐκ ἐθέλεσκε μάχην ἀπὸ τείχεος ὀρνύμεν Ἕκτωρ.

So long as I was fighting alongside the Achaeans, Hector was unwilling to
start a battle away from the wall.

The lines suit Achilles exactly. But they do not suit Meleager so well.
Meleager was among the *defenders* of Calydon; the Curetes were the
attackers (531–2). It is awkward to say that while Meleager was
fighting the Curetes could not remain outside the walls of Calydon;
but that is what the Greek appears to mean, and that is how the older
commentators naturally took it.[27] In the twentieth century scholars
have without any warrant assumed that it was their own city of
Pleuron (not mentioned at all by Homer in this passage) that the
Curetes were unable to remain without.[28] This implies a strangely
mobile war, where first one city and then the other was besieged.
Both explanations of 550–2 are awkward. It is most likely that here
we have a momentary carelessness. Achilles' situation has had its
effect on Meleager's and thereby slightly muddled the story.[29]

(ii) 565–72. So Meleager stayed out of the battle brooding on his
anger, which had been caused by his mother's curses. Althaea had
cursed her son with death because of the death of her brother, and
'the fury that walks in darkness heard her from hell'—heard, and
took note of her appeal, so that Meleager's death is here implied. The
death of Althaea's brother (in other versions, of two brothers) was
always part of the legend. Meleager killed him or them (unwittingly,
according to Bacchylides) in a fight over the spoils of the boar.

(iii) 573–99. The Curetes attacked more and more strongly in
Meleager's absence. Successive appeals were made to him by the
priests of the town, offering a great reward, his old father Oeneus,
his sisters and mother, and his dearest friends. He refused them all.

---

[27] e.g. F. H. Bothe (ed.), *Homeri carmina* II (Leipzig, 1833), J. U. Fäsi (ed.), *Homers Iliade* II (6th edn., Berlin, 1888), A. Pierron (ed.), *L'Iliade d'Homère* I (Paris, 1869), ad loc.

[28] Leaf (n. 9) ad loc., Robert (n. 1), 90, Howald (n. 1), 406, Öhler (n. 1), 15, Van der Kolf (n. 1), 447, Kraus (n. 1), 15. [29] So Noé (n. 1), 78.

Finally, when his own house was being struck by missiles, he gave in to the appeal by his wife Cleopatra and returned to the fighting. He saved the Aetolians, but no longer got the reward that had been offered by the priests.

Kakridis has much on the 'scale of affection', the natural order of the suppliants who come to ask Meleager to give up his anger.[30] The discussion is very useful, because it enables us to see the passage, not in isolation, but as typical of such scenes. It becomes clear that the mother has her natural place in an order of suppliants, and that we should not be surprised by her appearance here when a short while ago she was praying for the death of her son. The inconsistency in her behaviour which has worried a number of critics is caused by the fact that the poet is using a stock theme. Moreover, Kakridis shows us that the *Iliad* poet has altered the usual order of suppliants in one particular. He has placed the friends of the warrior, his *hetairoi*, as high in the scale as he could, even after members of Meleager's own family (585–6). The reason is that it is Achilles' own *hetairoi* who are appealing to him at the moment. Once again the situation in the Greek army at Troy has affected the detail of the paradeigma.

It is clear that Meleager's situation is very close to that of Achilles, not only at this stage of the *Iliad*, but in the whole plot of the epic. And the final solution is in essence that of the *Iliad*, Cleopatra taking the place of Patroclus as the person who made the last appeal, which caused the hero's return (although the two solutions differ in detail— Patroclus had to die first, and Achilles did get most of the promised gifts).[31]

Discussion has centred on the assumption that the coincidences between the two stories are not a matter of chance, but that the one was modelled on the other. In preparation for that problem we must consider how the Meleager story appears in our other ancient sources. It is immediately obvious that Homer's version is eccentric.

---

[30] Kakridis (n. 1), 19–25 and Appendix III.

[31] Howald (n. 1: 411) first suggested that the name Patro-klos was an invention formed from the elements of the name Kleo-patra. Öhler (n. 1: 16) was pleased with the suggestion, but had to reverse it, because he (rightly, as I think) made the *Il.* story the original, this part of Phoenix's tale of Meleager the copy. Thus he argued that Kleo-patra was an invention based on Patro-klos. This startling theory was accepted by Schadewaldt (n. 1), 140 and even by W. Theiler ('Die Dichter der Ilias', in *Festschrift für E. Tièche* (Berne, 1947), 164 n. 61); Kakridis (n. 1), 29 and Kraus (n. 1), 17 argue against.

Althaea's curse and the consequent withdrawal of the hero from the fighting do not appear in any other version of the Meleager story except where a mythographer is directly copying Homer.[32] The only full-scale versions of this legend in ancient poetry are Bacchylides 5. 94 ff. and Ovid *Metamorphoses* 8. 270 ff.; neither has any reference to the mother's curse or Meleager's withdrawal from the battle. Nor could they have any reference to the latter at least, because in them, as in all other allusions except one that will be mentioned in the next paragraph, Meleager's death is caused immediately by sympathetic magic. When Althaea heard the news of the killing of her brothers, she took out of the box the half-burnt piece of wood which represented Meleager's life, and threw it on the fire. Meleager collapsed at that moment.

A very different version quoting a new and unexpected cause of death is given by Pausanias.[33] He says that in the *Ehoeae* (the pseudo-Hesiodic *Catalogue of Women*) and the *Minyas* (a lost epic poem) Apollo, on the side of the Curetes against the Aetolians, himself killed Meleager. This statement has been supported by four finds among the papyrus fragments.[34] It is clear that there was an epic version in which Apollo was responsible for Meleager's death.

Heroic poetry, to judge from Homer and what we can see elsewhere, avoided magic and the supernatural. Notoriously, even the gods in the *Iliad* behave like human beings. It is therefore not surprising if one or more epic versions took the folk-tale of Meleager and cut out the motif of the brand, substituting for it a more epic motif. And what more epic than the killing by Apollo?[35] It is now generally agreed that the folk-story of the brand was the oldest version of

---

[32] Apollodorus I. 8. 3; Antoninus Liberalis 2 (from Nicander).

[33] Paus. 10. 31. 3 ἐς δὲ τοῦ Μελεάγρου τὴν τελευτὴν Ὁμήρῳ μέν ἐστιν εἰρημένα ὡς ἡ Ἐρινὺς καταρῶν ἀκοῦσαι τῶν Ἀλθαίας καὶ ἀποθάνοι κατὰ ταύτην ὁ Μελέαγρος τὴν αἰτίαν· αἱ δὲ Ἠοῖαί τε καλούμεναι καὶ ἡ Μινυὰς ὡμολογήκασιν ἀλλήλοις· Ἀπόλλωνα γὰρ δὴ αὗταί φασιν αἱ ποιήσεις ἀμῦναι Κούρησιν ἐπὶ τοὺς Αἰτωλούς, καὶ ἀποθανεῖν Μελέαγρον ὑπὸ Ἀπόλλωνος. (As to the end of Meleager, Homer's version is that the Fury listened to Althaea's curses and this was the cause of Meleager's death. But the collection called the *Ehoeae* and the *Minyas* are in agreement with each other; these poems say that Apollo defended the Curetes against the Aetolians, and Meleager was killed by Apollo.) [34] For discussion of these, see the Appendix.

[35] Apollo in the *Il.* is the defender of Troy. When Diomedes rushes on the god at 5. 432 ff., Apollo pushes him back three times, and the fourth time he says (440), φράζεο, Τυδεΐδη, καὶ χάζεο (Think, son of Tydeus, and go back). Again, when Patroclus attacks the wall of Troy, carried away by his success, in 16. 698 ff., Apollo

Meleager's death.[36] The story that he was killed by Apollo looks like an epic rationalization.

The version in Phoenix's speech is incompatible with the brand. The brand allowed no time for Meleager to withdraw from the battle in anger. There remains the possibility that the story as told in Homer might have ended with Apollo acting (as it were) as the agent of the Erinys, and killing Meleager in fulfilment of his mother's curse. Such a theory does, however, run counter to the explicit words of Pausanias, who distinguishes between the *Iliad* and the Apollo version.[37]

Nevertheless, a number of scholars of this century, who have assumed a Meleager epic earlier than the *Iliad* containing the detailed story given by Phoenix, have believed that that epic ended with Apollo killing Meleager.[38] Under the circumstances it is not surprising that some have reached the further conclusion that the *Iliad* itself is modelled on this pre-existing 'Meleagris'.[39] It is this that

pushes him back three times, and the fourth time he says (707), χάζεο, διογενὲς Πατρόκλεες (Go back, Zeus-born Patroclus). I have no doubt that in one version at least of Achilles' death (dare one say the *Aethiopis?*) Apollo pushed Achilles back three times, and the fourth time said, χάζεο, Πηλεΐδη, or φράζεο, Πηλεΐδη, καὶ χάζεο. (Quintus of Smyrna agrees: χάζεο, Πηλεΐδη, says Apollo just before Achilles' death (Q.S. 3. 40)). But Achilles, unlike Diomedes and Patroclus, disobeyed the god. Finally, it would not be surprising if, in some epic version of the fight between the Curetes and the Aetolians, Meleager came up against Apollo in the battle and heard the words of the god, χάζεο, Οἰνεΐδη or φράζεο, Οἰνεΐδη, καὶ χάζεο. Although Apollo's clash with Achilles had a much more central significance in the Trojan legend than that with either Diomedes or Patroclus, it is not the purpose of this note to add support to the theory that the *Aethiopis* provided the themes of the *Il.* (on which see U. Hölscher's admirable review of W. Schadewaldt's *Von Homers Welt und Werk* in *Gnomon* 27 (1955), 391–8; and, more recently, D. L. Page's review of G. Schoeck, *Ilias und Aithiopis*, in *CR* 13 (1963), 21–4); but to suggest how composition by theme might involve certain formulas associated with that theme.

[36] Only Bethe (n. 1), 7 seems to have cast doubts. Robert (n. 1), 88, Schadewaldt (n. 1), 139, Noé (n. 1), 56, Kraus (n. 1), 14, and Kakridis (n. 1), 14–16 are quite certain. Kakridis's arguments are particularly convincing on this point.

[37] 10. 31. 3, quoted in n. 33.

[38] e.g. Howald (n. 1), 408, Kraus (n. 1), 11, Von der Mühll (n. 1), 177 n. 49.

[39] Finsler (n. 1), 41 put this theory forward: 'Ohne den Zorn des Meleagros gäbe es keinen Zorn des Achilleus' ('Without the Wrath of Meleager we would have no Wrath of Achilles'). He has been followed by Howald (n. 1), 409, Cauer (n. 1), 265, and Sachs (n. 1), 20. Wilamowitz (n. 1), 335 and Page (n. 1), 329 n. 9 are sympathetic, but personally non-committal. Kakridis (n. 1) argues that this pre-existing 'Meleagris' was the model for several different incidents in the *Il.*, but (60 n. 22) 'does not dare to express a view' on the main question of the connection between Meleager's wrath and Achilles'.

makes the discussion of Meleager so central for the Homeric Question in the twentieth century. The theory concerns the genesis of the *Iliad* itself.

The opposite point of view is that of those who consider that Meleager's position in Book 9 is so like Achilles' in the *Iliad* precisely because the poet has made it like.[40] They stress the fact that it is a paradeigma—i.e. an argument or a lesson, not a separate tale. They infer that the details in it are there not for their own sake, but for the parallel with Achilles.

Our previous discussion has made it clear that the poet was perfectly prepared to invent even the central details of his paradeigma, to assimilate it to the situation to which it is being adduced as a parallel. That has happened in the Meleager story also. Meleager withdraws from the battle and is appealed to to return, *because* Achilles has withdrawn from the battle and is now hearing an appeal. The cause of Meleager's withdrawal is inevitably anger (because Achilles had withdrawn through anger), and the cause of Meleager's anger is given as his mother's curse. These two are stock motifs. The parent's curse has been used earlier in Phoenix's speech (in line 454, where Amyntor cursed his son), and it is familiar from other Greek myths (Oedipus and Theseus). As to anger, 9. 524–6 does seem to be a statement of fact, that there were *cholos* (anger) poems before the *Iliad*. And evidence in the Homeric poems and elsewhere suggests that this was a particularly popular theme;[41] perhaps this psychological interest was a feature of the final flowering of heroic poetry which may be assumed to have taken place in the eighth century.

One cannot therefore deny that there may have been a *cholos* of Meleager—indeed the squabble about the spoils of the boar could be so described. But the story in the *Iliad* is unconvincing. As many scholars have seen, it is not really logical that he should withdraw from the battle out of anger because his mother had cursed him. Her

[40] Robert (n. 1), 91, Drerup (n. 1), 66, Bethe (n. 1), 11, Schadewaldt (n. 1), 141 n. 4, Noé (n. 1), 75, Von der Mühll (n. 1), 176.

[41] Withdrawal from the battle because of anger is ascribed in the *Il.* to Paris (6. 326) and Aeneas (13. 460) as well as to Achilles and Meleager. (In *PCPS* 184 (1956/7), 23–4, I argued that the unmotivated *cholos* of Paris in 6. 326 was caused by the regularity of the *cholos* theme as a reason for a hero being absent from the battle.) Famous quarrels among the Greek heroes at Troy (in addition to Agamemnon–Achilles) are: Agamemnon–Menelaus (*Od.* 3. 136); Achilles–Odysseus (*Od.* 8. 75); Ajax–Odysseus (*Od.* 11. 544); Diomedes–Achilles (Q.S. 1. 768). One might add the sudden outburst between Ajax son of Oïleus and Idomeneus in *Il.* 23. 450–98.

sympathies, if anything, were on the side of the enemy.[42] It seems
most probable that here also, as in the Niobe story and others that we
have seen, Homer produced his parallel by the use of any traditional
motif that lay to hand.

That Meleager was the subject of heroic poetry before Homer is
certain; and the allusiveness of the background to Phoenix's story
may be due to compression from some previous version. But this does
not carry with it the mother's curse, the withdrawal from the battle,
and the appeals of his relations and friends. The mother's curse may
have existed in a previous epic version, but we have no evidence that
it did. The *cholos* of Meleager and all that followed and resulted from
it bear clear signs of being a paradeigma invented to fit the *Iliad*
situation.

APPENDIX

The papyrus fragments which come from versions in which Apollo
killed Meleager are *P. Mus. Berol.* 9777, with the addition of *P. Oxy.*
2075 fr. 1 and *P. Oxy.* 2481 fr. 5 (b) col. 11 [= Hesiod, *Cat.* fr. 25
M–W] and *P. Ibscher*, published by R. Merkelbach in *Studi italiani
di filologia classica* 24 (1950), 255–63 [= Hesiod, fr. 280 M–W].

P. Berol. 9777 = Hesiod fr. 135 Rz.[3] There is enough surviving
at the beginnings of the lines to show that it described the death of
Meleager at Apollo's hands, when he was fighting against the
Curetes (12–13):

$$\text{ἀλλ' ὑπ' Ἀπόλλωνος χερ[}$$
$$\text{μαρνάμενος Κου[}$$

Line 13 was completed by Wilamowitz as follows

$$\text{μαρνάμενος Κου[ρῆσιν ὑπὲρ Καλυδῶνος ἐραννῆς}$$

fighting against the Curetes for lovely Calydon.

P. Oxy. 2075 fr. 1 added the end of the second line, giving (with *P.*
9777)

$$\text{μαρνάμενος Κου[} \qquad \text{]ρ κεδνηι.}$$

---

[42] Bethe (n. 1), 10, Van der Kolf (n. 1), 449, Schadewaldt (n. 1), 139 ('ein sehr
unorganisches Etwas'), Kraus (n. 1), 15, and Von der Mühll (n. 1), 177 all make this
point.

With the new ending, Wilamowitz's old supplement would no longer do, and the *P. Oxy.* editor, Hunt, completed the line thus

μαρνάμενος Κου[ρῆσι, γυναικὶ δὲ πείθετ]ο κεδνῇ

fighting against the Curetes, for he was persuaded by his good wife.

This was a dangerous supplement, because it introduced the Homeric detail of persuasion by the wife to a version of the legend in which we have no reason to suppose that that detail was found. The line, with Hunt's supplement, was printed without question by A. Traversa, *Hesiodi Catalogi sive Eoearum Fragmenta* (Naples, 1951), p. 61, R. Merkelbach, *Die Hesiodfragmente auf Papyrus* (Leipzig, 1957), p. 18, and J. Schwartz, *Pseudo-Hesiodeia* (Leiden, 1960), p. 404.

Now, in the latest volume of the Oxyrhynchus Papyri (xxviii (1962), ed. Lobel), *P. Oxy.* 2481 fr. 5 (b) col. ii gives some letters from the end of our line, letters which show that Hunt's supplement could not have stood in that papyrus:

]ε[.]ρων[.] . ακ[

Lobel prints

μαρνάμενος Κου[ρῆσι περὶ Πλ]ε[υ]ρῶν[ι] μακεδνῇ

fighting against the Curetes around high Pleuron,

with some doubt about the adjective μακεδνός (usually of trees) describing a place. At all events, the wife motif is now removed from Hesiod's version; nor is there any recognizable reference to a mother's curse.

P. Ibscher contains some twenty-eight lines of a descent to Hell by Theseus and Pirithous. At the beginning Meleager is speaking. The significant lines from our point of view are 1–2:

]εσαιμεβιηφιτεδουρ ι τεμακρωι
]ι καιλητουσωλε[

which Merkelbach (*ed. pr.*) supplements as follows

ὀλ]έσαι με βίηφί τε δουρί τε μακρῷ
ἀλλά με μητρὸς ἀρα]ὶ καὶ Λητοῦς ὤλε[σεν υἱός

[No mortal's hand could] kill me by force and his long spear; but the curses of my mother and Leto's son killed me.

In this way Merkelbach introduces the mother's curse as a second reason for Meleager's death in addition to Apollo. But he admits in a note that this must be considered uncertain. He points out that the line is of the pattern of 16. 849 ἀλλά με μοῖρ' ὀλοὴ καὶ Λητοῦς ἔκτανεν υἱός (but my mortal fate and Leto's son killed me), 18. 119 ἀλλά ἑ μοῖρ' ἐδάμασσε καὶ ἀργαλέος χόλος Ἥρης (but fate and the harsh hatred of Hera caused his death),[43] where two grounds for a death are given. Neither these lines nor the uncertain iota read in the papyrus offers very strong support for Merkelbach's μητρὸς ἀραί.[44]

Whether *P. Ibscher* is actually the passage from the *Minyas* referred to by Pausanias is an open question. Merkelbach argues against it; Schwartz (p. 28) sees no reason why it should not be. One of the few things known about the *Minyas* is that it contained a descent to Hell (Paus. 10. 28. 2). If this really is the *Minyas* passage, then Merkelbach's μητρὸς ἀραί becomes less probable, because Pausanias in 10. 31. 3 (see n. 33) explicitly contrasts the Homer version, in which the Erinys heard Althaea's curse, with that of the *Ehoeae* and the *Minyas*, in which Apollo killed Meleager.

[43] Cf. also *Od.* 22.413 τούσδε δὲ μοῖρ' ἐδάμασσε θεῶν καὶ σχέτλια ἔργα (but fate sent by the gods and their own wicked deeds caused these men's deaths).

[44] [Additional note, 2000] In *Fragmenta Hesiodea*, ed. R. Merkelbach and M. L. West (Oxford, 1967), fr. 280, the line is printed ἀλλά με μοῖρ' ὀλο]ὴ καὶ Λητοῦς ὤλεσε[ν υἱός.

16

The Proem of the Iliad: Homer's Art

JAMES REDFIELD

In his proem (*Iliad* 1. 1–7) the poet of the *Iliad* asks his Muse for the *Iliad*, and in asking for it has to say what it is. The proem thus states in brief compass the whole of which it is the introductory part. It is a kind of lyric at the head of the epic, a masterpiece of compression; here, even more than elsewhere, every word is made to tell.

The proem has been the object of special attention by the philologists.[1] What follows incorporates much from those predecessors. I shall be concerned, briefly, with establishing and construing the text, and also, at greater length, with interpreting it. These problems require us to set the text within a context, to display its language as a use of epic diction, its emphases as a choice of epic themes, its devices as an exploitation of an epic genre. We thus examine, in this one instance, the interplay between the 'tradition' of the poet and his 'individual talent'.

T. S. Eliot reminds us, in the essay from which I draw these terms, that all poets are traditional. Nevertheless, Homer is a traditional poet in a special sense. The *Iliad* is, or at the very least is like, oral poetry, poetry created in performance by the rapid and relatively unreflective mobilization of traditional means. As we come to

Thanks are due to Paul Friedrich, to Gregory Nagy, and to the *CP* referee for many helpful suggestions; they are not responsible for this final version, which they have not seen.

[1] See S. E. Bassett, 'The Proems of the *Iliad* and the *Odyssey*', *AJP* 44 (1923), 339–48; B. A. van Groningen, 'The Proems of the *Iliad* and the *Odyssey*', *Mededelingen der Koninklijke Nederlandse Akademie van Wetenschappen, Afd. Letterkunde*, NS 9, no. 8 (1946), 279–94; W. W. Minton, 'Homer's Invocations of the Muses: Traditional Patterns', *TAPA* 91 (1960), 292–309; A. Pagliaro, 'Il proemio dell' *Iliade*', *Nuovi saggi di critica semantica* (2nd edn., Messina and Florence, 1963), 3–46; K. Rüter, *Odyssee-interpretationen* (Göttingen, 1969), esp. 28–34: 'Die traditionellen Elemente des Epenproömiums'. I have been particularly careful to acknowledge in detail my debt to Pagliaro; his brilliant commentary stimulated me to write the present chapter.

understand such poetry better, we begin to invent the philologies appropriate to it. Philology then reveals that the oral poet also is a creator. He handles his materials freely, and therefore meaningfully. I shall often draw attention to expressions atypical of epic usage: such expressions do not separate Homer from his tradition but rather display him as its master. The oral poet, like others, stretches his tradition as he puts it to use. I do not intend, therefore, a contrast between 'formulaic' and 'invented' language, but between more and less familiar or expected uses of the formulaic language, between (to borrow a contrast from the linguists) more marked and less marked expressions. Both have their place in epic art; both, indeed, appear in the proem.

I begin by setting out a text and offering an (unpoetic) translation:

> Μῆνιν ἄειδε, θεά, Πηληϊάδεω Ἀχιλῆος
> οὐλομένην, ἣ μυρί᾽ Ἀχαιοῖς ἄλγε᾽ ἔθηκε,
> πολλὰς δ᾽ ἰφθίμους ψυχὰς Ἄϊδι προΐαψεν
> ἡρώων, αὐτοὺς δὲ ἑλώρια τεῦχε κύνεσσιν
> οἰωνοῖσί τε δαῖτα, Διὸς δ᾽ ἐτελείετο βουλὴ
> ἐξ οὗ δὴ τὰ πρῶτα διαστήτην ἐρίσαντε
> Ἀτρεΐδης τε ἄναξ ἀνδρῶν καὶ δῖος Ἀχιλλεύς.

The wrath sing, goddess, of Peleus' son Achilles,
That cursed wrath, which inflicted countless pangs on the Achaeans;
Many potent shades she sent to Hades
Of heroes, and them she was preparing as prey to dogs,
And for birds a feast, and the word of Zeus was coming to completion
From that time when first those divided after quarrelling,
The son of Atreus, king of men, and bright Achilles.

Certain features of this translation will be explained in the course of the chapter, but there are two points which must be explained at the outset; on both points I follow Pagliaro. First, at the famous crux in line 5 I have adopted δαῖτα ('feast', the reading of Zenodotus, Athenaeus 12F), rather than πᾶσι ('all' sc. birds), the reading of the manuscript tradition. Δαῖτα is confirmed by passages in tragedy which seem to paraphrase the poem, especially Aeschylus, *Suppliants* 800–1: κυσὶν δ᾽ ἔπειθ᾽ ἕλωρα κἀπιχωρίοις | ὄρνισι δεῖπνον οὐκ ἀναίνομαι πέλειν (Then I do not refuse to be prey for dogs and dinner for the local birds). (Cf. also Euripides, *Hecuba* 1078, *Ion* 504–5.) Athenaeus reports ancient objections to οἰωνοῖσί τε δαῖτα (for birds a feast) on the ground that *dais* could be used only of human meals. Such objections could well have motivated the weak emendation πᾶσι, while it is hard to see why πᾶσι would have been replaced by δαῖτα. Furthermore, τεῦχε (was preparing) fits well with δαῖτα but would be odd with no object but ἑλώρια, since one is said, in the Homeric idiom, to 'make' a meal but not to 'make' prey.[2]

The second point has to do with the referent of ἐξ οὗ (from that time) in line 6. If we take it with ἐτελείετο (coming to completion) in line 5 (as did Aristarchus: schol. Arn/A ad loc.), then the plan or word of Zeus is represented as being in the process of fulfilment from the moment of the quarrel. If we take it with ἄειδε (sing) in line 1 (the choice of most moderns), the Muse is being asked to begin the story from the point of the quarrel. But elsewhere, when it is a question of beginning a story at a certain point, the adverb used is spatial: τῶν ἁμόθεν γε ... εἶπε ('tell of these things, from whatever point you will', Odyssey 1. 10), ἔνθεν ... ὡς ('from that point, how ...', Odyssey 8. 500); cf. οἴμης τῆς ('from that path of which...', Odyssey 8. 74) and the spatial metaphor in μετάβηθι ('shift', i.e. 'change your theme', Odyssey 8. 492). Ἐξ οὗ, by contrast, is a temporal expression, and is employed when a process has been going on, or a condition has obtained, since a certain moment.[3] An audience familiar with the Homeric idiom would thus take ἐξ οὗ with ἐτελείετο rather than with ἄειδε.

This interpretation of ἐξ οὗ gives us a proem which unfolds smoothly as a consecutive sentence, moving from the wrath, to its consequences, to its connection with Zeus, and then to the crucial moment when divine purpose and human action intersected. I now proceed to a detailed study of that sentence.

The first word, μῆνιν (wrath), states the topic of the poem. Three points about this much-studied word are fundamental to the proem.[4]

---

[2] These points are derived from Pagliaro's defence of δαῖτα in an essay first published in 1948, 'Un riflesso Pitagorico nella tradizione del testo Omerico', Saggi di critica semantica (2nd edn., Messina and Florence, 1961), 127–31, and from his restatement of his arguments in (n. 1), 35–7. The 'correct' emendation would be κύρμα; cf. the phrase ἕλωρ καὶ κύρμα: Il. 5. 488, 17. 151; Od. 3. 271, 5. 473 (Pagliaro (n. 1), 35 n. 21).

[3] Pagliaro (n. 1), 11–12, reviews epic usage of ἐξ οὗ and quotes, as the closest parallel to the proem, Od. 11. 167–8: ἀλλ' αἰέν ... ἀλάλημαι ... ἐξ οὗ τὰ πρώτισθ' ἑπόμην Ἀγαμέμνονι δίῳ (I have been wandering constantly, ever since I first followed bright Agamemnon); he also compares Od. 14. 379.

[4] E. Schwyzer, 'Drei griechische Wörter', RM 80 (1931), 209–17; H. Frisk, 'ΜΗΝΙΣ. Zur Geschichte eines Begriffes', Eranos 44 (1946), 28–40; J. Irmscher, Götterzorn bei Homer (Leipzig, 1950), 5–8; P. Considine, 'Some Homeric Terms for Anger', Acta Classica 9 (1966), 15–25; C. Watkins, 'À propos de ΜΗΝΙΣ', Bull. Soc. Ling. de Paris 72 (1977), 187–209.

First, *mēnis* (wrath) and its derived verb *mēniō* are used throughout the *Iliad* by both characters and narrator for Achilles' anger against Agamemnon (the noun occurs at *Iliad* 9. 517, 19. 35, 19. 75—and a peculiar derived form, *mēnithmos*, at *Iliad* 6. 62, 16. 202, 16. 282; the verb at *Iliad* 1. 422, 1. 488, 2. 769, 2. 772 = 7. 230, 9. 426, 12. 10, 18. 257, 19. 62); *mēnis*, among the various Homeric words for anger, is the specific name of Achilles' wrath.[5] Second, the noun is in epic diction restricted, except for Achilles, to gods (the verb is used of other humans);[6] Achilles' anger is godlike, and others fear him as they would an angry god. Third, *mēnis* includes an element of moral outrage; it is provoked by a bond broken, a hierarchy disrupted.[7]

---

[5] Achilles does not normally speak of his own rage as *mēnis* but rather as *cholos*—see esp. *Il.* 18. 107–10, where he speaks of the *cholos* that drips down sweeter than honey and rises like smoke. Other speakers and the narrator also use *cholos* and other words for anger far more frequently than *mēnis*. Watkins (n. 4), 194 notes that Homeric speakers never use *mēnis* for their own state of mind, and concludes that such usage is definitely taboo (although the taboo does not extend to the verb (*Il.* 9. 426, 19. 62) or to the derived form *mēnithmos* (*Il.* 16. 62, 16. 202)). It seems easier, however, to conclude that *mēnis* means an objective relation, an anger dangerous to someone (and therefore usually so classified from the outside), while *cholos* and *kotos*, 'bile' and 'rancour', are subjective conditions, experienced by the angry person. Achilles applies words derived from *mēnis* to his own frame of mind only when he is speaking of it as a definite position to which he is committed. Probably his rage does not become a *mēnis* until after Athena's intervention and his oath by the sceptre; at this point a flash of rage is transformed into a settled determination. The first use of the term after the poem applies it only indirectly to Achilles; after the oath. Ἀτρείδης δ' ἑτέρωθεν ἐμήνιε ('Agamemnon raged on the other side', *Il.* 1. 247). Agamemnon responds to *mēnis* with *mēnis*. The first application to Achilles is Thetis' imperative: μήνι' ('rage', *Il.* 1. 488). Evidently there is something settled and lasting about *mēnis*; it is 'colère durable' (P. Chantraine, *Dictionnaire étymologique de la langue grecque* III (Paris, 1968), s.v.).

[6] We must be alert to differences in the semantic range of nouns and their denominative verbs; in other cases also the range of the verb is the wider. For instance, *nemesis* is a human emotion, 'not used of the gods in Homer' (LSJ, s.v.), but the derived verbs *nemesaō* and *nemesizomai* are frequently used of the gods—of their outrage with one another and with men. *Aidōs* is a feeling evoked in men by their relations with other men or (twice) in a god by another god, but the verb *aideomai* is used also of human respect for the gods (cf. H. Ebeling, *Lexicon Homericum* (Leipzig, 1885), s.vv.).

[7] Zeus may feel *mēnis* against a god who disregards his authority (*Il.* 5. 31–4; *Od.* 5. 146–7) or who defies his thunderbolt (*Il.* 15. 122; cf. 15. 115–18). Men rouse the *mēnis* of Apollo if they dishonour his priest (*Il.* 1. 75; cf. 1. 94–5), think themselves equal to the gods (*Il.* 5. 444; cf. 5. 440–2), or defy fate (*Il.* 16. 711 = 5. 444; cf. 16. 707–8). The *mēnis* of an unnamed god may follow failure of sacrifice (*Il.* 5. 177–8), defilement of an enemy (*Il.* 22. 358; cf. 22. 338–43), or failure to bury a friend (*Od.* 11. 72–3). Zeus (*Il.* 13. 623–5; *Od.* 14. 283–4) or unnamed gods (*Od.* 2. 66–7) may be roused to *mēnis* against those who break the bond of hospitality. Similarly, human *mēnis* is provoked by offences against authority (*Il.* 1. 247) or merit (*Il.* 13. 460), against host (*Od.* 16. 376–82) or guest (*Od.* 17. 10–15).

Mēnis taps a cosmic power released by the disorder of a basic order. Achilles' anger thus has the demonic destructive power of a justified curse.

Achilles' anger is, of course, literally a kind of divine anger; with the help of his goddess mother he can bring the gods into action to avenge his wrongs. In so doing he lets loose in the world a power which is greater than himself and ultimately beyond his control. The proverb says: χαλεπὴ δὲ θεοῦ ἔπι μῆνις, 'the wrath of a god is harsh, when it comes' (*Iliad* 5. 178). Divine *mēnis* can bring the plague (*Iliad* 1. 75) or civil strife (*Odyssey* 3. 134–6); it can set a city in flames (*Iliad* 21. 522–4). Achilles' wrath is on such a scale; aimed at Agamemnon, it reaches out to bring destruction on his whole community.

Furthermore, Achilles, although he is half a god, is still a man; we are reminded in the second half of this line that he is son of Peleus. His wrath thus falls on his own people and ultimately, through Patroclus, on himself. The first line of the *Iliad* qualifies the hero in terms of his divine wrath and his human father, and thus places him between god and man. This ambiguous status is the source of his tragedy. The chosen starting point of the epic thus has implications which are unfolded in the poem's overall plot.

The words ἄειδε, θεά (sing, goddess) place the proem within a generic type, the invocation to the Muse.[8] At the same time the words chosen are atypical of the genre. Normally the Muse is asked, not to 'sing' but to 'say'.[9] The Muses are themselves singers, and sing among the gods as the bards sing among men (*Iliad* 1. 603–4; *Odyssey* 24. 60–1; *Theogony* 36–52), but the bard who invokes the Muse does not expect to bring their song into the world of men; rather the Muse, who gives song to men (*Odyssey* 8. 64, 8. 498; *Theogony* 104; Hesiod fragment 310 M–W; Archilochus fragment 1 West), will 'impel the bard to sing' (*Odyssey* 8. 73). The Muses 'teach'

---

[8] There are five invocations internal to the *Il.*: 2. 484–93, 2. 761–2, 11. 218–20, 14. 508–10, 16. 112–13. There are also the initial invocations of the *Od.* (1. 1–10), and *Works and Days* (1–10), and the *Eoiai* (Hes. fr. 1 M–W). The *Theogony* begins with a complex hymn to the Muses, which closes with an invocation of them (104–15). The invocatory first lines of the *Thebais* and *Epigonoi* are preserved: T. W. Allen (ed.), *Homeri Opera* v. 112.

[9] In Homer the verb is ἔννεπε if the Muse is singular (*Il.* 2. 761; *Od.* 1. 1), ἔσπετε if the Muses are plural (*Il.* 2. 484, 11. 218, 14. 508, 16. 112).

the bard (*Odyssey* 8. 488) and 'make to grow' in him the *oimai*, the paths of song—that is, themes and stories. They are the daughters of Memory (*Theogony* 54; Solon 1. 1 West) and remind the bard of what he might otherwise forget (*Iliad* 2. 492). They are a source of information, and their inspiration guarantees the truth of the song. But the voice which is heard is not that of the Muse, but of the bard. When, therefore, the bard asks the Muse not to 'speak' to him but to 'sing', a complex relation is somewhat simplified. The bard in effect claims that his song is the authentic voice of the goddess.

As the poet brings the Muse directly on the stage, so he addresses her, relatively informally, as *thea*. This vocative is proper, not to a prayer such as this invocation, but to face-to-face conversation with a goddess; in such a context the word has a tone of formal propriety.[10] Similarly, in a prayer a speaker who has already called a goddess by name may also call her *thea* (*Iliad* 10. 290; *Odyssey* 20. 61); we find this usage in the proem to the *Odyssey*, where *thea* (*Odyssey* 1. 10) is anaphoric to *Mousa* (*Odyssey* 1. 1). To pray to a goddess simply as *thea*, however, assumes a pre-existing relation between speaker and goddess. There are only two other instances of this form of address in Homer (*Iliad* 10. 462, 23. 770—the narrator tells us that both prayers are to Athena): both are by Odysseus to the goddess who is always close to him (cf. *Iliad* 10. 278–9; *Odyssey* 3. 221–2, 13. 314–15).

The first three words of the *Iliad* thus introduce us into a numinous world; a godlike wrath will be sung by a bard who is himself close to the divine source of song.

These first three words, with their consecutive trochaic word breaks, are metrically anomalous, and it has been held that they are 'nonformulaic'.[11] One can as easily think, however, that ἄειδε, θεά (metrical anomaly and all) was the regular expression in a proem after a trochaic topic word ending in a consonant, and this notion is confirmed by the only parallel case in early epic, the first line of the

[10] Vocative θεά (*thea*) is twice used by superior to inferior deities (*Il.* 15. 93, 24. 104)—perhaps to reassure them that their status will be respected, as Hermes says he will tell Calypso the truth, since she has asked him 'as one god to another', θεὰ θεόν (*Od.* 5. 97). Humans use it most often to signal their recognition of a goddess (*Il.* 1. 216, 5. 815, 18. 182; *Od.* 13. 312, 20. 37; cf. *h. Hom. Ven.* 185), or to signal the relevance of divine status as when Achilles calls Thetis' attention to her power (*Il.* 1. 401) or Odysseus tells Calypso why he cannot trust her (*Od.* 5. 173, 5. 178).

[11] By J. A. Russo, 'A Closer Look at Homeric Formulas', *TAPA* 94 (1963), 235–47, esp. 240.

Thebais: Ἄργος ἄειδε, θεά, πολυδίψιον ἔνθεν ἄνακτες (Allen,
Homeri Opera v, p. 112). Since, moreover, *mēnis* was the traditional
name for Achilles' wrath, since a proem usually began with a topic
word,[12] and since Πηληϊάδεω Ἀχιλῆος is the usual name-formula
for Achilles in the genitive case after the masculine caesura, we can
hold that the entire first line was 'dictated' to the poet from the
moment he chose his topic. And this conclusion would seem to
invalidate the analysis offered above, since the poet could not mean
anything special by words he had no choice about.

This view vastly overrates the rigidity of formulaic composition;
we should be cautious about deriving strict rules from evidence
which is after all fragmentary. Πηληϊάδεω Ἀχιλῆος (in violation
of the principle of economy) has, in fact, an alternative in this
position: μεγαθύμου Πηλείωνος (*Iliad* 18. 226, 19. 75—in the
second instance modifying *mēnis*). Invocations of the Muse, at least
in the *Hymns*, do not always begin with a topic word (*Homeric Hymn
to Aphrodite* 1; *Hymn* 19. 1). Another, less gifted, bard might have
begun, Μοῦσα μοι ἔννεπε μῆνιν Ἀχιλλῆος θείοιο... And in any
case formulae are meaningful. I concede that, as an adjective
becomes fixed in combination with a noun, and as the combination
becomes a normal unit in a specific metrical context, the two parts
lose independent meaning. The whole combination becomes 'lexicalized': ποδάρκης δῖος Ἀχιλλεύς (swiftfooted brilliant Achilles)
hardly means anything different from *Achilleus* (although even here
the greater length of the combined form adds an emphasis). But it is
also true that the latent implications in the most familiar combinations can be contextually evoked; if the context made us think of
Achilles' feet, we would notice *podarkēs* in a different way.[13] The first
line of the *Iliad* is rich in such implications. Whether we ascribe the
richness to the poet or to his tradition, it remains a poetic success.[14]

There is, however, a different, stylistic, point about formulaic
composition, which is exemplified by this first line. The first three

---

[12] See Van Groningen (n. 1), 284.

[13] We can observe the poet avoiding unwanted implications (and violating the
principle of economy) at *Il*. 23. 168, where the next line begins with a reference to the
feet of Patroclus, and Achilles is called (uniquely) *megathumos* (great-hearted) instead
of πόδας ὠκύς (swift-footed). See W. Whallon, *Formula, Character and Context*
(Washington, DC, 1969), 59.

[14] As Michael Nagler, *Spontaneity and Tradition* (Berkeley and Los Angeles, 1974),
61, says, 'It is necessary to recall... from time to time... that the art language cannot
compose for a poet or even, in the last analysis, restrict what he means to say.'

words are highly 'marked'; even if they are normal in a proem, a
proem itself is a highly marked environment, in contrast to the run of
the narrative. The second hemistich, which consists of the expression
most usual in this syntactic and metrical context, is less marked. The
first line thus exemplifies the familiar rule that hexameters become
more formulaic towards the end. We hear the line as composed from
left to right. The poet, having set himself a metrical problem in the
first part of his line, solves it with an item from his formulaic
repertoire. This involves a shift from relatively free, and therefore
relatively meaningful, syntagmata, to relatively lexicalized units. The
first hemistich consists of three lexemes; the second, in effect, of only
one. Information is thus transmitted at an uneven rate. The run of
the metre, with its alternation of asymmetrical hemistichs, is complemented by a variation of semantic density, and this contributes to
that correlation of semantics with phonology characteristic of poetic
utterance.

Similarly, phonology correlates with syntax. The first word of
line 2, οὐλομένην (cursed), an adjective in concord with the first word
of line 1, exemplifies another general stylistic feature: the tendency
towards ambiguous syntactic end-stopping of the line. What has
appeared to be a closed syntactic unit is, in effect, reopened by the
first item of the following line. Ἡρώων (of heroes) in line 4 works
much the same way. Milman Parry has called this feature 'unper-
iodic enjambement'.[15] It helps the singer to dramatize the process of
his thought; he seems to think one line at a time (as he no doubt often
did in the process of oral composition). Having established the *mēnis*
as his theme, he now finds something more to say about it.

From one point of view οὐλομένην adds little, since *oulomenos* is
a notably unspecific negative adjective, covering a range from
'inadequate' to 'unfortunate' to 'harmful' to 'outrageous'. It is a term
of general rejection. It is, however, also an adjective applied, exclusively in the *Iliad* and predominantly in the *Odyssey*, to persons
(*Iliad* 5. 876, 14. 84, 19. 92; *Odyssey* 4. 92, 11. 410, 17. 484, 18. 273,
24. 97). Four times in the *Odyssey* it is applied to objects, always
with a touch of personification: the things mentioned (Circe's drugs,
Odyssey 10. 394; Achilles' armour, *Odyssey* 11. 555; the belly,

---

[15] 'The Distinctive Character of Enjambement in Homeric Verse', *TAPA* 60 (1929),
200–20, esp. 205–7 [= *The Making of Homeric Verse* (Oxford, 1971), 251–65, esp.
255–6].

Odyssey 15. 344, *Odyssey* 17. 287) are more than mere instruments, and have a kind of life of their own. So we can say that οὐλομένην personifies the *mēnis*.[16]

We should also note that this adjective is used elsewhere in the epics exclusively in speeches; it has a tone of subjectivity, and expresses a personal rejection of another person or personified thing. The bard thus brings before us his own reaction to, almost his distaste for, his theme.

The personification is developed in the relative clause which follows: ἥ μυρί᾽ Ἀχαιοῖς ἄλγε᾽ ἔθηκε. Elsewhere the giver or sender of *algea* is a god or a curse.[17] It is once said that gods and men can inflict *algea* on each other (*Iliad* 5. 384), but the only particular human actor who inflicts *algea* is Achilles (*Iliad* 22. 422). Ἄλγε᾽ ἔθηκε thus has the same semantic range as *mēnis*; the relative clause reinforces our sense of the *mēnis* as a numinous agent.

In the next three lines the poet specifies the *algea*. The problem here is not what the poet means to say, but why he says it. We might expect at this point some foretaste of the plot; instead the fate of the heroes is stated in the most general terms. Their shades were sent to Hades, while they were left to the birds and dogs. This last statement, further, is puzzling because in the *Iliad* no bodies are ever left to the birds and dogs; such treatment of the dead, while often threatened, and even attempted, is never enacted.[18] The proem thus presents a scene which will not occur in the poem.

Let us begin by examining one puzzling phrase: ἰφθίμους ψυχάς (potent shades). *Iphthimos* (potent) is an obscure adjective; it may well be that by Homer's time it was an archaic word, used only in the epic language, and of uncertain meaning to the poet himself. But it does seem to have implications of potency—of physical strength, or fertility, or both.[19] The *psuchē*, on the other hand, is the typically impotent thing; it has no function for the living man except to leave

---

[16] This personification is noted by Pagliaro (n. 1), 5 n. 6.

[17] Zeus: *Il.* 2. 39, 2. 375, 18. 431, 24. 241; *Od.* 4. 722. Zeus and Poseidon: *Il.* 13. 346. Apollo: *Il.* 1. 96, 1. 110. The South Wind: *Od.* 12. 427. Unnamed gods: *Il.* 19. 264; *Od.* 14. 39. Curses: *Od.* 11. 279, 19. 330. It will be noted that the distribution of *algea* is close to that of *mēnis*; both are particularly associated with Zeus and Apollo.

[18] Cf. Pagliaro (n. 1), 29–33. For a sensitive review of all relevant passages, see C. Segal, *The Theme of the Mutilation of the Corpse in the Iliad*, Mnemos. suppl. 17 (Leiden, 1971).

[19] See J. Warden, "ΊΦΘΙΜΟΣ: A Semantic Analysis", *Phoenix* 23 (1969), 143–58; Pagliaro (n. 1), 21–3.

him at death, and its later fate is a mere existence, twittering and flittering in the dark underworld.[20]

Line 3 is similar to *Iliad* 11. 55, where, as Zeus sends down a rain of blood, we are told that he intended πολλὰς ἰφθίμους κεφαλὰς Ἄϊδι προϊάψειν (to send many potent heads [i.e. persons] to Hades). Similarly, in Hesiod fragment 204. 118–19 M–W, we are told of Zeus' intentions for the Trojan War:

> ... π]ολλὰς Ἀΐδηι κεφαλὰς ἀπὸ χαλκὸν ἰάψ[ει]ν
> ἀν]δρῶν ἡρώων.
>
> to despatch to Hades by means of bronze many heads
> of heroic men.

In the proem the subject is not Zeus but the *mēnis*; nevertheless, we are about to be told that all this was somehow a fulfilment of Διὸς ... βουλή (the word of Zeus). The poet seems in the proem to be drawing upon familiar language for Zeus' intention to produce destruction at Troy.

Ἰφθίμους κεφαλάς (potent heads) in *Iliad* 11. 55 is closer to normal Homeric usage than is ἰφθίμους ψυχάς (potent shades) in line 3 for two reasons: *kephalē* is a word elsewhere accompanied by adjectives (although nowhere else by the adjective *iphthimos*), and *iphthimos* is used with another word for 'head' in a fixed line employed four times in descriptions of arming: κρατὶ δ' ἐπ' ἰφθίμῳ κυνέην εὔτυκτον ἔθηκεν (on his potent head he set a well-made helmet). On the other hand, line 3 of the proem 'is the only instance in the *Iliad* or the *Odyssey* where *psuchē* is qualified by a descriptive epithet. This would suggest that of the two lines 11. 55 is the prototype'.[21]

The substitution was made easy for him by the close association of the *psuchē* with the head,[22] and by the fact that the *psuchē* of the dead man is regularly said to be sent to Hades, as in the formulaic phrase ψυχὴν δ' Ἄϊδι κλυτοπώλῳ ('his soul to Hades of the famous steeds', *Iliad* 5. 654, 11. 445, 16. 625). The poet is working with the resources of the formulaic language. Nevertheless, line 3 is odd. The oddity is not entirely semantic, for 'potent shades' is not much odder than 'potent heads'—the head is not a potent part of Homeric man,

---

[20] Cf. Pagliaro (n. 1), 22.

[21] Warden (n. 19), 154. Pagliaro (n. 1), 23–9 (not cited by Warden) reviews much the same material and comes to similar conclusions.

[22] R. B. Onians, *The Origins of European Thought* (Cambridge, 1951), 95 ff.; Warden (n. 19), 153–7.

whose power lies in his limbs and midriff. The real oddity is syntactic; the poet has produced a unique syntagm: *psuchē* + adjective. We must seek his motivation for including *psuchē* in the line at the expense of the normal syntactic privileges of that word. The explanation is to be found in the use of αὐτούς in line 4.

Autos is a pronoun which 'topicalizes' its antecedent. A person or object is marked as the focus of interest, in contrast to other items which, although they may be syntactically parallel, are of less interest to the speaker. Very often *autos* focuses attention on a person in contrast to his parts or possession.[23] Thus in lines 3 and 4 the *psuchē*, a part or possession, departs, while the dead hero remains on the field.

In the normal expression, κεφαλὰς Ἄϊδι προϊάψειν, the *kephalē* is in fact metaphorical for the *psuchē*.[24] The poet could not, however, use the normal expression followed by αὐτούς; the literal sense would have asserted itself. He would have seemed to say that a part of the body was sent away while the body remained on the field. The poet therefore inserted ψυχάς, not because he particularly wanted ψυχάς, but because he wanted an acceptable substitute for κεφαλάς.

Αὐτούς, then, motivates ψυχάς.[25] The dead bodies are spoken of as the heroes themselves, the *psuchai* as mere accessories. We should note that this notion is peculiar to the proem.[26] Usually the dead person goes to Hades and leaves his body behind.[27] With some perturbation of normal usage the poet here focuses our attention on

[23] Cf. P. Chantraine, *Grammaire homérique* II (Paris, 1963), 156; and Pagliaro (n. 1), 10 n. 7.

[24] Pagliaro (n. 1), 24–5, says (and I agree) that, even if the phrase reflects some earlier custom of decapitating the enemy, in the Homeric idiom 'to send the head to Hades' simply means 'to kill'.

[25] That αὐτούς in line 4 requires ψυχάς in line 3 has been seen since ancient times: cf. schol. ad 7. 330, 11. 55; it has been held (cf. G. M. Bolling, *The Athetized Lines in the Iliad* (Baltimore, 1944), 43–4) that ψυχάς was substituted for κεφαλάς when lines 4 and 5 were interpolated in the proem. My own interpretation is close to that of Pagliaro (n. 1), 23.

[26] Contra E. Rohde, *Psyche* (4th edn., Tübingen, 1907), 5 [Eng. trans. London, 1925]. The closest parallels are *Il.* 16. 856–8 = 22. 362–4 (with a difference of proper name in the last line). Here the *psuchē* goes off to Hades, while the victor continues to harangue the corpse: τὸν καὶ τεθνηῶτα προσηύδα. Τόν here is unemphatic; the victor speaks to the corpse as if it were not dead, treats it, irrationally, as a person. Rohde also cites *Il.* 23. 103–7, but this passage makes no reference to the dead body, only to the fact that Patroclus' *psuchē* looks just as he did in life.

[27] In similar phrases with προϊάψειν the object is a simple personal pronoun (*Il.* 5. 190, 6. 487; cf. 8. 367, 21. 47–8); the vanquished is sent to Hades. The *psuchē*

the fate of the dead bodies. This focus, I would suggest, looks forward to the last third of the epic. Achilles' *mēnis*, announced in the proem as the theme, is (in a narrow sense at least) concluded by the beginning of Book 16, when Achilles declares that his rage has passed (*Iliad* 16. 60–1). Thereafter Achilles' story centres on the deaths of two heroes and the fates of their bodies. Patroclus dies, his body is recovered from the enemy, and Achilles gives him an elaborate funeral. Achilles takes his revenge, kills Hector, and attempts to feed his body to the dogs. Finally Hector also is recovered by his city and properly buried. In its overall structure the *Iliad* moves from themes involving the social relations of the heroes—themes of honour and of the destruction which springs from dishonour—to themes involving the defilement and purification of the dead. The proem, formally, refers only to the first part of this story, to the destruction brought about by the *mēnis* on the Achaeans. Yet in its structure the proem shows a parallel development, as it traces the consequences of the *mēnis* from suffering (*algea*) to death to defilement.

The notion of defilement is made concrete in the words that follow: ἑλώρια τεῦχε κύνεσσιν | οἰωνοῖσί τε δαῖτα (was preparing as prey to dogs | And for birds a feast). The use of *teuchō* here, as a causative over an embedded nominal-predicate sentence (i.e. to mean 'made *x* into *y*'), is highly marked and unique in the *Iliad*; the normal Homeric causative is *tithēmi*.[28] *Tithēmi* is the verb in line 2, where, oddly enough, τεῦχε would have fitted comfortably (cf. ἄλγεα τεύχει at *Iliad* 1. 100 and related phrases at *Iliad* 13. 346 and *Iliad* 21. 585), just as θῆκε would have fitted in line 4.[29] If we

continues the adventures of the bodily person, as in Polydamas' rough joke: some Argive has been pierced with a spear 'and now I suppose he can use it as a staff while walking down to the house of Hades' (*Il.* 14. 456–7). The dead hero—that is, the dead body—must be protected, but at the same time he has gone away in the form of his *psuchē*. Thus Patroclus says: 'Bury me as quick as you can, that I may pass within the gates of Hades, for the *psuchai* keep me away' (*Il.* 23. 71–2). He is both there and here.

[28] Cf. Ebeling, *Lexicon Homericum* (n. 6), s.v. *tithēmi* 5. There are two causative uses of *teuchō* in the *Od.* (13. 190–1, 13. 397), but there also the normal causative verb is *tithēmi*. Perfect middle forms of *teuchō* are used in Homer as agentless passives, and thus as simple copulas; contrast *Il.* 6. 300 τὴν γὰρ Τρῶες ἔθηκαν Ἀθηναίης ἱέρειαν (for the Trojans had made her priestess of Athena), where we have a stated agent with *tithēmi*, with the agentless use of *teuchō* at *Il.* 16. 604–5 ὅς Διὸς ἱρεὺς ... ἐτέτυκτο (who was the priest of Zeus).

[29] Ἄλγε' ἔθηκε is a normal expression; cf. *Il.* 22. 422. The problem is not that ἔθηκε is out of place in line 2, but that τεῦχε is out of place in line 4. The whole sentence would be more normal if the two verbs were reversed.

seek a poetic motivation for τεῦχε, we find it, I think, in a further oddity: *teuchō* is not a normal verb with *helōria* (prey), since one is not said to 'make' prey but to 'leave' it (ἐᾶν, λείπειν). *Teuchō*, on the other hand, is one of the normal verbs for preparing a meal.[30] As we go through the chiastic series, prey-dogs, birds-feast, the choice of verb is justified only by the last item. *Τεῦχε* (in contrast to the more neutral θῆκε) thus serves to knit the whole expression together, and puts a special stress on δαῖτα (feast).

Δαῖτα has been the problem word in the proem since ancient times.[31] The association of dogs with birds is familiar in threats of defilement (*Iliad* 2. 393, 8. 379, 13. 831, 17. 241, 18. 271, 22. 42, 22. 335, 22. 354, 24. 411; *Odyssey* 3. 259), but the association of prey with feasting is not.

Elsewhere in the *Iliad helōr* (the developed form *helōria* is unique to the proem) is used of the dead body left to despoilment by the enemy (*Iliad* 5. 488, 5. 684, 17. 151, 17. 667, 18. 93), in the *Odyssey*, of bodies left as carrion for animals (*Odyssey* 3. 271, 5. 473, 24. 292).[32] The notion of *helōr* thus marks an intersection of the human and animal spheres. The warrior's 'catch' is sometimes mutilated with bestial playfulness (*Iliad* 11. 146–7, 13. 202–5, 14. 498–500, 20. 481–3). At war, as the *Iliad*'s similes often remind us, man becomes to man as man to beast or beast to beast; war negates society.

The *dais*, by contrast, is in Homer the institution wherein society pre-eminently becomes peaceful (cf. *Iliad* 1. 573–83, 9. 68–78). A *dais* is literally a 'sharing'; through the sharing of meat at the *dais* status is respected (*Iliad* 12. 310–21) and merit is recognized (*Odyssey* 8. 474–83). Here man is joined with man and with god through council, hospitality, song, sacrifice, and prayer.

The use of δαῖτα for the carrion meal of the beasts is thus a strong and (as the ancient critics complained) rather repulsive metaphor. While *helōria* points to an intersection between categories, δαῖτα suggests the deletion of the categorical contrast between men and

---

[30] Pagliaro (n. 2), 130, assembles the evidence for *teuchō* used with *dais*, *dorpon*, and *deipnon*, and for the verbs used with *helōr*, as part of his argument for reading δαῖτα as against πᾶσι. In none of the passages involving meals is the use of *teuchō* causative; in *Od*. 9. 291 and 9. 344, where we might have expected some such phrase as τοὺς ... τεῦχε ... δόρπον, we find instead that the material of the meal is made the object of a subordinate participial clause.

[31] The vulgate tradition, as we saw, emended it away; Zenodotus, who read δαῖτα, athetized lines 4 and 5; cf. Pagliaro (n. 1), 5.

[32] And once (*Od*. 13. 208) of property left abandoned.

beasts. The complex phrase suggests the analogies: warriors:
victims::dogs:prey and birds:carrion::men:meat.

More than once in the *Iliad* it is suggested that these two analogies
could be collapsed into warrior:victim::man:meat, that the perfection of victory would be actually to consume the vanquished (*Iliad*
3. 23–8, 13. 198–202, 18. 161–4, 22. 261–5, 24. 212–13). The most
explicit statement is by Achilles just before he kills Hector (*Iliad* 22.
346–54): 'If only I could cut you into raw meat and eat you myself,'
he says, but as it is κύνες τε καὶ οἰωνοὶ κατὰ πάντα δάσονται.
In this context we may hear in δάσονται an echo of the cognate
noun *dais*: 'the birds and dogs will share you out [as a feast]'.

At only one other place in Homer is *dais* used as in the proem for
the meal of an animal: Apollo says (*Iliad* 24. 33–54) that Achilles in
defiling Hector's body ἄγρια οἶδεν (knows wild things); he is like a
lion who came down on the flock ἵνα δαῖτα λάβῃσιν (to make a
feast). The lion feasts [like a man]; if we fill out the symmetrical
ellipses of what I take to be a complex comparison, we shall say that
Achilles is like a beast [who feeds on his prey].[33]

Achilles of course is no cannibal; rather the theme of cannibalism
represents, as a logical extreme case, the dehumanization of the
enemy, his reduction to a mere thing to be mastered. I have argued
elsewhere that such dehumanization is central to the terror of the
Iliad.[34] Here I add that δαῖτα in the proem (as in Apollo's simile)
suggests the same theme, as it were, inside out. In the poem men
become bestial; in the proem the carrion-eating beasts do a man-like
thing. What is presented in the proem as an objective fact about
beasts appears in the poem (where no bodies are ever eaten by the
beasts) as a subjective tendency of men, who in battle become
somewhat like predators or scavengers.[35]

---

[33] A pictorial reflection of this theme of latent cannibalism can be seen in Attic
vase-paintings, by Oltos and the Brygos painter, of Achilles feasting over Hector's
body; the blood from the meat of the feast (picked out in red paint by Oltos) runs down
on to the corpse beneath the table. These items are nos. 20*g* and 20*i* in K. Friis
Johansen, *The Iliad in Greek Art* (Copenhagen, 1967), 267.

[34] J. M. Redfield, *Nature and Culture in the Iliad: The Tragedy of Hector* (Chicago,
1975), 183–203.

[35] Pagliaro (n. 1), 29–34, gives a somewhat different account of the transformation: defilement, which appears in the poem as a threat (that is, as a rhetorical
element), appears in the proem as a fact of experience. The poet, he says, thus displays
his detachment from the literary tradition; he is able to revive a somewhat faded
rhetorical terror to vivid actuality.

The proem adds that all this was somehow according to the will of Zeus: $\Delta\iota\grave{o}s$ δ' $\grave{\epsilon}\tau\epsilon\lambda\epsilon\acute{\iota}\epsilon\tau o$ $\beta o\upsilon\lambda\acute{\eta}$. At least five interpretations of this much-discussed phrase[36] can be defended; while there are objections to them all, I shall be arguing my way through four in favour of the fifth.

First, the poet may have in mind no specific plan or intention of Zeus; he may mean simply that these events, like all events, were somehow 'god's will'.[37] Agamemnon and Achilles themselves speak of their quarrel this way: since it happened, Zeus must have willed it (Iliad 19. 86–90, 19. 270–4). But this way of talking is characteristic only of the characters in epic, not of the epic narrator, who, when he speaks of the boulē of Zeus (e.g. Odyssey 1. 86; Theogony 465, 730; Works and Days 71, 79, 99; Hymn to Demeter 9; Hymn to Aphrodite 23) means some definite plan or contrivance of the god.[38] Similarly, Zeus himself, when he speaks of the fall of Troy $\mathcal{A}\theta\eta\nu\alpha\acute{\iota}\eta s$ $\delta\iota\grave{a}$ $\beta o\upsilon\lambda\acute{a}s$ ('because of Athena's plan', Iliad 15. 71), means the contrivance of the Trojan Horse.

A second interpretation would hold that the quarrel between Achilles and Agamemnon was itself contrived by Zeus for some purpose of his own. The evidence for this interpretation is Proclus' reference, at the end of his account of the Cypria, to a $\Delta\iota\grave{o}s$ $\beta o\upsilon\lambda\grave{\eta}$ $\ddot{o}\pi\omega s$ $\grave{\epsilon}\pi\iota\kappa o\upsilon\phi\acute{\iota}\sigma\eta$ $\tau o\grave{\upsilon}s$ $T\rho\hat{\omega}\alpha s$ $\mathcal{A}\chi\iota\lambda\lambda\acute{\epsilon}\alpha$ $\tau\hat{\eta}s$ $\sigma\upsilon\mu\mu\alpha\chi\acute{\iota}\alpha s$ $\tau\hat{\eta}s$ $\mathcal{E}\lambda\lambda\eta\nu\iota\kappa\hat{\eta}s$ $\grave{a}\pi o\sigma\tau\acute{\eta}\sigma\alpha s$ ('plan of Zeus to relieve the Trojans by causing Achilles to withdraw from the Greek alliance', Allen, Homeri Opera v, p. 105).[39] This interpretation receives, however, no support from the text of the Iliad; there the quarrel is the result, not of divine contrivance, but of human error. Agamemnon refuses to return the priest's daughter and thus brings down the plague; the assembly called by Achilles (instigated by Hera, not Zeus—Iliad 1. 55) to correct this error is badly handled and brings about further error.[40]

[36] W. Kullmann, 'Ein vorhomerisches Motiv im Iliasproömium', Philologus 99 (1955), 167–92, includes extensive bibliographical notes referring to earlier discussions of the phrase.
[37] This position has been held: cf. Kullmann (n. 36), 167 n. 2. S. E. Bassett, 'The Three Threads of Plot of the Iliad', TAPA 53 (1922), 53, refers to it as 'today the most commonly accepted interpretation'.   [38] Cf. Kullmann (n. 36), 168 n. 1.
[39] Cf. ibid. 177–8, and Kullmann's Die Quellen der Ilias, Hermes Einzelschriften 14 (Wiesbaden, 1960), 210–11.
[40] Cf. A. Lesky, 'Göttliche und menschliche Motivation im homerischen Epos', SB Heidelberg, phil.-hist. Kl., 1961. 4, 16–17 [= this vol., Ch. 5 § 1 ad fin.]; and Redfield (n. 34), 91–8.

A third interpretation (probably now the most popular)[41] refers
Διὸς ... βουλή in the proem to the events which follow the quarrel
in the poem, to the intervention by which Zeus, in order to make the
Greeks feel the consequences of Achilles' *mēnis*, contrives a temporary success for the Trojans. Within the *Iliad* itself Διὸς βουλή
and related phrases usually refer to this intervention by Zeus (cf. *Iliad*
11. 79, 12. 235–42, 13. 347–50, 13. 523–5, 15. 592–602, 16. 121, 17.
331–2). I see, however, two objections to finding this meaning in the
proem. First, if we take ἐξ οὗ (from that time when) with ἐτελείετο
(was coming to completion), the statement will, by this interpretation, be untrue: the intervention of Zeus does not immediately follow
the quarrel but occurs only after a lapse of many days (cf. *Iliad* 1.
423–7). Zeus does not finally take charge of the battle until the
beginning of Book 8. (Perhaps this difficulty, as much as anything
else, has caused critics to take ἐξ οὗ with ἄειδε, 'sing', a syntactic
interpretation which, as we saw, is unsatisfactory on other grounds.)
Second, the contrivance of Hector's brief success originates, not with
Zeus, but with Thetis, who demands it of Zeus as an *eeldōr* ('favour',
Iliad 1. 504). The poet reminds us of this fact in the course of his
narrative (*Iliad* 13. 347–50, 15. 69–77, 15. 592–602), and Athena
says of Zeus: Θέτιδος δ᾿ ἐξήνυσε βουλάς ('he has accomplished the
plans of Thetis', *Iliad* 8. 370). But the language of the proem seems to
imply the initiative of Zeus himself; the Διὸς ... βουλή is mentioned
as a primary fact about the poem to follow, whereas within the poem
it is a secondary result of other events. Such misrepresentation of the
poem by the proem is (as we have seen) far from impossible, but it
should be motivated, and I see no clear motive for it here.

A fourth interpretation refers to the proem of the *Cypria*, where it
is said that Zeus determined to lighten the earth of her burden of
men; he therefore stirred up war against Troy where ἥρωες
κτείνοντο. Διὸς δ᾿ ἐτελείετο βουλή ('heroes were killed. And the
plan of Zeus was accomplished', Allen, *Homeri Opera* v, p. 118). The
view that Διὸς ... βουλή has the same referent in the identical
phrases of the proems of the *Cypria* and the *Iliad* has been
impressively championed by Wolfgang Kullmann, who has collected
from the *Iliad* more than a dozen passages where some general

---

[41] Kullmann (n. 36), 169 n. 1; this interpretation goes back to Aristarchus and was
championed by Bassett (n. 37), 54.

intention of Zeus to massacre the heroes may be implied.[42] This evidence is not quite persuasive; not one of these passages brings the implication to the surface. We can find Kullmann's meaning in them only if we read them with the *Cypria* (and other non-Iliadic passages—especially *Works and Days* 156–73 and Hesiod fragment 204. 96–119 M–W) in our minds.[43] The plan of Zeus to exterminate the heroes may be a latent theme in the *Iliad*, but it remains latent; the Homeric story is focused on the responsibility of the human actors for their own destruction. Even the intervention of Zeus on behalf of the Trojans (the $\Delta\iota\grave{o}s$ $\beta ov\lambda\acute{\eta}$ within the poem) is the result of Achilles' initiative to Thetis; the god, as it were, becomes an instrument of the man.

We may move towards a fifth interpretation by observing that our phrase occurs in one other place in early hexameter: *Odyssey* 11. 281–97 tells of a seer whose $\theta\epsilon o\hat{v}\ldots\mu o\hat{\iota}\rho a$ (god-sent fate) cast him in prison until the fated time was fulfilled; then Iphicles his captor released him, $\Delta\iota\grave{o}s$ δ' $\acute{\epsilon}\tau\epsilon\lambda\epsilon\acute{\iota}\epsilon\tau o$ $\beta ov\lambda\acute{\eta}$. The scholiast (ad loc.) explains the phrase: 'because Zeus had told the seer that he would be overcome by Iphicles'. In other words, the seer recognized the will of Zeus in the correspondence of the event to his foreknowledge of it.

This association of $\Delta\iota\grave{o}s$ $\beta ov\lambda\acute{\eta}$ with foreknowledge and prophecy is strengthened by passages in which that phrase means the content of an oracle (*Odyssey* 14. 328 = 19. 296; *Hymn to Apollo* 132; *Hymn to Hermes* 538). *Odyssey* 8. 73–82 suggests that $\Delta\iota\grave{o}s\ldots\beta ov\lambda\acute{\eta}$ may have this meaning in the *Iliad* proem also. Here Demodocus sings of the quarrel between Achilles and Odysseus which arose at a feast, and how Agamemnon rejoiced in his heart that the best of the Achaeans were quarrelling, since Apollo had spoken to him when he came to Delphi (*Odyssey* 8. 81–2):

$$\tau\acute{o}\tau\epsilon\ \gamma\acute{a}\rho\ \dot{\rho}a\ \kappa v\lambda\acute{\iota}v\delta\epsilon\tau o\ \pi\acute{\eta}\mu a\tau os\ \grave{a}\rho\chi\grave{\eta}$$
$$T\rho\omega\sigma\acute{\iota}\ \tau\epsilon\ \kappa a\grave{\iota}\ \Delta av ao\hat{\iota}\sigma\iota\ \Delta\iota\grave{o}s\ \mu\epsilon\gamma\acute{a}\lambda ov\ \delta\iota\grave{a}\ \beta ov\lambda\acute{a}s.$$

For then it was that the beginning of trouble was in motion
for the Trojans and the Greeks because of the plans of great Zeus.

---

[42] Kullmann (n. 36), 170–5 (citing *Il.* 2. 3–4, 2. 37–40, 11. 52–5, 12. 13–18, 12. 20–3, 13. 222–7, 19. 86–8, 19. 270–4, 20. 21); 190–2 (citing *Il.* 2. 110–15, 9. 17–25, 12. 231–50, 14. 69–70, 22. 208–12). The latter group are held to refer 'indirectly' to the plan of Zeus. Cf. also Kullmann's 'Zur $\Delta\iota\grave{o}s$ $\beta ov\lambda\acute{\eta}$ des Iliasproömiums', *Philologus* 100 (1956), 132–3, citing *Il.* 14. 83–7 and 17. 647.
[43] Cf. Kullmann (n. 39), 47 n. 2.

This story should belong to the first arrival of the Greeks at Tenedos,[44] and is most economically explained by assuming that Agamemnon had received an oracle that Troy would fall after the best of the Achaeans quarrelled. The oracle had a false and premature fulfilment in a quarrel between Achilles and Odysseus; the true fulfilment was the quarrel between Achilles and Agamemnon (the real 'best of the Achaeans') which opens the *Iliad*.[45] By this interpretation the words in lines 5 and 6 of the proem mean: 'the will of Zeus [as foretold] was [finally] coming to pass from the time those two divided...' (hence my translation: 'the word of Zeus'). The promise given long ago at Delphi when 'the beginning of trouble was in motion' (*Odyssey* 8. 81) was at last to be kept.[46]

In fact the train of events which originates with the quarrel in Book 1 of the *Iliad* leads to the death of Hector, which assures the fall of Troy (*Iliad* 24. 380–5); thus it is true that the *mēnis*, while it brings great suffering on the Greeks, also makes certain their promised victory.

This interpretation is subject to one mighty objection: no one in the *Iliad* ever speaks of the *mēnis* as the fulfilment of a prophecy. But we can say that this interpretation is not inconsistent with the poem, and is consistent with epic linguistic usage.

Within the proem $\Delta\iota\grave{o}\varsigma$ δ' $\grave{\epsilon}\tau\epsilon\lambda\epsilon\acute{\iota}\epsilon\tau o$ $\beta o\upsilon\lambda\acute{\eta}$ draws attention to the paradoxical relation between Zeus and the Achaeans. Zeus wills the victory of the Achaeans, but their victory comes about only because they endure a crushing disaster. The proem develops from wrath to suffering to death to defilement before it comes to Zeus. The frame continually widens; it begins with the single hero, then includes his living community, then the human dead, then the animals—birds and dogs. Finally it includes also the god; we move abruptly from the lowest to the highest. The association of Zeus with the carrion scavengers is reinforced by the aspect of the verbs.

[44] In other words, this was the quarrel portrayed by Sophocles in the *Syndeipnoi* (frr. 562–71 Radt).

[45] This is the interpretation of Pagliaro (n. 1), 17–20, except that he places the quarrel at Aulis; I also derive from him the interpretation of the proem in the light of Demodocus' story.

[46] Agamemnon may actually be referring to this oracle and its deceptive fulfilment when he complains that the promises of Zeus have not been kept (*Il.* 2. 110–18 = 9. 17–25). He cannot be referring to the omen described by Odysseus (*Il.* 2. 299–332), since this predicted success in the tenth year, and it is exactly the nine-year delay of which Agamemnon complains (*Il.* 2. 134–5).

Ἔθηκε and προΐαψεν are aorists, while τεῦχε and ἐτελείετο are imperfects; we are thus led to associate the verbs in pairs, and to see, not the death of the heroes, but their defilement, as the special accomplishment of Zeus.

Yet here also the proem is at odds with the poem. Zeus does not will the defilement of the dead; on the contrary, he arranges the funerals of Sarpedon (*Iliad* 16. 666–83) and Hector (*Iliad* 24. 110–19). If we take Zeus as the high god, representative of the gods in general, the contrast is even sharper; for, while the gods may require the destruction of mortals, they do not, as Hera explicitly says (*Iliad* 16. 450–7), require their defilement (although they may predict it: *Iliad* 8. 379–80). If we ask why the defilement of the dead does not occur in the *Iliad*, the simple answer is that the gods prevent it. Hera sees to it that the Trojans do not capture the body of Patroclus (*Iliad* 18. 165–86), and Thetis keeps the maggots from him (*Iliad* 19. 30–3). Aphrodite keeps the dogs from Hector (*Iliad* 23. 184–7) and Apollo protects his body (*Iliad* 23. 188–91, 24. 18–21).

But the implication of the proem is partly right: the gods desire and contrive the reciprocal violence which leads the heroes to fear and to intend the defilement of the dead. God sends war, and as war feeds on itself the heroes become more vindictive than even the gods. At one point, when Zeus says that Hera might wish to eat Priam and his children raw (*Iliad* 4. 31–6), the poet suggests that even the gods might be drawn into bestial impurity. At the end, with the gods' help, there is purity and healing, as there was for Niobe (*Iliad* 24. 613–14). But in the proem, by his association of Zeus with the vultures, the poet suggests the demonic power of the forces which Zeus lets slip.

From this point the proem winds down to its conclusion; lines 6 and 7 give the sense of an ending. We return to the human world, to a particular action and particular actors. Ἐξ οὗ δή (from that time when) focuses on a particular moment, which is then specified by the remainder of line 6. Διαστήτην (those two divided) while returning us to the theme (Achilles' withdrawal from battle), with which the proem began, introduces a development from the singular to the dual; what had appeared in line 1 as Achilles' solitary wrath now is shown to have its source in a quarrel between two parties. There is thus a shift from theme to plot, from the *mēnis* to its causes. In the process the wrath is somewhat 'demystified'; we shift from the numinous *mēnis* to the more mundane *eris* which underlies ἐρίσαντε (after quarrelling). *Diistēmi*, similarly, is a rather colourless verb, meaning

'divide' or 'go in opposite directions': its five other uses in Homer
(*Iliad* 12. 86, 13. 29, 16. 470, 17. 391, 21. 436) have no connotation
of hostility.

'Ερίσαντε, an aorist participle, states an event prior in time to
the finite verb it modifies;[47] we might translate the phrase, 'parted,
having quarrelled'. Line 7 names the subjects of the verb. The poet is
telling his story backward; the proem is not in narrative but in logical
order. It responds to the questions: What story is it? Why is it worth
telling? How does it begin and with whom?[48]

Line 6 is hardly familiar; there are no complex units in it which
recur, and the words of which it is made have no fixed places in the
line[49]—with the exception of τὰ πρῶτα (first), which appears here
in its normal place just before the caesura.[50] Line 7, on the other
hand, is entirely composed of familiar phrases, mostly in their
familiar positions. Ἀτρεΐδης (son of Atreus) occurs more than half
the time at the beginning of the line, and δῖος Ἀχιλλεύς (bright
Achilles) is invariably at the end of the line. The motion from free
composition to fixed language, and from compact to diffuse trans-
mittal of information (line 7 consists, in effect, of two proper names),
which, as we saw, is characteristic of the structure of the line, is here
expanded in scale, so that the motion is from a free line to a formulaic
line. Just as the familiar line-ending formulae give a sense of closure
to a particular line, so here the familiar phrases of line 7 give a sense
of closure to the proem as a whole.

Yet, just as there is a touch of the familiar in line 6, so there is
an unfamiliar touch in line 7. ἄναξ ἀνδρῶν (king of men), most
frequently used (as here) as an epithet of Agamemnon, occurs in

---

[47] Cf. R. Kühner, *Ausführliche Grammatik der griechischen Sprache* I (2nd edn.,
Hanover, 1869), 199.

[48] In actually beginning the story, the poet goes back one further step and asks:
who provoked them to quarrel? He then goes back one step further still, and tells how
Agamemnon angered Apollo, how Apollo's anger led to the plague, and how the
plague led to the quarrel.

[49] Of the sixteen instances of ἐξ οὗ cited by Pagliaro (n. 1: 11–12), about half occur
at the beginning of the line. I suggest, however, that it is misleading to take this as a
formulaic feature; more properly it is an outcome of the tendency in the Homeric style
for metrical and syntactic segments to correspond, so that items which open a clause
tend also to open the line. On the originality of διαστήτην ἐρίσαντε, see Russo
(n. 11), 246.

[50] Πρῶτον and πρῶτα (first) which, taken together, appear more than 140
times in Homer, appear more than twice as often just before the caesura as in all other
positions put together.

Homer some fifty times. Everywhere else, however, it occurs just after the caesura. Here and only here the phrase has been shifted to the first half of the line.[51] Our attention is drawn to the phrase, so that its latent semantics are brought to the surface. While Agamemnon is always ἄναξ ἀνδρῶν, the epithet has a special relevance here; the quarrel between Agamemnon and Achilles was so dangerous and insoluble precisely because Agamemnon was 'king of men'.

Since the verbal phrase in line 6 is in the dual, it requires two names to supply its subject; line 6 looks forward to line 7, and the syntax is not complete until the last word in that line: Ἀχιλλεύς (Achilleus). This completion of the syntax, when it arrives, also contributes to a sense of having reached a full stop. The proem as a whole moves from the accusative μῆνιν to the nominative Ἀχιλλεύς, from the hero's act as the object of the song, to the hero as actor. The link between the first word and the last frames the whole as a unity;[52] the proem is over and the poem is ready to begin.

In conclusion a few general remarks may be in order. The proem has long been admired for its clarity and compactness;[53] here we have also examined the poetic devices which make it expressive: personification—in the development of μῆνιν through οὐλομένην and ἄλγε᾽ ἔθηκε; metaphor—especially in δαῖτα; variation in tone—in the contrast between μῆνιν and ἐρίσαντε. We have found the proem to be a formed unity with a beginning, middle, and end, beginning and ending with Achilles, and centring on the dogs and birds, and on Zeus.

The proem does not tell us what the story will be, but suggests, by the elements chosen for inclusion, what the story will be about. The *Iliad*, it tells us, will explore the relations between man, beast, and god; it will be a story of suffering and death, and will go beyond this to tell of the ultimate fate of the dead. The fundamental device of the proem, as in all of Homer, is parataxis: the relevance of elements to one another is implied by their mere conjunction. This is an art of resonance and implication; precisely because the elements are familiar they come before us charged with meaning.

Where so much is familiar, further, every unfamiliar touch is meaningful—a fresh phrase like ἰφθίμους ψυχάς; a familiar word

---

[51] As noted by Pagliaro (n. 1), 38.
[52] Cf. Bassett (n. 1), 340; and Rüter (n. 1), 306 n. 6.   [53] Cf. Rüter (n. 1), 33.

used in an unfamiliar way, like τεῦχε; even a familiar phrase in an unfamiliar position, like ἄναξ ἀνδρῶν. The familiar itself, balancing the unfamiliar, could be used to give the style shape, and vary its pace. The epic tradition may be thought of as the ground against which Homer displayed the figure of his art.

17

Iliad 1. 366–92: *A Mirror Story*

IRENE J. F. DE JONG

I. INTRODUCTION

The insertion of another story into the main story is a well-known literary device,[1] and when the content of this inserted story reflects the main story, we may speak of a mirror story. The antiquity of this compositional technique has been demonstrated by Létoublon,[2] who discusses a number of examples from the *Odyssey* (e.g. Penelope's dream, 19. 536–53), and develops the following typology (slightly modified):[3] mirror stories (*a*) refer to events of the story;[4] (*b*) are either retrospective or prospective; (*c*) are either true or fictitious.[5]

In this chapter I want to examine a passage from the *Iliad* (1. 366–92), which can be described on Létoublon's criteria as a retrospective

I would like to thank M. Bal, J. M. Bremer, and S. R. van der Mije for their help and critical remarks in writing this chapter.

[1] For general discussions, see M. Bal, 'Notes on Narrative Embedding', *Poetics Today* 2 (1981), 41–59, and L. Dällenbach, *The Mirror in the Text*, trans. J. Whiteley and E. Hughes (Cambridge, 1989).

[2] F. Létoublon, 'Le Miroir et la boucle', *Poétique* 53 (1983), 19–36.

[3] (n. 2), 27.

[4] By 'story' I mean the events told by the primary narrator, i.e. in the case of the *Il.* the events of some 50 days, of the *Od.* of some 40 days. Létoublon also considers as mirror stories stories which refer to events of the 'fabula', i.e. all events recounted by both primary and secondary narrators. In the case of the *Od.* this would encompass the ten years of Odysseus' travels, and indeed earlier events such as incidents from the Trojan war and episodes from Odysseus' youth. I consider this an unhelpful extension of the term.

[5] Since the first publication of this chapter in 1985 I have arrived at an—even more (cf. n. 4)—restricted definition of a mirror story, which I now consider to be a clear and sustained echo of something also told by the primary narrator. Many inset tales in Homer reflect in one way or another the main story and these vaguer echoes I would analyse in connection with the 'key' function of these tales, i.e. their function for the hearers/readers (rather than the characters). See Ø. Andersen, 'Myth, Paradigm, and "Spatial Form" in the *Iliad*', in J. M. Bremer, I. J. F. de Jong, J. Kalff (edd.), *Homer: Beyond Oral Poetry: Recent Trends in Homeric Interpretation* (Amsterdam, 1987), 1–13.

mirror story, truthfully dealing with facts already told in the main story. In this way I shall add an example from the *Iliad* to the Odyssean ones discussed by her. At the same time I shall broaden the scope of the investigation by also taking into consideration the circumstance that most mirror stories in Homer are part of a speech, i.e. are told by one of the characters.[6] Létoublon only once draws attention to this fact, when discussing *Odyssey* 7. 241–66, a retrospective mirror story in which Odysseus tells the story of his stay with the nymph Calypso.

This same Ogygian episode has been related before (5. 1–261) by the omniscient narrator. The difference between his 'objective' version and Odysseus' subjective version is indicated by Létoublon as 'variation dans l'optique du narrateur'.[7] I think this point deserves further investigation. What exactly is the nature of this variation? Are the two versions more or less interchangeable? They are not: Odysseus could never present his story in exactly the same way as the narrator.

One example may illustrate this. When Odysseus tells Arete and Alcinous how suddenly, after seven years of involuntary exile, Calypso incited him to go home, he adds that she did so $Z\eta\nu\grave{o}s$ $\acute{v}\pi'$ $\grave{a}\gamma\gamma\epsilon\lambda\acute{\iota}\eta s$, $\mathring{\eta}$ $\kappa\alpha\grave{\iota}$ $\nu\acute{o}os$ $\acute{\epsilon}\tau\rho\acute{a}\pi\epsilon\tau'$ $\alpha\grave{v}\tau\mathring{\eta}s$ ('in obedience to a message from Zeus, or because her own mind changed', 7. 263).[8] What was her motive in letting him go? Odysseus does not know and therefore presents his audience with two alternative explanations. We, the hearers/readers, know the right answer, since in his version the narrator has told us how Hermes brought Calypso a message from Zeus to send Odysseus home (5. 29–148). Obeying these orders ($\acute{\epsilon}\pi\epsilon\grave{\iota}$ $\delta\grave{\eta}$ $Z\eta\nu\grave{o}s$ $\acute{\epsilon}\pi\acute{\epsilon}\kappa\lambda\upsilon\epsilon\nu$ $\grave{a}\gamma\gamma\epsilon\lambda\iota\acute{a}\omega\nu$, 5. 150), she went to Odysseus and told him to build a raft and sail home. The very fact that she did not mention Zeus' message made Odysseus' first reaction one of suspicion (5. 173–9). Calypso answered with a solemn oath that she had no harmful designs in store for him, but did not refer to Hermes' recent visit. Some verses later in this scene the narrator himself subtly reminds us of Hermes' visit: Odysseus sat down $\acute{\epsilon}\pi\grave{\iota}$ $\theta\rho\acute{o}\nu o\upsilon$ $\acute{\epsilon}\nu\theta\epsilon\nu$ $\grave{a}\nu\acute{\epsilon}\sigma\tau\eta$ | $\acute{E}\rho\mu\epsilon\acute{\iota}as$ (5. 195–6): 'on the seat from which Hermes had just risen'! With this small detail the narrator contrasts his own 'omniscient' knowledge with Odysseus' ignorance. Recounting this episode at the court of the Phaeacians, Odysseus is

---

[6] Létoublon (n. 2) 26.   [7] Ibid.
[8] All references are to the Monro–Allen (OCT) text.

still ignorant of Hermes' visit and at this point in his story gives two possible reasons for Calypso's change of mind: $Z\eta\nu\grave{o}s$ $\acute{v}\pi'$ $\mathring{a}\gamma\gamma\epsilon\lambda\acute{\iota}\eta s$, $\mathring{\eta}$ $\kappa a\grave{\iota}$ $\nu\acute{o}os$ $\acute{\epsilon}\tau\rho\acute{a}\pi\epsilon\tau'$ $a\mathring{v}\tau\mathring{\eta}s$.

This example shows us that the reflective qualities of a mirror story are conditioned by the identity of the subject of narration. In other words, the analysis of a mirror story has to be considered in the light of a larger complex: the relationship between speech and narrator-text. I propose to deal with this relationship first in order to create a framework for the investigation of *Iliad* 1. 366–92 as a mirror story.

II. THE PLACE OF DIRECT SPEECH WITHIN A NARRATIVE TEXT

In the following exposition I will make use of the theoretical model of the Dutch narratologist Mieke Bal.[9] Before entering on the subject of direct speech proper we have to define our position regarding the description of narrative texts as a whole. Bal's approach is a semiotic one: she describes a narrative text as a three-levelled structure, in which each level has its own agent, activity, and product. The text (first level) is the product of the narrating activity of a narrator. The content of this text is the story (second level) and the agent on this second level is the focalizer: it is with his/her eyes and in general through his/her perception that we, the hearers/readers, perceive the fabula (third level). This fabula consists of all events in chronological order, and the agents on this level are the characters. Although in theory we have to dissect the three activities from each other, in practice texts provide us with many combinations of two or three agents in one 'person'. Let me illustrate this with some examples from Homer:[10]

$\theta\mathring{v}\nu\epsilon\ldots$ $\mathring{a}\mu$ $\pi\epsilon\delta\acute{\iota}o\nu$ $\pi o\tau a\mu\mathring{\omega}$ $\pi\lambda\acute{\eta}\theta o\nu\tau\iota$ $\acute{\epsilon}o\iota\kappa\grave{\omega}s\ldots$
$\mathring{\omega}s$ $\mathring{v}\pi\grave{o}$ $T\upsilon\delta\epsilon\acute{\iota}\delta\eta$ $\pi\upsilon\kappa\iota\nu a\grave{\iota}$ $\kappa\lambda o\nu\acute{\epsilon}o\nu\tau o$ $\varphi\acute{a}\lambda a\gamma\gamma\epsilon s$.

He [Diomedes] was raging through the plain like a swollen river . . .
Thus the close ranks were routed by Diomedes. (*Iliad* 5. 87–93)

---

[9] See M. Bal, *Narratologie. Essais sur la signification narrative dans quatre romans modernes* (Paris, 1977) (partly translated into English in 'The Narrating and the Focalizing: a Theory of the Agents in Narrative', *Style* 17 (1983), 234–69) and *Narratology: Introduction to the Theory of Narrative* (Toronto, 1985).

[10] For a more detailed application of Bal's model to Homer, see I. J. F. de Jong, *Narrators and Focalizers: The Presentation of the Story in the Iliad* (Amsterdam, 1987).

We can analyse the presentation of this passage as follows: Homer narrates what he 'recalls' with the help of the Muses, viz. how the Trojans are routed by Diomedes; or, in narratological terms, the primary narrator-focalizer tells how characters are routed by another character.

A little later, this same event is presented once again, now through the eyes (focalization) of a Trojan:

> Τὸν δ' ὡς οὖν ἐνόησε Λυκάονος ἀγλαὸς υἱὸς
> θύνοντ' ἄμ πεδίον πρὸ ἔθεν κλονέοντα φάλαγγας,
> αἶψ' ἐπὶ Τυδεΐδῃ ἐτιταίνετο καμπύλα τόξα.

But as soon as the splendid son of Lycaon perceived him [Diomedes], raging through the plain and chasing the enemy in front of him, he quickly bent his curved bow at the son of Tydeus. (*Iliad* 5. 95–7)

Here the primary narrator-focalizer recalls and narrates how one of the characters, Pandarus, functioning as secondary focalizer, saw another character, Diomedes, rushing.

When the three agents are combined in one person (narrator = focalizer = character), we are dealing with autobiography, a Homeric specimen of which is Odysseus' account of his wanderings (*Odyssey* 9–12).

So far I have spoken of narrative texts as purely narrative, i.e. without considering the 'dramatic' element (monologue or dialogue) which in fact constitutes, together with the narrator-text, the epic genre or *genus mixtum*. It was Plato who first reflected on this mixed nature of narrative texts (*Republic* 3, 392c–394d) and distinguished διήγησις ἁπλή (simple narration, *diēgēsis*, i.e. when the poet Homer speaks as himself) from *mimēsis* (direct speech, i.e. when the poet speaks as one of the characters). His discussion and (part of his) terminology were transposed from the realm of philosophy (the role of literature in the educational system of the Ideal State)[11] to modern theory of literature by Genette in his influential treatise *Narrative Discourse*.[12]

[11] Plato's extended discussion of the co-existence of mimetical and diegetical parts in a narrative text serves the following purpose in his philosophical argument: from 376e onwards he is talking about the role literature should play in the education of the Guardians. Since all literature in antiquity was recited, and since the dramatic parts of the epic are particularly suited for dramatic recitation, the content of these mimetical parts had to be morally outstanding in order to provide the reciters with the right example.

[12] G. Genette, *Narrative Discourse*, trans. J. Lewin (Ithaca, NY, 1980), 162–71. I cannot agree with Genette's translation 'pure narrative' for διήγησις ἁπλή. The opposite of ἁπλοῦς (single, simple) in Greek is διπλοῦς (twofold) and this aspect of

What is the relation between narrator-text and direct speech? Considered strictly from a logical point of view, the narrating activity of the narrator[13] is permanent throughout the whole text: it is his voice which is responsible for the *diēgēsis* as well as the *mimēsis*. One glance at our text of the *Iliad* and *Odyssey* suffices to bear out this point, because we see one continuous flow[14] of dactylic hexameters. Plato, discussing a passage from the narrative text 'par excellence' of his time, the *Iliad*, touches on this point, when he says (393b): 'But the things after that he [Homer] tells as if he were himself Chryses and he tries as far as possible to create the illusion for us that it is not Homer who speaks, but the priest, an old man.' The words 'to create the illusion' exactly mark the point where narratology comes in, because the logical approach mentioned above does not suffice to describe what happens (in terms of the effect on the story) when the narrator-text changes into direct speech.

According to the theories of Genette and Bal, the relationship between narrator-text and speeches is hierarchical: the dramatic parts are embedded in the narrator-text.[15] The primary narrator stops narrating *about* actors and their events, but instead 'quotes' their own words, i.e. lets them speak for themselves. The characters thereby become secondary narrators in relation to the primary narrator. (The term secondary narrator is slightly misleading, since the content of what these actors tell is not always a narrative.) At the same time, the level of focalization changes, because the words of the characters in principle embody their view and interpretation of things. They become secondary narrator-focalizers.

doubleness is suggested by Plato in his term *mimēsis*—while reciting his part the reciter identifies himself with the character he impersonates; he is himself *and* the other at the same time. In the *diēgēsis* the narrator is only narrator. For a more detailed discussion, see De Jong (n. 10), 2–5.

[13] When I speak of the narrator, I mean the primary narrator-focalizer.

[14] This continuous flow of hexameters might account for the presence of so many transitional formulas introducing or concluding a direct speech: 'Then in answer to him spoke' and 'Thus he spoke'. Especially when we take into consideration the oral performance of the epics, these explicit markers of the transition from *diēgēsis* to *mimēsis* and vice versa seem indispensable. For an interesting general discussion of this so-called attributive discourse, see G. Prince, 'Le Discours attributif et le récit', *Poétique* 35 (1978), 305–13; for an application of his ideas to Homer, see De Jong (n. 10), 195–208.

[15] For a different model of description, see L. Dolezel, *Narrative Modes in Czech Literature* (Toronto, 1973), and W. Schmidt, *Der Textaufbau in den Erzählungen Dostojevskys* (Munich, 1973). They consider *diēgēsis* and *mimēsis* as equivalent parts of the text and use the term 'intertextuality'.

Returning to our starting point, I think we can now reformulate Létoublon's 'variation dans l'optique du narrateur' as a (funda-mental) difference in focalization between the primary and second-ary narrator.[16]

So far I have been occupied mainly with the question of *how* the information of *diēgēsis* and *mimēsis* is conveyed. My next concern is the information itself. What is the relation between the *content* of *diēgesis* and that of *mimēsis*?

III. DIRECT SPEECH AS THE CARRIER OF SECONDARY STORIES

Direct speech as such can be considered an event: 'x talks to y' stands on a par with 'x helps y', etc. And yet the act of speaking is different from all other acts, because it engenders another text within the primary text.[17] In this embedded text the character who speaks, can: (*a*) refer to the *hic et nunc* of the main story and thereby remain in his position as character (this is what happens in a conversation, a formal address, etc.); (*b*) tell a (secondary) story himself and thereby become a 'real' narrator. In the Homeric epics we never find a character who tells a story without referring beforehand or after-wards to the actual situation in which he finds himself.[18] We may conclude that secondary stories never appear in isolation, but always serve an argumentative function.

Now what kind of stories are told by these secondary narrators? One category is defined for us by Austin, the so-called digressions: 'anecdotes which describe action outside the time of the poem'.[19]

---

[16] In view of this, Létoublon's reference to Genette's category *voice* in this context seems to be beside the point: the question of focalization (as implied in the formulation 'l'optique') belongs to his category *mood* (Genette (n. 12), 161–211).

[17] Cf. E. Lämmert, *Bauformen des Erzählens* (Stuttgart, 1955), 195–202: 'Der Erzähler erzählt den Gesprächsakt wie ein anderes Geschehen des äußeren Vorgangs. Die Aussage der Personen aber vermag sich vom Fortschritt der Handlung zu lösen, ohne den Bezug zum erzählten Gegenwart zu verlieren' (196).

[18] It is interesting to note that the stories told by the professional story-tellers Demodocus and Phemius in the *Od.* are never presented as direct speech, but (at least initially) as indirect speech: Demodocus, see 8. 73–82 (indirect speech); 8. 267–366 (indirect speech, which after some lines changes into an independent construction); 8. 500–20 (indirect speech, then change into independent construction); Phemius, see 1. 326–7 (indirect speech).

[19] N. Austin, 'The Function of Digressions in the *Iliad*', *GRBS* 7 (1966), 296.

I think I can safely equate his 'time of the poem' with my own term 'story' (see note 4) and thereby create a useful criterion to distinguish digressions from mirror stories. After all, the latter reflect elements of the story and therefore stay, so to speak, within the time of the poem. Austin shows that the digressions serve as (hortatory, dissuasive, or apologetic) paradeigmata.[20] The function of mirror stories is not as easily generalized, but has to be determined in each separate case. Achilles' speech at *Iliad* 1. 365–412 offers me the opportunity to look at both a digression and a mirror story and although the interest of this chapter lies primarily with the mirror story, it will yet be illuminating to analyse the function of both.

IV. ACHILLES' SPEECH, 1. 365–412: THE FUNCTION OF THE NARRATIVES

To understand Achilles' speech, we have to recall briefly what precedes and follows it. The famous opening words of the *Iliad* ($\mu\hat{\eta}\nu\iota\nu$ $\check{\alpha}\epsilon\iota\delta\epsilon$, $\theta\epsilon\acute{\alpha}$) mention at once the theme of the poem, the wrath of Achilles. The circumstances which led to this wrath are told in the ensuing verses (1. 6–349, the moment when Achilles literally turns his back on the fighting community of which he used to be such a prominent member: $\dot{\epsilon}\tau\acute{\alpha}\rho\omega\nu\ldots\check{\epsilon}\zeta\epsilon\tau o$ $\nu\acute{o}\sigma\phi\iota$ $\lambda\iota\alpha\sigma\theta\epsilon\acute{\iota}s$). Sitting alone on the beach he prays to his mother, the sea-nymph Thetis, and briefly indicates the reason for his grievance: Agamemnon has dishonoured him by taking away his *geras* (special prize). On hearing this, Thetis immediately leaves the bottom of the sea[21] and, seating herself near him, asks him to tell her what has happened. Our speech (1. 365–412) is Achilles' answer to this question. At the end of it he urges his mother to go to Zeus and beg him to grant the Trojans a triumph in the war. In this way Achilles hopes that Agamemnon

---

[20] On the subject of digressions see also: Andersen (n. 5); J. H. Gaisser, 'A Structural Analysis of the Digressions in the *Iliad* and *Odyssey*', *HSCP* 73 (1969), 1–43; M. M. Willcock, 'Mythological Paradeigma in the *Iliad*', *CQ* 14 (1964), 141–54 [= this vol., Ch. 15].

[21] This voyage (1. 357–60) is described by the primary narrator-focalizer, who can actually see what Achilles himself cannot: Thetis sitting on the bottom of the sea (Achilles can only gaze at the sea: $\dot{o}\rho\acute{o}\omega\nu$ $\dot{\epsilon}\pi$ $\dot{\alpha}\pi\epsilon\acute{\iota}\rho o\nu\alpha$ $\pi\acute{o}\nu\tau o\nu$, 350). Thetis' speedy upward movement is compared to mist (359), presumably because mist was thought of as the evaporation of (sea)water.

will come to regret his mistake. Moved by his words Thetis consents
to go to Zeus (1. 414–27) and leaves.

This dialogue plays an important role in the development of the
plot of the *Iliad*, because here we find the transition from the human
level (quarrel between two leaders) to the divine:[22] Achilles' *mēnis*
will get its divine extension and intensification in the Διὸς βουλή
(plan of Zeus). Achilles himself brings about this transition by calling
for help from his divine mother and, through her mediation, from
Zeus, the mightiest god of all. In order to achieve this, he first has to
persuade his mother that her mission is at the same time crucial,
righteous, and possible. It is with this persuasive goal of the speech at
1. 365–412 in mind that we have to interpret its two narratives. The
second of these (396–406) is described by Austin as a hortatory
paradigm.[23] It is a story which Achilles has often heard Thetis herself
telling:[24] how she once helped Zeus, when he was attacked and
bound by three other Olympians. I will not go into the details of this
story, because they are discussed and explained most convincingly
by Willcock and Braswell.[25] There is, however, a flaw in the arguments of these three scholars regarding the precise function of this
story. Braswell argues that the myth of Zeus' salvation by Thetis,
which is otherwise unattested, was invented by the poet 'to equip
Thetis with a strong argument why Zeus should grant her request'.[26]
The underlying mechanism is the *quid pro quo* principle, found
everywhere in the epics and referred to by Achilles himself in his
speech (1. 394–5: εἴ ποτε δή τι ἢ ἔπει ὤνησας κραδίην Διὸς ἠὲ
καὶ ἔργῳ, 'if ever you gratified the heart of Zeus in word or deed').
Austin starts from the same assumption: 'This story is intended to
be the *hypomnesis* [reminder of past favours] of Thetis' prayer to

---

[22] For the causal relationship between Achilles' *mēnis* and the Διὸς βουλή, see
A. Lesky, *Göttliche und menschliche Motivation im homerischen Epos* (SB Heidelberg
1961. 4), 16–17 [= this vol., pp. 174–5].

[23] Austin (n. 19), 300.

[24] The presentation of the story remains with Achilles; Thetis does not become a
tertiary narrator. Achilles begins by quoting Thetis' own words in indirect speech:
ἔφησθα ... οἴη ... ἀμῦναι (397), but in 401 this form is abandoned—as usual in
Homer (see n. 18 above)—in favour of an independent construction: σύ ...
ὑπελύσαο.

[25] Willcock (n. 20), 143–4 [= this vol., pp. 438–40]; B. K Braswell, 'Mythological
Innovation in the *Iliad*', *CQ* 31 (1971), 18–19.

[26] Braswell (n. 25), 18. Willcock likewise stresses how details of the myth are
tailored to its intended recipient, Zeus.

Zeus ... '[27] But why then do we find this anecdote in Achilles' speech
to Thetis and not in Thetis' speech to Zeus (1. 503–10), where one
would expect it in the first place? The answer is, I think, that the story
functions primarily within the rhetorical context of Achilles' own
request: by supplying his mother with an excellent argument to back
up her request to Zeus, he greatly augments his own chances of
persuading her to go and make the request. A possible answer of
Thetis, 'I would like to help you, but I cannot', is hereby precluded.
Now the narrator might have *repeated* the story in Thetis' speech to
Zeus (after the cue εἴ ποτε δή σε μετ' ἀθανάτοισιν ὄνησα ἢ ἔπει ἢ
ἔργῳ, 503–4, cf. εἴ ποτε δή τι ἢ ἔπει ὤνησας κραδίην Διὸς ἠὲ
καὶ ἔργῳ, 394–5). Though a repetition of something the hearers/
listeners already know for the sake of the characters within the story
is not inconceivable (cf. the threefold repetition of the Bad Dream in
Iliad 2. 7–71), the narrator here seems to have let the knowledge of
his narratees prevail over that of his characters.[28] Moreover, he
wants Zeus to react hesitatingly to Thetis' request and hence makes
that request as sober as possible.[29] In sum, we get a more complete
picture of the function of this digression by extending Braswell's
formulation in the following way: the narrator equips Achilles (who
equips Thetis) with a strong argument.

Having explained the presence of this second narrative, I will now
turn to the first one, the mirror story of 1. 366–92. As a matter of fact,
Achilles himself is the first to comment on the repetitious character
of his story, as we see in his opening words (365): οἶσθα· τίη τοι
ταῦτα ἰδυίῃ πάντ' ἀγορεύω; (You already know; why should I tell
you all those things when you already know them?) It is interesting
to note that we encounter a similar remark by a speaking character
in the context of another mirror story. When Odysseus in his account
of his wanderings has reached the point in his stay with Calypso
which he had related the preceding night in the presence of Arete and

[27] Austin (n. 19), 300 n. 9.
[28] Cf. W. J. Wyatt, 'Homer in Performance: *Iliad* 1. 348–427', *CJ* 83 (1988), 295–7
('the first time we hear of Thetis helping Zeus, we need to be informed about her
service, the second time, that information would slow down the story too much');
Braswell (n. 25), 19 n. 2 ('more likely he [sc. the poet] regarded a general reference as
sufficient, since the audience would still have Achilles' speech in mind. In any case,
the myth is tacitly assumed in Zeus' granting of the request').
[29] Willcock's explanation (n. 20: 134 [= this vol., p. 439])—Thetis does not think it
worth while repeating the story to Zeus, because it is a mere invention of the
poet—confuses two levels, that of the historical poet and that of the characters in
the story.

Alcinous, he says (12. 450–4): τί τοι τάδε μυθολογεύω; ἤδη
γάρ ... ἐμυθεόμην (Why am I telling you these things? For I have
already told them ...). Following his own suggestion Odysseus there
ends his story. But Achilles' remark here is situated at the very
beginning of his story. Taking it at face value Aristarchus condemned
the ensuing verses (1. 366–92). His radical approach to the text has
found no following among other commentators (ancient or modern),
who instead have offered the following defences of 366–92. The first
defence is based on *poetic convention*: although the information
conveyed from 368 onwards is not really necessary for the hearers/
readers, 'the frequent verbal repetition of messages shows what the
epic poet and his hearers liked' (Leaf). This line of reasoning received
new life with the arrival of oral poetry theory, which explains and
condones the large amount of repetition in Homer (cf. e.g. Kirk, *Iliad
Commentary*, on 366–92). More particularly, it has been suggested
by Apthorp[30] that we are dealing here with a 'recapitulatory summary', 'a device ... to assist the audience to get their bearing when
the poet resumes after a break in performance'. A second form of
defence is *psychological* (bT scholia and Eustathius): talking about
one's grief to another person relieves the heart. The passage is also
defended on *rhetorical* grounds (A, bT scholia and Eustathius): we
are dealing with a so-called *anakephalaiōsis* (recapitulation by a
speaker at the end of his speech).[31]

The first argument is too much like a panacea. Nor is the comparison with the repetition of messages pertinent, since in those cases
the verbal repetition is functional: the message should be transmitted
as precisely as possible.[32] To think in terms of a 'recapitulatory
summary' is hardly relevant either, since the story is only four
hundred lines under way.[33] The second argument best fits the whole
context: Thetis asks Achilles to tell her about his *penthos* in order to
share his grief with him (ἵνα εἴδομεν ἄμφω, 1. 363). In his response

[30] M. J. Apthorp, 'The Language of *Odyssey* 5. 7–20', *CQ* 27 (1977), 7–8.
[31] Arist., *Rhet. ad Alex.* 1433[b]29, H. Lausberg, *Handbuch der literarischen Rhetorik*
(Munich, 1960), §§ 434–5, 442.
[32] Illuminating in this respect are Zeus' words to his messenger the 'Bad Dream' in
Il. 2. 10: πάντα μάλ' ἀτρεκέως ἀγορευέμεν ὡς ἐπιτέλλω (tell everything *very
precisely* just as I command it to you).
[33] Cf. Kirk, *Il. Comm.* 1 on 366–92: 'There is no obvious reason for denying that he
is the main composer himself, although the initial puzzle would remain; why did he
find a summary of this length necessary so soon after the events and arguments had
been set out *in extenso*?'

Achilles is at first reluctant to tell what happened (and relive his painful experiences),[34] but then starts his account, speaking in detail about the first phases and becoming increasingly concise towards the end. The third argument must be viewed in combination with and as evolving from the second one. Though 1. 366–95 would have to be considered a special case of *anakephalaiōsis* (since the recapitulation is found at the beginning not the end of the speech and events are summarized which were first told by the primary narrator-focalizer, not by the speaker himself), I think it serves the same function as an ordinary one, viz. to prepare for the conclusion, which can take the form of a verdict, a political proposal, or, as in Achilles' case, a request (393–5 and 407–12).[35] His account of what has happened is the answer to Thetis' request for information,[36] offers him the possibility to vent his frustration, and in the end serves the persuasive goal of his whole speech—to convince Thetis that the Greeks, and especially Agamemnon, deserve to be punished by Zeus for not honouring 'the best of the Achaeans' (cf. his concluding words at 410–12). Note that as in the case of Achilles' second narrative, Thetis will not repeat the mirror story to Zeus, confining herself to a pregnant summary (506–7). Thus the mirror story, too, functions primarily within Achilles' rhetoric towards his mother.

In conclusion: both narratives (mirror story (366–93) and digression (397–406)) function within the main rhetorical message of the speech, the first providing the *motivation*, the second an *instrument* for the service which Achilles is asking of his mother. The remainder of this chapter will be devoted to a more detailed analysis of the mirror story itself.

V. ACHILLES' MIRRORING OF 1. 6–349: THE LEVEL OF THE FABULA

We now know that Achilles has a definite purpose in recounting the origins of his present state of *mēnis*. But precisely *what* elements of the first version (1. 6–349) are mirrored, and *how* is this achieved?

---

[34] For reluctance to tell stories, see *Il.* 6. 145–51; *Od.* 4. 465; 7. 241–3; 9. 2–15.

[35] One might also consider 366–92 not so much a recapitulation as a full *narratio* in what is virtually Achilles' indictment of the Greeks.

[36] Achilles calls Thetis $\iota\delta\upsilon\iota\eta$ (knowing, aware of the facts) but is she really? When the plot so demands, gods are not omniscient: cf., in a very similar situation, *Il.* 18. 73–4 (= 1. 362–3), where Thetis again asks Achilles what has happened and where

The first question (to be dealt with in this section) arises chiefly at the level of the fabula: although Achilles' version is much shorter than the narrator's (27 vs. 343 verses), we find that he adds some new information. For the other question (§ VI) I must investigate the level of the story: the facts are represented from Achilles' viewpoint: where does this become apparent? Finally, on the level of the text I have to deal (also § VI) with a phenomenon which is typical of the Homeric oral style: the verbatim repetition 1. 372–9 = 1. 12–16 and 22–5.

I begin with the addition made by Achilles. In my introduction I stated that 1. 366–92 is a mirror story which reflects elements told before in the main story. I now have to adjust this statement and point out that the first four verses of Achilles' speech contain information which was not told before by the narrator. At the end of his proem, the narrator announced that he would begin his story with the quarrel between Achilles and Agamemnon (1. 6–7). The fulfilment of this announcement does not follow until 1. 54–304. In the intervening passage (1. 8–53) he twice recounts the steps which led to this quarrel. The first time, he does so cursorily, working back in time (8–12); the second time, he does so fully, in the progressive order of events (12–53). The pivotal scene is the arrival of Chryses, priest of Apollo, in the Greek camp and his request for the return of his daughter (12–24). This event is furthest removed in time from the narrator's point of departure, the quarrel.[37] Achilles commences his account at an even earlier point, viz. the moment when Chryseis was taken captive in a raid on Thebe.[38] He had announced (365) that he would tell everything, and it is therefore logical that he should begin at the very beginning, with the event which caused Chryses to come

---

63–4 and 74–7 make clear that she really does not know what *penthos* has reached her son; also 15. 521–5, where we are explicitly told that Ares did not know about the death of his son Ascalaphus. Achilles' insistence that Thetis knows seems expressive of his reluctance to tell his story.

[37] Cf. the analysis of this passage in W. F. van Otterloo, *De ringcompositie als opbouwprincipe in de epische gedichten van Homerus* (Amsterdam, 1948), 66–7.

[38] Ancient commentators were puzzled by the fact that Chryseis was taken captive in Thebe and not in her home city of Chryse. They offer all kinds of (imaginary) reasons (e.g. Eustathius: she went to a festival of Artemis; her father sent her to a hiding-place). If we try to give an explanation in terms of the story itself, I think we can say that the fact that Chryseis was not taken captive in her home city explains why her father had to come to the Greek camp later and beg for her release there, rather than doing so on the spot. One might even doubt whether Chryses would have survived a capture of Chryse, when we think of the fate of Eëtion, the father of Andromache, who was killed during the same (?) raid on Thebe (6. 414–16).

to the Greek camp and thereby set the following chain of events
in motion. There is one more reason why Achilles chooses to tell
what the narrator left out: he was himself one of the participants in
the raid (ᾠχόμεθ᾽, διεπράθομεν, ἤγομεν), and presumably its
leader.[39] It is significant that, when talking about the distribution of
the booty, he changes into the third person plural: δάσσαντο, ἕλον
(368–9). This small detail reflects his present mood: he bears the
brunt of the war efforts, but others (i.e. Agamemnon) reap the fruits
of his exertions. In the heat of his quarrel with Agamemnon Achilles
had expressed the same sentiment more explicitly (1. 165–8): 'But the
greater portion of the much-rushing war my hands perform: but
whenever the division of spoil comes, you [Agamemnon] get a much
greater prize, and I return to my ships with a small yet agreeable
prize, when I have worn myself out with fighting.'

   With this observation I am in fact already talking about Achilles
as focalizer, which means I have reached the next level, that of the
story.

VI. THE LEVEL OF THE STORIES AND THE TEXTS

I now have to describe more precisely the difference between the
narrator and Achilles as narrator-focalizers, a difference which is
the result of the direct speech being embedded in the main text. The
narrator and Achilles both cover more or less the same ground
(the same fabula), and yet as narrator-focalizers they belong to
completely different categories: the primary narrator-focalizer of the
Homeric epics is external, i.e. he does not play a part in his own story
and his story-telling is directed towards (anonymous) listeners/
readers. As focalizer he possesses great powers: he knows the future,
has access to the inner thoughts of his characters, and can transport
himself in no time from the world of human beings to that of the
gods.[40] Achilles, on the other hand, is a character in the story of the
narrator and plays an important role in his own story. He addresses
another character belonging to the world of the main story (Thetis).
His powers of observation are not greater than those of any other

---

[39] Two other references in the *Il.* to this raid both mention Achilles: 2. 688–93 and
6. 414–16.

[40] For the narrator's 'special abilities', see S. Richardson, *The Homeric Narrator*
(Nashville, 1990), 109–39.

human being. The worlds of the external primary narrator-focalizer and internal secondary narrator-focalizer are, therefore, two separate entities, which in principle have no contact with each other.[41]

Without implying that the version of the external narrator-focalizer must be 'objective',[42] we can expect Achilles' version to be somewhat more subjective, taking into account his own involvement and his motives in telling the story.[43] I first give a small example. Achilles, feeling responsible for the well-being of his men, characterizes the arrow shot by Apollo and carrier of the plague as a 'disastrous projectile' ($\kappa\alpha\kappa\grave{o}\nu$ $\beta\acute{\epsilon}\lambda os$, 382). The narrator for his part had drawn attention to the effectiveness of Apollo's shooting, calling the same arrow 'sharp' ($\grave{\epsilon}\chi\epsilon\pi\epsilon\upsilon\kappa\grave{\epsilon}s$ $\beta\acute{\epsilon}\lambda os$, 51).

A second, more complex example concerns Achilles' ordering and selection of events. The emotional climax of his story lies, of course, in his quarrel with Agamemnon. Surprisingly enough, he describes it in only two and a half verses (386–8), whereas the narrator devoted 250 verses to it! On reflection, this brevity on Achilles' part is very effective: with a few well-chosen words he contrasts his own sane advice (386: $\theta\epsilon\grave{o}\nu$ $\grave{\iota}\lambda\acute{a}\sigma\kappa\epsilon\sigma\theta\alpha\iota$) with Agamemnon's anger (387: *cholos*). To underline the contrast between the two reactions Achilles also places them in a chronological relation to each other ($a\grave{\upsilon}\tau\acute{\iota}\kappa$' . . . $\pi\rho\hat{\omega}\tau os$ . . . $\acute{\epsilon}\pi\epsilon\iota\tau a$), thereby suggesting that Agamemnon opposed his (Achilles') sane counsel of placating the god. In reality, the course of events was slightly different: Achilles' proposal to placate the god was made before, not after Calchas' speech (1. 59–76). It also

---

[41] Occasionally the two worlds are bridged by the narrator, when he addresses one of the characters in an apostrophe (e.g. *Il.* 4. 127, 146; 7. 104; and 13. 603, all addressed to Menelaus). See A. Parry, 'Language and Characterization in Homer', *HSCP* 76 (1972), 1–22; E. Block, 'The Narrator Speaks: Apostrophe in Homer and Virgil', *TAPA* 112 (1982), 7–22; N. Yamagata, 'The Apostrophe of Homer as Part of the Oral Technique', *BICS* 36 (1989), 91–103.

[42] Létoublon (n. 2), 25 uses this opposition 'objective'–'subjective', when comparing *Od.* 5. 1–261 (narrator's version) with 7. 242–66 (Odysseus' version). I do not think it right, however, automatically to describe the diegetical part of the epics as objective. For corrections of this persistent view, see S. E. Bassett, *The Poetry of Homer* (Berkeley, 1938), 81–113; J. Griffin, *Homer on Life and Death* (Oxford, 1980), 103–43; De Jong (n. 10).

[43] The interest of the differences between the narrator's and Achilles' version has been overlooked by Kirk, *Il. Comm.* 1 on 366–92: 'Competent and fluent though it may be within its chosen limitations, it is not, after all, very dramatic or interesting, at least compared with the fuller version.' Wyatt (n. 28), 291–2 only stresses the similarity of Achilles' and the narrator's version, failing to draw attention to the (revealing) differences.

was not Achilles but Agamemnon who first reacted to the words of
the seer, which is only logical, given his direct involvement in the
whole matter. Though angry at the seer, he declared himself prepared to give Chryseis back to her father and thereby (indirectly)
followed Achilles' advice to placate Apollo. Achilles omits all that
followed after this (Agamemnon's demand for compensation, his own
anger at this request, which made him the object of Agamemnon's
anger, and finally led to the latter's demand to be given Briseis,
Achilles' own *geras*); instead, in 387–92, he proceeds immediately to
the sad and unacceptable outcome of the quarrel and the fulfilment
of Agamemnon's threat of 182–7: Chryseis is on her way back
home, but Briseis has just been taken from him (note the echo of
ἀπειλήσω, 181, in ἠπείλησεν, 388).

Apart from this example of an effective arrangement of his material, I think we can say that Achilles presents a faithful picture of
what has happened. This faithfulness reaches its fullest extent in the
verses 1. 372–9, which are identical with the narrator-text 1. 12–16
and 22–25. Since Milman Parry's first studies the frequent recurrence of formulas or clusters of formulas has become a well-known
and accepted feature of the Homeric texts. Considered merely from
the point of view of poetic technique the passage 1. 372–9, therefore,
is neither special nor problematic.[44] Yet how am I as a narratologist
to deal with this phenomenon of verbatim repetition of diegetical text
within a character's speech? When we remember the different nature
and possibilities of the two focalizers, the primary narrator-focalizer
and Achilles as secondary narrator-focalizer, this automatic repetition seems to lead to grave inconsistencies. Achilles cannot read
other people's minds and yet he knows with what intentions Chryses
came to the Greek camp (λυσόμενος, 'in order to ransom [his
daughter]', 372 = 13) or what Agamemnon thought in his heart
about the request (οὐκ ... Ἀγαμέμνονι ἥνδανε θυμῷ: 'it did not
please him', 378 = 24). To explain Achilles' omniscience we have to
recall that he is narrating in *retrospect*: he recounts later what he has
seen and especially what he has heard before. In their speeches,
Chryses and Agamemnon themselves had clearly expressed their

---

[44] In his discussion of Homeric repetitions G. M. Calhoun ('Homeric Repetitions',
UCPCP 12 (1933), 20 n. 61) only draws attention to the end of the verbatim
repetition: 'the poet cheats our apprehensions... at *Iliad* 1. 379 ff., when Achilles
suddenly interrupts the verbatim repetition at the precise moment when we expect to
hear "μή σε, γέρον, ... ".'

motives and feelings (Chryses: λύσαιτε, 20; Agamemnon: οὐ λύσω, 29).[45] There is, therefore, no real obstacle to the re-use of these verses. I might even go one step further and consider this case of 100% mirroring as a *symptom* in the semiotic sense of the word, i.e. the unconscious emission of a sign.[46] To the hearers/readers as recipients of the sign, the recurrence of the same formulas *signifies* that regarding these events Achilles feels an external narrator's detachment; he is not yet emotionally involved, but considers himself only one of the many spectators, one of the assembled Greeks.

There is one more omniscient passage in Achilles' mirror story, this time the description of a scene at which he had not himself been present. I refer to the verses 380–1: having heard Agamemnon's harsh words the old man Chryses went away and prayed to Apollo. Now the narrator told us explicitly that the old man did not begin to pray until there was a safe distance between himself and the Greek camp (ἀπάνευθε κιών, 35). Achilles therefore cannot possibly have overheard this prayer and his version is a reconstruction. Having later heard (from Calchas, 93–6) that the plague was sent by Apollo because of the dishonourable treatment of his priest, he rightly infers[47] that Chryses must have prayed to the god to ask for divine revenge.[48] Once more the retrospective nature of the mirror story accounts for the knowledge of the person narrating it. There is one small detail in Achilles' reconstruction which characterizes it as such and at the same time betrays his focalization: according to the narrator, Chryses went away from the Greek camp frightened and in silence (I. 33–4), whereas Achilles describes him as angry at that

---

[45] A comparable case is found in *Od.* 10. 415–17, where Odysseus-narrator is able to tell what went on in the mind of his companions, because they expressed their feelings soon afterwards in speech (419–21).

[46] In semiotic pragmatics one makes a distinction between *symptoms* and *signals*. *Signals* are signs which are emitted *consciously* as such.

[47] Cf. E. Robbins, 'Achilles to Thetis: *Iliad* I. 365–412', *Echos du monde classique/ Classical Views* 34 (1990), 7, who speaks of 'logical inference on his [Achilles'] part'.

[48] Compare Achilles' first speech in the narrator's version: he then rightly concluded that Apollo was responsible for the plague (I. 64), but as yet did not connect the anger of the god with the events involving Chryses. His suggestions as to the causes of divine anger were of a general character (a promise to the gods not fulfilled or a hecatomb not offered). According to Robbins (n. 47), 7–9, Achilles had at this stage already guessed the connection between the plague and Agamemnon's dishonouring of a priest of Apollo, but chose to let another, more authoritative person, the seer Calchas, confront Agamemnon with this unpleasant information. This seems to me to be reading too much between the lines.

moment (380).[49] The first version is appropriate to Chryses' age and
defenceless position, whereas the anger in Achilles' version is more
in accordance with his own heroic temperament. In other words, he
patterns Chryses' behaviour on his own present behaviour, just as,
conversely, he will follow Chryses' example and—via Thetis—ask a
god to avenge him.[50]

VII. CONCLUSION

In this investigation I have approached an ancient Greek text with the
aid of modern narratological insights. The Homeric epic is a narrative
text comprising both narrator-text and speech. The narrator-text
contains the vision of the narrator (the *Iliad*) on a certain fabula
(events taking place in the last year of the Trojan war). The speeches
of characters in principle can contain any sort of information conveyed by human speech, including narratives. These narratives can
digress from the rest of the main story, in which the speech is
embedded, or *mirror* it.

One of these retrospective mirror stories is *Iliad* I. 366–92. By way
of preparation for his final, vengeful request to Thetis (to ask Zeus for
a temporary setback for his own comrades), Achilles tells his mother
the cause of his present anger and bitterness. This same story was
told just before in a much longer version by the narrator (I. 6–349).
Precisely because of this repetitive character scholarly interest in this
passage has been almost nil so far.[51] In this chapter I hope to have
illustrated that the comparison of I. 366–92 with its diegetical
counterpart can be illuminating in several respects: (*a*) because of the
retrospective nature of the mirror story a character can temporarily
assume the same omniscient position as the narrator (Achilles knows
the inner thoughts of Chryses and Agamemnon and reconstructs
the scene between the priest and Apollo, at which he had not
been present). (*b*) We get a clear picture of the mental state of one

---

[49] The narrator only attributes anger to Apollo: 9, 44, and 46.

[50] This is the main thrust of Robbins (n. 47), who in this context also draws
attention to ἐπεὶ μάλα οἱ φίλος ἦεν in 381: 'the mention of Chryses' being dear to
Apollo also establishes a paradigm for what Achilles hopes will happen' (p. 2).

[51] It is not analysed in D. Lohmann, *Die Komposition der Reden in der Ilias* (Berlin,
1970). Since the original publication of this chapter, two more studies have appeared:
Wyatt (n. 28) and Robbins (n. 47).

of the principal antagonists of the *Iliad*: Achilles feels badly rewarded for his contribution to the exertions of war (366–9); he looks back dispassionately on the dramatic confrontation between Agamemnon and Chryses (370–79),[52] but emotionally on his quarrel with Agamemnon, in which he considers himself the victim of Agamemnon's rash and unwise anger (380–92). That Achilles is given the chance to voice his evaluation of the quarrel and elicit a sympathetic reaction from a character within the story certainly contributes to the listeners'/readers' siding with him—at least at this stage of the story.[53] (c) It is shown that verbal repetition on a scale larger than that of the individual formula is not only explicable in terms of oral compositional technique, but also defensible in terms of narrative consistency, and indeed effective in terms of literary art. My preliminary theoretical discussion may appear to some to be inordinately elaborate compared to the harvest it yields on the exegetical level. To this objection I might respond—aside from the claim that any correct and consistent descriptive theory is to be welcomed—that I suppose that any Homeric mirror story may now be conveniently analysed and that, consequently, the insights here gained should be multiplied by the results of future analyses along the lines set out in this chapter.

---

[52] I think we have to interpret the words κακῶς ἀφίει (379 = 25) not as implying a moral judgement on Agamemnon (he dismissed him in a bad, intolerable way), but more as suggestive of the tone in which the words were spoken and their intended effect (rudely, insultingly). Cf. bT scholion ad loc.: κακῶς· αὐστηρῶς.

[53] Wyatt (n. 28) makes a strange detour to reach this same conclusion: he suggests that in I. 366–412 there 'is no fictitious audience', hence that Achilles directly addresses the hearers/readers, who in this way 'are moved and would like to help. Achilles wants us to understand and perhaps even approve his decision to ask Zeus to bring temporary defeat to the Greeks'. I disagree that there is no fictitious audience. (Wyatt, in my view, illogically restricts this term to groups of listeners, such as 'army, assembly, sailors'.) There is Thetis, and—as often in Homer and as Wyatt himself suggests in his n. 7—it is through the deployment of this sympathetic internal listener that the effect of a sympathetic response in the hearers/readers is created; for this device, see C. W. Macleod, 'Homer on Poetry and the Poetry of Homer', *Collected Essays* (Oxford, 1983), 1–15 [= this vol., Ch. 9].

ACKNOWLEDGEMENTS

1. Ian Morris, 'The Use and Abuse of Homer'. Revised from *Classical Antiquity* 5 (1986) 81–138, by permission of University of California Press. © 1986 by the Regents of the University of California.

2. Walter Burkert, 'The Making of Homer in the Sixth Century BC: Rhapsodes versus Stesichorus'. From *Papers on the Amasis Painter and his World* (Malibu, 1987), 43–62. Reprinted with minor revisions by permission of the author.

3. R. B. Rutherford, 'From the *Iliad* to the *Odyssey*'. From *Bulletin of the Institute for Classical Studies* 38 (1991–3), 47–54. Reprinted with minor revisions by permission of the editors.

4. Richard Gaskin, 'Do Homeric Heroes make Real Decisions?' Revised from *Classical Quarterly* 40 (1990), 1–15, by permission of Oxford University Press.

5. Albin Lesky, 'Divine and Human Causation in Homeric Epic'. Abridged from *Göttliche und menschliche Motivation im homerischen Epos*, Sitzungsberichte der Heidelberger Akademie der Wissenschaften, philosophische-historische Klasse, 1961. 4, by permission of the Heidelberger Akademie der Wissenschaften and Carl Winter Universitätsverlag. Translated by Leofranc Holford-Strevens.

6. Douglas L. Cairns, 'Affronts and Quarrels in the *Iliad*'. Revised from *Papers of the Leeds International Latin Seminar* 7 (1993), 155–67, by permission of Francis Cairns (Publications) Ltd.

7. Malcolm Schofield, '*Euboulia in the Iliad*'. From *Classical Quarterly* 36 (1986), 6–31. Reprinted with minor revisions by permission of Oxford University Press.

8. R. B. Rutherford, 'Tragic Form and Feeling in the *Iliad*'. From *Journal of Hellenic Studies* 102 (1982), 145–60. Reprinted with minor revisions by permission of the Society for the Promotion of Hellenic Studies.

9. C. W. Macleod, 'Homer on Poetry and the Poetry of Homer'. © Barbara Macleod 1983. Reprinted with minor revisions from Colin Macleod, *Collected Essays* (Oxford, 1983) by permission of Oxford University Press.

10. Jean-Pierre Vernant, 'A "Beautiful Death" and the Disfigured Corpse in Homeric Epic'. From J.-P. Vernant, *Mortals and Immortals: Collected Essays*, ed. F. I. Zeitlin. © 1991 by Princeton University Press. Reprinted with minor revisions by permission of Princeton University Press.

Originally published as 'La Belle Mort et le cadavre outragé', in G. Gnoli and J.-P. Vernant (edd.), *La Mort, les morts dans les sociétés anciennes* (Cambridge and Paris, 1982), 45–76, reprinted in *L'Individu, la mort, l'amour: Soi-même et l'autre en Grèce ancienne* (Paris, 1989), 41–79. Translated by Andrew Szegedy-Maszak. Translations of the *Iliad* are by Richmond Lattimore (Chicago, 1951).

11. Oliver Taplin, 'The Shield of Achilles within the *Iliad*'. From *Greece & Rome* 27 (1980), 1–21. Reprinted with minor revisions by permission of Oxford University Press.

12. Jasper Griffin, 'The Epic Cycle and the Uniqueness of Homer'. Abridged from *Journal of Hellenic Studies* 97 (1977), 39–53. Reprinted with minor revisions by permission of the Society for the Promotion of Hellenic Studies.

13. Wolfgang Kullmann, 'Past and Future in the *Iliad*'. First published as 'Vergangenheit und Zukunft in der Ilias', in *Poetica* 2 (1968), 15–37, and then in Wolfgang Kullmann, *Homerische Motive: Beiträge zur Entstehung, Eigenart und Wirkung von Ilias und Odyssee*, ed. R. J. Müller (Stuttgart, 1992), 219–42. Reprinted by permission of Franz Steiner Verlag, Stuttgart. Translated by Leofranc Holford-Strevens.

14. Laura M. Slatkin, 'The Wrath of Thetis'. Revised from *Transactions and Proceedings of the American Philological Association* 116 (1986), 1–24, by permission of the American Philological Association.

15. M. M. Willcock, 'Mythological Paradeigma in the *Iliad*'. Revised from *Classical Quarterly* 14 (1964), 141–54 by permission of Oxford University Press.

16. James Redfield, 'The Proem of the *Iliad*: Homer's Art'. Reprinted with minor revisions from *Classical Philology* 74 (1979), 94–110, by permission of University of Chicago Press. © 1979 by the University of Chicago.

17. Irene J. F. de Jong, '*Iliad* 1. 366–92: A Mirror Story'. Revised from *Arethusa* 18 (1985), 5–22, by permission of Johns Hopkins University Press. © 1985 Johns Hopkins University Press.

GLOSSARY

This is a list of Greek terms used in transliterated form in this book, and provides rough English equivalents (or explanations) as *aides-mémoire* only.

achos: distress, grief
aeikēs: unseemly
aeikeiē: unseemliness, disfigurement
aeikizō: I disfigure
agathos: good
agērōs (uncontr. *agēraos*): ageless
aglaos: shining
agnoia: ignorance
agōn: contest
agōnisma: competition-piece
aideomai: I feel shame/respect before
aidesis: pardon
aidōs: shame, respect
aisa: fate, due portion
aischron: ugly, disgraceful
aischunē: shame
aischunein: to shame
aisthēsis: perception
aition: cause
aitios: responsible
akleēs: without renown
akmē: peak, pinnacle
akrasia: weakness of will
alaston: unforgetting/unforgettable
alastōr: avenging spirit
alastotokos: miserable in motherhood
algos (pl. *algea*): pain
alkē: might
amēchania: helplessness
anagnōrisis: recognition
anaideiē: shamelessness
anakephalaiōsis: recapitulation

anēr: man
aoidē: song
aoidimos: worthy of being sung
aoidos: bard
aphēmōs: [*sense disputed*: 'anonymously', *acc. to Burkert, Ch. 2*]
aphradiē: lack of sense
aphthitos: immortal
apoikia: colony
aristeia: extended battle-sequence in which a single hero vanquishes
    a number of opponents
aristeus: exponent of excellence
archē: beginning
atē: delusion/disaster (personified: Ate)
athanatos: immortal
autodidaktos: self-taught
autos: self
barbaros: non-Greek
basileus: king
belteron: better
biē: force, vigour, violence
boulē: plan, counsel, council
boulēphoros: counsellor
chariestatos: most charming
charis: charm, grace, favour, gratitude
cholos: anger
chōrizontes: separatists
chronos: time
dais: feast
deipnon: dinner
dēmogerontes: elders of the people
dēmos: people
dēmosios: public, of the *dēmos*
didaskalos: trainer
diēgēsis: narrative
diistemi: I divide
dikē: justice
dolos: deceit
dorpon: meal
dusaristotokeia: miserable mother of an outstanding son
eeldōr: favour
eidōlon: ghost
eidos: appearance
ēmar: day

empedos: fixed
enargeia: vividness
epiklēsis: cult-title
epitaphios: funeral oration
epithumia: desire
erikudēs: very glorious
eris: strife
ethismos: habituation
ēthos: character
euboulia: excellence in counsel
eudaimonia: happiness
euētheia: 'goodness of character' (i.e. simple-mindedness)
euklēes: of good reputation
eukleia: good reputation
eumorphos: beautiful
eupraxia: doing/faring well
exaision: extraordinary, beyond *aisa* (q.v.)
gamos: marriage
geras: prize, mark of honour
gerontes: elders
goos: lament
guia: limbs
hamartia: error
hairein/haireisthai: to take/choose
hēbē: youth
hēdonē: pleasure
hekatoncheir: hundred-hander
helōr(ia): prey
hērōs: hero
hetairos: companion
homoiopatheia: sympathy
hoplopoiia: armour-making
hoplōteros: younger
hormē: impulse
horos: boundary-marker
hubris: self-indulgent disregard for the honour of others
huperbasiē: transgression of limits
iphthimos: potent
ischus: strength
kakoētheia: badness of character
kakos: bad, base
kalumma: covering, cloak, shawl, veil
keirō: I cut

kephalē: head
kēr: death-spirit
kerdion: more profitable
kērostasia: weighing of souls
kleos: fame, reputation, report
kommos: ritual lament
kotos: rancour
kouros: youth, warrior
kourotrophos: nurturer of youths
kratos: strength, power
krēdemnon: head-binder
kuanopeplos: dark-robed
kudos: glory
kurios: legal guardian
Litae: Prayers
lōbē: disfigurement
logos: word, speech, reason
loigos: devastation, disaster
mantis: prophet
maschalismos: a method of mutilating a corpse
medō: I plan, devise
megathumos: great-hearted
mēniō: I rage
mēnis: wrath
mēnithmos: wrath
menos: force, impulse
mesaipolios: grizzled, middle-aged
metanastēs: refugee
mētis: cunning intelligence
metopisthen: in future
mimēsis: imitation
minunthadios: short-lived
moira: portion, fate
Mousa: Muse
neikos: quarrel
nemesaō: I feel *nemesis*
nemesis: indignation
nemesizomai: I feel *nemesis*
nemessēton: occasion for *nemesis*
neos: young
neōteros: younger
noos (in classical Gk.: *nous*): mind, intention
nostos: return

oikos: household
oimē: path (i.e. theme) of song
ōkumoros: short-lived
opsimathia: late learning
orexis: desire, appetition
ostrakismos: ostracism
oulomenos: cursed, wretched, harmful
outidanos: non-entity, nobody
paideia: education
palaioteros: older
panēguris: festival
panta: all things, everything
pathos: suffering, affect, emotion
penthos: suffering
peripeteia: reversal
phēmē: report
philia: friendship
philos: (n.) friend, (adj.) dear
philotēs: friendship
phorminx: lyre
phrēn, phrenes: mind, wits
phronimos: wise, prudent
plēthus: multitude
poinē: blood price
polemos: war
polis: city-state
Poros: Way (personif.)
prooimion: prelude, preface
psuchē: shade, spirit, life, soul
rhabdos: staff
sēma: burial mound
skolion: drinking-song
sphairēdon: like a ball
sphragis: seal
sumpatheia: sympathy
sunhedria: assemblies
technitēs: skilled practitioner
Tekmōr: Sign (personif.)
temenos: precinct
teuchō: I fashion, prepare
tharsos: boldness, courage
thea: goddess
theama: sight

themis: right, custom-law, law-session; pl.
themistes: ordinances, judgements
theos: god
thumos: spirit
timē: honour
tithēmi: I put, make
tragōdos: tragic performer; *tragōdoi* (pl.):
tragedy, tragic performance